Roof Gardens,
Balconies and Terraces

Roof Gardens, Balconies and Terraces

Photography by Jerry Harpur

Text by David Stevens

Mitchell Beazley

Publisher: Jane Aspden
Art Director: Gaye Allen
Executive Editor: Guy Croton
Executive Art Editor: Ruth Hope
Editors: Alex Bennion, Cathy Lowne, Diane Pengelly
Art Editor: Glen Wilkins
Designer: Sarah Davies
Production: Rachel Lynch
Artwork: David Ashby

First published in 1997 by Mitchell Beazley,
an imprint of Reed International Books Limited,
Michelin House, 81 Fulham Road, London sw3 6rb

A cip catalogue for this book is available
from the British Library

isbn 1 85732 793 4

Reproduction by Colourpath, London
Produced by Mandarin Offset
Printed and bound in China

Half title page A carefully planned roof garden increases both your living space and your enjoyment of it.

Title page A roof garden has a drama all its own and gives you an opportunity to create a space entirely reflecting your personality.

Left The views from a terrace at ground level can be greatly enhanced by framing it, here with an arcade of softening plants.

Right Colour is a vital tool in garden design. Whether bold or muted, it should always be used coherently.

Contents

Introduction

To many people living in cities or towns, building a roof garden or redesigning an under-used balcony can be the only opportunity they will have to create a green oasis and an area of relative peace and privacy away from the urban bustle. Space is always at a premium in towns, so adding outside rooms to your home where you can sit, eat and entertain, or your children can play safely in the open air, is a wonderful means through which you can increase your living area. More than that, roof gardens and balconies have a major advantage over gardens that are at ground level: higher than many of the surrounding buildings, they can often provide beautiful and stunning views over day- and night-time cityscapes and these views can be exploited to form an integral part of the design of your garden.

Above left A warm colour scheme, vibrant planting and a distant glimpse of the landscape beyond all combine to create the ideal outdoor room, which can be sheltered, sunny and, above all, a private, restful haven.

Left Where views are important it is essential to invite them into your living space with a low boundary. If this is tempered with foliage, there will be a gradual transition between near and far.

Right Roofscapes are the stuff of aerial gardens – a kaleidoscope of windows, tiles and nearby balconies. A great joy of vernacular architecture is the sensitive use of traditional materials, something that modern designers should take heed of.

Above Comfortably furnished verandas provide the ultimate link between the inside and outside of your house, particularly in a hot climate where shade, combined with what breeze might be available, is often a necessity.

Above Exterior living space can be a vital addition to that inside the house. Here the link is reinforced in the colour scheme, paving materials and in the reflective quality of the pool.

Raised terraces are a perfect way of reworking the space in a garden at ground level. If there are areas that you feel are wasted, perhaps because they have too steep a slope to do anything except grass over them, a raised deck will provide a level platform on which you can create an entirely new part of the garden, with raised beds, seating, some plant-filled pots and perhaps a pond or a barbecue area. Like balconies and roof gardens, terraces can act as outside rooms, related to the inside of your home as much as to the rest of the garden. As such they may alter the way in which you use your garden: having somewhere pleasant to sit, eat or entertain will mean that you are able to spend more of your time out of doors.

In *Roof Gardens, Balconies and Terraces*, Jerry Harpur and I have set out with two specific aims. The first is to inspire you and to show you how some of the world's best garden designers have approached the unique problems of designing for the relatively small spaces occupied by roof gardens, balconies and terraces. Jerry has travelled across much of the world, including Italy, the United States, South America, the Netherlands, South and North Africa, Australia and Britain for the last year, tracking down and photographing many of the world's most beautiful and innovative roof gardens, balconies and terraces, each with its own character and style.

The book's aim is to provide guidance on all aspects of creating your own outdoor living space. The book is divided into five chapters: Design, Structure, Plants, Maintenance, and Accessories. Design focuses on what you may want from your garden, how to lay it out while making the best use of space and surroundings, and how to select an appropriate style. There is also an explanation of the basic rules of design, pattern, colour, size, texture and shape, as well as how to use them to manipulate the areas at your disposal.

Structure looks at the practical aspects of building a roof garden, balcony or terrace, including safety, structural and dimensional surveys, how to draw a scale plan, boundaries, flooring, where to place heavy beds and screens, and steps and overheads.

The chapter on plants shows you how to select plants that will suit the conditions in your garden and fulfil specific requirements such as focal points, screening, ground cover and colour. It gives clues both on how to arrange the plants in beds, pots and borders as well as on how to draw up a planting plan, so that the plants you buy not only form a coherent pattern but won't fall into the expensive mistakes category.

The section on maintenance offers advice on keeping both the hard landscape and the plants in the best condition possible. As well as stressing the importance of keeping the structural elements, boundaries, floors, screens and beds maintained and free of rot, rust and holes, I discuss the benefits of regular plant care – how often plants should be watered, how much food they should be given, how they should be trained, and when they should be pruned.

As accessories and ornaments are the most personal items in any garden, the final chapter simply gives advice on the different types avail-

Above The best gardens are an integral part of the architecture they adjoin. Arthur Erickson is a consummate designer and this composition is the perfect moulding of home, garden, mirror pool and the waters of Puget Sound in Washington State, USA.

able and how such items as statues, ponds and water features, urns, lighting, decorative trellis, *trompe-l'oeil* and garden furniture can best be used and positioned.

The greatest advantage of having a roof garden, balcony or terrace is that it will add an extra dimension to your home. It will be as much an outdoor extension of the inside of your home as it is a part of the garden. As well as providing extra space, all these additional areas are places for relaxation and enjoyment; you will find that eating breakfast on your balcony or roof garden on a Sunday morning can seem a world away from the usual weekday rush.

Design
in your mind's eye...

This is when you can really use your imagination. Spend a while considering how to use the new area of your garden. Reflect on the look and ambience that you want to create: modern, traditional, formal or informal. Think about plants, furniture, materials, tones and textures and how best to use them.

...and on paper

Repeat the process on paper. Visualize yourself and your family in it. Look at the areas of sun and shade, the views you want to exploit and those you need to hide. Move the screens, plants and furniture around until they feel right.

Left One of the most important design rules is that you should keep the layout as strong and simple as possible. Here, the strong line of the cacti forms a perfect border to the plain but beautiful terrace.

Planning the site

Design is a subtle business. Good design should combine strength of purpose, compatibility with the surroundings and, above all, simplicity. Overcomplication is the antithesis of good design and nowhere is this more apparent than in a garden. The vast array of materials, plants, containers and furniture in any garden centre, shop or nursery gives only a small idea of the kind of temptation facing the garden designer. A degree of self-control is essential if the space is not to become a jumble of unrelated objects. In many ways, the physical constraints of gardening above ground level can help, as they force the designer to begin with the essentials.

Design for your own needs

The whole subject of design is confusing to many people and suggests unattainable schemes in glossy magazines or coffee-table books. Nothing could be further from the truth: design is not just about fitting a particular scheme into a space; it is primarily about suiting and reflecting your own personality. You and your family or friends are the ones who will enjoy the space, and it is you who must determine how it is to be laid out. You should never copy exactly a scheme intended for a different garden; it may look fine where it is, but will, without doubt, prove unworkable for you.

Starting from scratch

The exact position and size of a roof garden or balcony is usually predetermined by the space already available. Occasionally, however, you can build a new balcony, or vertically extend a house so that there is fresh potential for living space outside. In such instances it makes good sense to work with the architect from the start. Explain to him or her what you want from the area, so that any favourable aspects, shelter and views can all be taken into account at the planning stage. The structural survey would then include the appropriate information and the building work would make provision for access and services such as electricity and water. There may be several areas and exit points that have potential, so ensure that both you and your designer take all these into account. Such an approach is far better – and inevitably cheaper – than trying to add the garden at a later date.

Above left Plants play a major role in any garden, but on a roof or balcony have a special function in softening austere surroundings. Strong foliage plants, like hostas, are ideal for this purpose.

Left Even the smallest balcony can provide room to sit and relax. Folding chairs save space, planting brings flowers and fragrance, while the sculpture echoes the line of London's Tower Bridge.

Right Simplicity of design is usually the key to tiny gardens and here the neatly-tiled floor is echoed in the squared trellis and white parasol. Burgeoning pots prevent any austerity and naturally lead you through the open area.

Above There should be a positive transition between inside and outside. Here the paving pattern encourages the eye to run down the garden to the simple planting screen.

Above Even the smallest and most uncompromising shape can provide room for sitting and dining if it is handled with flair. Continuity is achieved by the vertical boarding and handrail, while the backdrop of trees provides a green envelope.

Design constraints

The load-bearing potential of a roof or balcony will determine where beds, containers and other heavy features can be safely placed. The climate and aspect will dictate what provision is needed for shelter from winds or hot sun. High-level decks fall into much the same structural category as roof gardens and you should consult a specialist designer, architect or engineer.

A word of warning: few architects specialize in roof garden design, so choose your designer carefully, on recommendation if possible. Check the company has the necessary experience in specialized building codes, as well as what it takes to get the best out of the structure and available space.

Raised terraces or decks at ground level are a different matter, as there are fewer limits on space and weight, and there may be considerable scope for variation in where you put them as well as greater freedom in the choice of materials (see pages 40–43). Take your time over a basic survey that includes views, shelter, prevailing winds and the track of the sun throughout the day, both in summer and in winter.

In hot climates, potential terrace and sitting areas may virtually surround the house, allowing you to choose between sun and shade as the sun moves round during the day. Verandas are particularly successful in this regard. Terraces need not touch the building and it is often possible to put them in other parts of the garden where they can take on quite a different and perhaps more informal character. As always, they will need to be planned and sited carefully as they will almost certainly become major focal points within the overall composition and linkage with other parts of the garden will need to be taken into account.

On a roof, balcony or terrace there are often constraints of size and location and this basic planning process is important to ensure that you

Right Style is always difficult to define, but should always reflect the personality of the owner. This terrace is a cool, lush and relaxed refuge that relies on the careful use of natural materials and impeccable planting for its success.

do not make any expensive mistakes. At the start of all planning work you should assess what space you have and then plan into it everything you might need (how to carry out a structural and dimensional survey is covered on pages 52–58). Preparing a detailed plan will enable you to plot accurately both the dimensions of the area and all the factors that act upon it, including its orientation to the sun, good and poor views, prevailing winds, changes of level, access points, surrounding walls or roofs, available services, and existing floor coverings or other structures. Together these factors will determine not only just how the space is laid out but also the style of the garden.

One great advantage of preparing a design is that nothing is cast in stone. You can change your mind as often as you like, roughing out different ideas, trying different permutations and firming things up in order to progress towards a garden that is uniquely suitable to you and your needs. In other words, the first scheme you prepare should certainly not be the last; it is worth taking the time to rough out ideas as there may be different, but equally acceptable, solutions to any specific design problem.

What does the rest of the family want?

Bear in mind that as the garden is to be used by several people or a family, it is important to also listen to the other users' ideas. Elitist design that ignores the real function of a garden is usually sterile, so be open to suggestions.

Preparing the design

Initially, you should just rough out what you want to place where, whether it be sitting space, a dining or play area or features such as raised beds or water. At this stage it is immaterial whether the

PLANNING THE SITE

The finished garden scheme is drawn out to scale, taking into account the information gathered earlier.

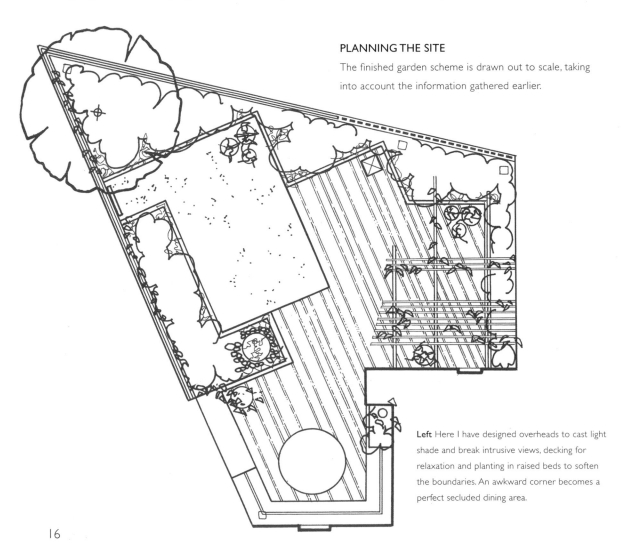

Left Here I have designed overheads to cast light shade and break intrusive views, decking for relaxation and planting in raised beds to soften the boundaries. An awkward corner becomes a perfect secluded dining area.

size of the area is large or small or at roof or ground level, although a small space will inevitably need to be thought about in simpler terms to avoid it looking crowded.

The importance of preparing a scale drawing of the area is clear: it allows you to see the exact proportions of everything and the space available for the various features. Make plenty of copies of the plan: this allows you to try different permutations, shifting the components about and seeing how they relate to each other. Some people make a simple model as this allows them to see the composition in three dimensions rather than two. Alternatively, if you want to see how things work out at full size, the area itself can be pegged or marked out with the shapes and the space simply divided with makeshift screens.

These techniques will allow you to visualize different ideas without actually undertaking any construction work. When you eventually arrive at a final layout you can prepare the design itself by filling in the detail, choosing materials and working out the pattern that best suits the shape of the area and is appropriate to the adjoining building or surroundings.

The design can then either act as the basis for a do-it-yourself project, be passed to one or more contractors for detailed quotations or act as your briefing document for a garden designer or architect. Whatever the final outcome, the exercise will allow you to gain a far better idea of how you will use the areas involved and be the basis for a fuller enjoyment of the finished garden.

Style considerations

A garden that lacks sympathy with the building it adjoins and with its environs rarely looks or works at its best. Good architects and designers create spaces that respect and are compatible with their surroundings. A problem often arises with the popularity of a style, whether it be 'cottage', 'formal', 'Japanese' or something else. While any of these may be appropriate, and indeed superb in the right setting, they can simply be a fashionable cliché in others. The incongruity of a traditional cottage garden adjoining a crisp contemporary façade would diminish the inherent charms of both house and garden. As a rule, a clean, modern composition will suit a newer building while something more traditional might be successful adjoining a period house.

Linking inside and out

Many people see the spaces inside and outside as two separate entities, when they should be linked as strongly as possible and carry on to use their immediate surroundings and more distant views to their advantage. In this way you can achieve a progression from inside to outside and beyond, drawing together materials, colour schemes, furnishing and plants into an all-embracing whole that will help to create a feeling of space at any point in the overall composition.

Doorways

Where doors give immediate access, the transition from inside to outside is often straightforward, but it can prove more difficult in the case of a roof garden, where narrow stairs or even ladders are more usual. Such a break in continuity makes it difficult to create a natural linkage and it

Above left The best rooms, whether inside or out, invariably have fine views, and this should work both from the house into the garden and from the garden towards the building.

Left Creating a successful living space has much to do with choice of compatible materials. Here floor tiles are complemented by the warm-coloured walls, vernacular buttress and traditional coping.

Above The organization of a formal space need not necessarily be rigid and in this case the centrally framed table is perfectly offset by the clipped balls that in turn frame the view.

may be worth considering how to improve it, both to facilitate access (especially while the building work is going on) and to allow a smooth visual transition from inside to out.

Having said that, there is an obvious and pleasing drama in climbing a well-constructed spiral staircase from one space to another, especially if this linkage is also themed with plants and compatible colour. Try to make the most of your

Above Steps are always an invitation to enter a garden. Here they have been further enhanced by simple planting in pots and by the plant-clad wall, which has been colour-washed to tone in with the doors and shutters.

Above These broad and generous steps are perfectly complemented by the introduction of the rounded domes of foliage that soften what might otherwise be an austere modern composition of shades of grey and geometric forms.

LINKING INSIDE AND OUT

The linkage between a house and the immediate area outside should be as seamless as possible.

Above The continuation of the decking patterns and planting either side of the glass doors smooths the transition from one to the other.

access points, using them to tie your interior and exterior spaces together.

The ideal is to have large areas of glass dividing inside and out, creating minimal visual disruption. Pots and containers can be grouped on both sides, disguising the dividing line.

Flooring

Just as doorways and how they are treated are important, so too are flooring materials. Here is an obvious opportunity to link inside and out by allowing similar surfaces to run together. A timber floor inside can be a cue for decking outside; tiles can relate to tiles; certain kinds of paving can look superb on both sides of a glass divide; while even more complex designs might involve the flow of water, lighting and planting from interior to exterior living space. When working out a pattern, try to make sure that modules, shapes or lines run continuously from inside to out. Paving or boards should be aligned rather than offset, with minimal visual disruption (*see above right*).

Ceilings and overheads

Although we tend to look down more often than up, the ceiling can be used as an additional link. The lines of a timber ceiling or beams can be echoed by overheads outside. This effect could be enhanced by installing subtle lighting strips on either side of the divide.

Shade and tone

Colour, often undervalued and underused, is another theme that can draw house and garden together. If you have a decorative scheme inside and an adjoining wall outside, why not paint the outside wall in the same shade? Awnings offer an ideal opportunity to pick up a fabric pattern from an interior scheme. Incidental features such as pots, containers and furniture can be chosen in much the same way, with a coherent and simple theme in mind.

Above Such a complicated, but beautifully detailed floor pattern, needs perfectly conceived geometry, immaculate construction and just the right setting to look at its best.

Below Overhead beams can provide the perfect link between inside and out, casting dappled shade, blocking a view from neighbouring windows and providing a frame for climbing plants.

Dividing the space

Roof gardens, balconies and raised terraces are generally far smaller than entire gardens at ground level. This means that they can be thought about and planned in much the same way as rooms inside the house and many elements can be addressed using the same techniques. Unlike their larger counterparts at ground level, roof gardens, balconies and raised terraces can be compared even further with rooms by the simple fact that they have floors, are partially or completely walled and may well have a ceiling in the form of overheads, beams or a canopy. Few people would think of simply scattering furniture, carpets, paintings or other features at random around a room inside the home, yet this so often occurs with furniture, ornaments, beds and pots outside. While we are conditioned to think about planning and allocating space in living areas, bedrooms and kitchens, I feel it is a great pity that those same perfectly valid rules are seldom applied to gardens.

Above left The subtle division of space is one of a garden designer's most valuable tools, providing the vital ingredients of tension, mystery and surprise. Just what those divisions are, and where they are positioned, will depend upon the individual setting.

Left Dividers need not be permanent structures, and moveable objects such as pots and furniture can effectively guide you through a space and create separate areas or rooms.

Above Dividing walls and an arch smothered with climbing roses invite you up the steps and into the partially hidden, more distant garden. The view is terminated by the central urn and there is a delightful transition between sunlight and shade.

What goes where?

The initial job, before choosing materials or creating a pattern, is to allocate space and to position the garden elements. This can be carried out roughly on copies of a scale drawing of the area. Look at your survey and identify the basic constraints and advantages of the site. What is the prevailing wind direction and does the wind need breaking or filtering in some way? Where does the sun track throughout the day and which are the shady areas? Your answers may suggest specific areas suitable for sitting, dining and entertaining. Just where are the good or poor views? They may need emphasis or they may need to be screened. Are you overlooked by a neighbour's window? A carefully positioned small tree in a container or the addition of overhead beams could improve your privacy. Are there any changes in level and,

if so, are they dramatic enough to necessitate steps or a ramp? Changes in level could perhaps be emphasized by a water feature, raised bed or carefully positioned focal point. Where are the doors and windows? You could use the former as the starting point for a main garden axis, and position a special feature within view of the latter to provide year-round interest from indoors.

Practical points

Most gardens have to serve practical functions as well as contain purely decorative elements: roofs and balconies are no different from their cousins on the ground in this respect. There is something immensely satisfying and visually pleasing about a string of brightly coloured washing, for example, which shows that your home belongs to real people rather than in a glossy magazine. Many a roof garden would benefit from a compost bin for trimmings and leaves (the resultant product would provide good plant nutrition), or there may be room for play equipment, a sand box or a well-designed storage area for toys.

On the plan, these features can be shown in an approximate position; there is little need for detailed design at this stage. The important thing is to position the various elements of the garden reasonably accurately.

Tension, mystery and surprise

These three elements are the key to creating a worthwhile garden design regardless of scale, whether it is a rolling landscape or the smallest balcony. Any space that can be seen at a single glance is far less interesting than one divided into different areas that can be discovered as you move through it. Obviously, in a small area there is less space available to create a number of different divisions, but a simple screen, a low planter or bench can still act as a divider on a roof garden or balcony and create greater interest.

If you have enough room, it can be delightful to allocate different purposes to different areas: a dining space, a play corner or an area for sitting, entertaining or barbecuing. If these areas are linked to their counterparts indoors, the whole design will be more coherent visually.

When each space has its own theme or purpose, the visitor tends to remain for a given length of time in each area, making the garden feel larger than its true size.

Screens

The way in which you divide the area will be determined by the surroundings; for example, high dividers or screens may be necessary in order to keep a particular area private, but low ones will be sufficient to create 'rooms'. Screens can be constructed to above eye-level and smothered with planting, or some areas can be defined by built-in seating at a lower level. Higher planting could involve trees and shrubs, while arches and overheads can all play a part. A combination of these features might be used, one linking with

Left Screens can be one of the most effective dividers, providing an excellent windbreak and ideal frame for climbing plants. Such a complex design benefits from the tempering effect of foliage.

Above As a general rule too many styles and materials make a garden look too 'busy', but here the design of the various screens and fences becomes all the more effective by echoing that of the surrounding architecture.

CREATING TENSION AND MYSTERY

The positioning of gaps in a screen is of great importance, as it can dictate how people walk through the space.

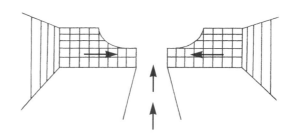

Above A narrow opening between two wings of trellis, hedging or other dividing material inevitably creates a feeling of tension and surprise for anyone walking through.

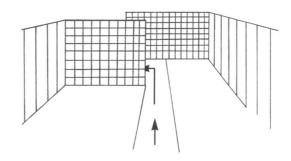

Above Where a path disappears from view there is always that question of mystery: just what does lie around the corner?

another and creating an overall subdivision of space at different points of the composition.

Dividers need not be above eye-level to be effective. Because your line of sight is lower when you are seated, even if you can see over a screen, it still defines spaces, giving it its own character.

Where you position the gaps in screens is important. Tension is created and increased as

Left Focal points always need careful positioning as they are purposeful eye-catchers. Remember that strong colour not only provides added vibrancy but brings a focal point towards you.

Below Too much white in a garden can lead to glare, but here it is tempered by the pastel furniture, planting and medium height raised bed that softens the higher wall.

you move towards an arch or a gap in a screen; as you move between the wings it is at its greatest, but releases with a surprise as you enter the new 'room' beyond to be greeted with a quite different theme or view. Mystery – just what lies beyond a wing of planting or a screen – is perhaps the most delightful element of garden design (*see p.25*).

Even on a balcony, particularly a long one, a short screen or subdivision can make the overall shape more attractive and manageable. Such dividers could be staggered along the balcony so that you zig-zag through the area (*see opposite page, above right*). This is a favourite trick of garden designers as it makes you walk slightly farther, thereby increasing the sense of space.

Focal points

Features such as water, statuary and urns can be used to draw the eye and form important focal points in the overall composition. Think about them in some detail when you are preparing the main design as they can provide directional emphasis, leading the eye across a roof. They can also be the focus of a vista on a long balcony or provide the sight and sound of water on a split-level terrace. Although some features may be occasionally moved or adjusted, many will form permanent or semi-permanent parts of the design. However, as the punctuation marks of the garden, they should always be used sparingly.

If you are concerned about the weight of an ornamental feature, return to your initial survey, check which parts of the roof or balcony are strong enough, and position the item accordingly. The best areas will normally be around the perimeter, or where a load-bearing member provides strength beneath the surface.

Right Steps will naturally lead the eye upward, and if the view can be terminated in some way then drama ensues. This fine urn gains greater importance by being placed on a plinth at the top of the flight of steps, to which your eye is led by the darker stripe of the brick path. The walls are simply constructed from well laid, pointed concrete blocks that provide a no-nonsense foil to the planting that tumbles over the edges.

Pattern and shape

Gardens come in all shapes and sizes and the patterns in which the various elements of the different areas are laid out have an enormous impact on how the space works in both visual and practical terms.

An obvious parallel can be drawn between how decorative effects are used indoors and how they are used on roof gardens, balconies and terraces. For example, indoors, wallpaper with a large, bold pattern tends to emphasize a surface, drawing the eye towards it and making the room feel smaller. On the other hand, a delicate, small-scale pattern, or a sponged or rag-rolled finish, tends to create a feeling of greater space. The same principle works in the garden, where a fence or screen of wide boards will seem closer than a fence or screen of narrow slats or a light trellis. The way in which you choose and use plants follows the same general rule: large, bold leaves will draw the boundary in, fine feathery shapes will push it out. The elements of your garden can be selected and positioned in order to manipulate the space visually.

Overheads

Heavy, large-section overheads seem to compress vertical space, while narrower and lighter timbers have an airy feel and are thus less oppressive. The same principle applies to the shadows that they cast onto the floor: thin, light shadow patterns will break the visual weight of a large expanse of paving as does sunlight that is filtered through the small-scale foliage of a tree such as silver birch or mountain ash.

Flooring

As well as the surface patterns and textures you choose, the way in which you lay or arrange the flooring materials has a bearing on apparent space, as strong lines tend to draw the eye in a particular direction. Long boards, laid so that they run away from a doorway or main viewing point, will tend to accelerate the view towards an imaginary vanishing point. As your eye travels

MOVEMENT THROUGH NARROW SPACES

In a long, narrow garden, entered at one end, dividers can be positioned to make the area seem shorter and wider.

Above A floor of just a single paving material can become bland or a little too 'heavy', but when teamed with another contrasting surface the end result is far more interesting. Keep things simple though, as three materials would distract from the simplicity.

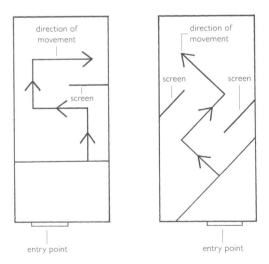

Above By taking a path up and across a garden, between screens or wings of planting, you introduce not only tension and surprise, but also force people to cover a greater distance.

Right Design continuity in this long, narrow balcony is achieved by matching the tone of the floor tiles with that of the old brick walls. Furniture also helps to dovode the area, although natural timber is far easier on the eye than painted furniture.

Above Any garden built up from strong flowing curves has a natural feeling of space and movement. In a reduced area, small modules on the floor, such as cobbles, can be laid up to the hedge and pool without cutting, and have no lines to distract from the main curves.

Left A rich paving pattern has much the same effect as a well-worked carpet inside the home, bringing scale and intimacy. Herringbone brick paving is both mellow and traditional.

along the uninterrupted shadow lines or joints, you tend to miss much of the detail along the way and the area might appear smaller. If, conversely, boards are laid across a view they will tend to slow the eye down and it will take longer to cross the area, so the space seems larger.

Broad deck boards will produce a more static visual effect than narrow ones will. I often vary board widths on a deck as I find that this can set up fascinating rhythms.

The scale of the paving or decking used also affects the perceived space. Small modules look and feel lighter than large ones, so the former should be used in an area where you want to maximize a feeling of space.

Most paving and hard landscape materials – boards, bricks, railway sleepers (ties), granite setts, wooden blocks or cobbles – can be laid to give directional emphasis, allowing you to manipulate the spaces at your disposal, and decking patterns can be arranged to lead the eye and help to disguise or emphasize the shapes around them.

Materials

You should also consider the number of different materials that are used in the garden. Remember that the old maxim 'less is more' makes good sense, particularly in small spaces where a busy pattern becomes obvious and obtrusive.

Using just a single boundary detail and one paving type will help to maximize the apparent space in a small area. In a larger garden there may be scope to increase the number of materials, but this should be done carefully, respecting the overall division of space, so that different treatments are found in the different 'rooms'.

This simplicity should run though all the main garden elements. When choosing additional furniture, pots, containers and statuary, try also to work to an overall theme in much the same way that you would when furnishing a room. Shape and pattern are infinitely variable tools, providing space and movement that can transform your outside living space.

Mind the gap

One further point is of great importance to the creation of any pattern. When drawing a scheme on paper, do not look in isolation at the shapes you are creating, but also consider the spaces that are left over; if you are not careful with the way you plant them or relate them to one another, the result can look uncomfortable or a mess of unrelated shapes. You should therefore think about the pattern of the area as a unified whole and not just about its most obvious parts.

Above Granite setts, or other small scale paving materials, can be laid to complex patterns, but attention to detail in both design and construction is absolutely vital because it will be very obvious if anything is misaligned.

Above Timber decking is an easily worked surface and can be cut and laid to an infinite number of patterns. As with any other paved surface, the pattern of the flooring should be kept as simple as possible; it will then add to the interest of the space rather than overwhelming the rest of it.

Manipulating shapes

The next thing for you to consider is the shape of the area with which you are dealing and how it can be used and manipulated visually to achieve its maximum potential. A designer's 'tricks of the trade' are simple devices that can be learned by anyone. The first rule is that the shape of a space generates movement in a particular direction: a long narrow garden, whether at ground level or in the air, will lead the eye down its space; a dog-legged area encourages you around the corner, and a square garden is static, at least within the confines of its boundaries.

Solutions for shapes

The key to most successful designs lies in being able to manipulate how people look at the area in question in order to get the best from it. You can use all of the elements of your garden to do this: the plants, dividers, focal points, features and floor patterns.

Long, narrow areas

In a long narrow space, laying a deck or paving pattern down its length and emphasizing the pattern by placing pots or seating down either side will make the garden look even longer and narrower as the eye rushes from one end to the other. In this case, the garden should be subdivided into a number of different areas, each with a different theme or purpose. If the spaces are large enough, this idea could be reinforced by giving each area different floor and boundary treatments. Such an approach will conceal the overall shape of the garden and superimpose a new and more visually manageable pattern.

The effect can be further enhanced through the way in which people are compelled to move through the space. If you are allowed to walk in a straight line from 'room' to 'room', the journey is a relatively fast one. If, however, the entry and exit points are staggered, it will take longer to negotiate the garden and the distance covered will be greater, thus increasing the apparent size of the garden.

The best design solutions to a garden of this shape will differ slightly depending on the exact position of the main view across and entry point

Above left Shapes, whether in two or three dimensions, have a positive role in how we perceive space. Here a contrasting paving leads the eye positively down and across the area.

Left Humour is an integral part of any design medium and mock wind socks on a roof make the sculptural point perfectly. They also check the view, before it moves on to the cathedral dome.

Right When you enter a long narrow roof or balcony from one end, the view opens up in front of you. To prevent the eye running straight to the opposite end, the area will need subdividing with points of interest to create more manageable spaces.

Above This self-contained dining area is framed by planting set at different heights in containers to either side, thus helping to disguise the long, narrow shape of the overall area.

Above Boards, bricks or any other surface laid across, rather than down a space, will emphasize the width and help draw the area apart. This can be reinforced by planting to create additional side-to-side movement as you walk through the garden.

into the garden. If you enter at one end of the area the space will stretch away from you, whereas if you approach the garden from the side there will be a shorter distance between you and the opposite boundary and the space will lead you away to either side.

In the second instance, if a major focal point is positioned exactly opposite the entry point, it tends to draw the eye immediately and make the short dimension seem even shorter. In a garden with the main view across the short axis, you should put a focal point to either side (*see below right*), at the edge of your vision, either from your viewpoint inside the house or from the main access into the garden. This will lead your eye away from the near point opposite toward the focal points that are farther away.

Angled areas

In a dog-leg garden, where the space either leads around the corner, or from area to area around a roof, there is obvious potential for floor, boundary and screening treatments to encourage you through the space. Flooring can be laid to echo a right-angled turn, so that your feet and eyes naturally follow the pattern. You will find that planting can be effective, with a sweep of vegetation that not only softens hard angles but leads you around the corner.

PLACING FOCAL POINTS

By using simple visual tricks, basic design rules can be used to manipulate space in any way that you wish.

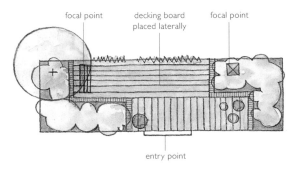

Above If you enter a long narrow space from the centre, focal points to either side will draw the eye away from the shorter dimension ahead. An additional way of softening the focal points is by the use of carefully-chosen plants.

The vertical space could be defined by overheads developed to form a pergola (as attractive on a roof as at ground level), provided that there is adequate space. Pergolas have enormous drawing power, containing the key design elements of tension, mystery and surprise.

The route that a pergola follows need not be simply in a straight line: it can pass through an angle or a series of angles, and is therefore an especially invaluable tool in reinforcing the basic pattern of the garden.

One of a pergola's functions is to engender expectancy: it creates tension as you enter at one end, with tantalizing views to either side as you move through it, and an enormous release of energy as you emerge from the far end. For this reason, it must have somewhere positive to go. A pergola is a device for movement and if a journey through it ends in anti-climax or, worse, at a bad view, then the feature is degraded.

Above Angularity in a design provides positive movement and, in the right setting, acts as a link with adjoining architecture. Minimal planting emphasizes rather than detracts from the overall pattern.

Below Diagonals, even though geometric, can offer a more gentle progression through an area. Here the underlying pattern has been emphasized by the raised beds and edging.

Square areas

Square gardens are the most difficult from the designer's point of view, as they lack any positive directional movement. There are a number of solutions to this problem. One is to employ a pattern that uses diagonals: a line that runs between opposite corners is longer than one going from side to side or top to bottom, so using a design that incorporates this principle makes the garden look larger than it is, and the eye is distracted from the underlying static shape (*see below*).

Many people avoid incorporating right-angles in the garden, fearing that it will become far too static and 'hard'. However, a series of overlapping rectangles, perhaps at different heights and using a variety of materials, softened and punctuated by planting, can form a fascinating backdrop that can be linked positively into the geometry and architecture of the immediate surroundings.

Curves have the potential to provide an enormous sense of movement but are often poorly conceived and fussy rather than vigorous. To avoid this, curves should be based on positive radii that are worked out on the drawing board.

CREATING MOVEMENT IN A SQUARE SPACE

The entire shape of this square area is negated by the strong diagonals of the decking and beds.

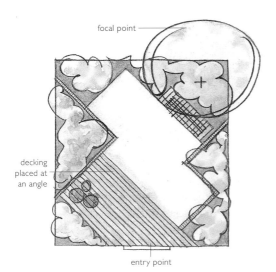

focal point

decking placed at an angle

entry point

Left Even in a comparatively small area you can create both space and movement by turning through an area. Decking is ideally suited to a change in direction and the eye is naturally led to the focal point formed by the urn.

Above Modern design is often based on a series of overlapping rectangles, based on an underlying grid. The resulting shapes can be given over to a combination of paving, planting, furniture and other incidental features.

Above A complex pattern such as this concentrates interest within the space, detracting from the surroundings. If you are faced with uncompromising boundaries or views which you wish to ignore, this can be a useful design tool.

Shapes based on a circle or a series of curves can form an effective disguise for a rectangular area. Most types of surfacing can be laid in a circular pattern and although it is difficult to shape raised beds to an exact curve it is not impossible, particularly if the roof is strong enough to carry brickwork. There is potential for manipulating such materials as artificial turf, gravels, stone chippings and glass beads, and circular shapes can also be echoed in arrangements of pots and containers.

Using your surroundings

On a roof garden you may have the wonderful addition of a fine view. This can be invaluable in drawing the eye out into a roof- or cityscape, which in turn lends itself to your composition. As such views are an integral part of the garden, you should encourage them in.

Framing the view

There is another design trick involved in the way that you go about framing the view, and it brings us back to the adage that 'less is more'. When I visit a garden with a fine view, either at ground level or on the roof, the clients often suggest that I should leave it exactly as it is. However, I think of a view in the same way as I would a good watercolour painting. This may look beautiful on a sheet of paper, but if you place it behind a mount it becomes sharper; if you select the perfect frame, although it is the same painting, your perception of it is immediately enhanced. In the garden we should think of framing the view, or several views, in some way.

A wide open view is often too expansive: too much to take in at one glance and therefore too dominant and all-encompassing. To 'improve' it you could, for example, blot out a less attractive area, perhaps bring in planting to one side and a screen to the other side, and finally use an overhead to define the upper limit.

Left Many fine views can be overpowering, but by partially hiding or framing them — perhaps with a wall and overhanging planting — you can make them even more effective.

There are infinite permutations, but the principle remains the same: if you heighten the drama and focus the view, you will have a powerful tool at your disposal. In this way you can 'borrow' a distant scene by drawing it into your space and keeping attention away from closer elements. You can also use the floor and boundary treatments as part of the focusing equipment. A board pattern can draw the eye towards a vista.

Above Containing a roof garden or balcony with planting not only acts as a safety measure but also softens the inevitable hard edges created by walls, fences and railings. In addition, the plants will bring colour, texture and interest to the composition.

Right A delicate, yet strong, boundary allows easy access to a view, framed by bars, that includes the island of Alcatraz. *Kniphofia* emphasizes the strong verticality of the pattern, its strong colour momentarily holding the eye within the garden.

Terraces: a wider choice

While the choice of materials is necessarily limited on balconies and roof gardens, because of space and weight constraints, a much wider selection is available for use on terraces at ground level. Suitable materials include stone of all kinds, pre-cast concrete, brushed aggregates, timber in the form of decking or railway sleepers (ties), gravel, wood or stone chippings, bricks and blocks. Avoid including a number of different surfaces: the point is to be selective, and while a single surface can seem bland or 'heavy', more than two may look too busy. Because one surfaces invariably lightens and balances another, two contrasting surfaces usually work well together.

Above left Containers not only offer endless opportunities for planting, they are also an integral part of the design, providing both division and focal points.

Left With their subtle shadow patterns, planting and surrounding screens can combine with decking and containers to form the basis for an ideal outdoor living space.

Above Steps should always be as broad and generous as possible, providing a gentle transition between different levels and tying terraced areas together in a positive way.

Right Pots are an ideal way of providing instant colour. In the form of bulbs and annual planting they can be changed from season to season and moved about the terrace at will, thereby altering the visual character of an area.

Materials, patterns and forms

Generally, areas near a building should be laid out in a crisp, 'architectural' manner in material that forms a natural link with the building. In this way a brick or stone house might suggest the use of brick or stone in the immediate terrace, while brushed aggregate or decking might be suitable near a contemporary concrete or timber building.

Paving

The way in which different paving materials are combined will depend to an extent on the basic pattern of the garden. This should be an extension of the building lines in order to help to link the house and garden together. You might have courses, or a grid, of brickwork that runs out from the building and is infilled with a contrasting material such as pre-cast concrete slabs, stone or brushed aggregate. Part of the pattern could consist of raised beds, planting at ground level, water, steps and built-in seating, all of which can be tied into the main modular pattern.

Many people like broken or 'crazy' paving, but the conflicting lines may clash with a cleaner

Left Colour need not be restricted to planting alone, although planting can help to tone down a vibrant floor that might otherwise dominate the situation.

Below Strength of purpose in architecture can often be successfully offset by equally strong terracing around the house, the one linking positively into the other.

façade. The answer here is to contain the paving within a contrasting grid or pattern that will help to stabilize the inherently busy surface.

Curves

Curves set close to a building need to be handled carefully if they are not to feel uncomfortable, but they can look superb if they are used in a positive way, with strong radii that link back to the underlying grid or building.

Terraces farther away from the house can be much more fluid in outline, echoing the possible informality of the garden at this point. Small modules or fluid materials, such as brick, granite setts, cobbles, wood chips or gravel, will conform to a curve without needing to be cut. Larger modules such as concrete slabs may need to be cut and this can be an expensive, time-consuming, noisy and difficult operation.

Overheads

In terraces as well as roof gardens, overheads and beams can form a particularly strong and attractive link with the building, extending the architectural lines into the garden and landscape.

Above Water in the natural landscape rarely runs in straight lines, but a curving pool, which in this case doubles as an occasional seat, has a natural feel.

Below One of the great advantages of small pots and containers in the garden is that they can easily be moved about to where they are needed at a particular time. Here they are disguising the hard right-angle formed by the larger planter.

Balconies

Balconies are in effect small roof gardens, and the same design guidelines apply, especially those concerning long, narrow spaces (see pages 33–34), as most balconies tend towards this shape. Their relatively small size means that designs should be kept as simple as possible: anything too 'busy' will be overpowering. The transition from inside to outside is usually uncomplicated, with no great changes in level, and so they can be linked easily through the use of pattern, materials, shade and tone. Balconies make ideal outdoor rooms.

Materials and features

Because the load-bearing potential of a balcony is limited, keep everything as light as possible and avoid grouping heavy items in one place. Also, because the space available is small, you will not have room for large numbers of pots and should keep special features to a minimum.

Flooring

Floors are usually straightforward, as they are already paved. It may be possible to resurface the floor, provided that the structure will accept the extra weight, and here there may be an opportunity to use a similar surface to that inside, perhaps sawn stone or tiles of some kind.

Screens and planters

One of the great charms of a balcony is the feeling of almost floating in space, but shelter and privacy are often at a premium. Screens, set to one or both sides can often help, with the style, shade and tone of these designed to reflect the

Above left Hanging gardens, such as these baskets, will naturally clothe vertical space. However, the containers will need to be securely fixed and regularly fed and watered to ensure that the plants are kept as healthy as possible.

Left Virtually every inch of space on this railing has been smothered with pot-grown plants. Although this arrangement will entail a high degree of maintenance, the end result will be worth the effort.

Above A decked balcony can dramatically increase your amount of living space. Not only will the railings act as a host to climbing plants but such a space is wonderfully light and airy.

building. Planters can often be built as a unit with the screens and, if set at either end of the balcony, they allow maximum space in the central areas for sitting and relaxation.

On a balcony that is both long enough to span the entire face of a building and accessible from a number of points, there may be an opportunity to subdivide the space with wings of trellis or screens. These can provide the key design elements of tension, mystery and surprise as you move through the space.

Awnings

Awnings on balconies, as on the roof, can cast soft swathes of shade but as wind may be a problem, they should be retractable. Fabric awnings can be used to extend the interior decorative scheme to the outside.

Using vertical space

On balconies, with their relatively limited floor space, explore the possibilities of hanging pots or planters on the walls, internal screens or railings. Planters could be built as an integral part of the railings, possibly with seating or other features. As with anything above ground level, all pots and planters must be securely fixed.

Above This simple paint scheme has the effect of unifying house and balcony, while the overheads set up fascinating patterns that will change throughout the day.

Above Most boundary structures, particularly those found on balconies, provide the ideal framework for all kinds of plants, especially climbers. The plants in turn help to reinforce the line of the underlying architecture.

Left The idea that a design should be kept as simple as possible applies equally to traditional or modern designs. In this case, the centrally placed pots add immeasurably to a classical composition.

Colour

While colour is usually understood and used with great sensitivity inside the home, the rules for using it are often forgotten or ignored outside. There are, obviously, a number of ways in which tone and shade can be used on most items in the garden, including the structural elements, the decoration, the furniture, the accessories, and the foliage and flowers of the plants. The whole scheme should be borne in mind when you are planning, so that a single element does not spoil the appearance of the whole garden by looking awkard or out of place.

Using shade and tone

Colour can be a wonderful tool for linking the interior and exterior spaces. An important consideration when using colour, however, is the effect of sunlight or naturally brighter light in washing out tones. A pale tone inside would be far less obvious in the garden. It may be necessary if you want to match tones inside and out, to slightly darken or strengthen the exterior shade.

White should be used carefully in the garden, particularly on a roof where it can glare without mercy. It would be far better to use a pale cream, which will appear softer and be more comfortable on the eye. This rule also applies when using colour on furniture and other features.

Visual effects with colour

Hot colours such as red or yellow draw the eye and tend to foreshorten space. Cool pastels do just the opposite. An orange parasol or tablecloth at the end of a roof or terrace will immediately draw your attention, causing the eye to ignore everything in between. A pastel scheme, however, will diffuse the light, be less obtrusive and increase the apparent space. Use bright hues with care, preferably close to the house or as part of a main viewpoint or point of emphasis.

Of course, these rules also apply to wherever you are placing plants in any garden, whether at ground level or on a roof or balcony. A multi-coloured bed of bulbs or bedding plants might look better near a plain wall than it would close to a brightly coloured wall.

Above left Colour can bring both drama and harmony to virtually any design situation. A patterned floor, shown here with both strong diagonals and apparent verticals, works in much the same way as do carpets inside the house.

Left A simple floor is undemonstrative and easy on the eye, allowing the visual action to take place elsewhere. This is a wonderfully quiet space, brought to life by those people using it.

Right Colour can be cool, hot, fun or simply asking for attention. Although this composition certainly belongs to the asking for attention group, it works well with the carefully chosen combination of planting in pots.

Structure

Planning…

The layout of your garden will depend to a large extent upon the underlying structure. Rather than regarding this as a constraint, you should look on it as a starting point and an opportunity to exercise your ingenuity to the full.

…and building

Once the layout is finalized the creative work itself can start. Whether you have designed your own garden, or it is being built for you by someone else, this is a fascinating process. The structure is the skeleton on which you will hang the plants at the next stage.

Left Where space is limited it is a real bonus if one major feature can double as another. A seat and a raised bed are not only the perfect combination, but also create an interesting visual feature.

51

Surveys

There are two types of survey: structural and dimensional. The primary function of a structural survey is to find out the load-bearing capacity of the underlying structures. A structural survey by an architect or structural engineer will show how your boundaries – walls, fences or railings – are fixed, what condition they are in and what you must do to meet local building, planning and safety codes. The survey may include a structural drawing detailing the areas involved and specifying the weight tolerances of each area. Avoid anyone who refuses to give you a detailed written report or employs such methods as jumping up and down on a roof to test its strength.

Elements of the survey

Safety is the first consideration when planning any kind of space above ground level. The purpose of the structural survey is to ensure that everything is as safe as possible.

Cost

Cost is always a major factor when taking on any project and a roof garden, area for area, will be more expensive than a garden at ground level. Budgets should therefore be set accordingly and, if necessary, phased over a period of time. Making an accurate estimate is so important that you may wish to seek professional advice.

Barriers

As well as checking the condition of any existing fences, walls and railings, it is imperative to determine how any new barriers can be built or fixed, taking into account the extra weight or leverage that will be imposed on them by the wind.

Load-bearing areas

These are generally around the edge and above internal supporting walls which can transfer the weight down to the ground. These are the areas where you will have to position such heavier items as planters, seating, groups of pots, dividers and water features: placing these on weaker areas of the roof may result in disaster.

The result of the survey

If the proposed surface looks unlikely to accommodate your plans, it may not mean that all is lost

Above left Water is a delightful element in any garden. Where there are weight constraints, small features, such as this spout tucked behind shiny Kiwi leaves, are an ideal compromise.

Left As a general rule the strongest parts of a roof are around the perimeter, where the main load-bearing structure connects with the walls. This is usually where the heavier elements can be positioned.

Right At ground level a sloping site can be terraced into a series of level platforms, each one of which can be paved or planted in a different way. Here, the verticality is emphasized even further by the overheads on the top terrace.

Above Structural elements such as walls, overhead canopies or pergolas can provide the perfect vehicle for a range of climbers, softening the outline of each plant.

or that it will be impossible to create a living space there. Where direct loadings onto the roof are inappropriate it may be viable to construct a surface that is completely or partly suspended on a separate floor, with the weight carried onto surrounding walls or other sufficiently strong areas.

If the survey is positive then you can start to think about just how you will plan your garden, although make sure that you follow advice on the load-bearing potential of specific areas.

The dimensional survey

A scale drawing prepared by a professional will inevitably save you a good deal of time, but doing a dimensional survey for yourself is not only a relatively straightforward and logical job but also a vital stage in the preparation of a design drawn to scale. You will need to measure the area and check a number of other factors that will determine the way in which you use the space.

Again, don't just draw a sketch on the back of an envelope and ignore anyone who suggests that such an approach is acceptable. If you intend to employ a professional, always ask to see examples or photographs of their work before you commission anything. If a professional comes with a recommendation, so much the better.

Tools

To undertake a dimensional survey, you will need certain tools. These include a 30m (100ft) tape measure, a shorter steel tape for measuring short runs or awkward details, a brick or other heavy object to anchor the tape in place as you unreel it, a clip-board and paper, a sharp pencil and a magnetic compass. If the project area is unsafe, perhaps without railings or walls, you may prefer to enlist the services of a professional surveyor.

What to include on the rough drawing

Start by sketching the area of the roof or balcony, noting the positions of doors, windows and projecting walls as well as any drains or drainage channels. Check whether there are any steps or changes in level and mark these as well as any overhanging structures that could affect headroom or planted areas below.

Access is a prime concern and while it may be fun occasionally to scale a ladder to the roof above, this cannot serve as a permanent solution. Remember too that materials for building works may have to come up through the house, so that a well-constructed stairway will make sense in terms of practicality and safety. When constructing the garden, it may be possible to haul materials up to the roof, but you not only need the correct tackle but it will have to be properly secured. A realistic appraisal of all access points to the area and the materials that it will be feasible to carry up through access points could make a big difference to the eventual cost of the project.

Nearly all roofs, even flat roofs, are built to a slope or 'fall' which is designed to carry rain water away, usually into drains or gullies. Check the direction of the fall, as it will almost certainly determine where the excess water from raised

beds will be directed and may even determine where the beds are sited. Nothing which might impede the flow of water must be placed over or in gullies. If water is allowed to stand on a roof it will eventually find its way through.

Services

There may well be existing taps or power points, which should be marked onto the plan since they represent important services that can be extended to other areas of the roof. Power and water are essential. They may be present on the roof before you start work but, if not, they must be installed. Power is needed for lighting and for features such as pool pumps, barbecues, automatic awnings or computerized irrigation systems. Water is the lifeline for planting, and as conditions can be harsh on a roof garden you will need easy access to it.

Both electricity and water should be installed by experts, although their positioning should be your decision. At this stage in the project your priority is ensuring that power is available.

Once you have completed the outline drawing you can start to take the measurements. This will involve setting out one or more base lines that

Above Large pots and containers can be very heavy, especially when full of wet soil. Here they are grouped around the edge of the roof, where they also help visually to soften the surrounding walls.

Below It is advisable that services, such as water and electricity, should be professionally installed. They should also be successfully concealed wherever they are installed on any roof, balcony or terrace. As an integral part of any scheme, lighting needs to be a subtle as well as valuable component.

MEASURING THE AREA

Whether undertaken by yourself or a professional, an accurate survey is vital to the planning of any space.

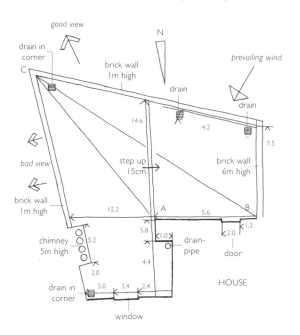

Above The survey plan should be drawn up in the garden to note down all the measurements taken and any other factors such as overhangs and wind direction that are likely to affect the finished scheme. Accuracy is all-important, as any discrepancies at this stage could lead to expensive mistakes later on.

MAKING AN ACCURATE PLAN

Triangulation is a simple exercise in geometry, used by surveyors in order to get an accurate fix on corners.

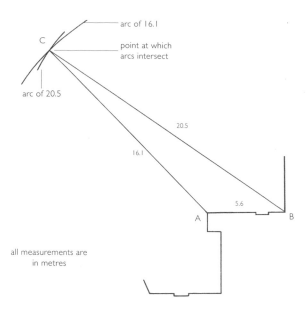

Above To position the third corner of a triangle, plot the two other corners and then, using a compass, draw an arc the correct length from each, i.e., 16.1m from A and 20.5m from B (*see detail above and plan above left*). Where the two arcs intersect is the position of C. Further corners can then be positioned using the same technique.

run along the faces of the building. Anchor the tape at one end of the run, reel it out in a straight line along the face of the building and continue to the end of the wall, across any open space, and fix at the opposite boundary. This is the first base line. Leave the tape on the ground and then take 'running' measurements along the line of the tape, taking in every salient point or feature – for instance, corners, pipes, steps, doors or drainage gullies – along the way. The tape can then be reeled in and re-positioned at right-angles to the position of the first base line, or elsewhere to set up a second base line running in another direction until the whole area is covered.

Roof gardens are quite often awkward in shape, with all kinds of nooks and crannies, which should all be carefully measured. The roof may also be out of square, as shown (*above left*). To fix the corners accurately you need to carry out the simple surveying technique known as triangula-

tion (*above right*). Any steps or sharp changes of level can also be noted and these drops are perfectly easily measured with the steel tape.

Once the basic measurements have been completed you can start to detail the rest of the area. Your surveyor may have indicated what the floor is made of, but if not, you should note it. It could be lightweight or conventional tiles of some kind, paving slabs, roofing felt, chippings, decking or artificial turf. Look at surrounding walls, screens or fences in a similar way, and as well as measuring exactly where the runs are and their height, note the materials they are constructed from.

Don't just survey within the confines of the area but look beyond where there may be good, or quite possibly unattractive, views. Indicate on your survey the exact direction of any such views. These may include a superb distant vista over the city, a neighbouring wall with windows which might compromise your privacy, or a wonderful roofscape that forms a geometric jumble of slates, tiles and chimneys. Chimneys might be an attractive addition to your landscape, but television aerials or satellite dishes will need to be shown on the survey so that they can be screened.

Overhanging roof structures can present particular problems in aerial gardens, as they can either create a 'rain shadow', which starves the area below it of moisture, or have the opposite effect, allowing water to pour onto a bed and create impossible growing conditions.

Another factor to take into consideration is the wind, which is usually stronger at roof height than at ground level. Wherever you live there is usually a prevailing wind that blows from a particular direction for most of the year. In a city, this direction may be modified by surrounding

Above Water is an infinitely variable medium, from grand pools at ground level to lightweight bowls and fountains on a roof. Here water spills from one level to another on a stone-clad terrace.

Below Barbecues and cooking areas should be carefully positioned in relation to the dining area and relevant services. Remember that any open fire is potentially dangerous on a roof.

roofs and buildings, but it will still come from a given point. However, those same buildings may funnel a wind, accelerating it, or creating buffeting as the air finds its way between various structures. Once you have established the direction of the prevailing wind, mark it on your survey, as this will determine how you site screens and organize the living spaces.

The final vital piece of information, and the one that will drive the whole scheme, is where the sun falls throughout the day. Make a note of this early in the morning, at midday and in the evening, drawing an arc on your survey so that you can see the sun's position at various times. Remember that the sun is lower in the winter, with longer shadows than on hot summer days. Note where surrounding walls or buildings cast shadows as this will determine the choice of planting and whether or not you sit in sun or shade at different times of the day. This survey should take you several days or more; it is sensible to take your time over the survey as design ideas often take time to formulate and the longer you spend looking at the space and surroundings, the more you will appreciate what they have to offer.

Above Gothic architecture in gardens is undergoing a revival at present. It is perfectly suited to heavy planting that can heighten the visual drama, such as this *Clematis* 'Prince Charles'. Make sure that any greenery can be moved away from walls for maintenance.

Making a scale drawing

Once you have completed the survey you are ready to transfer the information to a scale drawing. This will be the basis of your final design and allow you to plan the features, planting and furnishings in accordance with the limitations of the underlying structure. The plan will also be the basis of a total cost estimate.

As with the survey, the preparation of a scale drawing is a straightforward business, but one that confuses many people. Drawing something to scale is simply reducing in proportion all the dimensions of the object, in this case a garden, to a size that can be shown on a piece of paper. At its simplest, if you take a dinner plate that is 300mm (12in) across and draw it on a sheet of paper so that it appears to be 150mm (6in) across, then you have reduced the plate by a scale of 1:2. If you reduced it four times it would be a scale of 1:4, 20 times, 1:20, and so on.

There comes a point at which any further reduction results in an object on paper that is too small to be legible, so choose a scale that is small enough to fit on a sheet of paper but large enough to work on in some detail.

In the case of gardens this scale is usually 1:100 (10mm = 1m or ⅛in = 1ft), 1:50 (20mm = 1m or ¼in = 1 ft), or if the area is relatively small, 1:20 or 1:25. In other words, if you work at a scale of 1:50 the garden will be fifty times as large as on the drawing, but everything will be in proportion.

The easiest way to transfer the measurements you took on your survey to create a scale drawing is to work on a piece of tracing paper over a grid or sheet of graph paper. The latter may be a metric or an imperial grid, squared off in centimetres or inches. Use a grid appropriate to the method you chose for measuring the garden.

Before you start the drawing, make sure that the finished plan will fit on your piece of paper by checking the overall measurements and converting them to scale. If the garden measures 10m x 10m and you draw to a scale of 1:50, the finished drawing will measure 200mm x 200mm. If the garden measures 40ft x 20ft, then by using a scale of ¼in to 1ft the drawing will be 10in x 5in.

Tape the graph paper down on a board or table and then tape a sheet of tracing paper over it. Starting from near one of the corners, number the grid in metres or inches up and across the sheet. Now take your survey drawing and transfer the measurements you took onto your scale drawing. So, for instance, looking along that first base line running across one side of the roof, the door was 1m in from the boundary, the end wall 4.5m, the step 7m and the far boundary 12m. Now transfer the measurements that ran in the other direction, mark in the positions of the drains, angles of walls, taps and such things as a skylight set in the ceiling of the room below. Now mark the positions of the good and poor views, the direction of the prevailing wind, and of course the north point. Soon you will have a complete drawing, showing the roof area in miniature, but to scale. This will be the valuable basis for any design. Do not draw directly onto this survey

A SCALED SURVEY DRAWING

Smaller and especially awkward areas, such as corners, may need to be looked at in more detail.

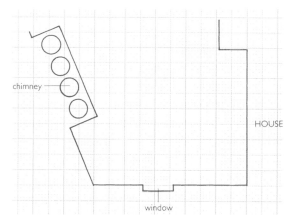

Above Because of their nature, many roof gardens have all sorts of awkward corners caused by such features as chimney stacks, that have to be measured and subsequently drawn up to scale. Such spaces can often form a self-contained area that could be given over to built-in seating, a dining area, raised beds or overhead beams, smothered with climbers.

Above At ground level, load bearing is far less of a problem than on a roof or a balcony. These heavy overheads and columns have been placed effectively in a classical setting to provide a break between the sitting area and the rest of the garden.

drawing but take plenty of photocopies and file the original away for safekeeping.

Like any garden or any room inside the house, the area will be made up of a number of separate elements: essentially the boundaries, floor and ceiling. While the first will be built to provide safety, screening from intrusive views and shelter, the second will provide a durable and decorative surface for all kinds of activities. Ceilings are less often considered, but they are an essential element of any roof area project. Normally the 'ceiling' takes the form of awnings or overheads that provide shelter and shade from the, sometimes intense, heat of the sun. The spreading canopies of trees planted in suitably large containers can also help to define the upper limit of an area.

Balconies

Balconies are usually smaller than roof gardens, and the main structural difference between them is that balconies are usually suspended out from the side of a building. This means that the weight constraints will be even more strict than they are for roof gardens, and that you should therefore avoid grouping heavy items in one place where they might put a disproportionate stress on one part of the supporting structure.

Adding a new balcony

It may even be possible, in certain circumstances, to build a completely new balcony without making major structural alterations to the exterior of your home. This is of course a highly technical job and would have to be undertaken by professionals. Such a structure would almost certainly be constructed from timber so as to remain as light as possible, and might be supported with wires from above or solid joinery from below. If construction is possible, it could give you a whole new living area, completely transforming the way in which you think of your space both inside and outside the home.

Left As a general rule, you should never mix architectural styles. Here the clean lines of this balcony perfectly complement the adjoining building.

Above Wrought iron is a strong material that can be fashioned into complex and delicate patterns. However, these railings are almost incidental, being completely smothered by a glorious riot of planting.

Right These tall, wrought-iron Gothic arched railings are simply designed. Their strong vertical emphasis forms the perfect foil for the delicious tumble of wisteria that droops from the balcony level to the ground level below.

Boundaries

The first considerations on any roof garden, balcony or terrace are the boundaries. It may be that these are already in place and have been passed by your architect or structural engineer as being completely safe. There are always local regulations or codes that must be complied with: if in doubt with any aspect of these, consult a professional. Safety is of course the prime concern, and any boundary must be high enough and strong enough to prevent possible accidents. But shelter and screening are also important. You will already have made a note of any prevailing wind. On a roof, wind speeds can be high, causing plants to be both physically damaged and to dry out quickly. Suitable screening, both on the boundaries and quite possibly within the garden, is therefore important, not just to break the force of the wind but also to provide necessary shade. The position and detailing of these screens is very much a part of the design process, although there are a number of other factors to bear in mind.

Above left For safety reasons, attention to detail is all-important on a roof. Make sure that all fixings are secure and regularly checked for wear and tear. If in any doubt repair or renew them immediately. All pots and ornaments near the edges should be fixed firmly.

Left The design of fences can be an art form in its own right and by varying the width and height of boards you can set up all kinds of fascinating rhythms, as well as echoing the background sky scraper! In addition, this fence neatly screens water and electric ducting.

Function and form

The design of a fence will have a considerable effect on a wind blowing against it. A solid fence or screen will force the wind over the structure and cause turbulence on the lee side, whereas a slatted boundary or screen will filter the wind and provide calmer conditions on the other side. The tops of fences can also be angled, which will affect the wind pattern and potential shelter.

While wind may affect the choice and design of a boundary, so will the need to embrace a fine view. This may mean that you keep the surrounding parapet at a relatively low level, high enough for safety but low enough to keep the view. This boundary could be stone or brick, a low slatted fence, a detailed timber or metal railing, or perhaps even plate glass. The boundary is, of course, solid but can be set slightly above the floor level so that at least air flows over and under the structure, thereby reducing turbulence to some extent.

Above Frosted or etched glass can provide maximum privacy, but allow ample light for both plants and people. The glass-topped table continues the theme, while foliage wraps the garden about, softening the boundaries.

An alternative, where the parapet wall is low and you don't wish to raise it further, is to build a raised planter in front of it. This will form a physical barrier, although safety is still a consideration, particularly if children will use the garden.

If the surface is a deck close to ground level, built-in seating may be ideal. The construction and fixing must be solid and secure, using materials that are as durable and resistant as possible to rot and wind. The fence or screen could be tied back to the main structure of the house, or internal trellising, by overhead beams, struts or wires. This will stiffen and strengthen the structure. A screen or fence forming a right-angle is stronger than a straight run. A fence, screen or trellis is

only as strong as the fixing that attaches it to the walls. Great care needs to be taken in doing this, especially if the parapet walls incorporate a weatherproof membrane or damp proof course carried up from the overall floor surface between the cement render and the stone or brickwork. Drilling, screwing or bolting through this may break the membrane, allowing dampness to work through. Although your surveyor may have noticed this, you should always check it yourself.

Posts might be metal, timber, or piers of stone, brick or concrete. Piers will be the most obtrusive as a screen is usually set between them. Timber and metal posts are less noticeable and may be hidden if the screen is carried across their face. Screens could also be firmly fixed into raised planters or seating, which would of course need to be strong or heavy enough to take the loads.

Materials

There is a wide choice of timber: colour and patterns of grain can vary enormously, so see what is available before making your choice. Certain types of timber are more resistant to rot or insect attack than others. Many tropical hardwoods are harvested from non-renewed resources: this destroys valuable rainforest, so always make sure that any timber you use comes from a properly managed resource. Softer woods vary in durability, but it is sensible to ensure that any timber you buy has been pressure treated with a suitable preservative. Additional durability will be provided by further treatment, with a non-toxic preservative such as a clear sealant, stain or paint. If you are in doubt over the timber to choose, the supplier should be able to give good advice, as should an architect or designer. The design of screens often lacks imagination – for inspiration, look at how they are used in restaurants and other public places. All kinds of patterns and thicknesses of wood are available, from chunky rectangular

Left Safety is always important above ground level, but boundaries and changes in level can be elegantly handled. Here timber trellis and posts are teamed with metal rails.

forms to the delicacy of bamboo. Modern treatments could include wire mesh in bright colours, plastic webbing, bent metal or wrought iron, in either contemporary or traditional patterns.

Construction

Slats, trellis or railings, whether vertical, horizontal or diagonal, will need to be set within or fixed to a secure framework that is in turn fixed to the adjoining building or internal structure. Timber railings, fences and screens have basically the same construction, with posts that are topped and bottomed with cross-pieces or rails laid flat. For fences and screens these are usually the same width as the posts, which should be no more than 1.8m (6ft) apart. In railings, the top rail is often

wider than the posts. The spacing of posts will depend on the overall length of the run, as will the size of the posts and rails, all of which will be defined by local building codes. Top and bottom rails can be notched or mortised into the posts.

Infill slats, which form the body of the fence or screen, may be butted together, which might result in turbulence and greater wind pressure, or fixed with gaps between. While the slat-bottoms are usually at the same level, the tops might be slightly varied in height to set up a rhythm. Trellis panels are usually set between posts. Because of the severe conditions on roof gardens, timbers should be fixed with rust-resistant galvanized, aluminium, stainless steel or copper nails, or with brass screws for ultimate strength.

FENCE STYLES

Boundary treatments should be planned and designed to fit in with the style of your garden.

wood and glass panels

wirebound slats

vertical louvres

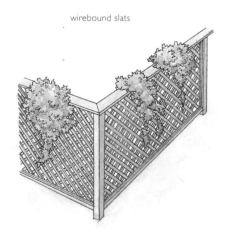

lattice

The floor

The floor is the basis of everything that happens over and under the roof and will have been checked for strength and stability by your architect or structural engineer. Apart from strength, the main purpose of the floor is to stop moisture from reaching the rooms below, and this is achieved with some kind of membrane or damp proof course. The roof's construction may have been carried out in a number of ways: its strength will determine the kind of flooring you use. The strongest roofs can take a conventional garden with all kinds of paving, walling, water features, seating, planting and lawns, although in most domestic situations the layout is much simpler.

Materials

There is a vast range of materials available for flooring and those that you choose should reflect not only the weight-bearing capabilities of your roof but also the amount of use that you may expect each area to receive.

Paving

Conventional paving is feasible if the roof is strong enough, and variations on this include all kinds of natural stone, which can be thinly sawn to reduce weight – various tiles, mosaics, gravels and chippings, and specialized lightweight tiles.

Paving slabs may either be set with open joints on a layer of free-draining gravel over a suitable roof surface, or set on pads or battens to lift them clear of the roof. Each method will allow drainage between the slabs and the roof to suitable outlets. Setting slabs on a continuous bed of mortar should be avoided, as expansion and contraction due to temperature variations might damage the roof membrane below. Smaller modules that are not affected by freezing temperatures can be bonded directly to the roof surface with various mastic adhesives. The gaps between the modules can either be left open or jointed with a flexible filler. Alternatively, expansion joints, which allow the overall surface to flex slightly, should be used no further than 3m (10ft) apart.

Fluid materials

Gravel and chippings of various colours and sizes can provide a low-cost and attractive floor for areas which are primarily decorative. Should access be needed it might even be possible to set

Above left Most floors should have a no-nonsense practical surface that is easy on the eye and does not dominate the surrounding design. Adjoining materials should be carefully detailed.

Left While optical illusions can be fun, they can often become boring and lose their point after a while, so be careful! These topiaried animals are weird and add to the somewhat offbeat composition.

Right Just occasionally you can break design rules with panache. In this situation, stepping stones would normally be neatly rectangular, but there is real power and drama in these rugged slabs.

Above Usually, the lawn and a gravel path would need to be separated to prevent the stones ruining the lawn mower. However, as this lawn does not need mowing, they can be run together.

Below Decking is a completely adaptable material, being easily shaped and fashioned, relatively light, and quickly laid, for both floors and surrounding features and furnishings.

stepping stones through the area. In a 'working' space used for sitting and dining, such an uneven surface would present problems.

More modern surfacing materials include roll-out plastics, plastic tiles, coloured imitation turf and glass beads, which are wonderful for 'non-walk' areas where the sun can make them sparkle.

Decking

Decking is a popular choice. It can be laid to all kinds of patterns and can even be suspended above the main roof structure if the surrounding walls and parapet construction are strong enough to accept the loads and fixings. In this case access should also be considered and simple steps from a doorway at roof level might be needed to reach the new surface. Such a 'suspended' floor might work best in a small area where the joist spans beneath the surface are not too long.

The visual effects achieved through different patterns (*see Chapter 1*) are important. The need to access the roof's surface through the flooring may

need consideration, so rather than building a continuous deck, it may be worth thinking about a deck that is laid in panels or modules. These can be lifted easily, should you ever need to maintain the waterproof membrane or reach drains and services below.

Such modules could be made in sizes from 450mm x 450mm (18in x 18in) to 600mm x 1.8m (2ft x 6ft), but the general rule is that, the larger the module, the more evenly any load is distributed across the roof. From your scale drawing you will be able to plan accurately the size and number of panels needed. If they are all of the same size the pattern will be a regular one, but by mixing sizes, or turning panels at right-angles to one another, you can set up all kinds of interesting patterns and rhythms.

The most straightforward modules use 50mm x 100mm (2in x 4in) boards and these should be of a structural grade and pressure treated. The cleats, to which the boards are nailed or screwed, should have the same dimensions.

If the roof has only a slight slope, the panels may be placed directly onto the surface, provided that drainage is maintained. If the fall is steeper, you can level the panels by using long lengths of 150mm x 50mm (6in x 2in) timber 'sleepers' beneath the cleats. These sleepers can be brought to level by using wedges or 'shims' fixed to the roof with exterior construction adhesive.

The maintenance of drainage beneath the deck is essential, so any sleepers or supporting structures must allow water to run into the drains provided, usually by running these parallel with the roof fall, but if necessary by leaving suitable gaps within the support network.

Of course an entire deck, rather than simply individual modules, can be laid, once again on a framework that will lift it clear of the roof and bring it to the same level. Such a framework of joists or bearers must be spaced closely enough to prevent the deck from sagging or flexing unduly when in use. The joists, which should be pressure treated with preservative, can also be laid upon strips of bituminized roofing felt, which will help to prevent them rotting.

LAYING DECKING

Above The basis of any deck is a strong underlying framework of timber joists that are spaced with regard to the thickness, weight and flexibility of the finished surface, and then positioned across the entire area to be covered.

Above In order to allow drainage beneath a deck, the joists can be lifted slightly proud of the roof surface on blocks or spacers. If the underlying roof slopes slightly, blocks or spacers can also be used to bring the deck level.

Above Boards are fixed last, with non-ferrous nails or brass screws, while removable spacers ensure even gaps. These deck boards are slightly ribbed, to provide extra grip in the wet, and as they are pressure treated they will last for many years.

Heavy elements

The placement of heavy items on a roof garden, balcony or raised terrace is an integral part of the design process, but these elements must be placed where the roof is strong enough to bear their weight. Whatever feature you are considering, all of the loadings should be checked with your architect or structural engineer. Involve professionals in the initial calculations and implementation of the project. Additionally, planters and raised beds, as well as water features, should be designed in such a way that the risk of leakage onto the substructure of the roof is minimized.

Raised beds and planters

Planting brings the roof garden to life but must be treated in quite a different way from planting at ground level: everything must be geared towards keeping the roof watertight and preventing the weight of wet soil from leading to structural problems. On large roofs and commercial projects, planting is often placed directly over the roof, but in such situations the substructure has often been planned specifically to accept it. Although a waterproof layer or membrane can last as long as the building, one leak could mean that the whole of the roof garden has to be removed to locate it. In a private roof garden, plants are often better in raised beds or containers that can be built or placed as units separate from the roof itself.

Layout

The layout will have been determined at the design stage, taking the result of the structural survey into account. As the beds will almost certainly be the heaviest items in the garden, they

Above left Water is a heavy element and needs positioning with great care on a roof or balcony. It makes sense, therefore, to choose a smaller feature that can be an attractive feature in itself.

Left While there are roof gardens that have been built to specifically handle heavy loads, this kind of composition, with substantial planting and water, belongs at ground level in a domestic setting.

Above Brick- or block-built raised beds can also be extremely heavy, although a lightweight soil or compost mix will reduce loadings on the roof. Advice from an architect or structural engineer will be vital before any construction is undertaken.

should, of course, be positioned over the strongest parts of the roof. If in any doubt, go back to your survey, or consult your engineer or architect.

Materials

Materials can echo those used elsewhere and could include brick, stone or concrete, with suspended bases to keep soil and drainage mediums clear of the roof. Timber can also be used in a wide range of designs, as well as plastic, metal and fibreglass boxes or containers. The bed will need

to be waterproofed and to allow drainage onto the floor below and into existing gullies.

Brick or stone can be painted on the inside with a bituminous sealer, which will help prevent water from working out through the wall with possible subsequent staining. These beds can be fitted with a false bottom of pressure-treated plywood, or galvanized metal sheet drilled to allow water to drain freely through. This base will provide protection for the roof surface should you need to empty the bed by using a spade or other tools. Lightweight concrete blocks can be cement-rendered and painted to match the colour scheme, and then painted inside with a bituminized sealer. All such beds should be built with drainage gaps or holes at the base to allow water to drain freely onto the roof. The height of the beds can vary and will depend on the strength of the roof. A good depth of soil or growing medium is between 300mm (1ft) and 450mm (18in), placed over a water-permeable woven plastic membrane that separates it from a drainage layer. This layer could be 150mm (6in) of lightweight expanded clay granules such as 'Leca'. All of this should be positioned over the perforated bottom of the bed which should sit above the roof surface by no less than 50mm (2in) to allow for free drainage. The height of these three layers results in a bed that is a comfortable sitting height.

A growing medium has recently been produced of light, easily handled fibre blocks, that can be fitted into any bed. One of its advantages is that it can be used in layers as thin as 100mm (4in), and still support excellent shrub growth. It is still placed over a drainage layer but is irrigated from below, unlike conventional soil mixes. A water pipe is laid into the bottom of the drainage layer with a float switch and overflow pipe about 40mm (1½in) above. The water is drawn through the fibre into the root system by capillary action. Such a technique could be used in a raised bed,

RAISED BEDS

Heavier and larger beds are possible at ground level

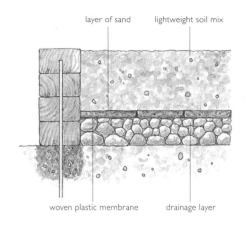

layer of sand   lightweight soil mix

woven plastic membrane   drainage layer

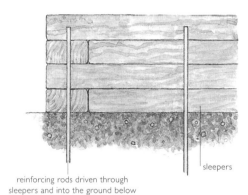

reinforcing rods driven through
sleepers and into the ground below

sleepers

Above Railway sleepers (ties) are naturally heavy, so they are best used at ground level. They should be overlapped, like bricks in a wall, and for added strength drilled to accept steel rods that can be driven into the ground.

Above Low-level raised beds can become part of an interesting floor pattern, and their relatively low weight can make them suitable for areas where load bearing is a problem.

Left Provided that the roof is structurally sound, you can certainly position relatively heavy features, especially around the perimeter. Overheads and planters have been colour-matched for continuity.

Above Until you notice that there is a fountain in the background, you might well mistake this pool for a more conventional raised bed. A contained water feature such as this provides the ideal environment for water-loving plantings, such as umbrella plants and water lilies.

CROSS-SECTION THROUGH A POND

A pump can introduce interest to any water feature.

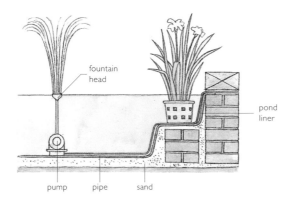

fountain head

pond liner

pump   pipe   sand

Above Most pumps recirculate water within the pool, cutting down on water use. However, ponds should still be topped up regularly.

with polystyrene blocks making up the height difference, or directly on the protected roof surface.

Timber beds provide the ideal visual link with a surrounding deck. They should at the very least be lined with heavy-duty polythene or butyl rubber, tacked to the inside and perforated at the bottom for drainage, but this is a temporary plan, unless carried out with care. Ideally, they should be fitted with fibreglass inserts, with drilled bases, that can be dropped into position and filled with layers of soil and drainage medium.

Built-in furniture

The last permanent feature, apart from incidental items such as water or barbecues, is any built-in furniture. This can often be a great space saver, being designed as an extension of the basic garden structure of raised beds, screens or boundary treatments. The style and materials should reflect those used elsewhere in the garden.

Water features

Any pool or water feature should be sited in an open position, away from overhanging trees. When first filled, pools will turn green with the action of algae, but will clear again once plants and fish are introduced and a balanced aquatic environment is achieved. Good aquatic or garden centres will sell collections of plants and fish to

Above Small water features are ideal for a roof garden or balcony, providing delightful focal points. Many of these can be bought ready-made and are easy to install.

suit a given size of pool. A submersible pump can be used to give the water movement and to provide aeration for plants and fish, so a power supply should be included on your plans. This will also allow for lighting.

Building a pond

Like raised beds, pools or water features are best kept as a self-contained unit separate from the roof, reducing the risk of leakage or accidental damage. Water features in the garden fit into two broad categories: conventional pools with an area of open water; or smaller features set on a wall or in the form of a 'millstone' type of arrangement.

Conventional pools can be either a preformed fibreglass type, in a wide range of shapes and sizes, or constructed from a tough butyl rubber liner. The former are often more successful on a roof as they are virtually indestructible and can be fitted within a raised area of lightweight concrete blocks, timber or brickwork, similar to the beds discussed on pages 71–74. Drainage holes should be incorporated in the base of the outer skin for any overflow or leakage from a puncture, so that water can run off into the roof drainage system.

Liner pools can also be constructed inside a raised area and should be laid over a false bottom suspended by battens clear of the main roof structure. Black is usually the best colour for both fibre glass pools and liners, as it sets up surface reflections which disguise the depth of the water. Steer clear of sky blue or imitatation pebbled finishes, which can discolour quickly with the effects of algae. A depth of 450mm (18in) is ample, and on a roof this can often be considerably reduced.

Pools should be designed as an integral part of the overall design. Where space is limited, the sides of the pool could serve a dual purpose: if built up to about 450mm (18in) and topped with a broad coping, they can double as an occasional seat, plinth for pots, ornaments or utility surface.

If the roof is strong enough, more exotic compositions can include split-level pools or a simulated rock outcrop. The latter can be constructed by specialists from light, painted fibreglass that is almost impossible to tell from the real thing.

CREATING A POND

A pond on a terrace can be larger than one on a rooftop.

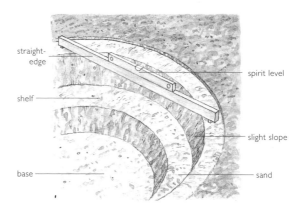

straight-edge

spirit level

shelf

slight slope

base

sand

Above The initial excavation will form the marginal shelf and basic outline. The soil should then be 'blinded' with sand and levelled.

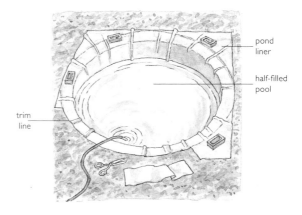

pond liner

half-filled pool

trim line

Above Water run into the loosely-fitted liner will mould it to shape. The edges can then be trimmed, allowing enough to hold it in place.

Above The final job is to lay securely the coping and any surrounding paving. The coping should overlap the edge in order to hide it.

Building a terrace

Whether your living space is at high-rise or ground level, it is essential to provide for well-laid, practical and aesthetically pleasing surfaces. The floor will be either bedded directly onto the ground or suspended above it. The materials you choose for flooring, beds, trellises and boundaries, and the design you implement, will have been considered during the conceptual stages (see Chapter 1). As a terrace will usually be larger than a roof garden and will be able to bear greater weights, you will probably have a wider range of materials to choose from.

Boundaries

Since any paved area or terrace needs to be contained, before you lay the floor you should think about the boundaries: walls, fences or raised beds, that will shelter, screen and define the space.

Safety is obviously important and walls of any material – brick, stone or timber such as railway sleepers (ties) or vertically set logs, should be built off sound foundations or 'footings'. These should be twice as wide as the finished structure and taken down to the 'undisturbed' ground. Topsoil should be removed as it is subject to decay, which could cause subsidence. Fences and screens are available in a wide range of styles and the posts can either be set in concrete (*see p.78*) or in spiked metal 'shoes' driven into the ground.

As raised beds at ground level are built differently from those on the roof, they can be set on solid concrete footings. Drainage is essential and pipes or gaps in the stone, brick, blockwork or timber should be incorporated every 900mm (3ft) at the base of the bed, above the surrounding surface. To allow water to percolate freely to the

Above left You can use a greater range of materials at ground level than on a roof, although the rules about simplicity still apply. Here, the grass sits slightly proud of the path so that it can be mowed.

Left Good design is often simple, which does not preclude subtlety. This terrace has all the necessary features: ample paving, a softly planted perimeter and overheads to give light shade.

Above Few of us can aspire to a swimming pool in this kind of setting, with the sight and sound of the sea beyond. Needless to say, sound construction is absolutely vital to retain this area and prevent it sliding into the ocean.

drainage points, a 150mm (6in) layer of broken stone or hard-core should be laid in the bottom. A porous geo-textile membrane between the stone and the upper layer of soil prevents this from washing into and through the drainage layer. A good-quality topsoil should be at least 450mm (18in) deep and can, if necessary, be improved with well-rotted manure or compost.

Retaining walls separate different levels in the garden. While it is possible to build low retaining walls yourself, it is advisable to employ a landscaper, who can work from a structural engineer's

FENCE POSTS

On terraces, one way to set posts is to bed them in concrete.

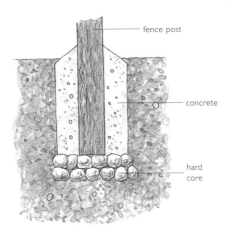

- fence post
- concrete
- hard core

Above Fence posts should be firmly bedded in concrete. Chamfer the concrete just above ground to shed water.

RETAINING WALLS

Retaining walls are ideal for beds at different levels.

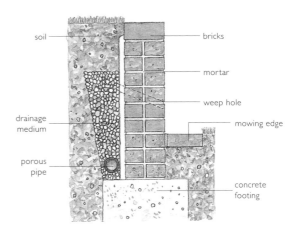

- soil
- bricks
- mortar
- weep hole
- drainage medium
- mowing edge
- porous pipe
- concrete footing

Above It is essential to relieve pressure behind a retaining wall by incorporating a vertical drainage layer above porous pipework.

drawings, for more ambitious projects. Retaining walls need extra strength because of the pressure-of soil and water, and sound foundations are essential. Equally important is the installation of regular drains or 'weep holes' in the wall. Behind the wall a layer of broken stone or coarse gravel allows water to reach the weep holes. Alternatively, a longitudinal perforated drain can be set behind the wall, at the base of the gravel to link into the face drains or to take any excess water away in either direction (*see above right*). For added strength, walls can be built from cast concrete with a 'toe' to act as a counterlever at the front face. Such walls can be faced with brick or stone.

Flooring materials

A wider range of materials can be used for a terrace than a roof garden or balcony because of the greater weight tolerances. Materials include cast concrete slabs, gravel, tiles and timber decking.

Paving

Most terraces will be paved, but you need to take a number of factors into consideration. Most houses have a damp proof course (DPC) to prevent ground moisture from percolating up the walls and into your home; if this layer is bridged by paving or other surfaces, such as earth banked up against the wall, damp will work through to the inside. To avoid this, the foundations of any paved area must be laid at least 150mm (6in) below the DPC and paving should be laid to a slope or 'fall' of about 1:100 away from the building. If a terrace is contained by walls or paving at a higher level, drains will need to be incorporated. All paving needs a firm foundation and the first job will be to dig deep enough to accept the finished paving. Allow 100mm (4in) foundation of

Above Solid timber railings that surround a timber deck or a raised terrace provide visual continuity of materials and are essential for obvious safety reasons.

hard-core or crushed stone, 25mm (1in) of mortar and the thickness of the paving. So if the slabs are 50mm (2in) thick, you will arrive at a depth of 175mm (7in) below the DPC. All of the topsoil should be removed, so you may need to dig further, making up the difference with the foundation layer of compacted hard-core or stone.

As the finished level needs to be laid to a slight fall, drive pegs into the ground to match this on a 1.8m (6ft) grid. Using a long straightedge and spirit level, bring the compacted foundation level with the pegs and 'blind' it with sharp sand or fine gravel to fill in larger gaps before laying paving.

Slabs should be bedded in mortar with four dabs at the corners and one in the middle (*see below*). First bed a slab close to the house, or at the highest point of a paved area, and another slab at the furthest point. Stretch a building line between the two and lay the intervening slabs along this, checking with a straightedge and spirit level as work progresses. A second line should be set up at right-angles to the first, running across the area.

There is a vast range of paving types available. Concrete block paving tends to look utilitarian and is not often chosen for intimate areas. Bricks can be superb provided they are frost-resistant. Special paving bricks can be bedded on a wet or a semi-dry mortar mix (*see p. 80*). In the latter case

Above The character of paving materials can vary enormously, from smooth, polished surfaces that encourage rapid movement, to detailed and textured paving that slow you visually and physically.

the area will need an edge to hold the overall surface firmly in place. This can take the form of bricks set or 'haunched' in mortar, or boards or heavier timbers firmly pegged in place.

Granite setts are cubes of granite once used as street paving. They are available second-hand or new and can make an excellent contrast within a paved area or an edging 'trim' around a terrace or feature, although their uneven finish makes them unsuitable for tables and chairs. They should be firmly bedded together in mortar.

Other small module materials include 'stable paviours', which are usually brick-sized and have an indented pattern; artificial pre-cast concrete

LAYING PAVING SLABS

Laying slabs is straightforward if you follow the rules.

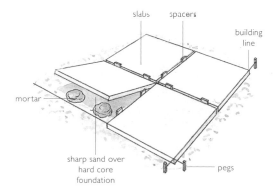

slabs   spacers   building line   mortar   sharp sand over hard core foundation   pegs

Above First a layer of crushed stone or hard core is compacted in. Then five spots of mortar are put at the corners and the slabs aligned with the builder's lines, before being spaced to allow for expansion.

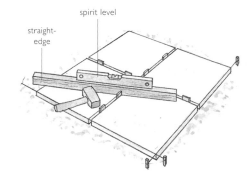

spirit level   straight-edge

Above To ensure that the slabs are at the correct height and are sloped at the correct fall (usually 1:100), use a spirit level on a straightedge and tap the corners down gently with a mallet.

Above Paving at ground level can usually be made of heavier materials than that on a roof and so can include all kinds of natural stone and concrete slabs.

BRICK PATTERNS

Special hard-wearing bricks are now available for paving.

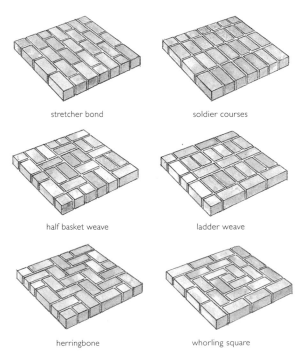

stretcher bond

soldier courses

half basket weave

ladder weave

herringbone

whorling square

Above Bricks can be laid in a variety of patterns, each with a different character. These can create different effects, from the straight lines of soldier courses to the intricate spiral of whorling squares.

'setts' and cobbles. These are egg-shaped stones found on river beds or beaches (it is illegal to remove them, so buy second-hand ones). They can again be ideal as an 'infill' surface and should be packed as closely together as possible.

'Fluid' materials

Materials such as gravel and concrete, which can be cast to virtually any shape, are regarded as 'fluid' and have enormous potential. Concrete can be both elegant and practical. It is a great pity that this material is often under-used and underrated. Its surface can easily be finished in a number of ways (*see p.82, top left*). Some manufacturers specialize in stamping patterns onto the surface of the concrete to imitate bricks, cobbles or other material. While this is often cheaper than laying the real thing, it rarely looks convincing.

Since concrete expands and contracts with changes in temperature, it should be cast as panels with 'expansion joints'. Such panels should be no greater than 3.6m (12ft) square and can become an integral part of the overall terrace design. The expansion joints can be strips of wood, brick, setts or paving slabs. Each panel of concrete must be able to flex independently.

Gravel, provided that it is laid over a well-consolidated base and bedded into a clay binder that is known as 'hoggin', can form an elegant surface, particularly in a traditional setting or small courtyard (*see p. 82, top right*). Gravels come in a range of colours and grades and the paler shades can be used to brighten a gloomy area.

Timber

Timber can be used for a further range of surfaces. Railway sleepers (ties) can form superb paved areas, either alone or contrasted with brick, paving of various kinds or gravels. They are solid and durable and would obviously link into a composition where they were used for raised beds or

Right The soft texture of timber decking always associates well with planting and the staggered pattern of the decking shown here leads you gently across the water to the sitting area.

CONCRETE FINISHES

Even materials usually thought of as plain can be decorative.

Above Concrete is, in fact, a wonderfully adaptable material and can be given all kinds of surface patterns by brushing or being exposed to show the small stones or aggregate in the mix. Even such articles as spades or a builder's float can create interesting textures.

Above Brick, provided it is hard and 'well fired', is one of the most versatile and long-lasting pavings. The austerity of this flight of steps is softened by the regular placing of pots.

THE STRUCTURE OF A GRAVEL PATH

The texture and colour of gravel make it an ideal surface.

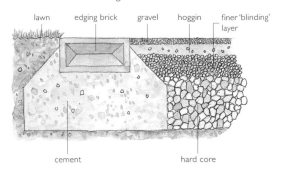

lawn   edging brick   gravel   hoggin   finer 'blinding' layer

cement   hard core

Above Gravel should always be laid on a clay binder, over firmly crushed hard-core, and usually edged to prevent it becoming loose.

steps. Select clean examples that are as free as possible from dirt or oil that can sweat out in hot weather and possibly be carried into the house.

Wood blocks that can be bedded on end in sand are sometimes available. These too are durable and can provide an interesting surface texture. Log slices, sections of tree trunks, approximately 150mm (6in) thick, can also be laid as paving and are usually bedded in sand over crushed stone or hard-core. Such a surface has an informal character and could blend into a more relaxed part of the garden away from the house.

Steps

Where there is a change of level between paved areas, access will be needed in the form of steps or a ramp. The cue for a choice of materials and style will normally be taken from the terrace, but sound construction is, as always, important.

Steps in a garden should be quite wide, as few things are less attractive or more dangerous than a narrow flight. Proportion is important too, both for the look of the flight and comfort. The ideal measurements are a tread of 450mm (18in) and a riser of 150mm (6in). If the tread is allowed to overhang the riser by about 50mm (2in), it will cast a shadow line and visually lighten the flight.

A long flight of steps may look and feel more relaxing if it has a landing or series of landings. These can often herald a change of direction as well as hosting pots, statuary or other ornaments.

Both planting and water can complement a flight of steps: it may be worth planning the whole feature as an integrated composition.

Methods of construction depend on the amount of traffic expected (*see p. 84*). If this is relatively low, and the ground firm, the bottom riser can be built off a solid concrete foundation with the treads bedded in mortar on excavated platforms running up the slope. A more durable flight can be built with a concrete substructure which is cast into a timber framework or 'shuttering'. Reinforcing rods can be incorporated for added strength. A different finish can then be laid using the concrete foundation as a base.

Steps can be built from different paving materials although timber can also be used. Railway sleepers could work well if used elsewhere in the terrace itself. Logs, firmly pegged, or set vertically into a slope, could provide a less formal look.

Decks

Decks at, or close to, ground level can be even more versatile than those on the roof because there is usually more scope and space available. In visual terms they can form the ideal link between a timber building or interior planked floor and provide an invitation to move outside.

There are also practical advantages, as timber is easily worked to form different angles and fits easily around shapes and into corners where paving might prove awkward.

Before you think about construction, assess your surroundings to see where the deck might best be situated. Microclimate is important, so check where the sun falls. Is a site too hot, or perhaps in the path of a prevailing wind?

As most garden boundaries are only 1.8m (6ft) high, even a low deck could raise you into view of neighbours or the street. You may wish to break the sight lines with screens, either as part of the deck or further away where higher planting could come into its own. Seating, screens and planting around or within the deck will provide a feeling of shelter and intimacy, making the space feel more comfortable. Overheads can be useful, giving privacy, supporting climbers, casting shade, and

providing a visual link between house and garden. When planning the layout make sure that the area is big enough: a deck should be larger than a corresponding room indoors, for ease of access around the space and because most garden furniture is rather larger than its interior counterpart.

It is a good idea to allocate different areas for different purposes, perhaps differentiated by a

Above Roughly hewn stone has been carefully laid to produce an informal flight of steps that allows room for low, cushion planting in between the individual stones.

STEPS

Sound construction is essential for steps.

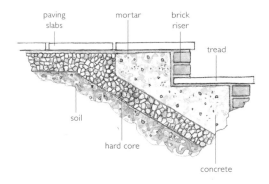

Above To achieve a strong, stable flight of steps the treads should be laid off brick risers, over solid concrete foundations, with a good layer of hard core underneath.

change of level, linked by broad steps or screened by raised beds and planting. If they lead out from the rooms inside, so much the better.

Decks can be the simplest and easiest of structures and are easy to build if, for example, they are laid upon bearers over an old paved area or existing unimaginative concrete terrace (*see p. 85*). They can be practical and low in cost, but realize a complete visual transformation of the space.

At the other end of the spectrum, decks can be complicated and sophisticated affairs, soaring

Below This long narrow raised deck is designed primarily to allow access. This function is emphasized by the strong directional nature of the boards and the timber railings.

over a sloping site where platforms could be extended out from the house, linked with steps and incorporate all kinds of features – from built-in seating, barbecues, hot tubs and, of course, planting. Trees and existing vegetation can be worked into the composition, with cutouts in the floor that allow stems or trunks access. A waterside home could provide a magical opportunity to span a deck across a lake or stream, either cantilevered from the building or built on piles from foundations driven into the underlying bed.

Like any structure, work needs to be carried out competently and with care, using professional design and building expertise. Safety and adequate strength are of course essential ingredients and the size and span of a deck will determine just how it is built. As always, timber should be carefully chosen and pressure treated against rot.

Where decks adjoin a building they can be hung from ledger rails bolted to the walls, but in other parts of the garden they may be free standing to form a separate living area. As with any paved area, a deck should always be set to a slight fall away from the building to shed water easily.

Verandas

Verandas are a practical and attractive feature, providing the perfect link between house and garden. In essence they are decks, often right around a building and covered by an extension of the roof. The front is usually left open and the space enclosed by a hand rail. As the height of the deck usually matches that of the floor inside, steps are often needed from the veranda down to the garden, but the change of level is usually slight and the number of steps correspondingly few.

In countries where the sun is high in the sky, it is essential to use any shade to cool both the immediate area and inside the house. If a veranda encircles the home, different parts can be used at different times, depending on the height of the sun. As the area is covered, furniture can be left out, although plants should be watered regularly and the area may be too shady for certain species.

As far as construction is concerned, a veranda is simply a low deck, usually suspended above the

ground on joists and timber piers, those set at the front being used as supports for the hand rails and continuing upwards to carry the roof. Decking patterns can vary, but on the whole should be simple, probably picking up the line and sizing of boards inside the house.

THE ELEMENTS OF A RAISED DECK

A stable, solid structure is essential for a raised deck.

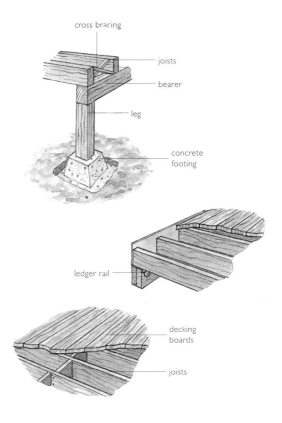

cross bracing
joists
bearer
leg
concrete footing

ledger rail

decking boards
joists

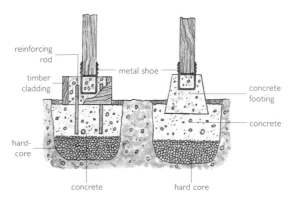

reinforcing rod
metal shoe
timber cladding
concrete footing
concrete
hard-core
concrete
hard core

Above A raised deck is an extremely versatile surface, which can create extra levels from a boring flat part of the garden, or turn an unusable sloped area into a valuable extra space. Decks can be placed either near the house or, more informally, away from it.

Overheads and awnings

In addition to wind, the hot sun can cause real problems on a roof – far more so than at ground level, where trees and constructed vertical elements can provide much-needed shade. In addition to providing this escape from the wind, or the sun in the heat of the day, overheads, canopies and awnings can also be useful for breaking the view from neighbouring windows. They can range from the simple to the complicated, from permanent structures with planting trained over them, to retractable awnings or even parasols.

Types of overheads

Overhead structures can be extremely simple, utilizing just a couple of uprights and a few cross members, or far more complicated, for exmple, using slats to echo the patterning of a deck below. They can incorporate screens, which could be set above planters to allow climbers to run over the screens and overheads.

Permanent structures

At their most complex, overheads can be completely roofed in to provide additional shelter, but this can allow debris to accumulate on top. Such debris can be difficult to remove and the result can sound like thunder when it rains.

In structural terms overheads can become part of the support structure for trellises and screens, which can in turn be linked into the boundaries, resulting in the whole fabric of the roof becomes integrated and stronger. Awnings that are reeled out from an adjoining wall can provide both shade and colour, but remember that as wind can be a real problem, fixings will need to be secure to resist especially strong gusts. Awnings should also be fully retractable so that they can be safely stowed away when the garden is not in use.

Movable overheads

At a simpler level any garden centre should stock a range of parasols and sunshades. These are usually sold with their own base and so require only a minimal amount of fixing, with the advantage that they can be moved if necessary.

Above left Overheads need not be complex to look good. The very simplest structures are often the most effective, with slats casting dappled shade below.

Left Many awnings can be automated so that they can be easily reeled in and out. A flexible canvas covering will be ideal for this situation as it will be unlikely to crack along the fold lines.

Right In the final analysis a straightforward manually operated awning may well be the easiest to use, but you should remember that this kind of feature is likely to be vulnerable to gusts of wind when situated on a roof.

Plants

Planning...

Plants are an integral part of your garden's design. They define the visual impact of each part of the garden: their colour, shape, size and texture can be used to bring an area to your attention or to make it fade into the background.

...and choosing

Which plant species you choose will, of course, depend on the style and size of your garden, as well as the climate. The plants form the clothing for the structural skeleton of the garden and your choice should be just as personal to you as your own dress sense.

Left Plants bring any garden to life. Whether the garden is large or small, on a roof or at ground level, plants will enhance the space with their colour, texture and fragrance.

Arranging the plants

Planting in small spaces, including roof gardens, balconies and terraces, is particularly important; too much and the whole area can be swamped, too little and the result can be meagre, emphasizing the harshness of the surroundings. Roof gardens and terraces each have their own particular problems which are largely to do with the severe weather conditions they may experience. However sheltered the space may be, wind will almost certainly prove troublesome at some point. This, combined with a hot sun, can make conditions difficult to deal with.

Plants to suit the conditions

This tends to suggest that certain species are more successful than others, although with care, and a lot of hard work, you can grow nearly anything on a roof or in a container. As a general rule, many Mediterranean plants do particularly well in these circumstances, being largely resistant to drought and adapted to thrive in hot, sunny conditions. Such plants often have felt-like or tough leaves that slow down their rate of transpiration.

Frost is far less likely to attack plants at higher levels. Although conditions may be tough, they are far from impossible, and you may even be able to grow species that would not survive in colder conditions elsewhere. One of the great joys of gardening lies in achieving something that others find difficult, so think and choose positively.

Nurseries and plant catalogues are very good sources of information on plants suitable for particular climates. Those plants which tolerate a specific range of conditions will naturally do better than those whose natural habitat is different from that of a proposed site. Bearing this in mind, a well-planted aerial garden is a joy, providing a rooftop oasis which thrives in spite of all the odds.

Successful planting

There is an enormous advantage in being able to choose your own ideal soil mix and in tailoring it to meet the particular needs of the plants you choose. You will, for example, be able to influence the acidity or alkalinity of the soil and so may be able to grow a wider range of plants than if you were in a garden at ground level.

Above left Formal floral settings work equally well inside or outside the home, acting as focal points that both draw the eye and link with the immediate surroundings.

Left Informal planting brings softness to the garden. It relies for its effect on the relationship of leaf texture, shape and form, as well as the overall outline of any given species.

Right Vertical planting will allow terraces to be gently moulded together without losing their architectural outline. The orange of the fruit brings a strong splash of colour to the white wall.

One of the secrets of successful planting is to make sure that beds and containers are as large and as deep as possible. The bigger their size, the more they can retain moisture and provide ample root room for the plants. A larger container also affords protection against extreme cold where the temperature drops below freezing. As well as having large enough containers, successful planting also requires you to spend time and trouble over both the selection and care of the plants.

Plants for all year round

Many people forget about the potential of a garden in winter, but since it can be several degrees warmer on a roof than at ground level, you can usually enjoy the space for a lengthy season. If, however, your garden is only used at certain times of the year, you will want a scheme that comes into its own at a given time, or at least does not look at its best when you are away.

Before we look at plant groupings it would be useful to review some of the principles of planting design that allow material to be put together attractively. Planting design styles can vary enormously. Some revel in the individual beauty of a

plant, others look at the broader appeal of form, shape and texture. Both approaches are valid, but concentrating on the beauty of specific plants will almost certainly use a greater number of species within the garden.

However, I personally prefer to concentrate on form, shape and texture. For me the flower is a seasonal bonus rather than the prime object of a species: as blooms can last only a short time, the rest of the plant has to provide interest for the remainder of the year. Whether you favour one style or the other, bear in mind that the planting of a garden, like the design, should reflect your personality and serve those who use the space.

Making a selection

You need only look at the range of plants at any garden centre or nursery, or in a catalogue, to see how potentially complicated plant selection can be. This can often be compounded by seemingly complicated professional advice. In fact, if the job is tackled in a logical sequence, it is straightforward and immensely rewarding.

The first difficulty is the distinction between classifying the plants and understanding the roles the plants can fulfil in the garden. To clarify this I have summarized below the types of plants available and just what they can do for you.

Trees

The largest plants are trees, and while you don't want something that dominates the area the smaller species can be extremely valuable. They can provide both vertical emphasis and shelter from a prevailing wind, as well as shade. Trees can be grown for their foliage, which can change dramatically from spring to autumn, as well as blossom, fruit, berries or nuts. Small-foliage varieties are often more appropriate in roof gardens as their canopies cast lighter shade and the leaves are less likely to be buffeted by strong winds. Most suitable species of tree are deciduous and therefore lose their leaves during the winter.

Trees occupy the highest storey of planting. They will need to be secured to prevent them from being worked loose by the wind. Shapes vary from fastigiate, or upright, to weeping, flat-topped, contorted or rounded, all of which have a different character and visual emphasis.

Above In this raised wooden bed, the designer has used the colour, texture, height, leaf size, shape and habit of the plants to create an area that always catches the eye. By concentrating on the whole plant, rather than just the flowers, the gardener has ensured that the bed will remain of interest for a much longer period.

RAISED BEDS AND PLANTERS

Raised beds perform a number of functions. As well as providing height so that smaller plants are not always at or below knee level, they allow the gardener to control the acidity of the soil and so grow plants that would otherwise not thrive. Planters for roof gardens are built differently to those for terraces in order to keep the weight down.

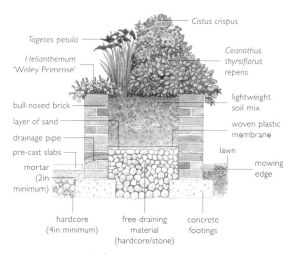

Above This raised brick planter is designed for use at ground level, with a layer of hardcore allowing it to drain into the soil. Root run and water will still be limited: species that enjoy hot, dry conditions will be ideal, as will a combination of medium height and lower-growing, sprawling plants, to soften the walls.

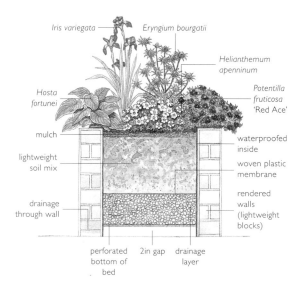

Above This bed is designed for use above ground level. Its rendered walls are made of lightweight blocks and water drains out through the wall. Irrigation is the key to rooftop planting. If carried out properly on a regular basis you can use a wide range of plants, including such water lovers as broad-leafed hostas.

Above Flowers should be a bonus, bringing colour at a particular time of the year. They should always be reinforced with a background of interesting foliage.

Above On a roof garden or balcony, where space is often quite limited, the planting will not only have to bring colour and interest and to clothe screens and walls, but should take up as little space as possible at the same time.

Shrubs

Shrubs have an enormous range of sizes, shapes and characteristics. They can be either evergreen or deciduous, and can be grown for their flowers, fragrance or foliage; they can also form a natural framework into which smaller and more colourful material can be woven. Many shrubs flower prolifically at different times of the year, including winter. While the foliage can provide enormous interest, particularly when contrasted with other species, many deciduous shrubs have an attractive branch structure that comes into its own during the winter, especially if it is set against a suitable background. Many shrubs can be successfully grown in pots and containers, which is a valuable bonus on a roof garden, balcony or terrace.

Hardy perennials

Shrubs have hard, woody stems but hardy perennials (or herbaceous plants) have far softer stems. The majority of hardy perennials die down in winter to reappear the following spring. These are the plants of the classic English herbaceous border and the term embraces a huge range, from stately spires smothered in mid-summer bloom to low ground cover. Although many are grown for their flowers, which can appear in winter as well as summer, many also have handsome foliage.

If a garden were laid out using only hardy perennials, there would be little winter interest, but adding shrubs can make an ideal combination. Hardy perennials can be used in a mixed bed or border to visually lighten the composition, while the shrubs' branch structure lends valuable support. Hardy perennials can also be planted in containers if they are fed and watered regularly.

Annuals

The term annual or, more correctly, half-hardy annual, is applied to plants propagated by seed

Right Box and other hedging plants can act as a wonderfully sculptural material that can take the place of hard landscape materials in an altogether softer context. This display will look equally good in summer or winter.

early in the year that flower during the same summer. Annuals are usually killed by frost at the onset of winter; they often originate in frost-free climates where they last from year to year. The pelargonium of South Africa is one such plant, and can be over-wintered in more severe climates if lifted and kept in a frost-free area.

Annuals are typically grown for their flowers, which can be spectacular and will last all summer if the spent blooms are removed before setting seed. They complement other planting, bringing instant colour and vibrancy, or can be used as 'fillers' in a young border where shrubs and herbaceous material have not knitted together. Their other use is in pots, containers, boxes and hanging baskets, which makes them an invaluable choice in a small area such as a balcony.

Bulbs

Bulbs can be treated either like hardy perennials, which die down and reappear, or annuals, which are removed once they have finished flowering. In the first approach – naturalizing – the bulbs are left in the ground from year to year, in a border where they can be mixed in with other planting to create a vibrant spring display. They are particularly valuable here as few other plants flower this early and many have not yet gained their summer foliage. When the bulbs finish flowering they are allowed to die down naturally before the foliage is removed. The alternative use is to plant them in pots and containers in autumn so that they flower the following spring. Once they have finished flowering they are allowed to die down before being lifted and stored. The pots can then be replanted with annuals for the summer. Different bulbs flower at different times of the year, most in spring but some in autumn. As a group, bulbs are enormously varied, ranging from tiny species only a few inches high to stately daffodils.

Climbers

This group of plants is especially useful in those areas partially or fully enclosed by walls, fences or screens. Most climbers are shrubby: they retain their branch structure in winter and they can be evergreen or deciduous. Although there is a climber for every situation, sunny or shady, they vary in their resistance to frost. Some are grown for their beautiful, often fragrant, flowers and some for their foliage, which varies enormously.

Left The marriage of hard and soft landscape can be both strong and subtle. Low planting has been used between these slabs to produce an interesting chequer-board effect.

There are two main types of climber – those that attach themselves and those that need to be supported. The support can be some kind of trellis fixed to the surface, which can also become an additional decorative element. Alternatively, climbers can be tied into horizontal wires, spaced every 450mm (18in) up a wall or stretched between fence posts.

Fruit, vegetables and herbs

Fruit, vegetables and herbs can be grown successfully in small areas, either in raised beds or pots, or in 'grow bags', which contain a well-balanced compost to ensure optimum growth. Vegetables are valuable as much for their decorativeness as for their culinary potential. Herbs in particular have long been grown for the quality of their flowers and foliage as well as their wonderful fragrance. Both fruit and vegetables can look handsome, especially when mixed with other planting.

Many people dismiss the idea of growing fruit trees in such a limited space as a roof garden, balcony or terrace as impractical, but they can

Above Raised beds and boxes can provide both definition and softness around a small garden, particularly if they spill over to disguise the containers below.

Above With tender loving care, reasonable room and regular feeding, even a roof can be lush and green, screening both surrounding walls and uncompromising views.

work very well in small spaces if miniature varieties are grown on a 'dwarfing' rootstock. Such trees can be grown as miniature bushes, trained as cordons, espaliers or fans or, a more recent development, in a pyramidal shape with a single main stem. If the branches are trained they will take up very little space and can be appropriate for even the smallest balcony. Apples and pears are particularly well suited to this treatment. The single-stem types, of which the 'Ballerina' varieties are a good example, are ideal for growing in a restricted area. As with any vigorous plant, the larger the pot the better. Regular feeding and irrigation is important during the growing season, as is some protection from frost during winter and early spring.

Few apple species are fully self-fertile and so for successful fertilization you will need at least two compatible varieties. Many varieties are partially self-fertile but (as is also the case with pears) a better crop will be formed if pollination is from another tree.

This brief guide classifies broadly the kinds of plants you are likely to use. There are other, more specialist, areas which you may be familiar with or will learn about as your interest develops.

Left A Mediterranean climate naturally brings enough warmth for citrus fruit to grow freely. Such trees grow well in containers, with regular attention, although being confined in containers will often limit their development.

Above Many vegetables have striking form and foliage and should be used in beds, borders and containers more often. Ornamental cabbages are particularly handsome in winter.

TRAINING FRUIT TREES

If space is limited, fruit trees can be trained on wires in a variety of shapes, including cordons, espaliers and fans.

Above Sticks can be used to support angled branches.

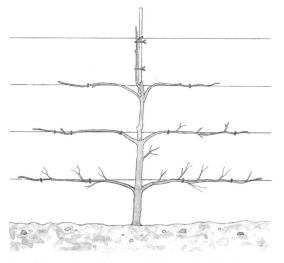

Above Side shoots should be pruned back to maintain the shape.

Pots and containers

Pots and containers play an especially important role in the smaller areas of a roof, balcony or terrace. Where it is difficult to build raised beds, pots can be packed together tightly so that almost the whole area is filled. They need not be at floor or ground level: boxes and baskets can be hung from walls, perched on ledges or placed on sills – always bearing in mind that they must be securely fixed to prevent accidents below. Window boxes can be wired back to the frame on either side or screwed to the sill. Parapet walls, if they are wide enough, sometimes offer the chance to construct integral boxes or troughs on top. Alternatively, long plant boxes can be built into the base of screens so that climbers can scramble up the surface. The plants can complement or enhance the container: an erect plant in a tall urn can act as a strong focal point; or colours could be used to make bold contrasts as, for example, when massed white flowers are set in a black pot.

Above left Pots and containers are the workhorses of roof gardens and balconies. Because of their mobility, they can be positioned to set up all kinds of fascinating patterns and rhythms.

Left Pots can often be grouped in generic types, in this case clay and terracotta. The contrast of different heights, textures and colours brings interest, as does the mix of exotic species, the aloe casting dramatic shadow against the wall.

Selecting containers

Any container, of whatever size, must have ample drainage. Pots bought from garden centres should have drainage holes, but always check. If necessary you will have to puncture the base of the container. Similarly, the bottoms of boxes should be drilled to allow water to drain away.

An enormous range of containers is available: your choice should be in sympathy with the overall style of the garden. The cost of the containers will be similarly variable, ranging from that of an expensive antique to the simplest bowl bought from the local garden shop or to 'found' items: some of the most effective containers started life as something quite different. Often the pot becomes an incidental feature, with foliage and flower spilling out to conceal all below. You don't have to spend a fortune for an attractive display.

While you can certainly mix styles and materials, do not overdo it, as a random collection of anything can tend to look fussy. Choose compatible materials: timber, terracotta and stone are of a similar type, looking quite at ease in a traditional composition. Modern materials such as fibreglass

Above Pots can either be a simple vehicle for plants or, as here, focal points in their own right. Careful positioning will be essential if the overall composition is not to become too 'busy'.

and plastic in bright primary colours are quite different, perhaps looking better beside polished metal or a contemporary concrete façade.

Positioning containers

Containers and other incidental features are an integral part of the design and must not be chosen and positioned in isolation, So that while there is room for some 'found' items, most containers should reflect the overall garden style.

This applies to positioning as well as materials, and while terracotta pots might look at home in a contemporary or traditional garden, they could be placed more formally in a contemporary setting and asymmetrically in a traditional setting (see p. 103). The same approach could apply to wall-hung containers: a formal approach might see identical boxes on either side of a doorway, while informally they could be grouped to one or both sides, in an irregular but pleasing pattern.

WOODEN PLANTERS

A wooden box will be lighter than a similar-sized concrete bed, but is filled in much the same way, with sufficient drainage material to prevent waterlogging.

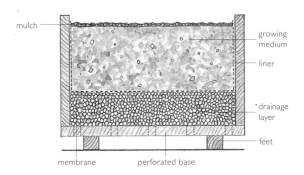

mulch

growing medium

liner

drainage layer

feet

membrane   perforated base

Above A waterproof liner protects the wood from the wet soil.

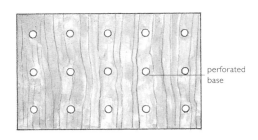

perforated base

Above Plenty of drainage holes should be drilled in the base.

Another guide to grouping pots is to use odd numbers, as three or five looks more comfortable than two, four or six. The classic arrangement of three containers uses one tall and narrow, one broader, medium-sized and a final small pot. This forms a triangular pattern, a familiar shape which is successful in many areas of design.

An advantage of most containers is that they can be moved: rearranging them can change the whole character of a space. Unfortunately, this is something we do indoors, but less often in the garden. Small pots can be moved easily but larger pots may need two people. Alternatively, fit them with castors or put them in a small wheelbarrow.

Size

The bigger the pot, the happier the plant will be, but feeding and watering will also need to be part of the maintenance programme in a way that is

Below The designer of this garden has used colour very cleverly to provide linkage between the building and the garden: white blooms echo the paint of the walls and the shutters reflect the terracotta pots. The muted tones of the paving mediate between the two.

not usually necessary with beds at ground-level. Any container, whether it is a raised bed, a planter or a pot, will tend to limit the eventual size of plants by restriction. Even with regular feeding and irrigation, in such a situation contained plants may fail to reach the size stated in a catalogue or planting encyclopedia. Exposure to especially cold or strong winds may also limit their development.

Large containers can accommodate either a vigorous shrub, a group of smaller plants, or a combination of both. Such an approach would be ideal to provide permanent colour and interest throughout the year, particularly in winter. The combinations of plants will necessarily be far simpler in a container than in a larger raised bed, owing to the limited space available.

ARRANGING POTS

How pots are grouped and positioned has a major effect on the perceived formality or informality of the area.

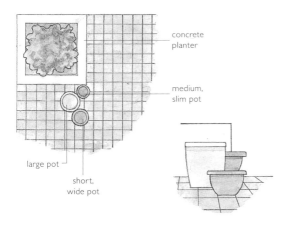

concrete planter

medium, slim pot

large pot

short, wide pot

Above The archetypal informal arrangement of three pots.

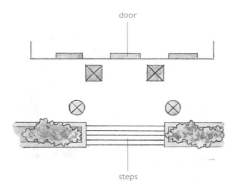

door

steps

Above A symetrical formal composition.

Above Comparable species of plants and similar-looking pots will always look good if they are grouped together. There is great empathy in this cluster of shallow bowls brimming with succulents that leads the eye down through the space.

Above Odd numbers of pots and plants always tend to look more comfortable than even numbers, although if three are all the same size they tend to look more static than an asymmetric trio.

Planting structure

The way in which you structure or arrange your planting is the key to clothing the garden and bringing it to life. Just how you carry this out is dependant on the space available: an expansive roof garden or terrace might have beds of ample size while a balcony may have room only for pots and containers. With a roof garden you can obviously grow a collection of different species, but on a balcony you will almost certainly be dealing with far smaller groups or single specimens. Even so, the pots and plants will need to be arranged in both a sensitive and practical way as the skill of planting design lies in the juxtaposition of shape and texture.

Arranging plants

Before preparing a planting plan check your scale drawing for details about wind, sun and shade, and establish what kind of soil you have or can bring in. A successful planting scheme will take all this into account so that groups and drifts of plants can be positioned so as to complement one another and make the best use of the site.

Drawing up a plan

While some people can plant a garden by eye, for most of us this is a recipe for disaster: it is almost impossible to remember all the details of height, spread, cultural requirements or the relationship of different leaf textures and flower colours.

To make life easier and avoid expensive mistakes, you should prepare a planting plan showing which plant goes where. Such a plan should be drawn to scale and will take your scale drawing (*see p. 56*) as its starting point. Working from a planting plan is essential if you want a sense of

Above left Small-leaved plants can provide infill, cover and colour. Plants such as variegated ivies are quite shade-tolerant, which makes them particularly useful in corners away from the sun.

Left One large plant can serve to soften a hard corner and block a view beyond, allowing lower-growing species either side to provide greater colour and interest.

Above There are some views and positions that should never be obscured, even at the expense of shelter. This bird's-eye view of Central Park in New York is a case in point.

cohesion in your garden. While the occasional impulse buy is undoubtedly fun, avoid making a habit of it, as it almost always leads to a disorganized scheme. Read the label before you buy and note the plant's flowering time, as well as its eventual characteristics and size, so that you can ensure that it will be suitable for the space. Every plant should be drawn on the plan at its final size, which ensures that the scheme will mature into a composition in which each plant has developed without encroaching on its neighbours.

A SUN PLAN

A plan should include details of sunny and shady areas, in both summer and winter.

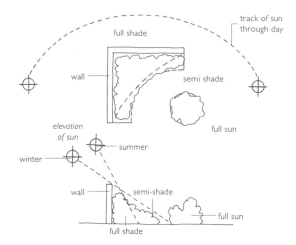

Above The areas of sun and shade dictate which plants go where.

Planting has practical functions, including shelter and screening from winds and poor views. The planting plan will determine the position of these plants as well as the maintenance they will need. A well-planned scheme can knit together and reduce work to a sensible minimum. In general, a scheme should follow the form of planting in a natural environment, with trees at the highest level, shrubs and some hardy perennials as a middle storey and finally a layer of ground cover. Obviously, the smaller the space available the more this approach may need to be modified.

A planting plan builds up logically. Framework plants come first, the trees and larger shrubs, followed by smaller shrubs and herbaceous material and finally the ground covers, annuals and bulbs.

Framework planting

The first and largest elements to position are any trees. In limited areas, choose smaller, less vigorous species, with light foliage to filter wind and block a view without being too dominant. In general these will need the maximum root run, in a raised bed or the largest possible container. While there will be room for only one, or at most a few trees, shrubs are a different matter. These range from larger species that grow to 2m (6ft) or more, down to ground-covers only a few inches high.

Initially you should position the main framework plants to provide shelter and screening and give an overall structure to the space. Many suitable framework plants are evergreen, ensuring winter interest and cover. These are often tough enough to form a protective 'outer envelope'.

A PLANTING STRUCTURE – THE PLAN

A planting plan should be based upon your original survey. It should always folllow a logical structure.

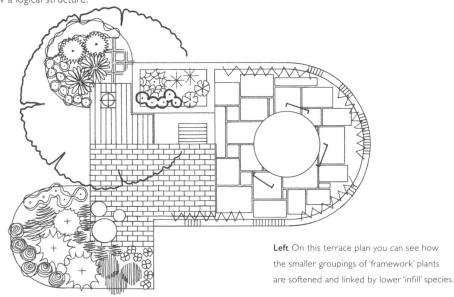

Left On this terrace plan you can see how the smaller groupings of 'framework' plants are softened and linked by lower 'infill' species.

Such planting will not encircle the garden, but will be placed only in key positions for specific purposes. Where you wish to retain a view, and shelter is unnecessary, planting can be lower.

It is important also to consider the outline formed by these larger specimens. It should be visually undemanding: most such plants should form an unobtrusive background on the boundary rather than be a focal point in their own right, which will simply draw attention to where your space ends. Framework plants should be 'softeners', disguising hard edges, breaking the angles of corners and even, if possible, linking with similar plants in an adjoining space or garden, thus making your plot appear a good deal larger.

Leaf size also is relevant here. Large, palmate leaves demand attention and draw a boundary in. Conversely, small, delicate foliage tends to fragment a boundary line and push it away, increasing the apparent space. It therefore makes sense to choose background 'framework' plants that make the plot feel as large as possible.

Above Leaf form is all important in planting design and a fine grass will help to break the line of a boundary by visually pushing it farther away. These grasses add further delight as they rustle in the wind.

Below There is nothing wrong with strong colour, as long as you are bold enough to use it and understand the relationship of the various ranges involved.

Climbers can form part of framework planting as they are often used on the perimeters of an area, helping to conceal the boundary. They are invaluable in clothing screens and dividers, blending them gently into the overall composition: climbers can also be allowed to run up and around the adjoining building; a green background is obviously more attractive to look at than brick or concrete.

FRAMEWORK PLANTS

Careful planning is needed to achieve a graduated arrangement of plants.

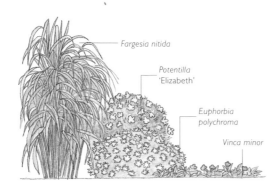

Fargesia nitida

Potentilla 'Elizabeth'

Euphorbia polychroma

Vinca minor

Above Many planting schemes work well with screening and structural plants towards the rear of a border, more colourful infill material in the middle and ground cover at the front. (*See also the plan on p. 106.*)

Above In a well-balanced garden border, whether at height or at ground level, there is a subtle contrast and grouping of species in layers that will provide interest over a long period, using texture, leaf form and shape as well as colour.

Filling in

Now consider how the intervening spaces can be filled with medium and small shrubs and herbaceous material. In drifts, the number of species can be higher, perhaps with one gently leading the eye through and past a sharp angle, or reinforcing a curve. Alternatively, plants can emphasize a geometric shape or underlying pattern, especially if they are clipped in a regular outline.

While framework shrubs are nearly all tall, infill plants can vary in height and shape and need not be rigidly graded from tall at the back to low at the front. Higher planting, often herbaceous, in the middle of the border, can highlight points of interest and give vertical emphasis. Ground-cover plants can include shrubs, hardy perennials or annuals, and can be used in greater numbers still, sweeping beneath taller material and linking areas containing several species.

Think about contrasts in leaf shape and texture, flowering lines and the difference between evergreen and deciduous material. The overall shape of the plant is important — is it rounded or spiky, feathery, prostrate or fastigiate? There are classic combinations such as a fastigiate or spiky shape behind a rounded outline, or sword-like leaves driving through large, round leaves. Finely divided leaves can look handsome with broad, bold foliage, while a horizontal sweep of ground cover can tie together complex forms above.

You can gain inspiration from many sources, the best of which are real gardens rather than flower shows where plants can be grouped unrealistically. Always carry a notebook and camera and make notes on plant height, spread, soil type, flowering time, etc., to build up a personal portfolio of plants. Botanic gardens are a useful resource for plant associations and accurate nomenclature, but you will often find that domestic plots similar to your own have other practical ideas to offer.

Right Architectural features benefit from the softening influence of plants. Here, in a courtyard, the arching lines of the delicate palms lead the eye up in sympathy with the rising staircase. There is no need for added colour in the plants here.

Colour

While colour is normally thought of in terms of flowers, bloom is usually the most vibrant feature and often one of the main reasons for choosing a particular plant in the first place. But you should not forget the bonus of the additional palette that leaves and berries provide with their changing colours at different times of the year. Colour, unfortunately, tends to be one of the most badly misunderstood and mismanaged elements in the garden, as a result of which one quite often sees gardens containing jumbles of unrelated hues with little or no continuity.

Above left Colour is one of the designer's most vital tools, drawing the eye or allowing a scheme to recede gently into the background. By demanding attention, these vibrant, urgent hues tend to foreshorten the space between themselves and the onlooker.

Left This scheme has been carefully worked in shape and texture, together with subtle colour grading, which is essentially cool with just a dash of hotter shades. It certainly would not benefit from any additional colour.

Above There is never just one, but literally thousands of shades of green, yellow or any other colour. This is why schemes that largely rely on foliage and cooler colours can be intricate as well as delicate.

Colour management

The basis of colour management is understanding the difference between the hot and cool ranges, and what these achieve visually. An understanding of the effects of different colours, shades and tones will help you to use them logically.

Positioning colours

Gertrude Jekyll was a painter before she took up gardening seriously and she brought with her an artist's understanding of colour in the landscape. It was her perception that hot colours – reds, yellows and oranges – are naturally vibrant and draw the eye. Conversely, blue, pink, mauve and pastels are cool and increase a feeling of space. It follows that hot colours at the furthest point of any area demand attention and the eye tends to ignore much of the intervening space. This has a foreshortening effect and the garden, or part of the garden, feels smaller as a result. The way to create the maximum possible feeling of space is then to grade the colours, from hot colour in the foreground or close to the house to the cooler colours in the distance.

Above This is a superb example of planting design at its best, with a glorious grading from white, through the flowering grass to the gorgeous warmth of the *Coleus* in the foreground.

Grey is a moderating agent that can link colour ranges and tone down vibrancy and settle it into cooler surroundings. A stunning red rose, which might be too dominant in a small area, could easily be tempered by the addition of grey foliage. Cream flowers would reinforce the subtlety and the result could be breathtaking. Paradoxically, toning down a striking colour in this way does not negate its effect but makes more of it, the addition of a secondary colour highlighting the first.

To prevent a pastel colour scheme becoming bland, add a measured splash of colour from the other end of the spectrum. You do not need a great deal: the amount is something you have to judge by eye and experience.

White can be used to add 'highlights' within a scheme, often to add sparkle to colours at the heavy end of a range. In this way a sweep of copper, purple or another dark colour can be given a delicious fillip with the purest white.

Tonal ranges

There are thousands of shades of red, yellow or green, each with a slightly different role. When studying landscape, I was taught to appreciate these subtle differences with a complex paint colour chart, trying to match a plant species to each. This was a nightmare exercise but it made me realize the diversity of the plant palette. The point here is that using colour to advantage in the garden is no different from using it well in any other sphere. There is no separate set of rules for outdoor designers: the same instincts which govern our choices at home and at work should be allowed free reign in outdoor spaces.

The effect of sunlight

Every gardener appreciates the effect that light has – not only on colour but on the garden in general. Anyone who has observed a climate different from their own will appreciate the effect that stronger or softer light has on a landscape. The stronger the light, the more it tones down colour. In very strong light, hot colours lose their vibrancy, or at least look less dominant. In tropical and sub-tropical countries there is a higher proportion of brightly coloured blooms, which would stand out in sharp relief in the more softly coloured landscapes of temperate areas. Where plants native to one country are introduced to others there is a possibility that they may clash with their surroundings. The misty backdrop of an English garden is often best suited to the subtleties of pastels, rather than the urgency of hot colours, but a plot in the Mediterranean could look very drab without the drama and vibrancy of its bright native blooms.

Light values are often higher in roof gardens and balconies, so you can use correspondingly stronger and harder colours without their necessarily dominating everything around them.

Above White is one of the most telling hues, with the ability to brighten a dark corner or highlight any part of a border. There is a purity about white that sets it apart from other colours.

Above Because pink and blue are in the same colour range, this tumbling pink fuchsia and the dark blue lobelia underplanting combine to make the perfect pair.

Left Spring is the season of hope and regrowth after the winter, with instant and welcome colour being provided by bulbs and other early flowers. Foliage is at its freshest and brightest with the vibrancy of youth.

113

Planting and care

All plants need a growing medium, water and nutrition. The first, soil, compost or rockwool, is the material in which plants anchor themselves and which carries the moisture and nutrients to the root systems. The medium you choose depends upon the load-bearing potential of the roof or by the ease with which material can be imported from ground level. Depths of soil will vary depending on the type of planting you choose, and while a large raised bed would need a depth of 450–600mm (18in–2ft), a pot of bulbs may need only half this amount or less. The amount of water and nutrition that your plants need will depend upon their size, as well as the size of their pots and the climatic conditions.

Planting media

Ordinary, good-quality topsoil is used only on the strongest roof gardens or those which have been purpose built to take heavy loads. It should be friable with an open structure and is best obtained from a reputable supplier. In most instances, you should opt for a compost based on peat or coir, both of which are much lighter. Bear in mind that composts straight from the bag are virtually dry, and when wetted down will be a great deal heavier, adding to the loading on the roof. Peat-based composts are slightly acidic and therefore best for plants that enjoy these conditions. There is, however, some controversy about the use of peat, as its extraction destroys environmentally sensitive sites. You can increase the acidity of any growing medium by adding proprietary acidifiers or buying a specially prepared 'ericaceous' compost.

Filling a bed or pot

Fill beds in layers, gently firming down each layer as you proceed. The soil will settle in the first six months and will need topping up occasionally. There is little point in mixing composts to your plant's requirements: commercial manufacturers prepare their blends with great care and are practised at achieving the correct nutritional balance.

For general use I usually recommend a multi-purpose peat-based compost. This will support a wide range of plant material and is well balanced and relatively light. If you need an even lighter compost, mix in no more than one part in five of horticultural vermiculite, or 'perlite'. Vermiculite has no nutritional value and the savings in weight

Above left On a wall or screen, many of the plants should be tied in at regular intervals. They should also be shaped carefully to prevent them becoming too rampant or swamping their neighbours.

Left The best planting schemes are planned taking the eventual size of species into account at the start. Even so, many plants will often need judicious thinning and sorting on an annual basis to keep them looking perfect.

Right Overcrowding can become a problem in small areas such as roof gardens and balconies, so take care when selecting plants, particularly when the view is as fine as this.

are minimal. It is almost certainly best to stick with a good multi-purpose compost but ensure that the weight of your garden is not in danger of exceeding the surface's load-bearing capacity.

Even the smallest pots can be filled with multi-purpose compost, but they still need a layer of drainage medium. This can be broken terracotta pots or 'crocks', or expanded clay granules. You can prevent the latter from dropping through the drainage hole in the bottom by covering the hole with a piece of crock, small stone or piece of slate. Standing pots on small 'feet' lifts them slightly clear of the surface. This helps drainage and the additional height gives slugs and snails a harder time if they try and reach the foliage above!

As compost tends to dry out quickly in a pot it can be useful to add a water-retentive gel to the mix. It swells when wet and holds water longer, so needs to be watered less frequently than the equivalent volume of compost. It can also be used in hanging baskets and window boxes. A planted bed will benefit from a 50–80mm (2–3in) thick mulch of medium-grade bark chips, which are heavy enough not to be blown away by a strong wind and help to retain moisture in the compost.

Above In this kind of paved area the tree pits will need to be deep and well prepared before planting is undertaken, and the trees will need regular irrigation while they are becoming established. The clipped hedges add immeasurably to this composition.

Rockwool

Using rockwool as a growing medium is a recent innovation which has its own advantages. It is relatively light, even when wet, since the slab needs to be only 100mm (4in) thick for average-sized container planting, or doubled over for larger plants and pots. It is placed over a membrane above a 50mm layer of expanded clay granules. Water is fed into the drainage layer at the bottom, where it is drawn upwards by the rockwool and roots. A drainage point to remove excess moisture is positioned at the top of the drainage layer.

Rockwool has no nutritional value, so after the first season when the plant has exhausted the nutrients placed within the rootball by the nurseryman, regular feeding is necessary. Mulching also helps to retain moisture. Rockwool products are usually only available through professional outlets and installation is normally carried out by specialist landscape companies.

FILLING A POT WITH SOIL

Like beds and containers, pots should be free-draining to prevent waterlogging.

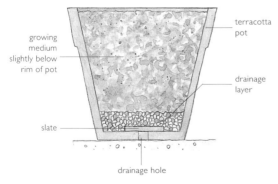

growing medium slightly below rim of pot

terracotta pot

drainage layer

slate

drainage hole

Above The drainage hole is covered with a piece of crock or slate, and the drainage medium and the pot filled with growing medium.

Buying plants

Nearly all plants are now available from suppliers 'container-grown'. Unless the ground is water-logged, they can usually be planted at any time, except the hottest parts of summer or during the winter. Some plants are more difficult to propagate and grow than others, and this is reflected in their retail price, as is their age and size. You are often paying for the length of growing time.

Checking that plants are healthy

When you buy a plant you should always check that it looks healthy, has clean foliage and shows no obvious signs of disease. If you buy plants in autumn, which is an excellent planting time, don't be put off by foliage that is starting to drop from deciduous shrubs, or dying down in the case of hardy perennials. Look at the bottom of the container: it's a bad sign if the roots are forcing their way through holes in the pot; it means that the plant is root-bound and has almost certainly been on the shelf or in the bed for too long.

Above Climbers grow in different ways: some self-cling to a wall while others use tendrils, or simply lean against a support. Recognize this fact when planning the bed and buying the plants and make sure that the right kind of support is available.

Below As long as they are fed and watered on a regular basis, many plants are particularly successful in pots. Acers grow very well in pots and can be complemented with low ground cover, which will in turn help to retain moisture.

Above By training plants against a wall in a decorative fashion, you can make a virtue out of necessity of keeping them tidy. Tied in carefully, and clipped regularly, the plants will become a feature, with strong directional emphasis.

Above Even the most uncompromising situation, in deep shade and damp conditions, can be suitable for certain types of planting, as borne out by the obviously healthy condition of the ferns perched on this piece of stone.

Implementing a planting scheme

If you have prepared a planting scheme it may be sensible to implement it in stages if the area is relatively large. This will also help to spread the cost.

The beds should be freshly prepared and moist without being waterlogged. Working from the plan, lay the available plants out in their positions in the beds. At this stage you can easily make minor adjustments. Bear in mind that no two plants, even of the same type, are ever alike: this may mean that one side looks slightly better facing in one or another direction.

Planting technique

With multi-purpose compost you should need only a trowel for planting. Excavate the holes one at a time, before easing the plant from its container, taking care not to damage the roots and teasing out any that are starting to grow around the rootball. Try the plant in the hole, bearing in mind that the top of the rootball should end up at the same level as the surrounding soil, and adjust the excavation accordingly. Finally, firm the plant into the compost and water it in gently.

Above Plants such as vines are both productive and decorative, but to be at their very best they need regular pruning and tying in to a supporting structure.

Supporting larger plants and climbers

Larger shrubs or small trees may well need to be staked into the edges of beds or other structures. Professional landscapers sometimes use an underground guying system; tied in to the rootball.

Climbers should be tied back to a trellis or on horizontal wires. The cane that is initially in the rootball for additional support can be left in place until growth is under way. If planted against a building, climbers should be spaced 150–230mm (6–9in) from the wall to maximize the amount of rainfall they receive.

Bulbs

Bulbs should be planted at specific depths in the soil. If bulbs are 'blind' – that is, they do not flower – this is usually because they were planted too shallow. They should be planted at about four times the depth of the bulb which, for a daffodil, for example, is 15cm (6in). Always ensure that the bulbs sit snugly on the bottom of the excavated hole with no air gap. In heavy soil they often need a little sharp sand under them, but in multipurpose compost this should not be necessary.

POSITIONING A ROOTBALL IN SOIL

It is important that container-grown specimens are planted at the correct depth.

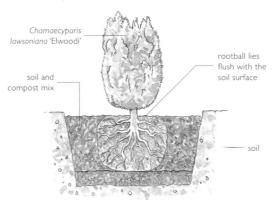

Chamaecyparis lawsoniana 'Elwoodi'

soil and compost mix

rootball lies flush with the soil surface

soil

Above Make sure that the top of the rootball is level with the surrounding soil. This provides both stability and the best possible conditions for the roots.

GUYING A LARGE PLANT UNDER SOIL

Trees and larger shrubs may need extra support when grown in containers.

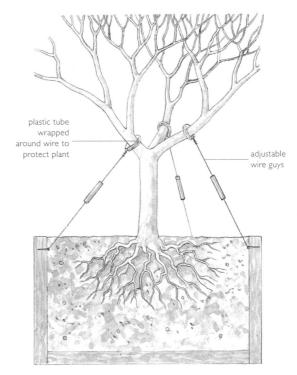

plastic tube wrapped around wire to protect plant

adjustable wire guys

Above Large plants should by guyed into the sides of the container to prevent them blowing over or damaging their root systems by moving in the wind.

Maintenance
Annual and...

Work that must be done each year will include making good any damage to structural elements, repainting, pruning and cleaning. All this work is usually undertaken while the garden is dormant in winter but will help to prolong its summer beauty for many years.

...daily care

Daily work in the garden need not be a chore. When done regularly, tasks such as deadheading roses or watering your plants can be a very relaxing way to spend summer evenings and increase your enjoyment and appreciation of your garden.

Left Maintenance is, of course, an integral part of gardening, but if it is done regularly, the workload need not be heavy. By choosing low-maintenance plants and fittings, you can keep the work to an absolute minimum.

Hard landscape

The hard landscape of a garden includes all the structural elements: the fences, railings and trellis, decking, paving or tiling, planters and beds, walls, paintwork, railings, and furniture. In order to prolong the life of these items and to ensure that they look their best and remain safe, a certain amount of winter maintenance is also necessary. Of course, if anything becomes apparent during the course of the summer that might prove hazardous, more expensive to repair if left undone until the autumn, or might spoil the look of the garden, it should be dealt with immediately. There will also be some regular, more frequent work to be undertaken, such as clearing drains and gutters in the autumn, or checking the pond's pump filter. On the other hand, some more complicated work may not need to be carried out so often: for instance, if you are lucky, the walls and chimneys may only need repointing once every thirty years or so.

Above left Water can be a feature as well as a necessity in any garden. Both decorative items such as fountain heads and practical items such as taps will need descaling with a non-toxic solution or by scrubbing from time to time to prevent a build-up of lime.

Left The most elegant and sophisticated design situations can also require minimal maintenance. This garden is a delightful study in the juxtaposition of materials in what must be the ultimate in low-maintenance gardening.

Boundaries

Whether they are on a roof or at ground level, boundaries may be subject to the vagaries of climate and can sustain weathering and possible structural weakening, or damage by wind. The boundary railing is your ultimate safety barrier and must be checked at all points to ensure that its strength and stability is never compromised.

Timber

Timber is particularly susceptible to weathering and will need regular attention. Stained fences and screens should be brushed down and treated with a non-toxic preservative annually or less frequently, depending on their condition. Do not use creosote as it is poisonous to plants.

Any plants on the boundary should be taken down carefully before the woodwork is treated or painted. Attaching plants to the fence with horizontal strands of wire allows them to be released, then refixed when the job is finished.

Fixings such as posts, brackets and straining wires should be checked carefully and tightened or renewed as necessary. On a terrace at ground

Above Where storage space is limited, furniture may need to be left outside throughout the year. In this case it may have been chosen for ease of care or minimal maintenance.

level, damaged posts can be cut away just above the surface and bolted onto new concrete spurs, but on a roof the whole post should be replaced and firmly bolted in position.

As the wind is stronger at roof level than at ground level, wear can be correspondingly worse. Replace any structural elements with the best-quality materials possible: non-ferrous screws or nails will last longer than steel ones and pressure-treated timber will prove a better investment than untreated wood. In an ideal world, worn boards or other timber would be replaced using similar timber which is equally weathered. In practice, however, there is a danger that new timber will look glaringly obvious. If you don't want to wait for it to blend in, it can be aged artificially.

Overheads with closely spaced beams or those that are roofed with sheeting, should be cleaned regularly to remove leaves or other debris. Check that the screw fixings of canopies have not worn

TAKING DOWN TRAINED PLANTS

With forethought, it is possible to plan your garden so that your plants remain unharmed during any necessary maintenance to nearby structures.

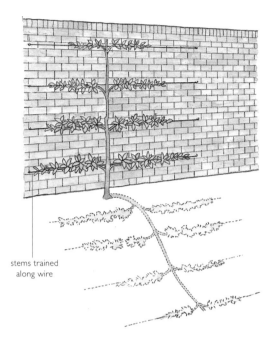

stems trained
along wire

Above If climbers are trained on wires they can be taken down, should the wall or fence need attention. The wires should be disconnected at either end and the plant lowered gently to the ground, ensuring that none of the branches are bent or strained. If you are doing anything with chemicals, make sure that you cover the plant until you have finished the job.

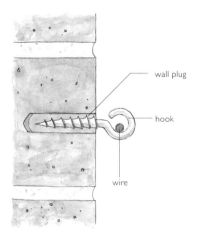

wall plug

hook

wire

Above Wires can be run through hooks that are screwed into wall plugs and simply lifted out as necessary.

or worked loose. Also check the framework of retractable awnings to ensure that all of the bolts and mountings are absolutely secure.

Painted metal

Painted metal fencing should be rubbed down and given a new coat. Plastic-coated surfaces can easily break down to expose the metal below which can then be liable to rust, so be sure to check for this problem.

Brickwork and rendering

Brickwork rarely needs attention, particularly if it is new, but check walls and chimney stacks where weathering may have weakened the mortar joints. Old brick chimneys can in extreme cases become dangerous: these should be removed or repaired urgently. Certainly removal, and even repointing, is best left to a professional, as it may involve scaffolding around a structure. Walls or raised beds that have been rendered will need to be repainted from time to time. If you have climbers trained on hinged trellis, this can be taken down as a unit to enable you to reach the wall behind. If the render does crack or break down it should be renewed before any blockwork below starts to deteriorate.

Glass panels

If the fixings of glass panels or screens become loose the panels could vibrate and finally break, so they should be checked regularly. They should either be cleaned with a detergent which does not harm plants, or else nearby plants should be removed while cleaning is in progress.

Floors

Decking, tiling, paving or other floor surfaces always receive a great deal of wear, but provided that the floor is well constructed and laid, maintenance should be minimal.

Drainage

Drainage channels and gullies should be cleaned regularly to avoid blockages. Standing water can quickly undermine the surface or, in roof gardens, leak into the rooms below. One of the advantages of decking made of removable panels is that these can be lifted for the removal of any leaves or litter. Drainage outlets or open joints in raised beds or containers should be accessible so that they can be checked and kept clear.

Paving and tiling

Any paved or tiled surfaces should be swept down regularly to remove dead leaves and other litter. If slippery green algae forms in shady areas, it can usually be removed by scrubbing with a stiff brush and detergent.

Removing and replacing individual paving modules is a delicate job on a roof, particularly if they have been mortared or fixed with mastic adhesive. Always be conscious of the waterproof membrane below: it may be better to leave it well alone if there is a likelihood of causing damage. Replacing any damaged paving in a terrace is straightforward as slabs, bricks or other modules can simply be chopped out and replaced.

Above This decorative tiling border is such a delicate and well-laid detail that is must be kept clean and properly maintained to be seen at its best.

Below While timber can be allowed to weather to an attractive finish, it nevertheless needs regular attention to prevent rot. Any damaged sections should be replaced immediately.

PREVENTING A POND FROM FREEZING OVER

A pond that supports fish or wildlife should never be allowed to freeze over in winter.

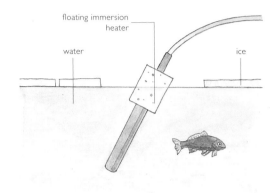

Above A small floating immersion heater will keep a circle of water ice free. It should not be allowed to touch the side of the pond.

Above Any open area of water, whether a swimming pool or a pond, needs to be kept clean. Leaves in particular can be caught in a net and removed once surrounding trees are clear. Pump filters should be cleaned regularly and any electrical fittings checked and, if necessary, repaired professionally.

Decking

Decks should be regularly checked for the safety of all components, particularly where they are built out over steep slopes. The railings and fixings close to ground level are perhaps the most important. The junction between posts and concrete pads, or where posts are bedded directly into soil, must be regularly checked. The timber should be treated with non-toxic preservatives and any damaged or weak components should be replaced immediately.

Beds, pots and containers

Timber raised beds should be checked inside and out for rot. Fibreglass inserts should prevent any internal damage, but if the beds have been lined with polythene there could be leakage and subsequent deterioration. Individual boards may need to be replaced or sections pieced in. Applications of preservative or paint should be carried out as for other surfaces in the garden: if this is done regularly, the beds should last for many years. Pots and containers should be examined annually and any made from timber treated as above. Since some terracotta is not frost proof and can flake or shatter in freezing conditions, these items should be brought inside or placed under cover away from the frost during winter.

Built-in furniture

Built-in furniture should be treated as for other timber features in the garden, but free-standing furniture should be rubbed down annually and teak oil or a proprietary preservative should be applied. Wrought iron or alloy furniture can be rubbed down, primed and painted, while plastics should be washed with detergent to remove algae, particularly if the items are left out all year.

Water features

Well-designed water features need relatively little maintenance. Leaves left in the water can cause toxins to build up in pools at ground level, but this is usually less of a problem on a roof. If leaves do fall in the area, it is easy enough to place a fine-mesh plastic net over the surface in autumn,

removing it with the leaves once the main drop is over. The bottom of the pool can be cleaned out from time to time, but only if there is a significant accumulation of debris. It should not be necessary to drain and refill the pool as this would destroy the natural balance which has taken time to develop. If necessary, drain about a quarter of the water and replenish with new water.

Pump filters should be cleaned regularly and electric cables and fittings checked. If there is any sign of damage, switch off the equipment immediately and seek professional help.

If a pool is allowed to freeze over in winter, toxic gases will quickly build up and these can be harmful or even fatal to fish. A small pool immersion heater will keep an area clear (*see p. 126*), or you can float a rigid inflatable ball on the surface to maintain a hole in the ice. Do not crack the ice with a hammer or other heavy object as the shock waves can stun any creatures in the pool.

Millstones, cobbles and boulders or similar small water features should need little attention except topping up in warm weather. Cables and pumps should be checked regularly. Limescale

Above Regular maintenance of swimming pools is vital, both for health reasons and to keep the feature looking at its best.

can slowly build up on water spouts. This should be carefully scraped away, as it could eventually block the flow or throw it off-centre.

Electric cables

Electricity is perfectly safe in a garden when it is installed and maintained correctly. Faults, particularly when water is present, are potentially fatal, so lighting and power circuits should be kept separate and should run through automatic circuit breakers. Installation and remedial work should be left to a qualified electrician, but always check the condition of cables and fittings, and take care when cultivating beds where lighting is installed.

Irrigation

Limescale should be removed from any drip-feed hoses or nozzles. Hoses should be checked periodically for splits or signs of perishing. Drip-feed systems should also be adjusted as plants grow and spread.

Soft landscape

The growth patterns of plants on a roof or within the confines of a raised bed or container are different from those of plants in the open garden. This means that some aspects of their maintenance are different. On a roof or balcony, the winds may be stronger and large plants and climbers may need to be supported on stakes or tied back to the wall or to trellis. Plants that are grown in containers are also dependent on the gardener for the majority of their water and all of their food and rarely grow to the full size indicated in catalogues or at the garden centre.

Support

Stakes can often be neatly screwed to surrounding timberwork. Any ties and supports should be regularly checked and adapted as plants develop. Shrubs, too, may also benefit from some support. Using the correct plastic ties is essential: avoid wire, string, cord or anything that may cut into the stem or trunk. Garden ties can be obtained from any good garden centre or landscaper.

Feeding

What, when and how much plants should be fed depends on the type of plants involved and the containers in which they are grown. Initially it is worth understanding what kinds of fertilizers are available and their characteristics.

All plant material needs food and once it has been consumed or washed out of the soil it needs to be replaced in some way. Some kinds of plants also need a specific level of acidity or alkalinity to take up nutrients effectively. Ericaceous plants such as rhododendron, azalea and heather thrive in an acid soil (one with a low pH value) and so should be grown in an ericaceous compost which may well contain peat or another acidifier.

Fertilizers

Fertilizers can be broadly categorized as quick acting, steady release and slow release. There are also different methods of application: powders or granules can be worked into the soil when planting or applied as a top dressing sprinkled around plants; liquid forms can be used as a foliar feed sprayed or watered onto leaves or watered in over

Above left The different ways that plants can be grown include pots or containers or in the open ground. In addition, they can be either free-standing or supported against a wall or fence.

Left Climbers can be tied back to trellis or by horizontal strands of wire. Attaching them to wires can be a slightly easier prospect for maintenance, as well as less visually intrusive.

Right Plants can also be used to support each other. Here, some of the tendrils of the clematis have wound themselves up through the tall, erect shrub behind.

Above Bulbs and annual bedding plants can provide instant colour and are particularly useful in a new garden while slower-growing material is knitting together.

the root system. Soil conditioners and mulches also add some nutrition to soil, but fertility should be boosted by other means from time to time.

Container-grown plants will contain a slow-release fertilizer incorporated by the nurseryman. This fertilizer can often be seen as small round granules on the surface of the rootball.

Shrubs and trees will benefit from steady- or slow-release fertilizers. However, steady-release types give up their nutrition faster in hot conditions, such as those often found on a roof garden, and may need to be supplemented with a liquid feed during the growing season.

Annual planting, including half-hardy bedding plants, will respond to liquid feeds around the roots and foliar feed through the leaves, while hardy perennials, or herbaceous plants, can be fed with both steady-release and liquid feeds. Bulbs benefit from a slow-release type such as bonemeal, which can be incorporated into the soil or compost in the autumn so that it is available when the bulbs need it in the spring.

How much food?

Avoid the temptation to over-feed plants, as it can cause scorching and even death. Always read the directions carefully and follow them to the letter. All garden chemicals should be kept in a locked cupboard, safely out of children's reach.

Certain sophisticated irrigation systems have the facility to incorporate a liquid feed and distribute it to plants automatically, but again the balance is critical: plants must not be over-fed.

Mulches are useful, particularly on a roof garden, to retain moisture. If sufficiently heavy they will also prevent lightweight compost being blown away. All organic mulches degrade over a period of time, rotting down to add a little nutrition and structure to the growing medium, so they need topping up on an annual or biannual basis.

Plants grown in rockwool will survive for two years on the slow-release fertilizer already in the rootball. From then on, a steady-release fertilizer should be added to maintain fertility, as well as liquid feed if necessary.

Annual maintenance

Some shrubs simply need to be pruned once each year to keep them neat and tidy, whereas others require a specific amount of pruning at a specific time of year to enable them to flower in following years; however, some shrubs need virtually no pruning at all. Herbaceous plants should be lifted

Above If you wish to grow food crops – such as apples, pears and citrus fruits – both in containers and on plants that last from year to year, regular feeding will be essential to maintain good yields.

Right As a general rule, the larger the pot, the happier a plant will be, revelling in having ample room for its roots. It also has the benefit for you that it will need to be watered less often. Even so, you should watch for extremes of weather, which can be detrimental.

Above left and above Plants can be trained to produce a formal or informal result. Large-leafed plants, with a sprawling habit, look best trained to ramble. Smaller-leaved plants with more compact habits can be encouraged into a controlled shape, such as an arch.

and divided, which produces more plants if you need them, or more attractive ones if you discard the older, less healthy parts. On the other hand, bulbs grown in containers need a little more care than those which are simply left in the ground in a larger garden.

Pruning shrubs

The pruning of shrubs, as distinct from the day-to-day deadheading and tidying of plants, is generally carried out on an annual basis. Many shrubs need little or no attention apart from the occasional removal of dead, weak or diseased wood. The practice of shearing over plants should be avoided, since it produces an artificial shape and can remove flowering wood. Shrubs which need to be pruned to keep them flowering at their best can be divided into separate categories.

Spring- and early-flowering deciduous shrubs that flower on stems developed in the previous season should be pruned immediately after they have flowered. The flowering stems should be cut back by about a third to strong lateral shoots. The resulting shape should be balanced since the plant will now produce new shoots that will flower the following year. Shrubs typical of this group include *Weigela*, *Philadelphus*, lilac and *Deutzia*.

Established shrubs that flower in late summer such as *Buddleia davidii*, *Lavatera* and *Perovskia* should be cut back in early spring to within two or three buds of the old wood to allow new wood to develop. The last group includes *Cornus* (dog wood), shrubby willows and elders. The first two have coloured stems that look superb in winter. The stem colour is strongest on the current season's wood: if the stems are pruned hard in early spring, they will grow through the summer and look at their best the following winter.

Climbers

As they give vertical cover, climbers are among the most useful plants on a roof garden, although they are untidy if left unpruned. The rules are generally the same as for shrubs: old wood on spring-flowering types should be cut back by about a third.

Wisteria, which is such a popular spring-flowering plant, should be pruned twice in the same year. In midsummer the side shoots can be cut back to within six leaves of the main stems and then during the following winter these same stems can be cut hard back to within three buds.

Passion flower, which flowers relatively late, can have its side shoots pruned back nearly to the main stems in spring, while honeysuckle can have some of the older stems cut out after flowering.

Some tender climbers can be successful in relatively mild rooftop conditions, but if you grow them it is best to remove frost-damaged shoots in spring, since these can die back and become infected with disease.

Clematis is another justly popular climber, but the rules for pruning it can be confusing, as pruning times vary according to when the flowering shoots develop. The real problem is that if you don't prune, the new growth which produces all the flower occurs progressively higher and farther from the base, leaving unsightly bare stems below. There are three major groups of clematis: those that flower before midsummer on the previous season's wood; those that flower in late spring or early summer and then come into bloom again in late summer; and finally, those that flower in late summer and early autumn on wood grown in that season. Examples of the early-flowering types are the popular *C. montana* and the wonderful blue *C. macropetala*, as well as the various *C. alpina*.

If you have sufficient room, vigorous varieties of the first group can be left unpruned and simply clipped back with shears after flowering. If you want to keep them really neat, then train them onto a framework straight from planting and cut all the flowering shoots back to a strong bud at the base in early summer.

Right Climbing and rambling roses will quickly form a tangle if not tied in and selectively thinned. Any training is best started when the plant is young and not left until it is mature.

Above Pots and containers do, of course, need regular irrigation, and this is best carried out in the early morning or in the evening, when the sun is not strong enough to scorch their foliage.

Above Provided that there is enough of the correct growing medium, there are few limits to what you can grow on a roof. Here, a virtual meadow has been created with succulent plants. Once established this kind of plant grouping will require very little maintenance and is ideal for carpeting large areas.

Those clematis that flower twice in the same season, such as *C.* 'Nellie Moser' and *C.* 'The President', should have between a quarter and a third of their stems cut back in late winter to the highest pair of strong buds. After the first flowering, cut back another quarter of the stems to produce flower early the next year. The last group, which includes *C. tangutica, C. viticella, C.* 'Jackmanii', *C.* 'Ernest Markham' and *C.* 'Hagley Hybrid', is easy to care for: cut each stem back in late winter to the lowest pair of well-developed buds. The new growth of clematis is brittle and should be tied back carefully in order to avoid wind damage.

Dividing herbaceous plants

Most herbaceous plants (or hardy perennials) should be lifted and divided roughly every three years in early autumn or mid-spring when the soil is warm enough to encourage root development. Lift the plants and then either carefully prise the rooted sections apart by hand or using two small border forks placed back to back. If the central section of the plant has become hard and woody, producing little growth, it can be cut out and discarded. Replant the new sections with a little steady-release fertilizer.

Bulbs

Bulbs that have been naturalized in raised beds should be allowed to die down naturally after they have flowered. Do not be tempted to cut off the green foliage before it goes brown. If you have bulbs grown in pots and containers, they too should be allowed to die down before being carefully lifted. The leaves should be cut off and the bulbs then stored in a dry, dark place to be replanted the following autumn.

Aquatic plants

Most aquatic plants die down in winter and if the situation is not too windy the brown foliage can be left in place to provide extra interest. If the foliage does get blown flat, it should be removed. Replanting aquatic plants is best done in late spring when the warmer water will encourage new growth.

Day-to-day maintenance

Day-to-day jobs become second nature to most gardeners and include deadheading spent blooms to sustain flowering, supporting hardy perennials as they grow, and tying in climbers. Such work is hardly time consuming and can again be enormously satisfying and restful.

Pests and diseases

Something else to keep a look out for is disease and insect attack, which can happen at virtually any time of the growing season. Blackfly, greenfly (aphids), caterpillars, and slugs and snails can be prevented with chemicals which should always be used according to the instructions. If you prefer not to use chemicals — I try to avoid them — there are a number of biological controls available, such as nematodes. Make sure that chemicals are stored under lock and key, away from children.

Disease is usually a viral or fungal attack of some kind such as black spot on roses, or mildew. Part of the solution is to ensure that plants are watered and fed correctly as disease can strike more easily if the plants are under-nourished or under stress. Again there are chemical treatments which are normally successful if they are applied early enough and exactly as directed.

Plants which are thriving in their growing conditions are generally far more resistant to pests and diseases than material that has to battle for existence. In my own garden I have little time to pamper plants and as a result I choose things which enjoy life rather than struggle for it, allowing me to do the same with my garden.

Irrigation and watering

All plants need water, although some species are more tolerant than others of the dry conditions on a roof, balcony or raised bed at ground level.

Irrigation systems range from simple hand-held devices to complex computer-driven systems that function under any conditions, whether you are home or not. All automatic irrigation works on the same principal, that of delivering the water almost directly to the roots of the plants. Watering should be carried out regularly and in the heat of summer, early in the morning, and in the evening to prevent leaf scorch and conserve water.

LOCALIZED IRRIGATION

Irrigation systems can remove the need for watering cans.

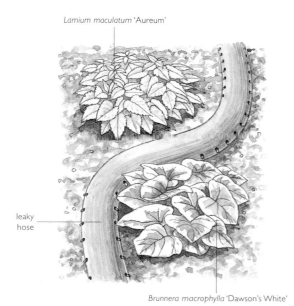

Lamium maculatum 'Aureum'

leaky hose

Brunnera macrophylla 'Dawson's White'

Above 'Leaky' pipe systems allow water to ooze around plants.

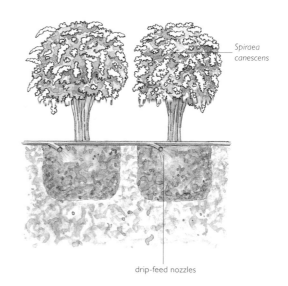

Spiraea canescens

drip-feed nozzles

Above Drip-feed irrigation ensures that water goes to the roots.

Accessories

Selecting...

The way in which your accessories are chosen and used is as important as the overall design: make sure that the design has a direct influence over the style of ornaments that you use.

...and positioning

Larger ornamental features should be put in place after the main structure of the garden or area of it has been laid out, but before the plants. There are no unbreakable rules, provided that an item is sited in keeping with the scale of its immediate surroundings.

Left Some pots are far too beautiful to plant up and rely on their sculptural outline for effect. A combination of planted and unplanted pots can be positioned to great effect in the garden.

Focal points

Major features such as water, statuary, urns and obelisks can be used to draw the eye and as important focal points in the overall composition. Think about them in detail while you are preparing the design as they will be permanent or semi-permanent parts of it, although I feel strongly that they should be moved from time to time. Features can give directional emphasis, be the focus of a vista on a long balcony or provide the sight and sound of water on a split-level terrace. They will be the punctuation marks of the garden, and so should be used sparingly.

Positioning and choice

An important initial consideration on a roof or balcony is the weight of any ornamental feature. If you are concerned about this, check your initial survey to see which parts are strong enough.

A wide range of synthetic materials is used to mimic traditional ones while still remaining lightweight. Fibreglass containers are manufactured to look like lead or terracotta, and it is becoming more difficult to tell the real thing, although there is an aesthetic argument against this use of synthetics to copy traditional materials. Plastics and synthetics are fluid, malleable materials which offer the chance of dramatic, contemporary and colourful shapes. Stone, terracotta and lead tend to be used in more traditional work, although they too can be featured in stunningly fresh ways.

Water features

Water is a significant element in any garden, in whatever position and whatever guise. It provides a feeling of movement, a cooling influence on a

Above left Sculpture comes in all shapes and sizes, alive as well as inert. Topiary is a fascinating art form: in this case, creeping plants are grown over a frame to create a fairground horse, creating a dramatic focal point.

Left Water is always both visually and aurally interesting. Although a grand feature like this entails considerable constructional skills, the end result is dramatic.

Above Even the tiniest bubble fountain can create a focal point in an intimate situation, such as a balcony. It really is all a matter of scale and positioning.

hot summer's day and, of course, a background sound which can be enormously soothing.

Small water features are often traditional in design. They vary from diminutive wall-mounted bowls with water cascading from one to another, to lion or fish heads that gush into a pool below.

On a contemporary note, you can buy rather more complicated, but still attractive, millstone or boulder features. The latter can be built within a raised area, possibly surrounded by planting, to provide a delightful focal point. Water is pumped

Above At first sight this appears to be a stunningly beautiful piece of free-standing sculpture, but if you look very closely you will see that it is, in fact, a water feature attached to a mirror.

Above Which came first, the gazebo or the framing columns? In any case the combination produces pure drama set against a rugged landscape. Keeping the balustrade clear of pots and planting might have heightened the focus onto the gazebo even further.

from a tank to play over the visible top surface. This can either be in natural or synthetic materials, which are often far lighter. These need not be imitations of natural materials: I have recently designed acrylic mirror pyramids of varying sizes which are a variation on this theme. Water is pumped from the sump to the top of the feature where it bubbles out to slide down over the sides and then back into the sump. The ever-changing reflections are fascinating. Variations on a watery theme are endless: found objects, pots, copper fish, barrels, glazed bowls and mini pools can all be incorporated into designs. They are also safer for children than areas of open water.

Water also attracts wildlife. Birds drink and bathe at most features while fish, dragon- and damselflies will breed and hatch in a larger, well balanced pool. A roof garden with water and plants can be a rich wildlife habitat anywhere.

Ornaments

Garden ornaments should not be used merely to dress up a garden: they should become part of it, as points of emphasis, interest or fun. The fun element is too often forgotten. Some people regard garden gnomes as icons of bad taste, but other animals and figures can be well modelled and add to a composition. If you like a piece and have a place for it, use it; it is, after all, your garden.

Sculpture

There are many classical statues to choose from, ranging from poor renditions in badly cast concrete through faithful replicas in reconstructed stone to original works of art. Prices vary, and an original piece could cost more than the entire garden. Size and, especially where conventional materials are used, weight can also vary greatly.

There are few good contemporary designs available and it is almost impossible to find these through a garden centre or shop. This is not for a lack of sculptors but rather from a lack of interest or of awareness on the part of the public. Good examples can sometimes be found at big garden shows, but because they are often especially made for the show the prices are high. Individual items are produced in a wide range of materials including wood, various metals – some of which are lightweight – bent wire, glass and acrylics. While the prices reflect the originality of the piece, genuine works of art do have investment value.

Scale is another important factor to consider. A relatively large piece may look correct in a garden at ground level, but in the smaller area of a roof or balcony could be out of place. Look at the space and choose carefully. Bear in mind also that the bigger the piece the more it will draw the eye and appear to diminish the surrounding space, so larger items should be sited particularly carefully.

Urns

Urns are usually large, often handsome classical pots that can be used as ornaments without the addition of planting, raised on plinths to increase their visual impact. Used singly they become focal points, but in pairs, to either side of a doorway or other feature, they focus the viewer's attention on

Above Just occasionally you can build something that is both unusual and has great charm. There is enormous power in this large pot built entirely from thin pieces of slate.

Below Because they can have personal associations that no one else would understand, items such as sculpture are best bought by the owner of the garden rather than the designer or architect.

the central object, so increasing tension as you approach. Classical examples are appropriate to a traditional garden design, although they can be used with panache alongside post-modern architecture. Many urns are suitable for interiors as well as outside and this creates an obvious opportunity for linkage, particularly if there is planting on both sides of the divide.

Terracotta

Terracotta is a popular material for ornaments, but in an exposed site, perhaps on a terrace at ground level, it should be checked for frost resistance. Because terracotta is clay-based, the modelling can be more detailed and sharper than on reconstituted stone. As it can be cast more thinly, a terracotta item is almost always lighter than a similar one in stone. It is usually a reddish brown, but the cream form – faience – can look superb in the right setting.

Obelisks

Obelisks draw the eye and act as punctuation marks in any setting: they can introduce a point of drama used either singly or in pairs. In a small space they should be proportionally small.

Other ornaments

These can include bird baths, sundials, boulders or 'found objects'. Many are intensely personal objects, and for this reason I very rarely choose these items for clients. You should use your imagination, both in the acquisition and the siting of such objects, and your garden will be richer for it.

In small areas, walls and screens can hold a wide range of ornaments, from classical plaques to various works in relief. Planters and baskets can add life and colour, while paintings, either directly on the wall or on a wide variety of materials, can be placed singly or as compositions.

Left and right The human figure is a popular subject for sculpture. Here the treatments of two classical figures are different: the modern setting sets off the vigour of the statue on the left, whereas the plant niche emphasizes the peaceful nature of the statue on the right.

Furniture

Garden furniture can be most uncomfortable. The golden rule is to try it out before you buy – sit on a chair for five minutes and check whether your knees fit comfortably under the table and don't be seduced by what looks attractive in the shop. Gardens are all about relaxation, and if you are not comfortable, you will not be able to relax. There are myriad styles and patterns, in a wide range of materials, including metal, plastic and timber. The key is to pick a style that complements that of the area and then to find a comfortable, practical example.

Materials

Which material or combination of materials you choose depends on a number of factors. Is the weather routinely good enough for you to leave your furniture out all year? Will you want to move it regularly? Do you mind hot plastic or cold metal? Is your garden going to be 'modern' or 'classical' in style? Does the furniture need to be hard-wearing enough for children?

Timber

Timber furniture is the most widely available, and styles in it range from the pure classicism of a 'Lutyens' bench that will stand alone as a superb focal point, to a homely, well designed and inexpensive set that will look good in most situations. As with most other things in the garden, it is important to keep furniture simple.

Most good, durable designs are made from hardwoods, which last longer than the softer pine. Some hardwoods are taken from non-renewable rain forest, so check before you buy that the timber comes from a properly managed resource.

Furniture on a roof garden or balcony may have to stand outside all year for lack of storage space, so bare timber will need to be maintained by using a 'teak' or other preservative oil on an annual basis. Painted furniture will need to be rubbed down and repainted from time to time.

Where space is at a premium, furniture sets that are either folding or that stack closely together can be invaluable, and free-standing loungers can be wonderful for quiet relaxation during the heat of the summer. To maximize your floor space, these can often be neatly and securely hung on a wall when they are not being used.

Above left The most important point about garden furniture is that it should be both comfortable and blend with its setting.

Left A modern roof garden deserves modern, bold furniture. Here, the curves of these metal and cloth chairs highlight the angularity and strong lines of the framework.

Right This built-in seating not only forms an integral part of the layout of the garden, it is also an effective way of adding colour.

Plastic

Not very long ago nearly all plastic furniture was considered to be cheap and nasty and the only colour available was white. There is now an enormous range of well-designed lightweight items in a huge range of colours and combinations. White is in fact a poor choice on a roof, as the glare can be almost intolerable.

One of the advantages of plastic furniture is that it can be allowed to stand outside all year. Loose covers can be brought inside, washed and stored at the onset of winter.

Metal

Metal furniture can be very uncomfortable to sit on. Many copies of traditional wrought iron or bent wire patterns are unusable for more than a few minutes. Again, do test furniture before you buy it. Some examples are, of course, perfectly comfortable to sit on or lounge in. Many of these are contemporary designs in a combination of metal and synthetics, both of which are usually extremely durable. Light tubular alloy is convenient and is also often used.

Above The final furnishings of any room help to bring it alive in a thoroughly personal way. Here you can introduce the details that make any composition both lived in and special.

On a more traditional note, park bench styles of iron with timber slats can look and feel particularly good: excellent reproductions are available.

Fabric

Fabric furniture comes in a variety of styles; my own favourite is the traditional deck chair. The folding wooden frames can be hung with the fabric of your choice, possibly one which echoes an interior colour scheme or pattern. Close relations are 'directors' chairs, which are nearly as comfortable and also fold up for easy storage.

Hammocks are another popular choice. They can be slung between any two secure fixings, although the strength of all the fixings should be checked regularly. On a roof or balcony there is often the opportunity to fix stout eyes into a wall and the hammock folds away when not in use. Hammocks with an integral frame are usually a little too large and cumbersome for a small area.

Bean bags are popular with young, old and pets alike. They are ideal for an additional influx of friends and are extremely comfortable – just try to get a dog out of one! There are waterproof materials now available so that the bags can be left in a shower of rain without going soggy.

Overheads and awnings

Awnings, shades and parasols are particularly useful on a roof or balcony where the light values are often higher and shade is scarce. Awnings are normally fixed to the building and can be unreeled from a housing or let down from a folded position. They usually cast soft shade, as the light is filtered rather than cut out altogether, and the many colours and patterns can link with the fabrics and cushions used elsewhere. Fixings should be secure, with no risk of the blind or awning unravelling in a high wind.

Parasols have become increasingly popular over recent years and are available in a range of sizes. Some just span a table, others are large enough to cover a complete terrace or balcony. Secure fixing is again vital on a roof: parasols are really suitable for use only on calm days. Plain colours are often best for a large area, although vibrant colours can form a focal point.

At ground level, on a terrace, an informal awning can be made that creates a pool of wel-come shadow by casting a sheet over the top of beams, or even over the low branches of a tree. The edges of the awning can be simply tied down and removed once the need for it is over. Scatter large cushions or bean bags underneath to complete the effect.

Above People rarely seem to take cushions into the garden, which is a shame, as they not only make garden furniture a good deal more comfortable, but they can extend a colour scheme from inside to outside.

HOW TO FIX A HAMMOCK

A hammock can be an ideal form of seating in limited space as it can be put away easily when it is not in use, thereby avoiding using unnecessary floor space.

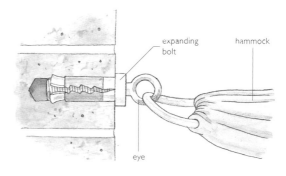

Above Hammocks are one of the most comfortable forms of garden furnishings, but need firm anchor points to ensure safety. Expanding bolts set into masonry are virtually indestructible, although the lashings should be checked on a regular basis.

Above Wooden furniture is durable and looks at home in most garden settings. It is immensely adaptable and is available in both traditional and modern styles to suit any garden design. Regular maintenance will ensure long life.

Lighting

Lighting can be used to transform the feel of a garden or outside living space, extending the length of time for which it can be used each day and bringing a different dimension to every aspect of its composition. It is only recently that specialist companies and consultants have begun to offer their services in the area of lighting garden areas and, so far, few schemes have been any more adventurous than having basic floodlights fitted to ground spikes. You can, however, achieve sensitive and dramatic effects by installing practical and decorative forms in such a way that they can be revised as the garden develops and the plants grow.

Above left Lighting can be functional, decorative, or a combination of both. If fittings are visible, they should be selected to match the adjoining architecture or garden style.

Left Drama is an essential part of lighting design and here the soft glow brings surrealism to the strongly clipped shapes, as well as clearly illuminating the steps.

Above Lighting set close to the wall and shining upwards 'grazes' the surface, highlighting the wall and throwing the arch into relief.

Utility lighting

First the utility lighting should be positioned. As well as lighting hazards, it also acts as a crime deterrent, although halogen floodlights can often leave pools of shadow. It can pay to have a system which effectively illuminates the area when you need it to, or you can programme it into a timer.

The obvious areas for illumination include doorways or French windows, any changes of level and steps, as well as the main routes around the area and its features. A soft floodlight system will provide an ideal working spread and can be positioned where it is needed most. This need not be at a high level: you seldom need to light the top of your head, so fittings should be recessed alongside steps or doorways to illuminate where you are going walk or what you might walk into, such as uprights for overheads and other structures, which can be nearly invisible if painted black. A gentle light at the top or bottom, shining up or down, will be delicate and practical.

Utility lighting usually has a visible source, so fittings should blend in with the area. Imitation coach lamps look ostentatious on a contemporary façade, as can cast-iron street lamps. Remember that the light is more important than the fitting. Something straightforward will probably be less expensive than an ornate reproduction. However, some fittings are striking as works of art; they are expensive but also a tempting buy.

Decorative lighting

In decorative lighting schemes, the illumination takes precedence and the fittings should be invisible. Subtlety is better than a garish display: this is a good example of 'less is more'. The approach to garden illumination is similar to that for other elements of garden design: a composition where the whole is immediately obvious is less interesting than one containing surprises or different areas. The parts and features of the garden should be brought to life in darkness and displayed differently from the way they appear during the day.

Colour

Many garden centres sell every colour of light bulb, which can lead to unfortunate results. Red and orange turn plants a sickly hue, while green tends to wash foliage out completely. It is best usually to have a simple white or blue light; blue often has the effect of sharpening colour.

Spotlighting

Perhaps the best-known form of garden lighting is where a relatively concentrated beam is thrown onto a single object, usually a focal point, thereby throwing it into sharp relief. The question of

height is an important one: a beam should be sited so that you do not cross it in walking around the space. The fitting should be concealed, comparatively high-powered, and set some way away from the feature. This dramatic technique should be used sparingly – too many spotlights might look overpowering.

Uplighting and downlighting

These involve lights that are positioned at the top or bottom of a feature such as a classical column, pergola, statue or tree. The aim of the effect is to highlight the feature alone, rather than to light the immediate area.

Below Lighting effects can be created with lanterns and candles, as they flicker with far more character than electricity. The source may be weaker, but you can quickly adapt to the lower light value.

Floodlighting

Here the beam is more diffused to give a pool of illumination far wider and softer than a spotlight. The source can be relatively close, but again should be concealed. The technique is a general rather than a specific one and can be used to light a group of plants, pots or another feature. The edges fade out into the surrounding darkness.

Grazing light

This fabulous technique places floodlights at the top or bottom of a wall so that the light skims or 'grazes' the surface, picking up surface detail. It allows any relief to be emphasized by shadows running away from the light source and can be used to enormous effect on a roof garden, where walls or chimney stacks above can be brought into the composition.

Moonlighting

This is my own favourite decorative lighting system and entails siting a relatively low-powered floodlight in the branches of a tree, or just above the slats of overheads, so that the pattern of the structure and branches moving in the wind are cast on the ground below. The effect can be magical, particularly when seen from inside the house, looking out through large windows.

Backlighting

This is the opposite of floodlighting. A light is set close behind a feature to throw it into sharp relief. The feature could be a specific focal point, such as a statue or other ornament. A screen or trellis clothed with planting can also look superb, its shadows thrown onto an opposite wall.

Water

Lighting techniques should be kept simple in relation to water features. Floating, rotating, multi-coloured lights do little to enhance the tranquil mystery of a garden feature. Underwater lights should be white or blue. The object can be simply lit to have a gently diffused glow from beneath the surface, or something rather more specific, possibly by backlighting a cascade or statue.

Above Uplighters, carefully set nearly flush with the paving, form the perfect illumination to highlight this simple modern setting of multi-coloured, polished stone columns.

Installing lighting

As far as the installation is concerned, you should always employ professionals. If mains voltage is used they will bury the cables or install armoured cable and waterproofed switch gear. Much garden lighting works on a low voltage system, wired back to a transformer and circuit breaker in the house. If cables are laid on the surface, care will be needed when you are digging or trowelling. The advantage of such a method is that it can be easily adjusted. Schemes are best set up by two people: one to move the fittings around, the other to direct operations.

The future

Most garden lighting is still fairly conservative, but some designers have experimented with lasers, fibre optics and holograms. The results with lasers (which should be installed by experts) can be both stunning and beautiful. Fibre optics, which are safer as light is transmitted down the fibre rather than power, can also look delightful.

Special effects

In a small area, especially, special effects such as trompe-l'oeil and murals can provide a feeling of greater space. In truth they rarely fool anyone, at least after the first glance, but they are fun and that in itself is a good reason to employ them. Trompe-l'oeil and the clever use of mirrors are particularly valuable in small spaces, as they can make the area appear larger. Although trompe-l'oeil and mirrors used to deceive the eye are simply a piece of fun, they still need to be planned carefully to ensure that they work correctly: otherwise they will simply fall flat like a joke with a poor punchline. Decorative trellis is another way of using creatively what is essentially a practical garden structure. It can be decoratively shaped, or coloured, or both. Even black-painted trellis has a quite different effect from that of a natural brown. Do bear in mind, however, that whatever special effect you choose should complement the style and feel of the rest of the garden.

Above left Visual trickery has been one of the designer's arts since time immemorial and should not be taken too seriously. Humour is an essential part of any garden composition.

Left This trompe-l'oeil is gloriously outrageous. It fools no-one but offers great charm and makes a real talking point. To make such compositions more effective they should, of course, be in the same style as the rest of the garden.

Trompe-l'oeil

Obviously trompe l'oeil involves trickery. The 'perspective' trellis with a central statue has become a cliché: there are more subtle ways of using the technique. A trellis 'window' with a view painted on the wall behind can be realistic and evocative, particularly if based on a romantic holiday vista. I have seen all sorts of permutations, from Mediterranean harbour views to a glimpse of a church spire and surrounding roofs.

Another version of trompe l'oeil that often works well uses a mirror instead of a statue inside a frame. The secret, when using mirrors in a garden to increase a feeling of space, is to ensure that they are angled so that you don't see yourself in them. They should be angled off into an area of planting so that it looks as though there is a new garden beyond. You can extend this trick by building a false arch or doorway; one of the best and most convincing I have seen involved a partially open false door with a mirror behind.

Mirrors can also be used in combination with water; behind a waterfall or within an arch with water flowing out in front. In both instances it looks as if the stream recedes back indefinitely. Another trick is to line the bottom of a very shallow pool with a mirror, which can make the water look far deeper. This could be invaluable on a roof garden. Some people are concerned about the possibility of birds flying into a reflective surface. I have found that the problem rarely arises as long as you partially cover the mirror with vegetation; this also enhances the illusory effect.

Decorative trellis

Trellis has been used in gardens as a divider and decorative element for hundreds of years. It has of late had something of a revival, but in classical rather than contemporary terms. As a result a wide range of classically inspired styles is available at most good garden centres. Alternatively, you

Right This delicate trellis provides a subtle backdrop to the more immediate action in front. The slats have the effect of breaking the light down, producing a real visual rhythm.

TYPES OF DECORATIVE TRELLIS

There are many different designs for trellises.

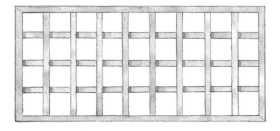

squares

diamonds

doubled diamonds

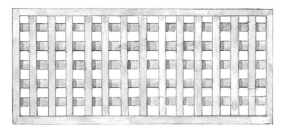

close squares

can have a specific design made to suit your own ideas and to fit a particular space. Basic patterns are normally based on squares or diamonds. Even so there is ample opportunity for variation in the detailing of posts and grouping and positioning of panels. Panels can have shapes cut out of them in a variation of the circular moongate principle, used at ground level to pierce a wall and allow a view into the landscape or next garden 'room'.

Above Mirrors can be enormously useful for increasing apparent visual space in a small garden. They need to be positioned carefully so that you cannot see yourself when you are walking towards them from the usual approach point.

While many people think of trellis in traditional terms, you can have a great deal of fun working in a more up-to-date style. Experiment with the positive and negative aspects of the material, cutting a pattern out of a run (a negative shape), or creating a pattern from the overall shape of the trellis, such as a tree or cloud (a positive shape). There are enormous possibilities since you can create virtually any shape or pattern ranging from regular cut outs running along a trellis, to a montage of shapes built up into a mural. As trellis is an ideal support for climbing plants, this adds to the fun. A climber could scramble up a trellis 'tree' or fill carefully shaped gaps. Pots grouped along a wall, beneath sections of a montage, could add to the effect. A striking composition, that I saw in the Far East, used clipped trees which precisely filled the shapes cut out of a long, complex run of trellis. At first it was difficult to see exactly what was going on, but the end result was intriguing.

Trellis is often the ideal medium for covering or disguising objects such as boiler flues, aerials or water tanks. Care is obviously needed near a flue, which can get dangerously hot. Ensure that the trellis continues a theme used elsewhere in the garden so that it does not draw attention to itself. A virtually invisible access door can be incorporated and climbers will complete the picture.

Colour is another important consideration with trellis, as it is with all garden accessories. At one time, only white or dark green were acceptable, but so many colours are now available that you can link the garden and interior colour schemes in numerous ways. While pale, bleached or dragged colours are in vogue, reds, yellows and oranges can be dramatic: used in the right place, with a festoon of climbers creating a restful colour break, they could provide the perfect splash or drama in a contemporary roof or balcony. Black is often thought of as an unlikely colour, but in fact it is extremely useful as it absorbs light and allows a view to pass through or beyond it. Black trellis can create a subtle counterpoint and look good with similarly painted overheads.

The features and furnishings that make up the incidentals of a composition are legion. Not only do they bring a composition to life, they also provide a personal signature, making the space uniquely and intimately yours.

Above Trellis should be coloured more often; just look what interior designers can do with it. This gives the opportunity to link it in with both the adjoining house and incidental planting.

Below By clipping the plants above and around the back of the seat, the sweeping lines of the seat are emphasized, bringing a rhythm that might be lost against more general planting.

Glossary

Aggregate The **gravel** component of concrete which varies in size and can be exposed by brushing the concrete when nearly dry to produce a textured finish

Annuals Plants that complete their entire life-cycle within one growing season

Aphids Plant pests such as greenfly and blackfly

Bark chippings Used to provide a soft, textured surface over pathways and beds. They also act as **mulch** and exclude weed growth

Bituminous sealer Asphalt

Cleat A piece of wood or iron bolted onto the roof or wall onto which decking is attached to stop it slipping

Cobbles Rounded, kidney-shaped beach or river-bed pebbles, either used loose or bedded in **mortar** to form a textured surface

Coir A growing medium made from coconut husks

Coping The top course of masonry in a wall. This is usually more weatherproof than the rest of the wall and can be decorative

Crocks Broken pieces of pot used to cover the hole at the base of a pot to provide drainage without allowing the soil to be washed out

Damp proof course (DPC) A layer of moisture repellant material in a wall (usually) near the ground, to keep water from permeating the building

Deadhead To remove a wilting or faded flower from a plant without allowing its fruit or seed to mature

Ericacious compost Compost which is acidic in nature and therefore suitable for acid-loving plants such as heathers, azaleas and rhododendrons

Faience A cream-coloured form of **terracotta**

Fastigiate With a conical or tapering outline

Fibreglass Material made of a lightweight plastic containing strengthening fibrous strands of glass

Friable Easily crumbled, especially when dry

Granite setts Blocks, usually the size and shape of bricks, used for 'cobbling' roads in the nineteenth century and for contemporary paving

Gravel Broken stone or small dredged pebbles used as a loose textured surface or as **aggregate** in concrete

Ground-cover Low-growing plants that spread out and knit together. Useful as a form of weed prevention

Hardy Describes a plant that will usually survive winter out of doors in a given climate

Hoggin A mix of clay and **gravel** used as a 'binder' in gravel paths and drives

Ledger rail A horizontal **timber** rail bolted onto the face of a wall to provide support for decking

Lumber *see* **timber**

Mastic adhesive A **bituminous** flexible sealer

Mortar A smooth mixture of cement, sand, water and plasticizer for joining or bedding stones or bricks

Mulch A soil covering which retains moisture, reduces erosion and prevents weeds. Organic mulches, such as grass cuttings, enrich the soil

Perennials Plants that should live under usual circumstances for at least three growing seasons

Pergola Arbour or covered walk, usually with climbing plants trained over it

pH The measure of acidity or alkalinity: soil above pH7 is alkaline, that below pH7 is acid

Plywood Strong, thin board made by gluing together layers of wood with the grains at right angles

Repointing Repairing the damaged **mortar** between bricks on a wall or chimney

Shrubs Woody-stemmed plants, smaller than trees and usually divided into separate stems near the ground

Terracotta Unglazed, brownish-red, fine pottery

Timber (lumber) Wood prepared for building by being weathered and treated with preservative

Top dressing Replenishing the upper layers of soil to provide nutrients for plants

Topsoil The fertile upper layer of soil

Trellis Wooden lattice work attached to a wall or fence, or sometimes standing alone, up which climbing plants can be trained. Decorative or painted trellis can be a feature in its own right

Trompe-l'oeil A painting or decoration designed to give an illusion of reality

Veranda A low, raised deck around a house, usually shaded by the roof being extended over it

Vermiculite Lightweight, water-absorbent granules used as a potting medium

Index

Photographic acknowledgments

All photos by Jerry Harpur, with grateful thanks to the following garden owners, designers and architects:
B = bottom, C = centre, L = left, R = right, T = top

DESIGNER R. David Adams, Seattle 52T, 67, 147T: Art Centre, Hong Kong 31T: DESIGNER: Daniel Bainuel, Marrakech 18B: DESIGNER Michael Balston 155T: DESIGNER Michael Balston & Arabella Lennox-Boyd 41 (Little Malvern Court, Worcs), 117B, 147B: DESIGNERS Martina Barzi & Josefina Casares, Buenos Aires 8B, 29, 47B, 80, 86T, 125B, 148T: DESIGNER Barbara Britton, NYC 22B: DESIGNER Robert Broekema, Amsterdam 37B, 103B: DESIGNER Tim Callis, Cape Cod 130T: Carillon Point, Seattle 131: DESIGNERS Tom Carruth & John Furman, LA 45, 81: DESIGNERS Ted Chaffers & Dennis Lochen, Jesus Pobre, Spain 132L: DESIGNER Robert W. Chittock, Seattle 155B: DESIGNER Brian Coleman, Seattle 5, 49: DESIGNER Belt Collins, Hong Kong Ltd. 21T, 138B: DESIGNER Codie Conigliaro back jkt C: DESIGNER Keith Corlett, NYC 72, 92: DESIGNER Stephen Crisp, London 12B, 31B, 36, 40BL, 55B: DESIGNER Davis Dalbok, Living Green, SF 100B,136 137: DESIGNER Grover Dear, Archasia, Hong Kong 43T, 60L, 70B: DESIGNERS Delaney & Cochran, San Francisco 32B (for Bank of America), 39B, 66B, 140B: DESIGNER Norbert Deppisch, Ranatur, Munich 134B: DESIGNER Tim Du Val, New York 21B, 33 (copyright Conran Octopus Ltd), 37T, 43B, 57B, 74T, 87, 101, 104B, 141B: DESIGNER Laurie Eichengreen, NYC 38: DESIGNER Cristina Erhartdel, Buenos Aires back jkt T, back jkt B, 10–11, 20T, 74B: ARCHITECT Arthur Erickson, Vancouver 9, 42R: DESIGNER George Freedman, Sydney 20B, 79L, 151 (for the Bank of New South Wales) : Palacio Ca Sa Galesa, Palma de Mallorca 109: DESIGNER Edwina von Gal, New York 144B: DESIGNER Sonny Garcia, San Francisco 23, 82, 112, 114B, 128B, 148B, 149: Generalife, Alhambra Palace, Granada 95: DESIGNER Val Gerry, NYC 115: DESIGNER Isobelle C. Greene, Santa Barbara 35T, 83, 91, 103T, 110BL: Greenwood, Sydney 118T: Xavier Guerrand-Hermes, Marrakech 48T, 52B: DESIGNER Paul Guerin, London 71, 90T, 146: DESIGNER Perry Guillot, NYC 34T: DESIGNERS Perry Guillot & Iris Kaplow, NYC 34B: DESIGNER Arnout ter Haar, Amsterdam 55T: DESIGNER Raymond Hudson, Johannesburg 98, 125T: DESIGNER Iris Kaplow, NYC 93, 11: DESIGNER Galen Lee, NYC 2–3: DESIGNER Mel Light, LA 70T, 154:

DESIGNER Leif Ljungstrom, Palma de Mallorca 46, 48B: DESIGNER Michael Love, Sydney 19: DESIGNER Mallory Kirk Marshall, Dark Harbor, Maine 8T: DESIGNER Christopher Masson, London 94T, 110BR, 153: DESIGNER Jim Matsuo, Santa Monica 57T: DESIGNER/ARCHITECT Rick Mather, London 63: DESIGNER/CERAMICIST: Keeyla Meadows, Berkeley, CA 26B, 117T, 129: DESIGNER Jeff Mendoza, NYC 25, 39T, 68T, 90B, 99, 107T, 122B: Fred Mengoni, NYC 1: ARCHITECT Urbis Travers Morgan, Hong Kong 62B: DESIGNER Camille Muller, Paris, 123 (a terrace in NYC): DESIGNERS Chapin & Cynthia Nolen, Montecito, CA 76B: DESIGNER Cynthia Nolen, Montecito, CA 18T: 'Ohinetahi', Christchurch, NZ 4, 27: DESIGNERS Marijke van Oordt & Robert Tjebbes, Amsterdam 134T: DESIGNER William J. Overholt, Seattle 68B: DESIGNER Henrietta Parsons, London 97B: DESIGNERS Andrew Pfeiffer & Leslie J. Walford, Sydney 142: DESIGNER Patrick Presto, San Francisco 40B, R: DESIGNER Mark Rios, LA 84: DESIGNER Chris Rosmini, LA 133: DESIGNER Mark Rumary, Yoxford, Suffolk 59: DESIGNER Antonella Daroda Sartogo, Rome 6T, 32T, 54, 86B, 132R, 144T: La Casella, Alpes Maritimes: DESIGNERS Claus Scheinert & Thomas Parr 30T, 53: DESIGNER John Sewell, London 94B, 108: DESIGNERS Lon Shapiro & Sonny Garcia, San Francisco 138T: DESIGNER Roberta Sherman, Seattle 6B,113T, 119: DESIGNER Mary Riley-Smith, NYC 97T: DESIGNERS Leslie Smith & Eric Eichenboom, Cape Town 120 121, 152B: Mirabel Osler/ DESIGNER Joe Smith, Dumfries 141T: Stellenberg, Cape Town 102, 107B: DESIGNER Rob Sterk, Amsterdam 88–89: DESIGNERS Barbara Stock & Stacey Hill, Seattle 14B, 24, 47T, 62T, 64, 100T, 122T: DESIGNER Stephen Suzman, San Francisco 35B, 73, 114T: Charlotte Temple, San Francisco 42L: Angela Theriot, San Francisco 50–51: ARCHITECT/DESIGNER Robert Tjebbes, Amsterdam 66T, 69T, 69C, 69B: Edmundo Tonconogy, Buenos Aires 30B: DESIGNER Jonathan Turner, London front jkt, 13, 14T, 143: Valdemossa, Majorca 140T: DESIGNER David J. Walsh, NYC 139: DESIGNER Donald J. Walsh, NYC 17, 145: Westbury Court 130B: DESIGNER John Wheatman, San Francisco 26T, 58, 118B: DESIGNER Anne Scott Wilkes, Sydney 96, 116: DESIGNER Albert Williams 113B: DESIGNER Robin Williams, Hungerford 15: Yacout Restaurant, Marrakech 150: DESIGNER Nadine Zamichow, NYC 105.

Marguerite Patten's
Step by Step
COOKERY

Hamlyn
London·New York·Sydney·Toronto

Making pancakes, see page 161

Contents

First published 1963; revised
edition 1973
Second impression 1974
© Copyright The Hamlyn
Publishing Group Limited 1973
Published by The Hamlyn
Publishing Group Limited
London · New York · Sydney
Toronto
Astronaut House, Feltham,
Middlesex, England
ISBN 0 600 37974 4
Printed in England by Cox and
Wyman Ltd, Fakenham

Cover photographs by John Lee
Line drawings by
Felicity Innes

Introduction

This book has been written for the many people who are new to cooking, but who want to produce interesting and nutritious meals with the minimum of time and expense.

I wanted this to be an exciting as well as instructive book, and so you will find colourful and special recipes in it, for I have found that, if you know the right procedure, it is no more difficult to make a luscious dish than a rather plain 'humdrum' recipe.

In order to give you an idea of how long to allow for making various dishes, not only the cooking time but the preparation time as well is given at the top of most recipes. However, do not be depressed if you take longer than the time suggested! It is almost unbelievable how practice in cooking enables you to become quicker, and to cut out some of the rather tiresome stages by dovetailing your preparations.

I am very grateful for all the co-operation given me in this book. Many Home Economists have been kind enough to produce practical step-by-step pictures of the basic principles in the majority of the recipes. Follow these carefully the first time you make the dish, for you will find that the handling of your ingredients plays a very big part in the success of the finished dish.

In several recipes I have mentioned the convenience foods of today. Whether frozen, canned or dehydrated, these are of a high standard, and quite frequently enable you to give more time to the more interesting aspects of cooking by cutting out or cutting down on some of the initial stages — for example, in soup or sauce making. Weights and measures, a guide to cooking terms, using your oven and basic methods of cooking will be found on the following pages. I would suggest that you read through the first part of this book before you start to cook. This does not contain recipes, but it does give information on equipment, food values, storing food and what to do with left-overs. I hope you will find this of value when you plan your household budget and your shopping. By careful buying, and a knowledge of how to make use of the left-overs that are found in every household from time to time, you will save money and avoid waste.

Good food plays a most important part in good health, and a well fed family is likely to be a happy one. Fortunately good food does not necessarily mean expensive food, and you will find a number of recipes using the cheaper cuts of meat and fish, and ideas for many delicious and economical dishes. I hope you will enjoy using this book, and that you find the family and friends enjoy your cooking.

Weights and measures

British imperial weights and measures have been used throughout this book.
3 teaspoonfuls equal 1 tablespoon. The average English tea cup is $\frac{1}{4}$ pint.
The average English breakfast cup is $\frac{1}{2}$ pint (10 fluid ounces). When cups are mentioned in recipes they refer to a B.S.I. measuring cup which does hold $\frac{1}{2}$ pint.
If you like measuring with a cup do buy one of these, or a very clearly marked jug.
Too much liquid, or too little, can spoil a recipe very easily.

American measures

The American pint is 16 fluid ounces, as opposed to the British Imperial pint and Canadian pint, which are 20 fluid ounces. The American $\frac{1}{2}$-pint measuring cup is therefore equivalent to $\frac{2}{5}$ British pint. In Australia the British imperial pint is used for liquids: solid ingredients are, however, generally calculated in American cups.

Imperial	American
2 tablespoons	3 tablespoons
6 tablespoons	$\frac{1}{2}$ cup
1 pint (20 fluid ounces)	$2\frac{1}{2}$ cups

Solid and dry ingredients	English	American
Butter or other fat	1 pound	2 cups
Flour	1 pound	4 cups
Granulated or castor sugar	1 pound	2 cups
Icing or confectioners' sugar	1 pound	$3\frac{1}{2}$ cups
Brown (moist) sugar (firmly packed)	1 pound	2 cups
Golden syrup or treacle	12 ounces	1 cup
Rice	14 ounces	2 cups
Dried fruit	1 pound	3 cups
Chopped or minced meat (firmly packed)	1 pound	2 cups
Lentils or split peas	1 pound	2 cups
Soft breadcrumbs	2 ounces	1 cup
Flour	1 ounce	$\frac{1}{4}$ cup
Sugar	1 ounce	2 tablespoons
Butter	$\frac{1}{2}$ ounce	1 tablespoon
Golden syrup or treacle	1 ounce	1 tablespoon
Jam or jelly	1 ounce	1 tablespoon

All U.S. standard measuring cups and tablespoons.

Metrication

For quick and easy reference when buying food it should be remembered that 1 kilogramme (1000 grammes) equals 2·2 pounds ($35\frac{3}{4}$ ounces) — i.e. as a rough guide, $\frac{1}{2}$ kilogramme (500 g.) is about 1 pound. In liquid measurements 1 litre (10 decilitres or 1000 millilitres) almost exactly $1\frac{3}{4}$ pints (1·76), so $\frac{1}{2}$ litre is $\frac{7}{8}$ pint. As a rough guide, therefore, one can assume that the equivalent of 1 pint is a generous $\frac{1}{2}$ litre.

A simple method of converting recipe quantities is to use round figures instead of an exact conversion: 25 grammes to 1 ounce, and a generous $\frac{1}{2}$ litre to 1 pint. Since 1 ounce is exactly 28·35 grammes and 1 pint is 568 millilitres it can be seen that these equivalents will give a slightly smaller finished dish, but the proportion of liquids to solids remains the same.

The following tables show exact conversions to the nearest whole number and alongside the recommended amount.

Solid and dry ingredients

Imperial	Exact conversion to nearest whole number	Recommended equivalent
Ounces	Grammes	Grammes
1	28	25
2	57	50
3	85	75
4	113	100
5	142	125
6	170	150
7	198	175
8	226	200
1 lb.	453·6	$\frac{1}{2}$ kilo (poor weight)
2 lb.	907·2	1 kilo (poor weight)

Liquids/fluids

Imperial	Exact conversion to nearest whole number	Recommended equivalent
Pints	Millilitres	Litres
1 pint (20 fl. oz.)	568	$\frac{1}{2}$ litre-generous
$\frac{3}{4}$ pint	426	$\frac{3}{8}$ litre-generous
$\frac{1}{2}$ pint	284	$\frac{1}{4}$ litre-generous
$\frac{1}{4}$ pint	142	$\frac{1}{8}$ litre-generous
1 fl. oz.	28·4	25 ml
B.S.I. tablespoon		18 ml
B.S.I. teaspoon		5 ml

Cooking terms

The way you handle tools and food is often the secret of a successful recipe. The following are some of the usual terms in the 'language of cookery'.

To beat

This means: quite a vigorous action, generally with a wooden spoon, for example:
you beat the ingredients for a batter;
you beat fat and sugar in creaming;
you beat a sauce as it thickens, i.e. stir very vigorously indeed, etc.

To blend

This means: mixing the ingredients together; the method of blending varies with the actual recipe. Liquids are blended as well as solid ingredients.

To blanch

This means: a) to whiten — as in the case of sweetbreads and tripe — put the meat into cold water, bring the water to the boil, strain the meat and throw away the water, thereafter cook the meat as the individual recipe; b) to remove the skins from almonds — put nuts into boiling water, leave a few minutes, strain and remove skins.

To chop

This means: to cut into small pieces. The best method of chopping with a knife is to hold the tip of the knife near the edge, between your left forefinger and thumb, and to hold the handle in your right hand. Put the food to be chopped on to the board and move the knife in a clockwise direction. This takes a bit of practice because as you move you chop down very firmly.

To fold

This means: a gentle flicking action. The importance of this is explained in the section on Sponges, on page 255. Most people are too vigorous to begin with, when folding. You do lessen the vigour if you hold the wrist of your right hand quite gently between the forefinger and thumb of your left hand. This restricts movement to a great degree and you achieve the proper folding action. A metal spoon or palette knife should be used.

To glaze

This means: to give a shine. Egg, or egg and milk, or egg and water glaze is used to brush over pastry before baking; fruit in a flan is glazed with a thickened or jelly mixture. Yeast buns have a glaze of sugar and water. Savoury dishes are sometimes glazed with aspic jelly.

To grate

This means: to rub food against a grater, and is used for a variety of things, such as cheese, suet and fruit rinds. When grating the rind of fruit be very careful not to grate too deeply. Take only the 'zest' (bright coloured part) of the fruit skin.

To knead

This means: a firm movement to produce a smooth dough. It is used for blending the ingredients in pastry, biscuits, yeast mixtures (gentle kneading is essential for pastry).

To pare

This means: to peel. You can buy a special knife which helps to remove peel in narrow strips from fruit or vegetables.

To prove

This means: to cause yeast dough to rise; the process is explained in the bread making recipe on page 264.

To remove juice

The easiest way to remove juice from citrus fruits is with a lemon squeezer. Halve the fruit and press on to the centre, giving sharp turns so that none is wasted. Modern juice separators, and separator attachments for some mixers, extract the juice from vegetables as well as from fruit.

To remove rind

This is done either by paring or grating, as above, or by peeling. If you wish to remove the rind of oranges for a fruit salad, cut it away, cutting into the fruit a little so that you get rid of all the white pith. Rind is easier to remove if the fruit has been warmed for about 1 minute in hot water.

To make a roux

This means: the fat and flour mixture which is prepared in a pan when making a sauce, see page 142.

To shred

This means: to cut into very narrow short strips. You shred almonds, cabbage, etc.

To stir

This means: a fairly brisk circular movement; unless stated to the contrary, a wooden spoon is the best utensil to use.

To whisk

This means: a rather more violent action. This is used for egg whites, etc. If whisking a drink, a small wire whisk is ideal, but for egg whites you need a larger whisk. Modern electric mixers whisk efficiently and quickly.

Using your oven

In most recipes in this book reference has been given to the oven temperature or the gas setting. *This is an approximate guide only.* Different makes of cookers vary, and it is a fact that even the same make of cooker can give slightly different individual results at the same temperature or setting.

If in doubt as to whether the temperature given is *exactly* right for your own particular cooker, do at all times refer to your own manufacturer's temperature chart. It is impossible in a general book to be exact for every cooker, but you will find that the following are a good average in every case.

Cool oven:	for meringues, keeping food warm
Very slow oven:	casseroles, some very rich cakes
Slow oven:	for rich cakes, casseroles and egg custards
Very moderate oven:	for rich cakes, casseroles, some biscuits
Moderate oven:	for reheating dishes, biscuits, some cakes
Moderately hot oven:	for some pastry dishes, some soufflés
Hot oven:	for pastry, tarts and small cakes
Very hot oven:	for rich pastry (puff)

Oven temperatures

The following chart gives the conversions from degrees Fahrenheit to degrees Celsius (formerly Centigrade) recommended by the manufacturers of electric cookers.

Description	Electric setting	Gas mark
very cool	225°F–110°C	$\frac{1}{4}$
,,	250°F–130°C	$\frac{1}{2}$
cool	275°F–140°C	1
,,	300°F–150°C	2
very moderate	325°F–170°C	3
moderate	350°F–180°C	4
moderate to	375°F–190°C	5
moderately hot	400°F–200°C	6
hot	425°F–220°C	7
,,	450°F–230°C	8
very hot	475°F–240°C	9

Placing food in the oven

Not only is it important to have the right temperature in the oven, but it makes a great deal of difference if the right position in the oven is used.

Electric ovens

The placing of the elements in electric cookers varies according to the different makes. On the whole one can say that in an electric oven the TOP and BOTTOM are the hottest parts. The TOP is generally slightly the hotter. This means when you cook the food, the dishes requiring the HOT part of the oven, i.e. meat, go to the BOTTOM. If you are roasting potatoes separately they can go to the TOP of the oven. A Yorkshire pudding goes to the TOP of the oven. A pie or pudding goes into the CENTRE of the oven.

When baking cakes in an electric oven, a large fruit cake goes into the CENTRE of the oven. Small cakes and scones go towards the TOP of the oven. Sandwich cakes go just above CENTRE of the oven. If you cannot get them side by side on the same shelf and are baking two or three sandwich cakes, put one just above CENTRE and one just above the BOTTOM of the oven.

Gas ovens

The TOP of a gas cooker is the hottest part and therefore is the right place for those foods that need a very HOT oven. If you are roasting meat and potatoes they will go towards the TOP of the oven. If you are making a Yorkshire pudding at the same time, the meat can be moved down in the oven and the Yorkshire pudding put in its place at the TOP. A fruit pie or pudding will go in the CENTRE or just below the CENTRE of the oven. The BOTTOM of a gas cooker is appreciably cooler than anywhere else: ideal for milk puddings, baked custards, slow casseroles.

Basic methods of cooking

Baking. Cooking in the dry heat of the oven; this is the method used for cakes, pastry, etc. You can also bake potatoes in their jackets. When baking, be careful to have the correct temperature and also the right position in the oven (see opposite).

Boiling. Cooking by immersing the food in a pan of liquid, which must be kept boiling all the time, i.e. quite a number of bubbles should be seen on the surface. You can boil vegetables and jam, for example, but many dishes, such as boiled bacon or boiled fish, are really simmered only.

Braising. A combination of stewing and roasting. The food is tossed in hot fat first, and then covered with a thickened liquid and cooked slowly, either in a covered casserole in the oven or in a covered saucepan. Meat and many vegetables are delicious if braised.

Casserole. Cooking slowly in the oven in a covered casserole dish — often meat, rabbit or vegetables.

Frying. 1. *Shallow frying*. This means cooking in a small quantity of hot fat in an open pan. On page 45 you will find detailed pictures of the right method of doing this. 2. *Deep fat frying*. Cooking by immersing food in a deep pan of hot fat. Page 46 gives full details of the right method of doing it. Frying is a process that needs care in the preparation of the food, in testing the temperature of the fat, and in timing the cooking, but if well done the results are delicious. It is used for meat, fish, vegetables, sweet dishes such as fritters, and cakes like doughnuts.

Grilling. Cooking quickly under a red hot grill: used for small tender pieces of meat, fish, and browning food, etc. Never try to grill tough meat or poultry, and keep food well moistened with a little oil or melted fat.

Poaching. Cooking gently in water which is just below boiling point — usually fish or eggs.

Pressure cooking. Cooking at higher temperatures than usual, in a special cooker, so that food is cooked much more quickly. Follow carefully the special directions for your own type of pressure cooker.

Roasting. True roasting is cooking meat on a turning spit, but this term is also used for cooking meat in the oven in its own fat or with additional fat. Good quality meat, etc., can be roasted in a hot oven, but the less good quality also can be roasted if a lower heat and a longer cooking time are used (see page 75).

Simmering. The rate of cooking used for stews — just below boiling point, so that the liquid bubbles gently at the side of the pan.

Steaming. Cooking either in a steamer over a pan of boiling water, or in a basin standing in (*not* covered by) boiling water. You can steam sponge puddings, suet puddings, egg custards, etc.

Stewing. Cooking slowly until food is tender. Use just enough liquid to cover the food, as the liquid is served with it and should be rich. Stews may be cooked in covered saucepans or casseroles, on top of the cooker, or in the oven — but always at a low temperature.

Microwave ovens

A Microwave oven gives very speedy cooking. The principle behind this form of cooking is that the heat 'goes through' the food immediately it is placed into the oven. In normal ovens the heat surrounds the food and penetrates gradually.
Microwave ovens are used to reheat ready-cooked dishes as well as cooking fresh food.

Pressure cookers

In a pressure cooker food is cooked very rapidly because pressure is 'built up' inside the pan, which looks very like an ordinary saucepan. Most foods can be cooked in a pressure pan, but I find the best use is for soups (these cook in a few minutes, instead of taking 30–40 minutes), for making stock (see page 63), for stews and root vegetables.

Refrigerator

A refrigerator is the safest place for storing perishable food, for the cabinet gives a temperature of between 40°F. and 45°F. Even so, be careful you do not keep fish, meat, etc. too long; see your manufacturer's instruction book.

Home freezers

In a home freezer you can store foods for a very long time; always check with your manufacturer's recommendations as to the maximum length of time. If kept too long the food will not 'go bad', but will lose texture and taste. Use this for storing cheaper bulk bought meat, ready-frozen foods, etc., and also to freeze your own fruit, vegetables and cooked foods.

Basic rules and equipment

How to follow the recipes in this book

You will find the recipes in this book easy to follow if you remember these points:

1 Quantities are for four people, unless stated to the contrary.
2 The preparation time is suggested at the top of each recipe. Please do not lose heart if you find it takes rather longer than the time given. After you have made the dish once you will find the preparation much more speedy on subsequent occasions.
3 After the preparation time you will sometimes find the term 'no delay'. This indicates that you can work straight through the recipe — when you have to let ingredients stand, cool, or set, etc., the time for this is indicated. There is nothing more frustrating than embarking on a recipe and then finding halfway through that it has to stand for two or three hours before you can continue!
4 Cooking times are a result of careful testing. Size of containers, individual cookers or the ripeness or tenderness of the foods being used can cause a slight variation, so do not be too worried if there is a little difference.

Rules for the good cook

1 Always see that your hands and utensils are kept scrupulously clean.
2 Assemble all ingredients for a recipe before you begin.
3 Clear up as you work.
4 Weigh or measure accurately.
5 Read the recipe very carefully. For example, when you are directed to 'fold' in flour this means a gentle flick of the wrist, not a heavy stirring! See page 7 for interpretation of basic cooking terms.
6 Always check oven settings against your manufacturer's instructions. Ovens vary considerably.
7 Learn to use herbs and spices in cooking.
8 Be adventurous — often you save time and money by trying out new foods and new recipes.
9 The first time you try a new recipe, follow the directions exactly. Afterwards you can decide on any alterations to suit your family's tastes.

Saving time when working

1 Collect utensils and ingredients on a tray before starting to make up the recipe; this saves footsteps and omissions.
2 Oven-to-table dishes cut down on the washing-up, and there are many from which to choose.
3 As you prepare food, put the used saucepans, etc., to soak; use cold water for milk or scrambled egg pans.
4 When you have finished the first course, put forks, knives, etc., into a jug filled with hot water. You will find the washing-up easy to finish.

Choosing kitchen equipment

There is one wise rule when choosing kitchen equipment, particularly the type you will use day after day — saucepans, cooker, etc. Buy the best you can afford. I have listed some of the things you will need when you first equip your kitchen.

Baking trays. You will need at least 2 flat baking trays of a size to fit comfortably in your oven for baking patties, etc. Make sure they are not so large that they come right over the heating elements, or the food at the edges will burn. Wipe baking trays very dry after you have washed them; leave in a warm place for an hour or so before putting away.
Basins and bowl. You will need 1 good sized mixing bowl, not less than 4–5 pints capacity (for mixing pastry and cakes), for too small a bowl hinders movement. You will need about 3 basins, approximately 1, 1½ and 2 pints in capacity — either china or oven and heatproof glassware (for mixing and cooking puddings, etc.).
Boards. While a formica working surface is excellent for rolling out pastry, etc., you need a board for chopping and cutting. Always wash wooden boards in warm — not too hot — water. Dry with a cloth, then store in a warm place for a while before putting away. If you ever have the opportunity to buy a marble slab for rolling pastry you will be very fortunate, for this keeps it exceptionally cool.

Brushes. You will need at least one small pastry brush, and since they are not expensive you may like to have two. Use one for greasing tins (a small quantity of fat for this purpose can be stored in a tiny basin, odd cup or earthenware jar, and heated over a pan of boiling water). The second brush should then be kept for brushing pies, etc., with egg and milk. Choose good quality brushes, of pure bristle if possible. Wash the brushes in warm, soapy water. Rinse in plenty of clean water. Dry well.

Cake tins. Most useful are 6-inch and 7-inch cake tins (cakes are easier to remove if tins have a loose base) trays of patty tins (for small cakes, tarts, etc.) two shallow sandwich tins (7–7½-inch is a useful size) loaf tins (for loaf cakes and bread); possibly you will also need a Swiss roll tin, and a ring tin for making angel cakes, etc. See page 237 for preparation of tins, etc.

Can opener. Choose a strong one, that will open most types of can. You can choose wall or electric can openers (that fit on to the mixer). Also buy a master 'key' for opening the type of can that requires a key. often those supplied break or get lost.

Casseroles. Casserole cookery is very popular and you will find a use for several casseroles. If possible, select those with lids which form a separate cooking utensil; ovenproof or flameproof (which may also be used on top of the cooker) are particularly practical. Oval and rectangular casseroles take up less room in the oven than round ones, but it is not always so easy to arrange food in them. Casseroles are easier to remove from the oven if you stand them on a metal baking tray; you can then pull out the whole tray.

Castle pudding tins. See Moulds.

Colander. Essential for draining and straining vegetables. It can be used as an emergency steamer.

Cutters. While the tops of glasses, etc., can be used for cutting rounds of pastry, a much more professional appearance is given by using proper metal cutters. All shapes and sizes can be obtained. Wash and dry as for metal baking trays.

Fish slice. Essential for lifting and supporting food and for draining away surplus fat. It is worthwhile having two slices, a light pliable one for lifting fairly solid foods such as fritters, and one of firmer construction to support eggs and fish.

Foil. This is very useful in the kitchen. See page 17.

Forks. Have one or two kitchen forks for mashing vegetables, sealing edges of pastry, etc.

Frying pans. Choose the heaviest one you can afford, for frying needs high temperatures, and cheap light pans quickly become uneven. After washing the pan, dry it well; this prevents food sticking. If you have a 'non-stick' (silicone type) frying pan, follow the manufacturer's instructions for cleaning this, i.e. never use abrasive cleaners. Even if you grill most foods, you will need an *omelette pan* for pancakes and omelettes. This should never be washed; wipe it out IMMEDIATELY after use with crumpled tissue paper. Buy a small pan with rounded edges for easy cleaning. A *deep fryer* consists of a pan rather like a saucepan with a wire basket that allows you to lower the food into and withdraw it from the hot fat. With care, you rarely need to turn the fat out of the fryer; clean as directed on page 46. For economy's sake, you could buy a frying basket to fit inside an ordinary saucepan.

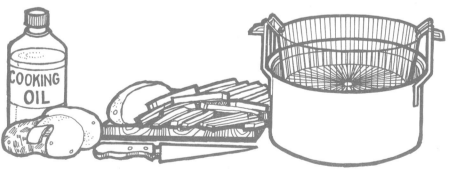

Deep fat fryer

Grater. Some kind of grater is essential and I would choose one with holes of several sizes for grating lemon rind, cheese, etc. Wash with a small scrubbing brush to clean all the holes, and dry in a warm place before putting it away. The liquidiser (blender) goblet can serve as a grater for making fine particles of cheese, breadcrumbs, etc.

Kettle. You must have some form of kettle; choose one of sufficient capacity, for a large kettle can always be half filled, while it is most annoying to have to wait for two lots of water. Buy light aluminium (which, while more expensive, wears best), enamel or light tin. Always buy a kettle big enough to cover the electric hotplate so that no heat is wasted. Look for a kettle with a heat-resisting handle and a good sized lid for easy filling. See that there is a vent for the steam, and that the lid does not fall off when pouring. It is a wise investment to choose an electric quick-boiling kettle.

Knives. A good selection of knives is essential. You will need:
Carving knife, as sharp as possible and have two if you can, for the heat of meat blunts the edge after carving for two to three people.
Kitchen knife, perhaps two for general purposes.
Palette knife, one of the most useful pieces of equipment for turning out pancakes, lifting food out of pans, cleaning out basins, etc.
Sharp knife, essential to have one at least for cutting and chopping.
Small vegetable knife, for preparing fruit, vegetables, etc.
Small rigid knife, for spreading butter, etc.
Stainless steel knives are now quite sharp; handle several patterns to find what suits your hand best.

Meat tin or roasting tin. Generally supplied with the cooker, for roasting meat. You may be interested in the covered self-basting tins that stop splashing of fat in the oven.

Mincer. When you begin to do more cooking you will find a mincer of some kind very useful for making good use of left-over meat, etc. Models available range from mincing attachments for electric mixers to quite cheap hand models; buy the best you can afford. A reasonably heavy mincer will stand without being screwed to a table. If you choose the screw-on type, make sure the nuts are insulated so that there is no fear of cracking enamel surfaces. Choose a stainless-bladed model. For very fine shredding, the Mouli shredder or grater is excellent; the food is passed through quickly and easily and it produces almost a purée. Wash and dry the mincer most carefully and stand it in a warm place to dry thoroughly before storing.

Moulds. Although you can use basins for setting jellies, etc., one or two attractively-shaped moulds assist in making your dishes look interesting. Many aluminium moulds can be used for baking cakes. Small castle pudding tins, or dariole moulds, are useful for cooking puddings quickly. Wash and dry carefully, leave in a warm place before storing.

Paper. Always keep a small stock of both greaseproof and absorbent paper, the former to line tins, wrap foods inside tins, etc., the latter for careful draining of fried foods. See page 17.

Pie dishes. You can use the bottom of oval casseroles, providing they have a good rim, for pies. Have at least two sizes — 1½ and 2 pints approximately.

Pie support. This keeps a meat or fruit pie a good shape. An egg cup makes a good substitute. Never use plastic egg cups though.

Potato peeler. There are a number of designs in the shops — handle them before buying; left-handed potato peelers are available.

Rolling pin. The modern glass or china rolling pins, while more fragile than wooden ones, are popular because they keep pastry cool, and are easy to handle and to clean. If your rolling pin is wooden, look after it in the same way as the board.

Sauce boat. An ovenproof glassware sauce boat is a useful extra for keeping sauces hot, since most dinner services seem to provide only one sauce boat.

Saucepans. The number you have depends very much on the amount of cooking you intend to do. If you are fond of sauces then you MUST have an extra pan, or you will find yourself seriously inconvenienced. Remember to choose pans with heavy bases if you have an electric or solid fuel cooker. In any case, a reasonably heavy pan is always a good investment, for it lasts for years.
You will need a small pan for small quantities of milk. Silicone (non-stick) pans are ideal for milk, although one can buy every size of pan in this finish. Look after them carefully (see frying pans, page 11). Also necessary are two saucepans for vegetables, approximately 4–5 pints capacity; a large pan for boiling pieces of beef, ham, etc.; and one that could be used for jam-making in small quantities. This should be large enough for the jam to boil without boiling over; minimum capacity 8 pints. A DOUBLE saucepan is ideal for making porridge, egg custards, Hollandaise sauce, etc.

Scales. Undoubtedly if you are to become a first class cook you must invest in a pair of scales, although you can measure by spoons or cups. Today it is possible to buy scales marked in both metric and imperial measurements, and in view of metrication this would be a wise investment.

Scissors. You will use these for removing bacon rinds, chopping parsley and cutting salad vegetables.

Sieves. In a number of recipes one is told to 'sieve' the ingredients, which means push them through the mesh of a fine sieve and so produce a smooth mixture. A hair or nylon sieve is ideal for vegetables and fruits, since there is no fear of metal dis-colouring the food. You also need a wire sieve or cooling tray to cool pastry and cakes, and a fine wire sieve for mixing flour and baking powder or aerating flour. Wash and dry sieves most carefully, for the hair mesh will rot if left damp, and metal ones may rust.

Spoons. As well as the ordinary kitchen metal spoons, you will need at least two WOODEN SPOONS. Develop the habit of using these spoons when you stir sauces, for they give a far better movement and are therefore less likely to allow the sauce or soup to become lumpy. Wash and dry like wooden boards. You may prefer to measure

dry ingredients in a spoon, in which case make sure you have the proper *measuring spoons*, made in plastic and conforming to the British Standard Institution's recommendations. You can also obtain a ½ pint or 1 pint measuring jug which, to a great extent, can take the place of scales.

Squeezer. A squeezer for extracting juice from citrus fruits is very important. Clean with a small brush.

Steamer. Although you can manage without a steamer in your kitchen, it is a most useful cooking utensil, enabling you to cook several dishes on one plate or ring, and giving very light puddings. If you buy a one-tier steamer, choose a model to which you can add later, a second, and perhaps even a third tier.

Storage jars, etc. You must plan a certain amount of storage equipment, i.e. tins for cakes, biscuits and pastry, which must all be kept separately. Bread can be stored in a bread bin, or wrapped in a cloth and put into a drawer where there is a certain amount of air circulation.

Strainer. You will need a small strainer for coffee and tea, and this would also be handy for straining any small lumps from a small amount of sauce, should they occur (see also Whisk, below).

Tongs. You can buy kitchen tongs which are extremely useful for picking up foods either too delicate or too hot to handle, and turning chops, etc.

Yorkshire pudding tins, etc. You can bake Yorkshire puddings in individual patty tins (see page 64) or buy an oblong or square tin. A *flan ring*, which is placed on a flat baking sheet or tray, is also a useful utensil, for the ring is easily removed from the baking tin, so lessening the chances of pastry breaking. Clean and store carefully.

Vegetable brush. A small hard brush is invaluable for cleaning vegetables.

Whisk. An egg whisk, flat, rotary or electric, is essential for beating egg whites quickly and easily. A flat whisk, used in a sauce, will help to prevent lumps forming, or remove most lumps

Note. Never use soda on any aluminium cooking utensil.

Foods the family need

A well balanced diet is a very important factor in keeping the family fit. Make sure, therefore, that you provide them with:

1 *Plenty of protein foods*. Meat, fish, cheese, eggs, nuts and the pulses (peas, beans, lentils) are the most important sources. Bread and milk contribute protein to the diet. Protein is the body-building food. Even on a slimming diet one should eat plenty of proteins.

2 *A reasonable amount of fat*, to help them to keep warm in cold weather: butter, margarine, cooking fats, suet.
Some doctors believe that TOO MUCH fat is unwise in our diet, particularly when approaching middle-age. Teenagers and schoolchildren often prefer fried foods to any other, but it is wise to try other methods of cooking, as too much fried food can cause over-weight and a poor complexion.

3 *Milk* is an essential food for children and excellent for adults. If not liked as a drink, use it in cooking as much as possible.

4 *Sugar* (sweets, jam, etc.) is a source of energy and as such must not be omitted from the diet – except when trying to lose weight. Children should be encouraged to clean their teeth after eating sweets and other sugary foods.

5 *Bread, cakes and other starchy foods*. While it is unwise to 'fill up' on bread, etc., so that you do not want to eat other foods, a certain amount is important, since it creates a feeling of well being. Bread and flour also contain the wheat germ which is an important source of vitamin B.

6 *Fruit, vegetables and salads*. Many of these provide the vitamin C that helps to build up resistance to colds, etc. Vitamin C is easily destroyed by cooking – so remember *not* to over-cook vegetables. Serve raw fruit and salads as often as possible.

Filling your larder

It is part of good housekeeping to store an adequate supply of foods in the house. Do not make the mistake of over-buying certain foods to begin with, for so many things deteriorate. In these pages you will find suggestions for the kind of food that it is helpful to have in the larder and the refrigerator.

Perishable foods

These are the foods that spoil easily, and should be stored in the coolest place possible. If you have a refrigerator, that is ideal for most of them.

Bacon. To store, keep the bacon well covered in greaseproof paper, polythene bag or foil, or in a polythene container. Keep towards the bottom of the refrigerator so it does not become too hard. If you have no refrigerator, and the weather is hot, moisten the paper with a little vinegar.

Cheese. There is a wide variety of cheese available; here is a selection.

For cooking and table:
Cheddar. Ask for a firm cheese (i.e. well matured) for easy grating.
Cheshire. Slightly stronger than Cheddar. Excellent for cooking when firm.

For cooking only:
Parmesan. Hard Italian cheese with very strong flavour. Can be bought in drums ready-grated.

For table use only:
Brie and Camembert. See that the cheese is soft; if it is hard it is not mature and lacks flavour. When mature it should be eaten within two days.
Blue cheese, Gorgonzola and Stilton. These should be slightly crumbly.
Processed cheese. Keep well wrapped — some processed cheese is excellent for cooking.

Cheddar and the firm cheeses can be stored in the refrigerator. Keep well covered (see bacon). Brie, Camembert, Danish Blue, Gorgonzola and Stilton are better kept at room temperature.

Eggs. Store in cool, dry place. An egg-box or rack helps to prevent cracking. They can be kept in the refrigerator if you have space. Ideally they should not be kept more than a few days; after that they should be turned daily. *Duck eggs* should always be cooked well before serving. They are better served hard-boiled or used in cakes — never use them for meringues or icings, as there might be a slight risk of food poisoning.

Fats

Butter. Salted butter will keep better than fresh. You can select from butter from many countries. Unsalted butter is better for butter icings and sweet sandwiches, but choice depends on personal taste.
Lard. Keeps very well. Ideal for frying meat, roasting potatoes and for pastry (mixed with margarine, if wished).
Margarine. There are many brands available at different prices, so try several. Salted margarine keeps better than unsalted. The unsalted margarine is better for cake fillings and sweet sauces. The luxury or soft type of margarine enables you to make cakes with the minimum of creaming, see page 244.
Suet. If you buy suet from the butcher, check it is fresh. When fresh it is faintly pink in colour. Chop or grate, then dust with flour. Store carefully, as it easily becomes rancid. Shredded packet suet is packed *with* flour so that it keeps well.
Vegetable fats or shortening can be used instead of oil for cooking fish, or in any dish where the 'meaty' flavour of lard or dripping is not desirable. In short crust pastry never use more than $3\frac{1}{2}$ oz. fat to 8 oz. flour, as it is very rich and causes pastry to crumble.
All fats must be kept in a cool place, with plenty of air circulation. Oil keeps well in a cool place (not necessarily the refrigerator, except in very hot weather). Put fats in a covered container in your refrigerator.

Fruit. Keep most fruit in a cool place, though it is not essential to store in the refrigerator. Bananas and melon should *not* be put into refrigerator, except to chill at the last minute before serving.

Meat. Keep raw meat uncovered in the refrigerator, but cover cooked meat to prevent drying. If you have no refrigerator, keep raw or cooked meat in a meat safe or covered with muslin, moistened with vinegar, with good air circulation.

Milk

Fresh milk. Jersey milk is slightly more expensive, but has a higher fat content and more cream; it keeps less well than other milk. In cooler weather milk will keep in a cool place with plenty of air circulation, but store in a refrigerator if possible. Long-life milk keeps some weeks when unopened.

Canned milk. Unsweetened evaporated milk is a good substitute for cream in sauces, etc., if used undiluted. Diluted (as instructed on the can), it can be substituted for milk in an emergency. Sweetened condensed milk can be used for the same purpose, but it *is* very sweet. Canned milk and cream should be stored in a cool cupboard, or refrigerator — when the can is opened.

Vegetables. Green vegetables should be used as soon as possible after purchase. Root vegetables may be kept longer. A well ventilated vegetable rack is best for storing. Salad vegetables can be stored in a covered container in the refrigerator, and cauliflower in plastic bags.

To store fish. Fish is such a highly perishable food that it is inadvisable to store it for any length of time.
Even if you possess a refrigerator, it is a good idea to buy fish freshly and store for not more than 24 hours, as near the freezing compartment as possible.

Less perishable foods

Although these are an easier group of foods to store, try to see they are kept in a dry, well ventilated pantry or store cupboard. It is advisable to store all spices in one place, condiments in another, and so on, for you save a great deal of time if you know exactly where to 'lay your hands' on a particular container.

Baking powder. You will not use this in general cooking if you buy self-raising flour. If you do buy baking powder, do not purchase too large a can at one time, since it deteriorates very slowly with keeping. It must stand in a DRY place.

Barley (pearl). This is used in some soups, such as Scotch broth, and forms a useful and filling addition to the dish. It keeps well in a dry place, but you will not use it very often, so do not buy too large a quantity: 8 oz. to 1 lb. will be plenty.

Bicarbonate of soda. In general cooking (as opposed to cake-making) you will need this rarely if using self-raising flour. Store like baking powder.

Biscuits. These should be stored in the wrappings in which you buy them and will keep in a dry place very well until you open the packet; the moment the packet is opened put into an air-tight tin. Store biscuits away from bread or cakes. Chocolate biscuits should be stored in a tin, apart from others, as they tend to make them soft.

Bread. Keep in a special bread container, a tin or wrapped in foil. Do not put it with cakes or pastry.

Bouillon cubes. These are often known as stock cubes and as you will see on page 63, they form an easy and very successful way of making a stock for soups, stews, etc.

Breadcrumbs, dried (or raspings). You can buy packets, or make your own breadcrumbs, see page 18. You will use them for coating fish, etc. (see page 44).

Cakes. These should be stored in an air-tight tin. Rich fruit cake can be wrapped in foil until required.

Crispbread. See Biscuits.

Cocoa or chocolate. This is used to flavour puddings as well as for drinks. Store in a dry place. Cocoa is better than chocolate powder in most cakes as it has a stronger flavour.

Coffee. You will find directions for making coffee on page 277; it is essential to buy coffee in small quantities for it deteriorates quickly. When you open a can or bag of coffee, transfer it to a covered air-tight jar. Even so, replace with fresh coffee as often as possible. There are many varieties available, but you need not be concerned with more than one or two unless your ambition is to become a connoisseur. Do, however, buy the best you can afford of a particular type. Breakfast coffee is usually a lighter roast than after-dinner coffee; it is sometimes called 'American roast'. For black coffee choose the darker kind, with a richer flavour, sometimes called 'Continental roast'. If you like your coffee with a strong bite, choose one to which a little chicory has been added.

Colourings. These are not essential, but a few drops can improve the appearance of many dishes, and they are needed in icing.

Cornflakes or other breakfast cereals. Keep packets sealed down tightly, and keep in a dry place.

Cornflour (and blancmange). This is used for making moulds, and a little can be used in place of flour (1 oz. in every 4 oz.) when making cakes or puddings, to give a finer texture. You can use cornflour in sauces as well; it thickens more readily — use ½ oz. cornflour in place of 1 oz. flour.

Crystallised cherries, etc. Cherries, angelica and peel are all useful commodities to have in the store cupboard, for they flavour cakes, puddings and sweets, and they give colour to the finished dish. Keep in tins or well covered, otherwise they either go very sticky or harden.

Custard powder. For custard sauce, see page 157.

Dried fruit. Currants, sultanas and raisins for cakes, puddings, etc. Since the fruit must be dry when used in baking, it is a good idea to wash it the moment it arrives from the grocer, unless ready-washed. Put it into a colander, and run hot water over until clean. Spread on flat trays and dry in the warmth of the kitchen for 48 hours. Store in a dry, cool place.

Flavourings

Anchovy essence, for fish sauces, etc.

Yeast extract, meat extract or bouillon cubes, for meat dishes.

Almond essence and vanilla essence, for sweets and puddings.

Flour. If you do a great deal of baking, you may prefer to have plain flour and adjust your baking powder to the particular dish you are making. But self-raising flour is excellent for most purposes. For pastry, I personally prefer plain flour, but you can make excellent short crust with self-raising. Store flour in a dry tin, drawer or jar. Never put fresh flour on top of stale.

Herbs. If you are a keen gardener you will probably grow your own herbs, but for most people a supply of dried herbs is extremely useful. Choose mixed herbs for stuffings, etc. (thyme, sage and marjoram). Fresh parsley and fresh mint should either be kept in the refrigerator or standing in a jar of water.

Macaroni. See Spaghetti.

Mustard. An essential condiment and flavouring for many savoury dishes.

Oatmeal or **porridge oats.** Store in cool, dry place.

Pepper. The most useful and usual is an ordinary white pepper, which can be used for the table and cooking. Black pepper is stronger, or use peppercorns in a pepper mill. Paprika has a sweet, rather than hot, flavour. It is bright red, see Goulash, page 69. Cayenne pepper, while looking like paprika, has a very hot flavour, so use it sparingly.

Rice. You will use this for savoury and sweet dishes. For curries, ask for long grain rice. For milk puddings use round (short grain) or Carolina rice. Store in a dry place.

Salt. Refined salt can be bought in drums or packets. The former is better, since it helps to keep salt dry. It may be wise to store away from the kitchen, since steam tends to make it soft and sticky. The block kitchen salt is cheaper to buy and better for preserving. Crush for table or kitchen use. Crushed cooking salt can also be bought.

Sauces. There is an unlimited number of made-up sauces on the market, and you will gradually discover those you like. I would have a small bottle of Worcestershire sauce in the store cupboard, for it is very useful in cooking.

Spaghetti or **macaroni.** Keep a small quantity in the cupboard for savoury dishes.

Spices. These are the most useful:

Savoury: *curry powder.*

Sweet: *allspice; mixed spice* (a combination of cinnamon, ginger and nutmeg); *cinnamon* — for cakes and puddings; *ginger* — also for cakes and puddings; *nutmeg* — whole or ground.

Sugar. There are several kinds of sugar. Castor is best for cakes and puddings, since it has a refined texture. Demerara is a dry, brown sugar, ideal for sweetening fruits, as it gives a rich flavour. It is considered more nutritious than white sugar. A soft, sticky brown sugar, known as 'moist sugar' is also available, and is recommended for rich, dark cakes and Christmas puddings. Granulated is the most usual for general purposes. Icing sugar is used for decorating cakes; it has a tendency to go lumpy, so keep in an air-tight tin. Loaf sugar is for table use and jam-making. Preserving sugar is used for jam-making.

Syrup and treacle. Golden syrup is an excellent sweetener and can also be used for sauces. It keeps well in a dry place. Black treacle is not so useful because of the pronounced flavour, but is an excellent source of iron; use for gingerbread, page 240.

Tea. This keeps well in a dry place. Most people prefer Indian to China tea for all occasions, but if you, or regular guests, like China tea, it is worth buying a little to serve with lemon instead of milk at tea-time. Store tea away from anything with a rather strong smell. Transfer opened packets to an air-tight tea caddy or tin.

Vinegar. Buy a good quality brown malt vinegar and a white vinegar. Wine vinegar is excellent in salad dressings.

Shopping for convenience foods

A considerable amount of time will be saved either by stocking convenience foods or buying these for quick and easy meals.

Frozen foods. There is an extensive variety of frozen foods, including vegetables, fruits, meat and fish products, desserts, cakes, ice cream, etc. If you have no refrigerator, use within a few hours. Store as directed on the packet in a refrigerator; the time varies according to the 'star' markings on your refrigerator. For long storage, put into a home freezer.

Canned foods. A selection of canned foods makes it possible for you to provide meals at short notice. Have one or two of the following:

Soups

Fish for hors d'oeuvre: sardines, anchovies, tuna, salmon (red salmon is the better quality)

Vegetables: mixed vegetables, peas, carrots, asparagus tips and tomatoes

Meat, such as corned beef and tongue

Pasta foods, e.g. spaghetti and ravioli

Fruit

Cream and/or evaporated milk

Canned fruits present few problems in storing, but make certain your pantry or cupboard is not too hot or very damp. If a can is 'blown', i.e. both ends are bulging, it is an indication that the contents are not in good order and, therefore, should not be used.

Dried foods. There are a number of very good dried or dehydrated foods on the market today. They take up less room than cans, and present few storage problems. They keep well, if stored in a cool, dry place.

Soups. Use for a stock in casserole dishes as well as a soup.

Fruits. Dried apricots, figs, etc. need soaking before cooking (see page 173).

Vegetables. The modern Accelerated Freeze Dried vegetables do not need soaking. They include peas, beans, etc. Dried onions are an excellent 'standby', for when a recipe needs very little onion, it is quicker, and cheaper, to use a teaspoon of the dried product.

Cake mixes. A great variety of cake mixes are on the market and do produce reasonably good results with the minimum of effort.

Kitchen papers

Cooking film. This can be wrapped round meat, etc., when roasting. It keeps the food moist and the oven clean and, since it is transparent, you can see whether the food is cooked.

Foil. Aluminium foil has become an invaluable part of kitchen equipment. It can be used:

1 For wrapping food. Many foods should be wrapped for storage in the refrigerator, see pages 14 and 15. Foil is excellent for this purpose.

2 Sandwiches wrapped in foil keep very much more moist than if wrapped in greaseproof paper.

3 Foil can be used to cover dishes in the oven; it takes up less space than a lid, and if tucked very tightly round the edges of the dish it keeps the contents much more moist.

4 Put foil at the bottom of the oven if you are afraid of something boiling over, i.e. juice in a fruit pie. Use it under radiant plates on the top of an electric cooker to make cleaning unnecessary. I find it a good idea to line the grill pan with foil when grilling food, so you dispense with the foil after use and have a pan that is easy to clean.

If you wipe foil carefully after use it can be stored and utilised once again, but it is inadvisable to wrap fish in it on one occasion and then, next time, use it for something with a rather more delicate flavour!

Plastic bags. These are most useful for wrapping foods in a refrigerator or freezer, keeping loaves of bread, sandwiches and salads fresh. They take up less space than containers and keep the food more moist. Do not use to cover dishes that are heated. PLASTIC BAGS MUST BE KEPT AWAY FROM SMALL CHILDREN, BECAUSE THEY CAN CAUSE DEATH BY SUFFOCATION IF A CHILD PULLS ONE OVER ITS HEAD.

Absorbent paper. Generally sold in rolls, ideal for draining fried food, wiping up spilt food; thicker paper can be used for lining drawers, etc. Wipe out greasy frying pans with kitchen paper to make it easier to wash the pans.

Tissue paper. This may also be used for draining fried foods. It is more fragile, so crumple it before putting on the dish to give it a little more body.

Greaseproof paper. For lining certain cake tins and covering dishes — though foil is better. Do not use greaseproof paper for draining fried foods, as it holds the fat rather than allowing it to drain through.

Roasting bags. Put joints or poultry into these bags — they keep the food moist in cooking.

Ways to use left-overs

Bread

1 Make your own crumbs for coating fish, etc. Cut the bread into cubes, put on to a baking tray and leave in a very moderate oven until golden brown. When crisp, roll between sheets of greaseproof paper to give finer crumbs. Store in a kitchen jar or tin.
2 Croûtons. Cut the bread into tiny cubes and fry in hot fat (see page 36). Serve with soup.
3 Puddings. See Caramel pudding (page 288); Fruit charlotte (page 165); Bread and butter pudding (page 179), etc.
4 Tartlet cases. Cut the bread into VERY thin slices. Press into greased patty tins. Bake until crisp and use instead of pastry cases.
Remember – stale bread can be freshened (see page 267); left-over *fresh* bread can be frozen, so it will *not* become stale.

Fish

1 Add to mashed potato for fish cakes; add to rice for kedgeree (pages 54, 234).
2 Add to diced vegetables, mayonnaise and rice for salads.
Remember – be very careful about using left-over fish; it deteriorates very rapidly. Cooked or uncooked *FRESH* fish may be frozen.

Jelly

1 Whisk lightly, add a little thick cream and use as a decoration for trifles.
2 Use instead of icing on cakes.

Meat

1 There are many recipes in this book for using left-over meat (see rissoles, shepherd's pie, etc.).
2 Mince cooked meat finely, blend with melted butter and seasoning for potted meat.
Remember – meat should always be kept well covered when cooked, to prevent drying.
Cooked meat may be frozen.

Potatoes

1 *Pommes gratinées.* Ingredients: approximately 1–$1\frac{1}{4}$ lb. cooked potatoes, $\frac{1}{4}$ pint milk, little margarine, 2 tablespoons grated cheese, salt and pepper. Method: cut potatoes into thick slices, arrange in greased pie dish, season well and add a small amount of margarine to each layer. Pour over milk – cover the top with cheese, cook for about 1 hour in very moderate oven, until milk is absorbed and the cheese gives a really thick crust on top.
2 *Potato croquettes.** Mash left-over potato until very smooth. Mix with yolk of egg and form into finger shapes. Roll in egg white and crumbs. Fry until crisp and brown (see page 137).
3 *Potato cakes.** Add grated onion or grated cheese or chopped parsley to mashed potatoes, and form into flat cakes. Flour lightly and fry until brown (see page 234).
4 *Duchesse potatoes.** Add plenty of margarine and egg yolk to mashed potatoes. Season well. Pipe into rose shapes or form into pyramid shapes and bake until crisp and brown (see page 139).
* these freeze well.

Rice

1 Cooked rice can be used as a savoury dish; mix it with fried onions, tomatoes, etc., for a quick risotto.
2 For a sweet dish, blend cooked rice with a little thick cream and serve with fruit.

Steamed puddings

1 Re-steam or cut into thin slices and fry.
Steamed puddings can be frozen.

Sandwiches

1 Dip in beaten egg and milk, fry, and serve at once.
Some sandwiches can be frozen, see page 222.

Vegetables

1 Mix with mayonnaise or French dressing and put into salads.
2 Mix with cheese or tomato sauce, cover with mashed potato and serve as a shepherd's pie.
3 Add to curry sauces and heat gently.

Left-over egg whites can be used for meringues, see page 166

Egg yolks
1 Add to pancake batters, or put into mashed or creamed vegetables.
2 Use the yolks only in egg custards; they are much richer. See recipe page 179.
3 Use, diluted with milk or water, for coating fish, etc.
   Remember — egg yolks keep much better if covered with cold water, to prevent a skin forming.

Egg whites
1 Use in meringues (see picture, and page 166).
2 *Fruit snow*. Add a very stiffly beaten egg white to each $\frac{1}{4}$ pint of thick fruit purée.
   Remember — egg whites should be kept covered so that they do not evaporate.

Cakes
1 Use plain cakes in trifles, see page 175.
2 Use plain or fruit cake as fritters. Cut into slices, dip in a little milk or egg and milk and fry. Sprinkle with sugar.
   Remember — cake should be kept in a separate tin from pastry, biscuits or bread. Cakes may be frozen.

Sour milk
1 Strain through muslin, add seasoning and a little butter to make curd cheese.
2 Use for mixing scones, see page 269.

Canapés and hors d'oeuvre

Simple canapés

A canapé is the name given to a small savoury piece of food. The simplest kind of canapé is to top pieces of toast, bread and butter or small biscuits, with a variety of interesting ingredients, see suggestions below. A variety of canapés are served at cocktail parties, where larger savouries would be difficult for the guests to manage. If you are planning a rather formal meal serve a tray of canapés with a pre-dinner drink and plan a light first course, since these are surprisingly satisfying.

Ready in minutes

Buy small cheese biscuits: spread with butter and top with pâté, or cream cheese and prawns, or sliced hard-boiled egg and rolled anchovy fillets, or tiny rolls of smoked salmon, or asparagus tips. You can make the cheese biscuit mixture below, cut into fancy shapes, bake as the recipe for cheese straws (page 22) and store until required.

Spike a grapefruit (or large apple or orange or cabbage) with: canned or fresh or defrosted frozen prawns; diced cheese and cubes of pineapple; small rolls of smoked salmon; gherkins; cocktail onions, etc. The food should be put on to cocktail sticks, then pressed into the grapefruit.

Cheese biscuit basic recipe

Preparation: 10 minutes
Makes: see recipe

Secret of success
Do not make the mixture too wet.

2 oz. flour	salt and pepper	1½ oz. cheese,* finely grated
pinch of mustard	1½ oz. butter *or* margarine	very little egg yolk *to mix*

1 Sieve the flour with the mustard, salt and pepper.
2 Rub the butter or margarine into the flour, add the cheese.
3 Bind with enough egg to make a rolling consistency.
4 Knead very thoroughly in order to handle the dough.
5 If storing for a while before baking, wrap well in polythene or foil.

   * the cheese can be grated Parmesan, which gives the stronger flavour, grated Cheddar, or Gruyère.

Cheese whirls

Preparation: few minutes
No delay
Cooking: 10 minutes
Makes about 18

Secrets of success
Knead well at stage 1
Cut very neatly at stage 3.

cheese biscuit basic mixture, *as above*

1 Using the basic cheese biscuit recipe, roll out the dough to ¾ inch in thickness, making this into a neat rectangle.
2 Spread lightly with yeast or beef extract or chutney.
3 Roll up like a Swiss roll, cut into thin fingers.
4 Brush with a very little egg or milk and bake for a good 10 minutes on a greased tin near the top of a hot oven (450°F., Gas Mark 7).

Cheese whirls
Quick canapés

Mix grapefruit and prawns for a cocktail, see page 27

Cheese straws

Preparation: few minutes
No delay
Cooking: 10 minutes
Makes about 18

Secrets of success
Knead thoroughly at stage 1.
Roll out firmly at stage 2, so the mixture does not break.
Cut neatly at stage 2.
Handle carefully at stage 6.

cheese biscuit basic mixture, *page 21*

1 Make the basic cheese biscuit mixture.
2 Roll out the dough and cut into thin straws, or cut straws and 2 or 3 circles of dough, see picture opposite.
3 Bake on a greased baking tray for approximately 10 minutes (425–450°F., Gas Mark 6–7).
4 When cooked, allow to cool on the baking trays, then arrange in a neat pile or pull the straws through the crisp circles, see picture opposite.
5 If wished, dip each end of the straws in mayonnaise or soft cream cheese; coat one end with chopped parsley and the other with paprika.
6 Handle carefully for they are very crisp.
7 When cold, store in an airtight tin.

Cheese butterflies

Preparation: few minutes
Cooking: 10 minutes
Makes 18

Secret of success
Do not pipe mixture on too soon before serving, as it softens biscuits.

cheese biscuit basic mixture, *page 21*

2–3 oz. cream cheese *or* savoury cheese spread, *page 222*

1 Make the basic cheese biscuit mixture.
2 Roll out the dough to $\frac{1}{4}$ inch in thickness.
3 Cut into small rounds, about 1–1$\frac{1}{2}$ inches in diameter.
4 Cut half the rounds through the middle to make 'wings'.
5 Bake on a greased baking tray near the top of a hot oven (425–450°F., Gas Mark 6–7) for 10 minutes.
6 When cold, pipe or spread a band of cream cheese or savoury cheese spread across the centre of the round.
7 Arrange the half circles to look like butterfly wings.

Devilled twists

Preparation: 10 minutes
Cooking: 10 minutes
Makes about 24

Secret of success
Do not stress the dough when twisting at stage 7.

4 oz. plain flour
shake of cayenne pepper
$\frac{1}{4}$ level teaspoon salt
1 level teaspoon paprika

2 oz. butter
1 egg yolk
1 tablespoon cold water

1 tablespoon French *or* mild mustard (less if wished)
Parmesan *or* dry Cheddar cheese, finely grated

1 Sieve flour, pepper, salt and paprika and rub in the butter.
2 Mix to a dry dough with beaten egg yolk and water, adding, if necessary, a few drops more.
3 Roll the pastry into a thin rectangular sheet.
4 Spread half with French or mild mustard, then fold the plain half over the half spread with mustard.
5 Press edges together and roll lightly again.
6 Cut into $\frac{1}{2}$-inch wide strips.
7 Twist and place on a greased baking tray.
8 Bake above the centre of a hot oven (425–450°F., Gas Mark 6–7) until crisp and pale golden, about 10 minutes.
9 While hot, sprinkle with a little cheese then return to the oven for 2–3 minutes. Cool on the baking tray. When cold, store in an airtight tin.

Devilled twists and Star shorties

Cheese straws

Star shorties

Preparation: 30 minutes
Allow pastry to cool before filling.
Cooking: 15 minutes
Makes about 36 small shapes

Secrets of success
Knead well at stage 3 so the minimum liquid is required.
Roll firmly at stage 4 so the dough binds together.
Do not add toppings, see below, until just before serving.

Topping for star shorties

Although the star shorties are delicious served without a topping, they can form the basis for interesting canapés. If you do not wish to make the biscuits, buy small cheese biscuits and use them instead. Try these toppings:

a) cream cheese and asparagus tips
b) grated cheese, grated carrot blended with a little mayonnaise
c) liver pâté and tiny cocktail onions
d) minced chicken mixed with chopped nuts and mayonnaise to bind
e) chopped prawns and cucumber blended with mayonnaise or scrambled egg
f) tiny pieces of smoked salmon, rolled round asparagus tips

½ teaspoon almond essence *or* ½ teaspoon vanilla essence
4 oz. butter

4 oz. plain flour
2 oz. fine semolina
2 oz. castor sugar
¼ level teaspoon salt

to glaze
½ oz. castor sugar
cinnamon, *optional*

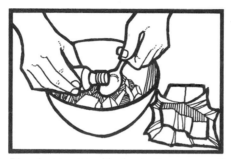

1 Blend essence with the butter very well to make sure it is evenly mixed.

2 Sieve the flour, semolina, sugar and salt.

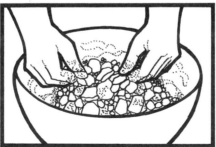

3 Rub in the butter (blended with essence). Knead the dough well, add a few drops of water if required to give a rolling consistency.

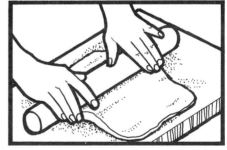

4 Roll out on a lightly floured board to about ⅓ inch in thickness; mark with a fork then cut into star shapes.

5 Bake on ungreased baking trays in the centre of a very moderate to moderate oven (350°F., Gas Mark 4) until crisp and pale golden, this takes 15–20 minutes.

6 While still hot, sprinkle with the sugar and cinnamon. Cool on the baking tray. Store in an airtight tin when cold. See picture on opposite page.

Cream yachts

Preparation: 15 minutes
Allow pastry to cool
Cooking: 12 minutes
Makes 12

Secret of success
Line the boat-shaped tins
carefully, otherwise you have a
poor shape – see stages 1–3.

6–8 oz. short crust pastry
(quantity depends on the
size of the boat-shaped
tins). *See page 184 for
recipe.*

rice paper
wooden cocktail sticks

1 Line boat tins with pastry. The easiest way to do this is to roll out the pastry to an oblong just under $\frac{1}{4}$ inch in thickness.
2 Arrange all the boat tins together on the table or pastry board, then carefully lift the pastry over the top.
3 Press it down over each shape to line it, then as you do this you will find the sharp edge of the tins cuts through the pastry. If not entirely cut through, press the rolling pin over the top – and the surplus pastry will fall away. Of course, if you prefer, you can cut neat oblongs and line each boat separately with the pastry.
4 Prick the bottom of the pastry boats. Stand the tins on a baking tray, bake for approximately 12 minutes just above the centre of a hot oven (425–450°F., Gas Mark 6–7).
5 Lift out of the tins when slightly cool – they are firmer then – and allow to cool completely before making the yachts.
6 To assemble the boats, first cut sails from rice paper with sharp scissors. The rice paper is obtainable in packets from good stationers. If by any chance you cannot get this, then use trimmings of pastry to make sail shapes, and bake them at same time as the boats. Make the fillings – see below.

Preparation: 5–6 minutes
No delay
Fills 6 boats

Secret of success
Do not exceed the amount of
tomato purée, etc., or the
delicate flavouring is spoiled.

Prawn filling

1 jar cream *or* $\frac{1}{4}$ pint double cream
4 oz. cooked prawns *or* shrimps

1 teaspoon concentrated tomato purée *or* ketchup *or* use the pulp from 1 large tomato

to garnish
parsley

Preparation: 10 minutes
No delay
Fills 6 boats

Secret of success
Do not over-whip the cream –
the filling must just hold its
shape.

Golden haddock filling

1 jar cream *or* $\frac{1}{4}$ pint double cream
4 oz. cooked smoked haddock, flaked

2 oz. Cheddar cheese, grated

to garnish
paprika
chopped parsley

1 Make the fillings in two bowls: whip the cream then add other ingredients.
2 Put into the boats, add the garnish on top, as given above.
3 Thread wooden cocktail sticks through the rice paper sails and press the point of the cocktail stick into the filling.
4 If using pastry sails, these are stiff enough to stand by themselves.

Left *Cream yachts*
Right *Ham and nut puffs*

Fish canapés

Fish boats

Preparation: 15–20 minutes
Cooking: 15 minutes
Makes 16

Secret of success
Try to mix the *hot* rice with fish, etc., at stage 4; this blends the flavours better.

6 oz. short crust pastry
1 oz. long grain rice, boiled, *page 147*

small can salmon *or* tuna fish
little mayonnaise, *page 207*

6 gherkins
small can anchovy fillets

1 Roll out pastry as page 184.
2 Line about 16 tiny boat-shaped tins – small patty tins would do (see page 24).
3 Prick the bottoms and bake 'blind' (empty – see page 190) for 12–15 minutes in the centre of a hot oven (425–450°F., Gas Mark 6–7).
4 Mix the rice with the salmon or tuna fish and enough mayonnaise to bind.
5 Chop the gherkins into tiny pieces and add to the rice mixture.
6 Split the anchovy fillets down the centre – allowing 1 strip per 'boat'.
7 Chop any that remain and add to the rice mixture.
8 Fill the 'boats' with rice etc., top with anchovy fillets.

Fish balls

Preparation: 15 minutes
Cooking: 8–10 minutes
Makes about 24

Secrets of success
Coat the little balls well with the egg and crumbs, and drain thoroughly.

ingredients as fish cakes, *page 54*

1 Use fish cake recipe on page 54.
2 Make into tiny balls, with well floured hands
3 Coat the balls with egg and crumbs; make certain they are well coated.
4 Fry, for 5 minutes only, in deep or shallow fat.
5 Drain on absorbent paper so they are not too greasy. Serve hot or cold.
6 If serving hot, keep warm on the dish with the absorbent paper until ready to serve.
7 To serve, transfer to a clean hot dish, lined with a savoury d'oyley or dish paper, pierce with cocktail sticks.

Variations
1 Use flaked crab meat, canned or freshly cooked salmon, in place of cooked white fish.
2 Roll the fish balls in a mixture of crumbs and finely grated Parmesan cheese, or crumbs and chopped blanched almonds.

Prawn and cheese rounds

Preparation: 15 minutes
Makes 12

Secret of success
Use really fresh bread.

4 slices of bread
1 oz. butter
2–3 oz. soft cream cheese

2 tablespoons finely chopped parsley
12 prawns *or* shrimps

to garnish
paprika

1 Cut the slices of bread into 12 small rounds using a pastry cutter.
2 Spread each round with butter and soft cream cheese.
3 Put a narrow border of chopped parsley around the edge.
4 Arrange a prawn or shrimp in the centre of each round, and dust with paprika.

Ham and nut puffs

Preparation: 10 minutes
No delay
Cooking: few minutes
Makes 36

Secret of success
Put the semolina in carefully and steadily at stage 1, otherwise the mixture becomes lumpy.

$\frac{1}{2}$ pint milk
2 oz. fine semolina
2 egg yolks
4 oz. lean ham *or* boiled bacon, finely chopped

2 oz. walnuts, finely chopped
1 teaspoon made-mustard
salt and pepper
1 egg white

for frying
oil *or* fat

1 Heat the milk, pour in the semolina and cook over a low heat, stirring until the mixture comes to the boil and thickens.
2 Simmer gently for 2 minutes, remove from the heat.
3 Stir in the egg yolks, ham, walnuts and mustard.
4 Season well to taste, then fold in the stiffly whisked egg white.
5 Drop heaped teaspoonsful of the mixture into deep hot oil or fat, and fry for about 1 minute, or till golden brown all over.
6 Drain on absorbent paper for 1–2 minutes only.
7 Serve hot, spiked with cocktail sticks. They are also delicious cold.

To vary
1 Omit the ham, add flaked crab meat.
2 Omit the ham, add 2–3 oz. finely grated cheese.

Hors d'oeuvre

Hors d'oeuvre are so varied in type that there will always be some kind to fit in with your menu. Some of the fish dishes in the chapter beginning on page 39 are suitable for hot hors d'oeuvre, but quite the easiest way of planning a meal is to have a cold first course. Some of the hors d'oeuvre in the following pages are filling enough for a light meal in themselves.

Left *Buckling pâté, see page 29*
Right *Prawn cocktail without mayonnaise*

Mixed hors d'oeuvre

There are many ingredients that can be used to provide a delicious and easy-to-make hors d'oeuvre. Try to have as much variety of colour and flavour as possible. Ideally your hors d'oeuvre should consist of:

Something with a fish flavour: sardines, anchovies, rollmop herrings, mussels, prawns, smoked salmon, fresh salmon, fish salads of any kind, cooked cod's or other fish roes. Dress the fish with mayonnaise or oil and vinegar and lemon, garnish with parsley.

Salad: choose between potato salad, Russian salad, tomato salad, cucumber, cooked corn on the cob, lettuce, watercress, celery, mixed vegetable. The salad should be tossed in mayonnaise or French dressing (pages 207, 208).

Meat: diced or sliced salami, chopped sausage, small cubes or rolls of ham, tongue, chicken, mixed with French dressing (page 208).

Eggs: sliced hard-boiled eggs, or hard-boiled eggs halved and the yolks mixed with anchovy essence, a little butter, then piled back into white cases.

Garnishes: in addition use some of the ready-prepared savoury ingredients which are such a good standby in the cupboard — pickled gherkins, cocktail onions, olives, pickled walnuts, etc.

Easy hors d'oeuvre

Asparagus: canned. Hot or cold, serve with melted butter or mayonnaise (page 207) and brown bread and butter.

Broccoli or cauliflower: frozen or fresh, cooked and served with grated cheese and melted butter.
Or serve little cauliflower flowerets, raw, with black olives as a side dish.

Egg Salad: hard-boiled eggs, halve and coat with mayonnaise (page 207) and serve with green salad.

Fruit: canned or fresh fruit juice, serve very cold;
grapefruit halved and sprinkled with sugar;
melon cut into portions, served with sugar and ginger;
sliced apple served with salami.

Smoked fish: eel or salmon, served with lemon, paprika and brown bread and butter.
Trout served in the same way, with horseradish cream.

Shellfish: prawns, shrimps or lobster on a bed of salad, top with mayonnaise (page 207) or tomato-flavoured mayonnaise (add a few drops tomato ketchup to mayonnaise).

Fish: sardines (see page 27).
Rollmop herrings (see page 29).

Vegetables: mustard pickles, pickled walnuts, pickled gherkins, onions, tomatoes, pickled cabbage.

Sardine and tomato hors d'oeuvre

Preparation: few minutes
No delay
Serves 4 as an hors d'oeuvre

Secret of success
Choose firm tomatoes

4 tomatoes
thick mayonnaise, *page 207*

large can sardines in
oil

to garnish
parsley

1 Cut the tomatoes into slices and sandwich these together with the mayonnaise.
2 Arrange with the sardines on a flat dish. Garnish with parsley.

To vary
1 Sandwich the tomatoes with scrambled egg blended with chopped chives and mayonnaise.
2 Serve on a bed of mixed green salad.

Shellfish cocktails

A simply made *Grapefruit and prawn cocktail* is shown in the colour picture on page 20.

Shrimps, prawns, lobster or crab can all be served as cocktails.
1 When making these prepare the lettuce (shred finely), the sauce and the fish.
2 Put together just before serving (making sure fish is well coated with sauce), so the mixture looks fresh. Serve as cool as possible.

Prawn cocktail
(without mayonnaise)

Preparation: few minutes
Serves 8

Secret of success
Add tomato juice gradually to give a smooth mixture. Use only $\frac{1}{2}$ can to $\frac{1}{4}$ pint cream to make a thicker and richer sauce.

$\frac{1}{4}$ pint thick cream
can tomato juice
    (approximately 16 fl. oz.)
Tabasco *or* Worcestershire
    sauce to taste

2 level teaspoons castor
    sugar
8 oz. prawns
lettuce

to garnish
paprika
few small lettuce leaves

1 Whisk the cream until thick.
2 Gradually whisk in the tomato juice, then fold in the Tabasco sauce and sugar.
3 This makes approximately 1 pint sauce, which should be chilled before using.
4 Mix in prawns and serve in tall glasses with shredded lettuce in the bottom; garnish with paprika and lettuce leaves.

Joppe's prawn salad

Preparation: few minutes
Serves 4

Secrets of success
Check the flavouring carefully. Add the Worcestershire sauce very gradually. This particular recipe is highly flavoured, but adjust it to personal taste.

for the sauce
4 tablespoons thick
    mayonnaise
1 tablespoon tomato ketchup
1 teaspoon finely chopped
    celery when in season *or*
    $\frac{1}{4}$ teaspoon celery salt

1 tablespoon lemon juice
salt to taste
1 teaspoon finely chopped
    onion
$\frac{1}{2}$–1 tablespoon
    Worcestershire sauce

4–6 oz. prawns *or* shrimps
lettuce

to garnish
whole prawns

1 Mix together all the ingredients for the sauce.
2 Arrange the prepared prawns on a bed of lettuce.
3 Spoon over the cocktail sauce.
4 Garnish with whole prawns and serve.

Joppe's prawn salad

Avocado pears

These have become a favourite hors d'oeuvre and can be served in a variety of ways. Allow half avocado per person

Secret of success
Choose really ripe avocados To test, feel *very gently* — they should be soft to the touch.

Avocado vinaigrette

2 avocado pears	French *or* vinaigrette dressing, *page 208*

Avocado pears discolour very easily, so always sprinkle with lemon juice or oil and vinegar as soon as the pear is halved.
1 Halve the avocado pears and remove the stones.
2 Fill the centres with French dressing (page 208). Serve at once, to avoid discolouring.

Sardine and avocado pear salad

1 avocado pear	little watercress	French *or* vinaigrette
small can sardines in oil	lettuce	dressing, *page 208*
1 tomato		

1 Halve the pear, remove the skin and stone.
2 Slice neatly and arrange on a dish with the sardines, sliced tomato, watercress and lettuce. Spoon oil and vinegar over the salad to prevent the pear discolouring.

Seafood avocado

2 avocado pears	mayonnaise, *page 207* or
4 oz. shelled prawns *or* shrimps	French *or* vinaigrette dressing, *page 208*

1 Halve the pears, sprinkle with lemon juice.
2 Fill the centres with prawns or shrimps, tossed in mayonnaise or dressing.

Walnut and soured cream salad

2 avocado pears	½ pint dairy-soured cream	seasoning
lemon juice	2 oz. walnuts	

1 Halve the pears, sprinkle with lemon juice.
2 Blend the soured cream and chopped nuts. Season well and put into the pears.

Melon cocktail

Preparation: 6–7 minutes
Allow to stand
Serves 6

Secret of success
Test that melon is just ripe; flesh should yield to gentle pressure.

1 medium melon	sugar to taste *or* syrup from jar preserved stem ginger	little preserved ginger

1 Dice melon, put into glasses and sprinkle with sugar, or cover with ginger syrup, and mix with stem ginger.
2 Allow to stand in a cold place, before serving.

To vary
Omit ginger. Mix the melon with mixed fruit, as grapefruit cocktail below.

Grapefruit cocktail

Preparation: 5–7 minutes
Allow to stand
Serves 4

Secret of success
Mix colourful fruits.

2 fresh grapefruit *or* large can grapefruit	8–12 oz. fresh fruit in season (diced melon, sliced orange, strawberries)	sugar to taste *to decorate* mint leaves

1 Remove sections from the grapefruit, or open the can of fruit and drain well.
2 Mix with other fruit and pile into glasses.
3 Sprinkle with sugar to taste.
4 Decorate with mint leaves. Put in a cool place until ready to serve.

Fruit cocktail

Preparation: 15 minutes

This is not only a delicious sweet but can be served as an hors d'oeuvre if wished.

1 pineapple	fresh fruit

1 Peel a pineapple carefully, trying to keep its shape intact. Replace the leaves, and arrange in a bowl.
2 Put a mixture of diced fresh fruit all round, and decorate with sprigs of mint.
3 To serve as a sweet, dust with sugar and moisten with a little fresh orange juice or Curaçao — or soak in a sugar syrup.
4 To serve as an hors d'oeuvre, use less sugar but add sprinkling dry sherry.

Buckling pâté

Preparation: 20 minutes
Serves 4–6 as an hors d'oeuvre
in lemon cases or up to 8–10 as
mixed hors d'oeuvre

Secret of success
Flavour well, see step 5.

To vary: use flaked cooked *fresh
herring* — add few drops anchovy
essence to ingredients. Or use
flaked canned salmon — mix with
mayonnaise and chopped
gherkins, season and flavour
with lemon juice.

4 large *or* 6 small lemons	seasoning	*to garnish*
2 large buckling	2 teaspoons lemon juice	parsley
2 oz. butter, softened		lettuce

1 Cut a thin slice from the 'stalk' end of each lemon, so the lemons stand upright.
   Save the slices to use for a 'lid' for the pâté.
2 Scoop out the centre pulp from each lemon, strain this and save the juice; any juice
   left should be put into a jar and stored in the refrigerator.
3 Cut the top in a 'van-dyke' fashion.
4 Skin and fillet the buckling, then flake the flesh and blend with the butter.
5 Add the seasoning and lemon juice; taste, add a little more juice if wished.
6 Pack the pâté into the lemon cases, replace the 'lids', to keep moist.
7 Serve the lemon filled pâté garnished with parsley and on crisp lettuce leaves.
   Illustration on page 26.

Chicken or veal pâté

Preparation: 15 minutes
Allow to stand 30 minutes
Cooking: 45 minutes

Serves 6–8 as an hors d'oeuvre
or up to 12–14 as part of a
mixed hors d'oeuvre

Secrets of success
Season and flavour well.
Blend ingredients thoroughly.
Do not cook too quickly.

Use for sandwiches, topping for
savoury biscuits, or as a first
course with thin buttered toast.

4–6 oz. cooked liver–chicken *or* calves', *see page 104*	2 oz. fresh white bread-crumbs, *to make these see page 268*	pinch of mixed herbs, *optional*
4 oz. cooked chicken *or* veal	½ teaspoon nutmeg	2 small eggs
	½ teaspoon onion salt, *optional*	3 tablespoons milk
		½ teaspoon Worcestershire sauce

1 Put the liver and chicken through a fine mincer.
2 Combine the liver and chicken with the breadcrumbs, nutmeg, onion salt and herbs
   if used.
3 Stir in eggs and milk, then leave to stand for 30 minutes to allow the mixture to
   soften slightly.
4 Add Worcestershire sauce, season further to taste then turn into a well greased 1-lb.
   loaf tin; cover with greased foil.
5 Bake in the centre of a very moderate oven (325–350°F., Gas Mark 3–4) for 45
   minutes.
6 Cool slightly, then turn out of tin, or allow to cool in the tin with a light weight on top.
   This cuts well into thin slices.

Liver pâté

1 For a stronger flavoured pâté: use 12 oz. uncooked liver; this can be all calves' liver
   or a mixture of calves' and pigs' liver. Put through a coarse mincer for a 'rough-cut'
   pâté, or a fine mincer for a smooth pâté.
2 Mince a small onion and clove of garlic with the liver.

Rollmop herrings

Allow 1 large rollmop herring
per person or 2 smaller pieces.
Buy jars of rollmop herrings as
a useful 'standby'.

Secrets of success
Choose ingredients that blend
with the sharp flavour.

jar rollmop herrings	lettuce	*for garnishes* see method

1 Open a jar of rollmop herrings and arrange them on a bed of lettuce.
2 Garnish with potato salad (page 204), diced beetroot, spring onions, sliced gherkins
   and Russian salad (page 205).

Rollmops with avocado
Mix diced rollmop herrings, diced tomatoes and diced avocado pears. Serve on
watercress and with French or vinaigrette dressing (page 208).

Rollmop hors d'oeuvre

Making your own soup

Thick filling soups

In these days when excellent ready-prepared soups are easily obtainable you may feel it is not worthwhile making your own. It is, however, worth considering that some soups can be a meal in themselves, and here are a few that would form a complete meal, with perhaps cheese and salad to follow.

Bacon soup

Preparation: 10 minutes
Allow 5 minutes afterwards to sieve soup
Cooking: 40 minutes
Serves 2 (good portions)

Secret of success
Cooking slowly at stage 6. Do not boil rapidly otherwise the soup will curdle.

Bacon soup

1 medium potato, peeled
1 medium onion
1 stick celery
1 oz. bacon fat *or* margarine

1 pint bacon stock
2 oz. bacon, diced
salt and pepper
¼ pint milk

1 egg yolk
2 teaspoons chopped parsley

1 Slice the potato, onion and celery. Toss for a few minutes in the hot fat.
2 Add the stock and simmer for 30 minutes.
3 Meanwhile fry the bacon, or cook under the grill, and chop this.
4 Sieve the soup and return to the pan, adding the diced bacon.
5 Season and when boiling, whisk in the milk blended with the egg yolk.
6 Lower the heat and cook for 2–3 minutes *without boiling*. If the soup should boil, the egg will curdle. The soup should thicken slightly.
7 Add the chopped parsley and serve at once.

Kidney and bacon soup

Preparation: 10 minutes
No delay
Cooking: 45 minutes
Serves 2 (good portions)

Secret of success
Careful thickening at stage 7 – stir all the time.

1 pig's kidney
1 good sized rasher bacon
1 leek

2 oz. mushrooms
¾ pint water
salt and pepper

½ oz. flour
toasted croûtons, *page 36*

1 Finely cut up the kidney, bacon, leek and mushrooms.
2 Fry the bacon first in the saucepan, until the fat runs out.
3 Add other ingredients and fry lightly. Do not let the leek brown.
4 Add ½ pint of the water and seasoning, cover the pan tightly.
5 Simmer for 35 minutes.
6 Blend the flour with ¼ pint water.
7 Add to the soup, stir as the mixture comes to the boil and cook for 4–5 minutes, stirring all the time.
8 Re-season if desired, and serve with toasted croûtons.

Tomato soup with dumplings

Preparation: 12 minutes
Soak lentils if wished
Cooking: 40 minutes
Serves 4–6

Secret of success
Make certain there is enough liquid in the pan at stage 6, before adding the dumplings. These absorb a great deal of liquid, so if the soup has become too thick it should be made slightly thinner.

Tomato soup with dumplings

12 oz. tomatoes
2 rashers bacon
2 oz. lentils
salt and pepper
1½ pints stock (preferably bacon stock)

knob of butter
bunch of mixed herbs

for the dumplings
2 rashers bacon

2 oz. flour (with plain flour add ½ teaspoon baking powder)
water *to bind*

1 Simmer the tomatoes, chopped bacon and the lentils (which can be soaked overnight in the stock) together with the well seasoned stock, until tender.
2 Rub through a sieve, or if you skin the tomatoes beforehand there is no need to sieve, just beat the mixture well with a wooden spoon.
3 *Meanwhile, make the dumplings:* chop the bacon into very tiny pieces.
4 Fry for 2–3 minutes, then add to the flour.
5 Make to a firm consistency with the water, and roll into tiny balls.
6 Put in the dumplings, knob of butter, seasoning and mixed herbs and cook for approximately 12–15 minutes. Remove mixed herbs before serving.

Dried pea soup

Preparation: 10–15 minutes
Overnight soaking
Cooking: 1½ hours
Serves 4–6

Secrets of success
Make sure the soup is well seasoned and flavoured. Dried peas must be well cooked, otherwise the soup loses its smooth texture.

8 oz. dried split peas
2 pints bacon stock (left from boiling piece bacon)

2 onions
1 carrot
1 turnip

salt and pepper
sprig of mint
1 teaspoon sugar

1 Soak the peas overnight in the bacon stock.
2 Put into a saucepan with the chopped vegetables, seasoning and mint, and simmer gently for approximately 1¼–1½ hours.
3 Either rub the soup through a sieve, or beat until very smooth, or pour into a warm liquidiser and emulsify.
4 Pour back into pan and reheat; add sugar and any extra seasoning if required.

To vary
If you have no bacon stock, use water and chicken stock cubes and add a very little yeast extract — which enhances the flavour of the soup.

Fresh pea soup

Simmer fresh peas (you will need about 1½ lb.) in the stock and cook for approximately 20 minutes, continue as recipe from step 2, above.

Lentil soup

Preparation: 10–15 minutes
Soak lentils if wished
Cooking: 1½ hours
Serves 4–6

Secrets of success
Lentils have an interesting flavour and texture, so do not over-cook.
Make sure the sauce is very smooth at stage 3.

8 oz. washed lentils
little chopped bacon
1 onion
1 carrot
1 pint stock *or* water

salt and pepper
little chopped thyme *or* parsley
1 oz. butter
½ oz. flour

½ pint milk

to garnish
chopped parsley

1 Put the lentils (soaked overnight, if wished), bacon, chopped onion, carrot and stock or water into a pan.
2 Add seasoning and thyme or parsley, then simmer gently for about 1½ hours.
3 Meanwhile, make a very thin sauce with the butter, flour and milk (see page 143).
4 Add the lentil purée and reheat.
5 Season to taste, and serve garnished with chopped parsley.

To give a more interesting flavour, add a little curry powder and an apple to the ingredients; use 3–4 tomatoes, skinned and chopped. Add these at stage 4; in which case heat the soup gently so the tomatoes do not make the mixture curdle.

Vegetable soups

Tomato soup

Preparation: 12–15 minutes
Cooking: 25 minutes
Serves 4–6

Secrets of success
Never over-cook the vegetables in any vegetable soup, otherwise you lose colour, flavour and texture.

1½ lb. tomatoes
1 pint water *or* white stock
½ small beetroot, preferably uncooked
small piece celery
few drops of Worcestershire sauce
1 teaspoon vinegar *or* lemon juice
salt and pepper
2 bay leaves

1 Put the ingredients all together in a large saucepan, and cook gently until the tomatoes are very soft. This should take about 25 minutes.
2 Remove the beetroot and bay leaves, then rub first through a sieve, and finally strain through muslin.
3 Reheat or serve cold.
4 If a slightly thickened soup is desired it will be necessary only to rub the mixture through the sieve, without straining afterwards, or put it into a liquidiser to emulsify.

To vary
Add one or two sticks of chopped celery to the soup after sieving; this gives a pleasing crisp garnish. If serving cold, top with soured cream or yoghourt, or small balls of cream cheese rolled in chopped parsley.

Mixed vegetable soup

Preparation: 12–15 minutes
Cooking: 8 minutes
Serves 4–6

Secret of success
Never put too much cheese on the soup, otherwise it could become tough; a light sprinkling only is required.

approximately 1¼ lb. mixed vegetables (choose a mixture for an interesting flavour)
1½ pints stock *or* water with bouillon cube
salt and pepper
to garnish
grated cheese
chopped parsley

1 Peel and grate the vegetables on a coarse grater.
2 Bring stock, or water and bouillon cube, to the boil.
3 Add vegetables and seasoning and cook rapidly for about 5–8 minutes until they are just tender.
4 Pour into hot soup cups and sprinkle with grated cheese and parsley.

If preferred, dice vegetables and cook approximately 15–20 minutes. At stage 3, sieve or emulsify mixture in a liquidiser, reheat and continue as stage 4.

Creamy potato soup

Preparation: 12–15 minutes
Cooking: 20 minutes
Serves 4–6

Secrets of success
Potato soup is excellent if well seasoned. Do not over-cook the soup for this would make the potatoes turn brown; the soup should be creamy in colour.

8 oz. peeled potatoes
1 large onion
1 bay leaf
1 pint white stock *or* water
1 oz. butter
1 oz. flour
½ pint milk
4–5 tablespoons thin cream *or* evaporated milk
salt and pepper
to garnish
cayenne pepper
chopped watercress *or* parsley

1 Simmer potatoes and onion with the bay leaf in stock or water until soft.
2 Rub through a sieve, or beat with a wooden spoon until very smooth.
3 Make a white sauce with the butter, flour and milk and add the potato purée.
4 Stir in the cream or evaporated milk and a little extra butter if possible.
5 Reheat gently after adding the cream, etc.
6 Season well and garnish with cayenne pepper and chopped watercress or parsley.

To vary
A few green peas added to the potatoes give an interesting colour and flavour. For a really smooth soup, proceed to stage 4, then emulsify in liquidiser.

Cream of spinach soup

Preparation: 10 minutes
No delay
Cooking: 12 minutes
Serves 4–6

Secret of success
Make sure the sauce is smooth.

Colour picture, page 37

1 oz. luxury margarine
1 oz. flour
1 pint milk
large packet chopped frozen spinach
salt and pepper
2–3 tablespoons thin cream, *optional*

1 Heat the margarine in a pan. Stir in the flour.
2 Cook for several minutes; remove from heat and gradually stir in the milk.
3 Bring to the boil and cook until thickened.
4 Add block of chopped frozen spinach. Heat in sauce, stirring from time to time.
5 When the spinach is quite defrosted, allow to simmer gently for approximately 3–4 minutes; do not over-cook.
6 If necessary, add a little extra milk.
7 Season well and, for a touch of luxury, add the cream.

Consommés

A consommé is considered quite a difficult soup to make perfectly, and therefore it is something you may feel you would prefer to buy rather than make yourself. You can buy cans of consommé or you can use bouillon cubes and water to make your own. If however, you would like to try the recipe, here it is — it can give you the basis for a number of first class thin soups.

Consommé

Preparation: 10 minutes
No delay
Cooking: 1 hour
Serves 4–6

Secrets of success
Allow a sufficiently long cooking time. Strain carefully, see stages 2 and 4.

12 oz. shin of beef
2 pints good stock
salt and pepper
1 onion

small piece celery
sprig of parsley
1 bay leaf

1 carrot
½ tablespoon sherry, *optional*

1 Cut the meat into small pieces and put these into the saucepan, together with the other ingredients.
2 Simmer very gently for 1 hour, then strain through several thicknesses of muslin.
3 Add sherry if desired.
4 To clear a consommé, put in a stiffly beaten egg white and clean egg shell and gently simmer again for 20 minutes, then re-strain.

Straining stock for consommé

Consommé chasseur

Preparation: 15 minutes
No delay
Cooking: 1 hour
Serves 4–6

Secrets of success
Do not over-cook the meat. Make sure the consommé is well seasoned.

ingredients for consommé, *above*

4–6 oz. cooked game *or* poultry

2 tablespoons port wine

1 Dice the meat very finely.
2 Make the consommé as directed above.
3 Cut the cooked game or poultry into neat small pieces which are easy to handle with a soup spoon. Heat the diced meat in the consommé, but do not cook for very long otherwise the meat loses flavour and texture.
4 When very hot, add the port wine to the soup and serve at once.

Garnishes for consommé
1 Tiny strips of cooked vegetables, known as julienne.
2 Mixed cooked frozen vegetables.
3 A little cooked long grain rice.
4 Sprinkle with chopped parsley.

Quick tomato consommé

Preparation: few minutes
No delay
Cooking: few minutes
Serves 4–6

Secret of success
Make sure the tomato juice is well seasoned, to make a good savoury clear soup.

1½ pints tomato juice
salt and pepper

2 tablespoons sherry

to garnish
grated cheese *or* croûtons, *page 36*

1 Heat the tomato juice.
2 Add seasoning and sherry. (As well as salt and pepper, you can add celery salt, cayenne pepper, a pinch of chilli powder and a few drops of Worcestershire sauce.) The tomato soup must have an interesting and piquant flavour.
3 Pour into soup cups and garnish with grated cheese, or with croûtons of fried bread.

To vary
Use half tomato juice and half consommé as recipe above.

Using prepared soups

The ready-prepared soups — whether canned or of the dehydrated packet types on the market — are an enormous help to the busy housewife. These are produced from very fine ingredients and give an excellent flavour. If, however, more individual results are desired, the ready-prepared soups can be used as a good base and additional flavourings put in.

Bouillon cubes are not only excellent flavourings for stock but also for consommé. Add a little sherry and individual garnishes (see page 36).

Creamed soups — asparagus, celery, etc. — are improved by diluting with a little cream or top of the milk, and can be used as the basis of creamed vegetable soup by adding a few extra fresh or frozen vegetables and simmering until these are tender.

Green pea soup can be given extra flavour by simmering a little chopped mint and bacon in it, or topping with cream and sprigs of chopped mint (as shown in the picture).

Chicken soup can be used in a variety of ways. Add diced cucumber and simmer until tender, or add mixed diced vegetables to a chicken noodle soup to produce a quick *Minestrone soup*.

Try a mixture of soups: mushroom and tomato soups mixed together are very good indeed — the *Confetti mushroom soup* (shown in the picture), is topped with tiny pieces of cooked parsley and pastry crescents.

Frozen vegetables also make soup-making easy. Use frozen spinach purée for soup (page 33) and the ready-prepared macédoine (mixed vegetables) for a *Vegetable soup*.

Add a knob of butter to most soups for a richer flavour.

Concentrated soups have to be diluted to serve as soup, but can be used just as they are as an excellent sauce — the packet soups can save you a great deal of time if you use them as the basis for casserole dishes or stews.

Quick prawn chowder

A prawn chowder is typical of some of the thick, almost stew-type soups so much enjoyed in America.
1 This is quickly made by heating chicken noodle soup, and adding a few prawns.
2 Heat gently for a few minutes, but do not over-cook.
3 If you have time, add chopped fried bacon and sliced uncooked vegetables to chicken noodle soup and heat for 15–20 minutes until tender — *then* add prawns and reheat. Lobster (canned or fresh) could be used instead of prawns.

Party seafood bisque

Preparation: 12 minutes — allow time after boiling the milk to let it cool *OR* to chill it thoroughly
Cooking: few minutes
Serves 6

Secret of success
Do not over-cook the shellfish at stages 3 and 4, for this toughens them.

medium can condensed tomato soup *and*
medium can condensed pea soup

medium can seafood (lobster, crab or prawns, or lobster tails) *or* use fresh fish, poached and flaked, *page 48*

small can evaporated milk
few drops Tabasco sauce
1 teaspoon Worcestershire sauce
good squeeze of lemon juice
seasoning

1 Dilute both the soups as directed on cans.
2 Add an extra ¼ pint water. Heat slowly.
3 Stir in flaked or chopped crab or lobster (or lobster tails).
4 Add the prawns, if used, whole. Make piping hot.
5 Whip chilled milk (page 174) and stir into the soup with flavourings and seasonings to taste.
6 Reheat but do not boil.
7 Toast one or two slices of bread and cut into squares or triangles. Serve separately in a dish, so everyone may sprinkle the top of the thick soup with the croûtons when ready to eat. This soup is excellent served chilled, and instead of toast I would then have crisp, hot, French bread.

To vary
Instead of condensed tomato and pea soup, use approximately 1½ pints of canned tomatoes or home-made tomato purée. To make this, chop tomatoes, warm for about 4 minutes then sieve (you will need about 2 lb. of tomatoes).

Hamburger chowder

1 Heat oxtail soup, and add to this either a small quantity of cooked minced beef, or dice 1 or 2 frozen meat cakes.
2 Simmer gently for a few minutes.
3 To make a more substantial and interesting chowder, long grain rice or diced vegetables can be simmered in the soup before adding the meat. Do not over-cook the meat.

Onion and potato chowder

Preparation: 6 minutes
No delay
Cooking: 20 minutes
Serves 4–6

Secrets of success
Dehydrated soups can become lumpy unless stirred as they thicken. Do not over-cook the potatoes at stage 2.

packet onion soup
2–3 potatoes

3 sticks celery

to garnish
parsley *or* cooked peas, *optional*

1 Make up the onion soup as the directions on the packet, but use approximately ¼ pint of extra liquid as the potatoes will absorb this during cooking.
2 Add diced raw potatoes and chopped celery, and simmer gently for about 15 minutes until the vegetables are tender.
3 Garnish with parsley or cooked peas, if wished.

To vary
If you do not wish to use onion soup, chop 4–5 large onions, toss in 2 oz. margarine then add 1½ pints of chicken stock, or water and stock cubes. Cook for approximately 15 minutes then add the potatoes, etc., and continue as the recipe above. Season well before serving.

Onion and potato chowder

To serve cold soups

A number of soups you make or buy can be served cold. A consommé is an example. This may form a jelly by itself, but if you are doubtful as to whether it will, and if you are using bouillon cubes and water which quite definitely will not jelly, then make *jellied consommé* as follows:

1 Soften 2 level teaspoons of powdered gelatine in 2 tablespoons cold consommé.
2 Pour over the hot consommé, and stir until the gelatine has dissolved.
3 Allow to set very lightly in a basin then whisk and pour into soup cups.

A tomato consommé can be set in the same way.
If you like a stiffer cold soup, then use about 3 teaspoons powdered gelatine.

Iced curry soup

Preparation: 10–12 minutes
Cooking: about 18 minutes, then allow time for freezing
Serves 4–6

Secrets of success
This soup is spoiled if it is lukewarm, so chill very well. Taste and adjust the seasoning when it is cold.

Curry paste is a useful alternative to curry powder; if not available use curry powder instead – add at stage 3.

1 large onion	2 beef bouillon *or* chicken	lemon rind
1 oz. butter	cubes	¼ pint thin cream
½–1 tablespoon curry paste	2 pints water	
1 oz. cornflour	seasoning	*to garnish*
	1 bay leaf	grated lemon rind

1 Chop the onion finely, or grate coarsely.
2 Heat the butter and cook the onion in this until soft but not browned.
3 Stir in the curry paste and cornflour and cook for 1 minute, stirring well.
4 Add the stock cubes and water, unless using the home-made stock. Bring to the boil, add seasoning as required.
5 Put in the bay leaf and a strip of lemon rind; continue simmering for a good 10 minutes.
6 Remove the lemon rind and bay leaf, then allow the soup to cool.
7 Stir in the cream and put into the coldest place possible – a few minutes in the freezing compartment of the refrigerator is an excellent idea.
8 Taste, add more seasoning if necessary, then serve in cold soup cups, garnished with grated lemon rind.

To vary
Add 2–3 oz. sultanas and a grated apple to the soup at stage 4. Top with desiccated coconut as well as grated lemon rind.

Cream of mushroom soup

Cooking: 15 minutes
Serves 6–8

Colour picture, opposite

Do not boil after adding cream.

1 Blend 2 oz. plain flour with 1 pint chicken stock, put into saucepan.
2 Add 2 oz. luxury margarine, 1 pint milk, 8 oz. finely chopped mushrooms 2 tablespoons chopped parsley and seasoning; simmer for 10 minutes.
3 Add 1 tablespoon lemon juice and 4 tablespoons cream, heat gently and serve.

Country vegetable soup

Cooking: 45 minutes
Serves 6–8

Colour picture, opposite

1 Chop 3–4 celery stalks, ½ white cabbage, 4 skinned tomatoes, 1 peeled turnip, 2 peeled onions and 4 peeled carrots.
2 Put into a saucepan with 2 oz. luxury margarine and 2 pints chicken stock, cover the pan and simmer gently for about 30 minutes.
3 Add seasoning to taste, 1 tablespoon chopped parsley and about 4 oz. fresh or frozen peas. Continue cooking for a further 10–15 minutes.
   If topped with a layer of grated cheese, this soup will make a most satisfying main meal.

Garnishes for soup

Soup always looks more attractive if served with a garnish on top. Here are some suggestions:

Chopped parsley: use this particularly on meat soups, and where it forms a contrasting colour.
Chopped hard-boiled eggs: use this on top of soups for invalids, and where it forms a contrasting colour.
Grated cheese: particularly good on vegetable soups.
Croûtons of fried bread: to make these, cut slices of bread about ¼ inch thick, removing crusts. Cut the bread into ¼-inch cubes. Heat a little butter in a frying pan and fry the bread until crisp and golden brown on both sides. Lift out of the frying pan, drain on absorbent paper, and keep hot until ready to serve with the soup. Either sprinkle on top at the last minute, or let people help themselves. Two slices of bread will give croûtons for 4–6 soup cups.
Toasted croûtons: toast slices of bread on both sides; cut into tiny squares.

Cream of spinach soup, see page 32;
Cream of mushroom soup and Country vegetable soup, above

Fish

Wise buying of fish

When you shop for fish, look carefully at prices, for they fluctuate a great deal. This is due to seasons, weather — which determines a good or bad catch — and the fact that at periods of the year you can have gluts of certain fish. The next thing is to look most carefully at the freshness of fish. You will see below details of how to tell if fish is fresh; sometimes stale fish may be reduced in price. If you shop at a good fishmonger and ask his advice he can help you.

How to tell if fish is fresh

There are a number of ways of telling if fish is fresh — firstly, its smell; this may not be easy to identify in a shop full of fish, but stale fish has a very definite smell of ammonia.

White fish, when fresh should be quite firm, the flesh should not look limp in any way, and the eyes and the scales should look bright and clear.

Oily fish, such as herrings and mackerel, have a bright silvery look about the scales and skin. If they are dull and the eyes cloudy, they are stale.

Smoked fish, such as haddock, keeps well, but it is stale if dry and dull.

With *shellfish*, it is fresh if a bright colour. In the case of lobsters and prawns, if the tails spring back after being pulled out, you know it has been freshly caught and cooked. It is of good quality if it feels weighty for the size; poor quality shellfish feels light because it is full of water.

Never keep shellfish long. Even if you have a refrigerator, it does deteriorate with storage.

Apart from the freshness of the fish, it is true to say they have the best flavour if eaten in season, and the fish buying guide on the next page does give you an idea of when to buy.

Various types of fish

Fish is divided into various types:

White fish: cod, haddock and hake are some of the most usual.

Oily fish: salmon is the most luxurious in this group, while herrings are one of the most economical.

Shellfish which includes crab, lobster, escallops (scallops), oysters, shrimps and prawns.

Freshwater fish is enjoyed by fishermen, and freshwater trout is particularly delicious.

Smoked fish: a number of fish are smoked: salmon, eel and trout — to be served as hors d'oeuvre; bloaters, kippers (both from herrings) — as light supper or breakfast dishes.

Quantities of fish to allow

Quantities do depend a great deal, of course, on individual appetites. However, as a general ruling, allow:

Filleted fish: either 1 large or 2 smaller fillets per person — the total weight should be approximately 5–6 oz. This may seem rather small but there are no bones, which weigh quite heavily.

Whole fish: a whole fresh haddock or codling will weigh approximately 2¼ lb. for 4 people. This sounds a lot, but remember the head is quite heavy.

Cutlets of fish: 1 cutlet per person, weighing approximately 7–9 oz. Some of this weight is accounted for by the fairly large bone.

Smoked fish: 1 large or 2 smaller kippers per person. A really good sized smoked haddock should be enough for 4 people.

Smoked salmon is served in thin slices; allow 1¼–2 oz. per person. Allow 4–6 oz. smoked eel per person, as the bone is fairly heavy. Allow 1 smoked trout per person.

Smoked haddock barbecue, see page 50

Fish buying guide

Name	Type	In season (Britain)	Best method of cooking
Bream	White	July–December	Baking or grilling
Carp	Freshwater	October–February	When young, grilling or frying; when older, baking
Cod	White	Throughout year; best October–March	All methods can be used. Excellent in 'made-up' dishes
Crab	Shellfish	May–August	Boiling (usually bought cooked) Dress and serve cold, or as a hot dish, see page 49
Dog fish or huss	White	September–May	Baking or frying
Dory or John Dory	White	September–early January	As for sole or turbot
Eel	Freshwater	September–May	Stewing or making into jelly
Eel	Smoked	Throughout year	Serve as an hors d'oeuvre with horseradish sauce and lemon
Flounder	White	November–March	As for plaice or sole
Haddock	White	October–February	As for cod
Haddock	Smoked	Throughout year	Poaching or as kedgeree
Hake	White	June–January	Frying or baking
Halibut	White	July–April	Poaching, grilling or baking; if under 3 lb. should be baked whole
Herrings	Oily	Throughout the year from various sources; British season June–February	Grilling, baking, and frying; or pickling and sousing (to serve with salads)
Herrings	Smoked	Throughout year	*Bloaters:* grilling or frying *Buckling:* as smoked trout *Kippers:* frying, grilling, baking, boiling
Lobster	Shellfish	February–October	Boiling (usually bought cooked); can be served hot or cold
Mackerel	Oily	March–July	As for herrings
Mackerel	Smoked	Throughout year	As for smoked trout
Mullet	Oily	April–October	Baking or grilling
Mussels	Shellfish	September–April	Boiling; serve in soups or as a savoury dish *Never use a mussel that is open and will not close* as you tap it for that means it is already dead
Oysters	Shellfish	September–April	Serve on shell – uncooked – or remove from shell and fry
Perch	Freshwater	May–February	Frying or poaching
Plaice	White	Late May–December	Baking, frying, or grilling; steaming or poaching
Prawns	Shellfish	*Small:* February–October *Large:* March–December	Boil to cook or obtainable ready cooked; serve hot or cold in main dishes. Excellent as an hors d'oeuvre

Name	Type	In season (Britain)	Best method of cooking
Salmon	Oily	March–August	Poaching or grilling, serve hot or cold
Salmon	Smoked	Throughout year	Not cooked – serve in thin slices as hors d'oeuvre or in sandwiches with lemon
Salmon trout	Oily	April–August	As for salmon
Scallops (Escallops)	Shellfish	June–March	In a cream sauce, or fried in egg and crumbs
Sole	White	Some kind available all year	Baking, frying, poaching, steaming, grilling. Serve with lemon, melted butter or sauces
Sprats	Oily	October–March	Baking or frying
Sprats	Smoked	Throughout year	Grilling or frying, or as smoked trout
Trout	Freshwater	April–September	Grilling, frying, baking
Trout	Smoked	Throughout year	Serve as hors d'oeuvre with horseradish and lemon
Turbot	White	April–early September	Baking, grilling, frying, poaching, or serving cold in fish salads
Whitebait	Oily	May–August	Frying in deep fat
Whiting	White	October–August	Poaching, baking, grilling, frying
Whiting	Smoked (golden fillets)	Throughout year	Same method as smoked haddock

Fish roes

The roes of fish are most nutritious. The ones you see in fishmongers are generally herring or cod's roes.

Herring roes. These can be obtained either as a soft (male) or hard (female) roe. For recipes, see page 52.

Cod's roe. You will find both fresh and smoked cod's roe available. The difference is very apparent for the smoked cod's roe is a rather bright pink colour. Serve this as a sandwich filling or with crisp toast as an hors d'oeuvre.

Fresh cod's roe. Many fishmongers cook this and all you need to do is cut it in slices and heat in a little hot fat. It is particularly good fried with bacon as a supper dish.

Uncooked cod's roe. This should be steamed gently for about 20 minutes and then used as above. It can also be blended with butter for a sandwich filling or heated in a white sauce (page 143) and served as a savoury dish.

How to clean fish

If you have bought the fish ready-filleted, etc., from the fishmonger, he will, of course, have washed it there. Even so, it is better to wash it in plenty of cold water yourself — pat dry on kitchen paper.

With whole fish you intend to bake, you may find there are loose scales on the skin. Scrape these off gently with a knife. You will find they come away more easily if you scrape towards the tail.

How to fillet and skin white fish

Most fishmongers will fillet and skin on request, but you may sometimes find you have to do it yourself. These step-by-step pictures show plaice being filleted and skinned; the same rules apply to any white fish of similar shape.

Note. If you dip the edge of your knife in a little salt, you will find you have a better cutting edge.

Picture 4 shows the correct way to skin fish, but if you are in a great hurry and you put the fillets under a hot grill for just a moment, the skin comes away with no difficulty.

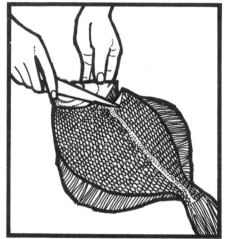

1 Cut off head with a sharp knife. (The head provides a great deal of flavour for fish stock.)

2 Make a deep incision down the back, i.e. on the side with the dark skin. Make a smaller cut round the edge of the flesh, avoiding the bones and fins.

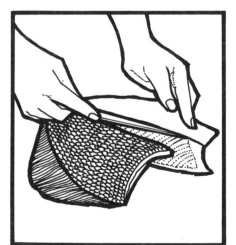

3 Insert the tip of the knife and gradually loosen flesh away from the backbone, folding it over gently with your fingers. Do not hurry or pull, or you may waste some by leaving it on the bone.
Turn the fish the other way and repeat process, working from the tail rather than the head. Then, turn the fish over and do the same on the white side, giving 4 fillets.

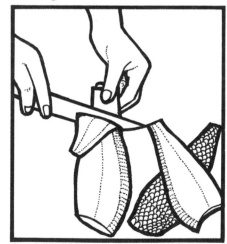

4 To skin, take hold of the fillet in your left hand, holding it by the tip. Make a very firm cut with a sharp knife just at the tip, then lift the fish with your knife away from the skin; continue like this until all the flesh is free.

To cook fish perfectly

Fish is one of the most delicious and easily digested foods, but it can be easily spoiled if over-cooked. Fish is ready when the flakes come away from the bone very slightly. Serve as soon as possible after cooking.

Grilled fish

Preparation: few minutes
Allow grill to heat up
Cooking: 4–10 minutes*

Most fish is suitable for grilling. Fillets of fish, unless very thick, can be grilled without turning. Whole fish and cutlets should be turned so that they are cooked on both sides.

Secret of success
Make sure that the grill is hot before you begin cooking.

*a very large whole sole may take longer than this, i.e. 12–14 minutes.

1 Brush the grid of the grill pan with a little melted butter or oil before cooking, so the fish does not stick, or put buttered foil over the grid, which makes it easier to clean the grill pan and grid.
2 Brush fish with a little melted butter, or oil, *before* cooking and season lightly with salt and pepper. A squeeze of lemon juice gives extra flavour.
3 For grilling thin fillets of fish – plaice, sole, whiting – allow approximately 4 minutes cooking time, turning the heat down after the first 2–3 minutes if desired.
4 For thicker fish, grill quickly for 2–3 minutes first on one side then on the other, to seal in flavour, then reduce heat for a further 3–4 minutes, brushing the fish once or twice with melted butter or oil.
5 When turning the fish, do this with a fish slice or broad-bladed palette knife so it does not break.
6 Mushrooms and halved tomatoes can be cooked in the bottom of the grill pan at the same time.

To vary
Whole sole is grilled as above; this is a very dry fish, so keep *well* basted with butter. When the fish is cooked the flesh may be removed from the bones before serving. Cut cooked flesh away from bones in same manner as shown opposite.

Devilled grilled fish

Preparation: few minutes
Wait for grill to heat up
Cooking: 4–10 minutes
Serves 4

Secret of success
Do not over-flavour with curry.

| 4 portions fish | ½–1 teaspoon curry powder | few drops Worcestershire |
| 1½–2 oz. butter | | sauce |

1 Spread the fish with the butter, blended with curry powder and a few drops of Worcestershire sauce.
2 Grill under hot grill, as directed above.

Tomato grilled fish

Preparation: few minutes
Wait for grill to heat up
Cooking: 4–10 minutes
Serves 4

Secret of success
Check tomato mixture is not too overpowering in flavour.

| 2–3 teaspoons tomato purée | 1½–2 oz. butter | 4 portions fish |

1 Add the tomato purée to the butter.
2 Spread this over the fish and grill under hot grill, as above.

Sauces to serve with grilled fish

Grilled fish can be served with a tomato, mushroom or white sauce, but one of the best accompaniments is parsley or maître d'hôtel butter, see page 44.

Parsley or maître d'hôtel butter

Preparation: 3 minutes
Wait for butter to cool
No cooking

Secret of success
Chill thoroughly.

.eeze of lemon juice   1–2 teaspoons chopped   seasoning
                         parsley   2 oz. butter

1 Work the lemon juice, parsley and seasoning into the butter.
2 Form into a neat block, allow to cool. If possible put in the refrigerator so that it becomes very firm.
3 Cut into neat pieces and put on the fish just before serving.

To prepare fish for frying

Preparation: 6–7 minutes
No delay

With egg and breadcrumb coating
1 Wash the fish and dry it well.
2 Dust lightly with a little flour; this is important as it makes certain the fish is quite dry.
3 Beat an egg lightly with a fork in a flat dish, then brush the beaten egg over both sides of the fish.
4 Put about 3 tablespoons crisp breadcrumbs in greaseproof paper and toss the fish in this until well coated. Shake each piece of fish lightly to get rid of surplus crumbs, since these might burn in the fat.

Note. This method can be used for cutlets, whole fish or fillets. Plaice is generally fried whole or filleted; ask the fishmonger to fillet it, or follow the directions on page 42. There is no need to remove the skin from the fish (or fillets) unless this is particularly disliked; again a good fishmonger will do this for you. Cod is a difficult fish to fry, for it has large flakes and is therefore inclined to break easily. Coat twice with flour before dipping in egg and breadcrumbs or batter. Handle carefully.

Preparation: 10 minutes
No delay

With a batter coating
1 Wash fish and dry it well.
2 Dust lightly with a little flour.
3 Make up batter (see below).
4 Pour batter into a shallow dish, then lay the pieces of fish in this just before frying. Drain well by lifting out of batter with your fingers and holding over dish for $\frac{1}{2}$ minute.

The batter: to coat 4 good sized portions.
This is suitable for fillets, cutlets or whole fish. If you like a very thin coating, add an extra tablespoon milk.

2 oz. plain *or* self-raising   1 egg   4 tablespoons milk *or*
     flour   pinch of salt   milk and water

1 Beat the flour, egg and salt until smooth.
2 Gradually stir in the liquid.

Preparation: 5 minutes
No delay

With a flour coating
1 Wash the fish and dry it well.
2 Put flour, with a little salt and pepper mixed with it, either in a bag of greaseproof paper (a nice clean method), or on a sheet of greaseproof paper or large plate. Allow about 1 dessertspoon flour to a good sized fillet.
3 Put the fish into the bag of flour and shake gently but firmly, or lift fish on to the plate or paper and using a palette knife press the flour into the fish.
4 Shake fish gently after removing from flour so that surplus flour drops off.

To fry fish

Use either a shallow frying pan or a pan of deep fat. Fish can be fried quite satisfactorily in shallow fat, especially when coated with egg and breadcrumbs or seasoned flour. A batter coating gives a better result in deep fat.

Importance of draining fried fish

Fish fried in shallow or deep fat MUST be well drained on absorbent paper or crumpled tissue paper. This absorbs the surplus fat.

44

To fry fish in shallow fat

Preparation: few minutes
No delay
Cooking: 4–10 minutes

Test heat of fat for frying by dropping in a small cube of bread; when the bread turns a pale golden colour in about 1 minute, the fat is ready. Always be careful not to overheat fat, or it burns before cooking the fish.

1 Choose a good solid frying pan, put 3–4 oz. whipped-up cooking fat (this is an excellent frying medium for fish) into the pan, or you can use 3–4 tablespoons oil. When melted the fat should come about halfway up the fish. For large pans or thick steaks you may need more fat. Heat STEADILY until you begin to see a faint haze, then test (see note at left).

2 When you are sure the fat is the right heat, carefully lower the fish into it and cook steadily for 4–5 minutes for whole fish or cutlets, then turn over carefully with a fish slice or palette knife and cook on the other side for the same length of time. When both sides are coloured, lower the heat for a minute to make sure the fish is cooked through.

3 Lift fish out of the pan and drain on crumpled kitchen or tissue paper put on a *hot baking tin* or dish, to make sure no surplus fat is left.

4 Garnish with parsley and lemon wedges. Serve on a dish paper (as in picture).

5 If any fat remains in the pan it can be strained into a container or basin — remember to let it cool slightly so the basin will not crack — and used again for fish within a day or so. For longer storage it must be cleaned (see page 46).

6 Wipe out the pan with paper to remove surplus fat, then wash in warm detergent solution. Dry well.

To fry fish and potatoes in one container

Deep fat
Give the potatoes the first frying, remove, then put in fish and cook. Drain and keep hot, then give final frying to the potatoes. Drain the potatoes on absorbent paper and serve.

Shallow fat
Fry the fish first, drain and keep hot, then cook potatoes; drain and serve. If there appear to be a lot of breadcrumbs in the pan it is advisable to wash this after frying the fish, and before cooking the potatoes.

To fry fish in deep fat

Preparation: few minutes
No delay
Cooking: 4–10 minutes

Points to remember: if you are fond of fried foods it is well worth investing in a deep fryer with a frying basket, for foods cooked in this way are much drier, and the results look more professional. To begin with it does mean a lot of fat — at least 1 lb. lard or whipped-up cooking fat or 1–1½ pints oil — to give any depth in a frying basket, but with care you can keep this fat for some time. Also, the amount of fat absorbed by food fried in deep fat is much less than in shallow frying, so in the end it is more economical. After using the fat, allow it to cool, then store in a COOL place, or strain into a container and store in a refrigerator. Should you not be using the fat for several days in hot weather you *must bring it to the boil*; this is best done daily.

AFTER USING THE FAT ONCE OR TWICE IT MUST BE CLEANED. Allow to become quite cold, cover with water, bring water and fat slowly to the boil, then allow to cool. Pour away the water which will carry off any impurities, leaving pure clean fat.

1 When cooking fish in deep fat, heat at least 1 lb. lard, whipped-up cooking fat or 1–1½ pints oil STEADILY in the pan. Test as for shallow fat (page 45).
2 Put in the basket, but lower the fish in gently by hand. The reason for this is to prevent any possibility of the coated fish sticking to the basket and being difficult to take out.
3 Cook as in shallow fat, but you need not turn the fish.
4 The moment the fish goes into the pan, lower the heat. NEVER OVER-FILL WITH EITHER FAT OR FOOD, otherwise there is a danger of the fat boiling over. Also too much food lowers the temperature of the fat and gives unsuccessful results.
5 Remove the fish with the basket, hold for a minute over the fat to drain, then transfer to crumpled tissue paper on a hot dish. This drains the last of the fat so the fish is perfectly dry and crisp.
6 Just before serving put the hot fish on to a hot dish, and garnish with lemon and parsley.

Oven 'fried' fish

Preparation: few minutes
No delay
Cooking: 15–25 minutes

1 Coat the fish in egg and breadcrumbs (see page 44), not batter.
2 Grease the baking tin. Put it into the oven to get very hot.
3 When hot, put the fish on to this and brush with a little melted fat.
4 Cook in a moderately hot oven (400°F., Gas Mark 5) for 15–25 minutes.

Although it takes a little longer to cook fish in this way it needs no attention and also far less fat is required.

To cook prawns or scampi

The very large prawns — so often called scampi — have become popular in both hot and cold dishes. Dublin Bay prawns are often sold as 'scampi', as well as those that come from the Mediterranean.
When sold cooked, they are peeled and used as ordinary prawns. Most scampi is sold deep frozen. It should be allowed to defrost sufficiently to separate the fish. *Never re-freeze* as this can be very dangerous.

Prawns, either fresh or ready-boiled or frozen and uncooked, should therefore be available throughout the year. They are delicious hot or cold in main dishes, or they can be added to a sauce to serve with white fish.

Fried scampi

Preparation: 10–15 minutes
No delay
Cooking: 3–4 minutes

Allow 6–8 per person for hors d'oeuvre (more for a main dish)

1 Dry the fish well, then carefully coat in batter, or egg and breadcrumbs (see full instructions on page 44).
2 Lower the coated scampi into hot deep fat and fry for 3–4 minutes only. Do not over-cook.
3 Lift out and drain well on crumpled tissue paper or absorbent kitchen paper.
4 Serve with lemon and tartare sauce (see page 207).

46

Baked fish

Preparation: few minutes
No delay
Cooking: as method

Most fish can be baked, but with fillets of fish care should be taken to keep them moist, as they dry more easily than whole fish.

1 Butter an ovenproof dish well, put in the seasoned fish.
2 Add a little stock, milk, or white wine to keep the fish moist. Afterwards use this stock in the sauce.
3 Cover with buttered greaseproof paper or foil.
4 Bake fillets for approximately 12–20 minutes. Bake fish cutlets for approximately 20 minutes. Bake whole fish for approximately 12 minutes per lb. (if stuffed, weigh with stuffing).
5 The heat of the oven should be moderate to moderately hot (375–400°F., Gas Mark 5–6).
6 Put halved tomatoes, mushrooms, etc., into the oven at the same time, covered with butter and/or buttered foil.

Marinated cod

Preparation: 15 minutes
Allow to stand 1 hour
Cooking: 35 minutes
Serves 4

Secret of success
A marinade keeps the cod moist as well as adding flavour to the dish.
The stuffing is an interesting one, for mustard blends well with cod.

for the stuffing
4 oz. fresh white breadcrumbs
1 rounded tablespoon chopped parsley
½–1 level teaspoon dry mustard
1 egg
2 tablespoons milk
salt and pepper

for the marinade
1–2 level teaspoons dry mustard
4 tablespoons cider, white wine, vin rosé, apple juice *or* orange juice
½ level teaspoon salt
shake of pepper
2 tablespoons olive oil

4 cod cutlets, each about 6 oz. in weight

for the topping
3 oz. cheese, grated

to garnish
tomato slices

1 To make the stuffing, mix together crumbs and parsley, beat the mustard into the egg, add the milk and stir into the crumbs, mixing thoroughly. Season to taste.
2 To make the marinade, blend the mustard with a spoonful of the liquid, add the salt, pepper and remaining liquid. Gradually whisk this into the oil.
3 Wash, dry and trim the cutlets (remove surplus skin).
4 Divide the stuffing equally between the 4 cutlets.
5 Secure each by tying round with thin string. (Continue as steps pictured.)

6 Put into an ovenproof dish and cover with the marinade. Leave at least 1 hour, turning the cutlets frequently.

7 Bake in the centre of a moderate oven (350–375°F., Gas Mark 4–5) for 30 minutes, basting every 10 minutes.

8 Remove from the oven and top with the grated cheese. Brown under a medium grill. Transfer to a warm dish, remove string.

9 Serve hot, garnished with sliced tomato if liked. Pour the liquid from the oven dish into a sauce boat and hand separately.

To poach fish

Preparation: few minutes
No delay
Cooking: see method, right

Poaching means just cooking very gently, either in salted water or in a fish stock, made from the bones and skin of the fish and flavoured with a bay leaf, onion and carrot. Never boil fish rapidly, for it is inclined to break and will certainly become very dry.

fish   salted water *or* fish stock

1 Put the fish into the cold liquid, bring to simmering point and cook as follows:
2 Allow 7 minutes per lb. for thin fillets of fish, and 10 minutes per lb. for thick cutlets.
3 If poaching in one piece, then allow 12 minutes for first lb., and 10 minutes after that for second lb.
4 For a very large fish, allow 7–8 minutes per lb. for any weight after the first 2 lb.

To steam fish

Preparation: few minutes only
No delay
Cooking: see method, right

This method of cooking is generally chosen when serving fish to children or invalids; the fish is then very light and nutritious.

1 Wash and dry the fish.
2 Put on to a heat-resistant plate.
3 Sprinkle *lightly* with salt and pepper.
4 Put a small knob of margarine or butter on top, and add 1 or 2 tablespoons milk, if desired.
5 Cover the plate with foil, or with a second plate.
6 Stand over a saucepan of boiling water and cook for approximately 15 minutes for thick fillets, slightly less for thin ones. Cutlets will take approximately 20 minutes.

Frozen fish

There are many excellent varieties of frozen fish on the market which are ideal when it is difficult to buy fresh fish. If the instructions say 'defrost before cooking', this means allow the fish to thaw out — preferably at room temperature. If in a hurry, put the fish, still in its packet or plastic covering, into a bowl of *warm* water only. Too rapid defrosting causes loss of flavour and texture. With shellfish, particular attention should be paid to slow defrosting.

To serve shellfish

As pointed out on page 39, it is essential that shellfish is eaten when very fresh. Much of the shellfish you buy is already cooked and deteriorates rapidly.

Crab: serve cold in salads. Details are given opposite for the preparation of crab. This is sometimes served hot, and if wished can be prepared, put into a shell or small dishes, covered with crumbs and a little butter and heated in the oven or under a hot grill. If by chance you catch or are given a raw crab, put into cold water, bring steadily to the boil and cook for approximately 15–20 minutes. It is advisable to tie the big claws together.
Escallops (*scallops*): these are sold uncooked and can be served in a cream sauce or covered with egg and crumbs (see page 44) then fried as white fish. They take approximately 5–6 minutes if small, a little longer if large.
Lobster: you will generally have this already cooked. One of the nicest ways is to serve it cold with salad (see page 50). It can be heated in a white, mushroom or cheese sauce (page 143). Make the sauce, put in the pieces of lobster, heat for a few minutes only.
Uncooked lobster: cook like crab, allowing approximately 20–25 minutes.
Mussels: these are always sold raw and alive (unless you buy them in a jar). To cook mussels: first wash well then put into a large pan of cold water, bring steadily to the boil and heat until all the shell is open. You then take away the top shell and the little weed, which is called a beard. The mussels can then be added to a white sauce or served in the liquid in which cooked. To make more interesting, add white wine, parsley and chopped onion to the water, before cooking, and season well. Always discard any mussels when the shells do not close when tapped, or any that remain closed after being heated.
Oysters: these are not cooked when you buy them and only rarely are they used in cooking. They are served raw as an hors d'oeuvre. Your fishmonger will open them for you; you serve them on the bottom shell.
Prawns or shrimps: although there are excellent frozen prawns or shrimps available, one can often obtain the fresh variety. These are already cooked. Prepare as page 46, and serve cold or heat in a cheese or white sauce. Do not allow more than a few minutes' heating. The very large shrimps and prawns, generally known as scampi, are best fried, see recipe page 46. Live shrimps or prawns should be cooked for a few minutes only in boiling salted water.

To prepare crab

Preparation: 15 minutes

One medium crab is enough for two people, one large one for four.
Feel the crab when you buy it. If it feels surprisingly light for its size, ask the fishmonger to break it open — for 'lightness' often indicates that it is 'watery' and you are not getting good solid crab meat. Either ask the fishmonger to dress the crab, or do this as shown.

1 Pull all claws off crab; if twisted towards you they come away easily. Wipe shell.

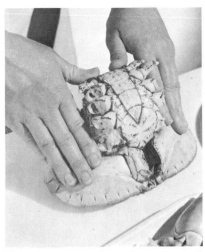

2 Take body away from the main shell.

3 Remove the stomach bag.

4 Discard this; IT MUST NOT BE EATEN

5 Take out all flesh, using a teaspoon handle, and put into one basin.

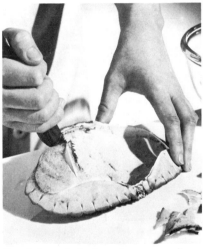

6 Crack top of shell and remove pieces so you have a flat surface to fill.

7 Discard grey fingers (dead men's fingers) from body; THESE MUST NOT BE EATEN. Also remove any flesh; put into second basin.

8 Crack the claws and remove the meat, add to the white flesh.

9 Arrange dark and light meat on the shell, and garnish with chopped parsley.

Lobster

Preparation: 12–15 minutes
No delay
No cooking time

Allow 1 small or ½ medium lobster per person

Lobster should be heavy for its size. Use as soon as possible.

1 Either ask the fishmonger to prepare the lobster OR split the lobster, remove the intestinal vein and lady fingers. These are found where the small claws join the body, and should not be eaten.
2 Crack the large claws very carefully and remove the lobster meat.
3 For lobster mayonnaise or salad, leave the meat in the shells and serve half a shell on each plate, piled with lobster flesh and with salad, mayonnaise (page 207), meat from the large claws and the small claws.
4 The second way of serving the salad is to remove all the meat from the body, dice this, mix with mayonnaise and arrange on a bed of lettuce.

Lobster with rice suprême

Preparation: 20 minutes
No delay
Cooking: 10 minutes, plus cooking time for rice
Serves 4

Secret of success
Do not over-heat at stage 6, or the fish will become tough.

2 small cooked lobsters
2 tablespoons chopped celery
1 onion, chopped

1 clove of garlic, *optional*
4 oz. butter
4 oz. cooked long grain rice

1 lemon
2 tablespoons pickle *or* chutney

1 Remove heads and claws from lobsters.
2 Remove flesh from claws as directed above – this can either be used for a separate salad or be added to this dish.
3 Cut each lobster tail into half, lengthways.
4 Remove meat, use shells for serving. Cut the meat into neat pieces.
5 Fry the vegetables in 2 oz. melted butter, then remove the clove of garlic and add the rice and lobster meat.
6 Heat, stirring gently, then pile the mixture into the shells and add a squeeze of lemon juice over the top.
7 Serve with a sauce, made by heating 2 oz. butter and then adding the chopped pickle or chutney.

Coquilles St. Jacques
(scallops in cream sauce)

Preparation: 12 minutes. See note about cooking potatoes
Cooking: 12 minutes (also cooking time for potatoes)
Serves 4

Secret of success
Do not over-cook at stages 1 and 7.

4 medium scallops
½ pint milk
8–12 oz. mashed potatoes*
1½ oz. butter

2 tablespoons flour
salt and pepper
1 tablespoon white wine *or* sherry, *optional*

1 tablespoon cream, *optional*
few crisp breadcrumbs
1 oz. cheese, grated

* these should be cooked earlier to give time to cool.

1 Simmer scallops in the milk for about 10 minutes, until quite soft. It is important to do this slowly; too quick cooking makes them tough.
2 When cooked, lift out of the milk and put in the centre of their shells.
3 Pipe round a border of mashed potatoes (see page 139).
4 Melt the butter in the pan, stir in the flour and cook gently for 3 minutes.
5 Gradually add the milk, made up again to 6 tablespoons.
6 Cook the sauce until thick, adding seasoning, the wine, and cream if used. Carefully cover the tops of the scallops with this.
7 Sprinkle with the crumbs and cheese, and either put into a hot oven or under the grill until heated through and crisp and brown on top.

To cook smoked fish

Although smoking or curing is not a method of cooking, it does make the fish very tender and care should be taken not to *over-cook* smoked fish. It is already salty so it is inadvisable to add any extra salt when cooking.
Kippers and bloaters: instructions for cooking these are on page 234.

Smoked haddock barbecue

Preparation: 15 minutes
No delay
Cooking: 30 minutes
Serves 4

Secret of success
This is highly flavoured, so taste as you go.

Colour picture, page 38

2 lb. smoked haddock
2 tablespoons oil
1 large onion
1 stick celery
4 tablespoons tomato ketchup

¼ pint fish stock
2 tablespoons brown sugar
2 tablespoons vinegar
1–2 tablespoons Worcestershire sauce
1 teaspoon made-mustard

salt and pepper
3 hamburger (or soft round) rolls

1 Cook the smoked haddock as recipe, page 51, divide into neat pieces.
2 Heat the oil in a pan and toss the chopped onion and celery in this.
3 Add all the ingredients except the fish and rolls; add the sauce and mustard gradually, tasting as you do so. Simmer for 20 minutes; add the fish.
4 Simmer for a further few minutes, stirring once or twice.
5 Split the rolls and toast until brown, top with fish mixture, serve at once.

Boiled finnan haddock

Preparation: 2–3 minutes
No delay
Cooking: 5 minutes

1 Cut off the side-fins and tail of the fish, then divide into the required number of portions.
2 Heat water in a saucepan, and when boiling put in the fish. Do not salt the water.
3 Simmer for about 5 minutes. Do not over-cook.
4 Strain well, using a fish slice, and put on to hot plates.
5 Put a good knob of butter or margarine on top before serving. Top with a fried or poached egg if desired.

Baked finnan haddock

Preparation: 2–3 minutes
No delay
Cooking: 10–12 minutes

1 Divide the fish into portions as above.
2 Place in a baking dish and half cover with milk.
3 Cover with paper greased with butter or margarine.
4 Bake in a moderately hot oven (400°F., Gas Mark 6) for about 12 minutes.

To cook oily fish

Because this group of fish contains a high percentage of fat in relation to other fish, they do not need a great deal of fat added during cooking. On the other hand, over-cooking or incorrect cooking can spoil the delicious taste and moist texture. This is particularly important when cooking salmon.

To bone herrings

Herrings are an excellent breakfast meal and can be cooked in a variety of ways.

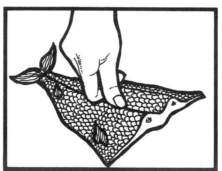

1 Remove the head and wash the fish thoroughly.

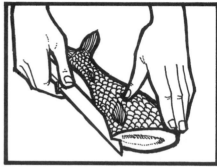

2 Remove scales by gently scraping, with a knife, from tail end towards the head. Split the fish down the stomach with a sharp knife.

3 Flatten the fish by laying it open-side downwards on a board and pressing gently with your hand.

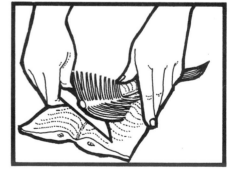

4 Turn the fish over and insert the point of the knife under the bone, from the tail end, and gently pull the bone away with your fingers, easing with the knife underneath. Trim the fins and tail.

To cook herrings

Preparation: few minutes
No delay
Cooking: 8–20 minutes

To fry herrings: use very little fat in the frying pan, or put in just a little salt and cook the herrings without any fat at all. Cook steadily on both sides until tender.
To grill herrings: season and brush with a little melted margarine. Cook under a hot grill to brown both sides, then lower the heat to cook through to the centre.
To bake herrings: put into a dish with seasoning, a squeeze of lemon juice plus a little margarine and bake in a moderately hot oven (400°F., Gas Mark 6) for approximately 20 minutes.

Herring roes

There are several ways in which herring roes may be cooked. They are one of the most digestible forms of food and can be served even to very young children.

Fried herring roes

Preparation: 5 minutes
No delay
Cooking: 15 minutes

Secret of success
Drain after frying only when serving to very young children or invalids.

2–4 oz. roe per person salt and pepper	1 oz. flour fat *for frying*	*to garnish* chopped parsley

1 Put the roes into a colander and wash under running water.
2 Dry and toss in well seasoned flour.
3 Fry in hot fat until pale golden brown. Do not drain — they *need* the little extra fat that clings to them.
4 Garnish with finely chopped parsley.

Steamed herring roes

Preparation: 3 minutes
No delay
Cooking: 15 minutes

Secret of success
Do not over-cook at stage 3.

2–4 oz. roe per person little milk seasoning	knob of margarine toast *or* mashed potato	*to garnish* paprika *or* cayenne, *optional*

1 Put the roes into a colander and let cold water run over them, then pat them dry.
2 Put on a plate, cover with the milk, seasoning and margarine.
3 Cover with a second plate and steam over a saucepan of hot water for about 15 minutes.
4 Serve on toast or with mashed potato; sprinkle with paprika or cayenne, if liked.

To grill mackerel

Preparation: few minutes
No delay
Cooking: approximately 12 minutes

Mackerel is excellent if served with a thick sweetened gooseberry purée.

1 Cut the heads off the mackerel and remove the bones, as for herring (see page 51). Heat the grill.
2 Fold the mackerel over again, after taking out the bones.
3 Put the fish on the grill grid with a small knob of margarine on each.
4 Sprinkle with salt and pepper, and cook rapidly for about 4 minutes.
5 Turn the fish, put a little more margarine on top with seasoning, and cook for a further 4 minutes.
6 Lower the heat of the grill to give a further 2 or 3 minutes' cooking. These are solid fish and take rather a long time to cook.
7 Serve on a hot dish, with any margarine that has dropped into the grill pan poured over the fish.
8 Garnish with rings of lemon and sprigs of parsley.

Soused herrings or mackerel

Preparation: 10–12 minutes
No delay
Cooking: 1 hour
Serves 4 as a main dish

Secret of success
Slow cooking blends the flavours.

4 large *or* 8 small herrings *or* mackerel 1 good teaspoon pickling spice	1 teaspoon sweet spice ½ teaspoon salt 1 small apple, sliced 1 small onion	1 teaspoon sugar ¼ pint water ¼ pint vinegar 2 bay leaves

1 Split the herrings.
2 Take out the backbones (see page 51) and roll the herrings.
3 Put into a covered casserole together with all the other ingredients and cook in a slow oven (300°F., Gas Mark 2) for 1 hour.
4 Leave until quite cold. Serve with lettuce, potato and beetroot salads.

Soused herrings

To cook sprats

Preparation: 5–10 minutes
No delay
Cooking: see method

Allow about 4–6 oz. per person. They are nicer fried or baked

Baked sprats

1 First cut off the heads, then wash and dry.
2 To bake, put in a greased casserole or baking tin and cover with greased paper.
3 Allow approximately 15–20 minutes in a moderate to moderately hot oven (375–400 °F., Gas Mark 5–6).

Fried sprats

1 Use little fat since they have a high fat content — just enough to cover the bottom of the pan.
2 Fry steadily for approximately 3 minutes on each side.

Salmon

As salmon is very substantial fish, allow from 4–5 oz. per person. Cook in one piece rather than slices, unless grilling the fish.

Salmon is probably more easily spoiled by bad cooking than any other fish. It is essential that it should not be over-cooked, for if it is you lose colour, flavour and moistness.
When buying salmon, make sure that the fish looks stiff and firm, with bright red gills, and the flesh a true salmon pink. The scales will be bright and shiny.

To poach pieces of salmon

Preparation: few minutes
No delay
Cooking: see method

With cutlets of salmon it is undoubtedly best to wrap them in well buttered or oiled paper.
To poach whole, do not wrap but put into cold salted water and time as stage 3, allowing 10 minutes per lb.

1 Season the salmon, add a little lemon juice if wished, and tie carefully in a neat 'parcel' of buttered paper.
2 Put into cold salted water with a little lemon juice and oil.
3 Bring slowly to boiling point, then simmer gently and allow 10 minutes per lb; or better still, bring just to boiling point, put a tightly-fitting lid on the saucepan and allow the fish to stay in the water until it is quite cold. This is an ideal way of cooking the fish to be served cold in a salad.

Grilled salmon

Preparation: few minutes
No delay
Cooking: 10 minutes

Buy slices (cutlets) of salmon.

1 Season the fish well and brush liberally with melted butter.
2 Cook steadily under the grill until just golden coloured on the top surface, turn and brush again with more melted butter; then grill on the second side, until just tender.
3 Serve with hollandaise sauce (page 143) or top with maître d'hôtel butter (page 44).

Baked trout with caper and mushroom sauce

Preparation: 10–15 minutes
No delay
Cooking: 30–40 minutes
Serves 4

Secret of success
Although the trout, etc., take longer to cook than many fish, do not over-cook.

Frozen trout do not need defrosting, but you will not be able to shape these at stage 2.

2–4 oz. mushrooms
4 medium trout
1 oz. margarine
½–1 tablespoon capers
grated rind and juice of
  1 lemon

for the sauce
1 oz. margarine
1 oz. flour
½ pint milk

to garnish
1½–2 lb. cooked potatoes
1 tablespoon milk
1 oz. margarine
salt and pepper
cocktail onions

1 Peel the mushrooms and slice thinly.
2 Wash and dry the trout and place together in a dish, curving the bodies into an 'S' shape. Brush with melted margarine.
3 Add the prepared mushrooms, capers, grated lemon rind and juice.
4 Cover the dish with foil, and bake in a moderate oven (350–375 °F., Gas Mark 4–5) on the middle shelf for 30–40 minutes.
5 Remove the liquid, mushrooms and capers to use for the sauce.
6 While the fish is cooking boil the potatoes, and make the sauce.
7 Melt the margarine in a saucepan over a low heat, then stir in the flour.
8 Cook until it bubbles, then remove from the heat, stir in the milk.
9 Bring to the boil and simmer gently for 2–3 minutes, stirring all the time.
10 Add the fish liquid, capers and mushrooms and reheat.

To serve the trout

11 Mash the potatoes, beat in the milk, margarine, salt and pepper, then pipe or pile on to a hot dish.
12 Arrange the trout on top, with cocktail onions to represent 'eyes'. Serve the sauce separately.

Fish pie

Preparation: 20 minutes
No delay
Cooking: 1 hour
Serves 4–5

Secrets of success
As the fish is later reheated in the oven, cook very lightly at stage 2.
Choose a fish with a definite flavour – cod, hake, haddock are excellent.

1½ lb. potatoes
1–1¼ lb. white fish
1–2 eggs

knob of butter *or* margarine
chopped parsley
salt and pepper

for the sauce
1 oz. butter
1 oz. flour
¼ pint milk
¼ pint fish stock
seasoning

1 Peel the potatoes and cook in boiling salted water for approximately 20 minutes.
2 Poach the fish in salted water until just cooked (see page 48).
3 Put the eggs on to boil for 10 minutes.
4 Drain the fish, keeping ¼ pint of the liquid.
5 *To make the sauce:* heat butter in the pan; stir in flour, cook for several minutes.
6 Gradually add the milk and the fish stock, bring to the boil and cook until thickened. Season with salt and pepper.
7 Mix the flaked fish with the sauce and the chopped hard-boiled eggs, put into the bottom of the dish.
8 Mash the potatoes, adding a little butter or margarine, 1–2 teaspoons chopped parsley and seasoning and spread over the fish mixture.
9 Bake for approximately 25 minutes, towards the top of a moderate oven (350–375 °F., Gas Mark 4–5).

Fish cakes

Preparation: 15 minutes
Cooking: 8–10 minutes
Serves 4

Secret of success
Any cooked fish can be used to make fish pies and fish cakes, but fish with a more definite flavour is best – cod, fresh haddock, turbot and hake are to be recommended.

Colour picture, opposite

Flavourings for fish cakes

Chopped herbs (parsley, thyme, chives, etc.) may be added to the mixture.
Add a few drops of anchovy essence or Tabasco sauce or Worcestershire sauce.

8 oz. cooked fish
8 oz. mashed potatoes
1 oz. butter
1–2 tablespoons milk*

mixed chopped fresh herbs
or pinch of dried herbs
seasoning
lemon

1 egg, beaten
crisp breadcrumbs *for coating*
fat *or* oil *for frying*

* use 2 tablespoons of milk if potatoes are dry or you could use egg or ¼ pint THICK panada, page 143.

1 Remove all small bones and skin from the fish. Cream the cooked potatoes until smooth.
2 Add some butter and a little milk.
3 Stir in the herbs and seasonings.
4 Add a little grated outer rind of lemon and a squeeze of juice.

5 Mix all ingredients thoroughly, then divide into portions.
6 Shape with floured hands into round, oval, or fish shapes, as in picture.

The picture opposite shows fish cakes, made as the recipe above. These can be fried, then frozen and reheated as desired, or the fish cakes may be prepared, coated with egg and crumbs, then frozen – cook from the frozen state.

7 Brush the shapes with beaten egg and coat closely with breadcrumbs, patting them firmly on, ready for frying (see page 45).
8 Heat a little fat or oil in a pan and fry the shapes, first on one side then the other, until golden brown. Drain on absorbent paper.
9 Lightly grill some thick slices of tomato, placing one on each shape, and serve with green peas, cooked and tossed in butter.

Meat

Wise buying of meat

Plan your buying of meat wisely. Many people tend to buy too large a joint which then has to be finished up in various ways, and obviously a family will become tired of the repetition of reheated meat.

Quantities of meat

Stewing: 4—6 oz. meat per person — weight without bone. Vegetables in stew help it to be filling.
Grilling: one good sized chop, or two small chops or cutlets per person. 4—8 oz. steak per person.
Roasting. for a small joint with large bone allow approximately 10 12 oz. per person. For a larger joint, where the bone is proportionately smaller, allow 8 oz. meat per person, or less if stuffing the joint.

How to tell if meat is fresh

You can rely on a good butcher to ensure you are buying fresh meat. Even so, it is wise to look at the meat carefully so that in time you become a good judge of its freshness and quality.
Beef: the lean should be a clear bright red and the fat firm and pale cream in colour. The very best joints MUST have a certain amount of fat on them.
Mutton or lamb: see that the lean is a dull red, but very firm. The fat should be white in colour. Lamb is paler in colour than mutton, but in many recipes either can be used, mutton needing longer cooking time in stewing.
Veal: be very critical, particularly in hot weather, as veal does not keep well. There is little fat to see, but what there is should be firm and white, the lean must look dry and be a pale pink.
Pork: the lean part of the meat must look pale pink, and the fat white and dry. Pork must never be served under-done. Avoid serving it in very hot weather.
Bacon and ham: see it looks moist and not too dry. Bacon may be blanched to remove excess of salt before adding to other dishes. Do not confuse ham and bacon — they have been cured in entirely different ways.

Various methods of cooking meat

As you will see from the charts on the following pages, it is important to choose the right piece of meat for the right cooking purpose. It is extravagant, for example, to choose an expensive cut of beef, such as sirloin, if you want to make a stew, and no good purpose is served because the flavour will not be that much better. Below are a few general rules to remember when cooking meat. You will find detailed instructions for cooking beef, lamb, pork, etc., on pages 64 to 108.
Roasting: remember if you put on too much fat when roasting meat it hardens the outside; too little fat on a lean joint will make it rather dry.
Grilling: since grilling is a very quick process you must choose really first class quality meat. Seal the outside as quickly as possible, so that the flavour is retained and meat keeps moist. Make certain that your grill is really hot before you start cooking. Because grilling is done under a really high heat, keep the meat well brushed with oil, fat or butter.
Frying: the same rules about quality apply as for grilling. It is better to use shallow fat for meat rather than deep fat. Seal the outside of the meat by putting into hot fat. Fry on both sides as directed in the recipes, then lower heat to make sure the meat is cooked through to the middle.
Stewing, casseroling, braising: the important thing is to realise that you are dealing with less tender pieces of meat, and in consequence need to cook them slowly. Do not try to hurry the cooking for you will only make the meat very tough. The heat in a pressure cooker enables a stew to be cooked in a short time.

Roast pork, see page 80
Uncooked rib of beef, see pages 58 and 64

Beef

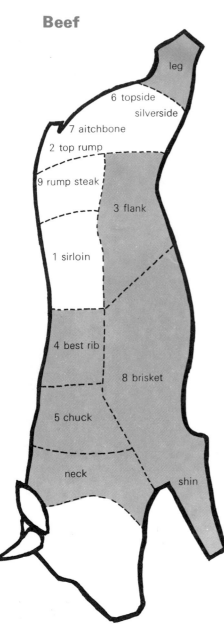

cheaper cuts

Meat buying and cooking guide

You use it for	Cut to choose	Cooking time	Accompaniments
Roasting	Sirloin on or off bone Ribs Fillet Aitch-bone (good quality) Topside Rump Leg of mutton cut*	15 minutes per lb. plus 15 minutes over. Well done, 20 minutes per lb. plus 20 minutes over, or 40 minutes per lb. in very slow oven (*see page 64*)	Mustard Horseradish sauce Yorkshire pudding Roast potatoes Thin gravy (*see page 64*)
Grilling or Frying	Rumpsteak Fillet Sirloin Entrecôte	5–15 minutes depending on thickness and personal preference (*see page 65*)	Chipped or mashed potatoes Salad Tomatoes Mushrooms (*see pages 65 and 136*)
Stewing or Braising	Skirt or chuck Bladebone Leg of mutton cut Brisket Flank	1½–3 hours; see also under Pressure Cooking (*pages 66–69*)	Mixed vegetables Dumplings Thickened gravy
Pickling or Boiling	Brisket Shin or leg Silverside Flank Aitch-bone	1½–3 hours (*see page 66*)	Vegetables or salad
Stock for Soup	Neck Shin or leg Clod Marrowbone Oxtail Flank	1½–3 hours (*see page 63*)	

* this is a piece cut from the shoulder and is best roasted very slowly (page 75).

Note. If doubtful about tenderness of any cuts of meat for roasting, roast slowly as instructed on page 75.

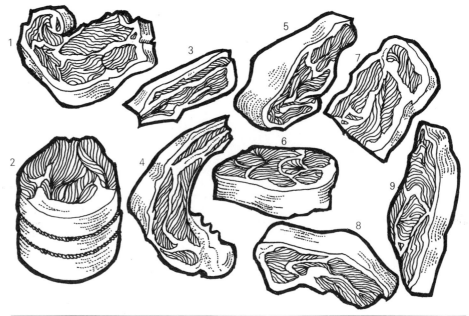

Lamb or mutton

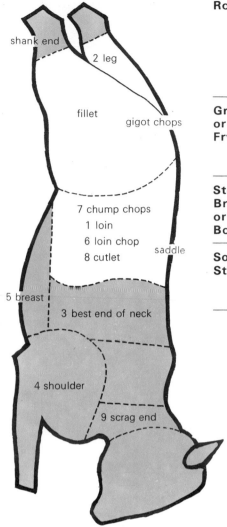

shank end

2 leg

fillet

gigot chops

7 chump chops

1 loin

6 loin chop

8 cutlet

saddle

5 breast

3 best end of neck

4 shoulder

9 scrag end

cheaper cuts

You use it for	Cut to choose	Cooking time	Accompaniments

Roasting	Leg
	Loin and saddle
	Best end of neck
	  (lamb)
	Shoulder
	Breast, stuffed and
	  rolled
		20 minutes per lb.
		plus 20 minutes
		  over
		(*see pages 71, 72*)
			Mutton:
			  redcurrant jelly
			Lamb: mint jelly or
			  mint sauce
			Fresh peas

Grilling
or
Frying
	Loin chops
	Gigot chops
	Cutlets (use as
	  part of mixed
	  grill)
		10–15 minutes
		(*see pages 75, 76, 77*)
			Chipped potatoes
			Tomatoes
			Mushrooms
			Peas
			Salads

Stewing **Braising** **or** **Boiling**	Neck Breast Leg Shoulder	1½–2½ hours (*see pages 78, 79*)	Mixed vegetables Creamed potatoes
Soups or **Stock**	Scrag end of neck Head Trotters	1½–2½ hours (*see page 63*)	

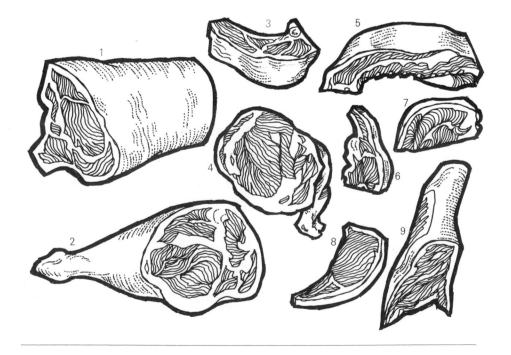

Pork

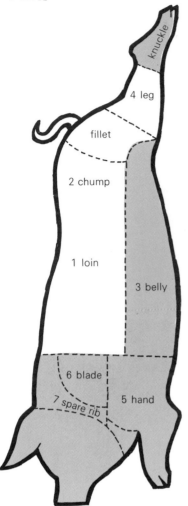

knuckle

4 leg

fillet

2 chump

1 loin

3 belly

6 blade

7 spare rib

5 hand

cheaper cuts

You use it for	Cut to choose	Cooking time	Accompaniments
Roasting	Loin Leg Bladebone Spare rib	25 minutes per lb. plus 25 minutes over (*see page 80*)	Sage and onion stuffing Mustard Apple sauce Orange salad
Frying or Grilling	Chops from loin Chump chops Spare rib chops	15–20 minutes (*see page 81*)	Apple sauce Apple rings Sage and onion stuffing Tomatoes Mushrooms
Boiling or Stewing	Head Hand and spring Belly Cuts given for roasting	2½ hours (*see pages 82, 83*)	Salads Mixed vegetables

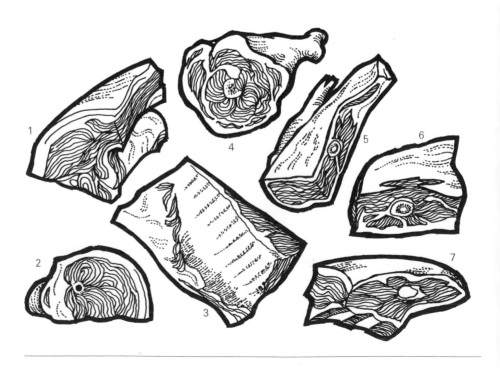

1 2 4 3 5 6 7

Veal

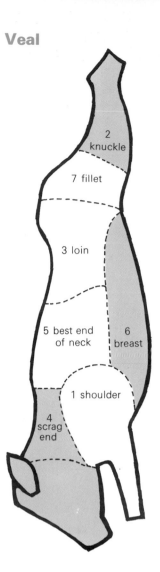

You use it for	Cut to choose	Cooking time	Accompaniments
Roasting	Shoulder Breast Best end of neck Loin Fillet Chump end of loin	25 minutes per lb. plus 25 minutes over (*see page 85*)	Sausages Veal stuffing or other well flavoured stuffing. Keep well basted
Grilling or Frying	Chops from loin Fillet Best end of neck chops Thin slices from leg — called fillets and when cooked escalopes	15–20 minutes (*see page 86*)	Chipped potatoes Tomatoes Mushrooms
Stewing or Braising	Breast Fillet Knuckle Middle or scrag end of neck	1½–2½ hours (*see page 87*)	Mixed vegetables Various sauces
Boiling	Head Feet Breast	1½–2½ hours (*see page 104*)	Mixed vegetables or salads
Stock for Soup	Feet Knuckle	1½–2½ hours (*see page 63*)	

 cheaper cuts

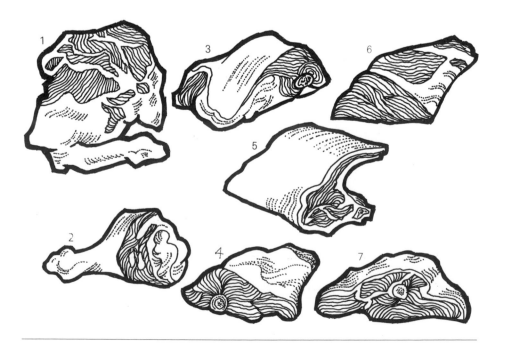

61

Bacon and ham

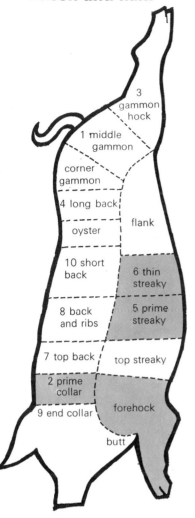

You use it for	Cut to choose	Cooking time	Accompaniments
Roasting or Baking	Gammon slipper Middle gammon Back and ribs Joint top streaky	20 minutes per lb. and 20 minutes over If well done cook like pork for 25 minutes per lb. (*see page 93*)	Mustard Salads Unusual garnishes such as baked apples, oranges, pineapple etc.
Grilling or Frying	Top streaky Prime streaky Thin streaky Gammon slipper Middle gammon Corner gammon Long back Short back Back and ribs Top Prime collar	Few minutes only for thin rashers but with thick slices of gammon cook outside fairly quickly then reduce heat to cook through to the middle Keep gammon well brushed with fat when grilling (*see pages 94–5*)	Eggs, tomatoes, mushrooms etc. for breakfast Vegetables or salads for main meals
Boiling or Braising	Forehock Prime streaky Flank back Gammon slipper Gammon hock Middle gammon Corner gammon Long back Back and ribs Top back Prime collar End of collar Oyster cut	Soak well if you want very mild flavour, then simmer gently for 20–25 minutes per lb. and 20–25 minutes over Do not boil too quickly A pressure cooker can be used (*see page 66*) Ham or bacon stock is excellent for soups	Any vegetables – beans and peas are particularly good with boiled bacon Salads, etc.

cheaper cuts

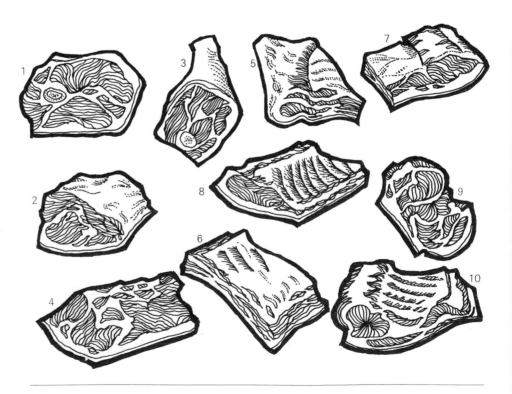

To help with cooking and serving meat

Well cooked meat depends a great deal on the fat with which it is roasted and the sauce or gravy with which it is served. Below you will find ways of making good dripping and a good gravy. If your joints are too small to produce dripping, then you may be able to buy some from your butcher, or use the lard or cooking fats that are available. Margarine, because it has a high percentage of water, is not a good fat to use when cooking meat.

Quickly made stock

Many recipes for soups and other dishes require stock. Below are very simple recipes for making stock in a saucepan or pressure cooker, but even if you use this, care of stock (it *must* stand in a cool place or be boiled daily) is a 'chore' for a person with little time. Here are some short cuts.

1 Make use of the excellent meat or yeast extracts or beef and chicken stock cubes available, for these give you good flavoured stocks within a minute.
2 By using smaller or larger quantities of flavouring to water you can obtain the strength desirable in a particular recipe.
3 Where a recipe requires 'white stock' use chicken stock or a small quantity only of yeast extract.

To make good dripping

Preparation: few minutes
Allow to cool and set
Cooking: 5–10 minutes

This is the fat that runs from meat or bacon during cooking. It is a valuable food and should not be wasted, for you will need it again to add to meat. It must be clarified before storing. Clarifying means cleaning, and the process is very necessary when using dripping.

To clarify dripping

dripping from the meat   water to cover

1 Cover dripping with cold water in a deep pan. Bring to the boil.
2 Allow fat and water to cool.
3 You will then be able to lift off the fat, leaving most of the impurities in the water.

To make bone stock

Preparation: few minutes
Cooking: 3–4 hours

Stock is not difficult to make, and a good stock will improve the flavour of many dishes. It is, however, considered quite dangerous to keep stock for long, unless stored in a refrigerator.

2 lb. bones – large marrow   1 bay leaf   salt and pepper
   bones if possible

1 Cover the bones of beef (for a brown stock), or veal and poultry (for a white stock), with cold water. Add the bay leaf, salt and pepper.
2 Simmer gently for several hours.
3 Vegetables can be added if wished, but they cause the stock to spoil more rapidly.
4 Strain stock.
5 When cold, lift off any fat from the top.
6 If stock has been kept for several days, even in a refrigerator, it must be boiled well before being used.

Stock in a pressure cooker

Preparation: 10 minutes
Cooking: 45 minutes at 15 lb. pressure

Secret of success
Store in a refrigerator or re-boil every other day to keep.

2 lb. bones – large marrow   1 carrot   1 onion
   bones if possible   1 turnip   1 teaspoon salt
2 pints water

1 Break the bones, or ask the butcher to do this.
2 Put into the cooker with all the other ingredients.
3 Bring slowly to the boil and remove scum from the top.
4 Fix the lid and bring steadily to pressure.
5 Reduce the heat and cook for 45 minutes.
6 Allow pressure to return to normal before removing the lid. Strain.
7 When the stock is cold, lift off any fat from top.
8 Potatoes and greens are unsuitable for this stock.

To roast beef

Preparation: few minutes
No delay
Cooking: see page 58

If you like a very lean joint, choose topside or rump or fillet. For a prime quality with a good distribution of lean and fat, choose ribs of beef (for a large joint) or sirloin. Aitch-bone of first rate quality can be roasted but is best roasted slowly.

Colour picture, page 56

Note. If you are doubtful about the tenderness of any cuts of meat for roasting, roast slowly as instructed on page 75.

If you like a crisp outside to the meat then *DO NOT* use a covered roasting tin — instead put a little well clarified dripping (page 63), or fat, on the meat — which can be seasoned lightly, if desired. Either put the meat *IN* a roasting tin or on a trivet (rack) in the tin, or cook it on a turning spit.

1 Put the meat into a hot oven (425–450°F., Gas Mark 7).
2 For joints under 4 lb. the heat need not be lowered a great deal — follow the times given on page 58, or in individual recipes.
3 For larger joints lower the heat after the first 1–1¼ hours to moderate (375°F., Gas Mark 4) or very moderate (350°F., Gas Mark 3), allowing longer cooking time.
4 There is then no need to add fat to sirloin or ribs of beef, but add a little to topside of beef.
5 If you are using a covered roasting tin or foil, add about 10 minutes to the cooking time.
6 Pour out all the fat except the amount for gravy (see below).
7 Make gravy as directed. Serve with mustard, horseradish cream or sauce, crisp roast potatoes and Yorkshire pudding.

To cook Yorkshire pudding

Preparation: few minutes
Batter is better if it is left to stand a while
Cooking: 35–40 minutes

Secrets of success
The correct consistency to the batter; a really hot oven, so the pudding rises well.

It may be necessary to raise the heat of the oven before putting Yorkshire pudding in to cook, and for the first 5–10 minutes of cooking time. If you are afraid the beef may be over-cooked, take it out for a few minutes.
1 Make pancake batter (page 161). You can use half quantities for two people.
2 When ready to cook, put a knob of lard or dripping into a Yorkshire pudding tin (measuring about 7 by 5 inches), and heat in a hot to very hot oven (450–475°F., Gas Mark 7–8) for a few minutes. For half quantity a tin measuring 4 by 3 inches is better.
3 Pour in the batter and cook for about 30 minutes in a hot to very hot oven. Lower the heat after 20 minutes to moderately hot.
4 In every type of cooker, use the top of the oven which is the hottest position.
5 To save cooking time, you can cook the batter in small patty tins. Put a piece of fat — the size of a large pea — in each tin; heat this.

Another way of cooking Yorkshire pudding is in the meat tin
1 Pour away most of the fat, then pour in the batter.
2 Stand the meat on a trivet and put on the rack above the pudding.
3 Cook the pudding for about 40 minutes, or 24 minutes for half quantity.

Roast potatoes

Preparation: 10 minutes
Cooking: 50–60 minutes

Secret of success
Do not use too much fat — 2 oz. per lb. of potatoes is plenty.

1 Peel and dry the potatoes.
2 Roll in the hot fat in the meat tin round the meat. Use two tablespoons to turn the potatoes round in the fat. Allow approximately 50–60 minutes' cooking. If preferred, the potatoes may be cooked in fat in a separate tin from the meat. The potatoes *must* be cooked in a moderately hot to hot oven. The latter is better to produce really crisp potatoes.
3 Another method is to cook for 5–10 minutes in boiling salted water first, drain well, then roast. This produces roast potatoes that are floury on the inside, yet crisp outside.
4 When cooked, drain with a perforated spoon before serving.

To make gravy for roast meat

Thin gravy
1 Pour away practically all the fat from the roasting tin, leaving the residue of meat to give flavour.
2 Add about 1 teaspoon flour and approximately ½ pint stock, or water flavoured with meat or vegetable extract, or a bouillon cube.
3 Bring to the boil. Cook until clear, then strain.

Thickened gravy
1 Leave about 1 tablespoon fat in the meat tin.
2 Add approximately 1 oz. flour. Cook together for several minutes.
3 Add just over ½ pint stock, or water flavoured with meat or vegetable extract, or a stock cube.
4 Bring to the boil, cook until thick, then strain.

Pot roasting

Preparation: few minutes
No delay
Cooking: as tables on pages
58 to 62

To pot roast meat, use roasting
joints (see tables on pages
58 to 62), or you can use the
less good cuts such as 'leg of
mutton cut' and brisket of beef,
or belly of pork, if 45–50
minutes per lb. are allowed.

1 Heat 2 oz. fat in a large saucepan.
2 Flour and season the meat, then cook in the hot fat until golden brown on the outside. After this, use one of the following methods:

Method 1
Put a very firmly fitting lid on the pan, turn the heat very low and cook, turning the meat from time to time, for about 40 minutes per lb. You can use this method only if the pan lid DOES fit tightly and the saucepan is very strong — or the meat will burn.

Method 2
Fit a trivet at the bottom of the pan.
Lift the meat on to this and add about 2 tablespoons water. Put a tightly fitting lid on and cook, allowing 40 minutes per lb. The liquid at the bottom of the pan makes delicious gravy.

Method 3
If you have no trivet, put a thick layer of well seasoned root vegetables — whole carrots, onions, turnips — at the bottom of the pan, and add 2 tablespoons water. Lift the meat on to the vegetables, put on the tightly fitting lid and cook as before. Do not cook potatoes with the meat, as they become too soft and would allow the meat to drop into the liquid at the bottom of the pan.

To grill steak

Preparation: few minutes
No delay
Cooking: 5–15 minutes

The most popular steaks for
grilling are:
Rump – an excellent flavour, a
little less tender than steaks
from fillet.
Fillet – particularly tender; the
fillet is limited so this is
expensive; it comes from the
undercut of sirloin.
Minute – a thin steak, generally
cut from fillet; needs cooking
only ½–1 minute on either side.
Sirloin – a steak cut from the
sirloin, not undercut; excellent
flavour.
Porterhouse – large piece of
sirloin steak.
Chateaubriand – a very large
fillet steak.

Secret of success
Make sure the grill is very hot
before cooking the meat.

1 Brush both the grid and steak with butter or olive oil.
2 Season the steak, and if in doubt as to whether it is tender, break down the tissues by 'banging' with a rolling pin or meat tenderiser; or marinate the meat by leaving it to stand for 1 hour in a mixture of oil and vinegar to which you add seasoning, including a pinch of salt or a crushed garlic clove.
3 Heat the grill, then put the steak on to the grid of the grill, with tomatoes and mushrooms at the bottom of the pan.
4 Cook rapidly on either side under a hot grill for 2–3 minutes on each side.
5 This is sufficient for people who like their steak 'rare' (underdone) in the centre, but if you like it well done, lower the heat and cook steadily for a further 10 minutes.
6 Garnish with watercress and maître d'hôtel or parsley butter (page 44; for steak you could add a dash Worcestershire sauce instead of lemon juice). For special occasions, garnish with asparagus tips, fried onion rings (page 137) or croûtons of bread (page 36).
7 Serve with mixed vegetables, potatoes, and try a really crisp salad with French dressing as an accompaniment.

Grilled T-bone steaks

To fry steak

Preparation: few minutes
No delay
Cooking: 5–14 minutes

Choose same quality and cuts
of steak as for grilling (see above).

1 Heat a good knob of butter or olive oil in the pan and put in the steak.
2 Fry quickly on either side to seal in the flavour.
3 Lower the heat and cook gently for about 10–12 minutes for well cooked steak, about 6–8 minutes for medium cooked, and 3–4 for underdone.
4 French or English mustard is the usual accompaniment; some people like Worcestershire sauce. Tomatoes, mushrooms, fried onion rings or watercress are the best garnishes.

To boil beef

The word 'boiling' is really incorrect, because the meat must cook very steadily, *not* rapidly. Keep the lid on the pan, and look from time to time to make sure that the liquid does not bubble too fast. Brisket or silverside are good for boiling, and the following recipes give full instructions.

Salted brisket of beef

Preparation: 10 minutes
Allow 1 or 2 hours for soaking
Cooking: 2–2½ hours
Serves 6–8

Secrets of success
It is a good idea to buy enough brisket to allow also for a cold meal, for it is delicious with salad.
If desired, more vegetables may be added halfway through cooking.

3–4 lb. piece of beef	4 small carrots	good pinch of pepper
4 small onions	1 beef stock cube	dry mustard

1 Soak the beef in cold water for an hour or two. If the butcher says it is very salt, soak overnight.
2 Put the beef into a large saucepan with the vegetables and half cover with cold water. Add the stock cube and a good pinch of pepper and mustard.
3 Bring to the boil quickly. Remove any scum that comes to the top.
4 Put the lid on the saucepan, lower the heat and simmer gently — allowing about 30 minutes to each lb. and 30 minutes over, i.e. a 4 lb. piece of meat will take 2½ hours to cook.
5 If wished, dumplings can be cooked with this, allowing them about 15 minutes' quick cooking in the liquid (for dumplings see page 67).
6 Do not thicken the liquid, but serve some in a separate sauce boat. To serve the meat, put it on to a large hot dish, with the vegetables and a little stock round, then garnish with dumplings and a few of the freshly cooked vegetables.

Salted silverside of beef

This is cooked in exactly the same way as brisket of beef (see above) and may be served hot or cold. It is a less fatty piece of meat and tends to be slightly more expensive than brisket.

Boiling fresh brisket or silverside

Unsalted brisket or silverside should be seasoned in the normal way for boiling, and needs no soaking. The great advantage of buying salted brisket or silverside, however, is that the meat not only has more flavour but a better colour.

To pressure cook brisket and silverside

Preparation: 10 minutes
Soak for several hours
Pressure cooking: 30 minutes at 15 lb. pressure
Serves 4

Secret of success
Time the cooking carefully.

2 lb. salted brisket *or* silverside of beef	2 large carrots	seasoning
1 small turnip	2 onions	½ pint water
	bunch parsley	

1 Soak the meat for several hours, or overnight if very salt.
2 Cut the vegetables into fairly large pieces.
3 Put into the cooker with the meat, parsley, seasoning and water.
4 Fix the lid and bring to pressure.
5 Lower the heat and cook for 25 minutes. Over-cooking will spoil the meat, so check times and pressure in your own pressure cooker book.
6 Allow pressure to drop gradually.
7 Serve the boiled beef with unthickened gravy (page 64).

Pressure cooking of other meats

Bacon, etc., can also be cooked in a pressure cooker. Allow approximately 12–15 minutes per lb. at 15 lb. pressure. Details will be given in your pressure cooker book, but good soaking of salt meat is essential.

Stewing steak

A stew is both an economical and satisfying dish, for you have an excellent blending of flavours, also if you are not a big meat eater you can use more vegetables and less meat with a very good result. Remember that slow cooking is the secret of a good stew, unless you are cooking in a pressure cooker.

Braising is a more complex method of stewing, but turns a family beef stew into a special occasion dish.
Any type of stew may be cooked in a covered casserole in a slow to very moderate oven, but about one-third *less* liquid should be used when cooking in the casserole, as there is less evaporation than in a saucepan.

Stewed steak

Preparation: 10–12 minutes
No delay
Cooking: 2 hours
Serves 4–5

Secret of success
Long, slow cooking.

1–1½ lb. beef steak
salt and pepper
1–1½ oz. lard *or* dripping

1 onion
½ bay leaf
nutmeg *or* mixed herbs

½ pint water
1 stock cube, *optional*

1 Cut the meat into neat squares or fingers.
2 Season with salt and pepper.
3 Heat the fat in a pan. Brown the meat on both sides in the fat, but do not over-cook.
4 Add the sliced onion and flavourings and ½ pint water. You can add a stock cube for extra flavour.
5 Cover the pan and stew slowly for 2 hours, adding a little extra liquid if required.
6 For a change of flavour: 2 teaspoons of vinegar can be cooked with this stew; or, for a thicker stew, roll the meat in seasoned flour instead of just salt and pepper.

Beef stew with dumplings

Preparation: 20 minutes
No delay
Cooking: approximately 2¼ hours
Serves 4

Secrets of success
Make sure the liquid boils before adding the dumplings. Check that you have plenty of liquid in the pan, as the dumplings absorb this. Never make the dumpling dough too dry, it should be firm enough to roll into balls (see stage 10) with floured hands.

1 lb. stewing steak
salt and pepper
2 level tablespoons flour
1 oz. dripping *or* fat
can condensed tomato soup
    and ¼ pint water
    OR ¾ pint brown stock

6 small onions
3 potatoes

for the dumplings
3 oz. flour (with plain flour
    use 1 level teaspoon
    baking powder)

¼ teaspoon salt
pinch of mixed spice
pinch of pepper
1 oz. suet *or* margarine
cold water

1 Cut the meat into 1-inch cubes, removing excess fat.
2 Mix the salt and pepper with the flour.
3 Put on a plate and turn the meat in the seasoned flour, or put the flour, etc., into a paper bag, drop the meat in this and shake. In this way you save any mess on the kitchen table.
4 Melt the dripping or fat in a pan. Don't get this too hot, otherwise it spoils the coating on the meat. Add the meat and turn in the fat until pale golden brown.
5 Add the soup and water or the brown stock.
6 Stir well, cover the pan and simmer gently for 1½ hours.
7 Add the whole onions and the potatoes cut in quarters. Replace the lid and simmer for a further 20 minutes.
8 *Make the dumplings:* sieve flour, baking powder (if used), salt, spice and pepper.
9 Rub in the margarine, or add suet, mix to a fairly firm dough with water.
10 Divide into 8, roll in balls, drop into the stew.
11 Allow the liquid to boil fairly rapidly for about 5 minutes so that the dumplings will rise and be light. Lower the heat and simmer for a further 10–15 minutes with the lid on the pan. Serve immediately.

Chuck wagon stew

Preparation: 10 minutes
No delay
Cooking: just over 2 hours
Serves 4

Secret of success
Cook slowly and steadily.

1 lb. stewing beef
salt and pepper
2 level tablespoons cornflour
3 tablespoons corn oil
    or fat

4–6 small onions
3–4 carrots, sliced
1 clove of garlic
4 oz. mushrooms, sliced
2 tablespoons red wine

½ pint water
1 beef stock cube
few black olives

1 Cut the meat into small pieces, coat with the seasoned cornflour and brown in the hot corn oil or fat.
2 Remove the meat and put it into a casserole.
3 Put the onions, carrots and garlic into the stewpan with any remaining cornflour, and stir all together for a few minutes until lightly browned.
4 Add the sliced mushrooms, wine, and ½ pint water mixed with the stock cube, then bring to boiling point, stirring.
5 Pour over the meat in the casserole, cover tightly and cook in a slow oven for about 2 hours.
6 Ten minutes before serving, add the olives.

Braising and casseroling beef

This method of cooking is ideal for family meals. You could use exactly the same recipes for a dinner party to save any last-minute dishing up.
For a richer flavour, add a small quantity of red wine to the stock.

Braised topside

Preparation: few minutes
No delay
Cooking: 1½ hours
Serves 6–7

You may like to serve some of the meat cold. In this case carve some of the hot portions from the top and some from the bottom, so that the centre of the joint, which is uncoated with the mirepoix, is kept as a cold dish.

½ oz. flour
salt and pepper
piece of topside beef,
    approximately 3 lb.

1 oz. lard *or* dripping
1 oz. butter *or* dripping
2 rashers bacon
2 onions

4 carrots
¼ pint stock
¼ pint red wine
bouquet garni

1 Mix the flour, salt and pepper. Coat the beef with the seasoned flour.
2 Brown on either side in the hot lard or dripping in a large pan.
3 Lift the meat out of the pan, heat the butter or dripping and fry the chopped bacon, sliced onions and carrots for 5–6 minutes.
4 Add the stock, wine, herbs (tied into a neat bunch) and seasoning.
5 Put the meat back into the pan, lower the heat and cover the pan.
6 Make sure the lid fits tightly so the small quantity of liquid will not evaporate.
7 Simmer gently for 1½ hours. *Check once or twice that mixture* (called *mirepoix*) *is not burning.* Add extra stock if necessary.
8 To serve, lift meat out of the pan — slice or carve as usual.
9 Sieve or emulsify the vegetables and liquid to form a thick sauce. Garnish the meat with the bacon and some of the sauce.

Note. A piece of beef cooked this way shrinks relatively little. Other vegetables (celery, tomatoes, etc.) may be added to the mirepoix.

Beef olives

Preparation: 20 minutes
No delay
Cooking: 1½–2 hours
Serves 4

Secrets of success
Do not over-cook at stage 4, as this hardens the meat.
Do not cook too quickly.
Keep well covered with sauce.

1 lb. stewing beef, cut very
    thinly
2 oz. dripping
¾ pint brown sauce *or* brown
    gravy, *pages 64, 142*

bay leaf

for the stuffing
2 oz. fine breadcrumbs
1 oz. suet or fat

¼ teaspoon mixed herbs
seasoning
½ teaspoon chopped parsley
few drops of lemon juice
yolk of 1 egg *or* a small egg

1 Cut the meat into neat pieces, about 4 by 3 inches.
2 Mix all the ingredients for the stuffing together, then divide between the pieces of meat and spread over.
3 Form into rolls, or, if the pieces of meat are sufficiently large, gather up into a dumpling shape, then secure with thin string or cotton.
4 Heat the dripping in a pan and fry the 'olives' in this until just brown on the outside.
5 Prepare the brown sauce or gravy.
6 Put the 'olives' in a saucepan or casserole.
7 Cover with the brown sauce, add the bay leaf.
8 Put a lid on the pan and simmer gently for 1½ hours, or put the covered casserole in a very moderate oven (325°F., Gas Mark 3), and cook for 2 hours.
9 To serve, arrange on a dish with a border of mashed potato, which can be piped round — see page 139 if you wish to pipe the potatoes — and as many cooked vegetables as possible, cut into small dice before cooking.

Braised chuck steak

Preparation: 12 minutes
No delay
Cooking: 2 hours
Serves 5–6

Secret of success
Do not over-cook at stage 5; this hardens the meat.

approximately 1½ lb. chuck
    steak
3 onions

4 oz. mushrooms
3 oz. lard *or* dripping
2 tablespoons flour

salt and pepper
¾ pint water *or* stock
1 beef stock cube

1 Cut the steak into four pieces. Slice the onions and the mushrooms.
2 Fry the onions in the hot lard or dripping until tender. Lift out.
3 Fry the mushrooms until tender. Lift out.
4 Mix the flour with the salt and pepper. Coat the steak with the seasoned flour.
5 Brown gently in the hot fat in the pan, for approximately 6 or 7 minutes on either side.
6 Lift the meat out of the pan, add the water and stock cube, bring to the boil and cook until you have a smooth but not too thick sauce. Taste and re-season if desired.
7 Put the meat into a baking tin or large casserole. Pour over the sauce, add the onions and mushrooms and cover with a lid, or plenty of foil.
8 Cook in a very moderate oven (325°F., Gas Mark 3) for 1½ hours.
9 Serve with the onions and mushrooms round the meat.

Beef goulash with scone cobbler topping

Preparation: 15–20 minutes
No delay
Cooking: 1 hour 45–50 minutes
Serves 4

Secrets of success
Keep the scone dough reasonably moist at stage 10. Cook quickly, at stage 14.

for the goulash
1 lb. stewing steak
1 *or* 2 onions
2 oz. beef dripping *or* fat
1 oz. flour
½ pint water

2 tablespoons concentrated tomato purée *or* ketchup
1 teaspoon paprika (sweet red pepper)
½ teaspoon salt
good sprinkling black pepper

for the topping
6 oz. flour (with plain flour use 1½ level teaspoons baking powder)
1 oz. butter *or* margarine
milk

1 Cut the meat into cubes. Slice the onions.
2 Heat the fat and quickly brown the meat on both sides.
3 Using a draining spoon, lift the meat into a casserole.
4 Fry the sliced onion and place over the meat.
5 Stir the flour into the fat and cook, stirring, until brown.
6 Stir in the water, tomato purée or ketchup, paprika, salt and black pepper.
7 Bring to the boil, stirring, and pour over the meat and onion.
8 Cover and cook gently in the centre of a very moderate oven (325–350°F., Gas Mark 3) for about 1½ hours.

To make the topping
9 Sieve the flour and baking powder, if used.
10 Rub in the fat, mix quickly and lightly with the milk to a soft but not sticky dough.
11 Turn on to a lightly floured board. Knead lightly and then press or roll out to about ½ inch thickness.
12 Cut into shapes.
13 Place over the *hot* meat mixture, brush with milk.
14 Increase heat of the oven to hot (425–450°F., Gas Mark 6–7) and bake, uncovered, for 15–20 minutes until the scones are risen and golden.

Making a stew in a pressure cooker

Preparation: 10 minutes
No delay
Pressure cooking time: 15–20 minutes at 15 lb. pressure

Your pressure cooker book will give you details of various recipes, but a simple stew is very satisfactory in a pressure cooker. Follow this method to prepare it.

1 Put the meat, vegetables, etc., into the cooker without the rack.
2 Use only half the quantity of water specified in an ordinary recipe.
3 Season lightly.
4 Put on the lid and bring to pressure as directed.
5 Allow 15 minutes for lamb, 20 minutes for beef.
6 Allow the pressure to drop at room temperature.
7 The stew can be thickened afterwards with a little flour, and, to give extra richness, a knob of fat.
8 If preferred, the meat can be tossed in fat at the beginning of cooking.

Using a pressure cooker to make a stew

Steak and kidney pudding

Preparation: 20–25 minutes
No delay
Cooking: minimum 3½–4 hours
Serves 4–5

Secret of success
Quick cooking at stage 12 so
the pudding rises well.

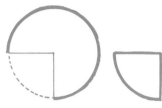

How to cut pastry to fit basin

*Tuck in edges of greaseproof
paper round pudding (foil may
be put over paper)*

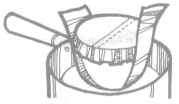

*Put strip of foil under pudding
so it is easily removed from
the steamer or pan*

for the suet pastry
8 oz. flour (with plain flour
use 1 teaspoon baking
powder)
good pinch of salt

4 oz. shredded suet
water *to mix*

for the filling
12 oz.–1 lb. stewing steak

2 lamb kidneys *or* 3–4 oz.
ox kidney
½ oz. flour
salt
water *or* stock

1 Put the flour, baking powder, if used, and pinch of salt through a sieve into a basin.
2 Add the shredded suet, mix with your fingers, then gradually stir in enough cold water to make a firm dough.
3 Roll out the pastry to ¼ inch thickness on a floured pastry board.
4 Make into a circle; cut out a quarter of the circle and put on one side for the lid. Lift the other piece of pastry into a lightly greased 1½–2-pint basin and arrange in this. You will find that it should fit very well indeed.
5 Press the two edges together and cut off the untidy pieces.
6 Cut the steak into thin pieces, and the kidney into small dice.
7 Put about ½ oz. (level tablespoon) flour and a good pinch salt on to a plate and mix them together.
8 Put a layer of meat into the pudding, then a sprinkling of seasoned flour. Fill the basin like this until all the meat is used.
9 Cover with enough water or stock nearly to fill the basin.
10 Re-roll remaining pastry and make into a circle large enough to cover the top of the basin. Put this over the pudding, damp the edges then press the edge of the lid to the edge of the side pastry.
11 Cover with a piece of greased paper, greased-side against the pudding.
12 Put into a steamer over a pan of boiling water and cook for a minimum of 3½–4 hours, or a little longer. For the first 2 hours the water must boil rapidly under the pudding. Fill up with boiling water as it gets low. If you have no steamer, stand the pudding in a saucepan with the water coming halfway up the basin. Fill up frequently.
13 When ready to dish up the pudding, lift carefully from the steamer on to the kitchen table. Dry the basin, then lift on to a hot plate and, to give the finishing touch, arrange a folded serviette round the basin. Never turn out the pudding.
14 Heat a little more stock, or water with a stock cube, and serve in a sauce boat. When the first slice of pudding is cut, pour in the stock to give more gravy.

Steak and kidney pudding

Steak and kidney pie

Preparation: 20 minutes
No delay
Cooking: 1 hour 55 minutes
Serves 4–5

Secret of success
Follow the recipe method to set pastry rapidly at stage 7, then lower heat to cook gently so the meat is tender.
If preferred, cook the steak and kidney first (see Stewed steak, page 67), cool, put into pie dish. Cover with pastry and cook for 35 minutes in a hot oven (reduce heat after 10 minutes).

12 oz.–1 lb. stewing steak
2 lamb or sheep kidneys *or* about 4 oz. ox kidney

good pinch of pepper
½ teaspoon salt
1 level teaspoon flour
water *or* stock

6 oz. short crust *or* flaky pastry, *pages 184, 193*
milk *to glaze*

1 Cut the steak and kidney into small pieces and roll in the well seasoned flour.
2 Stand a pie support or egg cup (not plastic) in the centre of the dish to support the pastry.
3 Put the meat into the pie dish, seeing that the kidney is well distributed.
4 Pour over enough water or stock to come halfway up the meat; any more would boil out in cooking.
5 Roll out the pastry and cover the pie. If you have any scraps of pastry left, form these into leaves, and a rose, to decorate the pie; it is traditional in cookery to ornament savoury pies in this way, but not sweet pies. *To make leaves:* roll out the pastry to a strip, then cut leaf shapes (approximately diamond), marking the 'veins' with the point of a knife. *To make a rose:* cut a narrow strip, then roll this round, and with your finger-tips depress at intervals to give a petal shape, OR see page 194 for *a tassel*.
6 Brush over the top of the pie with a very little milk, sticking the leaves and rose into position. Make a tiny slit in the pastry over the pie support to allow the steam to escape.
7 Bake in the centre of a hot oven (425–450 °F., Gas Mark 6–7) for about 25 minutes to allow the pastry to rise, then put a piece of paper over the top and lower heat to very moderate (325–350 °F., Gas Mark 3–4), to make sure the meat is cooked. Give it about a further 1½ hours.
8 For a steak and mushroom pie, use the recipe above but add 6 oz. mushrooms and omit the kidneys.

London beef bake

Preparation: 25 minutes
Cooking: 2 hours 45 minutes
Serves 4–6

Secrets of success
Cook the stewing steak and vegetables very slowly.
Use a little more water at stage 3 if cooking in a saucepan.
Do not over-cook the crumbs at stage 4, otherwise they will over-brown in the oven.

1½ lb. stewing steak
seasoning
1 oz. flour
1 oz. fat
2 medium onions

1 pint water
½–1 tablespoon tomato purée
2 carrots
pinch of mixed herbs

for the topping
1½ oz. butter
2 oz. white crumbs
8 oz. self-raising flour
seasoning
3 tablespoons oil
¼ pint milk

1 Dice the meat and toss in the seasoned flour, then fry in the hot fat for a few minutes, together with the peeled chopped onions.
2 Add the water, tomato purée, sliced carrots and herbs.
3 Either transfer to a casserole, cover and cook in the centre of a very moderate oven (325 °F., Gas Mark 3) for 2 hours, or simmer in the pan.
4 Heat the butter in a frying pan, toss the crumbs in this until golden.
5 Sieve the flour and seasoning, add the oil and milk, mix well.
6 Drop spoonfuls into the crumb mixture, turn until coated and form into balls.
7 Put the stew into a casserole (if it has been cooked in a pan), top with the balls of dough and bake in the centre of a moderately hot oven (375 °F., Gas Mark 4–5) for about 35–40 minutes.

London beef bake

To roast mutton or lamb

Preparation: few minutes
No delay
Cooking: as table on page 59

If you like a very succulent piece of lamb, choose shoulder or half shoulder, leg or half leg. The lower part of the leg is the leaner piece, whereas the shoulder contains more fat. Loin, or best end of neck, of lamb give you a good distribution of fat and lean, but of course you do have quite an amount of bone.

Breast of lamb is the most economical of all and very tender, but does, however, contain a very high percentage of fat. You can overcome this to a degree by using a stuffing such as veal (parsley), sage and onion, or sausage meat mixed with more crumbs. Mutton is less tender than lamb so it is best to use the slow method of roasting on page 75.

1 To roast the lamb or mutton, season lightly on the outside. There is no need to add any fat.
2 If using a covered roaster, or covering with foil, allow a good 10 minutes more than the time below.
3 Allow 20 minutes per lb. and 20 minutes over.
4 Remember, if stuffing breast of lamb, that you must count the stuffing in with the total weight. (Recipes for stuffings see pages 80 and 85.)
5 If you are using a covered roaster, take the lid off for the last 15 minutes to crisp the outside skin.
6 Lamb or mutton should be well cooked, so start in a really hot oven (425–450°F., Gas Mark 6–7), and reduce the heat slightly (400°F., Gas Mark 5) after the first 30–35 minutes' cooking.
7 The dripping you get from roast mutton or lamb is not as good as that from beef, and many people do not keep it, since it has a very distinctive flavour and cannot be used for other purposes.
8 If roasting potatoes with mutton or lamb they can be roasted round the joint (see page 64), but the fat from this meat is a little watery, so you do get a rather more crisp result if you roast the potatoes separately.

Roast lamb with garlic

If you are fond of garlic use this when roasting lamb.

1 Take one tiny section (clove) of garlic and halve it, then rub the cut surfaces over the lamb before roasting.
2 For a stronger garlic flavour, make a slit in the skin of leg or shoulder of lamb and insert the clove of garlic.
3 Remove before serving the lamb.

Preparing crown of lamb

Preparation: 15 minutes
No delay
Cooking: see method

Get the butcher to chop the bones at thick end of 2 best end of neck joints, and to chop through projecting bony structure; this is called 'chining'.

Pork or veal may be similarly roasted – time as for particular meat.

1 Use a sharp knife to cut part of the way through the sharp ends of the cutlets to separate them slightly (picture 1).
2 Cut flesh straight across on the skin side, remove fatty ends and trim the bones, scraping them free of flesh (picture 2).
3 Join together one end of each joint, using a thick needle and thin string. Bend joints round, skin-side inwards, and again sew to join, making a 'crown' shape (picture 3). Twist a piece of foil or greaseproof paper round the bony ends to check charring whilst roasting.
4 The crown roast may be cooked without any filling at all, or the centre of the crown can be filled with a stuffing. This can be sage and onion stuffing (page 80), or veal stuffing (page 85), or sausage meat stuffing (see above).
5 Roast the meat for 20 minutes per lb. plus 20 minutes over (the weight should include stuffing). Put the meat into a hot oven (425–450°F., Gas Mark 6–7) and reduce the heat to 375–400°F., Gas Mark 5, after first 30 minutes.
6 Garnish with parsley and cutlet frills, which can be bought from a good stationer. Serve like ordinary roast lamb.

Tips when making a crown roast
1 Protect the bones with foil during cooking so they do not scorch.
2 If you wish stuffing to remain soft, cover with a piece of greased foil. If you wish it to crisp, remove foil towards end of the cooking time.
3 If you wish to cook the meat without a filling, you can make it look more attractive by serving with the centre filled with cauliflower in a white sauce, with mixed cooked vegetables, or with cooked rice blended with cooked peas, carrots, or red and green peppers.

Crown roast of pork with orange rice, see page 147

Accompaniments to mutton or lamb

One does not serve mustard with mutton or lamb. Instead you have mint sauce with lamb, or you might like to buy mint jelly. With mutton you have redcurrant jelly or onion sauce (recipe below). The jelly is simply served in a small dish.

It is not an accepted thing to stuff mutton or lamb but there is no reason why it should not be done, especially if you are having breast of lamb. The gravy should be thin if you have not stuffed the meat, thick if you have. For details see page 64.

New or roast potatoes may be served with mutton or lamb.

Mint sauce

Preparation: 8 minutes
No delay
No cooking

Secret of success
Hot water dissolves the sugar and brings out the flavour of mint.

mint	sugar	vinegar

1 Chop the mint finely
2 Add sugar to taste, vinegar, and a little hot water if desired.

Note. Chopped mint or chopped mint and sugar may be packed in small waxed containers and frozen, so you may make mint sauce out of season.

Onion sauce

Preparation: 8 minutes
No delay
Cooking: 50 minutes
Serves 4

Secrets of success
Stir well as sauce thickens. Chop onions on a laminated surface rather than wood since it is difficult to get rid of the smell from a wooden surface.

3 onions	1 oz. flour	salt and pepper
1 oz. butter *or* margarine	$\frac{1}{4}$ pint milk	

1 Boil the onions in a covered saucepan until tender. Large onions will take about 45 minutes.
2 Chop the onions when cooked, and keep $\frac{1}{4}$ pint of the liquid.
3 Heat the fat in a pan, stir in the flour and cook for several minutes, stir well.
4 Remove from the heat and add the milk, the onion stock and seasoning; stir all the time.
5 Bring to the boil and cook until tender.
6 Add the chopped onions and reheat.

Slow roasting of meat

If in any doubt that meat is top quality, it will be advisable to roast slowly. To roast any meat slowly follow these times.

1 Set the oven at 275°F., Gas Mark 1, and allow 1$\frac{1}{4}$ hours for the first lb.
2 For each additional lb. up to 7 lb., allow an extra 25 minutes, i.e. a 4-lb. joint will take 2$\frac{1}{2}$ hours.
3 Pork and veal should be allowed 35 minutes to the lb.

OR

1 Set oven at 350°F., Gas Mark 3, and allow 50 minutes for the first lb.
2 Each additional lb. takes a further 20 minutes.
3 Pork and veal should be allowed an extra 30 minutes per lb.

To fry and grill lamb

Preparation: few minutes
No delay
Cooking: 12–15 minutes

Choose loin or best end of neck chops, or cutlets. Generally speaking, mutton is not suitable for frying or grilling, and even if tender will take considerably more time than lamb.

To fry
1 Since lamb contains a reasonable amount of fat, no extra fat need be added when frying or grilling.
2 Fry the chops or cutlets steadily rather than too quickly, to give a pleasant crispness to the outside fat.

To grill
1 Have the grill hot to begin with.
2 Brown the meat on either side.
3 Lower the heat to moderate, so that the meat can cook through to the centre.
4 Serve with grilled or fried tomatoes, mushrooms or tomato sauce (page 209).

Top *Spring lamb casserole, see page 78*
Bottom *Meat loaf, see page 287*

Frying lamb chops

Crumbed cutlets

Preparation: 10 minutes
Cooking: approximately 10 minutes
Serves 2

Secrets of success
Coating meat is not easy. Brush the cutlets thoroughly with the beaten egg, and pat the crumbs well at stage 2.
Drain on absorbent paper after frying, to prevent the cutlets being greasy.

| 4 lamb cutlets from best end of neck | 2 tablespoons crisp breadcrumbs (raspings) | *for frying* 1½–2 oz. fat |

1 Trim the fat from the cutlets and brush with beaten egg.

2 Coat cutlets with crumbs, patting them on with the knife-blade to coat closely.

3 Fry in the hot fat until golden brown on both sides, lower heat and cook until tender.

4 Drain on absorbent paper. Serve with buttered peas and grilled or fried tomato slices.

Lamb cutlets with cucumber

Preparation: 10 minutes
No delay
Cooking: 30 minutes
Serves 4

Cutlets from best end neck of lamb are small but delicious in flavour – allow 2 per person.

Secret of success
Make sure the fat is hot (stage 3) before the meat is put into the pan.

1 medium cucumber	1 egg	¼ pint gravy, *page 64*
2 oz. butter	1 oz. crisp breadcrumbs	
salt and pepper	2 oz. fat *or* butter *for frying*	*to garnish*
8 cutlets, from best end of neck, *or* 4 from loin	cutlets	chopped parsley

1 Peel the cucumber, remove the seeds and cut the flesh into dice.
2 Heat the butter in a saucepan, put in the cucumber, salt and pepper, cover closely and cook gently for nearly 30 minutes, or until tender.
3 Brush the cutlets with beaten egg, coat with the crumbs, then fry in hot butter or fat until brown on both sides, lower the heat and cook for 10 minutes.
4 Arrange the cutlets neatly on a dish with the cucumber in the centre, as shown, garnished with chopped parsley. Serve gravy separately, if you like this.

Lamb cutlets with cucumber

Grilled lamb cutlets with orange

Preparation: 5–8 minutes
No delay
Cooking: 12 minutes
Serves 4

Secret of success
Make sure the grill is really hot
before cooking the meat.

1 packet frozen mixed
  vegetables *or* 8 oz. diced
  mixed vegetables

1 small cauliflower
4 cutlets lamb from loin
1 orange

½ oz. butter

to garnish
chopped parsley

1 Put the vegetables on to cook.
2 Grill the lamb cutlets as directed until crisp and golden brown.
3 While the lamb and vegetables are cooking, slice the orange and cut into quarters, remove the pips.
4 Arrange the lamb on a hot dish with the orange slices, vegetables (drained and tossed in a little butter), and garnish with chopped parsley.

Mixed grill

Preparation: 10 minutes
No delay
Cooking: 10–20 minutes
Serves 1

This is a very substantial mixed
grill – most people would be
satisfied with say 3 meat
ingredients.

Secrets of success
Make sure the grill is really hot
before cooking the meat, so the
outside is cooked quickly and
the juices sealed in.

mushrooms
1–2 halved *or* whole
  tomatoes
seasoning

1 small cutlet *and/or* 1 piece
  rump *or* fillet steak
1 lamb's *or* pig's kidney

1 piece lamb's or calf's liver
1–2 sausages
1–2 rashers bacon

1 Put the mushrooms and tomatoes in the grill pan, seasoning well.
2 Start these under a hot grill for a few minutes.
3 Put the meat, well seasoned (with the exception of the bacon) on the grid, brushing with plenty of melted butter, margarine or fat.
4 Cook quickly, turning as necessary.
5 Add the bacon at the last minute, so this will not be over-cooked.
6 Arrange on a hot dish and serve with peas, French fried potatoes, chipped or sauté potatoes.
7 Accompany with a crisp green salad, if wished.

Baked stuffed lamb chops

Preparation: 10–15 minutes
No delay
Cooking: 30 minutes
Serves 2

Secret of success
Remember that stuffing meat
means extra cooking time, or a
higher temperature, to
compensate for the weight of
the stuffing.

for the stuffing
2 oz. soft white breadcrumbs
½ level teaspoon mixed herbs
1 level teaspoon grated
  lemon rind
shake of pepper

1 tablespoon finely chopped
  parsley
1 teaspoon finely chopped
  onion
good pinch of salt
1 egg yolk

½ oz. butter, margarine *or*
  dripping, melted

2 thick lamb chops

1 Mix all the dry ingredients well together and bind with the egg and melted butter.
2 Make a 'pocket' in each chop by cutting the meat away from the curved bone.
3 Fill the hollows with stuffing, then put the chops into a greased baking tin.
4 Cover with greased paper or foil, and bake in a moderately hot oven (400°F., Gas Mark 6) for 30 minutes.

Left *Lamb cutlets and orange* Right *How to stuff lamb chops*

To stew or casserole lamb or mutton

The cheaper cuts of lamb or mutton enable you to produce an economical and delicious meal.

If people dislike fat there are two ways in which you can overcome it:

1 Cut off some of the fat before making the casserole or stew; this is inclined to take away some flavour.
2 Make the stew some time before it is required. Allow to cool, when the fat will come to the top. Skim this off and then reheat to serve.

Lamb stew, basic recipe

Preparation: 15 minutes
No delay
Cooking: 2 hours
Serves 4–5

Secret of success
This is a very basic simple recipe; it can be delicious, if well seasoned.

1–1¼ lb. lamb, preferably from leg	1–2 onions	stock *or* water flavoured with little vegetable *or* meat extract, *see page 63*
2 carrots	salt and pepper	fresh *or* frozen green peas

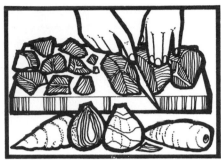

1 Cut up meat neatly and prepare carrots and onions, slicing or chopping them. Young New Zealand lamb is excellent for this stew.

2 Put a layer of carrots and onions at the bottom of a stewpan or casserole, then a layer of meat. Repeat the layers with a good dusting of seasoning between each, until all ingredients are in the pan.

3 Pour in stock to cover, put lid on the casserole or stewpan.
4 Cook gently until the meat is almost tender (about 1½ hours). Use very moderate heat in the oven (325 °F., Gas Mark 3).

5 Add the peas, cover the pan and continue cooking for a further 30 minutes.
6 Serve the stew in the casserole in which it was cooked.

Spring lamb casserole

Preparation: 25 minutes
Cooking: 45 minutes
Serves 4

Secrets of success
Make certain the vegetables are covered with the liquid so the potatoes do not discolour.
Do not over-cook.

Colour picture, page 74

1 lb. small new potatoes	1 pint beef stock *or* water and stock cubes	1 teaspoon Tabasco sauce seasoning
1 lb. small young carrots	2 tablespoons oil	
8 oz. shelled *or* frozen peas	8 lamb cutlets	*to garnish* chopped parsley *and/or* chopped mint

1 Scrape the potatoes and carrots, then put into an ovenproof casserole with the peas, *boiling* stock or *boiling* water blended with the stock cube.
2 Cover the casserole, put into the centre of a moderate oven (350–375 °F., Gas Mark 4–5) and commence cooking while frying the meat.
3 Heat oil in a pan and fry cutlets steadily for 4–5 minutes on either side; sprinkle with half the Tasbasco and season generously while cooking.
4 Remove the casserole from the oven, stir the rest of the Tabasco, any dripping from the pan, and a little seasoning into the stock.
5 Arrange the meat over the vegetables, replace the lid and continue cooking for 30–35 minutes.
6 Top with chopped herbs and serve from casserole with an unthickened gravy.

Lancashire hotpot

Preparation: 15–20 minutes
No delay
Cooking: approximately 1½–2 hours
Serves 4

Secret of success
Do not use too much water at stage 4, or the meat and vegetables will lose some of their flavour.

Lancashire hotpot

| 12 oz.–1 lb. lean middle *or* best end mutton, *or* stewing lamb | 1 lb. potatoes 2 large onions salt and pepper | hot water 1 oz. margarine chopped parsley |

1 Cut the meat into neat pieces.
2 Peel and slice the potatoes and onions. They should be about ¼ inch thick.
3 Fill a casserole with alternate layers of meat, onions and potato, sprinkling salt and pepper over each layer; ending with a layer of potato.
4 Pour in enough hot water to half-fill the casserole.
5 Put the margarine on top in small pieces, then put on the lid.
6 If the casserole has no lid, then spread the margarine over greaseproof paper and tuck this securely over the top.
7 Cook in the coolest part of the oven, either for 2 hours at 325°F., Gas Mark 3, or a good 1½ hours at 350°F., Gas Mark 4.
8 Take lid or paper off for the last 20 minutes, to brown the top.
9 Garnish with the chopped parsley, see picture.

Irish stew

Preparation: 15 minutes
No delay
Cooking: 2 hours 10 minutes
Serves 4

Secret of success
Cook *slowly* so the meat becomes tender and the whole potatoes, added at stage 4, keep their shape.

| 12 oz.–1 lb. scrag *or* middle neck of lamb 1 lb. potatoes | 2 onions about ¾ pint water salt and pepper | *to garnish* cooked peas cooked carrots |

1 Cut the meat into neat pieces. Cut either 1 or 2 new potatoes in halves, or old potatoes into slices. Slice the onions.
2 Put the meat, the pieces of potato and the sliced onions into the pan, add the water and seasoning.
3 Bring slowly to the boil, remove the scum, lower the heat and simmer gently for just over 1½ hours.
4 Add the rest of the prepared whole potatoes, season and continue cooking for about 40 minutes.
5 Pile the meat and stock in the centre of a hot dish, with the potatoes round, and a garnish of the freshly cooked peas and carrots.

Boiled mutton or lamb and caper sauce

Preparation: 10 minutes
No delay
Cooking: 1½–2 hours
Serves 4

Secret of success
Use half milk and half stock in sauce, to give a good flavour.

| 1–1¼ lb. scrag *or* middle neck of mutton *or* lamb 3 carrots 2 onions salt and pepper | *for the caper sauce* 1 oz. margarine *or* butter 1 oz. flour ¼ pint milk | ¼ pint meat stock salt and pepper 2 teaspoons capers 1 teaspoon caper vinegar |

1 Cut the meat into pieces, slice the vegetables; put both into a pan.
2 Cover with cold water, bring to the boil, skim off the scum.
3 Add seasoning, lower the heat and simmer gently for 1½–2 hours.
4 Lift the meat and vegetables on to a hot dish.
5 *Make the caper sauce:* heat the fat in a pan, stir in the flour and cook gently for several minutes, then gradually stir in the milk and the meat stock. Bring to the boil and cook until thickened. Add the seasoning, capers and vinegar. Heat, without boiling.
6 Serve the caper sauce in a separate sauce boat.

To roast pork

Choose loin, leg, shoulder, bladebone, spare rib.

Colour picture, page 56

1 To give pork a delicious flavour when roasting, mix a little finely chopped onion with salt, pepper and dry mustard, then rub the meat with lard or olive oil and sprinkle the onion mixture over this.
2 If roasting in a covered roasting tin, or in foil, remove the lid or foil a good 30–45 minutes before serving to allow the crackling to become crisp.
3 Always rub the fat of pork with melted lard, oil or butter, and season before roasting, to give a good crackling.
4 See that the skin is evenly and deeply cut (scored); this encourages it to crisp and makes the crackling.
5 Start in a really hot oven, and allow the time given in the table on page 60, *or* reduce the heat after the first 30 minutes to moderate and cook more slowly, allowing about 35 minutes per lb.
6 If cooking in a covered roaster, or covered with foil, allow an extra 10 minutes on the total cooking time.

Accompaniments to pork

Although it is a matter of personal choice, pork is generally stuffed with a sage and onion stuffing. To put this into a loin of pork, cut down the fat part and press the stuffing between the fat and the lean part of the meat. With leg of pork it is generally easier to bake the stuffing in a separate dish. If baking separately it will need approximately 35–40 minutes. To give more flavour to a sage and onion stuffing, add 1 or 2 teaspoons made-mustard.

Because pork is a fatty meat, fruit is an excellent accompaniment. Apple sauce is traditionally served with roast pork; you can add a teaspoon of mixed spice to this for a change. Or serve orange slices, or pears. These latter are given extra flavour if stuck with a few cloves before heating. Use canned pears; reheat in the syrup, drain and serve round meat as below. Roast potatoes and a thick gravy (page 64) may be served with pork.

Roast stuffed pork with pears

Add canned halved pears. flavoured with cloves, to the roasting tin about 10 minutes before the meat is cooked.

Sage and onion stuffing

Preparation: 7–8 minutes
No delay
Cooking: 20 minutes
Serves 4–6

2 large onions	1 egg	good pinch each salt
about ½ pint water	2 oz. breadcrumbs	and pepper
1 oz. shredded suet	1 teaspoon dried sage	

1 Put the onions into a saucepan and add the water.
2 Simmer steadily for 15–20 minutes; onions should be partly cooked only.
3 Remove onions from water on to a chopping board, and chop into small pieces.
4 Transfer to a basin, then add all the other ingredients, with a little onion stock if wished.

Apple sauce

Serves 6–8

1 Peel 1 lb. cooking apples and remove the cores.
2 Slice, put into a saucepan, add ¼ pint water, 1 oz. margarine *or* butter (optional) and 2 oz. sugar (white *or* brown).
3 This sauce can be cooked in a double saucepan, so eliminating any risk of scorching bottom of pan; in this case use 2 tablespoons water only.
4 Simmer until a soft purée, stir once or twice.
5 When the apples are cooked, beat with a wooden spoon until smooth, or sieve, or emulsify in a liquidiser; emulsifying tends to make mixture rather liquid, so use a little less water than given in stage 2.
6 If sauce is a little thin, let it boil rapidly to evaporate some moisture.

To fry and grill pork

Preparation: few minutes
No delay
Cooking: 15–20 minutes

Choose loin chops, cutlets or spare ribs.

Accompaniments
Serve grilled or fried pork with fried apple rings, i.e. slices of dessert apple cooked in a little hot margarine or butter; or apple sauce and orange salad; or just with grilled or fried tomatoes and mushrooms.

Grilling pork chops

To fry
1 Pork should be fried steadily so that you draw the fat from the meat, and no extra fat is then required.
2 Brown on both sides lightly in the pan, then lower the heat and cook steadily through to the centre.

To grill
1 Make sure the grill is hot before starting to cook.
2 Pork chops or cutlets (cutlets have the bone trimmed to look more attractive when serving – they are always cut from the loin) need little basting with fat, since there is generally a good distribution of fat and lean.
3 When once the outside of the meat has been sealed, turn the heat low to make sure the chops are well cooked through to the centre.

Pork cardinal

Preparation: 5–6 minutes
No delay
Cooking: 20–25 minutes
Serves 4

Secret of success
Make certain the pork is evenly coated (stage 2) and cook thoroughly at stage 3.

4 loin chops of pork	*for the sauce*	½ teaspoon powdered sage seasoning
1 egg	1 oz. plain flour	
1 packet ready-made sage and onion stuffing	3 level tablespoons concentrated tomato purée	*to garnish*
2 oz. bacon *or* pork fat	½ pint stock	slices hard-boiled egg few cooked peas

1 Remove the bones from the chops and trim the meat. Beat with a rolling pin.
2 Dip in beaten egg, then toss in the dry sage and onion stuffing.
3 Fry gently in the hot fat on both sides until browned and tender, then place on a hot dish.
4 *To make the sauce:* add the flour and tomato purée to the pan.
5 Stir while adding the stock. When thickened, add the sage and season well.
6 Pour this sauce round the pork, and serve with crispy fried potatoes and spinach. For a colourful garnish use rings of hard-boiled egg and cooked peas.

Pork chops with creamed corn

Preparation: 7–8 minutes
No delay
Cooking: 15 minutes
Serves 4

Secret of success
Pre-heat the grill so as to cook the meat quickly.

4 pork chops	small can unsweetened evaporated milk	2 cans sweet corn
for the sauce	¼ pint water	*to garnish*
1 oz. butter	salt and pepper	parsley
1 level tablespoon flour		

1 Grill the chops on both sides, as directed above.
2 While the chops are cooking, *make the sauce:* melt the butter in a pan and stir in the sifted flour, mixing well.
3 Dilute the evaporated milk with the water and the liquor from cans of corn.
4 Add this liquid gradually to the roux (the flour and butter mixture), stirring briskly until the sauce is smooth and creamy.
5 Adjust seasoning to taste, then stir in corn. Stir and simmer for 10 minutes.
6 Turn into a serving dish and arrange chops on top; garnish with parsley, as shown.
7 Serve with vegetables in season, or a salad of lettuce and onion rings.

Pork chops with creamed corn

Devilled rashers of pork

Preparation: 10 minutes
No delay
Cooking: 20–25 minutes
Serves 4

Secret of success
Taste the apple mixture when at stage 2. You may like to use more mustard – it should have a very definite flavour.

4 thick rashers belly of fresh pork
2 pickled walnuts
1 small cooking apple, chopped
½ teaspoon made-mustard
salt
large pinch of cayenne
2 large tomatoes

1 Grill the rashers on the grid of the grill pan until they are brown and fairly crisp (page 94), i.e. approximately 15 minutes.
2 Meanwhile, chop the pickled walnuts very finely and mix with the apple, mustard, salt and cayenne pepper.
3 Spread this on the rashers, heat through under a moderately hot grill for 7–10 minutes, and serve piping hot with grilled tomatoes – which can be halved and cooked under the rashers in the grill pan.

To stew, casserole or boil pork

Pork is not an ideal meat to casserole because of the high percentage of fat – it also needs plenty of flavouring. If people dislike fat, you can overcome this by cutting off some of the fat before making this casserole or stew, or boiling the pork. Or you can cook it some time before required, then allow to cool, when the fat will come to the top. Skim this, then reheat the stew to serve.

Porkoni

Preparation: 12 minutes
No delay
Cooking: 1¼ hours
Serves 4–6

This recipe is an excellent way of cooking fat pork, for the macaroni, etc., counteracts the fattiness.

2 onions *or* 6 spring onions
1¼–1½ lb. belly pork, diced
4 oz. cut macaroni
2 oz. brown sugar
2 tablespoons vinegar
½ pint stock
3 tablespoons wine *or* extra stock
dash of chilli sauce
2 tablespoons concentrated tomato purée*
salt and pepper

to garnish
small can asparagus tips, *optional*

* obtainable in cans or tubes.

1 Chop the spring onions, or slice large onions.
2 Place the raw pork, macaroni and onions in layers in an overproof dish.
3 Stir together the sugar, vinegar, stock, wine, chilli sauce and tomato purée.
4 Season and pour over the contents of the dish.
5 Cover with a lid, bake for 1¼ hours in the centre of a very moderate oven (325°F., Gas Mark 3).
6 Remove the lid and stir gently to blend all the ingredients.
7 Heat the asparagus tips, if used, in a pan, drain and arrange on top, as shown.

Porkoni

Pork balls in tomato sauce

Preparation: 10–12 minutes
Allow few minutes for soaking
bread
Cooking: 45 minutes
Serves 4

Secrets of success
Mince the meat well at stage 2
to give a smooth texture.
If condensed soup is not
available, use ordinary canned
soup undiluted, and boil for a
few minutes at stage 5 to
thicken.

1 small onion
8 oz. lean pork

1 thick slice bread, from
   a small loaf
1 egg yolk

salt and pepper
can condensed cream of
   tomato soup and ½ can
   water

1 Chop the onion finely.
2 Put the meat through a mincer.
3 *Make the meat balls:* soak the bread in water; squeeze it out, then add to it the pork,
  onion, egg yolk, salt and pepper.
4 Roll the mixture into large balls about 2 inches in diameter.
5 Mix the tomato soup and water and bring to the boil.
6 Drop the pork balls into this sauce, cover and simmer for 45 minutes. Serve in the dish
  as shown.

Pork balls in tomato sauce

Pork stew with dumplings

Preparation: 10 minutes
No delay
Cooking: 45 minutes
Serves 4

Secret of success
Check that there is sufficient
liquid before adding the
dumplings at stage 5, for these
absorb liquid very readily.

2 large potatoes
1 large onion
1 small turnip
1 stick celery
4 large pork chops
1 bay leaf

salt and pepper

for the dumplings
4 oz. flour (with plain flour
  use 1 level teaspoon
  baking powder)

pinch of salt
2 oz. chopped suet
water *to mix*

1 Place the quartered potatoes, onion, turnip and the chopped celery in a saucepan.
2 Place the chops on top and add the bay leaf, salt and pepper.
3 Cover with water, bring to the boil, skim, then simmer until tender.
4 *Meanwhile, make the dumplings:* sieve the flour, or flour and baking powder, with
  the salt, add the suet and enough water to give a slightly sticky consistency — yet dry
  enough to handle. Flour your hands and roll into small balls.
5 Drop the balls into the stew 15 minutes before serving, and simmer steadily.

Pork and apple pudding

Preparation: 20–25 minutes
No delay
Cooking: minimum 3½–4 hours
Serves 4

Secret of success
Cook the pudding rapidly for the
first 2 hours, so the suet pastry
is really light.

suet pastry, *page 70*

for the filling
12 oz.–1 lb. diced pork

3–4 oz. apple *or* onion, diced
½ teaspoon sage

½ oz. flour
salt and pepper
water *or* stock

1 Follow the recipe on page 70 for preparing a steak and kidney pudding, but instead
  of steak use diced pork, and instead of kidney use diced apple or onion.
2 Add a sprinkling of sage.
3 Cook as the instructions for steak and kidney pudding.

Raised pork pie

Preparation: 25 minutes
Cooking: 2–2¼ hours – plus time
to cool
Serves 6

Secrets of success
Unlike other pastry, handle this
while warm. Allow the pie to
cool before adding cool jelly, so
pastry stays crisp.

for the filling
1¼ lb. lean pork
2–3 rashers bacon, *optional*
¼ teaspoon powdered sage
salt and pepper

¼ pint stock*
1 level teaspoon gelatine

for the hot water crust
12 oz. plain flour

pinch of salt
3–4 oz. fat†
¼ pint water
milk *or* egg *to glaze*

* from boiling bones, or use water and ½ beef stock cube.
† clarified dripping or lard, or cooking fat, can be used in this pastry.

1 Cut the pork and bacon rashers into neat pieces.
2 Mix with the sage and seasoning.
3 *To make the pastry:* first sieve the flour and salt together.

4 Melt fat in warm water and add to flour.
   Mix with a knife and knead gently with
   your fingers; use when warm.

5 Roll out at once to approximately ¼ inch
   in thickness. Keep one-third for lid; put
   it in a warm part of kitchen until ready.

6 If good with your hands you can mould the pastry into the base and sides as shown,
   or mould round a 6½- or 7½-inch cake tin, lifting tin away and supporting with a band
   of greaseproof paper secured round the shape. When ready, put in filling with
   2 tablespoons stock.
7 Put on lid – DO NOT press down too firmly (*see picture above right*).
8 Seal edges and decorate with pastry leaves (make as for steak and kidney pie,
   page 70). Make a hole for steam to escape. Brush with milk or beaten egg.
9 Bake the pie in centre of a moderately hot oven (400°F., Gas Mark 5–6) for 45
   minutes, then lower heat to very moderate (325°F., Gas Mark 3), and cook for a
   further 1¼–1½ hours. ALLOW TO COOL.
10 *Meanwhile, make the jelly:* heat the stock and dissolve gelatine in this. Allow to cool
   and begin to stiffen VERY SLIGHTLY.
11 Make a little funnel with greaseproof or foil paper, similar to an icing bag (see page
   261). Insert into the hole in top of the cold pie.
12 Pour in the cold jelly. Leave the pie for jelly to set. Serve cold.

To roast veal

Preparation: few minutes
No delay
Cooking: see right

For roasting, choose shoulder, breast, best end of neck, loin, fillet or chump end of loin.

Secret of success
Veal is a very lean meat that could be tasteless and dry, so use plenty of fat in cooking.

1 The perfect way to roast veal is to use a larding needle (which can be bought in large ironmongers) and thin strips of fat from bacon. Insert these strips through the meat so that it is really kept moist during cooking. Otherwise wrap the veal in plenty of buttered foil when cooking, or cover the top with 1–2 oz. of fat.
2 If you have larded the meat, or covered it in fat, turn once during cooking so that both top and bottom are crisp. If covered in foil, remove this for the last 30 minutes.
3 Veal MUST be well cooked, otherwise it is very indigestible – allow 25 minutes per lb. and 25 minutes over. If covering the meat with foil, or using a covered roaster, allow an extra 10 minutes cooking.
4 If stuffing veal, weigh after stuffing, so that you include the weight of the stuffing.

Accompaniments to veal

Veal is generally stuffed. The traditional stuffing used with veal is given below. One of the very good joints, as suggested above, is breast of veal; you should ask the butcher to bone the veal. Put in the stuffing, roll it firmly, and tie with string.

With loin of veal, cut down the fat and insert the stuffing between the fat and the meat. Tie very firmly before cooking. Remember when the meat is stuffed to count this in with the weight of the meat.

You may find it more convenient to bake the stuffing in a separate dish; allow approximately 10 minutes. If you want the top of the stuffing crisp, leave the dish uncovered.

Serve veal with bacon rolls, roast or new potatoes and a thick gravy (page 64).

Veal stuffing

Preparation: 8–10 minutes
No delay
Cooking: as meat
Serves 4–6

Secret of success
Keep this stuffing moist; the suet or margarine, etc., does this. If you decrease amount of fat, add a little milk to bind.

4 oz. breadcrumbs	2 oz. shredded suet *or* melted	grated rind and juice of
1 egg	margarine	½ lemon
½ teaspoon mixed herbs	2–3 teaspoons chopped parsley	salt and pepper

1 Mix all the ingredients thoroughly together.
2 Taste, to make sure the mixture is well seasoned.

Note. Instead of mixed herbs use a little chopped fresh or dried thyme. This stuffing is then given the name of parsley and thyme.

Bacon rolls

Preparation: few minutes
No delay
Cooking: 15–20 minutes

Secret of success
Stretch the bacon to make it easier to roll, see opposite.

1 Buy rashers of long or streaky bacon, and if fairly big divide each rasher into half.
2 Roll the rashers of bacon, and put on to a metal skewer.
3 Put them into the oven for approximately 15–20 minutes.
4 To stretch bacon, hold the rashers, or halved rashers, with your left hand, pull a knife across them, then roll.

Note. If preferred grill the bacon rolls.

Pot-roasting in a pressure cooker

A pressure cooker can be used for pot roasting. Any meat that can be roasted in the normal way is suitable, and if by chance you have a less tender piece of meat, then try pot-roasting. The method is simple.

1 Put a little fat at the bottom of the cooker and heat this.
2 Brown the meat well in the fat, then lift the meat out of the cooker, insert the trivet and replace the meat.
3 Add water, allowing ½ pint for a joint that takes up to 15 minutes' pressure cooking time, and add an additional ¼ pint water for each 15 minutes over. For example, for a joint taking 45 minutes you need 1 pint water.
4 Beef needs 10 minutes per lb. at 15 lb. pressure. Lamb, veal, pork, need 12 minutes per lb. Roasting chicken needs 5 minutes per lb.
5 Allow pressure to drop at room temperature. The liquor makes good gravy.
6 If wished, the pressure can be allowed to drop and vegetables put in at the right time, so that the meal is cooked together in the one pressure cooker.

To grill or fry veal

Preparation: few minutes
No delay
Cooking: see opposite

Choose: chops from loin, fillet, best end of neck chops, thin slices from leg.

To grill veal

1 Brush the meat well with oil or melted butter. This will prevent veal drying.
2 Make sure the grill is hot, then put the veal underneath.
3 Allow approximately 3 minutes on either side to seal in the flavour, then lower the heat and cook for 6–7 minutes longer.
4 When turning the veal, brush the second side also with oil or melted butter.
5 Veal should be grilled on grid of the grill pan; cook tomatoes and mushrooms underneath to serve with it. Add bacon rashers when veal is half cooked.

To fry veal

1 The favourite way of frying veal is as an escalope (see below), but chops or cutlets can also be fried.
2 Use a fairly generous amount of fat — butter is ideal because it gives extra flavour. Cook steadily for 2–3 minutes on either side, then lower the heat and cook through to the middle for a further 6–7 minutes.

Escalopes of veal

Preparation: 8 or 9 minutes
No delay
Cooking: 10 minutes
Serves 4

Buy thin slices of veal cut from the leg.

Secret of success
Coat carefully for a crisp outside. The flour coating makes it easier to apply the egg and crumbs.

4 fillets veal	*to coat*	*to garnish*
salt and pepper	1 egg	see method, stage 4
1 oz. flour	1 oz. soft breadcrumbs *or* use crisp breadcrumbs	

1 Beat the veal slices gently with a rolling pin to flatten even more.
2 Coat with seasoned flour, then dip into beaten egg and cover with fine crumbs (see page 44).
3 Fry steadily in shallow fat, oil, or butter and oil mixed, until golden brown on both sides.
4 Garnish with wedges of lemon or, for a more elaborate garnish, top rings of lemon with freshly chopped hard-boiled egg and parsley, or egg and capers. Excellent served with green salad.

Variations on escalopes of veal

1 Top with fried or poached egg.
2 Serve with cooked spaghetti or macaroni and a tomato sauce.
3 Do not coat the veal with egg and crumbs, just toss in a little flour and then fry. Lift the veal on to a hot dish, add a squeeze of lemon juice to the butter in the pan, then pour over the pieces of veal.
4 Mix the breadcrumbs with 3 oz. grated Cheddar cheese plus seasoning, including a good pinch of mustard. Fry as above, then heat the butter until golden brown and pour over cooked meat. Top with chives and anchovy fillets as shown opposite.

To casserole or stew veal

Veal has a delicate flavour and therefore in all cooking, and particularly in stewing or casseroling, it is best if a very definite flavouring is added. A goulash made with veal is an ideal way of using it, because the paprika and onions give the desired flavour. Other ingredients to add to a veal casserole are plenty of tomatoes or sliced red or green pepper. Use a good knob of fat if stew lacks richness.

Veal paprika or goulash

Preparation: 15 minutes
No delay
Cooking: 2 hours
Serves 4–6

Secrets of success
The blending of flavours in this dish makes it successful. Taste as you season at stage 7 to make sure you have enough salt, etc.

2 onions	1 clove garlic, *optional*	1 beef stock cube
2 tomatoes	½ oz. paprika	salt and pepper
1–1¼ lb. stewing veal	½ oz. flour	¾ pint yoghourt
1 oz. fat	½–¾ pint water *or* stock	

1 Slice the onions. Skin the tomatoes.
2 Cut the meat into 1-inch cubes and brown quickly in the hot fat.
3 Remove the meat from the fat.
4 Lightly fry the sliced onions and crushed garlic, if used.
5 Add the paprika and flour and stir over low heat.
6 Pour in water and stock cube and bring slowly to the boil, stirring.
7 Return the meat to the liquid, add the chopped tomatoes and seasoning and simmer gently for 1½–2 hours.
8 Just before serving, stir in most of the yoghourt, heat gently.
9 Put into a hot dish and top with the remaining yoghourt. This is excellent served with cooked noodles.

Fricassée of veal

Preparation: 15 minutes
No delay
Cooking: 1½ hours
Serves 4–5

Secrets of success
This dish is delicious if cooked slowly to tenderise the meat. Do not omit the herbs; they provide a delicate flavouring.

1¼ lb. veal
1 onion
1 bay leaf
2–3 slices lemon
salt and pepper

bunch of mixed herbs
½ pint water
1½ oz. butter
1½ oz. flour
½ pint milk

1 tablespoon thick *or* thin cream

to garnish
chopped parsley

1 Cut the veal into neat pieces.
2 Put into a saucepan with the onion, bay leaf, lemon, seasoning and mixed herbs.
3 Add the water. Put the lid on the pan.
4 Simmer gently for about 1¼ hours.
5 Heat the butter in a separate pan, stir in the flour, cook for several minutes.
6 Gradually add the milk, bring to the boil and cook until thickened.
7 Lift the onion, lemon, bay leaf and bunch of herbs out of the veal, then add the meat and ¼ pint of the stock to the white sauce.
8 Heat together and add the cream.
9 Garnish with chopped parsley and serve with creamed potatoes.

Stewed knuckle of veal

Preparation: 20 minutes
No delay
Cooking: 2¼ hours
Serves 4

This is the famous Italian dish — *Osso buco*. When knuckle of veal is unobtainable use 1 lb. diced stewing veal instead.

1½–2 lb. knuckle of veal
salt and pepper
1 oz. flour
3 onions
1 oz. butter *or* 1 tablespoon oil
3 carrots

1 stick celery
3 tomatoes, skinned, *page 201*
bunch mixed herbs
grated rind and juice of 1 lemon
½ pint white wine *or* stock

1 level tablespoon concentrated tomato purée
½ pint water
dash Tabasco sauce, if liked

to garnish
chopped parsley

1 Cut the meat into neat pieces — fairly large for 4 servings.
2 Roll in seasoned flour.
3 Fry the sliced onions in hot butter or oil until pale golden.
4 Add the meat, diced carrots, celery, chopped tomatoes, herbs (tied in muslin) and seasoning. Toss the onions for 2–3 minutes.
5 Stir in the lemon rind and juice, white wine or stock, tomato purée diluted with the water and a dash of Tabasco sauce.
6 Cover and simmer for 2 hours.
7 Lift the meat on to a hot dish, discard the bag of herbs.
8 Rub the sauce through a sieve.
9 Pour over the meat and top with chopped parsley.

Variation
The recipe shown in the picture below gives a more piquant flavour to Osso Buco. Add a good amount of Tabasco (pepper) sauce to the stock, etc., at stage 5. Serve the meat mixture on a bed of cooked rice.

Left *Knuckle of veal (osso buco)*
Right *Escalopes of veal*

Veal and ham pie

Preparation: 25 minutes
Cooking: 2–2¼ hours – plus
time to cool
Serves 4

Secrets of success
Handle the pastry while warm.
Allow the pie to cool before
adding the cool jelly. This makes
sure the pastry remains crisp.

1 lb. veal
4–6 oz. bacon *or* ham
pinch mixed herbs
salt and pepper

hot water crust pastry,
page 84
2 hard-boiled eggs

¼ pint stock
1 level teaspoon powdered
gelatine

1 Cut the veal and bacon or ham into neat pieces. Mix with the herbs, salt and pepper.
2 Prepare the pastry case as directed in the recipe for raised pork pie (see page 84).
3 Put half the filling into pastry, add shelled hard-boiled eggs then rest of the filling.
4 Proceed as for raised pork pie, on page 84.

To use left-over meat

Great care must be taken when using meat that has been left from the joint.
If you have any doubts as to whether it is fresh, it is far better to discard it than run
the risk of food poisoning or an upset stomach.
If you want to reheat slices of meat in a gravy DO NOT OVER-COOK, otherwise the
meat will become tough and lose all its flavour. Make the gravy and then put in the
pieces of meat and heat for a few minutes only. You will find any recipe using left-
over meat is best if you add a little fat in the form of a sauce, because some of the
moistness of the meat is lost in cooking.

Durham cutlets

Preparation: 20 minutes
No delay
Cooking: 15 minutes
Serves 4

Secret of success
Do not over-cook the cutlets as
this dries the already-cooked
meat.

Uncooked minced stewing steak
may be used instead. Use ¼ pint
more liquid in the sauce at stage
3. Add the minced meat and
simmer gently for 30 minutes,
then add the crumbs, etc., and
proceed as recipe.

1 oz. margarine
1 oz. flour
¼ pint gravy, stock *or* water
    flavoured with a little
    meat *or* vegetable extract
salt and pepper
mustard

pinch mixed herbs
1 tablespoon chopped
    parsley
8 oz. cooked meat, minced or
    finely chopped
2 oz. breadcrumbs
2 oz. fat *or* lard *for frying*

to coat
1 egg
2 tablespoons crisp
    breadcrumbs

to garnish
parsley
fried tomatoes

1 Heat the margarine in a saucepan. You can if you wish fry about 1 tablespoon of
    chopped onion in this to give extra flavour.
2 Stir in the flour, away from the heat, then cook the roux (mixture) for about 5 minutes,
    until it begins to turn slightly brown. Be careful not to let it burn.
3 Remove from the heat, gradually stir in the gravy or stock. Bring to the boil and cook,
    stirring until thick.
4 Add seasoning, herbs, parsley, meat and breadcrumbs.
5 Let the mixture cool, turn out of the saucepan and form into 4 cutlet shapes.
6 Beat the egg on a flat plate, then, using a pastry brush, coat the outside of the cutlets
    with the egg.
7 Put the crisp breadcrumbs (or raspings) on a piece of greaseproof paper and turn the
    cutlets round in this gently until they are completely covered. Pat the crumbs into the
    cutlets, shake each cutlet to get rid of surplus crumbs.
8 Heat the fat or lard in a frying pan, put in the cutlets, fry steadily for 4 minutes until
    crisp and brown, turn with a knife and cook for the same time on the second side;
    lower the heat.
9 Allow a further 4 minutes so they are heated through to the middle.
10 To drain, lift on to crumpled tissue paper on a hot dish for about 2 minutes, then
    transfer to hot plates garnished with parsley and fried tomatoes.

Devilled beef rolls

Preparation: 10–15 minutes
No delay
Cooking: 10 minutes
Serves 4

Underdone beef is particularly
good in this recipe. You can also
use ham or tongue instead.

for the filling
1 small onion
2 oz. fat
1 oz. flour
1 teaspoon curry powder
¼ pint water

1 beef stock cube
salt and pepper
little chopped parsley
1 tablespoon chutney
2 tablespoons fine
    breadcrumbs

4 good sized slices cooked
    beef

to garnish
lettuce

1 Chop the onion very finely. Heat the fat.
2 Fry the onion in the fat and stir in the flour and curry powder.
3 Cook for 2–3 minutes, then gradually add the water and beef stock cube, stirring all
    the time. Bring to the boil and cook until thickened.
4 Add the salt, pepper, chopped parsley, chutney and breadcrumbs. Blend thoroughly.
5 Allow the mixture to cool, then spread over the slices of beef and roll firmly. Serve
    cold with lettuce.

Shepherd's pie

Preparation: 15 minutes
No delay
Cooking: 35–40 minutes
Serves 4

Secrets of success
This is excellent if the meat mixture is well flavoured and the potatoes browned well. If both meat filling and potatoes are very hot this dish will need only browning under a hot grill or near the top of a hot oven.

12 oz. cooked meat
1 oz. dripping *or* lard
1 large onion

2 or 3 tomatoes
$\frac{1}{4}$–$\frac{1}{2}$ pint gravy *or* stock
salt and pepper

good pinch of mi.
1–1$\frac{1}{2}$ lb. cooked po.
1 oz. margarine

1 Cut the cooked meat into small pieces or put through a mincer.
2 Heat the dripping or lard in a pan, and fry the sliced onion and tomatoes until tende.
3 Add the meat, gravy or stock, salt, pepper and mixed herbs. Vary the amount of stock according to personal taste. Place in the bottom of a pie dish.
4 Mash the potatoes and when they are very soft and smooth pile on top of the meat mixture.
5 Fork into an attractive shape.
6 Put the margarine in tiny pieces over the potato and bake in the centre of a moderately hot oven (400°F., Gas Mark 5) for 30 minutes, until the top is crisp and brown.

Madras shepherd's pie

The shepherd's pie pictured below is a pleasant variation on the traditional recipe. Prepare the meat and vegetable mixture as the recipe above, but stir 1–2 teaspoons curry powder into the meat mixture. Blend 6 oz. grated Cheddar cheese with the mashed potatoes, and cook as the traditional shepherd's pie above.

Note. If you wish to make this, or the shepherd's pie above, with freshly minced meat, increase the amount of stock slightly. Prepare as stage 3 above, but simmer gently in a pan for about 25–30 minutes, stirring well, until meat is nearly cooked, then complete the recipe as above, or as traditional recipe.

Madras shepherd's pie

Cornish pasties

Preparation: 25 minutes
No delay
Cooking: 50–60 minutes
Makes 4

The meat must be tender to use in these pasties. If you wish to take them on a picnic use 1 oz. LESS fat in the pastry. This makes it less fragile and so less likely to break when being carried. If using canned meat, shorten the cooking time to approximately 35 minutes.

10 oz. short crust pastry, *page 184*
6 oz. uncooked rump steak or good quality stewing steak*

2 medium potatoes *or* equivalent in small potatoes
1 large onion
salt and pepper

dry mustard
3 tablespoons stock *or* gravy *or* water flavoured with little yeast extract
milk *or* beaten egg to glaze

* canned meat can be used instead.

1 First make the pastry.
2 Roll this out to about $\frac{1}{4}$ inch thick, then cut into four rounds about the size of a large tea-plate.
3 Cut the meat into tiny pieces and dice the potatoes and onion.
4 Mix these together, adding seasoning.
5 Put a good pile in the centre of each round of pastry and moisten with a little of the stock. Brush the edges of the pastry with water, then bring these together in the centre.
6 Press them tightly so that there is no possibility of their opening during cooking, and stand the pasties on a baking tray.
7 Brush over with either a little milk or beaten egg to give a slight glaze.
8 Bake in the centre of a hot oven (425–450°F., Gas Mark 6–7) for 25 minutes. Lower the heat to moderate (350–375°F., Gas Mark 4–5) for a further 25–35 minutes, to make sure the meat is cooked inside.

To make a *good* curry you need a varied blending of flavours, and you get this by tasting during cooking and adjusting the flavour to suit yourself. On this and the next page you will find a basic recipe, with a number of suggested flavourings.

Part of a good curry is the interesting accompaniments that go with it.
Here are some of the things you can serve:

1 Chutney — a rather sweet type.
2 Desiccated or shredded coconut.
3 A sliced banana and/or apple.
4 A few nuts.
5 Shredded carrot mixed with raisins.
6 Poppadums, obtainable from good grocers.
7 Tiny onions and gherkins.

Curried lamb with savoury rice

Preparation: 15 minutes
No delay
Cooking: 1 hour 40 minutes
Serves 4

Secret of success
Perfect rice is essential in a curry. To rinse the rice and separate the grains, put the cooked rice on to a sieve, pour cold water through the grains. Shake well, spread on a flat plate and dry in the oven. If the oven is set to very moderate, use the coolest part of the oven. See the other method of cooking rice on page 147.

1–1¼ lb. lamb, preferably from leg
salt and pepper
1 oz. flour
1–2 dessertspoons curry powder
1 onion
1 apple *or* ½ large one
half a lemon

1½ oz. dripping *or* butter
1 tablespoon chutney
pinch sugar
about ¾ pint hot stock*
1 oz. sultanas

for the savoury rice
6 oz. long grain rice

1 onion
½ oz. butter
1–2 tablespoons chopped green and red peppers

to garnish
parsley

* or water in which a chicken stock cube has been dissolved.

1 Cut up the lamb into neat pieces and dust with seasoned flour, adding the curry powder as picture 1 below.
2 Slice or chop the onion and apple, sprinkling the latter with lemon juice.
3 Fry the onion and meat in heated fat until the meat is seared.
4 Stir in the chutney, sugar, a squeeze lemon juice.
5 Add the stock gradually, stirring until the contents of the pan are well mixed as picture 2.
6 Cover the pan and lower the heat. Simmer for 10 minutes.
7 Add chopped apple, sultanas and any remaining lemon juice, see picture 3.
8 Cover pan again and continue simmering in same pan, or transfer to a casserole in a very moderate oven (325°F., Gas Mark 3). Cook for about 1½ hours.
9 *To make savoury rice:* cook washed rice in salted boiling water containing 1 small onion, until tender (see page 147 for cooking rice). Drain well.
10 Rinse rice, then reheat on a dish in a cool oven.
11 Before serving round the curry, stir in the butter and some of the chopped raw peppers.
12 Use this rice to make a border for the dish of curry.
13 Sprinkle with the remaining chopped peppers. Put the curried lamb in the middle of the dish, and garnish with sprigs of parsley.

1

2

3

Lamb curry

Other meat curries

Beef: allow 2½ hours if using raw meat.
Mutton: allow 2½ hours if using raw meat.
Veal: allow 2 hours if using raw meat.
Pork: may also be used, but add extra chutney to counteract richness of the meat.

Other foods to curry

Most curries are made in a similar way to the lamb curry above. Fish can be curried very successfully, but instead of stock add water and a squeeze of lemon. For a vegetable or egg curry, use stock and 1 teaspoon of vegetable extract. If using cooked meat, make the sauce and add meat 15 minutes before serving.

Flavourings for curry

The lamb recipe is a fairly basic simple one. You can add interest and variation to curry by using some of these ingredients:

1 Coconut: 1 dessertspoon of desiccated coconut or 1 tablespoon of fresh.
2 Dried fruits: approximately 1 dessertspoon to 1 tablespoon currants or sultanas.
3 For a sweetened flavour, add 1–2 tablespoons jam.
4 For a hotter flavour, use 1–2 teaspoons curry paste as well as curry powder. Or add ½ teaspoon powdered ginger or a little chopped crystallised ginger.
5 For a very hot flavour, put in 1 or 2 chilli peppers and remove these before serving the curry. Tie in a piece of muslin so they are easy to take out.

Glazed bacon

The difference between ham and bacon

Most of the ham one sees in shops is cured and cooked, so no confusion can arise between this and bacon, but it is possible, occasionally, to buy uncooked ham. The difference in appearance is slight — there is a 'bloom' on ham, which might be confused with a faint mould. This should not be removed under any circumstances. Technically, the difference between ham and bacon is that bacon is cured as a whole side of the pig, whereas ham — which is produced from the gammon part only — is cut away from the rest of the pig and cured by a secret process.

Green bacon
This is the less salty type of bacon which has a delicious flavour, but does not keep as well.

To roast bacon or ham

Preparation: few minutes —
soaking advisable overnight*
Cooking: see method

Choose gammon, slipper, middle gammon: back and ribs, joint top streaky

* if using a sweetcure bacon, there is no need to soak this overnight.

1 Soak the joint overnight in cold water, for roasting 'keeps in' the salt flavour.
2 While you can roast bacon for the whole of the cooking, it is much more moist and delicious if boiled (or rather simmered) for half the time.
3 Allow 20–25 minutes per lb. and 20–25 minutes over; the slight difference in timing depends on the *shape* of the joint. A rather large flat joint needs 20 minutes only, while a thicker smaller one needs a longer period for the heat to penetrate, so for a 4-lb. joint, which needs a total of 5 × 20 minutes, i.e. 1 hour 40 minutes, the best result is obtained by giving 50 minutes' simmering and 50 minutes' roasting.
4 Instructions for glazing bacon or ham are given on page 96, but, for straightforward roasting, spread a little fat over the lean part of the meat and score (cut) the fat to encourage it to crisp.
5 If roasting for *all* the time, keep the joint in a covered roaster or wrapped in foil until the last 30 minutes. Use a moderate to moderately hot oven (375–400°F., Gas Mark 5–6).

Accompaniments to bacon or ham

Serve roast bacon with new or roast potatoes — roast these in a separate tin if you have simmered the bacon (details of roasting potatoes, page 64).
A thickened gravy, using some of the stock, can be served (see page 64).
Apple sauce and sage and onion stuffing (page 80) blend well with bacon or ham, or try *Baked apple rings:* core dessert apples, but do not peel, and allow 25–30 minutes in the roasting tin.

To grill bacon and gammon

Preparation: few minutes
No delay
Cooking: see method

Choose rashers of gammon, back or streaky bacon.
First remove rinds with a sharp knife or kitchen scissors — this makes bacon easier to cook and serve. Preferably put bacon on rack of grill pan, so surplus fat drains away.

Thin rashers of bacon should be just put under a hot grill and cooked quickly on both sides.

Bacon chops, i.e. back rashers of bacon cut rather thickly, are excellent grilled and served as a main meal. They need no extra fat, but grill steadily until crisp and brown on the outside and cooked through to the middle, see page 94.

Gammon is a very lean part of bacon so brush well with melted butter. Cut the fat at ½–1-inch intervals to encourage this to crisp and brown. Put under a COOL grill, i.e. do not pre-heat the grill; this prevents the bacon from curling up. Cook steadily to make sure it is tender through to the middle. If wished, glaze by sprinkling a little brown sugar on top and returning to the grill for 1 minute.
Serve grilled bacon and gammon with grilled tomatoes, mushrooms and vegetables, or with glazed pineapple rings, halved peaches or apricots, and green salad.

To fry bacon and gammon

Preparation: few minutes
No delay
Cooking: see method

First remove the rinds with a sharp knife or kitchen scissors.

Thin rashers should be put into a frying pan and arranged so that the lean of the second rasher is on top of the fat of the first. Continue filling the pan in this way. This makes sure that the fat keeps the lean part moist.

Bacon chops, i.e. thick back rashers of bacon, should be fried steadily to make sure they are cooked through to the centre.

Gammon should have the edges scored with scissors at ½–1-inch intervals to encourage the fat to become crisp. Heat a little fat in the pan and cook steadily, turning when the underside is well cooked. DO NOT cook too quickly.

To grill or fry ham

If using uncooked ham, fry or grill as bacon or gammon.
If using cooked ham, heat gently for a few minutes only, using plenty of melted butter when grilling to keep the ham moist.

Gammon Niçoise

Preparation: 5 minutes (if using packet stuffing), plus 15 minutes if making the stuffing
2–3 hours soaking for gammon if smoked
Cooking: 45 minutes (plus 20 minutes if making stuffing as page 80)
Serves 2

The amount of gammon is enough for 2 very generous portions. You can make the same amount of stuffing and anchovies cover 4 smaller pieces of gammon.

Secret of success
Do soak gammon if smoked, otherwise this dish is too salty.

1 packet sage and onion stuffing *or* recipe, *page 80*

2 thick gammon steaks, about 8 oz. each
small can anchovies

to garnish
watercress

1 Prepare the stuffing.
2 Soak the gammon in cold water for 2–3 hours (if smoked).
3 Trim the edges with kitchen scissors and place one steak on a greased fireproof dish.
4 On this, spread half the stuffing, then place the second steak on top.
5 Cover with the rest of the stuffing.
6 Arrange the drained anchovies in a criss-cross pattern over the top.
7 Cover with foil and bake in a moderate oven (350–375°F., Gas Mark 4–5) for about 45 minutes.
8 Serve garnished with watercress.

Gammon Veronique

Preparation: 10 minutes
Cooking: 20 minutes
Serves 4

Secret of success
Pre-heat the grill, although liquid is added in this particular recipe and the grill should not be too hot.
Snipping the fat prevents it curling in cooking.

Left *Gammon veronique*
Right *Grilled bacon chops*
(see page 93)

4 gammon steaks about ½ inch thick

½ pint dry *or* sweet cider
4 oz. white *or* black grapes

1 teaspoon cornflour

1 Cut the skin from the gammon with kitchen scissors or a sharp knife.
2 Snip round the edges of the fat with kitchen scissors or cut with a knife.
3 Remove rack from the grill pan, put the gammon and most of the cider in pan.
4 Grill under a medium heat for 6 minutes on either side.
5 Meanwhile skin, halve and de-seed the grapes.
6 Add the grapes to the gammon and cider and cook, for a further 3 minutes.
7 Lift the gammon and grapes on to a hot serving dish, keep hot.
8 Blend the cornflour with the remaining cold cider, pour the hot cider (from the grill pan) into a saucepan.
9 Stir in the cornflour mixture, stir over a medium heat until thickened.
10 Spoon over the gammon or serve in a sauce boat.

Note. You can cook gammon, etc., in a frying pan or the oven if preferred.

Hawaiian gammon rashers

Preparation: 5 minutes
No delay
Cooking: nearly 30 minutes
Serves 2

Secret of success
Do not increase the number of cloves, for this would spoil the pineapple flavour.
Stir the sauce as it thickens (stages 7 and 8) to ensure a smooth result.

2 slices gammon, 1 inch .thick
small can pineapple slices
4 cloves

little corn oil
1 level teaspoon dry mustard
1 level teaspoon cornflour

to garnish
4 glacé cherries
mint leaves
parsley

1 Trim the rind from the gammon, then arrange four slices of pineapple on top.
2 Press the cloves into the gammon fat, brush with corn oil, then place in an ovenproof dish.
3 Pour over the pineapple juice from the can, and bake for 20–25 minutes near the top of a moderately hot oven (400°F., Gas Mark 5–6).
4 When cooked, remove cloves and put gammon and pineapple on a serving dish.
5 Garnish with cherries, mint leaves and parsley.
6 Keep hot.
7 Mix the mustard and cornflour to a paste with 1 tablespoon water, then add to the juices from the ovenproof dish.
8 Cook for 3 minutes on top of the stove.
9 Season and serve as an accompanying sauce.

Bacon chops with rice stuffing

Preparation: 15 minutes
No delay
Cooking: 20 minutes (plus time for cooking rice)
Serves 4

Secrets of success
Do not over-cook the rice for the stuffing, and keep this moist when heating at stage 8.

4 bacon chops (thick back rashers)
1 lettuce

for the rice stuffing
2 oz. walnuts
1 onion

1 orange
2 oz. boiled rice, *page 147*
2 oz. raisins

1 Cut the rind from the bacon chops.
2 Put the rinds into a frying pan and heat for 5 minutes.

3 Arrange the bacon chops on grid on grill pan – heat grill for 2 or 3 minutes.
4 Cook under hot grill for a few minutes on either side, to brown outside. Then lower heat for a few minutes to cook through to centre (approximately 15 minutes in all). Keep hot.

5 Meanwhile, chop walnuts on a board.
6 Grate the onion, and squeeze out orange juice.
7 Toss rice, grated onion, walnuts, and raisins in the hot bacon fat in a frying pan, see picture.
8 Add orange juice and heat gently.

9 Wash and dry lettuce for the salad, and put into a serving dish.

10 Arrange the rice mixture in a shallow dish, then put the bacon chops on top.

To boil bacon or ham

Preparation: few minutes – allow to soak overnight or for several hours in cold water*
Cooking: see method

* sweetcure bacon does not need soaking.

Boiling is really an incorrect description, for it should be stressed that the liquid must *not* boil – only simmer.
1 Put the bacon or ham into a pan and cover with cold water.
2 Bring up steadily just to boiling point.
3 Skim if necessary, and take care that the liquid does not boil, but simmer. Put a lid on the pan.
4 Vegetables can be added if desired, but generally speaking the ham stock has sufficient flavour without them.
5 Allow 20–25 minutes per lb., and 20–25 minutes over.

IN PRESSURE COOKING allow 7 minutes per lb. at 15 lb. pressure, then let pressure drop to normal at room temperature.

To skin and glaze gammon

Preparation: 10 minutes
No delay
Cooking: 30 minutes, plus time of boiling

Do not over-cook the glazed gammon, otherwise the sugar will burn.

gammon   brown sugar   few cloves

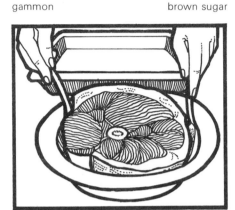

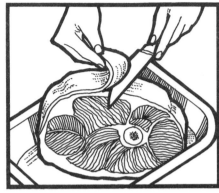

1 Lift the boiled gammon out of the pan and put into a roasting tin.

2 Slit skin at one end, then insert blade of a sharp knife under skin and cut carefully away from the fat.

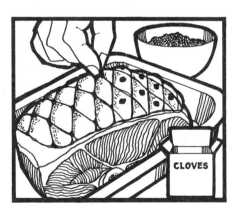

3 Sprinkle fat lightly with brown sugar. Score (cut lightly) the fat in diamond shapes. Press cloves into the fat.

4 Cook for 30 minutes in a moderate to moderately hot oven (375–400°F., Gas Mark 5–6). Serve with roast potatoes, brussels sprouts and grilled tomatoes.

Glazed gammon with cherries

Preparation: 10 minutes
No delay
Cooking: 30 minutes, plus time of boiling

If you think the vinegar in this recipe will give too 'sharp' a flavour for you, use 1 tablespoon only and substitute 1–2 tablespoons liquid from cooking the gammon.

boiled gammon
4 tablespoons brown (demerara) sugar
1–3 tablespoons dry mustard
3 tablespoons vinegar
maraschino cherries
cloves

1 Cook and skin the gammon as directed in previous recipe.
2 Score the fat surface in a criss-cross pattern to form diamond shapes.
3 Mix the sugar, mustard and vinegar to make the glaze.
4 Pat thickly over the fat surface.
5 Stud each diamond with a maraschino cherry fixed in place with a clove.
6 Put the gammon in an ovenproof dish and bake for 30 minutes in a moderate to moderately hot oven (375–400°F., Gas Mark 5–6). Baste several times with liquid from the joint and the glaze. Serve with new potatoes and peas.

To skin and glaze ham

Ham can be skinned and glazed in the same way as bacon. To give various flavours try the following:

1 Make a syrup by boiling 1 teacup pineapple or peach syrup (from can of fruit) with 1 or 2 tablespoons brown sugar. Brush all over skinned ham. Score fat, as for gammon: press raisins into fat. Bake for 30 minutes. Serve hot or cold, garnished with pineapple rings or halved peaches.
2 Make a similar syrup with cider and sugar.

To bake bacon or ham

Preparation: few minutes (slightly longer if using paste). Overnight soaking essential
Cooking: see method

Choose roasting joints as listed in the table on page 62.

Good soaking before cooking is essential, to prevent the meat tasting too salt. Sweetcure bacon does not need soaking.

1 Ham or bacon is baked either wrapped in foil, or in a flour and water paste; in this way all flavour is retained.
2 *To make the flour and water paste:* mix 1–1½ lb. flour (depending on size of joint) with enough water to make into a rolling consistency.
3 Roll out the pastry, put the joint on top and wrap the pastry round like a parcel. Seal the edges of the paste.
4 Bake in a moderately hot oven (400°F., Gas Mark 5) for 30 minutes per lb., and 30 minutes over.
5 Remove the foil or paste just before serving – the paste becomes brittle and can easily be taken off. Do not eat this.

To casserole bacon and ham

Preparation: few minutes.
Allow overnight soaking*
Cooking: see method

* sweetcure bacon does not need soaking.

Use joints given in the table on page 62 for boiling and braising. Cook these joints sufficiently slowly to make them tender.

Bacon blends very well with almost any vegetables and quite a number of fruits. These can be added during cooking if you have a very large joint.

1 Soak bacon or ham well, and put into the casserole.
2 Use water, stock or cider. Make sure you use plenty of liquid to cover the bacon and keep it moist.
3 Cover the casserole with a lid or foil during cooking.
4 Allow 35 minutes per lb., and 35 minutes over, in a very moderate oven (325–350°F., Gas Mark 3–4).
5 The liquid can be thickened, if wished, at the end of cooking, but this is not really necessary.

Vegetables that may be added: small peeled onions, carrots, peas, new or old potatoes (keep these fairly large so they do not soften too much); rings of red and green pepper.
Fruit that may be added: whole peeled apples or pears (allow about 1 hour cooking); soaked but *not* cooked dried prunes or apricots.
Herbs that may be added: a *bouquet garni* (bunch of mixed herbs); or chopped mint or parsley or chives.
Extra flavouring: may be given by using ginger ale instead of, or with, stock or cider, or by adding ½ teaspoon ground ginger or cinnamon to the stock.

Bacon and nut ring

Preparation: 20 minutes
No delay
Cooking: 1½ hours
Serves 4

The small quantity of peanuts in this recipe gives a pleasant texture to the dish.

3 oz. lard	1 small onion	1 egg
8 oz. flour (with plain flour use 2 teaspoons baking powder)	1 oz. salted peanuts, chopped	little milk
6 oz. raw *or* cooked bacon, chopped	salt and pepper	2 tablespoons brown raspings (toasted brown breadcrumbs)

1 Rub the lard into the flour and baking powder, if used, and then add the bacon, grated onion, nuts and seasoning.
2 Mix to a soft dough with the beaten egg and milk.
3 Well grease a 1-pint ring mould, or pudding basin, and coat this inside with brown raspings, turning upside down to remove the surplus crumbs.
4 Carefully fill with the dough, cover with foil and steam fairly rapidly for 1½ hours.
5 Turn out, and serve with brown gravy and green vegetables.

Cooking sausages

Ready-made beef or pork sausages have to conform to high standards of hygiene and meat content. Even so, it is important that uncooked sausages (or sausage meat) are cooked as soon as possible after purchase.

To grill or fry sausages

Preparation: few minutes
No delay
Cooking: 8–15 minutes
(depending on size)

While you can prick sausages as a precaution against skins bursting, today many sausages are in a skin that does not break in cooking, or are skinless. *If you prick them, use a fine-pronged fork gently.*

One has about 8 large sausages to 1 lb., 16 chipolata sausages to 1 lb., and about 32 tiny cocktail sausages to 1 lb.

To fry
1 Heat about 1–1½ oz. fat in a pan.
2 Put in sausages and cook until brown on the underside — turn with a fish slice (or kitchen tongs are ideal).
3 Cook on the surface until evenly brown.
4 Lift on to a hot dish.

To grill
1 Heat the grill for 1 minute only.
2 Put sausages on the grid of the grill pan.
3 Grill until brown, then turn round and continue cooking until an even brown all over.
4 Lift on to a hot dish.

Note. Sausages may be frozen — freeze separated, on a flat dish, so they do not 'stick' together; when hard, wrap neatly. Can be cooked from frozen state.

Always allow adequate cooking time — it is unwise to undercook these.

To bake sausages

Preparation: few minutes
No delay
Cooking: 20–30 minutes
(depending on size)

Prick sausages as above.

1 Grease the bottom of a baking or roasting tin.
2 Put in the sausages.
3 Bake in the centre of a moderately hot oven (400°F., Gas Mark 5) until crisp and golden brown. They should not need turning round.

Note. If you prefer to cook the sausages towards the top of the oven, allow a few minutes *less* cooking time. You may find they need turning.

Bacon and sausage plait

Preparation: 25 minutes
No delay
Cooking: 30–40 minutes
Serves 4–6

Secret of success
Slitting and overlapping the strips of pastry, stages 4 and 5, makes sure steam can escape and keeps the pastry crisp.

8 oz. streaky *or* back rashers bacon
2 hard-boiled eggs

12 oz. flaky *or* short crust pastry, *pages 184, 193*
salt and pepper

8 oz. pork sausage meat
1 teaspoon powdered sage *or* basil
beaten egg *for glazing*

1 Chop the bacon and the hard-boiled eggs.
2 Roll out the pastry to a 10-inch square.
3 Mix all ingredients together and place down the centre, leaving equal sides of uncovered pastry.
4 Cut the sides of the pastry obliquely in ½-inch strips (rather like fish fins) and brush with beaten egg.
5 Lift alternate strips over the sausage mixture, to form a roll resembling a plait.
6 Brush with egg and sprinkle with very little salt.
7 Bake in a hot oven (425–450°F., Gas Mark 6–7) for about 30–40 minutes.
This is delicious hot or cold with green salad.

Sausage casserole

Preparation: 10 minutes
No delay
Cooking: 45 minutes
Serves 4

Secret of success
Use a sharp cooking apple to give a pleasant 'bite' to this dish.

1 large onion
1 cooking apple
1 tomato, skinned
8–12 oz. skinless sausages

½ oz. lard
salt and pepper
scant ¼ pint water

medium can condensed cream of tomato *or* mushroom soup
potato crisps

1 Chop the onion, slice the apple and the skinned tomato.
2 Fry the sausages in the hot lard until golden brown on both sides.
3 Remove from the pan, then fry the onion until soft and golden brown.
4 Arrange the sausages, onion and apple in layers in a greased casserole, seasoning well between each layer.
5 Top with tomato slices and add the water and tomato (or mushroom) soup.
6 Cover and cook in the centre of a moderate oven (375°F., Gas Mark 4) for 45 minutes.
7 Serve with potato crisps — open the packet, tip on to a warmed baking tin and heat for a minute or two in the oven.

Baker's porkpot

Preparation: 15 minutes
Cooking: 1¾ hours
Serves 4–6

This makes use of cheaper pieces of pork in an interesting way. The pork and vegetable mixture can be prepared beforehand and reheated with the added mustard-covered bread.

1¼ lb. sparerib *or* shoulder of pork
8 oz. large pork sausages
1 onion
3 carrots
3 sticks celery
1 tablespoon flour
1 teaspoon soy sauce
1 pint chicken stock *or* water and stock cube
pinch dried rosemary
salt and pepper
for the topping
7–8 slices French bread
French mustard

1 Dice the pork and fry with the sausages until lightly browned.
2 Slice the sausages, then put with the pork into a 4-pint shallow casserole.
3 Chop the vegetables and fry in the remaining pork fat, add to the meat.
4 Blend the flour with the soy sauce and stock, or water and stock cube.
5 Bring to the boil and cook until thickened, pour over meat, etc., adding rosemary, salt and pepper.
6 Cover the casserole and cook for 45 minutes in the centre of a very moderate oven (325–350°F., Gas Mark 3–4).
7 Spread bread with mustard and put on top of the meat, etc. (mustard-side uppermost), then continue cooking for another 45 minutes; do not cover the casserole.

Baker's pork pot

Savoury lattice flan

Savoury lattice flan

Preparation: 30 minutes
Cooking: 40 minutes
Serves 4–6

Secret of success
Drain the fried foods well so they do not make the pastry greasy, see stages 3 and 4. Serve hot or cold with crisp salad.

6 oz. short crust *or* flaky pastry, *pages 184 and 193*
8 oz. pork sausage meat
pinch mixed herbs
1 tablespoon flour
1 oz. lard
1 large onion
2 large tomatoes
2 tablespoons brown table sauce *or* chutney
to glaze
1 egg *or* egg yolk

1. Roll out the pastry and use most of this to line a 7-inch sandwich tin, or a plain flan ring, on an upturned baking tray.
2 Mix the sausage meat and herbs, form into 12 flat cakes on a floured board.
3 Heat the lard and fry the cakes until brown on either side, drain.
4 Fry the thinly sliced onion and tomatoes in the remaining fat until soft.
5 Put the sausage meat cakes and vegetables into the pastry case, add the sauce or chutney, spreading evenly over the top.
6 Roll out the remaining pastry thinly, cut into narrow strips, then arrange on top of the filling in a lattice design and brush with the egg or egg yolk.
7 Bake in the centre of a hot oven (425–450°F., Gas Mark 6–7) for 15 minutes.
8 Lower the heat to very moderate, cook for a further 10–15 minutes.

Toad-in-the-hole

This popular English dish is an excellent combination of meat and a light batter mixture. Sausages, halved kidneys or chops may be used.

Yorkshire toad-in-the-hole

Preparation: 10–15 minutes
Allow batter to stand
Cooking: 40 minutes
Serves 4

Secrets of success
Make certain the meat, sausages, or whatever you are using, are REALLY HOT before pouring in the batter – or this will be heavy instead of light. Always keep the oven to a high temperature at beginning of cooking period.

for the batter
4 oz. plain flour, salt
1 large egg
½ pint milk
for the 'toad'
2 oz. lard
4 large pork sausages
4 streaky rashers
made-mustard

1 Sieve the flour with a pinch of salt into a basin, and drop the egg into the centre. Mix to a smooth batter with the milk.
2 Leave to stand for at least 2 hours.
3 Melt the lard in the roasting tin and wrap each sausage in a rasher which has been stretched with a knife and spread with a little made-mustard.
4 Place in the fat and cook for about 5 minutes, in a hot to very hot oven (450–475°F., Gas Mark 7–8).
5 Remove tin from oven, turn over the sausages and pour over the batter.
6 Replace in the hot oven, cook for approximately 35 minutes. Lower the heat to moderate after 20 minutes.

99

Cooking minced meat

Raw minced meat can be used in many ways — when choosing minced meat make sure it looks moist and not too fat.

Many recipes suggest frying minced meat first, before adding liquid — but *do not over-cook* as this dries the meat badly. Personally I prefer the method in the next recipe, i.e. adding the meat to the liquid (sauce, etc.).

When simmering the meat, break it into pieces once or twice at the start of cooking, or it forms solid 'lumps' which are most unpalatable.

Tomato mince

Preparation: 5–8 minutes
No delay
Cooking: 40–50 minutes
Serves 4–5

1 oz. lard *or* fat
1 medium onion, finely chopped

medium can condensed cream of tomato soup
1 lb. minced beef

1 rounded tablespoon oatmeal
salt
pinch of cayenne pepper

1 Melt the lard or fat, then gently fry the onion until tender.
2 Pour in the tomato soup, then add the meat, oatmeal, salt and pepper. Break up the lumps of meat carefully in the early stages of cooking.
3 Cover and simmer gently for 30–40 minutes.
4 Serve with roast or mashed potatoes.*

* if using mashed potato, pipe or fork this round the edge of the dish as an attractive edging.

Mince collops

Preparation: 10 minutes
No delay
Cooking: 1 hour
Serves 2

This gives a more moist mixture than if the meat is fried first of all; stir well to break up lumps at stage 5.
If adding rice (see Variations), make sure there is enough liquid in the sauce before adding this.

1 onion
1 oz. fat
½ oz. flour

$\frac{3}{8}$ pint stock *or* water with beef stock cube
8 oz. minced beef
salt and pepper

2 slices bread

to garnish
parsley

1 Chop the onion finely.
2 Fry in hot fat until tender, but not brown.
3 Stir in the flour and cook for several minutes.
4 Gradually add the stock, bring to the boil and cook until thick.
5 Stir in the meat and seasoning and cook steadily, breaking the pieces of meat with a fork or spoon for the first 10 minutes.
6 Simmer for the rest of the time, stirring occasionally.
7 When the meat is almost ready to serve, toast the bread and cut into triangles.
8 Arrange toast on a hot dish with meat in the centre.
9 Garnish with parsley.

Variations
1 Add 1 or 2 teaspoons curry powder to the flour. Stir in a few sultanas and 1 teaspoon chutney.
2 Add 2 sliced skinned tomatoes to the onion.
3 Use just over ½ pint stock or water, and add 1 oz. long grain rice, 30 minutes before serving.

Hamburger baps

Preparation: 7–10 minutes
No delay
Cooking: 40 minutes

This mixture is enough to fill 4 rolls, or use it for 2 hot rolls and save the rest as a cold filling for 2 plain buttered rolls to take for a packed meal.

Secret of success
Stir well at stages 2, 3, 4 and 7 to keep the mixture from burning. It is important that it becomes stiff.

1 medium onion
1 oz. lard
8 oz. minced beef

½ level teaspoon curry powder
1 level tablespoon flour

small can condensed vegetable soup
salt and pepper
4 baps *or* soft round rolls

1 Chop the onion very finely.
2 Melt the lard in a small saucepan and gently cook the onion until tender.
3 Stir in the minced beef and curry powder.
4 Cook until brown.
5 Sprinkle the flour over the meat, stir and cook until flour is brown.
6 Add the can of vegetable soup and seasoning.
7 Stir and cover.
8 Simmer gently until the meat is tender (approximately 30 minutes), and until a fairly thick mixture.
9 Split the baps, toast the cut sides and fill with the hamburger mixture. Serve at once.

Hamburger baps

To carve meat

Beef: carve thin large slices ACROSS the joint. Where sirloin of beef is cooked on the bone you should first remove the backbone or chine, then cut the first slices along the bone. Next turn the joint and cut slices at right angles from the bone.

Lamb or mutton: cut thickish slices DOWNWARDS, but with certain joints it is best to carve in the following way:
Saddle: cut very long slices first across the centre of the joint, cutting these downwards. Next cut slices from either end of the saddle, finally cut rather slanting from the remainder of the joint.
Shoulder: here one follows the contour of the bone and cuts slices round this. If the end of the shoulder bone is held in a napkin it gives one a firmer hold.

Pork: cut shoulder of pork like lamb, and also the leg. Loin of pork should be easy to cut, since the skin is scored before cooking to give good crackling and the butcher generally saws through the bones. Cut slices downwards.

Veal: the method of carving depends on the joint. Legs or shoulder are carved downwards or round the bone like lamb, loin is cut downwards into chops, fillet is carved across as beef.

THE HEAT OF THE JOINT QUICKLY BLUNTS A CARVING KNIFE – SO IF YOU ARE CARVING FOR A LOT OF PEOPLE IT IS WISE TO USE TWO KNIVES ALTERNATELY.

The correct way to carve pork

Cold meat dishes

Sliced cold meat with salad is one of the easiest of meals. Suggestions for serving cold meats will be found in the *Salad section* (page 201), but here are a few recipes for more unusual cold meats.

Beef brawn

Preparation: 10–12 minutes
No delay
Cooking: 2–2½ hours
Serves 4–6

Try making this brawn with a calf's head or lamb's head and only 8 oz. steak. Follow directions for preparing calf's head in recipe opposite, stages 1 and 2, do not remove brains. Simmer with the steak until tender. Remove the meat and continue as stages 5–9.

Beef brawn

1¼–1½ lb. stewing steak	2 carrots	1 beef stock cube
2 pig's trotters, *optional*	salt and pepper	2 level teaspoons powdered
1 onion	1 pint water	gelatine, *optional*

1 Cut the meat into neat pieces.
2 Leave the vegetables whole.
3 Put all the ingredients (except gelatine) into a pan, put on the lid.
4 Simmer gently for 2–2½ hours until the meat is tender.
5 Drain the meat, pack into a basin.
6 If you like the rather rich meat from pig's trotters, cut this away from the bones and mix with the steak.
7 Boil the remaining stock in an OPEN pan so it evaporates until only ¼ pint is left. If you do not use pig's trotters, dissolve 2 level teaspoons powder gelatine in the hot ¼ pint stock.
8 Strain over the meat.
9 Put a plate over the top with a weight on the plate. This pressing down ensures a good shape to the brawn.

Galantine of beef

Preparation: 15 minutes
Allow to cool before coating
Cooking: 1½ hours
Serves 4–6

Secrets of success
Keep the galantine mixture moist at stage 3. You can add 1–2 tablespoons extra stock, sherry or thin cream for a softer consistency.
Make certain the aspic jelly *has* stiffened slightly at stage 9, otherwise it will run off the galantine.

1 oz. dripping	1 lb. beef minced finely *or*	½ pint aspic jelly
1 oz. flour	8 oz. minced beef and	
¼ pint stock *or* water with	8 oz. sausage meat	*to garnish*
little beef extract added	1 oz. fine breadcrumbs	mixed vegetables
	1 egg, chopped	

1 Heat the dripping in a pan, stir in the flour and cook for several minutes.
2 Add the cold stock gradually, bring to the boil and cook gently until thickened.
3 Mix in all the other ingredients except the aspic jelly and mixed vegetables.
4 Put into a greased tin or mould and steam for 1½ hours. If no mould is available, form into a neat roll and wrap in greased paper or foil, then a cloth.
5 It is very important to cover with greased paper to keep the galantine as dry as possible when cooking.
6 Turn out carefully and allow to cool.
7 Coat with aspic jelly.

To coat galantine with aspic jelly
8 Make jelly. You can make this up from aspic jelly crystals — use 1 dessertspoon to ½ pint boiling water.
9 Allow to cool, and when just beginning to set, spread over the cold galantine with a palette knife dipped in hot water.
10 Garnish with brightly coloured pieces of vegetables, placing in position before the jelly is quite firm. Turn out and arrange sliced tomatoes round the dish.

Offal

It is impossible to generalise about cooking offal since each type varies, but do not make the mistake of avoiding offal, for it provides excellent meals — in some cases very cheaply.

Offal buying guide

Brains: calves', pig's or sheep's brains can be served in thick sauce on toast or as sauce. They are very nutritious.

Feet or trotters: calf and pig feet contain a great deal of gelatine, and are used to help set moulds and brawn.

Head: the head of a calf is considered the most delicate in flavour, but both sheep and pig heads can be used in exactly the same way. For recipe see this page.

Heart: the small heart of sheep, calf or pig can be stuffed and roasted. Ox heart is inclined to be tough but can be casseroled slowly in a thick brown sauce. Halve the heart, fill with sage and onion stuffing, wrap in buttered foil, cook for $1\frac{1}{4}$ hours in a moderately hot oven (400°F., Gas Mark 5).

Kidneys: these can be used in a number of ways, as a savoury dish by themselves, fried with bacon, or served on toast as a savoury. The kidneys from pig, calf or lamb are all very tender and can be cooked fairly quickly. All that is needed is to remove the gristle and skin, toss in seasoned flour and fry in butter for 10 minutes. Ox kidney, however, is much tougher and should be used in recipes with prolonged cooking.

Liver: this is a very important food and a rich source of food values, particularly for young children and invalids. Calves' liver is of the highest quality. Liver becomes tough by over-cooking, so fry or grill for 6–7 minutes only, using plenty of fat.

Tail: oxtail is used in soups and stews, or provides a first class meal (page 106).

Tongue: small tongues from calf, sheep or pig can be used in the same way as ox tongue. Recipes are given for cooking and pressing these on page 105. When boiled and skinned, tongue can also be heated in brown or Madeira sauce, and served with vegetables as a hot meal.

Tripe: whilst many people dislike tripe, it is a first class food and very economical. It comes from the stomach of the animal. (A recipe for cooking it is on page 105.)

Calf's head with brain sauce

Preparation: 20 minutes
No delay
Cooking: 3 hours
Serves up to 8

An excellent cold weather dish, this takes time in preparation, but it is well worthwhile.
To serve this dish, arrange the meat from the head on a hot dish. Pour over the brain sauce and garnish with croûtons of crisp toast. Pig's or sheep's head can be used instead of calf's head.

| 1 calf's head | herbs | 1 bay leaf |
| parsley | | |

1 Split the head down the centre.
2 Wash carefully in cold water and remove the brains.
3 Put the head, parsley, mixed herbs and bay leaf into a pan of cold water, just cover the head.
4 Bring just to the boil and remove any scum.
5 Put on the lid and simmer gently for about 3 hours.
6 When it is done, take out the head and dice the meat neatly.
7 The tongue can be served separately, or cut into neat fingers and added to the cooked meat when serving.

Brain sauce

| brain from calf's head | salt and pepper | $\frac{1}{2}$ pint white sauce, *page 143* |
| vinegar *or* lemon juice | | |

1 Soak the brain in cold water, to which should be added a few drops of vinegar or lemon juice. This will whiten it.
2 Simmer for 15 minutes in salted water.
3 Strain, chop and add to the white sauce; season well.

103

Braised kidneys and rice

Preparation: 10 minutes
No delay
Cooking: 25 minutes
Serves 4

This is a good way of turning a comparatively small quantity of lamb kidneys into a sustaining meal.

1 onion
1 tomato
2 oz. fat *or* butter
1 oz. flour

generous ½ pint stock *or* water and chicken stock cube
8 small lamb kidneys

seasoning
little red wine, optional
3 oz. boiled long grain rice, *page 147*

1 Chop the onion; skin and chop the tomato.
2 Fry the onion and tomato in hot fat until soft.
3 Stir in the flour. Cook for several minutes, then gradually add the stock or water and chicken stock cube.
4 Bring to the boil and simmer, stirring the sauce until smooth and thickened.
5 Add the halved or whole kidneys, with skin and gristle removed. Season well
6 Simmer steadily for nearly 20 minutes, adding a little red wine if wished.
7 Serve on a bed of hot boiled rice.

Fried and grilled kidneys

Preparation: few minutes
No delay
Cooking: 10 minutes
Serves 2

This makes a good breakfast dish. Pig or lamb kidneys are both excellent for frying or grilling.

4 kidneys
salt and pepper

½ oz. flour

2 oz. margarine *or* butter

To fry
1 Halve the kidneys — remove the gristle.
2 Toss the meat in seasoned flour.
3 Fry steadily in hot margarine or butter.
4 Serve on toast, with fried bacon and vegetables.

To grill
1 Prepare as for frying, except that the kidneys will need no flouring.
2 Brush with plenty of melted butter.
3 Grill steadily.
4 Serve with grilled mushrooms, tomatoes, etc.

Fried and grilled liver

Preparation: few minutes
No delay
Cooking: 4—8 minutes

Choose calves', lamb's or pig's liver. Calves' liver is the most expensive and the most tender.

Secret of success
Never over-cook or it becomes hard and dry, instead of moist and tender.

liver
salt and pepper

flour
bacon

fat, *optional*

1 Coat the liver with a very little seasoned flour, then fry with the bacon, adding a little extra fat if necessary; or brush with melted butter and grill.
2 Allow 2—4 minutes' cooking on either side, depending on thickness.
3 Serve as soon as possible after cooking.

Pig and lamb tongues

Preparation: few minutes.
No delay as no soaking required
Cooking: 1¼—1½ hours

Allow 1 pig's tongue for 2 people or 1 lamb's tongue per person.

These are very tender and ideal for small families.
Pig or lamb tongues are prepared and cooked in the same way as ox tongue. You rarely will find that a butcher sells them salted, so add seasoning while cooking. They take about 1¼—1½ hours to cook; press as ox tongue.

Calves tongues

Preparation: few minutes
No delay as no soaking required
Cooking: 1—1¼ hours

One calf's tongue serves 2—3.

These have a very delicate taste, and can be cooked in the same way as ox tongue, but will need seasoning during cooking as they are rarely sold salted. They take about 1—1¼ hours to cook. Press as ox tongue.

Pressed ox tongue

Preparation: few minutes. Some hours necessary for soaking, and standing when cooked
Cooking: 2–3 hours
Serves about 12–18

Ask for a salted tongue and soak for several hours, or overnight, in cold water. If it is not possible to obtain a salted tongue, then cook *at once*, adding salt to taste — the colour is never as good, though, as when salted or pickled.

ox tongue	1 carrot	6–8 peppercorns
1 onion	1 bay leaf	1 level teaspoon powdered gelatine

1 Put the tongue into cold water, bring to the boil and add the onion, carrot, bay leaf and peppercorns.
2 Simmer very gently in a covered pan, allowing 40 minutes per lb.
3 At the end of this time, lift the tongue out of the stock and allow to cool until you can handle it. Discard the vegetables.
4 Meanwhile, boil the stock in an open pan until there is only just over ¼ pint left.

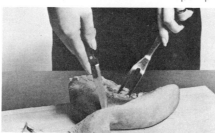

5 Remove the skin from tongue and any tiny bones at the root of the tongue.

6 Lift into a round cake tin, saucepan or dish, curling it round to give a good shape. It needs to be a fairly tight fit.

7 Dissolve the powdered gelatine in the stock and strain over the tongue.

8 Cover with foil, put a plate or weights over top to press into shape, leave until cold.

9 Remove the weight and foil, dip base of tin or saucepan into hot water for ½ minute to loosen the jelly round the meat, and turn out; garnish with salad.

Creamed tripe and onions

Preparation: 10 minutes
Allow time for blanching tripe
Cooking: just about 1¼ hours
Serves 4

Secret of success
Blanch as directed.
Season the sauce very well.

1½ lb. tripe	salt and pepper	*to garnish*
½ pint milk	1 oz. flour	chopped parsley
2 large onions	1 oz. butter *or* margarine	paprika

1 Cut the tripe into neat pieces. Blanch as the directions for creamed sweetbreads, stage 2 (page 106).
2 Put the tripe with ¼ pint milk, ½ pint water, the thinly sliced onions and seasoning into a pan, and simmer gently until tender; this takes about 1 hour.
3 Blend the flour with the remainder of the milk, add to the tripe, bring to the boil and cook until smooth.
4 Add the butter or margarine and a little extra seasoning.
5 Garnish with chopped parsley and paprika.

Oxtail

Preparation: 15 minutes
No delay unless removing fat —
see method
Cooking: 3½ hours
Serves 4–6

Secret of success
This is one of the best stews
possible. Its only disadvantage
is the rather rich, 'fatty' flavour.
It is a good idea to cook as the
method, allow to cool, leave for
24 hours, then remove the fat
and reheat.

Braised oxtail

1 large oxtail *or* 2 medium	1 beef stock cube	2 carrots
1 oz. flour	bunch of mixed herbs *or*	1 turnip
salt and pepper	pinch of dried herbs	2 oz. peas
1 oz. fat	2 sticks celery	*to garnish*
1 pint water	1 onion	chopped parsley

1 Ask the butcher to cut the oxtail into pieces.
2 Coat the meat in flour, which should be well seasoned.
3 Melt the fat in a pan and fry the oxtail until pale golden on both sides. Remove any fat from the pan.
4 Add the water and stock cube, bring to the boil and stir until slightly thickened.
5 Put in the fresh herbs, tied in muslin, or pinch of dried herbs, and the chopped vegetables.
6 Simmer in a covered saucepan for just over 3 hours. The peas should be added towards the end of the cooking period.
7 Serve garnished with parsley.

To vary
Add cooked or canned haricot beans towards the end of the cooking period.

Creamed sweetbreads

Preparation: 10–15 minutes.
Allow 1 hour for soaking, then
time to blanch sweetbreads
Cooking: 25–30 minutes
Serves 4

Secret of success
Sweetbreads are one of the most
digestible of all meals; do not
omit to 'blanch', see stage 2.

12 oz.–1 lb. sweetbreads	little lemon juice	1 tablespoon milk
3 tablespoons white stock *or*	salt and pepper	2 tablespoons thick *or*
white stock and milk	1 oz. flour	thin cream

1 First soak the sweetbreads in cold water for 1 hour.
2 Put into a saucepan, cover with more cold water, then bring the water to the boil and throw it away. This process is known as 'blanching' the sweetbreads, and whitens them.
3 Return the sweetbreads to the saucepan with the liquid, lemon juice and seasoning. Simmer gently for about 15–20 minutes.
4 Remove the sweetbreads, and take off any skin.
5 Blend the flour with cold milk, add to the stock, then bring to the boil and cook until thickened.
6 Stir in the cream, return the meat to the sauce and heat.

Fried sweetbreads

Preparation: 10–15 minutes
Allow 1 hour for soaking
Cooking: 25–30 minutes
Serves 4

This method of cooking sweetbreads disguises the white,
somewhat unattractive
appearance of this very delicious
meat.

12 oz.–1 lb. sweetbreads	crisp breadcrumbs	*to garnish*
salt	butter *for frying*	chopped parsley
1 egg		

1 Soak and blanch the sweetbreads as described above, then simmer in salted water for 15–20 minutes.
2 Skin and, if wished, press between 2 plates, then dry well, brush with egg and roll in crisp breadcrumbs.
3 Heat the butter and fry the coated sweetbreads until golden brown.
4 Drain on kitchen paper; serve garnished with chopped parsley. An excellent accompaniment is tartare sauce, page 207.

Canned and frozen meats

Canned meat has become of very much higher quality during recent years. The following are well worth keeping in store:

Bacon: pre-packed bacon in polythene bags keeps longer as a standby. Once the pack is opened, though, the bacon must be used in the normal time.

Corned beef: canned corned beef can be served hot or cold with salad. There are several recipes for this in the book.

Ham: small cans of ham or chopped ham can be used in place of the fresh variety.

Steak: cans of stewed steak are the basis of quick and easy meals. You will find ways of varying them below.

Tongue: ox tongue or small cans of calves' tongue can be served hot or cold. Be careful with this meat when once the can is opened, as it deteriorates very quickly.

Frozen meats and chickens: these should be defrosted at room temperature before cooking. The ready-chopped chicken saves time and can be used in a variety of ways. Ready prepared steak or hamburgers (frozen meat cakes) that need just a few minutes' cooking are also useful.

Steak au gratin

Preparation: 8 minutes
No delay
Cooking: 15 minutes
Serves 2

The crisp topping is a pleasant contrast to the tender steak.

medium can stewed steak   2 oz. soft breadcrumbs   2 oz. grated cheese

1 Heat the canned steak steadily for about 10 minutes.
2 Tip into a pie dish.
3 Cover the top with a layer of breadcrumbs and grated cheese.
4 Brown under the grill for 5 minutes.

Curried steak

Preparation: 10 minutes
No delay
Cooking: 15–20 minutes
Serves 2

Secret of success
This should not be over-cooked – canned meat is very tender.

1 onion   2–4 teaspoons curry powder   1 tablespoon chutney
1 oz. fat   medium can stewed steak   1 tablespoon sultanas

1 Fry the sliced onion in the fat.
2 Add the curry powder and cook for a few minutes.
3 Stir the canned steak into the onion mixture.
4 Bring to the boil and heat the steak gently for 10 minutes.
5 Add the chutney and sultanas to the sauce.

Hasty goulash

Preparation: 5 minutes
No delay
Cooking: 15 minutes
Serves 2

Paprika, or paprika pepper as it often is called, is NOT hot; it is a sweet flavouring.

medium can stewed steak   ½–1 tablespoon paprika   1 tablespoon water
small can tomatoes

1 Put the steak into a pan and heat for 10 minutes.
2 Tip the tomatoes in with the steak, together with the paprika blended with the water.
3 Heat for a further 5 minutes.

Steak and marrow

Preparation: 10 minutes
No delay
Cooking: 15–20 minutes
Serves 3–4

This makes an interesting meal. Other vegetables (such as peppers or aubergines) could be stuffed in the same way.

1 marrow   medium can stewed steak   1 oz. butter *or* margarine
salt and pepper   2 oz. soft breadcrumbs

1 Peel a small marrow and cut into rings; remove the seeds.
2 Steam or boil until just tender, season lightly.
3 Meanwhile, heat the canned steak.
4 Strain the marrow rings and put on to a heat-resistant dish.
5 Top each ring with steak and breadcrumbs.
6 Dot with a little butter or margarine and brown under the grill.

Steak and dumplings

Preparation: 10 minutes
No delay
Cooking: 20 minutes

1 Heat the canned steak with 1 pint water.
2 Make tiny dumplings by adding 1 oz. shredded suet to 2 oz. self-raising flour and a pinch of salt. Mix with water to a rolling consistency.
3 Roll into tiny balls, drop into the liquid and cook for 15 minutes.

Using canned soups as sauces

Canned soups make excellent, easy sauces.

Asparagus: an excellent basis for simmering veal and chicken.
Consommé: excellent for heating beef.
Chicken: dilute with milk and use for reheating slices of cooked ham or veal.
Mushroom: an ideal sauce for veal or pork.
Tomato: a most versatile soup that can be used as a sauce for stewing beef, lamb, veal or bacon.

Dilute concentrated soup for long cooking, to prevent evaporation making the liquid too thick.

Veal birds

Preparation: 12 minutes
No delay
Cooking: 1¾ hours
Serves 4

Colour picture, opposite

1 lb. veal, sliced very thinly	salt and pepper	*to garnish*
stuffing (*as for beef olives, page 68*)	1 oz. flour	olives
	2 oz. margarine	mushrooms
	can condensed tomato soup	pickled walnuts
		fried bread

1 Flatten the slices of veal.
2 Fill rolls of veal with stuffing, secure with cocktail sticks or string.

3 Mix salt and pepper with flour on a plate, and coat the rolls of veal in this seasoned flour.

4 Fry in a little hot fat until golden brown all round.
5 Dilute the can of soup with an equal amount of water.
6 Put veal olives into casserole, cover with the tomato liquid. Put lid on the casserole.

7 Cook for just over 1½ hours in centre of a very moderate oven, or for 1 hour in the pan.
8 Garnish with olives, fried mushrooms, and — for an unusual touch — pickled walnuts on fried bread. Coat with the tomato sauce. Or serve with broccoli spears, Duchesse potatoes and garnish with cooked mixed vegetables, as colour picture, opposite.

Veal birds

Wise buying of poultry

You will find that a little knowledge in buying poultry is a very valuable thing. It may sometimes be worth your while to look around several shops, for poultry varies a great deal in price at certain times of the year. For example, just before Christmas roasting chickens are very expensive because they are being fattened up for the traditional meal, and you will be well advised, therefore, to look for a boiling fowl or a young chicken that can be fried, grilled or roasted.

Good quality poultry is firm and, if the heads are left on, the beak should still look quite bright in colour and the combs a good clear red.

When buying a duck or goose do not choose one that is obviously very fatty, for this is wasteful.

Look out for birds with good solid breast meat, for this is more economical to cut.

Poultry buying and cooking guide

	Method of Cooking	Timing	Accompaniments
Chicken			
Large roasting chickens or capons	Roast	Allow 15–20 minutes for each lb. and 15–20 minutes over. If very large allow longer time, if smaller and not very fat shorter time (*see page 113*)	Thick gravy; veal stuffing; bread sauce; sausages; bacon rolls; green salad; green vegetables; roast or other potatoes
Young chickens	Roast	15 minutes per lb. and 15 minutes over (*see page 113*)	Thick gravy, bread sauce; fried crumbs (*page 124*). No stuffing; other accompaniments as capon
Frozen chickens	Roast, fry, grill	As fresh chicken	As fresh chicken
Very young spring chickens	Grill or fry	Allow approx. 20 minutes	Thick gravy or tomato sauce; grilled or fried mushrooms or tomatoes, or as Chicken Maryland (*page 120*)
Fowl	Boil	About 3 hours (*page 122*)	Boiled rice; creamy white sauce (*page* 122) or other sauces
	Casserole or slow roast	About 3 hours (*see page 117*)	As roast chicken, except impossible to roast potatoes when cooking poultry by this method
Turkey			
Small bird under 12 lb.	Roast	Allow 15 minutes per lb. and 15 minutes over: weigh with stuffing in	As chicken, or serve with cranberry sauce
Large bird over 12 lb.	Roast	Allow only 12 minutes per lb. for extra weight over 12 lb.	Chestnut, forcemeat or giblet stuffing
Duck			
Young bird	Roast	15 minutes per lb. and 15 minutes over	Thick gravy; sage and onion stuffing; apple sauce; orange salad
Older bird	Casserole	2½ hours (*see page 122*)	Boiled chestnuts; onions; olives
Goose			
Young bird	Roast	15 minutes per lb. and 15 minutes over	Thick gravy; sage and onion stuffing; apple sauce; green salad
Older goose	Slow roast	*See page 117*	As above
Guinea fowl			
When young	Roast	As chicken	As chicken
Older	Casserole	As chicken	As chicken

Frozen poultry

There is a great deal of frozen poultry on the market today and since it is prime quality it is worth buying. Best results are obtained if the poultry is allowed to thaw out gradually. Do not defrost by immersing in hot water, and do not cook when it is frozen.

Quantities of poultry to allow

Chicken
Really large chickens give 6–8 portions and should be carved in slices.
A smaller chicken gives 4–5 portions. You can either carve in slices, or divide the bird into two and serve two wing and breast portions and two leg portions. For very small or spring chickens, split in two.

Turkey
A large turkey can be calculated at 12 oz. per person, as you get a greater proportion of meat than bone on the bird.
With a smaller turkey you may have to allow just a little more than this. Never attempt to give people joints of turkey. One carves and serves light and dark meat.

Duck
A large duck is generally assumed to give 4 portions, but this can be rather disappointing sometimes as the breast of a duck, even a seemingly large bird, can look big and yet have relatively little meat. You are safe in assuming that it will give 3 good portions and you may be lucky and get 4. Give breast and wing as one portion, leg as another, and do not try to carve a duck into slices. A small duck cuts into 2 portions.

Goose
Again this can be very deceptive in that often a goose has a very small breast. Allow approximately 1 lb. per person.

Guinea fowl
Serve like chicken.

To prepare poultry for cooking

A great deal of the poultry one buys today is already prepared. If, however, you are given poultry still with the head on, and undrawn, i.e. the giblets, etc., not removed from the body, it is not a particularly difficult job to draw and truss it as directed.
The weight of the bird is very important in cooking, and if you have no big scales make sure the poulterer gives you the weight *when trussed*. Remember in the case of fresh (not frozen) poultry, you will be charged for the weight with the head on, and you may be surprised what a drop in weight results when the bird is trussed. It is the trussed weight that determines the cooking time. As stressed, frozen poultry MUST be defrosted before being cooked. Wash and dry the poultry well.

How to draw poultry or game
1 First cut off the feet, and, if necessary, draw the sinews from the legs.
2 Hold the bird by the legs and singe, if desired.
3 Cut off the head, leaving about 3 inches of neck.
4 Insert a small pointed knife at the end of the spine and split up the skin of the neck. Pull away loose skin, then cut off neck close to the windpipe.
5 Cut round the vent. Put in fingers and loosen the inside. Do this carefully so that the gall bladder (attached to the liver) is not broken.
6 Firmly draw out the inside.
7 Cut gall bladder from the liver.
8 Put the neck, liver, gizzard, heart and kidneys into a bowl of cold water. Wash thoroughly, then simmer these gently to make stock for gravy.
9 Wipe inside of bird with a clean damp cloth.

To truss poultry and game
The purpose of trussing the bird is to keep a good shape while cooking.
Stuffing should be done first.
1 Put the stuffing in the bird at the breast end. If two kinds of stuffing are used, then one kind can be put the other end. Fold skin firmly over the back at the neck end.
2 Press the legs down firmly at the sides of the bird.
3 Put a skewer right through the bird, just under the thighs. Turn the bird over and pinion the wings with the skewer. Pass string under the ends of the skewer and cross over at the back. Turn the bird over and tie the string round the tail, securing the ends of the legs.

Preparing giblets for stock

1 Wash the giblets, remove any surplus fat; check that the green gall bladder is not still on the stomach; this gives a bitter taste to the stock.
2 Check the liver, make sure there is no green on this from the gall bladder.
3 Cover giblets with cold water, season well, simmer for 1–2 hours until tender, or allow about 30 minutes in a pressure cooker.

Roast chicken

Preparation: 25 minutes, depending on stuffing, etc.
No delay
Cooking: see method

A good size capon serves 6–8. A medium sized chicken serves 4. A small chicken serves 2 (half this).

Chicken should either be covered with fat bacon or with fat of some kind, as it is very important for the breast to be kept really moist. Use cheap bacon — or butter gives an excellent flavour.

1 With a small chicken, use one kind of stuffing in both neck and body. With a large bird, you can use veal stuffing at one end and a forcemeat stuffing, as with turkey, at the other. Small spring chickens are not stuffed, and because there is no fat on them they should be covered with plenty of butter or fat during cooking; a small knob of butter put inside during cooking helps to keep them moist. A sprig of fresh rosemary gives a delicious flavour if put in with the butter.
2 If using frozen chicken make sure it is thoroughly defrosted before cooking.
3 Many people like to use a covered roasting tin, or to wrap the bird in foil to keep the oven clean and the bird moist. If you want crisp brown skin, take off foil or lid for the last 30 minutes' cooking.
4 For roasting, allow 15–20 minutes per lb. and 15–20 minutes over. Always include weight of stuffing with this. Start in a hot oven (425–450°F., Gas Mark 6–7). Lower heat to moderate, (375°F., Gas Mark 4) after first 35–40 minutes. If using a covered roaster or foil, allow an extra 10–15 minutes' cooking time. Do not over-cook.

Accompaniments for roast chicken

Some people like a thickened gravy with roast chicken, in which case strain off the giblet stock and use as recipe on page 64. If you like a thin gravy, blend the stock with the residue left in the roasting tin and heat.

Veal stuffing is most popular with chicken; this and bacon rolls are described on page 85. For a large chicken, use double amount of veal stuffing. An unusual pineapple walnut stuffing is given below, also a bread sauce.

If you like sausages with the chicken, they can be put round the bird about 30 minutes before dishing up.

If roasting potatoes, these can be cooked separately or roasted round the chicken. The latter will not be possible if you have the bird covered in foil, since the potatoes will not crisp.

Bread sauce

Preparation: 6–7 minutes
No delay. Time to infuse
Cooking: 10 minutes
Serves 4–6

Secret of success
The margarine or butter produces a richer and more pleasant sauce. 1 or 2 tablespoons thick cream may be added at stage 4.

1 small onion	½ pint milk	2 oz. breadcrumbs
2 or 3 cloves, *optional*	salt and pepper	1–2 oz. margarine *or* butter

1 Peel the onion. If using cloves, stick them firmly into it.
2 Put the onion into the milk, together with the other ingredients. Bring the milk slowly to the boil.
3 Remove from the heat and stand in a warm place for as long as possible – this makes sure the milk absorbs the flavour.
4 Just before the meal is ready, heat sauce gently, beating with a wooden spoon.
5 Remove the onion before putting the sauce in a sauce boat.

Pineapple walnut stuffing

Preparation: 10 minutes
No delay
Cooking: 1–1½ hours
Serves 4–6

This is a delicious change from the usual stuffings. Vary by adding 1–2 tablespoons raisins.

1½ oz. butter	2 oz. walnuts, chopped	little pineapple juice,
2 oz. white breadcrumbs	1 level teaspoon salt	*if required*
4 oz. canned pineapple, chopped	finely grated rind of ½ lemon	

1 Melt the butter in a saucepan, add the breadcrumbs and stir and cook for a minute or so.
2 Stir in all remaining ingredients. If required, add 1–2 tablespoons pineapple juice to give a moist consistency.
3 Pack the stuffing loosely into either the neck or body cavity of the chicken, prepared for roasting as described above. This amount will stuff a 4-lb. chicken.
4 Secure the neck flap in position under the wing tips.
5 Spread the chicken all over with softened butter, then cook as directed above.
6 Serve with pineapple rings around; top each with walnut half, and watercress.

Roast turkey

Preparation: 35–45 minutes (if making 2 stuffings). No delay
Cooking: see method

Allow about 12 oz. meat per person (including bones, etc.) Turkey dries easily, so if not covering the bird, it needs frequent basting. To do this, spoon hot fat over the bird, especially the breast, from the fat in the tin – be careful in handling; the tin will be heavy and fat very hot.

Colour picture, page 110

1 Make the stuffing or stuffings. Pack one stuffing into the neck end of the bird, second stuffing into the body end. Tie or skewer the neck skin into position to prevent stuffing coming out.
2 Put the turkey into the roasting tin. Cover well with fat. This can be cheap fat bacon; some grocers sell bacon pieces which are ideal.
3 Weigh the bird – or, if your scales are too small, add weight of the stuffing to weight of the trussed bird.
4 In order to keep the oven clean the turkey can be wrapped round in foil: cover the whole of the bird and tuck round the edges of the tin.
5 Allow 15 minutes per lb. and 15 minutes over for a bird up to 12 lb. After this weight allow only 12 minutes per lb. extra. If covering with foil or using a covered roaster, allow an extra 10 minutes' cooking time, or use the slow roasting method (page 117), particularly if you are going out and there is a danger of the turkey being over-cooked.
6 Start in a hot oven (425–450°F., Gas Mark 6–7). Lower the heat to very moderate (350°F., Gas Mark 3) after the first 45–60 minutes (depending on size of the bird). Remove foil 45 minutes before serving if you like a crisp skin.

Accompaniments to turkey

These are very similar to chicken, but below you will find suggestions for a change of sauce and stuffing. Since it is quite likely that you will be having turkey when you entertain, it is a good idea to simmer the giblets the day before so that the stock is all ready for gravy.

Cranberry sauce

Preparation: 1–2 minutes only
Cooking: 15 minutes
Serves 6–9

The 'bite' of cranberries is excellent with turkey.

Colour picture, page 110

| 8–12 oz. cranberries | 2–3 oz. sugar | knob of butter |
| ¼ pint water | | |

1 Simmer the cranberries in the water.
2 Rub through a sieve, add sugar to taste and a little knob of butter.
3 For an unsieved sauce make a syrup of water and sugar.
4 Drop in the cranberries, cook until you have a thick mixture, then add the butter.

Note. You can use a little port wine instead of all water.

Chestnut stuffing

Preparation: 20–25 minutes
Skin after 10 minutes while warm
Cooking: 25 minutes
Serves 6–8

You can use 1 lb. canned unsweetened chestnut purée instead of fresh chestnuts

1 lb. chestnuts	4–8 oz. cooked ham,	little milk
½ pint stock *or* water and	chopped	2 oz. butter
1 chicken *or* beef stock	2 oz. breadcrumbs	
cube		

1 Split the chestnuts and boil for 10 minutes in water.
2 While warm, remove skins and simmer nuts in the stock until very tender.
3 Rub through a sieve, then add to all the other ingredients.
4 This stuffing can be varied by adding chopped onion, mixed herbs or parsley, but do not use too strong flavours to obscure the delicious chestnut taste.

Forcemeat stuffing

Preparation: 8–10 minutes
No delay
Cooking: as poultry
Serves 4

Use a mixture of beef and pork sausage meat.

8 oz. sausage meat	1 egg	mixed herbs
1 tablespoon chopped		
parsley		

1 Mix all the ingredients thoroughly.
2 If desired add finely chopped cooked liver and stomach of the poultry.

To vary
2–3 oz. seedless raisins and 1–2 oz. chopped walnuts can be added to the stuffing, or add a few tablespoons chopped celery and 1 small grated onion.

Giblet stuffing

Make veal stuffing (page 85) and add the finely chopped cooked giblets to this. You can also use the meat from neck of the bird as well as the liver.

To vary
The finely chopped liver may be added to sage and onion stuffing (page 80) for a savoury stuffing. This is a very good second stuffing, if you are also serving veal or chestnut stuffing.

Cutting an orange

Roast duck

Roast duck

Preparation: 25 minutes
No delay
Cooking: see method

1 large duck serves 4
1 medium duckling serves 2

It is important that duck is not greasy — see suggestions in method.
You can place the duck on a grid (rack) in the roasting tin.

1 Put stuffing into body of the duck. This does become somewhat richer from the fat from the bird, so be careful not to add too much fat to the stuffing.
2 Put the duck into the roasting tin — for a crisp skin it is better uncovered. Allow 15 minutes per lb. and 15 minutes over, plus 10 minutes extra if covering with foil or a lid.
3 Start in a hot oven (425 450°F, Gas Mark 6–7); lower the heat to moderate (375°F., Gas Mark 4) after 45 minutes.
4 After the duck has been cooking for 30–45 minutes (depending on size) and the skin is beginning to brown, take a fine skewer and break the skin at intervals. The purpose of this is to allow the surplus fat to run out and to give you a crisp skin. Be careful not to push the skewer in too far, otherwise you will make the fat run into the bird and spoil the texture of the flesh.

Accompaniments to duck

Simmer the giblets to give stock for a thickened brown gravy (see page 64) — 1 tablespoon orange juice and port wine gives an excellent flavour.
Orange salad gives a pleasing contrast in texture; if you do not make this, then serve slices of orange round the duck.
Sage and onion stuffing and apple sauce (page 80).
Fresh or frozen peas and new or creamed potatoes.

Orange salad

Preparation: 8–10 minutes
No cooking
Serves 4

Do not mix other salad ingredients with orange, etc., otherwise you will spoil the flavour of this salad.

2 large oranges	good pinch of salt and	1½ tablespoons oil
1 lettuce	pepper	1½ tablespoons vinegar,
1 teaspoon made-mustard	½ teaspoon sugar	preferably white

1 Peel the oranges. As you do so cut into the fruit very slightly, so you remove outside pith as well as skin.
2 Cut sections from the oranges with a sharp knife; with practice, you can cut between the skin so you have just flesh. Discard the pips.
3 Arrange the well washed and dried lettuce on a dish. Top with the orange.
4 Put the mustard on a saucer, add the seasonings and sugar and gradually blend in the oil and vinegar. Pour over the salad.

Casserole of duck

Preparation: 25 minutes
No delay
Cooking: 2½ hours plus time for cooking giblets and chestnuts
Serves 4

This is a very good way to cook older birds.

8 oz. chestnuts	1 oz. flour	pinch of dried sage
4 onions	¾ pint giblet stock	1 duck
1½ oz. fat *or* butter	salt and pepper	few olives, *optional*

1 Slit the chestnuts, boil for 10 minutes, then remove skins *while warm*.
2 Peel the onions and toss in the fat, lift into a casserole.
3 Stir the flour into the fat and cook for several minutes.
4 Gradually add the stock, bring to the boil and cook until slightly thickened. Season and add the sage.
5 Put the duck, with the breast side uppermost, and the peeled chestnuts, into the casserole. Cover with a lid or foil.
6 Cook for 2½ hours in the centre of a very moderate oven (325°F., Gas Mark 3). To brown skin on the breast, lift off the lid and raise the heat of the oven to 425°F., Gas Mark 6, for the last 15 minutes.
7 Add olives, if used, just before serving.

Roast goose

Preparation: 25 minutes
No delay
Cooking: see method

Allow about 1 lb. per person
(i.e. an 8 lb. goose when trussed
serves 8 people only)

See suggestions for encouraging
the surplus fat to run from the
goose (stage 3), or stand the
goose on a grid (rack) in the
roasting tin.

1 Prepare the goose like duck (page 115).
2 Allow 15 minutes per lb. and 15 minutes over. Do not cover goose during roasting.
   Start in a hot oven (425–450°F., Gas Mark 6–7), then lower the heat after the first
   45 minutes to very moderate (350°F., Gas Mark 3), or use the slow roasting method,
   page 117, for some geese are inclined to be tough.
3 Because goose is considered by many people to be ultra 'fatty' it is important that it
   is pricked after 45 minutes' cooking, after 1¼ hours' cooking, and 30 minutes before
   serving.
4 If there is a great deal of fat running into the tin you can pour some of this away —
   it keeps the oven cleaner and enables the goose to crisp better.

Note. The goose may be put on a trivet in the roasting tin so it does not come into
contact with the fat.

Accompaniments to goose

These are exactly the same as for duck (page 115) but you can try a new stuffing —
the one below is excellent. Some people do not make sage and onion stuffing or
apple sauce. They actually cook the apples and/or onion in the body of the goose.
A few prunes can be heated in the gravy, if wished.

Apricot and raisin stuffing

Preparation: 7 minutes
No delay
Cooking: depends on size of
roast. Several minutes' heating
of apricots and raisins
Serves 8–10

This can also be used for stuffing
joints of pork, veal or lamb. Use
half the quantity.

4 oz. dried apricots	12 oz. breadcrumbs	6 oz. diced green pepper
4 oz. seedless raisins	1 teaspoon salt	*or* celery, *optional*
		4 oz. butter

1 Place the apricots and seedless raisins in a saucepan, cover with cold water and
   bring to the boil.
2 Strain, then cut the apricots into small pieces.
3 Mix the rest of the ingredients, except the butter, together.
4 Melt the butter and pour on to the crumbs.
5 Mix well and bind together.

To vary
Dried prunes or peaches may be used in place of apricots.

To carve poultry

Chicken
The method of carving depends on the size of the bird.
For very tiny spring chickens serve one per person, or, if slightly larger, cut into halves
— if you cut firmly down, slightly to one side of the centre of the breast bone, it is
quite easy to do.
Medium chickens can be jointed, rather than carved, making one or two joints of
each of the legs and two joints of the breast and wings, or, if serving children, each
breast and wing could be divided into two portions. A large chicken is carved like a
turkey.

Turkey
Either cut off the leg on one side or pull it well away from the body. This enables you
to cut really large slices from the breast. When sufficient meat from the breast has
been cut, then carve the meat from the leg.
Give each person a little light meat, dark meat and stuffing.

Goose
As turkey.

Duck
Small ducklings can be cut into halves, like tiny chickens, for there is not a lot of
meat on the breast. Cut the large birds into four joints — 2 from breast and 2 from legs.
For a very large duck, rather thick slices can be cut from the breast instead of serving
the breast uncut.

Game
Small birds are served whole or halved — larger birds carved or jointed like chicken.
Venison is carved like lamb.

**The heat of the joint quickly blunts a carving knife — so if you are carving
for a lot of people it is wise to use two knives alternately.**

Slow roasting of poultry

Poultry, like meat, can be roasted very slowly. This gives tenderness to older birds and the flesh shrinks less.

Use a very cool oven (275°F., Gas Mark 1).

Allow: $1\frac{1}{4}$ hours for first lb., no matter how large or small the bird; 25 minutes for every extra lb. up to 7 lb.; 20 minutes per pound above that weight. The disadvantage about this, if you are having a big turkey for a mid-day meal, is that the oven has to be turned on so many hours before the meal. However, an automatic cooker can be set to switch itself on.

How to joint a chicken

So many exciting new dishes can be made with a jointed chicken — grilled chicken, fried chicken, casserole dishes.

Choose a $2-2\frac{1}{2}$ lb. bird to provide 4 generous portions. Thaw bird sufficiently, if frozen, to remove the parcel of giblets from the body cavity, then proceed as follows:

1 Place chicken on chopping board and, with a strong, sharp knife, cut through lengthwise all along the breastbone.

2 Open bird out, then cut through along length of backbone. Tap knife sharply with a heavy weight where necessary.

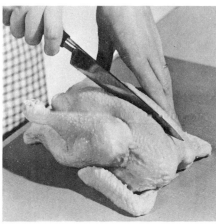

3 Lay halves of chicken on board and divide each in half again by cutting diagonally across between wing and thigh. This gives 4 portions.

4 To make 6 joints, divide each thigh and drumstick portion in half again, by cutting through at ball and socket joint.

To joint a chicken French style

This method of jointing a chicken produces a large number of joints and is, therefore, economical. Choose a bird $2\frac{1}{2}-3$ lb. in weight. Remove the giblets and thoroughly clean the inside of the bird; trim the wings and legs.

1 Cut off the legs — pull gently from the bird and cut through joint. Cut each leg into 2 pieces.
2 Cut off the wings — pinch up a piece of flesh between the thumb and first finger before cutting.
3 Cut the body in half, cutting through the rib cage.
4 Cut the breast diagonally across into 2 pieces. Tap the knife gently with a heavy weight to cut through the bone.
5 Cut the back (undercarriage) into 3 pieces. The undercarriage pieces are cooked and used to build up the centre of the dish when serving. They would not normally be served as portions.
6 Flesh from these pieces can be used in dishes where small chicken pieces are required.
7 Use the chicken joints for a variety of fried and casserole dishes.

To fry chicken

Preparation: few minutes plus time for jointing chicken
No delay
Cooking: 20 minutes

The very popular young spring chickens are ideal for frying, for this retains the maximum of the rather delicate flavour.

Colour picture, page 127

1 First joint the chicken (see previous page) or buy jointed chicken.
2 Dry the joints well.
3 To give a very crisp outside, coat either with seasoned flour or egg and breadcrumbs.

To coat in flour
1 Put 2 tablespoons flour into a bag, with a good pinch salt and pepper.
2 Drop in joints of chicken and shake in flour until coated.

To coat in egg and breadcrumbs
1 Brush joints with beaten egg.
2 Put 3 tablespoons crisp breadcrumbs into a bag and shake joints in this until thoroughly coated. Shake each joint slightly before cooking.

To fry chicken in shallow fat

1 Heat about 3 oz. butter or cooking fat or 3 tablespoons oil in a frying pan until really hot — a finger of bread should brown in 1 minute.
2 Put in the joints of chicken.
3 Cook for about 4 minutes on one side, turn and brown on second side for the same time, until chicken is golden brown — but NOT too dark.
4 Lower the heat so that the chicken continues to cook through to the centre. This will take about 10 minutes; turn the chicken once or twice during cooking.
5 Lift out on to kitchen paper or a dish to drain. Keep hot.
6 Fry halved tomatoes or mushrooms in the pan if wished.
7 A crisp green salad is an excellent accompaniment.

Shallow fried chicken

To fry chicken in deep fat

1 It is better to coat joints with egg and breadcrumbs for this method, or with batter as one does fish (see page 44).
2 Heat the fat in your deep fryer until a cube of bread turns golden brown in ½ minute.
3 Insert the frying basket so that this gets hot and the chicken will not stick to it.
4 Put in the pieces of chicken and fry for 4–5 minutes until golden brown. WATCH THAT THE FAT DOES NOT GET ANY HOTTER — DECREASE HEAT WHEN NECESSARY.
5 Fry steadily for a further 8–10 minutes. You must watch the heat carefully during this time, so that the outside of the bird does not become over-cooked before it is tender through to the middle.
6 Another way of doing this is to fry for 4–5 minutes only, then lift out the joints of chicken and put into a tin and cook for 25 minutes in a moderate oven (375°F., Gas Mark 4).
7 Drain and serve in a napkin-lined basket, garnished with watercress. Deep-fried chicken can be served hot or cold.

Chicken casserole with dumplings

Preparation: 25 minutes
No delay
Cooking. 1 hour
Serves 4

The sustaining texture of dumplings helps to make a comparatively small chicken serve a greater number of people.

1 frying chicken, about 2–2½ lb.
salt and pepper
1 oz. cornflour
2 tablespoons corn oil
3–4 small carrots, diced
1 onion, sliced

1 chicken stock cube
1 pint boiling water
small can or tube concentrated tomato purée
2 tablespoons white wine, *optional*
1 bay leaf

4 oz. mushrooms, sliced
few cooked green peas
dumplings, *recipe below*

to garnish
chopped parsley

1 Joint the chicken (see page 117).
2 Add the salt and pepper to the cornflour and coat the chicken joints thoroughly.
3 Heat the corn oil in a pan or frying pan.
4 Brown the chicken in the corn oil, and then transfer to a casserole with the carrots and onion.
5 Dissolve the chicken cube in the boiling water and mix in the tomato purée.
6 Add the wine, if used, and bay leaf, then pour over the chicken and vegetables.
7 Cover tightly and cook gently in the centre of a very moderate oven (350°F., Gas Mark 3) for approximately 30 minutes.
8 Add the mushrooms and peas, and continue cooking for a further 30 minutes.
9 Meanwhile put the dumplings to cook – recipe below
10 Arrange the cooked dumplings on the stew and sprinkle all with chopped parsley.

Dumplings

3 oz. plain flour
pinch of salt

1 level teaspoon baking powder
½ oz. cornflour

1 tablespoon corn oil
just under ⅛ pint milk

1 Sift the dry ingredients together.
2 Mix the oil and milk and stir in.
3 If necessary, add enough extra milk to form a soft dough, then form into small balls with floured hands.
4 Arrange in a single layer in a steamer, allowing enough space between the dumplings for them to rise and expand.
5 Make sure the water in the pan is boiling.
6 Steam for 30 minutes over boiling water.

Chicken in a blanket

Preparation: 25 minutes
Cooking: 2 hours 15 minutes
Serves 4–6

Secrets of success
A boiling fowl must be cooked slowly, so flesh becomes really tender.
Do not boil sauce at stage 3 after adding the cream.

1 small boiling fowl *or* 4–6 joints boiling chicken
2 large carrots
1 large onion
2 sticks celery

1 oz. butter
1 bay leaf
1 blade of mace
1½ pints water

salt and pepper
pinch of dry mustard
mushroom sauce (see stage 2)
fried bread *for garnish*

1 Simmer the jointed fowl with the sliced vegetables, butter, herbs and seasoning for about 2 hours, or until tender.
2 Make a coating sauce with 2 oz. butter, 2 oz. flour and ¾ pint chicken stock.
3 Add 4 oz. button mushrooms and simmer for a few minutes, then stir in ¼ pint thin cream and seasoning; do not boil. Coat the drained chicken with this.
4 Garnish with triangles of bread, fried in butter or fat, and a few mushrooms.

Chicken in a blanket

Chicken Maryland

Preparation: 25 minutes
No delay
Cooking: 25–30 minutes
Serves 4

Secret of success
This favourite chicken dish is easy to cook, but needs careful timing to ensure all the 'bits and pieces' are ready together.

corn fritters, *recipe below*
3 rashers streaky bacon
2 bananas

1 2–2½ lb. frying chicken
egg and breadcrumbs *for coating*

fat *for frying*

to garnish
watercress

1 Make the corn fritters and allow to stand.
2 Make bacon rolls and put on metal skewers.
3 Peel the bananas and split lengthways.
4 Cut chicken into four joints; coat each with egg and breadcrumbs (page 118).
5 Heat sufficient fat in a frying pan to give a depth of ½ inch. When hot, fry the joints of chicken quickly until golden brown on each side, then reduce the heat and cook gently until tender for about 25 minutes, turning once. Put in the bacon rolls for the last 7 minutes and turn in the fat.
7 Dust the bananas with a little flour, or any egg and crumbs left, and fry for a few minutes.
8 Drain the chicken, etc., on absorbent paper.
9 Serve the chicken on a hot dish with the corn fritters, fried bananas, bacon rolls, and garnished with watercress.

Chicken Maryland

Corn fritters

Preparation: 5 minutes
No delay
Cooking: 5 minutes
Serves 4–6

Secret of success
Do not exceed the amount of flour; these should not be too solid.

1 egg, beaten
2 level tablespoons self-raising flour

salt and pinch of cayenne
1 teaspoon Worcestershire sauce

small can corn kernels
fat *for frying*

1 Make a batter with the egg, flour and seasoning and beat well.
2 Mix in the sauce and the drained corn.
3 Gently fry tablespoons of the mixture in a little hot fat, turning once, for 4–5 minutes, until golden brown.

Sweet-sour chicken

Preparation: 15 minutes
Cooking: 15 minutes
Serves 4

This combination of sweet ingredients with chicken makes a very pleasant change.

Colour picture, page 127

4 joints young chicken
2 oz. butter
small can pineapple cubes
¼ pint chicken stock

1 oz. cornflour
1 tablespoon white vinegar
2 teaspoons soy sauce
1 teaspoon made-mustard

2 teaspoons honey
2 dessert pears
few fresh *or* canned cherries

1 Fry or grill the chicken with the butter, as page 118 or 121.
2 Meanwhile, open the can of pineapple cubes, drain the syrup, add to the chicken stock. If necessary add a little water or stock to give ½ pint.
3 Blend the cornflour with the stock and syrup, then put into a saucepan with the vinegar, soy sauce, mustard and honey.
4 Stir over a medium heat until it thickens and is smooth.
5 Peel and slice the pears, put into the sauce with the pineapple cubes and cherries.
6 Keep hot, stirring from time to time, until ready to serve.
7 Arrange chicken on dish and top with the sauce, as colour picture page 127.

To vary
Use the above recipe, but omit the pears and cherries.

Vineyard chicken: fry or grill the chicken in the usual way. Meanwhile, make a sauce with 1½ oz. chicken fat or butter, 1½ oz. flour, ½ pint chicken stock, ¼ pint white wine. Add seasoning and the finely grated rind of 1 orange, the orange juice and about 2–4 oz. skinned de-seeded grapes.

Chicken and tomato bake

Preparation: 10–15 minutes plus time to defrost chicken if frozen
No delay
Cooking: 1¼–1½ hours.
Serves 4

1 spring chicken
2 oz. button mushrooms
1 oz. butter *or* margarine

1 large onion, finely chopped
1 oz. flour
salt and pepper

2 large tomatoes, sliced
medium can condensed kidney soup

1 Cut the chicken into four joints (see page 117).
2 Gently fry the mushrooms in the melted butter until tender. Remove from the pan.
3 Fry the onion until tender and golden brown.
4 Add the chicken joints coated with flour, to which should be added a little salt and pepper, then fry until brown on all sides.
5 Place the onion, chicken, mushrooms and tomatoes in a greased shallow oven-proof dish.
6 Blend the soup with ½ can water and seasoning, and pour over the chicken.
7 Cover closely; bake in very moderate oven (350°F., Gas Mark 3) for 1¼–1½ hours.

To grill chicken

Preparation: 7 minutes
No delay
Cooking: 20 minutes

Keep the chicken well basted during cooking. Grilled bacon, sweet corn, peas or green salad also blend very well with grilled chicken, and a rather spicy tomato sauce (page 209) is an excellent accompaniment.

young chicken
2 oz. butter

salt and pepper
little lemon juice

little sugar, *optional*

1 Joint the chicken as directed on page 117.
2 Put the joints of chicken on to the grid of the grill pan if you can get this a reasonable distance away from the grill. If your grill compartment on the cooker is very shallow, then it is better to put the chicken into the actual grill pan.
3 Brush with a little melted butter and season lightly; a squeeze of lemon and sugar adds flavour.
4 Heat the grill, put the chicken underneath.
5 Allow 4–5 minutes on either side with the grill at maximum heat.
6 Turn the heat lower and allow a further 8–12 minutes, baste several times with butter.
7 Mushrooms and tomatoes can be grilled at the same time. If grilling whole mushrooms and tomatoes they can, in some cookers, be put in the grill pan with the joints on top, in which case you can put them in the pan at the beginning of cooking. If, on the other hand, you are cooking the chicken in the grill pan add the tomatoes and the whole, or sliced, mushrooms halfway through cooking; add a little extra butter to these if desired.
8 Serve the joints of chicken with mushrooms, etc., arranged round the dish or over the top.

To grill chicken – brush all over with a little melted butter

Barbecued or spit roasted chicken

Barbecued
The modern fashion for barbecues gives many occasions on which young chicken can be served. They should be jointed (see page 117), brushed with melted butter or oil, seasoned well, then cooked over the barbecue fire in exactly the same way as if grilling.

Spit roasted
Choose young chickens for this. Insert the chicken on the spit and brush with melted butter or oil. Cook according to the time given on page 113. If during cooking the breast begins to look a little dry, stop the spit and brush the chicken once more with extra fat.

To boil a fowl

Preparation: few minutes
No delay
Cooking: see method

A boiling fowl can very often be a very wise investment, and also a much more easily digested meal than even roast chicken. There are several ways of cooking it. Never try to cook a real boiling fowl too quickly – it will be very tough on the outside if you do.

Very slow treatment
1 Put the bird into a large container; a metal bread bin is admirable when a large saucepan is not available.
2 Completely cover with water and add seasoning to taste.
3 Steam, without boiling, allowing 30 minutes per lb. plus 2 hours over.
4 Make certain the lid fits tightly: look once or twice to see that the water has only an occasional bubble on the surface.

Quicker treatment
1 Put 1 or 2 potatoes inside the bird; the steam from these helps to make it tender and keep it moist.
2 Put into a steamer over a pan of rapidly boiling water.
3 Sprinkle over a little seasoning.
4 Allow 40 minutes per lb. Keep the stock for a sauce.

If you wish to serve fowl as roasted bird
1 Use the slow roasting method – working out approximate time for weight of bird and adding 1 hour, or the following:

1 Cook as the quicker method above for two-thirds cooking time.
2 Lift out of the liquid, drain well.
3 Brush with melted fat, cook for rest of time in hot oven (425–450°F., Gas Mark 6–7).

Accompaniments to boiling fowl

If serving as roast chicken, then you can have the same accompaniments. If serving as a boiled or creamed chicken, cut into joints or slices and serve with a border of creamed potatoes or boiled rice (pages 138 or 147). Serve a cream sauce or hard-boiled egg or liver and parsley sauce (recipes below).

Cream sauce

Preparation: few minutes
Cooking: 8 minutes

Left-over pieces of cooked chicken and ham can be heated in this sauce.

1 oz. butter	$\frac{1}{4}$ pint stock from boiling chicken	1 tablespoon cream (or top of the milk will do)
1 oz. flour	salt and pepper	
$\frac{1}{4}$ pint milk		

1 Heat the butter in a pan. Stir in the flour, cook for several minutes.
2 Take pan off the heat and gradually add the milk, then the stock, stirring all the time.
3 Return to the heat and bring to the boil, stirring well.
4 Cook until the mixture coats the back of a spoon.
5 Add seasoning and cream or top of the milk.

Hard-boiled egg sauce
As above, but add 1 or 2 chopped hard-boiled eggs. The whites only could be added, and sieved or chopped yolk used as a garnish.
Do not over-boil the eggs; this produces a dark line round the yolk and a strong flavour.

Liver and parsley sauce
As above, but add 1 tablespoon chopped parsley and chopped cooked chicken liver. Add the liver just before serving, so it does not darken the sauce.

Chicken casserole

Preparation: 10 minutes
No delay
Cooking: see method
Serves 4–6

The frozen or fresh younger chickens are excellent in this dish, but an older boiling fowl is ideal as it has more flavour.

4–8 potatoes	4 onions	1 pint hot water
4 carrots	1 chicken or fowl	salt and pepper
little chopped celery	1 chicken stock cube, optional	herbs, optional
2 oz. mushrooms		1 oz. butter

1 Prepare and cut the vegetables into neat pieces, or they can be left whole.
2 Wash and dry the chicken.
3 Put the chicken, vegetables, giblets and stock cube, if used, dissolved in the hot water, into the casserole.
4 Add seasoning – herbs such as thyme, bay leaves, etc., can also be added.
5 Spread butter over the breast of the chicken.
6 Put lid on casserole or cover with foil.
7 Cook in the centre of a very moderate oven (325°F., Gas Mark 3), allowing $1\frac{1}{2}$–$1\frac{3}{4}$ hours for a younger chicken, or $2\frac{1}{2}$–3 hours for older fowl.
8 Lift chicken and vegetables on to serving dish, keep hot; prepare a sauce. The stock can be used in a cream sauce – see recipe above, or make a thickened brown sauce (page 142).

Game

During the season, watch for game in your shops, or you may be fortunate enough to have it sent to you. People's taste in game varies — some like it very 'high', i.e. kept for some days so that it is very strong, but if you are in doubt do not hang it for too long. Never cook game on the day it is shot — it is better if several days old. Here are some of the more popular game:

	Method of cooking	Timing	Accompaniments
Young	**Grouse** Roast	15–20 minutes per lb., 15–20 minutes over (*see page 124*)	Thickened gravy: bread sauce or redcurrant jelly. Fried breadcrumbs Game (potato) chips Watercress or salad
Older	Casserole	2½ hours (*see page 125*)	Vegetables
Young (an old hare is not very pleasant as the flavour is too strong)	**Hare** Roast as rabbit (*see page 126*) Casserole (jugged)	20 minutes per lb. plus 20 minutes over 2½ hours (*see page 125*)	Sage and onion stuffing Redcurrant jelly Forcemeat balls
Young	**Partridge** Roast	15–20 minutes per lb. plus 15–20 minutes over	As grouse
Older	Casserole	2–2½ hours (*see page 125*)	Vegetables
Young	**Pheasant** Roast – keep well basted	15–20 minutes per lb. plus 15–20 minutes over	As grouse
Older	Casserole	2–2½ hours (*see page 125*)	Vegetables
Young	**Pigeon** Roast – keep very well basted	25–30 minutes in all	As grouse
Older	Casserole	1½ hours (*see page 125*)	Vegetables
Young	**Rabbit** Roast	1½ hours (*see page 126*)	Sage and onion stuffing Bacon Vegetables
Older	Boil, casserole	1½–2 hours (*see page 126*)	Vegetables
Young	**Snipe** Roast – handle carefully as the skin may break	25 minutes	As grouse
	Venison As veal (*see page 85*)	As veal (*see page 85*)	As veal
	Woodcock Roast or fried. Do not draw, as intestines delicious	25–30 minutes	As grouse

Other game birds you may buy include teal, widgeon, etc., and these can be cooked in the same way.

To roast game

Preparation: few minutes
No delay
Cooking: as chart on page 123

Secret of success
Use plenty of fat, as game is
inclined to dry easily. Do not
over-cook.

Roast game

1 Wash and dry the game.
2 Put into a roasting tin.
3 Cover the breast with fat; bacon or butter can be used.
4 You can wrap the game in foil or use a covered roaster, if wished, in which case add 10 minutes to the cooking time.
5 Start in a hot oven (425–450°F., Gas Mark 6–7), lowering the heat to moderate (375°F., Gas Mark 5) after the first 25 minutes.
6 Allow the time given in the chart on page 123.
7 Remove the bacon, foil, or lid of the roaster for the last 15 minutes, to brown the breast.

Accompaniments to game

Serve with thickened gravy. Quite frequently you will not have giblets of game, so use water and beef stock cube to make stock. Use any residue from the roasting tin to give flavour.

Some people serve game on slices of toast so that all the rich flavour is retained. Serve bread sauce (page 113) or redcurrant jelly, fried crumbs, game (potato) chips and watercress or salad, or a green vegetable and roast or creamed potatoes.

Fried crumbs
Make *large* crumbs (i.e. fairly coarse) from the bread, and fry in butter until crisp and golden brown. This can be done the day before, or earlier in the day, and the crumbs reheated gently in the oven.

Game chips
Game chips or potato crisps are wafer-thin slices of potato, fried until crisp and brown. However, bought potato crisps are so satisfactory that it is hardly worthwhile making game chips. Tip crisps on to baking tray and heat for 10 minutes in a very moderate oven, or 2–3 minutes in a hot oven. Allow to cool for 2–3 minutes to regain crisp texture.

Some new accompaniments for game
Diced peeled dessert apples may be put into the roasting tin about 15 minutes before the game is cooked, then served with the game — see picture.

Stuff game with skinned and de-seeded grapes, or with grapes and cream cheese. Roast in the usual way.

Game casserole

Preparation: 15 minutes
No delay
Cooking: see below
Serves 4 if good sized bird

This is a good way of tenderising the meat, if the game seems rather old.
Partridge, pheasant or several small pigeons can be used instead of grouse — the larger birds take approximately 2–2½ hours to cook; pigeons need only 1½ hours.

2 large tomatoes
1 *or* 2 onions
3 oz. dripping *or* fat
1 grouse
1 oz. flour

¾ pint brown stock *or* water
  with beef stock cube
seasoning
2 tablespoons burgundy *or*
  claret, *optional*

little chopped celery
fried bread
few glacé cherries

1 Skin and slice the tomatoes, slice the onions.
2 Heat the dripping or fat in a pan and fry the game until pale brown.
3 Put into a casserole.
4 Toss the sliced tomatoes and onions in the fat.
5 Blend the flour with the onion mixture, cook for several minutes, add the stock, bring slowly to the boil, stirring all the time to keep the mixture from becoming lumpy.
6 Season well.
7 Add the burgundy or claret and chopped celery.
8 Pour the sauce over the game, put a lid on the casserole and place in a very moderate oven (325°F., Gas Mark 3).
9 Cook for 2½ hours.
10 Serve with small pieces of fried bread, and to give an unusual touch of colour and flavour, add the cherries.

New flavourings for game casseroles

Casserole using variation a) of game casserole above
Casserole using variation b) above

Use the basic recipe above, but:
a) omit the sliced onions (stage 1), use about 16 small onions or shallots and 4 oz. sliced mushrooms plus the tomatoes. Omit the fried bread and glacé cherries and top with chopped parsley. If the game is jointed, allow only 1½ hours cooking time. Jointed guinea fowl can be used in this recipe, see picture below left, or whole pigeons;

b) omit the sliced tomatoes from the basic recipe (stage 1), add 8 soaked prunes. Towards the end of the cooking time, add 8 small frankfurter sausages and 2 cooking apples, peeled and cut into fairly thick slices. Omit the fried bread and cherries. Whole guinea fowl can be used in this variation as well as grouse, pheasant, etc. (see picture, right), or use whole pigeons.

Casseroled or jugged hare

1 This is cooked very much like casserole of game. Ask the poulterer to joint the hare and give you the blood, if available.
2 Cook the liver separately, and if possible sieve and add to the liquid together with a little port wine and the blood. If using blood you have slightly *less* stock. Cook for 2½ hours.
3 Serve with redcurrant jelly and forcemeat balls.
4 To make forcemeat balls use veal stuffing (page 85) or forcemeat stuffing (page 114); form into tiny balls. Put on to baking tin and cook for 25–30 minutes in a moderate to moderately hot oven, 375–400°F., Gas Mark 5–6.

Boiled rabbit

Preparation: 15–25 minutes
No delay
Cooking: just over 1½ hours
Serves 4–6

Secret of success
Rabbit looks much more
appetising if the flesh is white,
so follow directions in stage 1.

1 rabbit	salt and pepper	¼ pint milk
4 oz. fat bacon	1 pint water	
1 large onion	1 oz. flour	*to garnish*
10 oz. mixed root vegetables, diced		*chopped parsley*

1 Soak the rabbit in cold water to which a little vinegar has been added, to whiten the flesh — see quantities below.
2 Cut into neat pieces. The poulterer probably will do this. Dice the bacon and put into pan with chopped onion, vegetables, rabbit, seasoning and water.
3 Put on the lid and simmer gently for about 1½ hours, until the rabbit is tender.
4 Blend the flour with the milk and stir into the liquid.
5 Bring to the boil, stirring well, and cook until smooth and thickened.
6 Taste and re-season if necessary. Garnish with chopped parsley.

Roast rabbit

Preparation: 15 minutes
No delay
Cooking: 1½ hours
Serves 4–6

The flavour of the rabbit when
roasted is excellent, provided it
is well cooked and you have
been careful to choose a young
rabbit; older rabbits are better
stewed, as recipe above.

1 small young rabbit	2–3 rashers bacon	2–4 oz. dripping
sage and onion stuffing, *page 80*		

1 Soak the rabbit for about 2 hours in vinegar and water (1 tablespoon vinegar to 1 pint cold water). This improves both colour and flavour.
2 Wash the rabbit in fresh water and dry it.
3 Put the stuffing into the rabbit and lay the rashers of bacon on top.
4 Place the rabbit in the roasting tin with the dripping.
5 Cook for about 1½ hours, starting in a hot oven (425–450°F., Gas Mark 6–7) for the first 25–30 minutes, then reducing the heat to moderately hot (400°F., Gas Mark 5).

Ideas for using up cooked poultry or game

1 Heat in a brown gravy or curry sauce. Use same sauce as for lamb (pages 64, 90).
2 Use instead of meat in shepherd's pie (page 89).
3 Use diced and mixed with mayonnaise (page 207) in salad.
4 Use instead of turkey in the following recipe.
5 **Chicken or turkey croquettes:** make a thick white sauce with 1 oz. chicken fat or butter, 1 oz. flour and ¼ pint chicken stock or milk, season well. Add 8–12 oz. minced cooked poultry and 2 oz. fine breadcrumbs, together with a good pinch of mixed herbs. Cool the mixture, form into finger shapes, coat with beaten egg and crumbs and fry until crisp.

Minced game may be used in the same way, but make a brown sauce instead of a white sauce. These croquettes should be well drained after frying, and served hot with gravy or cold with salad.

Turkey pie

Preparation: 20 minutes
No delay
Cooking: 30–40 minutes
Serves 6–8

The filling of this pie is fairly
heavy and substantial — that is
why it is advisable to cook and
serve on the same dish.

12 oz. short crust pastry (made with 12 oz. plain flour, 6 oz. fat)	*for the filling* ¾ pint moderately thick white sauce, made from 2 oz. butter, 2 oz. flour, ¾ pint milk, *page 143* 4 oz. mushrooms	1 lb. cooked turkey 4 tablespoons finely chopped celery seasoning beaten egg *or* milk *to glaze*

1 Prepare the short crust pastry, and make the sauce.
2 Grill or fry the mushrooms, then chop them.
3 Chop the turkey fairly coarsely.
4 Add turkey, mushrooms and celery to sauce and season well. Cool slightly.
5 Roll out nearly two-thirds of the pastry and with it line a lightly greased 8–9-inch ovenproof pie plate. Spread with the turkey mixture.
6 Moisten edges of the pastry with cold water, then cover with the rest of the pastry, rolled out to form a fitting lid.
7 Press edges well together to seal, knock up with the back of a knife, then press into flutes (see page 194 for pastry edges).
8 Brush top with beaten egg or milk; decorate with pastry leaves, made from trimmings (page 194). For a festive touch shape as holly leaves.
9 Bake the pie just above the centre of a hot oven (425–450°F., Gas Mark 6–7) for 10–15 minutes, when it should just be colouring; reduce heat to moderate (350–375°F., Gas Mark 4–5) and cook a further 20–30 minutes, or until the pastry is crisp and golden. Serve hot or cold.

Top *Sweet and sour chicken, see page 120*
Bottom *Fried chicken, see page 118*

Vegetables and basic sauces

Importance of vegetables in the menu

Well cooked vegetables make all the difference to a good meal. They make it more interesting, they save money by 'eking out' the more expensive meat or fish, and they add valuable vitamins to your meal.

Wise buying of vegetables

A great deal of money can be wasted by inefficient buying of vegetables. Remember the following points:

1 When you buy green vegetables, look closely to see that the outer leaves are not yellow and wilting. You may find just one or two on cabbages. This is relatively unimportant, but if a great number of the outer leaves are yellow it is a sure sign that the vegetables are stale.
2 Good quality cabbage, brussels sprouts, etc., should feel firm in the centre — if they do not there is very little heart, and you will have to buy a much bigger quantity.
3 Cauliflower should look white, although certain types of cauliflower are more creamy white than others.
4 Root vegetables are an extravagant buy if thickly coated with soil. On the other hand, although they look much more attractive if washed before selling, they are much more inclined to spoil, so must be used up quickly.
5 After a very bad frost and snow spell it is almost certain that fresh vegetables will be affected, and it is therefore advisable to choose canned or frozen vegetables at these times.
6 When buying fresh peas, watch to see that the pods look fairly plump. If, however, they are very yellow in colour, the peas are either stale or very old.
7 Beans that are too enormous in size are quite likely to be rather tough. A good runner or French bean will break in half quite easily.

Quantities to allow

It is very difficult to be too dogmatic about the amount of vegetables to allow, since individual tastes vary a great deal. Here is a very approximate guide:
Potatoes: the amount of potatoes people eat varies so much that no definite quantity can be advised. As an average allow 2–3 small potatoes per person.
Green vegetables: approximately 4 oz. prepared but uncooked.
Root vegetables: approximately 3 oz. prepared but uncooked.

Canned vegetables

The quality of canned vegetables has improved a great deal and they are a very useful standby.
Remember that a quite high degree of heat is used when canning and the vegetables have, therefore, already been cooked. They need reheating only.

Frozen vegetables

Frozen vegetables have an extremely good flavour but this can be lost by over-cooking. During processing frozen vegetables are 'blanched', which means that they are subjected to a certain amount of heat. This has partially cooked them. To obtain a good result, therefore, it is important to follow the manufacturers' instructions and to under-cook rather than over-cook. Remember, NEVER store frozen vegetables longer than the recommended time.

Dried vegetables

Instructions for cooking dried vegetables are on page 141. The Accelerated Freeze Dried (A.F.D.) vegetables need little soaking and cook very quickly.

Baked stuffed potatoes, see page 135

How to prepare and serve vegetables

Detailed instructions for the correct cooking of vegetables by various methods will be found on pages 133–142. Below is a general guide to the set method of preparation for individual varieties.

Artichokes, globe: cook steadily in boiling salted water for about 30 minutes. Serve with a little melted butter, or white, cheese, or Hollandaise sauce (page 143).

Artichokes, Jerusalem: scrub well and peel or scrape. Soak in a little cold water, adding a few drops of vinegar. Cook for about 30 minutes in boiling salted water, adding a few drops of vinegar. Serve with melted butter, white, cheese, or Hollandaise sauce (page 143).

Asparagus: wash carefully, then cut off a little of the thick white base of stalks. Either steam or boil the bunch in salted water in a tall pan for 20–25 minutes. Serve with melted butter or Hollandaise sauce (page 143).

Aubergines: wash and remove any hard stalk. Bake in a casserole with a knob of margarine and little milk for 30 minutes. Aubergines can also be stuffed or sliced and fried.

Beans, broad: shell and wash, unless very young, when they can be cooked whole. Cook in boiling salted water for about 20 minutes. Serve with a little melted butter and chopped parsley.

Beans, butter: generally purchased dried. Soak overnight in cold or, better still, boiling water. Drain, cover with cold salted water and simmer gently for 2–3 hours. Drain and toss in butter and chopped parsley, or serve with white sauce (page 143). Excellent cooked in a pressure cooker.

Beans, French or runner: wash and string. French beans can be left whole but runner beans are better thinly sliced. Cook steadily in boiling salted water for about 15 minutes.

Beans, haricot, and flageolets (green haricot beans): prepare and cook like butter beans.

Beans, Lima: prepare and cook like butter beans. Add to a casserole.

Beetroot: wash carefully; cook in boiling salted water until soft. Time will vary according to size, but test by pressing gently. Beetroot is usually served cold with salads, but is delicious hot with parsley or Hollandaise sauce (page 143).

Broccoli: cook large heads and sprouting broccoli like cauliflower; serve with melted butter or white sauce (page 143). Broccoli spears are cooked carefully like asparagus to retain firmness; serve with melted butter or Hollandaise sauce (page 143).

Brussels sprouts: mark a cross with sharp knife at base of each sprout. Remove loose outer leaves. Boil rapidly like cabbage.

Cabbage, spring, summer or savoy: shred finely with sharp knife and boil rapidly for about 10 minutes in salted water. Serve raw in salads.

Cabbage, red: cook like green cabbage. Can be pickled.

Capsicums: see Peppers.

Cardoons: these look like tall celery. Cut away outer stems; cut inner stems into short pieces, but leave the heart whole. Put into boiling salted water with 1 tablespoon lemon juice or vinegar, cook steadily for $1\frac{1}{2}$–2 hours until tender. If the skin is rather tough, cook for about 20 minutes, drain, rub off skin, then put back into fresh water and finish cooking. Serve with melted butter, or a white or Hollandaise sauce (page 143).

Carrots: scrub well or scrape, cook in boiling salted water until soft.

Cauliflower: cut off thick stalks and outer leaves, divide head into small sprigs, cook rapidly in boiling salted water. Serve with white, parsley, or cheese sauce (page 143).

Celeriac (turnip-rooted celery): the large ugly root needs peeling and dicing. Cook like celery; it tastes delicious.

Celery: this is generally eaten raw and in salads, but is also good cooked. Divide into neat pieces and cook in boiling salted water for about 20 minutes. Serve with white, parsley, or cheese sauce (page 143) or braise (page 142).

Chard: cook like cabbage.

Chestnuts: slit skins, boil 10 minutes then remove outer and inner skins. Finish cooking in boiling salted water. Serve as purée with melted butter, or mixed with brussels sprouts.

Chicory: cook like celery. In France and America this is called endive.

Chives: use chopped to give a mild onion flavouring.

Choucroute: see sauerkraut

Corn-on-the-cob or sweet corn: wash corn, strip off outer green leaves, and boil in salted water for about 20 minutes, until the corn feels soft. Serve with a little melted butter. Do not boil too quickly or for too long, otherwise the corn becomes tough again.

Courgettes: see vegetable marrow.

Cucumber: cucumber is generally served raw with vinegar, but can be boiled in pieces in salted water or braised like celery.

Dandelion leaves: wash well. Cook like spinach or serve in salads.

Eggplant: see aubergines.

Endive: known as chicory in France and America. Cook like lettuce or serve in salads.

Fennel: a little, cut finely, flavours a salad, but it can be cooked like other vegetables in boiling salted water and served with a white sauce (page 143). It is particularly good served with fish.

Garlic: use very sparingly, crushed or finely chopped, as a flavouring — a clove is one small portion.

Gumbo: see okra.

Kale: cook like cabbage or spinach.

Kohlrabi: cook root like turnip; the stems can be cooked separately.

Leeks: cut off roots and outer leaves; split down middle so they may be thoroughly washed. Use in place of onions in soups and stews, or boil for 30 minutes in salted water. Serve with a white or cheese sauce (page 143).

Lentils: dried pulse; soak and cook in main dishes.

Lettuce: although normally served in salads, lettuce can be cooked like cabbage or in a little butter in a covered pan until soft, or braised.

Mushrooms: can be fried or grilled in butter or baked in a covered casserole for about 30 minutes. Mushrooms can also be stewed in milk, then the remaining liquid thickened with a little flour or cornflour. Champignons, or button mushrooms, are the small round type, cèpes the larger flat type of mushroom.

Nettles: when young these can be cooked like spinach — when preparing grasp firmly in gloved hands.

Okra (gumbo): pea-like vegetable in pod, obtainable canned if not fresh; slice, boil and serve with butter.

Onions: put into soups or stews, fry with meat or savoury dishes. As a separate vegetable boil for a good hour in salted water and serve with white sauce (page 143).

Parsley: eat raw, use as garnish or fry.

Parsnips: boil, steam or put into soups and stews, but as their flavour is rather dominating, do not use too large a proportion. Very good roasted round a joint.

Peas: shell and cook steadily in boiling salted water for 10–15 minutes. Serve with a little melted butter. Mint and 1 teaspoon of sugar improve the flavour.

Peppers, sweet red or green (capsicums): shred and use raw or in various ways, fried, added to sauces, egg dishes or a casserole, or as main dish stuffed whole (page 145).

Peppers, hot red or green (chillis): very pungent. Use sparingly for flavouring.

Potatoes: always put into BOILING salted water and cook steadily until soft. They can also be fried, roasted, baked in their jackets or steamed.

Pumpkin: use like vegetable marrow.

Radishes: serve in salad or cook in place of turnips.

Rutabaga: Swedish turnip, yellow or white fleshed. Cook like turnip.

Salsify (sometimes called oysterplant): wash or scrape well, then cook like Jerusalem artichokes. Serve with a little melted butter and chopped parsley.

Sauerkraut: make by fermenting cabbage. Can be obtained ready-prepared; heat with butter and flavourings.

Seakale: cook like celery — it is rather bitter if served raw.

Shallots: use like onions.

Sorrel: generally used in soup; it can be cooked like spinach.

Spinach: wash leaves in several waters. There is no need to add water to spinach, so just put into a strong pan with a little salt and boil rapidly until tender — about 15 minutes. Either rub through a sieve or turn on to a board and chop finely, then return to the pan with a little milk and butter, and reheat.

Spring greens: cook like cabbage.

Sweet potatoes or yams: cook like potatoes.

Squash: cook like vegetable marrow.

Swedes: cook like turnips.

Tomatoes: delicious raw, or can be used in every way cooked; they add flavour to all savoury dishes.

Turnips: put into stews and soups. When young they are very good cooked in boiling salted water, then mashed. Turnip tops can be cooked like cabbage.

Yams: see sweet potato.

Vegetable marrow (when small known as courgettes): peel, cut into neat pieces and either steam over boiling water, adding a little salt, or bake, stuffed, or boil in salted water until tender. Serve with cheese or white sauce (page 143). Marrows are also used in sweet dishes and jam. Courgettes (baby marrows) are delicious cooked with garlic in butter and oil.

Correct cooking of vegetables

By boiling

This is the most common way of cooking vegetables, and also the way in which they can be very readily spoiled by over-cooking.

To boil green vegetables
1 The quicker green vegetables are cooked, the more vitamin content they retain. It is important, wherever possible, to shred them or break into small pieces.
2 To shred cabbage, or other green vegetables, wash in cold water, add a little salt if wished, shake reasonably dry, put on the chopping board and cut into very fine shreds with a knife.
3 Put approximately 1 inch of water into a saucepan and add between $\frac{1}{4}$ and $\frac{1}{2}$ teaspoon of salt, depending on personal taste.
4 BRING THE WATER TO THE BOIL.
5 Always take the vegetables to the boiling water so that it does not go off the boil. Add the vegetables gradually to the water so the water continues to boil.
6 PUT A LID ON THE PAN AND COOK AS QUICKLY AS POSSIBLE.
7 You may have to look once or twice the first few times you cook by this method, which is known as the conserved method of cooking, since you conserve both flavour and goodness. The only difficulty is that in using such a small amount of water you must be careful to see that the liquid does not boil away completely. Adjust your heat to prevent this.
8 Serve as quickly as possible after cooking, straining, and mixing with a knob of butter or margarine.

To boil root vegetables
1 These can be cooked as quickly as green vegetables and should go into boiling water.
2 There used to be a rule that everything that grew above the ground went into boiling water and everything below the ground, which includes root vegetables, of course, went into cold. Modern dieticians have disproved this theory and have found that all vegetables are better cooked in boiling water.
3 Use about 2 inches of water and cook steadily, rather than rapidly, until tender.

To boil pulses
1 Peas, beans and lentils are the pulses and these have quite a lot of protein in them. They are, therefore, ideal to cook when you are having a meal with only a little meat or fish.
2 Put peas into boiling salted water, add a pinch of sugar and a sprig of mint.
3 Do not boil peas too rapidly, otherwise they toughen.

Pressure cooked vegetables

1 Your pressure cooking instruction book will give you details of the correct cooking of vegetables.
2 I must stress that over-cooking in a pressure cooker can ruin vegetables; 1 minute under this very high temperature counts as 5–6 in an ordinary pan.
3 Use less salt in a pressure cooker: the natural mineral salts are retained.
4 Green vegetables retain both flavour and vitamin content in a pressure cooker. Always put on the rack to keep crisp.
5 Root vegetables and pulses can also be cooked in a pressure cooker.
6 When you are cooking a selection of vegetables, separators are ideal.

Oven cooking of vegetables

It is possible to cook vegetables by various methods in the oven, and this is extremely useful if you have an automatic electric or gas cooker for it means that your complete meal can be cooked in the oven.

Boiling in a casserole

1 NEVER COOK GREEN VEGETABLES THIS WAY OTHERWISE YOU DESTROY ALL THEIR GOODNESS.
2 Prepare the vegetables as for boiling. The size will determine the cooking time, so if you have a meal which is being cooked for a long time keep the pieces of vegetable as big as possible.
3 Put into a casserole, adding about 1 inch of water, seasoning, a knob of butter or margarine.
4 Cover the top tightly. Foil tucked very firmly round the edges is excellent.
5 Cook for 1–2 hours in a moderate oven (375°F., Gas Mark 4), although the heat will be determined by the rest of the meal.
6 Strain and serve in the usual way.
7 As a little flavour may be lost by this method of cooking, a clove or spices can be added to give a change of taste.

Roasting vegetables

By cooking in hot fat in the oven you can keep in a great deal of the flavour. Unfortunately only certain vegetables are suitable for cooking by this method; onions, parsnips, potatoes and swedes are all good.

Roast onions

Preparation: 5 minutes
Cooking: 1½ hours

Secret of success
Choose large, firm, mature onions.
Good with lamb, veal or pork.

1 Peel the onions, season lightly.
2 Sprinkle with a little flour.
3 Put into really hot fat, either in a separate roasting tin or round the joint.
4 Roast for approximately 1½ hours in a moderately hot oven (400°F., Gas Mark 5–6), or 1 hour in a hot oven.

Note. If the onions are lightly sprinkled with sugar 15–20 minutes before they are cooked, they will have a delicious flavour.

Roast parsnips

Preparation: 10–12 minutes
Cooking: 1–1½ hours

Secret of success
Choose fairly young parsnips.
Excellent with beef.

1 These can be roasted raw in hot fat, or to give a better flavour first boil for 15–20 minutes in salted water.
2 Drain, pat dry in a cloth or kitchen paper and then put into hot fat.
3 They will take approximately 1¼–1½ hours if raw, and about 1 hour if partially boiled, in a hot oven (425–450°F., Gas Mark 6–7).

Note. The texture of parsnips which are boiled for 15–20 minutes before being roasted is rather better than those roasted from the raw state.

Roast potatoes

1 Details of roasting potatoes with meat are given on page 64.
2 If roasting potatoes for an automatic meal, i.e. where they are put into a cold oven, they must be coated with melted fat to keep them a good colour.

Roast swedes

1 Swedes can be roasted in just the same way as parsnips, above.
2 They are best simmered for 30 minutes, drained, then put into hot fat.

134

Baking vegetables

To bake vegetables means cooking them in the oven without liquid or fat. Obviously the vegetables must have a good skin, like potatoes or onions, so they don't spoil or dry. They can be wrapped in foil.

Baked potatoes

Preparation: 5–6 minutes
No delay
Cooking: 45 minutes–1 hour, or for slower method 1½–2 hours

Allow 1 potato per person

You can hasten cooking if you push a metal skewer through the middle before baking.

1 Scrub large potatoes, wipe them dry and rub with a little melted fat or oil. This makes the skin thick, shiny and delicious to eat.
2 Place on a baking tray or on the oven shelves.
3 The cooking time varies from 45 minutes to 1 hour in a hot oven (400–425°F., Gas Mark 6–7).
4 If wished, the potatoes can be cooked in a moderate oven for 1½–2 hours, or in a moderately hot oven for 1–1½ hours. To test if potatoes are cooked, press firmly; when soft they are tender. Make a small cross on top and, holding the potato in both hands, squeeze gently until the cross opens in four points and allows the steam to escape.
5 Serve with butter or margarine and seasoning.

Baked stuffed potatoes

Preparation: 10 minutes
No delay
Cooking: as baked potatoes plus a few minutes for reheating

This is one of the very best ways to serve a potato either as an accompaniment to the main dish or a light supper dish.

Colour picture, page 128

1 Prepare and bake the potatoes as above.
2 Cut off the tops, being careful to hold each potato firmly with a cloth, as it is very hot.
3 Scoop out the centre of the potato and put it into a basin.
4 Add salt and pepper and the filling. Choose one of the alternatives below.

5 Mix the potato pulp with the filling and a good knob of margarine or butter.
6 Pile back again into the potato case and reheat in the oven for about 10 minutes.

Filling: this could be grated cheese *or* chopped cooked fried bacon *or* a little yeast or beef extract *or* chopped cooked kidneys *or* a small quantity of chopped or minced cooked meat *or* canned or cooked corn on the cob.

Baked onions

Preparation: 7 minutes
No delay
Cooking: 1½ hours

Secret of success
Choose large, firm, mature onions.

1 Put the onions into a dish with a little butter, milk and seasoning.
2 Cover with buttered-paper if desired.
3 Cook in the centre of a moderate oven until tender. This will take approximately 1½ hours for medium sized onions.

Note. The onions can be sprinkled with grated cheese, or cheese and crumbs, about 15–20 minutes before serving. Do not cover the onions again.

Frying vegetables

Frying is a very good way of cooking certain vegetables, to keep maximum flavour. Directions for potatoes are given in full, but swedes, parsnips and aubergines can all be fried in a similar way.

Fried or chipped potatoes
(in deep fat)

Preparation: 10 minutes
No delay
Cooking: 5 minutes

Using deep fat or oil is the better way of frying potatoes; they crisp and brown more easily.

1 Peel potatoes, then cut into long even fingers.

2 Wash these, dry well in a cloth and keep in cloth until ready to cook, to keep as dry as possible and prevent discolouration.

3 Heat and test the fat as for fish (page 45). If preferred, use a chip instead of a cube of bread. The fat should bubble immediately, and the chip should stay at the top. If it sinks and there is no movement of fat, the temperature is too low.
4 Put enough chips into the frying basket to fill about one-quarter of it.
5 Lower carefully into fat. Make sure it does not overflow. Cook for about 3 minutes.

6 Remove potatoes with the basket and stand them on a plate.
7 Just before serving, reheat fat, test for temperature. Fry chips rapidly for about 2 minutes, until crisp and brown. Drain on absorbent paper.
8 Serve on a dish paper if possible; this makes certain the chips are well dried and crisp.

Frying potatoes in shallow fat

Cooking: 5–8 minutes – depending on thickness

1 Wash and dry the potatoes as described above. They can be cut into chip shapes, but when using less fat fairly thin slices are best.
2 Heat enough cooking fat, lard, oil, or well clarified dripping in the bottom of a frying pan to give a good $\frac{1}{4}$ inch depth. Test for correct temperature (see above).
3 Fry steadily for approximately $2\frac{1}{2}$–3 minutes, turn, cook on the other side, then drain.

Sauté potatoes

Preparation: few minutes
No delay
Cooking: 5–6 minutes

For sauté potatoes, use potatoes that have been boiled. Make sure they are not over-cooked, so that you can slice really neatly.
1 Cut boiled potatoes into neat slices.
2 Put the slices of potato into a small amount of hot fat and cook for 2–3 minutes on either side.
3 Drain as for chipped potatoes. Sprinkle with parsley.

Potato croquettes

Preparation: 12 minutes
No delay
Cooking: several minutes

Deep fat or oil browns the finger shapes more evenly.

1 Mash potatoes as directed on page 138.
2 Add seasoning and margarine but NO milk.
3 Form mashed potatoes, which should be smooth but firm, into the desired shapes.
4 Coat the outside with a little flour; the easiest way is to put some flour on a plate and roll the croquettes in this.
5 Brush with beaten egg and coat in crisp breadcrumbs.
6 Heat the fat. Put the croquettes into the frying basket.
7 Fry for several minutes; drain well on absorbent paper, as potato chips.

Fried onions

Preparation: 10–12 minutes
No delay
Cooking: few minutes deep fat; 6–8 minutes shallow fat

An excellent accompaniment to many dishes, particularly fried or grilled steak and fried liver.

1 Peel and cut onions into slices, then separate into rings.
2 Dry well, then coat each ring with a little seasoned flour.
3 Shake away surplus flour and put onions into deep hot fat.
4 For testing the temperature of the fat see page 136.
5 For very crisp fried onions, remove from the fat when golden brown, heat the fat for a few minutes longer then put the onions back in for another minute.
6 Drain on crumpled tissue or kitchen paper.
7 If using shallow fat, the onions need not be coated but just fried steadily in a little hot fat until tender.

Onion fritter rings

Preparation: 10–12 minutes
No delay
Cooking: few minutes
Serves 4

These look, as well as taste, delicious.

| 4 medium onions | ¼ pint milk | 3 oz. plain flour |
| 1 egg | good pinch of salt | lard *for deep frying* |

1 Peel and cut onions into ¼-inch slices and separate into rings.
2 Beat egg and stir in milk and salt.
3 Add a few onion rings at a time to this mixture and coat thoroughly.
4 Place flour in a polythene or paper bag and add onion rings, a few at a time, and shake to coat.
5 Fry in deep lard, as above, until delicately browned. Drain on absorbent paper.

Fried mushrooms

Preparation: few minutes
Cooking: 6–8 minutes

To prepare mushrooms, cut off base of stalks. If of prime quality, wash very well in plenty of cold water. Big field mushrooms must be skinned. To do this: lift edge of skin with point of knife, or your fingers, and pull off, being careful not to break the cap of the mushroom.
1 Heat a knob of fat in a frying pan.
2 Cook on the white side of the mushroom first, then on stalk side, until just tender. Do not have fat too hot so that the mushrooms brown.
3 Lift out and drain with a fish slice or on paper.

Note. If the mushrooms are fried in beef dripping they have an excellent flavour. Toss in finely chopped chives and parsley before serving.
They make an excellent after-dinner savoury served on toast or fried bread.

Fried tomatoes

Preparation: few minutes
No delay
Cooking: few minutes

1 Halve or slice the tomatoes.
2 Heat a very little fat in the bottom of a frying pan, put in the tomatoes.
3 Sprinkle lightly with a pinch of salt, a shake of pepper, and some people like a pinch of sugar.
4 Fry steadily for just a few minutes. Do not over-cook.

Note. 1–2 crushed cloves of garlic add an excellent flavour to the tomatoes. Add the garlic to the hot fat.

Bubble and squeak

Preparation: few minutes
No delay
Cooking: approximately 10 minutes

A good way to use left-over potatoes and cabbage.

1 Use approximately the same amount of cooked potato and cooked green vegetable.
2 Mash the potatoes with a fork until very smooth.
3 Put into a basin with the cabbage, a knob of fat, and, if rather dry, a very little milk or stock.
4 Heat enough fat in a frying pan; dripping gives the best flavour.
5 Put in the mixture and flatten.
6 Cook *steadily* for about 5 minutes: lift edge of mixture to see if browning. If it is, turn the heat very low until mixture is heated through.
7 If possible, fold in half rather like an omelette and place on a hot dish.

Mashing and creaming vegetables

This method is an ideal way of serving older potatoes. *To mash* simply means beating with a fork until there are no lumps and the mixture is very smooth. For a small child, or invalid, it is always a good idea to rub the vegetables through a sieve.

To cream means first to mash and then to add a little milk or cream, butter and a small amount of extra seasoning. Below you will find a recipe for creaming potatoes — carrots, swedes and parsnips are all creamed in the same way.

Creamed potatoes

Preparation: 7–8 minutes
No delay
Cooking: 20–25 minutes
Serves 4

To make a change from the familiar white of potatoes put them under a very hot grill for a few seconds to brown the top.

1¼–1½ lb. potatoes*	¼ pint milk	*to garnish*
1–2 oz. margarine	salt and pepper	parsley

* new potatoes cannot be mashed or creamed.

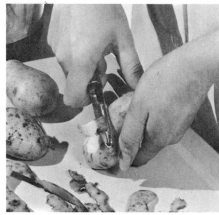 

1 Peel potatoes thinly with a potato peeler or sharp knife.
2 Put the potatoes into boiling salted water and cook until just tender – do not boil too quickly.
3 Strain through a colander – return to pan.
4 Mash with a fork, then beat with a wooden spoon. Try to do this near an open window or door; it will whiten the potatoes.
5 Heat the margarine and milk together, then gradually add to the potatoes, beating as you do so. Season.

6 Pile into a dish, fork into a neat shape and garnish with a sprig of parsley.

Creamed mushrooms

Preparation: few minutes
No delay
Cooking: 10 minutes
Serves 4

If you wish a more attractive colour to this dish
a) make a white sauce;
b) fry the mushrooms in butter, and
c) blend sauce and cooked mushrooms.

8 oz. mushrooms	1 oz. flour	1 oz. butter
½ pint stock	2 tablespoons milk	salt and pepper

1 Prepare the mushrooms as directed on page 137.
2 Put into a saucepan with the stock (or use water and a little yeast extract), and simmer steadily for about 6 minutes. *You can use milk instead of stock here but the appearance of the finished dish is much better if stock is used.*
3 Blend the flour very carefully with the milk.
4 Add to the mushrooms and liquid with the butter and seasoning.
5 Bring to the boil, stirring all the time: cook until smooth, then serve.

Creamed mushrooms – cooking mushrooms in a little stock

Less usual ways of serving vegetables

Since vegetables are served so regularly in the average home, you will find it worthwhile trying new ideas with them from time to time.

Duchesse potatoes

This is the name given to creamed potatoes when made richer by the addition of more butter and egg.

1 To every 1 lb. potatoes beat in at least 1 oz., and preferably 2 oz., butter, but do not put in any milk.
2 You should also add the yolks of 1 or 2 eggs — a good way of using up an egg yolk if you have used the white in a sweet.
3 Beat together and reheat in the pan, but for a professional touch pipe as shown in the picture.

Piping Duchesse potatoes

Piped potatoes

If you have aspirations to become good at piping and decorating the very best thing for practising with is mashed potato.

1 Use a duchesse potato mixture or creamed potatoes, but do not put in too much milk or the mixture will be too soft.
2 If you have any doubt as to whether the mixture is smooth, the potatoes must be rubbed through a sieve *before* creaming.
3 Use a cloth piping bag and a potato pipe.
4 Insert the pipe into the bag.
5 Half fill with the potato; this is easier to handle if reasonably warm.
6 Press steadily and firmly through the pipe, either as a border for dishes or in small shapes.

Honeyed pineapple carrots

Preparation: 15 minutes
Cooking: 30–35 minutes
Serves 4

The combination of sweet flavours and carrots is very pleasant.

15 small long carrots*
2 tablespoons canned pineapple cubes *or* chopped fresh pineapple

2 oz. butter
2 tablespoons honey

1 tablespoon lemon juice

* canned carrots could be used instead.

1 Cook whole carrots in a small quantity of boiling, salted water until just tender — see page 133. If using canned carrots, heat only.
2 Meanwhile chop the pineapple.
3 Drain the carrots in a colander.
4 Melt the butter in the pan.
5 Add the honey, lemon juice and pineapple.
6 Add the carrots and turn to coat evenly.
7 Tip into a shallow baking tin.
8 Bake for about 8 minutes in a moderate oven (375°F., Gas Mark 4).

Using canned beans and peas

When time is short one is often tempted to open a can of peas or beans. With a little imagination they can be transformed into quite exotic dishes. Here are a few ideas.

Peas New Orleans

Preparation: 8 minutes
No delay
Cooking: few minutes
Serves 4–6

The mint flavour is very strong, particularly if using dried mint. You may like to use a little less.

Peas New Orleans

2 oz. butter *or* margarine
2 oz. chopped fresh mint leaves *or* 1 teaspoon crumbled dried mint leaves

½ medium orange
2 teaspoons sugar
¼ teaspoon salt
large can garden peas

to garnish
orange segments

1 Melt the butter or margarine in a pan.
2 Add the mint and grated orange rind.
3 Simmer gently for 3 or 4 minutes.
4 Stir in orange juice, sugar and salt.
5 Drain the peas.
6 Add the peas to the sauce and mix lightly.
7 Cover and cook until the peas are hot. Turn into a serving dish.
8 Garnish with orange segments, see picture.

Country style bean bake

Preparation: 8 minutes
No delay
Cooking: 10–25 minutes
Serves 4

Children enjoy baked beans which are a good source of protein.
This is a very pleasant way to serve them.

2 onions
1½ oz. butter

large can baked beans
1 tablespoon treacle *or* molasses

1 teaspoon made-mustard
pinch of powdered cloves

1 Peel the onions and cut into rings.
2 Heat the butter in a pan.
3 Lightly brown the onion in the butter.
4 Mix most of the onion with the beans, treacle or molasses, prepared-mustard and a pinch of powdered cloves.
5 Top with the rest of the onion rings and heat in a saucepan for about 5 minutes, or bake in a casserole in a very moderate oven (325°F., Gas Mark 3) for about 20 minutes, or until bubbling hot.

Beans in round dogs

Preparation: 12 minutes
No delay
Cooking: 15–30 minutes
Serves 6–8

8 frankfurter sausages
little fat *for frying*

for the bean mixture
1 onion

1 apple
2 large cans beans in tomato sauce
sprinkling brown sugar

½–1 tablespoon chilli *or* Worcestershire sauce
1 teaspoon made-mustard
2 tablespoons chutney

4 rolls *or* 8 slices toast

1 To twist the frankfurters, slash at intervals on one side and place them in hot fat in a frying pan. They curl as they heat.
2 Grate the onion and apple.
3 Mix the beans thoroughly with all the other ingredients and cook for about 10 minutes in a saucepan, or 25 minutes in a moderate oven (375°F., Gas Mark 4).
4 Arrange the frankfurter sausages on sliced hot rolls, or rounds of toast, and fill with the hot bean mixture.
5 Put the extra bean mixture into a serving dish.

Zippy beans

Preparation: 12–15 minutes
No delay
Cooking: 35–40 minutes
Serves 6–8

Secret of success
Be sparing with the Tabasco
sauce – it *is* very strong.

2 onions
1 green pepper

2 large cans beans in
    tomato sauce
2 teaspoons made-mustard

dash Tabasco sauce,
    optional
grated cheese

1 Grate or chop one of the onions finely and cut the other into rings.
2 Chop the green pepper, discarding the seeds.
3 Mix all the ingredients except the onion slices and cheese.
4 Place in a baking dish and heat in the centre of a moderate oven (375°F., Gas Mark 4)
   for 25–30 minutes.
5 Arrange the onion rings on top and sprinkle generously with cheese.
6 Return the dish, uncovered, to the oven for about 10 minutes, or until the cheese is
   lightly brown.

Dried vegetables

To prepare dried peas, beans, lentils:
1 Soak overnight in cold water.
2 Add a good pinch of salt and simmer very gently in the same water for approximately
   1½–2 hours.
3 Remember dried vegetables 'swell' a great deal during cooking, so therefore allow
   plenty of water and not too great an amount of vegetable, i.e. 1 oz. dried peas or
   beans is generally a fairly ample portion for each person.

Pressure cooking of dried vegetables

A pressure cooker is an ideal way of cooking dried vegetables, for it cuts out an
enormous amount of cooking time and does give you a more tender vegetable.
1 Soak overnight in cold water then put the water, with salt to taste, into the pressure
   cooker.
2 *Never have the pressure cooker more than half filled with dried vegetables.*
3 Allow 15 minutes at 15 lb. pressure for peas and lentils, 25–30 minutes for beans.
4 Allow pressure to drop at room temperature.

Grilling vegetables

Not many vegetables are suitable for cooking under a grill, but mushrooms and
tomatoes can be cooked in this way.
1 Prepare vegetable, i.e. halve tomatoes, etc.
2 In order to keep the vegetables moist, put them in the grill pan rather than on the grid.
3 Put plenty of margarine or butter on top.
4 Season lightly and cook for about 10 minutes.

Grilled mushrooms on toast.

To braise vegetables

Braising vegetables, like any other food, means serving them in a really good brown sauce. The vegetables most suitable for cooking by this method are onions, celery and leeks. The easiest way to braise vegetables is as this method.

1 Peel onions or cut celery or leeks into even-sized lengths.
2 Fry lightly in just a little fat.
3 Lift into casserole and coat with brown sauce (recipe below).
4 Use a coating consistency of brown sauce, as some juice comes from the vegetables and this will thin the liquid down.
5 Cover the casserole very well.
6 The time for cooking varies with the vegetables. *Onions* will take approximately 1½ hours, *leeks* approximately 1 hour, *celery* approximately 1–1½ hours, in a very moderate oven (350°F., Gas Mark 3).
7 If by chance the sauce is a little too thick, when serving add 2 or 3 tablespoons of stock or hot water, stirring it well.

Vegetables as a main meal

Cauliflower cheese (recipe on page 144)

Vegetables can be served as a main dish providing some form of protein food is added to them. For flavouring they can be sprinkled with grated cheese or topped with an egg.

One of the best ways of turning vegetables into a satisfying meal is to coat them with a sauce. In order that the vegetables are not over-cooked, start making the sauce just before straining the vegetables.

The right way to make a sauce

People often say that making a sauce is extremely difficult. In actual fact it is very simple providing you follow the method carefully for the first few times.
1 Use a wooden spoon. This gives you greater control over the liquid.
2 Make sure that the butter or fat heats gently, but does not over-heat and discolour.
3 *Take the pan off the heat before stirring in the flour.*
4 Do not over-cook the roux, i.e. fat and flour, otherwise the flour will discolour. Keep it moving with the wooden spoon all the time it is cooking. It is ready for the addition of liquid when it looks very much drier, or see brown sauce.
5 Take the pan off the heat before adding the milk.
6 GRADUALLY stir the cold milk or liquid into the roux.
7 Continue to stir as the sauce comes to the boil and begins to thicken.
8 *If by chance the sauce goes a little lumpy in spite of all your care, give it a really sharp whisk using a proper egg whisk.*

Brown sauce

Preparation: 5 minutes
Cooking: 10 minutes

* if using the brown sauce for *meat* this should either be meat stock, see page 63, or use water and beef extract or stock cube. If using brown sauce for *vegetables* this can be meat stock, see page 63, or use water and yeast extract.

coating consistency (sauce)
1 oz. cooking fat *or* dripping

1 oz. flour
½ pint brown stock*

salt and pepper

panada (binding consistency)
as above but use ¼ pint brown stock*

thin sauce
as above but use 1 pint brown stock*

1 Heat the fat or dripping in a pan. For a better flavour, fry a little chopped onion, celery and carrot, in which case use 2 oz. fat.
2 Add the flour and cook steadily in the fat until brown in colour. Be careful not to over-brown this.
3 Add the stock, carefully stirring all the time. Bring to the boil, season and cook until thick and smooth. If vegetables have been used, strain.

White sauce

Preparation: few minutes
Cooking: 5–8 minutes
Serves 4

Secret of success
If this, or any other sauce, appears lumpy, whisk sharply at stage 5 or emulsify in a warmed liquidiser goblet.

coating consistency (sauce)
1 oz. butter *or* margarine   ½ pint milk   salt and pepper
1 oz. flour

panada (binding consistency) ·   *thin white sauce for soups*
as above but use ¼ pint milk   as above but use 1 pint milk

1 Heat the butter or margarine gently, remove from the heat and stir in the flour.
2 Return to the heat and cook gently for a few minutes, so that the 'roux', as the butter and flour mixture is called, does not brown.
3 Again remove the pan from the heat and gradually blend in the cold milk.
4 Bring to the boil, then cook, stirring with a wooden spoon, until smooth.
5 Season well and serve.

Using white sauce with vegetables

Use a coating consistency for serving with vegetables. For a good flavour use less milk and make up the quantity with vegetable stock.

Cheese sauce

Preparation: few minutes
Cooking: 5–8 minutes
Serves 4

1 Make white sauce as directed above.
2 When thickened, stir in 3–6 oz. grated cheese and a little mustard.
3 Do NOT boil too long as the cheese will become 'stringy' and tough.

Good cooking cheeses to select: Cheddar, Gruyère, Dutch, Emmenthal, or Parmesan.

Parsley sauce

Preparation: few minutes
Cooking: 8 minutes
Serves 4

1 Make the white sauce as directed above.
2 Add 1–2 tablespoons chopped parsley.
3 Cook for several minutes if you like the milder taste of *cooked* parsley, or add the chopped parsley to the sauce and serve at once, to retain flavour and firm texture of the uncooked herb.
4 This is excellent with fish or vegetables.

Mushroom sauce

Preparation: 10 minutes
Cooking: 12 minutes
Serves 4

For a paler-coloured sauce, fry mushrooms in a separate pan, then blend with sauce and serve.

ingredients as white sauce above, but use ½ pint and 2 tablespoons milk and add 2–4 oz. mushrooms

1 Prepare the mushrooms and slice – see page 137.
2 Put on to cook with the milk, and simmer for 5 minutes.
3 Make a 'roux' with the butter and flour as in white sauce, in another saucepan.
4 When the flour has been cooking for several minutes, gradually add the milk and mushrooms, stirring all the time until the sauce thickens.
5 Season well.

Shrimp sauce

Preparation: few minutes
Cooking: 5–8 minutes
Serves 4

1 Make white sauce as directed above.
2 Add about 2–4 oz. chopped prawns and a little anchovy essence just before serving; do not over-cook, otherwise this toughens the fish.
3 If using fresh prawns, simmer shells and use ¼ pint stock instead of the same amount of milk.
This sauce is excellent with fish and with cauliflower.

Hollandaise sauce

Preparation: few minutes
Cooking: approximately 10 minutes
Serves 4

Secret of success
This is *not* an easy sauce, for it is essential to whisk hard (see stage 2) and to keep the sauce from becoming too hot.

2 egg yolks   pinch of cayenne pepper   2–4 oz. butter
salt and pepper   1–2 tablespoons lemon juice
           or white wine vinegar

1 Try to use a double saucepan. Put the egg yolks, seasoning and lemon juice or vinegar into the top.
2 Whisk over hot water until the sauce begins to thicken.
3 Add the butter in very small pieces, whisking in each pat and allowing to melt before adding the next.
4 DO NOT ALLOW TO BOIL, otherwise it will curdle.
5 If too thick, add a little thick cream.

Cauliflower cheese

Cauliflower au gratin

Preparation: 10 minutes
No delay
Cooking: 20 minutes
Serves 4

If wished, use half milk and half cauliflower stock for sauce.

1 medium cauliflower
½ pint cheese sauce, *page 143*

1 oz. Cheddar cheese, grated

1 tablespoon crisp breadcrumbs

1 Cook the cauliflower in a little boiling water in a covered pan until tender. Drain.
2 Arrange neatly in buttered scallop shells or an ovenproof dish.
3 Make the cheese sauce.
4 Coat the cauliflower with the cheese sauce, this gives *Cauliflower cheese* (*mornay*) (picture page 142).
5 Sprinkle with cheese mixed with crisp breadcrumbs and brown under a hot grill or in a hot oven (425°F., Gas Mark 6), this dish is called *Cauliflower au gratin*.

Seafood cauliflower

Preparation: 10 minutes
Cooking: 20 minutes
Serves 4

If using frozen shrimps, allow these to defrost at room temperature. Prawns may be used instead. Do not over-cook the cauliflower.

1 small cauliflower
1 oz. cornflour
¾ pint tomato juice
few canned, fresh *or* frozen shrimps

2 oz. cheese, grated
1 oz. butter
little chopped parsley
1 teaspoon Worcestershire sauce

squeeze of lemon juice
salt and pepper
pinch of sugar

1 Trim cauliflower and remove some of the hard stem with a circular cutting motion.
2 Prepare a sufficiently large pan of boiling salted water.

3 Cover and cook steadily until tender.
4 *Meanwhile make the sauce:* mix cornflour smoothly with a little of the tomato juice, put the rest on to heat. Add the mixed cornflour, stir until boiling and boil for 3 minutes.

5 Add the shrimps, cheese, butter, parsley, Worcestershire sauce, lemon juice, seasoning, sugar. Heat for 1–2 minutes.

6 Drain the cauliflower, place on a serving dish and pour the sauce over.

Stuffed vegetables

Certain vegetables can be stuffed in order to turn them into a more substantial dish. You can use:

Veal stuffing (*page 85*)
This goes very well with peppers but is rather flavourless for marrow.

Sage and onion stuffing (*page 80*)
This is very good for marrow.

Savoury meat stuffing
1 Make ½ pint brown sauce as directed on page 142.
2 Add to this 8 oz. minced meat, cooked or fresh, and a beef stock cube.
3 Stir in a pinch of mixed herbs and 2 oz. breadcrumbs.

Rice stuffing
1 Boil 2 oz. long grain rice as directed on page 147.
2 Mix with 3 oz. grated cheese, 2 skinned and chopped tomatoes and seasoning.
3 Add a little chopped parsley or mixed herbs.

Stuffed marrow

Preparation: 20 minutes
No delay
Cooking: 1½ hours
Serves 4–6

This dish makes an appetising and economical main meal.

| 1 medium vegetable marrow | stuffing, *see above* | 2–3 oz. fat |

1 Peel the vegetable marrow and halve lengthways.
2 Remove the seeds.
3 Press stuffing into one half of the cavity and put the second half over the top.
4 Tie with string.
5 Heat the fat in a roasting tin for approximately 5–6 minutes.
6 Put in the stuffed marrow, and bake for 1¼–1½ hours in the centre of a moderately hot oven (400°F., Gas Mark 5–6).
7 Spoon the hot fat over the top of the marrow from time to time during cooking to brown it.

Stuffed peppers

Preparation: 20 minutes. After boiling, allow peppers to cool for a few minutes
Cooking: approximately 55 minutes
Serves 4

These vegetables are ideal to serve with a stuffing, for they look and taste interesting.

| 4 green *or* red peppers | stuffing, *see above* | little fat |

1 Cut the tops off the peppers.
2 Scoop out the centre core and pips. Discard these as they are inclined to be very hot.
3 Cook the peppers in boiling salted water for 5 minutes only, lift out, cool slightly.
4 Pack with the stuffing and bake for approximately 35–40 minutes in the centre of a moderate oven (350–375°F., Gas Mark 4–5).
5 A savoury meat stuffing is one of the best fillings for peppers.

Stuffed peppers

Vegetable pie

Preparation: 30–40 minutes
No delay
Cooking: approximately 1 hour
Serves 4

This is a nutritious as well as appetising meatless main dish.

1 lb. potatoes
approximately 1–1¼ lb.
  mixed root vegetables (not
  potatoes)

4–6 oz. cheese, grated

for the sauce
1 oz. butter

1 oz. flour
½ pint milk *or* milk and
  vegetable stock
salt and pepper

1 Prepare the potatoes and put on to cook. When cooked, drain and cream them as directed on page 138.
2 Peel and cut the vegetables into small pieces. Cook until tender, then drain.
3 Make the white sauce as directed on page 143.
4 Mix the diced cooked vegetables with the sauce and most of the grated cheese. Put into a pie dish.
5 Top with the creamed potato and the remaining grated cheese.
6 Put into a moderately hot oven (400°F., Gas Mark 5) for approximately 15 minutes.

Vegetable cutlets

Preparation: 15 minutes
Allow mixture to cool before shaping
Cooking: 30 minutes
Serves 2

To add to the food value of this dish use peas or beans among the vegetables and/or add grated cheese to the sauce.

8 oz. root vegetables

for the sauce
1 oz. butter

1 oz. flour
¼ pint milk
salt and pepper

1 egg
1 oz. crisp breadcrumbs
fat *for frying*

1 Peel and dice the vegetables. Cook until *just* tender; drain.
2 Make the white sauce (panada consistency) as directed on page 143.
3 Mix the sauce and vegetables together and allow to cool.
4 Form into cutlet shapes.
5 Brush with beaten egg and coat in breadcrumbs.
6 Fry in shallow fat for approximately 3–4 minutes on either side.
7 Drain on absorbent paper and serve hot or cold.

Egg and vegetable cutlets

Recipe as above, but add 2 chopped hard-boiled eggs to the vegetable and sauce mixture.

Rice and vegetable cutlets

Recipe as above, but add 1 oz. cooked long grain rice and 2 oz. grated cheese to the vegetable mixture.

Corn toasties

Preparation: 10 minutes
No delay
Cooking: 10 minutes
Serves 4

Corn is a very pleasant and sustaining vegetable and the canned corn keeps the flavour and texture of the fresh vegetable very well.

3 oz. butter
½ onion
2 tomatoes

2 oz. mushrooms, optional
large can corn and sweet
  pepper mixed

2 oz. ham
4 slices bread
1 oz. cheese, grated

1 Heat the butter in a pan and gently sauté the finely chopped onion, chopped tomatoes and mushrooms, if used.
2 Drain the can of corn and pepper and add to the mixture in the pan.
3 Heat gently and stir in the chopped ham.
4 Toast the bread.
5 Arrange the corn mixture on slices of toast.
6 Sprinkle with grated cheese and grill until golden brown.

Corn stuffed potatoes

Bake 2 really large potatoes in their jackets, see directions on page 135. When cooked, halve carefully to keep the skin intact. Scoop out the centre pulp, mash with a little butter, seasoning. Open a can of corn kernels, drain this. Blend the corn and 3 oz. grated cheese with the potato pulp. Moisten with 2 tablespoons milk or thin cream. Pile back into the potato cases. Heat for a few minutes, top with more grated cheese and serve.

Savoury rice dishes

Using rice in the menu

Secret of success
Use long grain rice for all savoury dishes.

Rice is a very pleasant addition to a number of dishes. It blends extremely well with vegetables just as it does with fish, meat, or cheese dishes. It is essential to choose the correct rice for a specific purpose. As you will see under puddings (page 163) round grain rice is ideal because this becomes slightly sticky in cooking and so thickens the pudding. For savoury dishes, on the other hand, one generally wants the rice to remain fairly firm, with each grain separate, and so it is best to choose long grain rice, sometimes known as Patna rice, although today this grain is produced in many other countries.

Boiled rice

to serve with curries and savoury dishes

Preparation: few minutes
No delay
Cooking: 10–16 minutes

Secret of success
Use long grain rice for all savoury dishes.

| 4 oz. long grain rice | 2 pints water | $\frac{1}{2}$–1 teaspoon salt |

1 Wash the rice well.
2 Bring the water to the boil, add salt and rice.
3 Boil steadily for 10–16 minutes (or time stated on the packet).
4 Test most carefully to see if *just soft but firm*.
5 Strain, then rinse the rice in the strainer. To use at once, pour boiling water through the grains to free them from starch. If you have time to reheat the rice, pour cold water through the grains, then spread out on a baking tray covered with muslin or kitchen paper and reheat in a slow oven (275–300°F., Gas Mark 1–2), stirring once or twice.

One-Two method of cooking rice

Preparation: few minutes
Cooking: 20 minutes

If using *quick-cooking* rice use twice the amount of water to rice, i.e.
1 oz. rice, 2 fluid oz. water; 1 cup rice, 2 cups water.
If using *slower-cooking* rice, use $2\frac{1}{2}$ times amount of water.
1 Put the rice and cold water, with salt to taste, into a pan.
2 Bring the water to the boil as quickly as possible, stir briskly, cover pan.
3 Simmer gently for 15 minutes, by which time the water will have been absorbed.
4 Serve at once.

Steamed rice

Preparation: few minutes
No delay
Cooking: 1 hour

Secret of success
Use long grain rice for all savoury dishes.

1 Wash the rice very well; use long grain rice unless serving it as a sweet.
2 Cover with water, then stand the basin in a steamer or in a pan of boiling water. Make sure the rice and water only half fill the basin.
3 Put a piece of greased paper over the basin if standing it in a saucepan of water, or put the lid on the steamer.
4 Cook very slowly for about 1 hour, by which time the rice will have absorbed all the water and each grain should be fluffy and white. It does not need rinsing.

Fried rice

Preparation: few minutes
No delay
Cooking: 10–16 minutes for boiling, about 5 minutes for frying.

| 4 oz. cooked long grain rice | 2 tablespoons oil | *to garnish* chopped parsley |

1 Dry the cooked rice very well, then toss in the hot oil and fry for several minutes until golden brown.
2 Garnish with chopped parsley.

Orange rice

Melt 2 oz. butter in a pan, add 8 oz. celery and 2 onions, finely chopped, 1 lb. rice and teaspoon salt; mix well. Pour over $1\frac{1}{2}$ pints stock, $\frac{1}{2}$ pint orange juice. Bring to boil, stir, lower heat and simmer 15 minutes, uncovered. Add 4 oz. raisins and grated rind 1 orange before serving. Garnish with orange segments.

Garlic rice

1 Heat 1–2 oz. butter in a pan.
2 Add 1 or 2 crushed cloves of garlic.
3 Toss in the butter until softened, then add to steamed rice (*see above*).

Rice with shrimps and peppers

Preparation: 8–10 minutes
No delay
Cooking: 15 minutes plus time
for boiling or steaming rice
Serves 2–3

Secret of success
Do not over-cook the shrimps,
etc.; this toughens shellfish.

1 onion
½ green pepper
½ red pepper

2 tablespoons oil
4 oz. shrimps *or* prawns
4 oz. boiled *or* steamed
  rice, *page 147*

1 tablespoon soy sauce
2 eggs
salt to taste

1 Chop the onion coarsely and slice the peppers, removing seeds.
2 Heat the oil in a frying pan, fry the onion until brown.
3 Add the shrimps or prawns, and sliced peppers, then fry until semi-cooked.
4 Add the cold rice and fry gently, stirring continuously, until the mixture begins to brown.
5 When the mixture is hot, add the soy sauce, then the eggs, beaten with salt to taste, and fry gently for 2–3 minutes.

Rice with mushrooms

Preparation: 8–10 minutes
No delay
Cooking: 10 minutes plus time
for boiling or steaming rice
Serves 2–3

1 onion
4 oz. mushrooms
2 tablespoons oil

4 oz. boiled *or* steamed
  rice, *page 147*

1 tablespoon soy sauce
salt and pepper

1 Chop the onion finely and the mushrooms rather coarsely.
2 Heat the oil in a frying pan, add the chopped onion and fry until brown, then add mushrooms and fry until semi-cooked.
3 Add the cold rice and fry gently until the whole begins to brown, stirring occasionally. Take care not to burn mixture.
4 When the mixture is hot, add the soy sauce and pepper and salt to taste.

Saffron rice

Preparation: few minutes
No delay
Cooking: 10–16 minutes for
boiling, 1 hour for steaming
Serves 2–3

4 oz. boiled *or* steamed
  rice

½–1 teaspoon saffron
  powder*

1 oz. butter

* the amount of saffron powder is very generous. Reduce to ¼ teaspoon if wished.

1 Boil or steam the rice as directed on page 147; add the powdered saffron blended with a little water, or use a few drops of saffron.
2 Strain the rice, if necessary, and toss in butter.
3 This is an excellent accompaniment to fish.

Stuffed onions

Boil 5 or 6 large onions until nearly tender. Remove from the salted water, cool, remove centres and chop these. Mix chopped onion with 2–3 oz. chopped fried mushrooms, 2 oz. cooked rice, seasoning, 1–2 oz. margarine or butter and a good pinch of sage. Fill the onion cases, then put into a greased dish with 2–3 tablespoons onion stock. Bake for 40 minutes in centre of a moderate oven. Serve with fried mushrooms, tomato rings; garnish with parsley, as shown.

Stuffed onions

Chocolate steamed
sponge pudding

1 Cream fat and sugar; beat in eggs.

2 Fold in sieved flour and cocoa.

3 Turn into greased pudding basin. Cover with greased greaseproof paper, see pages 70 and 154.

4 Shake pudding out on to hot dish.

5 Serve with hot orange sauce.

Puddings and sweets

A good pudding makes a meal

Today puddings tend to be lighter, because so much stress is laid on the importance of watching one's weight, and the value of fresh fruit in the diet. A good pudding can make a meal a well balanced one; for example, if you have had a rather light salad as a first course then a steamed pudding containing fats, eggs and flour is a very good choice.

On the other hand, if you have had a substantial first course, a light sweet, probably some kind of fruit recipe, prevents a feeling of being over-fed.

To make a perfect steamed pudding

In this book you will find a number of recipes for steamed puddings of various kinds. Remember that:

1 The water must be boiling when the pudding goes on to cook, and it must keep boiling fairly rapidly for the first hour.
2 There are a number of fats that can be used for making a sponge type of pudding. Choose between margarine, whipped-up cooking fat or butter.
3 Some of the modern whipped-up cooking fats (shortenings), and certain types of margarine, cream very quickly indeed, and if you are in a hurry it is a good idea to choose these.
4 Watch the water under the pudding to make sure it *is* boiling; when you have to fill up the pan below the steamer fill up with boiling water.
5 Cover the top of the pudding very well; use foil or a pudding cloth over paper.
6 Make sure the lid of the steamer fits very tightly so that the steam does cook the pudding.

Chocolate steamed sponge pudding

Preparation: 15 minutes
No delay
Cooking: 1–1¼ hours
Serves 4–6

Secret of success
Make quite certain the water boils very rapidly for the first 1 hour. This ensures the pudding rises well.
The pudding may be prepared in an electric mixer if wished.

4 oz. butter *or* margarine
4 oz. castor sugar
2 eggs

4 oz. flour (with plain flour use 1 level teaspoon baking powder)

1 tablespoon cocoa
about 1 tablespoon warm water

1 Cream the fat and sugar together until light and fluffy. Do this exactly as recommended for sponge cake (page 242), and see picture below.

2 Beat in the eggs a little at a time, (*colour picture 1, opposite*).
3 Fold in the sieved flour, baking powder, if used, and cocoa, adding sufficient warm water to form a soft dropping consistency, i.e. so that mixture drops readily from the spoon, (*colour picture 2*).
4 Turn into a greased pudding basin (greased with cooking fat, margarine or butter), filling only three-quarters full to allow room to rise, (*colour picture 3*).
5 Cover with a greased greaseproof paper cap and seal by folding under rim of basin. To make this cut a round of double greaseproof paper, grease on underside, place over top of basin and tuck in edges very lightly. See pages 70 and 154.
6 Steam about 1–1¼ hours over boiling water.
7 Turn on to a hot dish. Notice how to hold basin, so you can shake pudding out without breaking it. If it appears to stick, loosen round the edges with a palette or round-bladed knife, (*colour picture 4*).
8 Serve at once with hot chocolate or custard sauce, or with an orange sauce containing 1 orange cut into pieces as shown (*picture 5*). For sauce recipes see page 157.

To cook a pudding without a steamer

1 Stand basin on an upturned saucer in a pan, which should be half filled with boiling water.
2 You will find it safer and easier to take the pudding in and out of the pan if you tie the paper round with string and then make a string handle of double thickness over the top, or support the basin with a double band of foil.
3 Keep water boiling rapidly and look at fairly frequent intervals to make sure it has not boiled away.
4 Fill up with boiling water, but make sure level of the water is not so high that it might boil into the pudding.
5 Cook for same time as when steaming.

Steamed jam sponge pudding

Preparation: either 15 minutes or 5 minutes if using quick method. No delay
Cooking: 1½ hours
Serves 4–6

Secret of success
Make quite certain the water boils very rapidly for the first hour. This ensures the pudding rises well.
The pudding may be prepared in an electric mixer if wished.

3 oz. margarine
3 oz. castor sugar
2 eggs

4 oz. flour (with plain flour use 1 level teaspoon baking powder)

1 tablespoon milk
½ oz. margarine, melted
2 level tablespoons raspberry jam

1 Either follow the directions for Victoria sandwich (page 242), adding the milk at the end, or place all the ingredients, except the jam, in a large mixing bowl (this is possible only when using the quick-creaming luxury margarine).
2 Beat well for 1–2 minutes (pressing the margarine to the sides of the bowl if re-frigerated).
3 Brush a 1½-pint pudding basin with the melted margarine.
4 Place the 2 tablespoons of jam in the bottom and the pudding mixture on top.
5 Cover with greaseproof paper or foil (see instructions for covering puddings on pages 70 and 154) and put in a steamer over a saucepan of rapidly boiling water.
6 Steam for a good 1½ hours, then turn on to a hot dish and serve immediately.
7 If desired serve extra jam sauce (page 157).

For 2 servings use half quantity. Steam for 1 hour only in a smaller basin.

Variations on sponge puddings

Richer pudding: use 4 oz. margarine, 4 oz. sugar, omit milk. *Economical pudding:* use only 2 oz. margarine and 2 oz. sugar, and 2 tablespoons milk.

All variations are cooked as the basic recipe.
Fruit puddings can be served with custard sauce or sweet white sauce, page 157.
Other sauces are suggested in the variations.

Fruit pudding
1 Fold 4–6 oz. mixed dried fruit into the mixture.
2 Omit the milk, as the mixture should be of a stiffer consistency.

Ginger sponge pudding
1 Sieve 1 level teaspoon ground ginger with the flour.
2 Add 1–2 oz. diced crystallised ginger with the flour (this could be omitted).
3 Put golden syrup at the bottom of the basin, then add the sponge mixture.
4 Serve with golden syrup sauce (page 157).

Golden cap pudding
1 Use apricot jam instead of raspberry.
2 The finely grated rind of 1 lemon can be added to creamed margarine and sugar.

Blackcap pudding
Use blackcurrant jam instead of raspberry.

Lemon sponge pudding
1 Add finely grated rind of 1 lemon to the creamed margarine and sugar.
2 Mix with 1 tablespoon lemon juice instead of milk.
3 Put lemon curd or lemon marmalade in basin instead of jam.
4 Serve with lemon sauce (page 157).

Prune sponge pudding
1 Soak about 8–10 prunes overnight.
2 Drain and put at bottom of basin instead of jam.
3 Mix 6 tablespoons liquid in which prunes were soaked with 2 level teaspoons cornflour, 1½ oz. sugar, 1 tablespoon lemon juice; boil together until thick and clear. Serve as a sauce.

Orange sponge pudding
1 Add finely grated rind of 2 oranges to creamed margarine and sugar.
2 Mix with 1 tablespoon orange juice instead of milk.
3 Put orange marmalade in basin instead of jam.
4 Serve with hot marmalade or orange sauce (page 157).

Sultana sponge pudding

Preparation: 15 minutes or 5 minutes if using quick method
No delay
Cooking: 1½ hours
Serves 4–6

This, and several other recipes in this section, 'highlight' the ease of making puddings with the quick-creaming fats.

3 oz. margarine
3 oz. castor sugar
2 eggs

4 oz. flour (with plain flour use 1 level teaspoon baking powder)

1 tablespoon milk
2 oz. sultanas
½ oz. margarine, melted

1 Either follow directions for Victoria sandwich (page 242), adding milk and sultanas at the end, OR place all ingredients in a large mixing bowl, beat well for 1–2 minutes (pressing the margarine, if refrigerated, to the sides of the bowl).
2 Put mixture into a 1½-pint pudding basin previously brushed with melted margarine.
3 Cover with greaseproof paper or foil (see pages 70 and 154 for instructions for covering puddings); steam for a good 1½ hours.
4 Turn on to a hot dish and serve immediately with custard sauce (page 157), or fresh cream, see picture below.
For 2 servings, use half quantities and steam for 1 hour only in a smaller basin.

Steamed apricot pudding

Preparation: 12 minutes
No delay
Cooking: 20 minutes OR
1¼ hours
Serves 4

Secret of success
Make quite certain the water boils very rapidly for the first 50 minutes. This ensures the pudding rises well.

2 oz. good quality dried apricots
4 oz. flour (with plain flour use 1 teaspoon baking powder)

pinch of salt
2 oz. butter *or* margarine
2 oz. castor sugar
1 egg

¼ pint milk
2 tablespoons orange marmalade

1 Cut all but one of the apricots into pieces. If they are very hard and dry, soak in water for 1–2 hours, drain well and shake in a kitchen cloth or absorbent paper before chopping.
2 Sieve flour, baking powder, if used, and salt.
3 Rub in the fat, add the sugar.
4 Mix to a soft batter with the egg and milk.
5 Stir in the chopped apricots.
6 Spoon the marmalade into a well greased 1-pint pudding basin, or into 4 individual dariole or castle pudding tins, and place the whole apricot on top, two-thirds fill with the pudding mixture and cover with greased paper or foil.
7 Steam steadily for 1¼ hours, or for 20 minutes in dariole moulds.

Mandarin sponge pudding

ingredients as chocolate sponge pudding, *page 151,* plus 1 oz. extra flour

small can mandarin oranges

1 Make the chocolate sponge pudding as page 151, using the extra 1 oz. flour to give a stiffer mixture.
2 Open the can of oranges, drain well. Use half the mandarin oranges to line the bottom of the basin.
3 Chop the remainder of the oranges, add to the chocolate mixture.
4 Cover and steam as recipe page 151, allowing 1½ hours cooking time; turn out carefully to serve — see picture below.

Left *Sultana sponge pudding*
Right *Mandarin sponge pudding*

Coconut castle puddings with orange sauce

Preparation: 20–25 minutes
No delay
Cooking: 20–30 minutes
Serves 4

Castle pudding tins (dariole moulds) are very useful, for they can be used for baking cakes as well as steaming puddings. The jam-topped sponge, recipe page 152, and other puddings, can be cooked as individual puddings. Use dariole moulds or castle pudding tins as picture 4, and cook as recipe, right.

4 oz. flour (with plain flour use 1½ level teaspoons baking powder)
2 oz. butter *or* margarine

2 oz. castor sugar
1 oz. desiccated coconut
1 egg
3 tablespoons milk

few drops of vanilla essence

to decorate
4 *or* 8 glacé cherries

1 Sieve flour and baking powder, if used, into a bowl.

2 Rub in fat until the mixture resembles fine breadcrumbs.
3 Add the sugar and coconut.

4 Mix to a stiff dropping consistency with the egg, milk and vanilla essence. Beat well.

5 Transfer mixture to 4 well greased individual pudding basins, or 8 castle pudding tins. DO NOT FILL more than two-thirds.
6 Cover with greased waxed paper or foil. The 'pleat' in the paper is a good idea, in case the puddings rise slightly above tin tops.

7 Steam steadily for 20 minutes if using castle pudding tins, 30 minutes if using individual basins.
8 Turn out on to a warm serving dish, and top each pudding with a glacé cherry.

9 Serve with orange sauce, which can be prepared while the puddings are cooking.

Orange sauce

juice of 2 oranges
1 heaped teaspoon arrowroot

finely grated rind of
1 orange*

2 rounded tablespoons castor sugar

*do not use any white pith when grating the orange rind. Take only the top yellow 'zest

1 Make orange juice up to ½ pint with water.
2 Blend arrowroot to a paste with a little of the liquid.
3 Heat the remainder with the rind and sugar, then pour on to paste.
4 Return to the pan and cook, stirring, until sauce comes to the boil and thickens.
5 Simmer gently for 3 minutes.

Lemon sauce
Use lemons instead of oranges.

Suet puddings

There is a great variety of suet puddings one can make, and, while satisfying, they need not be too heavy.

If you buy suet from the butcher, remove all skin and gristle. Put on to a chopping board and chop firmly – this is easier to do if the suet is dusted liberally with flour. Packet shredded suet is, however, an excellent product.

Suet puddings MUST be cooked for the full time given in the recipe.

Fruit pudding

Preparation: 15–20 minutes
No delay
Cooking: 2 hours
Serves 4–6

This pudding can be served throughout the year, for the fruit filling is varied according to the season.

for the suet pastry
8 oz. flour (with plain flour
  use 2 level teaspoons
  baking powder)
4 oz. shredded suet

water *to mix*

for the filling
approximately 1 lb. prepared
  fruit

2–3 tablespoons sugar
little water

1 Sieve the flour and baking powder, if used.
2 Add the suet and enough water to make a soft rolling consistency.
3 Roll out the pastry, use two-thirds to line a greased basin. (For details of cutting pastry see page 70, steak and kidney pudding.)
4 Prepare the fruit. *Rhubarb* should be cut into neat pieces. *Apples* should be peeled, cored and sliced. *Blackcurrants* should be stalked. *Plums* should be halved and stoned if very large. *Gooseberries* should be topped and tailed.
5 Add sugar and about 2 tablespoons water, according to juiciness of fruit.
6 Roll out the remaining pastry and press over the top of the pudding. Dampen edges of pastry before sealing.
7 Cover with greased greaseproof paper or foil – a 'pleat' in the paper as shown on facing page is a good idea.
8 Steam over boiling water for approximately 2 hours, making sure the water really does boil.
9 Turn out on to a hot dish, and serve with cream or custard sauce (page 157).

Pressure cooking of puddings

Your pressure cookery book will give you special directions for your own make of pressure cooker – but generally speaking the best results are at 5 lb. pressure, although a Christmas pudding can be cooked at 15 lb. pressure.

In order to make the pudding rise, allow the first third of the cooking time *without pressure*. Then put on a 5 lb. weight, bring to pressure and cook for rest of time.

Making a rhubarb pudding for pressure cooking: aluminium or enamel pudding bowls are best

Jam roly poly

Preparation: 12 minutes
No delay
Cooking: 2 hours when steaming; 1½ hours when baking
Serves 4–6

When suet is not available, rub 4 oz. margarine into the flour.

suet crust pastry, *recipe
  above*

jam

1 Prepare the pastry, roll out into a neat oblong about ¼ inch thick.
2 Spread with jam, being careful not to take the jam right to the edges of pastry.
3 Turn in the side edges, and roll lightly like a Swiss roll.

To steam
1 Wrap lightly in greased greaseproof paper (allow space for pudding to rise), then in a floured cloth.
2 Put into steamer, cook for 2 hours over rapidly boiling water.

To bake
1 Put on to greased baking tin.
2 Bake just above the centre of a moderately hot oven (400°F., Gas Mark 5) for 25 minutes.
3 Reduce the heat to moderate (375°F., Gas Mark 4) for the rest of the time.

Christmas pudding

Preparation: approximately 1 hour. Mixture is better if allowed to stand overnight.
Cooking: 6–8 hours
Serves up to 12

A Christmas pudding is probably one of the easiest things to make. The preparations take a long time, but they are not in any way difficult.

Secret of success
Try to make the pudding 4–6 weeks, at least, before Christmas. This gives it a chance to mature in flavour.

2 oz. breadcrumbs	4 oz. shredded suet	4 oz. sultanas
4 oz. grated apple	4 oz. brown sugar	2 oz. prunes *or* dried
¼ pint ale, beer, stout *or* milk	1 small carrot, grated	apricots, chopped
	4 oz. mixed candied peel	grated rind and juice of
4 oz. flour	4 oz. chopped blanched	½ lemon
2 eggs	almonds	grated rind of ½ orange
1 teaspoon mixed spice	4 oz. currants	1 tablespoon golden syrup
1 level teaspoon cinnamon	8 oz. raisins	*or* black treacle
1 level teaspoon nutmeg		

1 Make sure that the bread is not too stale. It is easier to make breadcrumbs if the bread has become firm, but on no account should it be over-stale otherwise it might become 'mouldy'.
2 A good cooking apple gives the best flavour in the pudding.
3 The ale or beer does not prove too strong in taste, but gives a richness to the pudding.
4 Mix all the ingredients together, stir well and leave overnight if possible.
5 Place in 1 large or 2 smaller basins and cover well with cloth or paper (see pages 70 and 154).
6 Steam or boil for 6–8 hours.
7 Remove wet coverings and cool. When pudding is cold put on dry covers.
8 Steam for 2 hours on Christmas Day.

Christmas pudding in a pressure cooker

1 If you have a pressure cooker, allow 2–3 hours at 15 lb. pressure.
2 To prevent the top of the pudding becoming too wet it is a good idea to make a flour and water paste.
3 Mix about 8 oz. flour with enough water to make a firm dough, and roll into a round the size of the top of the basin.
4 Place this mixture over greaseproof paper on the pudding, cover with more grease-proof paper, then the pudding is ready to cook.

To store the Christmas pudding
Be very careful to store the pudding in a cool, dry place. It must not be stored near an excess of steam — so the kitchen cupboard is not a good place.

Date and orange pudding

Preparation: 12 minutes
No delay
Cooking: 1¼ hours
Serves 4

Secret of success
The addition of breadcrumbs in this pudding gives a pleasant light texture.

3 oz. dates, unstoned weight	1 oz. white breadcrumbs	grated rind of 1 small orange
3 oz. plain flour	2 oz. finely chopped *or*	1 egg
1 rounded teaspoon baking powder	shredded suet	approximately 2 tablespoons
	2 oz. castor sugar	milk

1 Well grease a pudding basin or mould, and place half the stoned dates round the base and sides.
2 Chop the remainder.
3 Sift the flour and baking powder into a bowl.
4 Add the breadcrumbs, suet, sugar, chopped dates and orange rind.
5 Mix with the egg and enough milk to form a soft consistency, so the mixture just drops from the spoon.
6 Turn the mixture into the prepared basin or mould, cover the top with greased greaseproof paper or foil, then steam steadily for 1½ hours.
7 Turn out on to a warm plate and serve with fresh orange slices, and orange sauce or custard (page 157).

Brandy butter or hard sauce

Preparation: 10–15 minutes
Allow to stand
No cooking
Serves 6–8

This can be stored in a refrigerator or freezer for several weeks if wished.

4 oz. unsalted butter	4–8 dessertspoons brandy *or*	*to decorate, optional*
6 oz. icing sugar	rum	glacé cherries
		angelica

1 Cream the butter until white.
2 Gradually add the sugar and the brandy or rum.
3 Stand the mixture for some little time in a cold place to get really hard.
4 Pile or pipe into a pyramid shape, and decorate with cherries and angelica, if wished.

Variations
1 Add the finely grated 'zest' from 2 oranges; be careful not to use any bitter white pith.
2 **Rum butter:** use brown sugar (demerara or moist brown) in place of icing sugar, and rum in place of brandy.

Sweet white sauce

Preparation: few minutes
Cooking: 5–8 minutes
Serves 4

Secret of success
Stir well at stages 4 and 5, to
keep the sauce smooth.

1 tablespoon cornflour	1 oz. sugar	½ oz. butter
½ pint milk	little vanilla essence	

1 Blend the cornflour with a little cold milk.
2 Bring the rest of the milk to the boil.
3 Pour over the cornflour, then return to the pan with the sugar.
4 Stirring, continue to cook steadily until smooth and thick.
5 Add vanilla essence and butter; serve with steamed puddings.

Almond sauce: flavour with almond essence; this is excellent with fruit puddings.
Liqueur sauce: flavour with 1 tablespoon liqueur, or a few drops flavouring essence (rum, crème de menthe, cherry or apricot brandy are particularly good). Serve with sponge pudding.

Jam sauce

Preparation: 1–2 minutes
Cooking: 4–5 minutes
Serves 3–4

Secret of success
Do not leave this sauce while
heating; it burns easily.

good 4 tablespoons jam	juice of 1 lemon	2 tablespoons water

Boil all the ingredients together until the jam has melted.

To vary
1 Use marmalade or apple or redcurrant jelly in place of jam.
2 Use a sweetened fruit purée in place of jam.

Golden syrup sauce

Preparation: 8 minutes
Cooking: few minutes
Serves 4

Secret of success
Do not omit the lemon from this,
otherwise the sauce is lacking in
flavour.

grated rind and juice of 1 lemon	3 tablespoons golden syrup	¼ pint water

1 Mix all the ingredients together in a saucepan.
2 Heat gently for a few minutes.

Treacle sauce: use all black treacle (an excellent source of iron) instead of syrup, or use half treacle and half syrup.

Chocolate sauce

Use recipe for sweet white sauce above, but measure out cornflour, remove 1 level dessertspoon and replace it with 1 dessertspoon cocoa. Another chocolate sauce recipe is given on page 180.

Custard sauces

Preparation: few minutes
Cooking: 10–12 minutes

Secret of success
It is essential that the egg
custard sauce does not boil, so
check that the water is only hot,
and stir during cooking.

1 egg	1 tablespoon water	½ pint milk
or		
custard powder	sugar	milk

With egg
1 Beat the egg and sugar.
2 Pour on the milk, which can be warm.
3 Stand the sauce in a jug in a saucepan of water, or in the top of a double saucepan or a basin over hot water, and cook very gently until the mixture just coats the back of a wooden spoon. Stir nearly all the time as it cooks.

With custard powder
Follow the directions on the packet or can, remembering that it must cook for several minutes, otherwise it will have a taste of uncooked custard powder.

157

Baked sponge puddings

A sponge pudding can be baked in the oven instead of steaming it, and served with jam sauce. It tends to be less light. It may be served over fruit, as in Eve's pudding, below, or as an upside-down pudding.

Eve's pudding

Preparation: 15 minutes
Cooking: 45–50 minutes
Serves 4

This is an excellent pudding. The cooking time assumes a fairly large pie dish, so the sponge topping is a thin coating only. If baking in a smaller deeper dish, allow at least 1 hour.

for the filling
1¼ lb. apples
2 oz. sugar
2 tablespoons water

for sponge topping
3 oz. margarine
3 oz. castor sugar
2 eggs

4 oz. flour (with plain flour use 1 level teaspoon baking powder)

1 Peel, core and slice the apples.
2 Put into a 2-pint pie dish with the sugar and water.
3 Put into the centre of a moderate oven (350–375°F., Gas Mark 4–5), for approximately 10 minutes.
4 Cream together the margarine and sugar until soft and light. Gradually beat in the eggs.
5 Fold in the flour and baking powder, if used. ADD NO LIQUID.
6 Spread over the hot apples; if by chance the fruit has made a lot of juice, spoon out 2 or 3 tablespoons before spreading over the sponge.
7 Bake in the centre of the oven for 35–40 minutes until firm.
8 Sprinkle the top with sugar before serving.

Variations
1 The apple can be mixed with dried fruit.
2 Soft fruit can be used, in which case there is no need to heat it first, simply put the sponge over the top and cook for approximately 40 minutes.

Spiced pear upside-down pudding

Preparation: 20 minutes
No delay
Cooking: 40–50 minutes
Serves 4

The method is based on the assumption that one of the quick-creaming margarines is used. To give a lighter pudding, ½ teaspoon baking powder may be mixed with the flour, etc., at stage 3.

for the topping
1 oz. margarine
1 oz. soft brown sugar
8 canned pear halves

8 canned *or* glacé cherries

for the pudding mixture
4 oz. margarine

2 eggs
4 oz. soft brown sugar
4 oz. self-raising flour
1 rounded teaspoon cinnamon

1 *To make the topping:* cream the margarine with 1 oz. soft brown sugar. Grease a 7-inch square tin and line the bottom with a piece of greaseproof paper.
2 Spread the creamed mixture on the bottom of the tin and arrange the pears on top of this, flat-side downwards.
3 *To make the pudding:* mix all the ingredients together in a mixing bowl, then beat well with a wooden spoon for 1 minute. Spread mixture on top of the pears.
4 Carefully smooth the top of the mixture.
5 Bake in the centre of a moderate oven (350–375°F., Gas Mark 4–5) for 40–50 minutes. Test to see if cooked by pressing firmly on top. Look at the pudding after about 25 minutes, and if becoming rather brown reduce heat to 325°F., Gas Mark 3.
6 Remove from the oven, turn on to a hot dish and place a cherry in the centre of each pear.
7 Serve hot with cream or custard.

Upside-down puddings

Use the sponge mixture as Eve's pudding, or the recipe above, and bake over any raw or well drained canned fruit.
The glaze given by creaming margarine or butter and sugar (stage 1, above) is important in keeping the fruit moist and giving a good shine, so use this with all fruits.
Arrange the fruit on the glaze in an attractive design, top with the sponge or pudding mixture, and bake as the recipe above.

Spiced upside-down pudding

158

Crunchy apple cobbler

Preparation: 20 minutes
No delay
Cooking: 35–40 minutes
Serves 4–6

Secret of success
A cobbler uses a scone-like mixture as a topping, and this *must* be baked quickly.

for the apple mixture
3 oz. brown sugar
½ level teaspoon lemon rind
½ level teaspoon cinnamon
1 oz. seedless raisins

3 tablespoons water
12 oz. cooking apples

for the scone mixture
4 oz. self-raising flour

pinch of salt
1 oz. butter
3–4 tablespoons milk
1 oz. butter, softened
2 level tablespoons brown sugar

1 Combine the sugar, lemon rind, cinnamon, raisins and water in a saucepan.
2 Peel, core and quarter apples, and then simmer in the syrup until tender.
3 Turn into a wide shallow earthenware dish.
4 While the apples are cooking, sift the flour and salt, rub in the butter and add the milk. Knead lightly.
5 Roll out on a floured board to an oblong shape, spread with softened butter, sprinkle with brown sugar and roll up like a Swiss roll.
6 Cut into 16 thin pinwheels. Arrange on the apples.
7 Bake for approximately 15–20 minutes near the top of a hot oven (425–450°F., Gas Mark 6–7).
8 Serve with cream or custard.

Spiced apple crumble

Preparation: 15 minutes
No delay
Cooking: 45 minutes
Serves 4–6

Secret of success
Semolina, used with flour, as in this recipe, gives a crisp 'nutty' texture to the crust.

for the apple mixture
12 oz. apples, peeled and sliced
2 oz. sugar
very little water

3 oz. raisins

for the crumble
3 oz. butter
1½ oz. sugar

3 oz. flour (with plain flour use 1 level teaspoon baking powder)
3 oz. fine semolina
1 level teaspoon cinnamon

1 Simmer the apples and sugar with very little water until soft.
2 Melt the butter in a saucepan. Stir in the sugar and flour, baking powder, if used, sifted with the semolina and cinnamon.
3 Press half the flour mixture into a loose-bottomed 8-inch sponge sandwich tin or small pie plate.
4 Top with the apple purée and raisins.
5 Sprinkle the remaining crumble on top and dust with cinnamon.
6 Bake in the centre of a moderately hot oven (400°F., Gas Mark 5–6) for 30 minutes.
7 Serve with cream.

Note. This is good hot or cold.

Left *Crunchy apple cobbler*
Right *Spiced apple crumble*

Fruit crumbles

Most fruit is suitable for topping with a crumble mixture. Use recipe above which gives a sandwich effect to the fruit; for a top layer only use half quantity and cook for 30 minutes.

Another fruit crumble mixture (enough for top only)
2 oz. butter *or* margarine*
4 oz. plain *or* self-raising flour
2–3 oz. sugar

* do not exceed the amount of butter or margarine in the crumble mixture, otherwise it does not become crisp.

1 Rub fat into flour until like fine breadcrumbs.
2 Add the sugar, then sprinkle over fruit.
3 *Soft fruits* need little liquid, just sugar and about 1 tablespoon liquid.
Hard fruits — apples, rhubarb, firm plums or gooseberries — can be cooked for about 10 minutes before putting crumble on top. Do not use too much water or the crumble mixture will 'sink-in'.

Try a dessert pudding

A very special gâteau is suitable for a sweet, and has the advantage that it can be prepared beforehand.

Redcurrant layer dessert

Preparation: 20 minutes. No delay with cake. Fruit must cool
Cooking: 20–25 minutes
Serves 5–6

If using quick-creaming margarine, put all the ingredients into the basin plus ½ teaspoon baking powder (to compensate for the lack of creaming), and beat for 2–3 minutes.
Use an electric mixer for stages 1 and 2, but add the flour by hand.

Left *Berry trifle gâteau*
Right *Redcurrant layer dessert*

for Victoria sandwich mixture
4 oz. butter *or* margarine
4 oz. castor sugar
2 eggs
4 oz. flour (with plain flour use 1 level teaspoon baking powder)

for the filling
12 oz.–1 lb. red *or* blackcurrants (reserve 8 sprays *for decoration*)

4 oz. sugar
thick cream, whipped
icing sugar

1 Cream the fat and sugar until soft and fluffy, add the eggs and flour carefully — page 242 gives details of correct mixing.
2 Divide the mixture equally between 2 well greased 6–7-inch sandwich tins.
3 Bake above the centre of a moderate oven (350–375°F., Gas Mark 4–5) for 20 minutes, or until well risen and golden, then turn out on to a wire tray and cool.
4 Stalk the currants, wash and put into a pan with the sugar but no water.
5 Cover the pan, cook very slowly just until the sugar melts, then strain the fruit, and cool both this and the juice.
6 Cut each cake into two layers, sandwich with whipped cream and currants.
7 Dust the top with sieved icing sugar and decorate the edge with sprays of fresh fruit. Chill. Serve with the strained juice.

Berry trifle gâteau

Preparation: 15 minutes. It is better if left 24 hours after cooking before filling and serving
Cooking: 20–25 minutes
Serves 5–6

This very unusual cake is based on the Greek halva. Fold the semolina, etc., into the egg whites very carefully at stages 3 and 4, so you do not lose the fluffy texture.

4 eggs
pinch of salt
3 oz. sugar
3 oz. fine semolina
1 oz. ground almonds
1 level teaspoon baking powder
1 oz. butter

for the syrup
4 oz. sugar
¼ pint water
¼ pint Marsala, sherry *or* a mixture of orange and lemon juice

for the filling and topping
½ pint thick cream
little sugar
1 lb. raspberries, loganberries *or* blackberries

1 *First, make the cake:* separate egg whites and yolks.
2 Whisk the whites and salt to a stiff froth and gradually whisk in the sugar.
3 When stiff, whisk in the egg yolks; when thick and creamy, *fold* in the sieved semolina, ground almonds and baking powder.
4 Fold in the melted butter.
5 Turn into two greased 7- or 8-inch sandwich tins.
6 Bake above the centre of a moderately hot oven (400°F., Gas Mark 5–6) for about 20–25 minutes, until the cakes feel firm when pressed lightly.
7 Boil the sugar and water for syrup for 3–5 minutes (stirring until the sugar is dissolved) until just beginning to thicken, but remove before it changes colour.
8 Add the wine or fruit juices. Pour over the cakes as soon as they come from the oven and have been turned out on to a cooling tray. Cool and leave for some hours.
9 Before serving, sandwich together and top with whipped cream and sugared berries.

To make good pancakes

See step by step colour pictures, frontispiece

1 Do not have the batter too thick.
2 Put enough fat in the pan to give a covering over the base — about ½ oz. lard should be enough in a small pan, or use oil. It is better to put in a fresh amount of fat for each pancake.
3 Pour only enough batter in the pan to give a light covering — it is easier to do this if you transfer the batter to a jug, see picture 3, frontispiece.
4 Cook steadily on the bottom side for about 2 minutes, then turn or toss.
5 TO TURN PANCAKE, insert a palette knife or fish slice under pancake. Feel a good grip on the handle, then turn over gently.
6 TO TOSS PANCAKE, shake the pan before attempting to toss. If the pancake moves freely it is thoroughly cooked on the bottom side. Hold the pan loosely, with your hand and wrist quite relaxed and pointing downwards. Give a very sharp upward flick and the pancake will rise out of the pan and turn, so make sure pan is in the right position to catch it, see picture in frontispiece.
7 Roll or fold the pancake *away* from the handle and tip on to a hot dish — see below for details of serving.
8 ALWAYS look after your pan for pancakes as carefully as you do an omelette pan (see page 11).

Pancake batter

Preparation: 7 minutes
No delay although batter can stand
Serves 4–6

Use half quantity only for 2 servings, or make up batter and store remainder in a COOL PLACE until next day, when it could be used either for more pancakes or a Yorkshire pudding. After storing, whisk well before using.

standard batter	1 egg	½ pint milk *or* milk and water
4 oz. flour		
pinch of salt		

rich batter	2 eggs	1 tablespoon olive oil
4 oz. flour	just under ½ pint milk *or*	
pinch of salt	milk and water	

1 Sieve the flour and salt, add egg or eggs and enough liquid to give a sticky consistency, see pictures 1 and 2, frontispiece.
2 Beat well, then gradually add the rest of the liquid.
3 Add oil last, if using this.

Stacked pancakes

Preparation: 10 minutes
No delay
Cooking: 10–15 minutes
Serves 4–6

This way of serving pancakes is most attractive. Cut into slices, like a cake.
Remember pancakes can be wrapped and stored in the freezer.

pancake batter, *recipe above*	*for the filling* lemon curd	*for the topping* 1 egg white 2 oz. castor sugar ½ oz. blanched almonds

1 Make and cook the pancakes as directed above.
2 Pile as they are cooked, in a folded napkin to keep warm.
3 Sandwich together with lemon curd.
4 *Make the meringue topping:* whisk the egg white until very stiff.
5 Beat in a little of the sugar very gradually.
6 Fold in remainder of the sugar.
7 Spread the meringue over the top of the pile of filled pancakes.
8 Decorate with almonds then put in a very hot oven (475°F., Gas Mark 8) for 1–2 minutes only, or until meringue is lightly browned. Serve warm.

To serve pancakes

Pancakes can be served in a variety of ways but the traditional way is with lemon and sugar.
1 Tip the pancake (you can roll or fold) on to a hot dish, dust with castor sugar and serve with thick slices of lemon or halved lemons.
2 If you like a very 'sugary' pancake, tip the pancake on to a sheet of greaseproof paper covered with sugar, and coat thoroughly, then fold over.
3 You can fill pancakes with hot jam — it is easier to do this if you put the cooked pancake on to paper. Put in the hot jam and roll or fold *or* fill with fruit (see next page) *or* arrange as a cake (see picture).

Fruit-filled pancakes

Make the pancake batter and cook as directed on the previous page. While the pancakes are cooking prepare the fruit.

1 Soft fruits (raspberries, strawberries, etc.) need mashing with a little sugar. Heat gently if wished, although they are very pleasant if served raw. Decorate with whole fruit and top the pancake with thick cream JUST BEFORE serving.

2 Apples, plums, etc., should be halved and sliced, then simmered until just soft with very little sugar and water, and then put into pancakes.

3 Canned fruits should be drained of most of the syrup and heated. The syrup makes an excellent sauce.

The picture below shows an interesting way to serve the fruit pancakes. Keep the cooked pancakes hot then fold in half, arrange rather like a pleated fan, and top with the sugared fruit.

Storing and freezing pancakes

As mentioned on page 161, the batter may be stored in a refrigerator. Cooked pancakes may be stored in the refrigerator for several days. Make the pancakes, separate each one with a piece of greaseproof paper. When all the pancakes are cooked, make into a foil parcel.

When freezing cooked pancakes follow the same procedure as above. This means the pancakes do not stick together, and you may remove as many or as few as required.

Note. In order to prevent frozen pancakes having a slightly 'tough' texture, add 1 teaspoon olive oil to the batter before cooking. Refrigerated or frozen pancakes can be heated in the oven or in a greasy frying pan.

Raspberry pancakes

To keep pancakes hot

It is not easy to cook pancakes at the last minute, so cook before the meal and keep on a hot dish standing over a saucepan of boiling water OR on a hot dish in a very cool oven, do not cover the dish.

Fruit fritters

Preparation: 6—8 minutes
No delay
Cooking: 7—10 minutes
Serves 4

Apples. Choose good cooking apples. Peel, core, cut into thin slices, coat with batter. It is a good idea to flour apples before coating as the batter then 'sticks' well.
Pineapple. Drain rings of pineapple well, then proceed as for apples.
Bananas. Halve if wished, and add a little rum essence to the batter.

fritter batter
4 oz. flour (with plain flour use 1 level teaspoon baking powder)

1 oz. sugar
2 eggs
$\frac{1}{4}$ pint milk

1 oz. butter *or* margarine, melted, *or* olive oil

1 Sieve the dry ingredients, add the eggs and milk.

2 Lastly add the melted fat or oil — this is not essential but helps to give a crisp fritter.

3 For a very light fritter batter the egg yolks should be put in first, and when you have a very smooth thick batter fold in the stiffly beaten egg whites at the very last.

4 Coat the fruit and fry STEADILY in shallow fat or in deep fat if preferred. (See page 136 for frying.) This makes sure that the outside is brown and the fruit hot and well cooked, whereas if fritters are fried too quickly they become too brown on the outside before the middle is cooked.

5 Drain on kitchen paper and dredge well with sugar.

To make a good milk pudding

There are many recipes for making a good milk pudding, but it is important to realise that slow cooking for a baked milk pudding is essential. If you like a very rich result, add to the pudding about 1 oz. butter, or the same amount of suet, and stir it in after about 30 minutes' cooking. Some people like the flavour that evaporated or condensed milk gives, in which case dilute with a little water, and if using condensed milk, you will not need sugar.

The following recipe is for rice pudding: other milk puddings such as sago and tapioca are made in much the same way.

Rice pudding

Preparation: few minutes
No delay
Cooking: approximately 2 hours
Serves 4

Secrets of success
The longer and slower the cooking the better the flavour. ½–1 oz. butter, added at stage 4, or even earlier at stage 1, gives both colour and richness to the pudding.

| 2–3 oz. round grain rice | 1–2 oz. sugar | butter, *optional* |
| 1 pint milk | | |

1 Wash the rice, put into a pie dish and cover with the milk. Add the sugar.
2 Cook for at least 2 hours in a very slow oven (275°F., Gas Mark 1), stirring after the first 30 minutes.
3 The larger quantity of rice gives a much more solid pudding.
4 If you are in a great hurry, you can cook the milk pudding for a shorter time at a higher temperature but the flavour is not as good. Just before serving, stir in the butter, if used.

To vary
Add 2–4 oz. dried fruit; stir once or twice during cooking, see also page 164

Boiled rice
(for a thick milk pudding)

Preparation: few minutes
No delay
Cooking: 45 minutes upwards
Serves 4

Boiled rice is a very adaptable pudding. Instead of milk, cook the rice in canned orange or pineapple juice.

Secret of success
Since rice is inclined to stick, it is advisable to cook this in a double saucepan over boiling water; in this case the pudding will take approximately 1 hour at least, and is improved with even longer cooking.

| 2–3 oz. round grain rice | 1–2 oz. sugar | lemon rind *or* vanilla pod |
| 1 pint milk | | *to flavour* |

1 Wash the rice well.
2 Bring the milk and sugar to the boil, add the flavouring then shake in the rice.
3 Lower the heat and cook very gently for about 45 minutes, until the rice is very tender.
4 Remove the rind or pod.
5 Serve with fruit, jam or syrup.

To vary
In addition to the variations suggested at left and on page 164, try cooking the rice in a fairly thin apple, rhubarb, or other fruit purée. Serve hot, or spoon into a mould and allow to cool, then turn out and top with whipped cream.

Using canned rice

The canned rice and other milk puddings available are a good way of having a milk pudding with the minimum of trouble. They can be reheated in a short time in the oven, in a pie dish, to give an attractive brown on top, or used as the basis for more elaborate puddings like the one below.

Christmas meringue

Preparation: 8 minutes
No delay
Cooking: 50 minutes
Serves 4–6

Home-made rice pudding could be used instead of canned pudding.

| 2 eggs | 6–8 oz. mincemeat | 2 oz. castor sugar *for* |
| large can creamed rice pudding | | *meringue* |

1 Separate the egg yolks from the whites.
2 Put the yolks into a basin, open the can of creamed rice and pour in with the yolks, mixing together well.
3 Put into pie dish and bake for 30 minutes in centre of very moderate oven (325°F., Gas Mark 3). It should feel quite firm on top when taken from the oven.
4 Spread with a good layer of mincemeat.
5 Whisk the egg whites until very stiff, fold in the sugar.
6 Pile on top of the pudding and return to the oven for a further 15–20 minutes, until the meringue is golden brown. Serve hot.

Making semolina puddings

A semolina pudding is better if it is cooked on top of the stove before cooking in the oven.

Preparation: few minutes
No delay
Cooking: see method
Serves 4

Secret of success
Semolina can become lumpy very easily, so shake it into milk steadily, and stir at same time.

| 1 pint milk | 2–3 oz. semolina | 1–2 oz. sugar |

1 Bring the milk to the boil.
2 Shake in 2–3 oz. semolina, stirring briskly all the time so that it does not become lumpy.
3 Cook for about 3–4 minutes until the pudding thickens, add sugar to taste, then pour into a pie dish and continue cooking for about 35 minutes in a slow oven (300°F., Gas Mark 2).
4 If preferred a semolina pudding can be cooked for about 10 minutes on top of the stove. Stir all the time.

Flavouring milk puddings

Milk puddings can be flavoured in a variety of ways.
1 Blend about 1 oz. chocolate powder with the milk.
2 Stir in 1 dessertspoon coffee essence with the milk.
3 Give a caramel flavour by making a caramel sauce as directed on page 179, then stir in the milk very slowly so it does not curdle.

Baked lemon chiffon

Preparation: 15 minutes
No delay
Cooking: 50–55 minutes or about 1½ hours
Serves 4

Secrets of success
Semolina can become lumpy very easily, so shake it into the milk steadily. Stir all the time you do this.
If serving cold (see picture 3), you can increase the amount of sugar added to the meringue from 2 to 4 tablespoons.

½ pint water
2 oz. finest semolina
2 oz. butter *or* margarine
juice of 2 lemons

grated rind of 1 lemon
3 tablespoons sugar
3 eggs

to decorate
maraschino cherries
angelica
split blanched almonds

1 Warm the water, remove from heat and sprinkle in the semolina.
2 Return to heat and bring to the boil, stirring.
3 Add the butter or margarine.
4 Cool slightly and beat in the lemon juice and grated rind.

5 Stir in 1 tablespoon sugar and beat in the yolks of eggs and 1 stiffly whisked egg white.
6 Pour into a greased ovenproof dish and bake in a very moderate oven (325°F., Gas Mark 3) for about 30 minutes.

7 Whisk 2 egg whites stiffly with the remaining sugar (see page 166 for instructions on correct making of meringue mixtures).
8 Pile on to baked mixture.

9 Decorate with cherries, angelica and almonds.
10 Return to the oven to brown and crisp. Serve hot or cold.

If you wish to serve this pudding hot, it will need only 10–15 minutes in a very moderate oven. If on the other hand you wish to serve it cold, you achieve a better meringue if you lower the heat to 275°F., Gas Mark 1, and allow approximately 45 minutes.

Fruit charlotte

Preparation: 12–15 minutes
No delay
Cooking: 50–55 minutes, but allow extra time for cooking fruit if necessary
Serves 4–6

I prefer fairly coarse breadcrumbs in this recipe. It gives a more interesting texture.

3–4 oz. margarine *or* butter
6 oz. breadcrumbs*
3 oz. sugar (brown is best)

for the filling
1 lb. fruit
water *if required*

sugar to taste

* make the breadcrumbs rather big *or* remove crusts and cut bread into fingers.

1 Heat the margarine or butter in a frying pan, and cook the breadcrumbs or fingers of bread until they are golden brown and crisp on both sides.
2 Tip bread into a basin and mix with the sugar.
3 Prepare the filling — see below.
4 Put one-third of the crumbs and then half the filling into an ovenproof dish.
5 Cover with the second third of crumbs, rest of the filling and final layer of crumbs.
6 Bake in the centre of a very moderate oven (325–350°F., Gas Mark 3–4), for approximately 45–50 minutes.

To prepare fillings for fruit charlottes

1 *Apples:* slice very thinly and use raw, with a sprinkling of sugar OR simmer with a little water and sugar until a thick pulp. Currants can be added, or a little grated orange or lemon rind.
2 *Plums of all kinds:* halve and stone. If very ripe, use raw. If firm, simmer with sugar and water first, like apples.
3 *Gooseberries, currants, etc.:* use raw only if very ripe, otherwise simmer to a thick pulp.
4 *Soft fruits:* these can be used, but their flavour is rather 'lost' in this pudding.

Apple charlotte

Fruit amber

Preparation: 20 minutes
No delay
Cooking: 1 hour or longer — see recipe
Serves 4–6

Fruit ambers often have a border of *pastry*. Line the edge of dish and bake in a hot oven until golden brown. The correct pastry edging is made of puff pastry, but flaky or short crust could be used.

1¼ lb. fruit
2–3 oz. sugar
very little water
2 egg yolks

2 oz. fine breadcrumbs

for the meringue
2 egg whites

2–4 oz. castor sugar, *see below*

1 Prepare the fruit. Peel and slice apples thinly, halve and stone plums, top and tail gooseberries.
2 Put into a saucepan with the sugar and very little water, simmer gently until a thick pulp. Stir occasionally.
3 Beat the purée until very smooth, or sieve if wished.
4 Stir in the beaten egg yolks and crumbs.
5 Bake in the centre of a very moderate oven (325–350°F., Gas Mark 3–4), for 25 minutes.
6 Whisk the egg whites until very stiff.
7 Fold in 2 oz. sugar using a metal spoon.
8 Pile on top of the pudding, and cook for a further 20 minutes at same temperature.

Meringues on puddings

Meringues on puddings cause little bother if serving hot. Make certain the egg whites are very stiff, before folding in the sugar. If serving cold, certain rules must be followed.
1 Use more sugar, i.e. 2 oz. sugar to each egg white; this ensures that the meringue is crisp when cold.
2 Spoon or pipe on to pie, and make certain the meringue touches the edge of the dish or flan case – this prevents it becoming 'sticky' round the edge.
3 Cook very slowly – 1 hour at 250–275°F., Gas Mark ½–1.

Meringues

Preparation: 15 minutes
No delay
Cooking: several hours
Makes 8–12 large or 24 small

Secret of success
The same 'rules' apply when using an electric mixer, although you will find you *can* add all the sugar with the machine switched to low speed. *Do this carefully and gradually* and switch off as soon as the sugar is incorporated.

| 2 egg whites | 4 oz. castor sugar *or* 2 oz. castor sugar and 2 oz. icing sugar, sieved | little oil *or* butter, melted |

1 Place the egg whites in a clean and dry bowl. Whisk until very stiff.
2 Beat in about ½ oz. of the sugar, then another ½ oz.
3 Continue like this until *half the sugar* is used; stop beating in the sugar if the eggs become at all 'damp' looking.
4 *Fold* in the rest of the sugar carefully.
5 Brush the baking tins with oil or butter. Use only a thin layer of oil, or melt the butter and brush on with a pastry brush.
6 Take a teaspoonful of the egg white mixture, and with a second spoon put this on to the tray. If you hold the first spoonful in your left hand, then 'roll' the mixture on to the tray with the help of the second spoon, you get a good shape; OR you can pipe through a large piping bag and tube as for potatoes (page 139).
7 Bake for 2–3 hours in a very cool oven (225–250°F., Gas Mark 0–½), until crisp but not coloured.
8 Cool for a few minutes, then slip off the tins with a palette knife first dipped in hot water, then shaken dry.
9 Cool completely on wire tray, then store in airtight tins – they keep for weeks.

Fillings for meringues
Sandwich together with jam and/or thick whipped cream *or*
Meringues Chantilly: whip thick cream until it holds its shape, flavour with vanilla essence and sweeten; sandwich the meringues with this, and pipe a border of cream, if wished.
Meringues glacés: sandwich the meringues together with ice cream and decorate with whipped cream.

Normally there is no point in freezing meringues because they store so well in an airtight tin. However, if they have been filled with cream or ice cream, and there are any left, freezing is the perfect way to store them.

Chocolate mousse

Preparation: 10 minutes
No delay
Cooking: few minutes
Serves 2–3

Secrets of success
Do not have the water too hot under the chocolate.
Make sure the egg whites are very stiff. Fold into the chocolate very carefully.

| 2 oz. plain chocolate | 2 eggs |

1 Break chocolate into pieces and melt slowly in a basin over a pan of hot water. *Do not allow to become too hot.*

2 Remove the basin from the heat. Separate the egg whites from the yolks and beat the yolks into the melted chocolate.

3 Whisk the egg whites until very stiff.

4 Carefully fold the egg whites into the melted chocolate. Use a tablespoon or a plastic spatula to retain lightness. Pour into serving dishes, allow to set. Chocolate mousse is better eaten the same day that it is made. Allow at least 1½ hours for setting if putting in refrigerator.

5 Here are a few ideas for serving and decorating chocolate mousse: topped with cream and a cherry; with cream, grated chocolate and nuts; with mandarin orange sections and cream; with cream, walnuts and chocolate buttons; plain, in a shallow bowl; with pineapple pieces, cherry and cream.

Chocolate mousse

Rhubarb fool, see page 172

Using fruit in sweets

Fresh fruit in itself is one of the most time-saving of foods, for it makes a perfect dessert with no effort involved at all. There are, however, endless varieties of canned fruits which will save a great deal of time. Apple purée is excellent for sauce or sweets where one is told to sieve the fruit. Canned fruit salad makes a sweet if you add sliced apples, bananas or oranges.

Frozen fruits can be almost as good as fresh. The secret is to use them when they are still very slightly frozen. They lose both colour and taste if defrosted too much.

Dried fruits such as apricots, apples, figs, prunes, etc., are an excellent standby in the larder. Good soaking in cold water shortens the cooking time.

Fresh fruit

However carefully fruit is cooked the vitamin content is very largely destroyed, and it is therefore a wise thing to serve fresh fruit as a dessert from time to time, or if you have had a fairly substantial pudding it does give a refreshing end to a meal. For a formal meal, always provide fruit knives and forks, and your guests will feel more comfortable if small bowls of water are provided so that they can wash their fingers. The old-fashioned 'finger bowls' are rarely obtainable today but a pretty soup cup, filled with cold water and topped with a flower, does very well.
Oranges can be sliced either into rings or segmented. Cut off the peel, cut deeply to remove the white pith.
Pineapple can be peeled and cut into rings.
Apples and pears are rather better if not prepared beforehand, because of loss of colour.

Hints on stewing fruit

There are several ways of stewing fruit. You cook it as directed below in a saucepan, but remember the following points:
1 Do not use too much water. Some watery fruits, e.g. rhubarb, and raspberries, need practically no water; others should be only half covered.
2 If you wish to keep the fruit a good shape, always boil sugar and water together first, then add the fruit and simmer gently.
3 Always cook the fruit slowly, otherwise it breaks badly before being softened through to the middle.

If preferred, fruit can be cooked in the oven.

Compote of fruit

Preparation: 5–8 minutes
No delay
Cooking: 5–15 minutes
Serves 4

Apples should be peeled, cored and sliced.
Plums, apricots, etc., can be halved and stoned.
Soft fruit is just washed.
Gooseberries need topping and tailing, i.e. remove stalks and flower ends. Kitchen scissors are the easiest to use.
Blackcurrants can be prepared in the same way, although most people find removing stalk ends sufficient.
Redcurrants should be stalked. If you hold the stalks in one hand and pull currants off with the prongs of a fork you will find this the easiest method.

2–3 oz. sugar

¼ pint water for soft fruit; ⅜ pint for medium ripe fruit; just under ½ pint for hard fruit

1 lb. prepared fruit

1 Put the sugar and water into a saucepan and simmer until the sugar has dissolved.
2 Add the prepared fruit; see left.
3 Cook *gently* in the syrup until tender.

Try mixing fruits together and cooking them in the oven as the recipe below.

Stewed apricots and cherries

8 oz. apricots
8 oz. cherries

2 oz. sugar *or* golden syrup

water

1 Halve the apricots and remove stones.
2 Put the apricots and cherries in a sieve or colander and wash under running water.
3 Dry, then put into a pie dish with the sugar or golden syrup and half cover with water.
4 Put a piece of paper over the top of the fruit, or a lid on the dish, and cook for 45–50 minutes in a very low oven (275–300°F., Gas Mark 1–2).

Hot apple sweets

Choose a good cooking apple
One of the most famous cooking apples in the world is the Bramley seedling, but there are many others which cook as well. Choose a firm, hard apple. A rather soft apple will go to pulp before the inside is cooked.

Baked apples
Plain baked apples are cooked exactly as the recipe below; there is no need to stuff them. If you loosen the skin, as described, it is easier to remove.

Baked stuffed apples

Preparation: 6–7 minutes
No delay
Cooking: approximately 1 hour
Serves 4

Secret of success
Choose a really good cooking apple that remains a good shape when cooked. Some apples become a soft pulp on the outside before the centre is cooked.

4 large cooking apples	2 tablespoons sultanas *or* currants	½ oz. margarine
for the stuffing	1 tablespoon breadcrumbs	
2 tablespoons golden syrup *or* honey		

1 Wash and dry the apples and then, using a sharp knife, split the skin round the centre; this makes it very easy to remove when the apples are cooked.
2 Using an apple corer, take out the cores.
3 Stand the apples in a baking tin or dish, then divide the syrup between them, pouring this into the centre hole.
4 Add the dried fruit, breadcrumbs and a tiny knob of margarine on top of each.
5 Bake for approximately 1 hour in the centre of a very moderate oven (325–350°F., Gas Mark 3–4).
6 Serve with any liquid in the dish, and cream or top of the milk, or custard.

Almond apples

Preparation: 10 minutes
No delay
Cooking: 45 minutes
Serves 4

To blanch the almonds, put into boiling water for 2–3 minutes, lift out, cool and remove the skins.
Stage 5 is a fairly 'tricky' job; if preferred, dredge the apples with the cornflour.

Almond apples

4 medium cooking apples	2 egg yolks	1 oz. cornflour
2 oz. blanched almonds	2 oz. soft breadcrumbs	1 oz. butter
3 oz. sugar		

1 Peel and core the apples.
2 Chop the almonds and mix with half the sugar.
3 Beat the egg yolks with the rest of the sugar and stir in 1 oz. breadcrumbs.
4 Coat the apples with this mixture.
5 Put the cornflour on a plate or in a paper bag and roll the apples in this; use two spoons to do this.
6 Melt the butter in an ovenproof dish, put in the apples and fill the centres with the almond and sugar mixture.
7 Sprinkle with the remaining 1 oz. breadcrumbs, and bake in the centre of a moderate oven (350–375°F., Gas Mark 4–5), until tender, about 45 minutes.

Chocolate apple meringues

Preparation: 10–15 minutes
No delay
Cooking: 40 minutes
Serves 4

If the apples are small in size use 4; do not halve at stage 1. See comments about making meringues, page 166.
Take care the chocolate mixture does not burn, stage 8. Stir well and keep the heat low.

2 large cooking apples
juice of 2 lemons
1½ oz. sugar *to sweeten apples*
1 tablespoon redcurrant jelly

2 egg whites
4 oz. castor sugar

for the chocolate sauce
3 oz. plain *or* unsweetened chocolate

1–2 oz. sugar
1 teaspoon cocoa
¼ pint water
vanilla essence
2 egg yolks

1 Peel and core the apples, cut them in half and simmer for about 10 minutes in water with a squeeze of lemon juice, until just tender — see page 169 for poaching fruit. DO NOT ALLOW TO BREAK.
2 Place in a buttered ovenproof dish.
3 Put the rest of the lemon juice, sugar and redcurrant jelly into a saucepan and bring to the boil.
4 Pour over the apples.
5 Whip the egg whites stiffly (see page 166) and fold in the castor sugar. Pipe in circles round the top of the apples.
6 Bake for approximately 30 minutes in the centre of a slow to very moderate oven (300–325°F., Gas Mark 2–3).
7 *Meanwhile, prepare the chocolate sauce:* break up the chocolate and reserve a small piece.
8 Put the rest into a small pan with the sugar, cocoa and water.
9 Stir over a very low heat until the chocolate has melted.
10 Simmer for about 5 minutes until thickened. Add the vanilla essence, then take pan off the heat and stir in the beaten egg yolks.
11 Fill the centres of the apples with this sauce, grate the reserved chocolate and put on top.

Left *Apple islands*
Right *Chocolate apple meringues*

Apple islands

Preparation: 5–7 minutes
No delay
Cooking: 1 hour
Serves 4

This method of cooking a milk pudding and apples is delicious, for the flavours blend during cooking.
Use home-made *cooked* boiled rice, page 163, instead of canned rice.

4 medium cooking apples

2–4 tablespoons bramble *or* redcurrant jelly

large can creamed rice
about ¼ pint milk, *optional*

1 Peel and core the apples, put into an ovenproof dish.
2 Fill the centre of each apple with jelly or jam.
3 Open the can of creamed rice and pour this round the apples.
4 If you like a fairly liquid milk pudding, then add the extra milk to the rice.
5 Bake in the centre of a moderate oven (325–350°F., Gas Mark 3–4), for approximately 1 hour, until the apples are just soft.
6 Decorate with extra jelly or jam, if wished.

To serve apples cold

Apples can be served cold if stewed (see compote of fruit on page 169). Make sure the fruit is covered with syrup to prevent discolouration.
Some people like cold baked apples; these are very pleasant if topped with cream or ice cream.

171

Apple fool

Preparation: 15 minutes
No delay
Cooking: 15 minutes
Serves 4

The easiest way to prepare this is to emulsify the fruit purée and custard together in the liquidiser goblet.

1 lb. apples
2 tablespoons water
1–2 oz. sugar
good squeeze of lemon juice

½ pint thick sweetened custard, made as directed with custard powder

to decorate
few glacé cherries
tiny pieces of angelica

1 Peel, core and slice the apples.
2 Put them into a saucepan with the water and sugar.
3 Cook gently so they do not burn.
4 When the apples are smooth, beat well with a wooden spoon, adding the lemon juice.
5 When the custard and apple are both cold, beat them together with a wooden spoon.
6 Put into four glasses; decorate with cherries and angelica.

Other fruit fools

Most fruit can be served as a fruit fool (recipe above), but soft fruit such as strawberries, etc., needs no cooking, just mashing or sieving then sweetening. Other fruits particularly good in fruit fools are:

Gooseberries and blackcurrants. These should be pressed through a sieve, after cooking, to remove skins.

Plums. Stone and halve before cooking so that the minimum of water is required.

Rhubarb. Cook with the minimum of water, sieve if wished, see colour picture page 168.

Flamenco orange cups

Preparation: 20 minutes
No delay
Cooking: few minutes
Serves 6

Secret of success
Makes of gelatine vary; some can be dissolved in hot liquid very easily, others are better if soaked in the cold liquid and dissolved over a pan of very hot water; if in doubt as to the way any gelatine behaves, use this latter method.
Soak oranges in boiling water for 10 minutes (this makes insides easier to remove from the skins).

6 medium oranges
3 level teaspoons powdered gelatine
½ pint milk

2 oz. fine semolina
2 oz. castor sugar
1 egg yolk
1 egg white

to decorate
mint leaves or chopped nuts

1 Dry the orange skins after soaking, and cut off tops. Carefully scoop out the flesh from each orange and squeeze the juice. You should have about 6 tablespoons; if necessary add a little water to give this quantity of liquid.
2 Strain and heat the juice. Dissolve the gelatine in the hot juice, stir thoroughly and leave in a cool place to thicken.
3 Heat the milk, sprinkle in the semolina and, stirring carefully, bring to the boil. Boil gently for 3 minutes.
4 Remove from the heat, whisk in the sugar and egg yolk, cover and leave until cold.
5 Whisk the thickened gelatine until frothy, gradually beat in the creamy semolina mixture, then gently fold in the whisked egg white.
6 Pile equal amounts of the mixture into the orange 'cups' and chill.
7 Before serving, decorate each with a crisp mint or other leaf, or a sprinkling of chopped nuts.
8 Serve with shortbread biscuits.

Flamenco oranges

Banana fluff

Preparation: 12 minutes
No delay
No cooking
Serves 4–5

Secret of success
Add the lemon juice to the bananas, at stage 2, with the minimum delay. This prevents their turning brown.

¼ pint thick cream	5 bananas	little lemon juice
2 egg whites	2 tablespoons icing sugar, sieved	sponge fingers

1 Whisk the cream until just stiff. DO NOT OVER-BEAT otherwise it will curdle. Beat the egg whites until *very stiff*. Use two separate basins.
2 Mash 4 bananas with sugar and lemon juice — fold the cream into this, then add egg whites.
3 Line a shallow dish with the sponge fingers, then pile the banana mixture on top.
4 Decorate with the remaining banana, cut into slices.

Note. Try this also with fresh raspberries, loganberries or strawberries.

Baked bananas

Preparation: few minutes
No delay
Cooking: 15 minutes
Serves 2

You can use rum or brandy over the bananas, in place of lemon juice.

4 small ripe bananas	knob of butter	2 tablespoons brown sugar
lemon juice		

1 Slice or halve the bananas and then put into a shallow dish.
2 Squeeze the lemon juice over the fruit, dot with butter, cover with the sugar.
3 Bake for about 15 minutes in a hot oven (425°F., Gas Mark 6).
4 Serve hot with cream.

To vary
1 Add a little rum or orange juice to the bananas at stage 2.
2 Top with grated fresh or desiccated coconut halfway through baking (stage 3).

Cardinal peaches

Preparation: 5 minutes
No delay
Cooking: 10 minutes
Serves 4

Secret of success
Use a large saucepan to give plenty of space to turn the peaches in the syrup.

4 large *or* 8 small fresh peaches	2 oz. sugar	4 oz. raspberries
	½ pint water	1 tablespoon redcurrant jelly

1 Choose rather firm peaches.
2 Skin them after dipping in hot water for ½ minute.
3 Heat the sugar, water, mashed raspberries and jelly.
4 Put the peaches in this and cook gently, turning them round until pale pink and soft.
5 Lift out the peaches, put on a dish and coat with the syrup.
6 If wished, make a blancmange, arrange the peaches round this and coat with the syrup, or serve round a block of ice cream.

Making a good fruit salad

Preparation: 10–12 minutes
No delay
No cooking

Secret of success
Choose a good mixture of colours and flavours of fruit. Add chopped nuts and dried fruit sometimes.

1 Prepare the fruit, cutting it into neat but not too small pieces. *Grapes* should be halved and pipped. They can be skinned if wished. *Peaches* should be skinned by putting into boiling water for ½ minute. *Apples* and *Pears* should be peeled and cored. *Oranges* should be divided into sections, removing pith and pips.
2 If using canned fruit as a basis, no syrup need be made.
3 If you wish to make a syrup, put the peel of 1 or 2 oranges with water and a little sugar into a saucepan, simmer for about 5 minutes, cool slightly and strain over the fruit.
4 Add a little kirsch to the syrup for special occasions.
5 If slimming, use fresh orange, or orange and lemon juice, instead of syrup.

Dried apples and other dried fruit

When fresh fruits are not available, dried fruits are a good standby in the larder. They keep for a long time if stored in a cool, dry place.

1 Wash the fruit very well.
2 Soak fruit overnight in cold water.
3 Cook for 1½–2 hours in the same water in which the fruit was soaked. Add sugar to taste; OR allow approximately 12 minutes in a pressure cooker at 15 lb. pressure.
4 A little lemon juice can be added to apples or apricots, or to peaches.
5 Figs and prunes have a very good flavour if cooked in weak tea or coffee rather than water.

To vary
1 Mix together several types of dried fruit to make a fruit salad.
2 Use soaked lightly-cooked dried fruit in upside-down puddings, see page 158.

To whip evaporated milk

Preparation: 1 minute. Milk must be allowed to cool
Cooking: 15 minutes

If the can of milk is very cool you can whip lightly without boiling it, but most people find it more satisfactory to boil as described in the method.

1 Boil the can of milk for about 15 minutes in a pan of water, then chill thoroughly for several hours.
2 Turn the evaporated milk into a large bowl and whisk.
3 For *very thick* cream from evaporated milk, turn the milk out of the can after the 15 minutes boiling (open the can *carefully* so the milk does not spurt out).
4 Stir the milk on to 1 teaspoon powdered gelatine, dissolved in 2 tablespoons very hot water. Cool as before, then whip. Or omit the gelatine and add a little lemon juice instead.

Note. Do make certain the can is covered with water at stage 1, and that the water does not evaporate.
Open the can *carefully* as the hot milk tends to 'spurt out'.

Pineapple and strawberry scoop with shortbread biscuits

Preparation: 15 minutes
Allow to chill
Cooking: 20 minutes for biscuits
Serves 4–6
Makes 20 biscuits

A melon could be used instead of a pineapple.
The method assumes you are using one of the soft margarines.

| 1 medium pineapple | 8 oz.–1 lb. strawberries *or* other fruit | little sugar |

1 Wipe the pineapple with a damp cloth and cut in half lengthways.
2 Remove centre flesh from inside the pineapple halves, leaving the skin intact.
3 Cut flesh into small cubes; discard the centre core.
4 Wash and hull the strawberries.
5 Mix together the strawberries and cubed pineapple, add sugar to taste and fill the pineapple halves with the fruit.
6 Leave in a cool place, preferably a refrigerator. Serve with cream and shortbread biscuits.

Shortbread biscuits

| 6 oz. plain flour, sieved | 4 oz. margarine *or* butter | 2 oz. castor sugar |

1 Place the sieved flour in a mixing bowl, add the fat and sugar and knead together with your fingers to form a smooth dough.
2 Roll out the dough on a lightly floured board to about $\frac{1}{4}$ inch thick, and cut into various shapes.
3 Place on a greased baking sheet and bake in the centre of a moderate oven (325–350°F., Gas Mark 3–4) for 20 minutes.
4 Remove and allow to cool on the tin.
5 Sprinkle with castor sugar when cold; store in an airtight tin until ready to use.

Pineapple and strawberry scoop

174

To make a trifle

Preparation: 20 minutes
Allow layers to cool
Cooking: time required for making custard

If you cover the trifle with a plate as it cools you will prevent a skin forming on the custard.
To make a lighter cream topping, blend 1 stiffly whisked egg white into ¼ pint whipped cream, or see under 'To whip cream'.

There are a number of ways of making trifles. The simplest is as follows:
1 Buy sponge cakes and split these, fill with jam, and put at the bottom of a dish.
2 Allow approximately 3–4 sponge cakes for four people.
3 Soak with a little sherry, or fruit juice, or white wine.
4 Cover with 1 pint custard sauce (page 157), but make this a little thicker than usual. Allow to cool, then decorate with whipped thick cream, or whipped evaporated milk (page 174), glacé cherries and pieces of angelica.

Trifle with jelly
1 A more elaborate trifle is made by putting chopped fruit over the sponge cakes and then adding liquid jelly. Allow this to set.
2 Make the custard and allow it to cool, stirring from time to time so that it does not become too set.
3 Pour the cold custard over the set jelly.
4 Chopped blanched almonds or tiny ratafia (macaroon) biscuits can be added to the custard. Decorate as before.

Milk moulds and cold sweets

Milk is just as nourishing if served in a sweet as when drunk from a glass, and it is a very wise rule to make sure the family have their pint of milk per day in some form or other. If they are not fond of milk puddings, a great deal of nourishment is obtained by giving them cream on sweets, etc.

To whip cream

1 You must use thick cream to be sure of whipping successfully.
2 Put into a basin and whisk firmly.
3 Use a flat whisk or a fork and whisk until thick.
4 A large rotary whisk will do the job well, but there is a danger of it over-whipping the cream; over-whipped cream becomes buttery and separates.
5 A little sugar and a few drops of flavouring may be added *when* the cream has thickened.
6 For a lighter cream: a) whip ¼ pint thick cream until it just holds its shape, then gradually whip in as much thin cream as possible. If you wish a light piping cream you will be able to add 4–5 tablespoons, but if you just wish to pile the cream over a dessert you may incorporate ¼ pint thin cream. b) whip ¼ pint thick cream in one basin and 1 egg white in another, fold together just before serving. This mixture does not pipe well.

To make a blancmange

Preparation: few minutes
Allow to set
Cooking: 8 minutes
Serves 4

Instructions for making blancmanges are given on the packets. You will get a better flavour if a small knob of butter is put in as the blancmange thickens. If you have no flavoured-blancmange make as recipe.

1¼ oz. cornflour *or* use a little less cornflour and ½ oz. cocoa *or* use ¾ pint milk and ¼ pint strong coffee	1 pint milk 1–2 oz. sugar	flavouring butter, *optional*

1 Blend the cornflour with 2 tablespoons cold milk.
2 Put the rest of the milk on to boil.
3 Pour the boiling milk over the blended cornflour and return it to the saucepan to thicken.
4 Add the sugar and flavouring and cook steadily until really thick. Add a knob of butter, if wished.
5 Pour into a rinsed mould or basin, and cover with a plate to prevent a skin forming.
6 Turn out when quite cold.

Junket

Preparation: 2–3 minutes
Allow to clot
Cooking: few minutes
Serves 4

The reason 'undisturbed' is stressed in stage 3 is that sharp movement could break the junket and make it 'watery'.

1 pint milk 1 oz. sugar	1 teaspoon rennet*	cream *or* grated nutmeg

* if using pasteurised milk use 2 teaspoons rennet.

1 Heat the milk and sugar to blood heat, i.e. so the mixture feels tepid when touched.
2 Stir in the rennet, then pour into a dish or dishes.
3 Leave in room temperature, UNDISTURBED, until clotted.
4 Top with cream or a little grated nutmeg; chill after junket clots.

Variations on plain junket
Flavour the milk with a little chocolate or coffee powder, or use flavouring essences.

Preparing moulds for jellies

1 A jelly will turn out very much better if the mould is brushed very lightly with a little olive oil. If you do not wish to do this, always rinse the mould out in *cold* water before putting in the jelly.
2 If the jelly seems disinclined to turn out when set, dip the mould for a FEW SECONDS ONLY in warm water.
3 Hold the dish on which you mean to turn the jelly over the mould. Grip tightly, then turn upside down.
4 If you damp the serving dish very slightly before putting on the jelly you will find it easy to slide the jelly into the centre of the dish.

Semolina mocha royale

Preparation: 6 minutes
No delay
Cooking: 7–8 minutes
Serves 4

Secret of success
Add the semolina *gradually* at stage 3, whisking or stirring as you do so.

Note. 1 egg white, whisked until stiff, can be folded into the mixture just before pouring into the mould.

Orange mould

1 pint milk	1 dessertspoon cocoa	canned *or* stewed pears
3 tablespoons sugar	4 tablespoons fine semolina	few glacé cherries
1 teaspoon instant coffee	½ teaspoon vanilla essence	

1 Heat the milk to boiling point, add the sugar and mix well.
2 Remove from the heat. Blend the instant coffee powder and cocoa with a little extra milk or water and stir into the milk.
3 When smoothly blended, return to the heat and add the semolina, gradually stirring all the time until the mixture is thickened.
4 Cook gently for several minutes, then stir in the vanilla essence.
5 Pour the mixture into a lightly oiled or buttered mould, rinsed in cold water. Leave in a cool place until set.
6 Turn out, and arrange cooked or canned pear halves round the mould.
7 Decorate each portion of pear with a glacé cherry.

Vanilla mould: omit the coffee and cocoa from recipe above.
Orange mould: use only ¾ pint milk at stages 1–3, then whisk in ¼ pint syrup from canned mandarin oranges at stage 4, and continue cooking. Decorate with mandarin oranges and cherries as picture below.

To make jellied sweets

The excellent packet jellies produce easy sweets.
1 They can be made more interesting by adding chopped fruit. *Never use fresh pineapple in a jelly as it prevents it setting.* Canned pineapple is perfectly satisfactory; be sparing with the liquid if using moist fruits.
2 Flavour can be added by using fruit juice as part of the total liquid.

Milk jellies

Preparation: few minutes
Cooking: 2–3 minutes only
Serves 4

¼ pint water	1 fruit-flavoured jelly	¾ pint milk

1 Boil the water and dissolve the jelly in this. If it is slow to dissolve, stand the basin over a saucepan of boiling water.
2 Allow to cool; when cold whisk in the cold milk (this prevents curdling).
3 Pour into a mould and allow to set.

Raspberry lemon mould

Preparation: few minutes
Allow to set
Cooking: 2–3 minutes only
Serves 4

Secret of success
The jelly must be cold before adding the milk.

1 lemon-flavoured jelly   ¾ pint milk   8 oz. raspberries
¼ pint water

1 Dissolve the lemon jelly in the boiling water as above.
2 Allow to cool, then whisk in the cold milk. If jelly is not cold before adding milk the mixture will curdle.
3 Pour into a rinsed ring mould and leave to set.
4 Turn out and fill the centre with fresh raspberries.

Raspberry mousse

Preparation: 8 minutes
Allow time to set
Cooking: few minutes
Serves 4

Secret of success
Do not try to add egg whites to jelly mixture until this stiffens, or the mixture separates.

small can raspberries *or*   ¼ pint lightly whipped thick   *to decorate*
  6 oz. fresh fruit   cream *or* whipped   raspberries, *optional*
1 raspberry-flavoured jelly   evaporated milk, *page 174*
3 tablespoons milk   2 egg whites

1 Drain the fruit and measure the juice.
2 If necessary, add enough water to give ¼ pint.
3 Thoroughly dissolve the jelly in this, and when cool add the cold milk.
4 Allow to stiffen slightly and then fold in the whipped cream or evaporated milk; lastly fold in the stiffly beaten egg whites.
5 Pour into a rinsed mould. When firm, turn out and decorate with the raspberries, if wished.

Lemon and coconut mould

Preparation: 10–15 minutes
Allow time for jelly to set before adding egg whites
Cooking: few minutes for heating water
Serves 4

Secret of success
Do not try to add egg whites to jelly mixture until this stiffens, or the mixture separates.

1 lemon-flavoured jelly   2 oz. desiccated coconut   *to decorate*
2 eggs   2 oz. sponge cake crumbs   glacé cherries
1–2 oz. sugar   blanched almonds

1 Dissolve the jelly in just over ¾ pint boiling water; cool.
2 Beat the egg yolks and sugar with a whisk until light, add the coconut, crumbs and the lemon jelly.
3 Leave until beginning to set lightly, then fold in the stiffly beaten egg whites, using a metal spoon.
4 Put into a rinsed mould. When quite firm, turn out and decorate with glacé cherries and nuts.

Marshmallow jelly

Preparation: 5 minutes
Wait for jelly to cool
Cooking: few minutes for heating water
Serves 4

The marshmallows would melt if added to warm jelly.

1 lemon *or* orange-flavoured   few pieces fresh fruit   2–4 oz. marshmallows
  jelly

1 Make the jelly with 1 pint water as instructed – allow to cool but not to set.
2 Add the fruit and the marshmallows (pink and white if possible), cut into small pieces.
3 Pour into a rinsed mould. When set, turn out.

Carnival mould

Preparation: 15 minutes
Wait for setting between layers
No cooking
Just heating liquid
Serves 4

If you stand the mould on a layer of ice at stage 3, it sets almost immediately.

small can cherries *or*   small can mandarin oranges   1 orange-flavoured jelly
  maraschino cherries   2 oz. marshmallows

1 Strain the juice from the fruits and add just enough water to make nearly 1 pint.
2 Dissolve the jelly in this, as instructed on the packet.
3 Pour a thin layer of jelly into the mould and allow to set. The rest of the liquid jelly should be kept in a warm place to keep it liquid until required.
4 Add a layer of chopped cherries, oranges and marshmallows. Cover this with jelly, and allow to set.
5 Continue to fill the mould like this, allowing each layer to set before adding the next.

Cold lemon soufflé

Preparation: 20 minutes
Allow mixture to stiffen before
adding egg whites
Serves 4–6

Prepare a soufflé dish by tying
round it a band of greaseproof
paper, greased with butter, so
that it stands about 2 inches
above the top of the dish.

Secrets of success
Make quite certain the gelatine
mixture has stiffened slightly
before adding the whipped
cream, or evaporated milk, and
egg whites.
Serve soufflés when freshly
made. They do not improve with
keeping for any length of time.

½ pint cream *or* evaporated
milk
2 large *or* 3 small eggs
juice of 1 large *or* 2 small
lemons

2 oz. castor sugar
½ oz. powdered gelatine
2 tablespoons water
few drops of vanilla essence

to decorate
thick cream, whipped
nuts, angelica, *or*
crystallised violets

1 Whip the cream or evaporated milk (pages 174, 175).
2 Separate the egg yolks and whites, and put the yolks into a basin with the lemon juice and sugar.
3 Stand the basin over a pan of hot water, beat until creamy. Remove and beat until cold.
4 Dissolve the gelatine in the water.* Add to the egg yolks.
5 When partly set, fold in most of the whipped cream and vanilla essence.
6 Whip the egg whites until very stiff, fold into the soufflé mixture.
7 Pour into the prepared soufflé dish. Leave until set, then gently remove the paper. Decorate the top with piped whipped cream and nuts, or tiny pieces of angelica or crystallised violets.

* gelatine dissolves more readily if: a) it is first softened in *cold* liquid in a basin; b) the gelatine and cold liquid are either stirred into a hot mixture or the basin containing the softened gelatine is put into a pan containing a small quantity of very hot liquid (use this method in the recipe above), and left until the gelatine has dissolved.

Quickies

5-minute sweets and ideas for
summer fruits

1 Wash and dry bunches of red or white currants, brush with egg white then coat with castor sugar. Leave in the air to dry out. These are lovely as a table decoration and dessert.
2 Mash redcurrants with a little sugar and vanilla essence or vanilla-flavoured sugar (obtainable from good grocers). Leave for several hours, then serve with top of the milk or thin cream.
3 Halve strawberries or use raspberries. Put a block of ice cream into a bowl, stir in the fruit, leave for about 30 minutes in a cold place for the flavours to mingle, then serve.
4 For ice cream sodas, put a good layer of slightly sweetened soft fruit in tall glasses, then a spoonful of ice cream. Top with soda water and serve with straws and spoons.
5 Use redcurrants and strawberries in salads — they are particularly good with cream cheese or cold lamb salads. Toss in mint sauce for lamb.
6 Add raw blackcurrants, raspberries, etc., to fruit jellies, stirring in when the jelly is cold but not set.

Yoghourt desserts

One of the easiest desserts is to
serve yoghourt with fruit or
mixed with sugar.

Serves 4–6

Lemon yoghourt whip
Dissolve a lemon jelly in just ½ pint water.
Chill until slightly stiffened, fold in the juice
of half a lemon, four 5 oz. cartons of natural
yoghourt and 2 whisked egg whites. Spoon
one-third of the mixture into 4–6 glasses,
allow to stiffen, cover with halved
strawberries. Continue like this, top with whole
fruit.

Yoghourt apricot crunch
Soak and cook 8 oz. dried apricots with
1 oz. sugar and water to cover, until tender.
Sieve or emulsify with 4 tablespoons of the
liquid. Dissolve ½ oz. gelatine in 4 more
tablespoons of the liquid. Whisk a small can
evaporated milk until stiff (see page 174).
Fold the gelatine and apricot purée into the
whisked milk together with four 5 oz.
cartons of natural yoghourt. Divide between
4–6 glasses and allow to set.

Stir ½ oz. butter and 2 oz. demerara sugar over a
low heat until the sugar has melted. Add 2 oz.
blanched chopped almonds, mix well then
cool. Sprinkle over the dessert.

Egg custard
(baked or steamed)

Preparation: few minutes
No delay
Cooking: 1¼ hours
Serves 4

Secrets of success
The method, right, gives the precautions necessary to prevent the custard curdling.

| 2 eggs | ¾ pint milk | little grated nutmeg |
| 1 level teaspoon sugar | | |

1 Beat the eggs with a fork, add the sugar and warmed milk.
2 The milk MUST NOT BOIL, otherwise it will curdle the eggs.
3 Pour into a greased pie dish or basin, grating the nutmeg on top.

Baked custard
1 Half fill a dish, slightly larger than the pie dish, with cold water.
2 Stand the pie dish in this, then bake for about 1¼ hours in the centre of a slow oven (275–300°F., Gas Mark 1–2) until firm. Too great a heat causes curdling and will spoil the custard.

Steamed custard
1 Put the basin into the steamer over very hot water, and cook steadily for about 1¼ hours. The water must never boil, otherwise the custard will curdle.
2 Test with your finger; if you can just bear it in the water the heat is right.
3 Cool slightly, then you can turn out the custard.

Bread and butter pudding

Preparation: 10 minutes
This is better if allowed to stand before baking
Cooking: 1 hour
Serves 4

Secret of success
You use a slightly hotter oven than for an ordinary baked custard, so top of the pudding becomes golden brown, but care must be taken that the pudding does not 'curdle', or become 'watery' at the bottom. If the pudding appears to be cooking too quickly after 45 minutes, lower the heat.

| 2 large *or* 4 small slices | 2 oz. dried fruit | little extra sugar |
| bread and butter | ingredients as egg custard | |

1 Remove the crusts from the bread and butter and cut the bread into neat squares or triangles.
2 Arrange in a pie dish with the dried fruit.
3 Prepare the egg custard as above; pour into the dish.
4 If possible allow to stand for 30 minutes.
5 Sprinkle the top of the pudding with a little sugar.
6 Bake for approximately 1 hour in the centre of a very moderate oven (325°F., Gas Mark 3). If necessary, lower heat after 45 minutes.

Caramel custard

Preparation: 12–15 minutes
Allow caramel to set slightly before adding custard
Cooking: see right
Serves 4–6

Secrets of success
If you do not stir as the sugar dissolves, stage 1, the liquid evaporates and leaves dry sugar behind.
If you stir continually, or even frequently, when the sugar has dissolved you lower the temperature and hinder the sugar reaching the right temperature.

4 eggs *or* 4 egg yolks*	1 pint milk *or* ½ pint milk	*for the caramel*
1 oz. sugar	and ½ pint evaporated milk	3 oz. castor sugar
		3 tablespoons water

* using all egg yolks gives a very rich custard. You can use 2 whole eggs and 2 yolks if wished.

1 *First, make the caramel sauce:* put the sugar and water into a small heavy pan, place over a low heat and allow sugar to melt, stirring until it has dissolved – do not allow the syrup to come to the boil until all the sugar is melted.
2 Increase the heat and cook, stirring very occasionally, until it is a good deep golden colour.
3 Remove from the heat, and pour into a warmed buttered soufflé dish or cake tin, turning it this way and that until the sides and the bottom are evenly coated with the caramel.
4 Beat the eggs and sugar with a fork, heat the milk to just UNDER boiling point and pour on to the beaten eggs.
5 Stir and strain into the caramel-coated mould.
6 Stand in a baking tin with enough hot water round it to come halfway up the sides, cover with a piece of buttered paper or kitchen foil and bake in a slow oven (300°F., Gas Mark 2), for about 1 hour until quite set, or in a very slow oven (275°F., Gas Mark 1) for about 2 hours, or steam for 2 hours, making sure the water never boils.
7 Let the custard get cool before turning it out. (It is important to fill the dish in which the custard is baked quite full, or the custard may break when it is turned out.)

Ice cream sweets

The ice cream one buys can be the basis of a number of very good sweets. Ice cream will keep for some hours in the freezing compartment of a refrigerator. If you have no refrigerator, then the ice cream block keeps better if wrapped in newspaper.

Sundaes

These can be made simply by putting ice cream and fresh or canned fruit into sundae glasses and topping with Melba sauce. For a chocolate sundae, use chocolate or coffee ice cream and top with hot or cold chocolate sauce and a few chopped nuts.

Easy Melba sauce

Preparation: few minutes
Cooking: few minutes
Serves 2

2 good tablespoons redcurrant jelly	2 tablespoons water	2 good tablespoons raspberry jam

Heat all ingredients together, cool before using.

Using fresh raspberries: heat 4–6 tablespoons crushed sieved fruit with the jelly and water, add a little sugar. Cool before using.
Fruit Melba: arrange fresh or drained canned fruit (peaches, pears, pineapple, etc.) on top of ice cream, and coat with the sauce.

Easy chocolate sauce

Preparation: few minutes
Cooking: few minutes
Serves 2

Secret of success
Do not over-heat the mixture.

2 oz. chocolate	1 tablespoon water

1 Break the chocolate into pieces. Place in a basin.
2 Add the water and heat over a pan of hot water.
3 Keep hot and spoon over ice cream. If you need to keep sauce hot for some time, use 2 tablespoons water; check that water in the pan is not too hot.

Pears Hélène: this is the best known use of hot chocolate sauce. Arrange halved and cored dessert pears, or well drained canned pear halves, on top of ice cream. Coat with hot chocolate sauce.

Home-made ice cream

Preparation: 15 minutes
Cooking: 10–20 minutes, dependent upon type of custard used
Freezing: 1–1½ hours
Serves 6–8

Secrets of success
Freeze mixture quickly. In modern 3-star refrigerators or home freezers there is no need to turn to coldest position; with an older refrigerator turn to coldest setting ½ hour before putting mixture into freezing compartment.
Do not over-sweeten the mixture.

½ pint custard sauce – using custard powder *or* 2 egg yolks, ½ pint milk and 1 oz. sugar	flavouring, *see below* 1–2 oz. sieved icing sugar	½ pint thick cream 2 egg whites

1 Make the custard sauce, cool and stir to prevent a skin forming.
2 Add the flavouring and sugar, and then the lightly whipped cream.
3 Spoon into the freezing trays and freeze for 35–40 minutes, until the mixture is beginning to stiffen, then remove from the trays into a cold bowl.
4 Whisk well, then fold in the stiffly whipped egg whites.
5 Return to the freezing trays and freeze until firm. If the refrigerator has been turned to fast-freezing re-set to normal.

Flavourings
1 Add 1 teaspoon vanilla or other essence; blend 1–2 tablespoons sieved cocoa or 2 teaspoons instant coffee powder with the sauce.
2 Add about ⅓ pint thick fruit purée to the mixture.

Rich ice cream

Preparation: 10 minutes
No cooking
Freezing: 1–1½ hours
Serves 3–4

¼ pint thick cream ¼ pint thin cream	1½–2 oz. sieved icing sugar flavouring, *see above*	2 egg whites

1 Whip the thick cream until it just holds its shape, then gradually whisk in the thin cream and sugar.
2 Add the flavouring, see above (but use only half quantities), then fold in the stiffly whisked egg whites.
3 Freeze until firm; there is no need to beat this mixture during freezing.

Baked Alaska

Baked Alaska

Preparation: 15 minutes
Allow time for oven to heat
Cooking: 3 minutes
Serves 6

Secret of success
You must have a very hot oven and very short cooking time to brown the meringue, otherwise the heat penetrates through to the ice cream.

large block ice cream*
1 raspberry jam sponge
  sandwich

firm fruit: fresh, canned,
  stewed *or* frozen

for the meringue
3 egg whites
3 oz. castor sugar

* enough for 6

1 Turn on the oven and heat to 475°F., Gas Mark 8.
2 *Make the meringue:* whisk the egg whites until stiff.
3 Fold in the castor sugar.
4 Place the ice cream on the sponge, then surround and cover with pieces of well drained fruit.
5 Spread the meringue over, making sure it covers the ice cream completely.
6 Brown in a very hot oven (475°F., Gas Mark 8) for approximately 3 minutes. Serve at once.

Raspberry cream tartlets, see page 191

Amounts of pastry to allow

Please take this as an approximate guide, for the thickness of pastry makes a great deal of difference to the amount used.
As you become more expert you will find that you waste less pastry when making a pie, etc.

8 oz. pastry should be enough for a 7-inch pie, i.e. pastry above and below.
5–6 oz. pastry makes a 7–8 inch flan.
5–6 oz. pastry makes a pie for 4 or 5 people.
6 oz. pastry makes 6–8 really deep individual patty cases.*
4 oz. pastry makes 9 small tarts.

* patty tins are obtainable separately or in sets of 6 or 8, or more usually 9 or 12.

Note. *When a recipe says '6 oz. pastry' it does not mean the total weight* but pastry made with 6 oz. flour, etc.

182

Pastry

To make good pastry

Basic rules

1 Keep ingredients, utensils and hands as cool as possible.
2 Use a large bowl rather than a small basin for short crust pastry so that there is plenty of air space.
3 Sieve the flour with the salt before mixing. This lightens the dough.
4 When rubbing fat into the flour, lift hands as much as possible so that air is introduced into the dough.
5 Rub in fat only with forefinger and thumb. Too much pressure when rubbing in fat will make pastry too sticky.
6 It is undoubtedly better to use plain flour for all pastry. Many people, however, prefer self-raising flour for short pastry, especially when the proportion of fat is decreased. If you are successful with self-raising flour, do not change. For richer pastry, i.e. flaky or puff pastry, it is wise to use plain flour.
7 The consistency of the dough is all-important. Be careful not to make it too wet, as this produces a hard pastry. If the dough is too dry, it will be difficult to roll out. Generally speaking the dough is the right texture when it rolls into a large ball with very little handling. Short crust pastry needs on an average 2—3 tablespoons water to each 8 oz. flour.
8 Pastry should be baked quickly. Correct temperatures are given in the various recipes.
9 When using very hard fat (perhaps straight from the refrigerator) which is almost impossible to rub into the flour, you will find it helpful to grate fat on a coarse grater, or to soften it by working with a knife. When making a flan pastry the fat can be slightly warmed and creamed.
10 When rolling out pastry, remember never to roll the rolling pin backwards and forwards. It should roll one way only — straight ahead. The pastry should be turned at right angles.
11 When rolling the pastry, lift the rolling pin from time to time. This helps to keep the dough light.

Fats to use in pastry

There is a great deal of discussion as to what is the best fat to use in pastry. Since there is such a variety of fats on the market today it is a little difficult to decide, but in this chapter you will find recipes and pictures for pastry using practically every type of available fat. If used correctly, all of these make successful pastry.

Whipped-up cooking fat or shortening (see pages 84, 184, 185, 188, 191, 193)	partially in puff partially or entirely in short crust or flaky entirely in quick short crust entirely in hot water crust
Pure lard (see pages 84, 184, 198)	partially or entirely in short or flaky entirely in hot water crust
Pure cooking fat (see pages 84, 184, 186, 189, 193)	partially or entirely in short, flaky or sweet short crust entirely in hot water crust
Margarine — hard type (see pages 184, 190, 193, 194, 195)	partially or entirely in short or flaky entirely in puff entirely in flan or biscuit crust
Margarine — softer type (see pages 189, 190, 195)	partially or entirely in quick type pastry entirely in flan or biscuit crust
Butter (see pages 184, 189, 190, 195, 196)	partially or entirely in short or rich short crust or flan or biscuit crust entirely in puff

Short crust pastry

Preparation: 10 minutes
No delay
Cooking: as recipe

Secrets of success
Keep all ingredients and utensils as cool as possible.
Incorporate as much air as possible at stage 1, by lifting the mixture as you rub in the fat.
Do NOT use too much water at stage 2; makes of flour vary in the amount of liquid they require, so this is an average amount only. Do NOT over-handle the dough at stage 4.
Roll quickly and lightly at stage 5, and when using the pastry.

3½ oz. whipped-up cooking fat *or* 4 oz. other fats   8 oz. plain flour (*or* self-raising flour can be used)   ½ level teaspoon salt
2–3 tablespoons cold water

1 Rub whipped-up cooking fat or other fat into sieved flour and salt, using the fingertips, until the mixture looks like fine breadcrumbs. Rub quickly and lightly, lifting mixture up all the time to get as much cool air in as possible.

2 Add freshly drawn cold water (or iced water if there is a refrigerator), using a tablespoon to be accurate. Sprinkle the water evenly over the mixture.

3 Take a palette knife or any round-bladed kitchen knife and mix together lightly, cutting through and pressing together. A knife is used to keep the pastry cool.

4 Put down the knife and quickly bind the mixture into a smooth dough with the hand (holding the bowl with the other hand), leaving the bowl clean.

5 Place the dough on a LIGHTLY-floured board or table top, and remove cracks by kneading lightly. Flour the rolling pin lightly and, using short sharp strokes, roll the pastry to whatever shape is required. Roll in one direction only and turn as necessary, taking care not to stretch it. Bake as directed in recipes.

Other fats to use in short crust pastry

The step by step pictures opposite have shown pastry made with the modern type of whipped-up cooking fat. You will use exactly the same method for a mixture of margarine and cooking fat or lard, or all margarine, all butter, etc. Whipped-up cooking fat produces the best result if 3½ oz. only is used to 8 oz. flour. When using other fats allow: 2 oz. margarine plus 2 oz. cooking fat (either pure cooking fat or the whipped-up type, or 2 oz. lard). If using all lard you get a very short pastry, but 4 oz. can be used; 4 oz. margarine or 4 oz. butter should be allowed to 8 oz. flour.

Use short crust pastry to make
fruit pies and flans; sausage rolls; small tarts.

Quick method of making crust pastry

Preparation: few minutes
No delay
Cooking: as recipes

Because the modern cooking fats soften so quickly you can use this quick method to make pastry. The soft (often called 'luxury') margarines can be used in the same way. Use just under the 3 tablespoons water if using margarine, then test the dough at stage 3; if necessary add a few drops more water.

3½ oz. whipped-up cooking fat *or* 4 oz. soft margarine

3 tablespoons water
8 oz. plain *or* self-raising flour

pinch of salt

1 Place the cooking fat or margarine in one piece with water, 2 rounded tablespoons of the sieved flour, and salt in a mixing bowl.

2 Whisk together with a fork for about ½ minute until well mixed and fluffy.

3 Add the remaining flour and, stirring, form into a firm dough.

4 Very lightly knead on a lightly floured board, moulding to a smooth ball. Roll out; use in same way as short crust pastry.

Banana twirls

Preparation: 18–20 minutes
No delay
Cooking: 15–20 minutes
Makes 4 small portions

Choose firm, fairly under-ripe bananas for this dessert.

Secret of success
Do not be over-generous with butter or margarine and sugar at stage 6.

4 small bananas
1 tablespoon lemon juice
short crust pastry made with 4 oz. flour, etc., *page 184*

for the topping
½ oz. butter *or* margarine, melted
½ level tablespoon castor sugar

¼ level teaspoon cinnamon

1 Peel the bananas, divide each into two and sprinkle with lemon juice; this keeps them a good colour.
2 Make the short crust pastry as directed.
3 Turn out on to a lightly floured board, knead quickly then roll out fairly thinly into an oblong.
4 Divide into 8 strips, each 10 inches by 1 inch.
5 Moisten the strips with cold water and wrap round banana pieces.
6 Brush the tops with melted butter or margarine, and sprinkle with sugar and cinnamon.
7 Transfer to a well greased baking sheet, and bake towards the top of a hot oven (425–450°F., Gas Mark 6–7) for 15–20 minutes, until crisp and brown.
8 Serve hot or cold with whipped cream or vanilla ice cream.

185

To make a plate pie

Preparation: 25 minutes
No delay
Cooking: approximately
40 minutes
Makes a 7-inch plate pie

The way in which pastry is
handled is shown clearly in the
pictures. Do not stretch the
pastry in rolling, lifting, cutting,
etc.

Secrets of success
Do not use more than a few
drops of water with the fruit.
To make sure the bottom layer
of pastry stays firm and crisps
during baking, sprinkle this with
a little cornflour or flour or fine
semolina before adding the fruit.
Make sure the edges of the
pastry are sealed well, see
picture 2, so the juice from the
fruit will not boil out during
cooking.

| 8 oz. short crust pastry, page 184 | 12 oz.–1 lb. fruit | sugar to taste |

1 Make the pastry; roll out half into a neat round.
2 Put this over the pie plate. The easiest way is to lift the pastry with the rolling pin.
3 Cover the pastry with the prepared fruit, add sugar and a few drops of water.

4 Roll out the second half of pastry. Put over the top of the fruit.

5 Press the edges together and cut away surplus pastry. Cut away from you as shown in the picture, for this prevents the pastry stretching.

6 Flake the edges together. To do this press the forefinger of your left hand against the rim of the pastry. Hold a knife in your right hand and cut into the pastry to make several layers.

7 Brush top of the pie with a little water or milk, and make a fine slit in the centre for any steam to escape.

8 Bake in the centre of a hot oven (425°F., Gas Mark 6) for 20 minutes, then lower the heat to moderate (375°F., Gas Mark 4) for a further 20 minutes, until the pastry is cooked. Sprinkle with sugar if wished.

Cinnamon apple pie

Preparation and cooking as
above
Serves 6

If wished to give an attractive
'shine', brush pastry with a little
milk or water, and sprinkle
lightly with castor sugar.

| 10 oz. short crust pastry good 1 lb. apples | 1–2 teaspoons powdered cinnamon | 3–4 oz. brown sugar squeeze of lemon juice |

Method as recipe above, adding the cinnamon with the sugar to make sure it is evenly distributed. Use a shallow oval plate, about 9 inches long and 6 inches wide, instead of the usual round one, and pile the apples high, or use an 8-inch pie plate.

To vary
1 Omit the cinnamon and add sultanas and grated lemon rind to the apples.
2 Blend the sliced apples with 1–2 sliced bananas, or orange segments (omit the lemon rind if using orange segments).

To store pastry

1 The best way to store short crust pastry is in the form of crumbs. Rub fat into flour and put into a screw-topped jar or plastic bag in the refrigerator.
2 To store the richer pastries, wrap in foil or greaseproof paper and keep for several days in the refrigerator, or some weeks in a home freezer.
3 Store cooked pastry in a tin away from cakes or biscuits.
4 Cooked pastry freezes extremely well.

Rich raisin pie

Preparation: 20–25 minutes
Cooking: 30 minutes
Serves 6

For extra richness, add 1
dessertspoon of rum or sherry to
the raisin mixture, stage 3, and
another to the whipped cream,
stage 7.

short crust pastry made
   with 8 oz. flour, etc.,
   page 184
8 oz. seedless raisins

1 small orange
1 tablespoon golden syrup
1 tablespoon demerara sugar
¼ pint thick cream

halved shelled walnuts
2 dessertspoons rum *or*
   sherry, *optional*

1 Roll out about two-thirds of the pastry and line a 7-inch flan ring or tin, as directed on page 190.
2 Wash the raisins in very hot water. Drain and dry.
3 Mix them with the orange juice and grated orange rind and golden syrup, then spread in the prepared pie shell.
4 Cut the remaining pastry into ¼-inch wide ribbons, preferably with a serrated-edged wheel cutter.
5 Criss-cross the raisin mixture in a neat lattice of small squares.
6 Scatter with demerara sugar and bake the pie just above the centre of a hot oven (450°F., Gas Mark 7) for about 30 minutes, or until the crust and lattice ribbons are golden brown.
7 When cold, drop a spoonful of stiffly whipped cream into alternate lattice squares: top with half a walnut.

Rich raisin pie

Custard tart

Preparation: 15 minutes
No delay
Cooking: 30 minutes or 35–45
minutes, depending on method
Serves 6

Many people find difficulty in
keeping the pastry from rising in
a custard tart. This will not
happen if
a) you use plain flour in the
pastry;
b) you bake the pastry 'blind'.
or brush with egg white.

5–6 oz. short crust pastry,
   page 184

2 eggs *or* 1 egg and 1 egg
   yolk

1 tablespoon sugar
½ pint milk
little grated nutmeg

1 Line a 7- or 8-inch flan ring or tin, as directed on page 190.
2 Bake the pastry 'blind' in a hot oven for 10 minutes (425–450°F., Gas Mark 6–7). This sets the bottom.
3 Beat the eggs and sugar, pour over the hot, *not* boiling, milk.
4 Pour into the pastry case, then bake for a further 20 minutes in the centre of a moderate oven (350–375°F., Gas Mark 4–5).
5 When set, top with grated nutmeg.

Many people bake pastry and custard together, in which case:
1 Line a flan tin or ring with pastry.
2 Brush liberally with egg white to prevent it rising.
3 Pour in the egg custard mixture, *using cold milk*.
4 Bake for 35–45 minutes in a moderate oven (350–375°F., Gas Mark 4–5).
5 Top with grated nutmeg.

Individual custard tarts

Cooking: 15–20 minutes

1 Line deep patty tins with short crust pastry, brush with egg white.
2 Pour in the cold custard mixture (see above).
3 Top with grated nutmeg before baking.
4 Cook for 15–20 minutes just above the centre of a moderately hot oven (400°F., Gas Mark 5).

187

To make a fruit pie

Preparation: 20–25 minutes
No delay
Cooking: approximately 30–35 minutes
Serves 6

Always use a pie dish that is sufficiently small so the fruit can be piled fairly high. If you have not enough fruit, then put in a pie support or an egg cup. Never use a plastic egg cup as it will melt in cooking. If using very juicy soft fruits, such as raspberries, blackcurrants, etc., you can omit the water. If using fruit that cooks very quickly, keep the pastry particularly thin.

1–1½ lb. fruit
very little water

sugar to taste

5–6 oz. short crust pastry,
page 184

1 Put the prepared fruit into a pie dish with a small amount of water and sugar to taste.
2 Roll out the pastry to the shape of the pie dish, but make it 1–1½ inches bigger all round than this.
3 Cut off a long narrow strip.

4 Moisten the edge of the pie dish with a pastry brush and press the strip of pastry to the rim.

5 Lift up the remaining pastry with the help of your rolling pin and lay it over the top of the pie. Press the edges together.

6 Flake and flute the top of the pie. Brush with a little water. Shake on a very small quantity of sugar.

7 Bake in the centre of a hot oven (425–450°F., Gas Mark 6–7) until the top of the pie is golden brown. Turn the heat to moderate for a further 15 minutes, to make sure the fruit is cooked.

8 It is advisable to stand the pie dish on a baking tray, just in case any fruit juice boils out in cooking.

Fillings for fruit pies
Use any fruit that is in season: the following are particularly interesting ways to vary fruit pies. Also there are many canned fruit pie fillings which can be used in place of fresh fruit.

Apple and raisin pie: add 4 oz. seedless raisins to each 1 lb. apples. If the raisins are fairly dry, heat for a few minutes in water, then use this liquid in the pie. Add normal amount of sugar.

Apple and prune pie: allow 4 oz. dried prunes to each 1 lb. apples. Soak overnight in water or water and orange juice to cover. Put with apples in the pie dish, or if rather hard simmer gently for a time, then add to apples and sugar.

Cherry and almond pie: add about 2–3 oz. blanched almonds to each 1 lb. cherries

Sweet short crust pastry

A little sugar can be added to short crust pastry, and this blends very well with fruit tarts, etc. Use no more sugar than recommended in the recipe, or about 1 oz. sugar to 8 oz. flour; see also special flan pastry, page 190.

Strawberry and banana tart

Preparation: 20–25 minutes
Wait for pastry to cool
Cooking: 20–25 minutes
Serves 4–6

Secret of success
It is important to allow the glaze to cool, stage 12, before adding to the tart, otherwise this softens the pastry.

* do not slice the bananas until ready to glaze, otherwise they discolour. If you do wish to slice early, sprinkle with a little lemon juice.

for the sweet short crust pastry
8 oz. plain *or* self-raising flour
pinch of salt
½ oz. castor sugar

4 oz. cooking fat
2–3 tablespoons water

for the filling
12 oz. strawberries
2 bananas

¼ pint water
1 rounded tablespoon castor sugar
1 rounded teaspoon arrowroot

1 Make the pastry as short crust pastry (page 184) but sieve the sugar with the flour and salt.
2 Roll out on a lightly floured board into a round large enough to line a 9-inch ovenproof pie plate.
3 Trim off surplus pastry with a sharp knife.
4 Finish pie edge by cutting pastry ¾ inch from the outside edge towards the centre, and at ¾-inch intervals around the plate.
5 Damp the edge with water and fold one corner of the cut pastry over diagonally, press down firmly with the fingers and continue the process around the plate.
6 Prick all over the bottom with a fork.
7 Bake on the second shelf from the top of a hot oven (425°F., Gas Mark 6) for 20–25 minutes.
8 Cool, remove from the pie plate on to a serving dish.
9 Prepare and halve the strawberries, slice the bananas.* Fill the tart with these.
10 Mix the water, sugar and arrowroot together.
11 Bring to the boil in a small saucepan, stirring all the time, and boil gently for 3 minutes.
12 Cool, and then pour over the fruit. Serve cold.

Mincemeat tart

Preparation: 12 minutes
No delay
Cooking: 25–30 minutes
Serves 4–6

Soft margarine enables pastry to be made very quickly and easily. You can also make a similar tart using chopped well drained canned pineapple, instead of the apple purée.

for the one-stage rich or biscuit pastry
4 oz. soft margarine
1 level tablespoon castor sugar

6 oz. plain flour
1 tablespoon cold water

for the filling
8 oz. mincemeat

2 tablespoons sieved apple purée
1 tablespoon brandy *or* rum, *optional*

1 Put the margarine, sugar, 2 tablespoons flour and water in a bowl.
2 Cream with a fork for about ½ minute, until well mixed.
3 Stir in the remaining flour to form a firm dough.
4 Knead lightly on a floured board.
5 Roll out to line a 9-inch ovenproof plate or tin.
6 Trim the edges, flake and flute (page 190).
7 Roll out the remaining pieces, cut 6 thin strips for the top.
8 Mix together the mincemeat, apple and brandy or rum (if used); put on to the pastry case.
9 Place the pastry strips on top in a criss-cross pattern.
10 Damp the edges and press to the sides of the pastry.
11 Bake on the second shelf from the top of a moderately hot oven (400°F., Gas Mark 5–6) for 25–30 minutes. Serve hot or cold.

Left *Mincemeat tart*
Right *Strawberry and banana tart*

Flan pastry or biscuit crust

| 5 oz. butter *or* soft margarine | 8 oz. flour | cold water and 1 egg yolk |
| 2 dessertspoons sugar | pinch of salt | *to bind* |

Preparation: 10–12 minutes
No delay

This rich pastry needs firm handling when rolling out, as it is inclined to break. Knead rather more than short crust.

1 Cream the fat and sugar together until light in colour.
2 Sieve the flour and salt together and add to the creamed fat, mixing with a knife.
3 Gradually add enough water, or egg yolk and water, to make a firm rolling consistency.
4 Use the fingertips to feel the pastry (page 183).

To make a flan

Preparation: 15–20 minutes
Allow to cool before baking
Cooking: 25 minutes

If the flan ring is placed on an upturned baking tray or sheet it is easy to slide the flan off the tin.

Flan base pricked with a fork (stage 5)

Roll out the flan pastry. There are two ways of making a flan.
1 Roll the pastry to a size a good 1½ inches larger all round than the flan ring. Lift the pastry with the help of the rolling pin and drop carefully into the tin, on a baking sheet.

 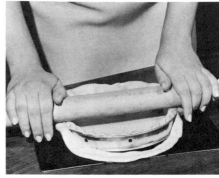

2 Mould and flute the edges with your fingers, as shown.

3 Trim the pastry by passing the rolling pin across the top, as shown.

4 Put foil or greaseproof paper into the flan case, then put crusts of bread or haricot beans inside.
5 The other way to bake 'blind', i.e. empty, is to prick all over the base of the flan, to prevent the pastry from rising.
6 Bake for approximately 25 minutes in the centre of a moderately hot oven (400°F., Gas Mark 5–6).
7 If you have put beans or bread in the flan case, lift these out, and remove the tin, for the last 10 minutes of baking.

The second way to make a flan, is to use a baking tin.
1 You then lay the tin over the pastry, allowing 1½ inches all round. Turn the tin the right way up and lift the round of pastry into this, moulding it to fit.
2 Either cut away the surplus pastry, or roll very firmly with the rolling pin until you get a clear cut edge.
3 Bake as above, removing beans, etc., if used, after 15 minutes.

To fill a flan with fruit

1 The flan must be cold. If using *canned* fruit, drain away the syrup. The easiest way to do this is to put the fruit in a sieve or strainer placed over a basin.
2 Arrange the fruit in the bottom of the flan case.
3 Measure the syrup, and allow 1 teaspoon arrowroot or cornflour to each $\frac{1}{4}$ pint syrup.
4 Blend smoothly and boil until thick and clear.
5 If using stewed fruit, cook very carefully as directed under compote of fruit (page 169), and proceed as for canned fruit.

Ice cream flan

Preparation: few minutes
No delay
No cooking
Serves 4–6

1 Spread the bottom of a cooked flan case with a little jam or lemon curd.
2 Put spoonfuls of ice cream over this.
3 Pile the ice cream high and serve within a few minutes.

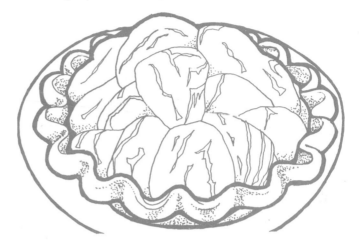

Fruit tartlets

These are some of the more delicious ways of combining fruit and pastry.
Choose short crust, sweet short crust or flan pastry (pages 184, 189, 190).

1 Roll out the dough and line small patty tins.
2 Prick the base of the little cases, so the pastry will not rise, or put a small piece of foil or greaseproof paper and a crust of bread into each tartlet case, then bake 'blind'.
3 Choose a hot oven for short or sweet short crust pastry, i.e. 425–450°F., Gas Mark 6–7, and allow about 12–15 minutes towards the top of the oven, but only a moderately hot oven for flan (often called biscuit crust) pastry.
4 When the tartlets are cooked, lift out of the patty tins and let the pastry cool on a wire tray.
5 Fill with a little whipped cream or jam or redcurrant jelly or sweetened crushed fruit, then top with whole fruit.
6 The fruit may be glazed as suggested above (filling a fruit flan) or left plain and topped with whipped cream, see colour picture page 182.

Lemon meringue pie

Preparation: 30–35 minutes
No delay
Cooking: approximately 55 minutes
Serves 4–6

If baking the meringue to serve cold, you can add an extra 2 oz. sugar to the egg whites.

Colour picture, page 199

6 oz. short crust pastry, *page 184*	water	4 oz. sugar
	1 level tablespoon cornflour	2 eggs
for the filling	1 oz. butter, margarine *or*	
juice and rind of 2 lemons	cooking fat	

1 Line a flan ring and bake as directed on page 190.
2 Add enough water to the lemon juice to give 6 tablespoons liquid.
3 Blend the cornflour with this.
4 Put into a pan with the fat, 2 oz. sugar and the lemon rind.
5 Cook steadily, stirring well until thick and smooth.
6 Take off the heat and then when the lemon mixture is no longer boiling, beat in the 2 egg yolks.
7 Put in the pastry case, and set in the centre of a moderate oven for 15 minutes.
8 Whisk the egg whites until very stiff, then fold in most of the remaining sugar.
9 Pile on top of the lemon mixture, sprinkle with rest of the sugar.
10 Either set quickly for 15 minutes in the centre of a moderate oven (375°F., Gas Mark 4) – ideal when serving the sweet hot – or to give a really crisp meringue, for about 1 hour in a very low oven (275°F., Gas Mark 1). In this way the meringue will stay crisp when served cold, see colour picture page 199.

To make sausage rolls

Preparation: 25 minutes
No delay
Cooking: 20–25 minutes

Makes 8 large or
     16 medium or
     32 cocktail size
Naturally the smaller sized rolls need a shorter cooking period.

It is easier to form the sausage mixture into one long roll as suggested under stage 2. Choose the centre of the oven, see stage 8, to ensure that the sausage meat is adequately cooked.

12 oz. short or flaky pastry,
   pages 184, 193

for the filling
1 lb. sausage meat or
  skinless sausages

to glaze
egg or milk

1 Roll out the pastry thinly on floured board. Cut into oblongs about 4 inches wide and 10–12 inches long.

2 Lay sausages or rolls of sausage meat down centre of oblong.
3 Dampen the edges of the pastry.

4 Fold the edges together, pressing them securely together.

7 Brush over with beaten egg or milk.

5 Cut the strip into 4 equal lengths.
6 Snip holes in tops of rolls with scissors, or prick with a fork.

8 Bake in a hot oven (425–450°F., Gas Mark 6–7) for 20–25 minutes, until a golden brown, turning the heat down after 12–15 minutes if necessary.

Sardine rolls

These can be made in exactly the same way as sausage rolls, but use mashed sardines instead of sausage meat.

Flaky pastry

Preparation: about 40 minutes
Delay for setting pastry
Cooking: as recipe

The pictures show the right way to put the fat on to the dough and to fold the pastry, etc. Do not pull or stretch this.

Secrets of success
Plain flour gives a better result in this pastry, although you can use self-raising flour if no plain is available.
Do not use very hard fat; take this out of the refrigerator for some time before using so it is easy to handle.
Keep everything cool as you work. Do NOT have the dough too dry at stage 4
Do not be impatient if the pastry seems rather sticky and difficult to handle; simply allow it to cool, and you will then find it quite easy.

| 5–6 oz. fat | ½ level teaspoon salt | 2 teaspoons lemon juice, |
| 8 oz. plain flour | 7–8 tablespoons cold water | *optional* |

1 Divide fat into 4 even portions.
2 Sieve flour and salt into the mixing bowl.
3 Rub one portion of fat into flour and salt.
4 Add water and lemon juice, mixing with a knife to a smooth, non-sticky dough. If it is too stiff, or some flour is unabsorbed, add an extra teaspoon of water and mix until smooth.
5 Sprinkle lightly with flour and leave to rest in a cool place for 30 minutes, covering with a damp cloth.

6 Turn on to a floured board and roll out to an oblong 12 by 6 inches.
7 Dab small pieces of second portion of fat evenly over top two-thirds of dough, leaving a margin of ½ inch all round.

8 Fold the bottom third of the pastry upwards and the top third down to cover it.
9 Brush off all the surplus flour.

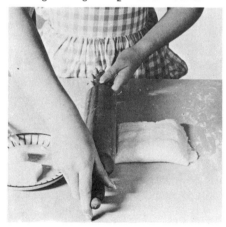

10 Seal the 3 open edges with a rolling pin.

11 Give the pastry a half turn (always to the left), and start rolling out by pressing pastry gently twice with the rolling pin to trap in as much air as possible.

12 To complete making the pastry, roll out to a rectangle 12 by 6 inches.
13 Add third portion of fat, dabbing it on as before.
14 Fold in three, seal, give a half turn and roll again.
15 Repeat once more with the last portion of fat.
16 Roll out, fold and seal for the fourth time without fat.
17 Cover and leave for 30 minutes in a cool place before use.

Using fat for flaky pastry

The pictures show the method of making flaky pastry with modern cooking fat. It is advisable to use 5 oz. only to 8 oz. flour. You can use any of the following fats:
1 All butter; use 6 oz. to 8 oz. flour.
2 All margarine. A rather hard type is best; use 6 oz. to 8 oz. flour.
3 Two-thirds margarine or butter and one-third cooking fat, whipped-up cooking fat or lard; use a total of 5½ oz. to 8 oz. flour.

To decorate pies

It is traditional that a fruit pie has no decoration whatsoever on top, but with a savoury pie you can have quite an elaborate decoration.

To make leaves, cut diamond shaped pieces from pastry as shown. Mark 'veins' on the leaves with a knife.

An easy decoration for a meat pie is to make a tassel. Cut strips of pastry and then cut into the pastry as shown in the picture to within about $\frac{1}{3}$ inch. Roll loosely so pastry has room to rise. Moisten with a little water or egg, and press on top of pie.

To trim pastry

Instead of a knife you can use a pastry wheel. This not only cuts away the pastry without fear of stretching it, but also marks it into an attractive design.

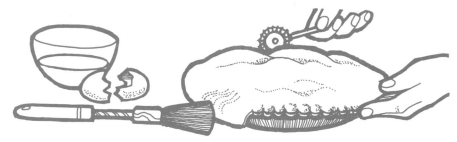

To glaze pastry

Mention is made in various recipes of brushing the pastry with water, egg, etc. This is done with a small pastry brush and it gives an attractive shine to the pastry. Always wash and dry the brush after use.

Fillings for vol-au-vent cases

1 Vol-au-vent cases can be filled with chopped chicken or meat in a thick white sauce. Use the panada consistency given on page 143.
2 Flaked fresh or canned salmon mixed with mayonnaise (page 207) is another good filling.
3 Creamed mushrooms (page 138) are extremely good.
4 The chicken vol-au-vent illustrated below (recipe on the opposite page) are easily made for a special occasion.

Chicken vol-au-vent

Puff pastry

Preparation: 30–40 minutes
Allow time to put pastry in cool place between rollings

Secrets of success
Read the comments given under flaky pastry, for the same points are important when making the richer puff pastry.
Do not make the pastry too thick for it rises very drastically, see stage 11, and the picture.

*you have a good choice of fats here. Use: butter, *or* table or luxury (soft) margarine, *or* ⅔ table margarine and ⅓ modern whipped-up light fat or lard.

8 oz. plain flour
good pinch of salt

cold water *to mix*
few drops of lemon juice

7–8 oz. fat*

1 Sieve flour and salt together.
2 Mix to a rolling consistency with cold water and lemon juice. Roll to an oblong shape.
3 Make the fat into a neat block and place in the centre of the pastry. Fold over it first the bottom section of pastry, and then the top section, so that the fat is covered.
4 Turn the dough at right angles, seal edges and 'rib' carefully (page 193) and roll out.
5 Fold the dough into an envelope, turn it, seal the edges, 'rib' and roll again.
6 Repeat 5 times, so making 7 rollings and 7 foldings.
7 Rest the pastry in a cold place once or twice between rollings, to prevent it becoming sticky and soft.
8 Always put it to rest before rolling it for the last time, and before baking.
9 Bake in a very hot oven.
10 Bake for the first 10–15 minutes at 475–500°F., Gas Mark 8–9, then lower to Gas Mark 5–6, or turn electric oven right out, or re-set to 400°F. to finish cooking at lower temperature.
11 Well made puff pastry should rise to 4 or 5 times its original thickness.
12 When making vol-au-vent cases it may be necessary, after baking, to remove a little soft dough and return the cases to the oven to dry out.

How to make vol-au-vent or bouchée cases

Preparation: 15 minutes
No delay
Cooking: 10–25 minutes according to size of case

Puff pastry (recipe above) made with 8 oz. flour, etc., will produce:
1 really large vol-au-vent case enough for 6–8 portions when filled
or
6–8 large individual cases
or
12 medium cases
or
24 tiny cocktail bouchées

1 Roll out the pastry to ½–¾ inch thick.
2 Cut into rounds, with a fluted or plain pastry cutter.
3 With a smaller plain cutter – about half the diameter of the pastry cases – mark firmly into the pastry; this should press about halfway through the dough. Lift out gently so you have marked a smaller ring in the pastry.
4 Bake on ungreased trays in a hot or very hot oven (see recipe above for temperature, etc.) for 15–25 minutes, depending on size, until quite brown. Tiny cases for cocktail parties need about 10 minutes.
5 Lift the cases off the tins, and with the help of a palette knife carefully take out the centre ring of pastry – you will find this has shrunk during cooking and it is not difficult to remove.
6 Put the outer cases back in the oven for a few minutes to dry out. Reduce the heat to moderate for this.
7 See page 194 for fillings.

Chicken vol-au-vent

Preparation: 10 minutes
Cooking: few minutes, plus time for cooking pastry cases if home-made

When filling vol-au-vent cases:
if wishing to serve HOT, put HOT filling into HOT pastry at the last minute;
if wishing to serve COLD, allow both pastry and filling to cool before putting together.

1 small onion
2 oz. mushrooms
½ green pepper
1½ tablespoons oil *or* 1½ oz. butter

1 level tablespoon cornflour
¼ pint milk *or* chicken stock
salt and pepper

squeeze of lemon juice
2 tablespoons cream
8 oz. cooked chicken, diced
12 vol-au-vent cases, *see above*

1 Peel and chop the onion and mushrooms.
2 Remove the seeds from the green pepper and cut the flesh into narrow strips.
3 Heat the oil or butter, then fry the vegetables gently.
4 Put the cornflour into a basin, blend with the milk or stock.
5 Add seasoning and lemon juice.
6 Bring to the boil and cook until thickened – stirring all the time.
7 Stir in the cream and chicken, and heat for a few minutes.
8 Put into the vol-au-vent cases.

French apricot flan

Preparation: approximately 40 minutes, with delay for pastry and filling to cool
Cooking: 20 minutes pastry; 10 minutes fillings
Serves 6–8

This pastry is particularly crisp and pleasant. It can be used in place of flan, short, or sweet short crust pastry, in other recipes.
The filling is one form of confectioner's custard and useful for filling tarts, cakes, etc.

Secret of success
Make sure the pastry and the topping are cool before putting together.
To form a richer topping, make as stages 11–14, then fold in about ¼ pint whipped cream.

for the rich sweet pastry
8 oz. plain flour
1½ oz. icing sugar
4 oz. butter
2 egg yolks*
1 tablespoon milk
little egg white *to glaze*

for the cream filling
1 egg
1 oz. castor sugar
½ oz. flour, preferably plain
few drops of almond *or* vanilla essence
¼ pint milk

for the topping
large can apricot halves
2 level dessertspoons apricot jam
1 scant dessertspoon water

* 1 whole egg could be used instead.

1 Sift the flour and icing sugar into a bowl.
2 Rub in the butter until the mixture resembles fine breadcrumbs.
3 Mix to a pliable paste with egg yolks and milk.
4 Knead lightly until smooth, and then leave, covered, in a cool place for at least 30 minutes.
5 Turn on to a board dusted with flour, and roll out into an oblong, about 13 by 7½ inches.
6 Cut two ¾-inch wide strips from the long sides, and brush with egg white.
7 Put back on top of the oblong, along both cut edges, to form a raised border.
8 Press gently to seal and carefully knock up the edges with the back of a knife (page 190).
9 Prick the base well with a fork, brush the borders with egg white, then bake towards the top of a moderately hot to hot oven (400–425°F., Gas Mark 5–6), for 20 minutes.
10 Cool on a baking tray, then lift on to a wire tray.
11 *For the filling:* put the egg and sugar into a basin over a basin or saucepan of hot water, and whisk until thick and white.
12 Fold in the flour, add the essence, then stir in the milk by degrees.
13 Turn into a saucepan and heat slowly, stirring, until the mixture just comes to the boil.
14 Remove from the heat AT ONCE and cool.
15 When quite cold, spread thickly over the pastry base.
16 Arrange rows of apricot halves over the cream filling, then brush them with cool glaze.
17 *To make the glaze:* heat the jam with the water.
18 Strain, then reheat until the liquid just starts to boil.
19 Allow to cool and thicken *slightly* before using, for a hot glaze would spoil the pastry.
20 Finally, cut across and serve in slices.

French apricot flan

Using frozen pastry and pastry mixes

Ready-prepared frozen pastry is very good if used exactly as directed. Remember that once defrosted it keeps no longer than ordinary pastry.
There are also pastry mixes on the market and these can be used in place of the recipes given in this section.

Using ready-cooked pastry
If buying pastry from a shop, either with a filling or ready for filling, you may find it has become a little soft due to exposure to the air. You will improve it a great deal if you heat it for a few minutes in the oven.

Mince pies

Preparation: 15–20 minutes
No delay
Cooking: 20–25 minutes
Makes 12

Secret of success
Do not be too generous with the mincemeat or this will boil out in cooking and make the tarts sticky.

8 oz. short crust *or* flaky pastry, *pages 184, 193*   approximately 6–8 oz. mincemeat

1 Roll out the pastry.
2 Cut into 12 rounds for the base of the pies, using a cutter a little bit larger than the size of the patty tins. Press rounds of pastry into the tins.
3 Put on a spoonful of mincemeat.
4 Cut out 12 rounds for the lids. These need to be a little smaller than the previous ones.
5 Press the edges together; make a slit on top with kitchen scissors or a sharp knife.
6 Bake for 20–25 minutes just above the centre of a hot oven (425–450°F., Gas Mark 6–7); if necessary reduce the heat after 15 minutes.

Making mince pies – use a small palette knife or ordinary table knife to remove from tins

Jam tarts

Preparation: 5 minutes
No delay
Cooking: 15 minutes
Makes 12

If you bake the tarts empty they are very crisp, but the jam does tend to have a 'not belonging' taste. The best way is to bake the tarts with a very little jam in, so there is no danger of it boiling over. The moment that the tarts come from the oven put in some extra jam.

4 oz. short crust pastry, *page 184*   3–4 tablespoons jam

1 Roll out the pastry and line patty tins; add some jam.
2 Bake for 15 minutes just above the centre of a hot oven (425–450°F., Gas Mark 6–7). Add more jam.

Crisp topped jam tarts: make the tarts as above, but bake for 10 minutes only; remove from the oven, add a little more jam and a topping of fine breadcrumbs, crushed cornflakes or chopped nuts. Return to the oven for a further 5–6 minutes.
Fruit purée tarts: fill the tartlet cases with very thick sweetened fruit purée instead of jam. Top with whipped cream when cooked and cool.

Treacle tarts

Use exactly the same recipe as for jam tarts, but add golden syrup and a squeeze of lemon juice. Put this into the tarts and top with just a few breadcrumbs or crushed cornflakes.
A large treacle tart is often difficult to bake, for the pastry tends to rise slightly in baking. I suggest you follow the suggestions for a custard tart (page 187), i.e. partially bake the pastry 'blind', remove from the oven, then add the treacle and topping.

To prevent pastry from sticking

Because pastry has a relatively high percentage of fat, it is less inclined to 'stick' to tins, etc., than cakes, so if the tins are well looked after (page 237) no difficulty should be experienced.
If using the flan pastry or biscuit crust, which is rather rich and inclined to crumble easily, a little fat brushed over the tins before baking is a good idea.

To remove tarts from tins and plates

1 Even if serving the tarts hot, always wait for about 3 minutes before removing from tins, for this gives the pastry a chance to 'set' and become more firm.
2 Do not use a pointed knife; this may break the pastry and certainly could damage the tins. Use a small palette knife or an ordinary table knife.

197

American pies and tarts for special occasions

Lemon chiffon pie

Preparation: 25–30 minutes
No delay
Cooking: 25 minutes for flan
Serves 6–8

Open can of evaporated milk and chill in freezing tray for about 30 minutes, then turn into a bowl and whip lightly. If not possible, follow directions for whipping evaporated milk, page 174.

8 oz. short crust pastry, *page 184*
large can evaporated milk

water
grated rind, juice of 1 lemon
1 lemon-flavoured jelly

2 oz. sugar
little desiccated coconut

1 Roll out the pastry, line a 9-inch flan ring or fairly deep tin, and bake 'blind', as directed on page 190.
2 Whip the evaporated milk.
3 Add enough water to the lemon juice to make 6 tablespoons. Heat this and pour over the jelly, stirring until dissolved. Add the sugar.
4 Allow the jelly to cool until just beginning to set, then stir in lemon rind.
5 Fold the whipped milk into the half-set jelly.
6 Put into the baked COLD flan case; leave until firm.
7 Spread 1 or 2 tablespoons desiccated coconut on to a baking tin and brown a few minutes in the oven. Allow to cool, then sprinkle over the top of the filling.

Peach and lemon chiffon pie

Preparation: 30 minutes
No delay
Cooking: 30 minutes (add 15 minutes if making chocolate biscuits)
Serves 5–6

Secret of success
Make certain the jelly mixture is lightly set, stage 6, before adding the egg whites and sugar. This gives an even texture. If the jelly is too liquid the egg whites rise to the top.

Colour pictures on cover

approximately 24 chocolate biscuits, *page 273*
3–4 eggs
3–4 oz. castor sugar
3 tablespoons lemon juice

1 teaspoon grated lemon rind
4 tablespoons water with 4 eggs *or* 3 tablespoons water with 3 eggs
½ oz. powdered gelatine

to decorate
sliced canned *or* fresh peaches
sprig of mint

1 Line a 9-inch pie plate with the chocolate biscuits, breaking and fitting them, so they cover the entire bottom of the plate. Place them round the sides too.
2 Separate the egg yolks from the whites.
3 Put the yolks into a basin with 2 oz. sugar, lemon juice and rind, and whisk over a pan of boiling water until thick and creamy.
4 Heat the water and dissolve the gelatine in this; if necessary stand this in a basin over a pan of boiling water to dissolve perfectly.
5 Add the dissolved gelatine to the egg yolk mixture and stir well until blended.
6 Allow to cool and set lightly.
7 Whisk egg whites, fold in rest of the sugar; add to lemon and egg mixture.
8 Spoon into the biscuit-lined dish and when quite firm, decorate with the peach slices and mint.
If preferred, make a flan ring, as recipe for Lemon chiffon pie above, and continue from stage 2.

Orange meringue pie

This pie, like the better known Lemon meringue pie, is an American favourite.
Follow the directions for the pastry as page 191. When making filling, use the juice and rind of 2 medium oranges (probably you will need no extra water). If you like a rather sharp flavour, add the grated rind and juice of ½ lemon. This does not detract from the orange taste, but enhances this.
Deep-dish lemon or orange meringue pies: the recipe on page 191 gives only a shallow layer of lemon mixture, but one with a very definite flavour. If you wish a deeper pie, then use a really deep tin (increase the amount of pastry slightly or roll the 6 oz. out thinly). Use the grated rind and juice of 2 lemons plus ¼ pint water (or use the grated rind of 2 lemons and the juice of 3 lemons plus ¼ pint water). Blend with 1 oz. cornflour and thicken, then continue as the recipe on page 191. Taste and add a little extra sugar if desired.

Using bottled cream

It is wise to have one or two bottles of cream available, for they help to 'dress-up' a sweet. If the cream is unopened it keeps for a long time in a cool place. Directions for whipping are given on the bottle. Generally, you are advised to pour off the 'whey' or liquid.

Using canned cream

Canned cream is perhaps easier to store than bottled cream, since there is no possibility of the cans breaking. The cream thickens easily, and can be substituted for fresh cream in most recipes; pour off 'whey' as suggested above.

Lemon meringue pie, see page 191

Stuffed egg salad

Salads and savoury dishes

To make good salads

A good salad depends very largely on the ingredients being really fresh, so take care to store them carefully so that the lettuce, etc., is crisp and attractive looking. Colour makes a great deal of difference to a salad – include as varied a selection of ingredients as possible to give this. Arrange them carefully, so it does not look a 'muddle', but has a definite pattern.

If you are fond of salads be imaginative about them – include fruit sometimes, particularly with meat or cheese.

To prepare green salads

Lettuce
1 Be very careful how you handle lettuce, particularly the forced and imported ones obtainable in winter.
2 Wash and dry very gently and very carefully. Do not squeeze very hard.
3 Remove the outer leaves with your fingers, or with a stainless steel knife.
4 Separate the leaves and wash in cold water to which a little salt has been added.
5 Lift out of the salt water and put either into a salad shaker and shake quite dry, or into a teacloth and pat dry. Kitchen paper can be used instead of the teacloth.
Other green vegetables, endive, etc., are prepared in the same way.

Watercress
1 Cut off the bottom stalks.
2 Divide into sprigs.
3 Wash as lettuce.

Mustard and cress
1 Take off the mustard and cress from the stalks, if you buy one of the containers in which it is growing.
2 If not, then you will buy it in a small bunch.
3 Lift out of this, and wash in a tiny sieve or colander under running cold water.
4 Remove any of the tiny seeds. Dry in a teacloth or kitchen paper.

Egg salads

Preparation: few minutes
Allow time for eggs to cool
Cooking: 10 minutes

Secret of success
Do not over-cook the eggs. When they are cooked, crack the shells at once, then plunge into cold water. This prevents a line forming round the yolks.

See colour picture opposite

eggs   lettuce   mayonnaise
garnish, *see method*

1 Cook the eggs in boiling water for 10 minutes, cool (see left) then shell.
2 Serve whole, halved or sliced on lettuce, top with mayonnaise and garnish with paprika, chopped parsley or tomatoes, cucumber and radishes.

To slice eggs: hard-boiled eggs crumble easily, so use a very sharp knife or a proper egg slicer (keep this carefully so the wires do not break).

Stuffed egg salad: hard boil 4 eggs, cool, halve lengthways, then remove the yolks into a basin. Mash with seasoning and 2 tablespoons mayonnaise and a pinch of curry powder. Serve on a bed of endive (sometimes known as chicory), then garnish with small pieces of red pepper (capsicum), sliced cucumber and chopped parsley.

Note. Mashed sardines, grated cheese, chopped vegetables may be used instead of curry powder.

201

Making a quick salad

A salad can be prepared in a very short time if you make use of the ready-prepared or convenience foods available.

For green salads it is time-saving to wash and prepare lettuce, watercress, etc., when purchased, so they are all ready for use. Store them in the salad container or plastic bags in the refrigerator or in a cool place. Mustard and cress can often be purchased in containers — still growing — so cut and use as desired.

An unwashed lettuce keeps well in a biscuit tin or covered saucepan.

To prepare lettuce, etc., in a hurry, wash in cold water, lay it flat on teacloths and pat gently until dry, or shake well in a salad container.

For Russian salads use the frozen prepared vegetables and cook as directed, drain well, then toss while still hot in mayonnaise (page 207).

Canned Russian salad is a good standby — top with a little paprika pepper and/or chopped parsley.

Potato salad can be bought ready for use in a can. It is improved by adding a little extra seasoning.

Canned beans — peas — asparagus all add interest to salads; also use sliced apples, oranges, etc., which are very easily prepared and combine well with all salad ingredients.

To make a mixed salad

Preparation: few minutes
No delay
No cooking

Secret of success
Do not add the dressing to the salad, as suggested in stage 3, *unless* this is being eaten fairly soon. The dressing will make the salad 'limp' if it stands too long.

lettuce and/or endive	French dressing	radishes
watercress	tomatoes	hard-boiled eggs
mustard and cress	cucumber	

1 Prepare the green salad ingredients, shredding the lettuce finely.
2 Put either on a plate, dish or into a salad bowl.
3 You may like to toss this in French dressing (page 208) before going any further.
4 Top with tomatoes, cucumber, radishes and sliced hard-boiled eggs; see page 201 regarding hard-boiled eggs, since it is very important that you do not get a dark rim round the edge of the yolk.
5 The hard-boiled eggs should be sliced at the last minute, or cut into quarters so they do not dry. Use an egg slicer; failing this use a sharp knife.

Ham with mixed salad

Ham with mixed salad

The photograph shows how attractive it is to serve the meat on the same large dish with the salad. Instead of cutting slices, try cutting the ham (or other cold meat) into neat narrow strips. This is very practical when you are coming to the end of the joint and have a rather untidy piece left.

To prepare tomatoes

Preparation: few minutes
No delay
No cooking

To skin tomatoes
Dip tomato into boiling water for approximately 30 seconds. Lift out carefully, put into cold water and then pull away the skin; *or* put a fine skewer through top of the tomato to support it, then hold over a low gas flame until the skin goes 'pop'. Pull off with your fingers. *or* if the tomatoes are very fresh and quite ripe you can remove the skin without heat. Rub the back of a knife quite hard over the tomato; the skin then comes away without any difficulty.

1 If you like the skin of tomatoes, just wipe and dry them and remove the stalks.
2 Cut into thin slices or make into a water lily: with a sharp knife cut a zig-zag line round the tomato, taking each cut to the centre, then pull the halves apart.
3 If you do not like the skin, remove it as instructions on the left.

New ways to serve tomatoes
Tomato and pepper salad: slice the prepared tomatoes thinly, and cut red and green peppers into thin rings (discard core and seeds). Arrange the peppers and tomatoes on flat dishes, top with French dressing (page 208), chopped parsley and chopped chives.

Tomato garlic salad: crush or chop 2–3 cloves of garlic finely. Slice 4 or 5 tomatoes thinly and toss in French dressing with chopped parsley and cloves of garlic. Chill well and serve on a bed of endive or lettuce.

Corn stuffed tomatoes: cut a slice from small skinned tomatoes, remove the centre pulp, chop and mix with mayonnaise and cooked or canned corn. Pile back, top with chopped chives.

To de-seed tomatoes

Preparation: few minutes
No delay
No cooking

1 Skin the tomatoes (see above).
2 Cut the tops off the tomatoes and squeeze firmly with your fingers. The seeds then drop out.
3 You can scoop round the centre of the tomato with a teaspoon to make sure none have been left. Well season the tomato cases before filling.
4 You can use the pulp of tomato for adding to mayonnaise, etc., but one very rarely needs to be quite so drastic in removing all the pips (seeds) in this way.

Stuffed tomato salad

Preparation: 12–15 minutes
No delay
No cooking
Serves 4–6

Added flavour can be given with a small amount of chopped mint – and if preferred French dressing (page 208) can be used instead of mayonnaise: or use diced or grated cheese, chopped hard-boiled eggs or flaked fish, instead of lamb.

8 medium tomatoes	few cooked carrots	lettuce
salt and pepper	few cooked peas	endive
mayonnaise, *page 207*	about 6 oz. cooked corn *or*	1 small red pepper
6–8 oz. cooked lamb	canned corn	

1 Cut the tops off the tomatoes.
2 Scoop out the centre pulp, put this into a basin and chop into small pieces.
3 Shake a little salt and pepper into each tomato case.
4 Mix about 2 tablespoons mayonnaise with the tomato pulp and add the lamb, cut into small cubes.
5 Dice carrots and add to the lamb mixture, with peas and some of the corn.
6 Arrange a bed of crisp lettuce and a little endive on a flat dish.
7 Pile the lamb mixture into the tomato cases and put on to the lettuce.
8 Cut the red pepper into half, remove *all the seeds and core,* for these are very hot.
9 Cut the pulp of the pepper into narrow shreds and top each tomato with this.

To prepare cucumber for salads

Preparation: few minutes
No delay
No cooking

Below is the way to give a serrated effect to cucumber.

1 If you like the skin of cucumber, just wipe it but do not remove.
2 Cut into thin slices with a very sharp knife and put either into a little vinegar with salt and pepper on top, or into French dressing (page 208).
3 If adding to a mixed salad, lift out of the dressing just before the salad is prepared.
4 If you do not like the skin, remove this with a very sharp knife so you do not waste the flesh.
5 Cut into thin slices and put into dressing as above.
6 For a serrated effect – see sketch – draw the prongs of a fork sharply down the skin; this tears away alternate strips. Cut into slices in the usual way.

Cucumber boats: cut a peeled or unpeeled cucumber into lengths of about 1½–2 inches. Halve lengthways, then remove the centre part and chop finely. Mix this with flaked fish, or chopped ham, or chopped hard-boiled eggs and mayonnaise to bind. Pile back into the cucumber cases and top with paprika or chopped parsley and chives.

To prepare radishes

Preparation: few minutes
No delay
No cooking

To make a radish rose cut as indicated in the sketch opposite, put into ice cold water for 1 hour or longer and leave to open out.

1 Cut away from the stalks, and take away from the base the fine wisp of root.
2 Wash very well in cold water.

Radishes in salads
Radishes add both flavour and crisp texture to salads. One of the most interesting is when combined with rice, as in the colour picture on page 149.

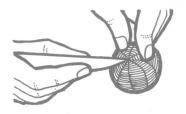

Spanish salad

Colour picture, page 149

Boil long grain rice in salted water until just tender, drain if necessary, and blend with finely chopped onions and chopped radishes while still warm. Toss in either French dressing (page 208) or mayonnaise (page 207), then add cooked diced or thinly sliced red and/or green peppers, crushed garlic, diced cooked fish and anchovy fillets, or chicken and diced ham. Diced dessert apple and/or oranges may be added. Serve with rings of cucumber, rings of radish and onion.

Ham and egg salad

Preparation: 15–20 minutes
Allow eggs to cool
Cooking: 10 minutes for eggs
Serves 4

Most fruit blends well with cooked ham; try prunes, apples, pears, peaches.

2 *or* 3 hard-boiled eggs	small can mandarin oranges	radishes
lettuce	mayonnaise, *page 207*	1 red *or* green pepper
4–6 oz. cooked ham* *or* boiled bacon	chopped parsley	

* buy the ham in one thick slice so it can be cubed.

1 Shell the hard-boiled eggs, and cut into neat slices.
2 Arrange the lettuce on a flat dish.
3 Cut the ham into neat cubes, and mix with the well drained mandarin oranges (save the juice to mix with a jelly), and a little mayonnaise.
4 Pile into centre of dish; top with a spoonful of mayonnaise and parsley.
5 Wash, dry, then cut the radishes into slices, and arrange on top of the sliced eggs.
6 Cut one end off the pepper, remove the seeds and core, then cut the pulp into neat rings. Arrange on the lettuce.

Raw vegetable salad

Preparation: 10 minutes
No delay
No cooking
Serves 4–6

Choose the white Dutch type cabbage, if possible, for salads. This is more crisp than an ordinary cabbage. Raw brussels sprouts, spinach or cauliflower may be used instead of cabbage.

½ small cabbage	1 medium raw beetroot	French dressing, *page 208*
2 carrots	2 tomatoes	watercress
1 small young turnip	salt and pepper	

1 Shred the cabbage and grate the carrots, turnip and beetroot.
2 Slice the tomatoes.
3 Arrange in an attractive design on a flat dish, and add seasoning and dressing to taste. Garnish with watercress.

To vary
1 When young turnips are not available, use chopped radishes instead.
2 Diced celery, grated or chopped celeriac (celery root), or chopped chicory may be added to the salad above.

Potato salad

Preparation: 10–15 minutes
No delay
Cooking: approximately 25 minutes
Serves 6–8

For a salad the potatoes must not be over-cooked. If using old or new potatoes it is quite a good idea to boil them in their jackets, skin and dice while hot.

1 lb. potatoes	2 teaspoons finely chopped onion *or* chives	3 teaspoons finely chopped parsley
approximately ¼ pint mayonnaise, *page 207*		salt and pepper

1 A good potato salad should be mixed when hot, then eaten when very cold.
2 Cook the potatoes in salted water until just cooked – be careful they do not become over-soft.
3 Strain, and leave until just cool enough to handle – BUT NOT COLD.
4 Cut into neat dice and toss in the mayonnaise, adding onion or chives, parsley and seasoning.
5 Leave until cold, then, if desired, garnish with a little more chopped parsley. If preferred, toss in oil and vinegar instead of mayonnaise.

Russian salad

Preparation: 20 minutes
No delay
Cooking: 20 minutes
Serves 4

Try to have a good variety of vegetables: carrots, potatoes, turnip, a little swede. In addition use a few peas.
Frozen mixed vegetables can be used instead. Do not over-cook these, as the salad tastes best if vegetables are slightly firm.

| approximately 1 lb. mixed root vegetables | 1 tablespoon vinegar | salt and pepper |
| 1 tablespoon oil | 3—4 tablespoons mayonnaise, *page 207* | |

1 Cut the vegetables into neat dice.
2 Put into boiling salted water and cook steadily until tender. If using fresh peas, these can be added after the other vegetables have started cooking since they do not take so long to cook.
3 Strain and allow to cool.
4 Put into a basin and mix with the oil and vinegar, then add the mayonnaise. Season to taste.

To vary
Add chopped hard-boiled eggs and chopped herbs at stage 4.

Meat salads

Preparation: few minutes
No delay
No cooking

An English platter, or Assiette Anglaise, means a selection of cold meats, and this makes a most pleasant salad.
Never leave cooked meat exposed to the air for too long or it becomes very dry.

Beef: when making the salad dressing or serving it, you may like to add a little mustard or horseradish cream. Many people like mustard pickle with cold meat salad.
Corned beef: this dries very quickly, so open the can at the last minute. Slice or flake the corned beef.
Ham: make sure you have plenty of crisp lettuce with this. A little mustard added to the mayonnaise (page 207) gives a good 'bite'. Apples or apple sauce are also excellent with ham.
Lamb: a French dressing (page 208) blended with a little chopped mint is the best accompaniment to cold lamb.
Tongue: this dries very quickly and so should be arranged on a dish or plates at the last minute. Serve with green salad. Chutney or a sweet pickle is good with tongue.

Tongue and pear salad

Fruits in salads

Fruit is an excellent accompaniment to green salads.

Apples: these are good added to coleslaw, or mixed with nuts, etc.; leave the peel on if possible to give a touch of colour. Apples discolour very quickly, so either prepare at the last minute or coat with French dressing (page 208), mayonnaise (page 207) or lemon juice.
Bananas: these blend very well with a cheese salad. Toss in mayonnaise (page 207) or lemon juice to keep them a good colour.
Dried fruit: any dried fruit goes well in a salad, particularly with cheese or ham.
Grapefruit: excellent in green salad or with rather rich ingredients.
Melon: this is very pleasant served with ham or chicken. Cut into cubes or use a melon baller.
Oranges: a perfect ingredient in a salad to serve with duck or goose, to counteract the richness. Prepare the orange as directed on page 115 and toss in a little French dressing (page 208).
Peaches and apricots: canned or fresh peaches are excellent with ham, apricots with tongue or salami.
Pear: fresh or canned pears can be filled with mayonnaise (page 207) and served with a cheese or meat salad. An avocado pear, however, which is quite different from an ordinary pear, is best with the stone removed, and served with French dressing (page 208).

Cheese salads

Preparation: few minutes
No delay
No cooking

Note. Cheese blends well with fruit (page 205), as well as other salad ingredients.

1 The cheese can be grated, or cut into neat pieces.
2 Arrange on a bed of lettuce and garnish with slices of tomatoes, cucumber and radishes.

Blend cheese with other ingredients in salads, e.g.:
Diced cheese can be mixed with potato salad (choose cream, Cheddar or Danish Blue cheese).
Grated cheese may be blended with coleslaw (page 208) — add at the last minute so the cheese retains its texture.
Mix two different cheeses together in salads, e.g. Danish Blue plus cream cheese, Gruyère and cottage cheese, etc.

Fish salad

Preparation: 10 minutes
Allow fish to cool
Cooking: 10–15 minutes
Serves 4

1 lb. white fish	1 small onion	*to garnish*
diced cucumber	2 hard-boiled eggs	cucumber and beetroot
2 oz. chopped celery *or* chicory	mayonnaise, *page 207* lettuce	slices

1 Cook the fish gently — do not over-cook. Flake it and mix with diced cucumber, chopped celery or chicory, chopped onion, chopped eggs and mayonnaise.
2 Serve on a bed of lettuce.
3 Garnish with sliced cucumber and beetroot.

Savoury crab salad

Preparation: 15–20 minutes if dressing crab
No cooking
Serves 4

Rice helps to make the fairly expensive shellfish into a more substantial dish.

1 large dressed crab, *page 49*	salt and pepper	1 tablespoon oil
2 oz. cooked long grain rice	1 oz. finely chopped celery	lettuce
1 dessertspoon lemon juice *or* vinegar	1 teaspoon chopped parsley	
	2 teaspoons chopped gherkins	

1 Mix together all the ingredients, except the lettuce, and season well.
2 Serve on individual dishes on a bed of lettuce; garnish with small claws of the crab.

Canned salmon salad

Canned salmon makes a very pleasant salad.
Take care how you turn the salmon out of the can — if you open the can completely the salmon falls out more easily.

Canned salmon salad

canned salmon	mayonnaise	black olives
lettuce	capers	cucumber
lemon		

1 Arrange the salmon on a bed of lettuce and garnish with rings of lemon.
2 Pour mayonnaise over the salmon — in the photograph the home-made mayonnaise on the opposite page was used.
3 Put a few capers on top of each round of salmon and add black olives if desired, or use rings of cucumber.

Shrimp salad

Preparation: few minutes
Allow time for frozen shrimps
to defrost
No cooking
Serves 4

4–6 oz. fresh *or* frozen
    prawns *or* shrimps

mayonnaise
lettuce

to garnish
tomatoes, cucumber, lemon

1 If shelling the fish, put into hot water for 1 minute; shells then come away easily. If using frozen prawns or shrimps, allow these to defrost very gradually.
2 Toss the shellfish in mayonnaise. Serve on a bed of lettuce and garnish with tomatoes, cucumber and lemon.

To vary
Mix the mayonnaise with curry powder or tomato purée.

Mayonnaise

Preparation: 10–15 minutes
No delay
No cooking

To keep the basin firmly in position while making the mayonnaise, place it on a damp cloth; this will prevent it from slipping on the table.

2 egg yolks
1 level teaspoon dry mustard
1 level teaspoon salt

$\frac{1}{4}$ level teaspoon pepper
$\frac{1}{4}$ level teaspoon paprika

4 tablespoons vinegar
8 tablespoons salad oil

1 Put the egg yolks into a basin, add the mustard, salt, pepper and paprika and mix thoroughly together (the mustard helps to emulsify the dressing and prevent curdling).

2 Slowly add 2 tablespoons vinegar and stir well.
3 Add the oil drop by drop, as in the picture.

4 Stir hard with a wooden spoon until the mayonnaise is thick and smooth.
5 Add the remaining vinegar *gradually* and beat vigorously.

Ways to flavour mayonnaise

Preparation: few minutes only
No delay

Mayonnaise can form the basis of a number of new salad dressings. Try these:

Cheese mayonnaise: cream 2 oz. soft cheese with 2 tablespoons milk. Add $\frac{1}{4}$ pint mayonnaise. Serve with vegetable salads.
Curried mayonnaise: blend 1–2 teaspoons curry powder with 1 or 2 tablespoons milk. Stir in $\frac{1}{4}$ pint mayonnaise. Serve with meat or potato salads.
Green mayonnaise: add chopped fresh herbs to mayonnaise. Serve with fish salads – if mint is used it is excellent with lamb salad.
Horseradish mayonnaise: blend 1 tablespoon horseradish cream with $\frac{1}{4}$ pint mayonnaise. Serve with cold beef salad or canned salmon salad.
Lemon mayonnaise: add grated rind and juice of 1 lemon to $\frac{1}{4}$ pint mayonnaise. Serve with cheese or fish salads.
Spiced mayonnaise: add a little grated nutmeg and a few drops Worcestershire sauce to $\frac{1}{4}$ pint mayonnaise. Serve with potato and vegetable salads.
Tomato mayonnaise: add a dessertspoon tomato ketchup or a teaspoon tomato purée to $\frac{1}{4}$ pint mayonnaise. Serve with shellfish salad.

Tartare sauce

Preparation: few minutes
No delay
No cooking

$\frac{1}{4}$ pint mayonnaise
2 teaspoons chopped parsley

1 teaspoon capers

2 teaspoons chopped
    gherkins

Mix all the ingredients together.

Bought mayonnaise

A recipe is given on page 207 for making your own mayonnaise, but as you will see this does take a long time. There are very many good kinds of mayonnaise and salad dressings on the market. They keep well and their flavour suits most people, so they can be used in any of the recipes.

Sharp sauce

Preparation: 5 minutes
No delay
No cooking

For shrimp or lobster cocktails.

¼ pint (5 fl. oz.) soured cream*
3 tablespoons finely chopped onion

1 tablespoon mayonnaise, *page 207*
1 tablespoon capers

¼ teaspoon dry mustard
cayenne pepper
lemon juice

* dairy soured cream gives an interesting 'bite' to sauces, etc.

1 Blend the soured cream with the finely chopped onion, mayonnaise, capers, mustard and a pinch of cayenne pepper.
2 Lemon juice can be added to taste.

French dressing

Preparation: few minutes
No delay
No cooking

A French dressing is easy to make. The only difficulty could be that it might curdle slightly if the ingredients were not blended carefully.

pinch sugar, salt and pepper
1 teaspoon made-mustard

1 tablespoon salad oil
½ tablespoon vinegar

1 tablespoon finely chopped parsley *or* chives, *optional*

1 Put the seasonings and mustard into a flat saucer or basin and very gradually blend the oil in, stirring all the time. A small spoon is the best utensil to use.
2 When the oil is thoroughly mixed, add the vinegar.
3 Finally, add the chopped parsley or chives.

To vary
Add 1–2 crushed cloves of garlic to the dressing.

Coleslaw

Preparation: few minutes
No delay
No cooking

This is the name given to a salad which primarily consists of shredded raw cabbage; the Dutch white cabbage is the best type to buy.

1 cabbage heart

French dressing, *recipe above or* mayonnaise, *page 207*

1 Wash and dry the cabbage, cut into very fine shreds.
2 Put into a basin and add French dressing or mayonnaise. Mix together.

To vary
1 Add a little grated dessert apple and raisins.
2 Add chopped celery and a few chopped dates.
3 **Peach coleslaw.** Arrange coleslaw at the base of the dish; top with peaches and ham, formed into rolls, and olives. Garnish with parsley.
4 Mix cabbage with chopped gherkins, capers and French dressing.

Mandarin rice and ham salad

Preparation: 12 minutes
No delay
Cooking: none if rice is cooked previously
Serves 4

If you prefer the green pepper to be softer, blanch for 5 minutes in boiling water, drain, cool, then cut into strips.

6–8 oz. cooked ham
1 small green pepper
4–6 oz. cooked long grain rice

1 tablespoon finely chopped onion
2 teaspoons sugar
2 teaspoons soy sauce*

2 tablespoons French dressing, *above,*
can mandarin oranges

* obtainable from stores that sell Chinese food.

1 Cut the ham into ¼-inch strips.
2 Dice the green pepper, removing all seeds.
3 Combine the rice with the pepper, onion, sugar, soy sauce and French dressing. Toss in basin, arrange in dish with drained orange and ham strips.
4 Crisp lettuce should be served separately.

To vary
Canned luncheon meat may be substituted for the ham.

Mushrooms in salads

Raw mushrooms are delicious in salads. Wash tiny mushrooms, trim ends of the stalks, but do not peel. Toss in mayonnaise and serve on crisp lettuce.
Sliced mushrooms may be added to salads. Toss in French dressing (above), and mix with chopped chives and chopped parsley. Or mix with orange segments.

Savoury dishes

Pasta is the name used to describe the macaroni foods, which include spaghetti, cannelloni, etc.

To cook pasta

1 It is very important to make sure that the pasta is put into a sufficient quantity of boiling salted water.
2 If you use too little water it becomes sticky and is inadequately cooked.
3 Use at least 2 pints water to 4 oz. pasta.
4 Do not over-cook. The pasta is cooked when it feels just tender, and if you bring a piece out there should be no white uncooked flour on it.
5 Serve as soon as possible after cooking.
6 There are varieties of quick-cooking pasta on the market and these are of good quality. Their shape has just been adjusted to make them cook more rapidly.

Macaroni cheese

Preparation: 15 minutes
No delay
Cooking: approximately
40–45 minutes, unless grilling —
when it will be about
25 minutes
Serves 4

If you like a more moist macaroni cheese, then use $\frac{3}{4}$ pint cheese sauce to the same quantity of cooked macaroni.

3 oz. macaroni	2 oz. grated cheese	1 oz. margarine *or* butter
$\frac{1}{2}$ pint cheese sauce, *page 143*	1 tablespoon crisp breadcrumbs	

1 Put the macaroni into about $1\frac{1}{2}$ pints boiling water, to which you have added 1 level teaspoon salt.
2 Cook steadily until the macaroni is just tender. Do not over-cook; elbow length quick-cooking macaroni takes only 7 minutes.
3 Drain in a colander, arrange it in a hot dish and pour the cheese sauce over it.
4 Sprinkle the cheese and breadcrumbs on top, and put the margarine or butter on in several small pieces.
5 Either bake for about 25 minutes near the top of a moderately hot oven (400°F., Gas Mark 5) until crisp and brown, or put under a hot grill.

Spaghetti

Spaghetti is quite easy to cook if you remember the rule above, i.e. use plenty of water according to the quantity of pasta.

1 Put the water on to boil.
2 Add the salt; allow about $\frac{1}{2}$ teaspoon salt to each 2 pints water.
3 Hold the spaghetti quite firmly in your hand with the pieces standing upright.
4 Lower one end into the boiling salted water. Wait for a minute or so until you see this end has become softened, and then twist the spaghetti until more of the pasta is in the water.
5 Wait again until this part seems softened, when you should be able to lower the rest of the spaghetti into the water.
6 Allow to boil steadily for a few minutes, then stir very gently with a wooden spoon or a fork to separate the pieces of pasta.
7 Spaghetti will take about 15 minutes (see above for way to test if cooked).
8 Strain through a colander, or sieve, and then lift the pieces with two forks to separate them slightly.
9 A little butter can be added, and chopped parsley.
10 Serve with tomato sauce (recipe below).

Tomato sauce

Preparation: 10 minutes
No delay
Cooking: 10 minutes
Serves 4

This particular tomato sauce does not need sieving.

1 oz. butter *or* margarine	1 small tube *or* can	$\frac{1}{2}$ pint water
1 small onion	concentrated tomato purée	salt and pepper
1 small apple	2 level teaspoons cornflour	good pinch of sugar

1 Heat the butter or margarine, fry the chopped onion for a few minutes, then add the peeled and grated apple.
2 Add the tomato purée, the cornflour blended with the water, and seasoning.
3 Bring to the boil and stir until smooth.
4 Simmer gently for about 10 minutes, taste and re-season, adding sugar if necessary.

Canned, frozen and quick-cooking pasta

Canned macaroni, ravioli and spaghetti are extremely popular, and with good reason, for they provide a quick meal and a sustaining one. The canning process tends to make the pasta very soft, so do not over-heat.
Frozen pasta foods such as ravioli can be purchased. They are generally better cooked from the frozen state.
Do not over-cook the quick-cooking pasta foods; check cooking times on the packets.

Using convenience foods

Mention has been made in this book of the convenience foods that are available, i.e. frozen, canned, dehydrated and packet foods. While no-one would suggest you use these entirely, it is a good idea to have some of them available as a standby, for they can form the basis of many quick dishes.

Dehydrated foods

There is quite a selection of dehydrated or dried foods on the market:
1 Mixed vegetables, which can be put into soups or stews.
2 Onions, which can be used in the same way, or added to savoury dishes.
3 Complete meals: spaghetti, curry and dried meat dishes are obtainable. You will find that if the right directions for cooking are carried out the food is extremely good, and very useful to store since it takes up little space and keeps for a long time.

Frozen meat cakes

These can be used in a number of ways.
Follow the directions for cooking on the packets and, above all, observe the directions for storing. Never attempt to keep frozen meat for a longer period than recommended. Do not over-cook the meat, for it is minced.

Fry meat cakes in a little hot fat and sandwich together with rounds of crisp fried bread.

Grill or fry and serve with salad.

Top meat cakes with a little stuffing and slices of tomato and bake in the oven.

Grill or fry meat cakes and arrange with lettuce on slices of bread, garnish with radish, cucumber, hard-boiled egg, beet-root, tomato, etc., and serve as open sandwiches.

Sausages pomodonia

Preparation: 10 minutes
No delay
Cooking: 15 minutes
Serves 4

To skin the tomatoes, stage 3,
put into boiling water, cool,
then pull off the skin.
Use the bacon rinds as easiest
'nibbles' instead of potato crisps.
Fry in a pan until very brittle
and crisp.

Secret of success
Turn the sausages as they cook,
so they are evenly browned.

| 2–3 rashers bacon | 4 large tomatoes | 1 bay leaf |
| knob of lard | 1 lb. pork sausages | 1 packet frozen peas |

1 Cut the bacon into small dice, removing the rinds — this is easiest to do with kitchen scissors.
2 Heat a knob of lard in a frying pan.

3 Skin the tomatoes and cut into small pieces.

4 Put bacon and sausages into pan, fry until bacon is crisp and sausages golden brown.

5 Add the bay leaf and tomatoes.

6 Cook gently until the tomatoes are soft.

7 Cook the frozen peas in a small quantity of boiling salted water.

8 Arrange the tomato and bacon sauce at the bottom of a dish and top with the sausages. Drain and serve the peas separately.

211

Baconburgers

Preparation: 15 minutes. Allow about 1 hour for mixture to stiffen before cooking
Cooking: 6–8 minutes
Serves 4

This is an excellent way of using inexpensive bacon pieces.

Secret of success
Allow the mixture to set, stage 4, so the bacon cakes are easy to handle yet moist inside.

12 oz. cold boiled bacon
   or ham
1 medium onion
3 oz. cheese, grated
seasoning

2 tablespoons breadcrumbs
1 small egg
flour
about 1–2 oz. bacon fat *or*
   cooking fat *for frying*

to garnish
spring onions

1 Mince the bacon or ham and onion finely.
2 Mix the bacon, onion, cheese, seasoning and breadcrumbs together lightly. Bind with the beaten egg.
3 Roll out into flat round cakes, about ½ inch thick, on a floured board.
4 Leave in a cold place or refrigerator to become firm.
5 Coat with seasoned flour just before frying.
6 Heat the fat (just enough to cover the base of the pan) in a thick frying pan.
7 Fry the baconburgers for 3–4 minutes on each side.
8 Drain well. Serve between split baps or soft rolls and garnish with spring onions.

Bacon pan bread

Preparation: 12 minutes
No delay
Cooking: approximately
25–30 minutes
Serves 4

This dish provides both the meat course and the bread to serve with it.

Secret of success
Do not use too small a container – see stage 5.

Left *Bacon pan bread*
Right *Stuffed pancakes*

4 oz. bacon rashers
2 oz. plain flour
4 oz. fine semolina
3 level teaspoons baking
   powder

½ level teaspoon salt
½ level teaspoon dry mustard
1 dessertspoon castor sugar
1 dessertspoon chopped
   onion
2 eggs

4 tablespoons milk
poppy *or* dill seeds, *optional*
2 oz. butter

1 Cook the bacon in a small frying pan until crisp.
2 Drain and reserve the dripping, chop the bacon.
3 Sift together the flour, semolina, baking powder, salt, mustard and sugar, add the onion and bacon.
4 Beat the eggs and blend with the milk and 2 tablespoons bacon fat.
5 Stir this liquid into the dry mixture, and put into a well greased 7- or 8-inch sandwich or baking tin, or ovenproof dish.
6 Sprinkle, if liked, with poppy or dill seeds.
7 Bake in a hot oven (425–450°F., Gas Mark 6–7) for about 20 minutes, until golden and firm; put just above the centre of the oven.
8 Cut into wedges and serve hot with a crisp salad. Place a knob of butter on each serving.

Stuffed pancakes

Preparation: 7–10 minutes
No delay
Cooking: 10–15 minutes
Serves 4

To keep pancakes hot, put on a dish over a pan of boiling water or on an uncovered dish in a low oven.

6 oz. ham
small can condensed cream
   of mushroom soup

for the pancake batter
4 oz. flour
pinch of salt

2 eggs
½ pint milk (less
   2 tablespoons)

1 Chop the ham finely and add to half the can of soup. Heat gently.
2 Make the pancakes in the usual way (see above).
3 Stuff each pancake with the ham and mushroom filling, roll up and put into a hot dish.
4 Heat the remaining soup and pour over the pancakes.
5 Serve the pancakes and the sauce as soon as possible after cooking.

Curry stuffed pancakes

Preparation: 25 minutes
No delay for sauce,
batter 30 minutes
Cooking: 30 minutes
Makes 4 pancakes

This is a fairly complicated recipe, so you may like to make a large amount of mixture and store both the sauce and the cooked pancakes in the refrigerator or freezer. To store pancakes put a piece of greaseproof paper between them so they do not stick, wrap in foil.

The curry sauce given on the right is excellent as a sauce over hard-boiled eggs, or mixed with meat or fish, etc.

Secret of success
Allow the curry sauce to cook for the long period suggested so that you produce a good blending of flavours.

1 small onion
1 small apple
1 tomato, skinned, *page 203*
1 oz. margarine
1 rounded dessertspoon curry powder
1 level teaspoon curry paste, *optional*
salt and pepper
1 oz. sultanas
½ pint stock *or* water

4–6 oz. shelled prawns

4–6 whole prawns *to garnish optional*

for the batter
2 oz. plain flour
pinch of salt
1 egg
¼ pint milk
oil *or* fat *for cooking*

for the rice
4 oz. long grain rice
½ level teaspoon salt
1 pint boiling water

accompaniments
little chutney
1 sliced banana
sliced green pepper
½ lemon

To make the curry sauce
1 Chop the onion and apple finely, chop the skinned tomato.
2 Melt the margarine in a medium sized saucepan, add the onion, and fry gently for 5 minutes.
3 Add the curry powder, then fry slowly for 5 minutes.
4 Add the remaining ingredients, except the prawns, and simmer gently for about 1 hour.
5 Add the prawns about 5 minutes before serving, and reheat slowly.

To make the batter
6 Sieve the flour and salt into a bowl.
7 Make a well in the centre, add the egg and half the milk.
8 Beat well for 5 minutes.
9 Leave to stand for 30 minutes. Add remaining milk and re-beat before using.
10 Heat fat or oil in a medium sized frying pan until fairly hot.
11 Pour sufficient batter into the pan to make a thin coating, cook until golden brown.
12 Toss or turn and cook on the other side. For further instructions on pancakes see page 161.
13 Turn out on to kitchen paper and keep warm.

To cook the rice
14 Place the rice in boiling, salted water, cover the pan with a very tightly fitting lid and cook until tender (about 15–20 minutes), then strain.
15 Rinse the rice under the cold tap.
16 Place a piece of greaseproof paper on a baking tray, put the rice on this and put into a cool oven until the rice is dry. This will take about 20–25 minutes. (See page 147 for correct cooking of rice.)
17 Place the rice on an oval serving dish.
18 Fill the pancakes with the curry mixture, roll up and place on top of the rice.
19 Cut wedges of lemon for each pancake, garnish with whole prawns, if used. Serve immediately with suggested accompaniments.

Curry stuffed pancakes

Californian risotto

Preparation: 10 minutes
No delay
Cooking: 30 minutes
Serves 2

Secret of success
Do not over-cook the rice; it should retain its texture.

If preparing some time before serving this dish, use a little more liquid when cooking the rice, for this absorbs liquid as it stands.

1 small onion, finely chopped
1 oz. butter
4 oz. long grain rice
approximately ¾ pint hot chicken stock *or* water and 1 chicken stock cube

salt and pepper
1 tomato, skinned, *page 203*
2 oz. seedless raisins

3 oz. cooked ham, bacon *or* chicken, finely chopped
2 oz. Cheddar cheese, grated
Cheddar *or* Parmesan cheese *to serve separately*

1 Cook the onion lightly in the butter, stir in the rice and cook for a few minutes.
2 Add the chicken stock, or water and stock cube, seasoning and chopped tomato pulp, and bring to the boil.
3 Simmer gently, stirring occasionally until all the liquid has been absorbed and the rice is just tender — 15–20 minutes.
4 Add the raisins, meat or chicken, and grated cheese; mix quickly and lightly, heat for about 5 minutes and serve at once, handing grated cheese separately.

Turkey à la king

Preparation: 15 minutes
No delay
Cooking: 15 minutes
Serves 3–4

Secret of success
This is an excellent way to serve cooked turkey. Heat carefully and season well.

Chicken or game or cooked veal can be used instead of turkey.

1 small onion
2–4 oz. mushrooms *or* can mushrooms
8–12 oz. cooked turkey

small can peas *or* packet frozen peas
1 oz. butter
1 oz. flour

large can evaporated milk
salt and pepper
1 small loaf of white bread

1 Grate the onion, chop the mushrooms finely, cut the turkey into small pieces.
2 Cook frozen peas for 3 minutes, or drain canned peas, without cooking.
3 Heat the butter in a pan.
4 Stir in the onion and cook for several minutes.
5 Gradually add the flour and blend thoroughly; cook for 2–3 minutes.
6 Take the pan off the heat and add the evaporated milk.
7 Return to the heat and bring to the boil, stirring all the time.
8 Put in the mushrooms (and mushroom liquid if using canned mushrooms), peas and turkey. Season well. Heat gently for just a few minutes.
9 Split the loaf through the centre, put in half the filling.
10 Cover with the rest of the bread and top with the remaining filling.

Turkey puffs

Preparation: 20–25 minutes
No delay
Cooking: 30 minutes
Makes 9–12

Secret of success
Make sure the oven is sufficiently hot when the puffs start cooking. This will make the pastry rise well.

These puffs are excellent as a picnic dish.

8 oz. flaky pastry, *page 193*
8 oz. cooked turkey

few pieces left-over stuffing
2 eggs

salt and pepper
egg *or* milk *to glaze*

1 Roll out the pastry to approximately ¼ inch thick.
2 Use just over half of this to line patty tins.
3 Cut the turkey into small pieces.
4 Put into a basin, add pieces of stuffing, eggs, seasoning.
5 Divide this mixture between the pastry cases.
6 Cut the rest of the pastry into rounds for the tops of the puffs.
7 Seal the edges and make a slit in the centre of each puff with a sharp knife or a pair of scissors.
8 Brush with egg or a little milk, cook in centre of a hot to very hot oven (450–475°F., Gas Mark 7–8) for 15 minutes, lower the heat to moderate for a further 10–15 minutes.

Ham rolls with peaches and sweet corn

Preparation: 10 minutes
No delay
Cooking: 10 minutes
Serves 4

The addition of cheese makes this a particularly nourishing dish. Instead of peach halves you could choose pineapple rings.

6 oz. Cheddar cheese
6–8 slices ham
2 tablespoons milk

dash of salt and pepper
can creamed sweet corn
6–8 canned peach halves

to garnish
parsley

1 Cut the cheese into fingers and allow 1 finger per slice of ham.
2 Place one on each ham slice and roll up.
3 Place the rolls in a shallow ovenproof dish.
4 Stir the milk, salt and pepper into the sweet corn.
5 Spoon over the rolls.
6 Lift the peaches from their syrup; arrange round the ham rolls.
7 Heat in a moderate oven (350–375°F., Gas Mark 4–5) for 10 minutes, to soften the cheese. Garnish with parsley to serve.

To vary
Use rings of fresh or canned pineapple, or whole canned or cooked apricots, or small cooked dessert apples (simmered in lemon-flavoured syrup).

Left *Ham rolls with peaches and sweetcorn* Right *Ham gnocchi*

Ham gnocchi

Preparation: 12 minutes
Allow mixture to cool
Cooking: 10–12 minutes
Serves 4

Secret of success
Add the semolina gradually at stage 2, stirring well to keep the mixture from becoming lumpy. This is both an economical *and* very pleasant savoury.

Do not attempt to cut the mixture into rounds until completely cold.

This makes a very good hors d'oeuvre.

1 pint milk
¼ level teaspoon salt
pinch of pepper
4 oz. fine semolina
3 oz. ham, chopped

1 dessertspoon chopped parsley
3 oz. Parmesan *or* Cheddar cheese, grated
2 oz. butter

½ teaspoon made-mustard
2 eggs

to garnish
parsley

1 Heat the milk with the salt and pepper.
2 Sprinkle in the semolina and bring to the boil, stirring.
3 Cook gently for about 3 minutes, until the mixture thickens.
4 Stir in the chopped ham and parsley.
5 Remove from the heat, stir in 2 oz. of the grated cheese, 1½ oz. butter and the made-mustard.
6 Beat the eggs, add to the mixture and stir over a low heat for 1 minute, without boiling.
7 Turn out on to a greased or wetted shallow oblong tray, spreading about ½ inch thick.
8 Leave until quite cold. Cut into 1½-inch rounds with a wetted cutter.
9 Arrange in overlapping rounds on a greased shallow casserole or baking dish.
10 Top with the remaining cheese and dot with the remaining butter.
11 Heat under grill, slowly at first to heat through, then more quickly to brown, or bake in a hot oven (425–450°F., Gas Mark 6–7) until hot and golden. Garnish with parsley.

Ham with peanut rice stuffing

Preparation: 15 minutes
No delay
Cooking: 40 minutes
Serves 4

Secret of success
Nuts give an unexpectedly crisp texture to the stuffing; do not over-cook at stage 6, otherwise they become softened.

6 spring onions
2 *or* 3 sticks celery
2 oz. butter *or* margarine
2 oz. uncooked long grain rice

½ pint chicken stock*
1 teaspoon dry mustard
1 apple
1 oz. salted peanuts

8 thin slices cooked ham
2 tablespoons cider, *or* use more chicken stock

* or use water and 1 chicken stock cube.

1 Chop the onions and celery very finely. Use the green part of spring onions.
2 Fry the celery and onions in the butter or margarine until tender.
3 Add the rice. Cook until lightly browned, *stirring frequently.*
4 Add the chicken stock and dry mustard; bring to the boil, stir well.
5 Cover and cook over low heat for 15 minutes.
6 Add the chopped apple and salted peanuts.
7 Cook for a further 5 minutes, making sure the rice does not stick.
8 Place a little filling on the centre of each ham slice.
9 Fold the ham over the filling, secure with wooden cocktail sticks.
10 Place in a baking dish, add the cider or more chicken stock.
11 Cover the dish with foil, or a lid, and bake in a moderate oven (350–375°F., Gas Mark 4–5) for 15 minutes.

Zucchini pilaf

Preparation: 15 minutes
No delay
Cooking: 30—35 minutes
Serves 4

Zucchini is another name for courgettes or small marrow. If the zucchini are very small, allow 2—3 instead of the 1 listed in the ingredients.

Secret of success
Do not over-cook this dish; the rice, etc., should be tender but not too soft in texture.

approximately 8 oz. cooked lamb
1 small clove of garlic
1 onion
2 oz. butter *or* margarine
3 oz. uncooked long grain rice
2 tablespoons chopped celery
2 tablespoons diced green pepper
1¼ pint stock *or* water and chicken stock cube
1 tablespoon Worcestershire sauce
1½ teaspoons salt
pinch of pepper
1 diced unpeeled young marrow (zucchini *or* courgette)
2 oz. cheese, grated

1 Cut the lamb into neat squares and chop the garlic and onion.
2 Melt the butter or margarine in a large saucepan and add the lamb, rice, onion, celery, green pepper and garlic.
3 Cook, stirring frequently, until the rice is golden.
4 Stir in the stock, Worcestershire sauce and seasonings. Bring to the boil; stir.
5 Cover the saucepan with a lid and cook over VERY LOW heat for 20 minutes. Look once or twice to make sure the rice is not absorbing too much liquid.
6 Stir in the diced marrow and cook, covered, for 10 minutes longer, by which time you should have a moist but not too wet mixture.
7 When ready to serve, sprinkle with the cheese.

Creamy beef pie

Preparation: 25—30 minutes
No delay
Cooking: 25—30 minutes
Serves 4

This recipe is very unusual, for the meat is made into the 'pie-crust' instead of ordinary pastry

Secret of success
Cook the sauce well at stage 6, so that it becomes fairly stiff in consistency.

can corned beef
4 oz. sausage meat
3 tablespoons rolled oats
1 dessertspoon curry powder
1 onion
½ teaspoon salt
pinch of pepper
1 egg

for the filling
3 oz. butter
3 oz. flour
1 pint milk
can sweet corn *or* packet peas and carrots
salt and pepper
¼ teaspoon grated nutmeg

to garnish
parsley
cucumber

1 Mash the corned beef with a fork, or mince.
2 Combine with the sausage meat, rolled oats, curry powder, grated onion, salt and pepper.
3 Add the beaten egg and mix.
4 Press the mixture on the sides and base of an ovenproof dish to resemble pie-crust.
5 Melt the butter in a saucepan, add the flour, cook for 3 minutes.
6 Add the milk gradually and stir over the heat until the mixture boils and thickens.
7 Add the sweet corn or peas and carrots, seasoning and nutmeg.
8 Pour into the meat crust, cover with greaseproof paper, bake in the centre of a moderate oven (375°F., Gas Mark 4) for 25—30 minutes. Serve garnished with sprigs of parsley and slices of cucumber.

Beef fondue bourguignonne

Preparation: few minutes
Cooking: few minutes
Serves 4—6

Secret of success
Choose really tender fillet steak for this dish. Do not cook until quite ready to eat the food.

Take great care that the pan of very hot oil is placed in a safe place, and protect a polished table from the heat of the table heater and the pan of oil. See note about removing meat from fondue forks.

Colour picture, opposite

1¼—1½ lb. fillet steak
corn oil
seasoning
various sauces, *see below*

1 Cut the meat into neat cubes, about ¾ inch. Keep in a cool place until ready to cook, then arrange on an attractive plate or in a dish.
2 Heat the oil in the fondue pan over the heat of a hotplate or boiling ring, until it reaches 375°F., (i.e. a small piece of bread turns golden brown within ½ minute).
3 Transfer the oil to a table heater, make sure it is quite steady.
4 To serve the beef fondue, spear the pieces of meat on to wooden or metal fondue forks. Dip in the oil and cook until tender; this takes from about 1 minute, if you like underdone beef, to 3 minutes if you like it well cooked. Season if wished.
5 Slide the cooked meat off the fondue fork with the help of an ordinary fork (*this is essential as naturally the fondue forks become ultra hot*) and put on to a plate, then dip into one of the sauces below and eat at once. Salad can also be served.

Sauces to serve
Cold creamy sauces form a better contrast to the very hot meat than hot sauces. Choose from the following, and also have a dish of natural yoghourt.
Curry mayonnaise: blend a little curry powder or curry paste with mayonnaise.
Horseradish mayonnaise: blend horseradish cream with mayonnaise.
Mustard mayonnaise: blend French mustard with mayonnaise.
Tartare sauce: blend chopped gherkins, chopped parsley and capers with mayonnaise. Add a little lemon juice if wished.
Tomato mayonnaise: blend either tomato ketchup, fresh sieved tomato pulp or concentrated tomato purée with mayonnaise.

Beef fondue bourguignonne

1 The complete recipe for a soufflé is on page 230. The particular soufflé illustrated here is flavoured with Dutch cheese. This picture shows the grated cheese being added to the thick sauce.

2 In this picture the stiffly whisked egg whites are folded into the cheese-flavoured sauce. Note the large size of the pan which enables one to mix all the ingredients.

3 The cheese soufflé mixture being spooned into the soufflé dish.

4 The cooked cheese soufflé. This is how a soufflé should look, i.e. well risen and golden brown.

Cheese soufflé

Cheese savouries

Welsh rarebit

Preparation: 10 minutes
No delay
Cooking: few minutes
Serves 4–6

A Dutch Gouda or Edam makes a soft creamy Welsh rarebit, or use Cheddar or Cheshire, or a Double Gloucester.
This Welsh rarebit mixture can be stored in covered jars for some days in a refrigerator.
A more substantial meal can be made by topping the Welsh rarebit with crisp rolls of bacon, which should be cooked under the grill. Roll the bacon, put on a skewer as directed on page 85, and cook steadily. Garnish with parsley.

1 oz. butter
1 oz. flour
¼ pint cold milk
1 teaspoon made-mustard

salt and pepper
1 tablespoon beer *or* ale *or* Worcestershire sauce

8 oz. cheese, grated
4–6 large slices toast
butter *for toast*

1 Heat the butter in a saucepan, stir in the flour, cook for several minutes, gradually add the cold milk.
2 Bring to the boil and cook until smooth and thick.
3 Add the mustard, salt, pepper, beer or Worcestershire sauce, and most of the cheese.
4 Heat steadily, without boiling too quickly, until the cheese has melted.
5 Spread over hot buttered toast, sprinkle with the remainder of the cheese and brown under a hot grill. Serve at once.

Buck rarebit: top the prepared and grilled cheese mixture with a poached egg.
Vegetable rarebit: put cooked tomato slices, cooked mushrooms or celery on the buttered toast, top with the rarebit mixture and continue as stage 5.

Welsh rarebit with bacon rolls

Cheese pudding

Preparation: 10 minutes
Allow milk to cool
Cooking: 30–40 minutes
Serves 4

If the mixture is allowed to stand for 30 minutes after stage 4, you have a softer textured pudding.

4 oz. white bread
2 oz. butter

¾ pint milk
2 eggs

4–5 oz. cheese, grated
salt and pepper

1 Cut the bread into neat dice and put into a basin.
2 If preferred, make the bread into crumbs.
3 Heat the butter with the milk, pour over the bread.
4 Allow to cool slightly, then add the beaten eggs and most of the grated cheese. Season well.
5 Pour into a pie or entrée dish, cover the top with the remainder of the cheese.
6 Bake for approximately 30–40 minutes in the centre of a moderate oven (350–375°F., Gas Mark 4–5).

Fish savouries

Crab Newburg

Preparation: 5 minutes
No delay
Cooking: 10 minutes
Serves 2–3

This mixture can also be used as a filling for omelettes, pancakes or vol-au-vent. See page 195.

Crab Newburg

small can condensed cream of mushroom soup
4 tablespoons milk

6-oz. can crab *or* a small dressed crab

1 tablespoon sherry
2–3 slices toast

1 Heat the mushroom soup and the milk.
2 Meanwhile, flake the crab meat, add it to the soup and bring to the boil, stirring. *Do not over-cook.*
3 Add the sherry and serve with toast in individual dishes.

To vary
1 Serve the crab meat mixture in small vol-au-vent cases as shown below.
2 Blend the crab meat with a creamy white sauce plus the sherry, instead of soup.

Breton fingers

Preparation: 12 minutes
No delay
Cooking: 10 minutes
Serves 4

This is also an excellent after-dinner savoury. Cut the 4 slices of toast to give 8 fingers and serve 8 people.

small can sardines in oil
salt and pepper
½ teaspoon made-mustard
1 heaped tablespoon breadcrumbs

1 teaspoon Worcestershire sauce
2 oz. Cheddar cheese, grated
little margarine *or* butter, *if necessary*

4 slices buttered toast

to garnish
tomato

1 Mash the drained sardines very well and season.
2 Mix oil from the can of sardines with the breadcrumbs, seasoning, Worcestershire sauce and cheese.
3 If there is not enough oil to give a soft mixture, add a little margarine or butter, and cream well.
4 Spread mashed sardines on slices of toast and cover with the crumb mixture.
5 Put under a hot grill for a few minutes until crisp and golden brown.
6 Garnish with a small piece of tomato.

Fish and crab mélange

Preparation: 5–10 minutes
No delay
Cooking: 10 minutes
Serves 2–3

Secret of success
Wrap the fish, see stages 2–6. This retains maximum flavour.

If using frozen cod, do not wait for the fish to defrost, cook at stage 5 as fresh fish.

8 oz. cod
salt and pepper
lemon juice
½ oz. butter
1 small red pepper

lettuce
mayonnaise, *page 207*
4 oz. crab meat (meat from 1 small fresh crab *or* frozen *or* canned)

to garnish
asparagus tips

1 Season the cod with salt, pepper and lemon juice.
2 Place it on a piece of greaseproof paper, dot with butter.
3 Fold the edges of the greaseproof paper over, to make an envelope.
4 Place in a steamer over a saucepan of boiling water.
5 Cook for 10–12 minutes, until the flesh comes easily away from the bone.
6 Empty the envelope of fish into a small basin. Remove skin and centre bone; cool.
7 Flake the fish with its own cooking liquor.
8 Halve the pepper, remove the seeds and core, dice the flesh, mix with flaked cod.
9 Make a bed of shredded lettuce on a shallow dish, put a border of flaked cod and pepper all round the edge.
10 Stir a rounded dessertspoon of mayonnaise into the crab meat, then arrange in a smaller circle inside the cod. Garnish with asparagus tips.

Anchovy pie

Preparation: 15 minutes
No delay
Cooking: 15 minutes
Serves 2–3

An unusual supper savoury.

Secret of success
Stir briskly at stage 3, since
cornflour mixtures thicken
rapidly.

1 small onion
1 clove of garlic
1 oz. butter
1 oz. cornflour
½ pint milk

small can *or* tube
   concentrated tomato purée
small can anchovy fillets
1 oz. cheese, grated

8 oz. mashed potatoes

to garnish
8–10 black olives

1 Chop the onion and garlic finely.
2 Fry the onion and garlic in the hot butter until tender but not browned.
3 Add the cornflour and cook for a minute, add the milk, mix well and cook for 3 minutes, stirring constantly. Remove from the heat.
4 Stir in the tomato purée, most of the anchovy fillets cut into small pieces, and the grated cheese.
5 Pour into a 6-inch pie plate, pipe the top with a lattice of potatoes (page 139), then brown under the grill.
6 Garnish with black olives and the remaining anchovy fillets.

Matthew Flinders flan

Preparation: 25–30 minutes
No delay
Cooking: 25 minutes
Serves 4

If serving this cold, allow sauce
and filling to cool before putting
into flan case, otherwise the
pastry will become soft.

6 oz. short crust pastry,
   page 184

for the filling
1½ oz. butter

1½ oz. flour
½ pint milk
salt and pepper
squeeze of lemon juice

large can tuna fish
1 teaspoon finely chopped
   parsley
small can anchovy fillets

1 Roll out the pastry to ⅛ inch in thickness, and line a 7- or 8-inch flan ring on an upturned baking tin.
2 Bake 'blind' in a hot oven (425–450°F., Gas Mark 6–7) for 20–25 minutes (see page 190 for details of lining flans).
3 *To make the filling:* melt the butter in a saucepan and add the flour.
4 Stirring constantly, gradually add the milk and bring to the boil; cook until thickened.
5 Season with salt and pepper, cook for 2 minutes.
6 Whisk in the lemon juice AWAY from the heat, then add the flaked tuna fish and parsley.
7 Fill the flan and arrange anchovy fillets on top like the spokes of a wheel.
8 Serve hot or cold with grilled tomatoes.

Seafood jambalaya

Preparation: 15 minutes
No delay (less time if you buy a
dressed crab or frozen crab
meat)
Cooking: 30 minutes
Serves 2

Secret of success
Do not over-cook at stage 8.

1 *or* 2 sticks celery
1 onion
2 oz. butter *or* margarine
2 tomatoes

½ pint water
salt and pepper
2 oz. long grain rice
1 small crab

2 oz. peeled shrimps *or*
   prawns

to garnish
lemon

1 Chop the celery and onion into small pieces.
2 Toss the onion and celery in the butter or margarine, and when tender, add the chopped, skinned tomatoes. Allow to simmer for 5 minutes.
3 Pour in the water, season well. Bring to the boil.
4 Put in the rice and cook for 15 minutes.
5 Season with more salt and pepper if necessary.
6 Add the crab meat (see page 49 for directions on removing crab from shell).
7 Add the shrimps or prawns.
8 Simmer for 5 minutes only, making sure the mixture does not stick.
9 Garnish with lemon.

Cheese and prawn tartlets

Preparation: 20 minutes
No delay
Cooking: 10 minutes, plus time
for cooking tartlet cases
Makes 12

Secret of success
Prick pastry cases before
baking. Do not over-cook; they
go back into the oven at stage 6.

12 cooked tartlet cases
   baked 'blind', *page 190*

for the filling
½ oz. butter

½ oz. plain flour
¼ pint milk
salt and pepper
pinch of dry mustard
6 oz. Cheddar cheese, grated

3–4 oz. picked prawns
1 small fresh *or* canned
   red pepper
½ oz. fresh breadcrumbs
1 egg, lightly beaten

1 *To make the filling:* make sauce in the usual way with butter, flour and milk (page 143), remove from the heat, stir in the seasoning, mustard and cheese.
2 When the cheese has melted, stir in all but 12 prawns.
3 If using fresh red pepper, blanch it in hot water for 5 minutes, drain.
4 Slice 12 thin strips from the pepper, chop the rest finely.
5 Stir the chopped pepper into the sauce with the breadcrumbs and egg.
6 Divide the filling between the pastry cases, bake in a moderate oven (350–375°F., Gas Mark 4–5) for 10 minutes, until golden brown.
7 Garnish with the whole prawns and strips of red pepper. Serve hot or cold.

To make good sandwiches

One often hears complaints about dry and rather dull sandwiches. This is quite unnecessary, since properly made sandwiches can be most appetising. The following are useful points to remember:

1 Use reasonably fresh bread.
2 If the butter is hard, soften this by standing the plate over a pan of boiling water, then putting the chopped-up butter on the hot plate. Never oil the butter, since it spoils the flavour and soaks into the bread.
3 Use a fairly moist filling if the sandwiches have to keep for a time.
4 Never leave sandwiches exposed to the air for any time — cover with either a damp cloth or foil.
5 Sandwiches keep overnight if wrapped in foil or polythene, or if put into the salad container and then stored in the refrigerator.
6 Freezing sandwiches: all fillings freeze well except salad ingredients, hard-boiled eggs and mayonnaise. Wrap the sandwiches and freeze on lowest temperature.
7 When you have a large quantity of sandwiches to make, use a sandwich loaf lengthways, so giving larger slices of bread.
8 Do not be conservative about your choice of bread — use a bottom slice of white bread and a top slice of brown, for a change.

Open sandwiches

These are not only very attractive in appearance, but also particularly good to eat. Open sandwiches can be made substantial enough for a main meal — or small and neat enough for a cocktail savoury: there is an infinite variety of ingredients that can be used.

1 Use split bridge or other rolls for the base, or brown, white, rye or crispbread.
2 Butter the bread.
3 Put on the filling — here are some suggestions:
crisp lettuce, prawns or shrimps, mayonnaise (page 207) and sliced hard-boiled eggs;
ham formed into neat rolls and topped with red cabbage (bought in jars), sliced tomatoes and gherkins;
slices of beef, garnished with horseradish cream, sliced cucumber and sliced tomatoes;
slices of tongue, garnished with watercress, and scrambled egg;
rashers of bacon — fried or grilled until very crisp — on top of lettuce; garnish with scrambled egg or sliced hard-boiled egg and gherkins;
liver sausage on lettuce, garnished with cooked prawns;
canned corn can be combined with any of the above.

10 savoury spreads for toast or sandwiches

1 Grated cheese, grated carrot and a little chopped parsley, mixed together with mayonnaise (page 207).
2 Creamed butter, chopped watercress and a squeeze of lemon juice — seasoned well.
3 Creamed cheese and finely chopped celery; use a small amount of the green leaves too.
4 Creamed cheese and chopped boiled bacon or ham, then just a touch of chutney.
5 Chopped hard-boiled eggs, crisp chopped bacon and a little mayonnaise to bind.
6 Chopped soft-boiled eggs, knob of butter, little chopped parsley or watercress, pinch of celery salt and seasoning.
7 Chopped hard-boiled eggs, pinch of curry powder and a little chutney.
8 Chopped tongue, chopped beetroot and a little mayonnaise to bind.
9 Flaked cooked haddock, chopped lettuce and chopped gherkin — bind together with butter.
10 Flaked cooked kippers — be careful to take out all bones — little butter, squeeze of lemon juice and lots of pepper.

Ribbon sandwiches

The picture opposite shows ribbon sandwiches. To make these, butter slices of brown and white bread; spread a slice of white bread and butter with filling, top with buttered brown bread, more filling, then white bread. Cut into fingers or other shapes.

Savoury cheese spread

Preparation: few minutes
No cooking

If a very soft creamy consistency is desired, add a little milk or thin cream to the mixture.

2 oz. butter | 2–3 oz. grated cheese | seasoning

Cream the butter, add the grated cheese and seasoning.

To vary
1 For a more definite flavour, use crumbled Danish Blue cheese.
2 Add finely chopped ham, chicken or shellfish to the mixture above.
3 Blend chopped watercress and/or grated raw carrot to the spread.

Double filled sandwiches

Preparation: few minutes
No cooking

The two lists at the right show happy partnerships in fillings. Choose one from list 1 and the filling opposite from list 2.

filling 1	filling 2
shrimps in mayonnaise, *page 207*	scrambled egg mixed with little curry powder and chutney
minced boiled gammon *or* ham	finely shredded cabbage in mayonnaise, *page 207*
peanut butter	crisp fried bacon sliced apple
sliced liver sausage	apple chutney and grilled bacon
sardines with sliced cucumber	sliced beetroot
chopped hard boiled eggs with anchovies	mayonnaise, *page 207* and chopped celery heart
pickled herring, sliced onion	sliced tomatoes

1 Butter 1 slice of bread, then cover with the selected filling from the list named *filling 1*.
2 Butter *both* sides of a slice of bread, put over the filling.
3 Cover with a filling from the second list and a slice of buttered bread. Press down, cut into fingers or triangles.

Toasted sandwiches

Preparation: few minutes
Cooking: few minutes

Make sure the grill is very hot so the bread toasts quickly. Serve as soon as possible after the sandwiches are prepared, for toast quickly spoils and loses its crispness.

Left *Ribbon sandwiches*
Right *Hot and cold double decker toasted sandwiches*

1 Make sandwiches in the usual way, filling with cheese, fish, meat, or rashers of grilled bacon.
2 Put under the grill, brown on both sides, serve at once.
3 The double decker toasted sandwiches in the picture were made by toasting three slices of bread per person.
4 While still hot the bottom layer of toast was topped with grilled bacon, then a second layer of hot toast put on top.
5 This was covered with a slice of cheese and sliced tomatoes, heated under the grill until the cheese softened, and topped with a slice of toast and a slice of grilled tomato.
6 The second double decker sandwich was made of cold toast — use this while still crisp.
7 Spread with butter and fill the first layer with sliced ham and cheese, the second layer with tomato and lettuce.

223

Sandwich layer gâteau

Preparation: 20 minutes
Better if allowed to stand
No cooking
Makes 20 slices

Suggested fillings
3 eggs, scrambled, mixed with
1 rounded dessertspoon chopped
anchovy fillets, 1 level
dessertspoon chopped capers

2 oz. each lean ham, and cooked,
minced or chopped liver: bind
with 3 dessertspoons evaporated
milk, thin cream, top of the milk
or mayonnaise, page 207, and
season well to taste

4 oz. finely grated Cheddar
cheese mixed with 2 tablespoons
salad cream and 2 tablespoons
chopped watercress

1 Remove all crusts from a day-old sandwich loaf.
2 Cut into four long slices.

3 Sandwich with suggested fillings (see left).

4 Spread top and sides of filled loaf with a light coating of softened butter, or margarine, or cream cheese.
5 Cover with chopped walnuts or peanuts. You need about 4 oz. nuts for a large loaf, 2½ oz. for a small loaf.

6 Cover the top with a central row of sliced radishes, or stuffed olives, or wedges of tomato.
7 Chill before serving, as this makes it easier to slice.

Fried sandwiches

Preparation: few minutes
Cooking: few minutes

As a filling for fried sandwiches
try:
thin slices of ham and cheese
together
grated cheese mixed with grated
carrot
flaked cooked fish or chopped
meat mixed with a little sauce
to keep it moist

1 Make sandwiches in the usual way.
2 Fry steadily in a little fat on one side until brown, and then turn and fry on the second side.
3 Drain and serve

Note. The sandwiches should be drained on absorbent paper, i.e. kitchen roll or crumpled tissue paper.

Egg-coated sandwiches: make the sandwiches in the usual way, cut into neat fingers, then dip in beaten and well seasoned egg and fry as above.

Sandwich bake

Preparation: 12 minutes
Allow to stand 30 minutes before cooking
Cooking: approximately 1 hour
Serves 4

Secret of success
Do not use too hot an oven, for this would make the mixture curdle.

The purpose of using a dish of water, stage 7, is to prevent the bread mixture becoming too crisp.

3 oz. ham
4 thin slices of bread
8 oz. cottage cheese
1 teaspoon chopped onion

2 eggs
good sprinkling of pepper
½ level teaspoon salt

¾ pint milk
1 oz. butter
paprika, *optional*

1 Chop the ham finely.
2 Cut the crusts from the bread.
3 Blend cottage cheese, chopped ham and chopped onion and spread over 2 slices of bread, top with remaining slices.
4 Cut each sandwich into four, arrange in an ovenproof dish.
5 Whisk the eggs, pepper and salt and mix in the milk; pour over the sandwiches.
6 Dot the top with butter, dust with paprika, if used, and leave to stand for 30 minutes
7 Stand in a pan of hot water to half the depth of the dish of sandwich bake.
8 Cook in a slow oven (300°F., Gas Mark 2) for about 1 hour, until lightly set.
9 Garnish with parsley; serve hot with green vegetables or a crisp green salad.

Hamburger supper loaf

Preparation: 8–10 minutes
No delay
Cooking. 30 minutes
Serves 4

Secret of success
The method of heating the loaf at stage 8 makes sure this does not become over-browned.

1 onion
1 clove of garlic
12 oz. sausage meat
1 oz. butter

1 beef cube
¼ oz. cornflour
¼ pint water
1 tablespoon chopped parsley

1 French loaf, split lengthwise

to garnish
apple and tomato slices

1 Chop the onion and garlic very finely.
2 Fry the onion, garlic, and sausage meat in the melted butter, until golden brown.
3 Crush the beef cube and add to the meat mixture in the pan.
4 Stir in the cornflour and cook gently for a minute, then add the water.
5 Bring to the boil, cook for 1 minute, stirring constantly.
6 Finally, add the chopped parsley.
7 Divide the mixture in half, spread on the two halves of bread.
8 Garnish each portion with apple and tomato slices, then wrap in cooking foil.
9 Place on a baking sheet, and bake for about 20 minutes in a moderate oven (350–375°F., Gas Mark 4–5).

Carnival bacon flan

Preparation: 30–35 minutes
No delay
Cooking: 25 minutes
Serves 4–6

This can be served hot or cold; if serving cold, add the cold filling to the cold pastry.

8 oz. short crust pastry, *page 184*
4 oz. tiny button mushrooms
1½ oz. butter

2 tomatoes
6 oz. streaky bacon
2 hard-boiled eggs
few cooked peas

for the white sauce
1½ oz. butter
1½ oz. flour
salt and pepper
¾ pint milk

1 Roll out the pastry and line a Swiss roll tin.
2 Bake 'blind' in a hot oven for 20–25 minutes (425–450°F., Gas Mark 6–7).
3 Prepare the mushrooms, fry in the butter. Slice the tomatoes.
4 Cut the bacon into about 2-inch lengths. Form into bacon rolls (page 85) and grill.
5 Make the white sauce (page 143).
6 Slice the hard-boiled eggs.
7 Remove the pastry from the tin, and place on a serving dish.
8 Pour the white sauce on the base, then arrange all the above ingredients in lines lengthways.

Left *Sandwich bake*
Right *Carnival bacon flan*

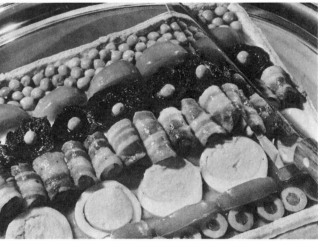

Egg dishes

How to cook eggs well

Most egg dishes can be spoiled by over-cooking, so make sure the family are ready before starting to cook the straightforward egg dishes.

Many people new to cooking find difficulty in cracking an egg without breaking the yolk — this is because they are afraid to give a sharp enough tap to the outside shell. If you have too small a crack on the shell, you need to exert too much pressure in opening the egg, and the chances are that the yolk WILL be broken. Tap the egg on the edge of a saucer, cup or basin and this will give you a clean break — or crack with a sharp knife.

Boiled eggs

No preparation
Cooking: 3½ minutes

Most people like their eggs just set, in which case they will take 3½ minutes. Allow 4 minutes if you know the eggs are very fresh. An egg required to be rather under-set and liquid should have about 3 minutes. A very firm egg, i.e. hard-boiled, needs about 7–10 minutes.

1 Put enough water into a small saucepan to cover the eggs.
2 Bring to the boil, then lower the eggs into the water.
3 Time the cooking carefully and serve at once. If you find the egg shells cracking, immediately put about 1 tablespoon vinegar into the water; this prevents the egg coming out of the shell and spoiling. You can adjust the cooking time according to taste.
4 When hard-boiled eggs are cooked, crack the shells and lower the eggs immediately into cold water. This prevents a dark ring forming round the yolk.

Note. The cooking time, left, produces a very lightly boiled egg.

Scotch eggs

Preparation: 12 minutes
Allow eggs to cook
Cooking: 15 minutes, plus time for boiling eggs
Serves 4

This makes a simple but pleasant hors d'oeuvre.

Secret of success
The flour-coating round the eggs makes sure the sausage meat clings to the eggs.
Do not under-cook the Scotch eggs at stage 5.

4 eggs	1 egg *for coating*	breadcrumbs
2 tablespoons flour	2–3 tablespoons milk *for*	deep fat *for frying*
12 oz. sausage meat	*coating*	

1 Hard boil the eggs, cool them. Shell, and then roll them lightly in flour.
2 Divide the sausage meat into four, press round the lightly-floured eggs.
3 Coat these with the egg and milk beaten together; roll each firmly in breadcrumbs.
4 Fry steadily in fat and drain.
5 Remember that the sausage meat has to cook, so do not hurry the frying process.
6 Cut each Scotch egg in half with a sharp knife dipped in hot water.
7 Serve hot with tomato sauce (page 209), or cold with salad.

Note. If taking Scotch eggs for a packed meal, do not halve as stage 6, for they keep a better shape if left whole.

Scotch eggs

226

Poached eggs

Preparation: 1 or 2 minutes
Cooking: 3½–4 minutes

Like all egg dishes, poached eggs must be served the moment they are cooked, so it is advisable to toast the bread while they cook.
Stages 1–4 give a neater looking but less light egg than stages 7–10.

| eggs | salt | butter and toast |
| margarine *or* butter | | |

1 Crack the shells and pour the eggs into a cup or saucer.
2 If you have a proper egg-poacher put a piece of margarine or butter, about the size of a hazelnut, into each cup, adding a pinch of salt, if wished. Heat the poacher over water — the margarine or butter MUST be hot before the eggs are added. Gradually add eggs.
3 Put on lid and allow water in the pan to boil steadily for about 3½–4 minutes.
4 Slide the eggs on to buttered toast.
5 *Or:* put a small piece of margarine or butter into an old cup and stand it in a pan of boiling water to melt.
6 Pour in egg, put a lid on the saucepan and cook as before.
7 *Or:* this method is preferred by many people as it gives a lighter result; bring a good ½ pint water to the boil in a saucepan or frying pan.
8 Add 1 dessertspoon vinegar, if wished, for this prevents the egg whites from spreading. Put in a good pinch of salt.
9 Slide eggs into boiling water, leave for 3 minutes, or until white is set.
10 Insert spoon or fish slice, drain the eggs carefully and put on toast.

Poached eggs with mushrooms

Preparation: 5 minutes
Cooking: 5–6 minutes

1 Fry sliced mushrooms in hot butter.
2 Pile on toast.
3 Top with a poached egg. For methods of poaching eggs see above.

Note. If mushrooms are fresh and of good quality, do not peel, simply trim ends off the stalks, wash well, dry, then slice. An excellent breakfast dish.

Poached eggs in cheese sauce
(eggs mornay)

Preparation: 12 minutes
Cooking: 12 minutes
Serves 4

Secret of success
Make sauce before poaching eggs, so these are not over-cooked.

| 4 poached eggs | 4 slices of toast | ½ pint cheese sauce |
| 1 oz. butter | | |

1 Put the poached eggs on buttered toast, or into a heatproof dish.
2 Cover with a cheese sauce (page 143).
3 Sprinkle with grated cheese.
4 Brown very quickly under a hot grill; this dish is often known as eggs mornay.

Poached eggs au gratin: proceed as above, then top the sauce with breadcrumbs and grated cheese and brown under the grill.

To separate egg whites

Preparation: 1 minute
No cooking

There are several ways in which the yolk and white of an egg can be separated.

1 a) Crack egg shell, then pull the two halves gently apart. Do this very slowly so that the egg white falls into a container.
b) When you have broken the egg, if you think there is any white left in the shell, tip the yolk from one half to the other of the shell — all the time allowing white to drop out.
c) Put the yolk into another container, then run your little finger round the inside of both halves of the shell to remove any egg white inside.
2 a) Break the egg carefully on to a flat plate or saucer.
b) Put an egg cup over the yolk and hold this down firmly.
c) Pour the white into a separate container.

Scrambled eggs

Preparation: 2–3 minutes
No delay
Cooking: few minutes

Allow 1 egg per person, or for more generous helping 3 eggs for 2 people

Secret of success
Since scrambled eggs continue cooking in the hot pan, it is a good idea to have the toast all ready before you start to cook the eggs, and to remove the pan from heat before the eggs are completely set.

| eggs | milk, *optional* | margarine *or* butter |
| salt and pepper | | |

1 Beat the eggs lightly, adding a good pinch of salt and pepper. Add 1 dessertspoon milk for each egg; some people prefer a firmer mixture with no milk added.
2 Heat a piece of margarine or butter, the size of a small walnut, in a saucepan, pour in the eggs, cook gently, stirring well from the bottom until the mixture starts to thicken.
3 Turn the heat very low and continue cooking.

Scrambled egg with chicken
1 Chop tiny pieces of chicken, allow 1 tablespoon to each egg.
2 Heat the chicken in the milk and butter.
3 Add the beaten seasoned egg: cook as before.

Scrambled egg with ham
As with chicken, but as ham is slightly salt, reduce quantity of seasoning.

Scrambled egg with tomatoes
1 Allow a good sized tomato for each 2 eggs.
2 Skin, thinly slice and heat in the butter.
3 Beat the eggs; use no milk: season and cook as before.

Eggs in baked potatoes

Preparation: 8 minutes
No delay
Cooking: 1¼ hours
Serves 2

Secret of success
Season potatoes well.

| 2 large potatoes | ½ oz. butter | 1–2 oz. cheese, grated |
| salt and pepper | 2 eggs | 1 oz. breadcrumbs |

1 Scrub and bake large potatoes (page 135).
2 When cooked, take off a slice and scoop out the greater part of the inside. Put into a basin, mash this, season well, add no milk but a little butter, if wished; press back into the case, making a neat shape.
3 Break the eggs carefully and put an egg into each case.
4 Top with grated cheese, seasoning, breadcrumbs; add a few tiny pieces butter.
5 Place in a hot oven (425–450°F., Gas Mark 6–7) until the cheese is brown and the eggs set. This takes approximately 15 minutes.

Mushroom omelette

Preparation: 10–12 minutes
Cooking: about 10 minutes

Secret of success
Cook quickly: serve at once.

allow for each person:	2 eggs	knob of butter
2 oz. mushrooms	salt and pepper	
milk *or* butter *for cooking*		

1 Wash and skin the mushrooms if desired (see page 131), then cut into slices.
2 Either simmer in a little milk for approximately 5–6 minutes and season well, or cook in butter until tender.
3 Continue as recipe, putting the *hot* mushrooms into omelette; *or* the cooked, well drained mushrooms can be mixed with the eggs before cooking.

Ham omelette

Preparation: few minutes
Cooking: 5 minutes

Cheaper quality ham can be used, or this is a good way to use up canned luncheon meat.

allow for each person	salt and pepper	good knob of butter
1 oz. ham		
2 eggs		

1 Chop the ham or luncheon meat and mix with the beaten eggs and seasoning.
2 Heat a knob of butter and pour in the egg mixture.
3 Allow about ½ minute for it to 'set' in a skin at the bottom, then tilt the pan and push the egg liquid backwards and forwards, so that it drops to the bottom of the pan. Continue until set (see opposite).
4 Fold or roll away from handle, and tip on to a hot dish.

Tortilla

Preparation: see method
Cooking: see method

To make tortilla (Spanish omelette) choose the ingredients to add to the eggs, i.e. left-over vegetables, ham, shellfish, etc. If preferred, prepare fresh vegetables for this omelette. Dice potatoes, chop or slice onions, crush garlic, chop red and green pepper, etc. Toss in a little oil, add a small quantity of stock and simmer until tender, season well. Add to the beaten eggs and cook as an ordinary omelette, opposite, but do not fold, serve as a flat omelette.

To make a perfect omelette

Preparation: 4–5 minutes
Cooking: 3–4 minutes for plain omelette

Secret of success
Make sure the butter is hot at stage 3.
Cook the omelette quickly, otherwise it will be tough,
Serve as soon as cooked,
Fillings and flavourings should be prepared BEFORE you start to cook the omelette.

Herbs: add a good pinch of dried herbs or 1 or 2 teaspoons freshly chopped herbs – thyme, sage, mint, parsley – to eggs *before* cooking.

Cheese: either add about 1 oz. grated cheese to each egg before cooking, or, to give a more moist filling, put grated cheese into omelette just before folding or rolling.

Chicken: as ham omelette, opposite, using chicken.

Tomato: fry skinned tomatoes until soft, season well, and put most of the tomato mixture into the omelette before folding or rolling; top the omelette with the remainder.

Prawn or Shrimp: heat shrimps or prawns in a little butter or white sauce, drain, and put into omelette before rolling or folding.

eggs
water
      salt and pepper
      butter

1 Break the eggs into a basin. Allow 3–4 eggs for 2 people. To give a light omelette a small amount of water can be used, and if you rinse out the egg shells with the water no egg is wasted.

2 Season and beat the eggs lightly.

3 Heat a good knob of butter in an omelette pan. Allow 1 oz. for a small sized omelette.
4 Pour in the beaten eggs.

5 Allow egg mixture to set into a thin skin, then, using either a fork or palette knife, push egg away from the sides, at the same time tilting omelette pan so the liquid egg from the top falls into the pan.

6 Put in the filling (see left and page 230 for suggestions).

7 Take a palette knife and insert it under the omelette, near the handle. Either fold in half, as illustrated, or roll slightly; the thickness of the filling determines which you will do. Always fold, or roll, away from the handle for easy removal from the pan.

8 Hold the hot plate or dish in your left hand and tip the omelette on to this.
9 Serve as quickly as possible.

229

To make a soufflé

Preparation: approximately
20 minutes. No delay
Cooking: approximately
35 minutes
Serves 4

Prepare soufflé dish by greasing it well with butter. You need a 7-inch soufflé dish to make sure mixture will not rise above level of the dish without needing any support. If using a 6-inch soufflé dish, it is a good idea to tie a band of buttered greaseproof paper above the top of the dish, to support the soufflé as it rises.

Secret of success
Do not use too great a weight of filling otherwise the soufflé will be heavy.

Colour picture, page 218

for an economical soufflé	½ pint milk	filling, *see below*
2 oz. butter	salt and pepper	3 eggs
2 oz. flour		

for a lighter soufflé	salt and pepper	3 egg yolks
1 oz. butter	filling, *see below*	4 egg whites
1 oz. flour		
¼ pint milk		

1 Heat the butter in a large saucepan.
2 Stir in the flour and cook for several minutes.
3 Gradually add the milk, bring to the boil and cook until thickened. This will produce a really thick sauce (panada) so stir vigorously. Season.
4 Add the prepared filling, see below and colour picture 1, page 218, which shows the grated Dutch cheese being added.
5 Separate the yolks from the whites of the eggs. Beat yolks and add to mixture.
6 Beat the egg whites very stiffly. Fold the egg whites into the mixture in the saucepan, see picture 2, page 218.
7 Spoon the mixture into the soufflé dish, see picture 3, page 218.
8 Bake in the centre of a moderately hot oven (400°F., Gas Mark 5) for about 35 minutes, until well risen and brown. The lighter soufflé will take about 5 minutes less to cook. *Serve at once*, see picture 4, page 218.

Fillings for soufflés
Mushrooms: 3–4 oz. mushrooms, 1 oz. butter. Chop the mushrooms and cook until tender in the butter.
Cheese: use a strong Parmesan cheese or grated Cheddar cheese. Allow 2–3 oz. Parmesan, 4 oz. Cheddar, or use all Dutch cheese for a creamy texture.
Ham: chop 3 oz. cooked ham very finely.
Fish: about 3 oz. cooked finely flaked smoked haddock is excellent.

Sweet soufflé fillings
Chocolate: use ½ oz. flour and ½ oz. cocoa instead of 1 oz. flour. Add 1–2 oz. sugar and no seasoning.
Coffee: use ¼ or ½ pint strong coffee and 2 oz. sugar. Omit milk and seasoning.
Pineapple: use ¼–½ pint pineapple juice (from canned pineapple) together with 1 oz. sugar. Omit milk and seasoning. Add 3 oz. finely chopped canned pineapple.

Soufflé omelette

Preparation: few minutes
Cooking: see method

This produces a very light impressive looking omelette that can be served as a sweet or savoury.

Sweet fillings
Banana and nut: heat sliced banana in a little butter with chopped walnuts or hazelnuts. Sprinkle with sugar, see picture.
Jam: add a little sugar to taste before cooking, then fill omelette with hot jam. Fold and dust with sieved icing sugar.

Separate the egg yolks and whites. Beat the yolks with a small quantity of water, milk or cream (see quantities under plain omelette, page 229). Add seasoning or sugar to taste. Fold in stiffly whisked egg whites. Heat butter in the omelette pan, as page 229, add eggs and allow to cook for 2 minutes. Since this mixture is very thick, the best results are obtained if the pan is placed at this stage under a moderate grill. When egg mixture is set on top, add filling, fold and serve. *Savoury fillings – page 229.*

Sweet soufflé omelette with banana and nut filling

Breakfast dishes

While the dishes on the next pages are particularly associated with breakfast time, they can of course be served at other meals. In the same way, many of the recipes in other parts of this book are very suitable for breakfast.

Speed is often of more importance at breakfast time than anything else, so it is advisable to lay the table and prepare as many things as possible the night before, but do not leave perishable foods exposed.

To prepare grapefruit

Preparation: 6–7 minutes
No delay
No cooking

1 Cut the grapefruit in half, allowing half per person.
2 Using either a small pair of scissors, or a sharp vegetable or fruit knife, slit between the sections of fruit, so making them easy to remove with a spoon.
3 Take out the centre pith and 'core' and serve.

If you are sure everyone likes sugar, sprinkle a little over the fruit and let it stand for as long as possible; this will give it a better flavour. Remember though, that the fruit will lose Vitamin C.

To prepare fruit juices

You can buy cans of fruit juices which taste best if well chilled, so if you have a refrigerator put the unopened can in this the night before.

Fresh fruit loses its Vitamin C content as a result of exposure to the air for long periods, so do not squeeze oranges for breakfast the night before.

To prepare cereals

These can be served with hot or cold milk, but are also extremely good if topped with cooked, fresh or canned fruit.

Make sure you close the packets of cereal as much as possible after use, since the contents will soften if in contact with the air. If by chance they have become soft, spread the cereal out on to a flat baking tray and heat for 6–8 minutes in a moderately hot oven (400°F., Gas Mark 5). Allow to cool on the tray, then return to the packet.

Porridge

Preparation: few minutes
No delay
Cooking: see below and method

The modern quick-cooking rolled oats are so popular that most people today make their porridge with them.
If you wish to make porridge with oatmeal, use 3 oz. to 1 pint of water. Cook very slowly, adding salt to taste, for approximately 40 minutes. A double saucepan prevents any possibility of the porridge burning. This makes a thick porridge. You may like to use more water or less oatmeal.

| 2 cups quick-cooking rolled oats | salt to taste | 5 cups milk *or* water |

1 Add the rolled oats and salt to the boiling milk or water.
2 Boil for 50–60 seconds, stirring continuously if using milk.
3 When water is used, stir occasionally.
4 Turn off heat, cover and allow to stand for 5 minutes.
5 Stir and serve.
6 For thicker porridge use more oats; for thinner porridge use less oats.
7 For creamier, smoother porridge, boil for 2 or more minutes, stirring as necessary.

Muesli: mix the uncooked rolled oats with chopped nuts, diced fresh fruit, dried fruit and natural yoghourt or milk, and serve cold. This may be prepared overnight if desired.

To make good toast

Preparation: 1 or 2 minutes
No delay
Cooking: few minutes

1 Put bread on grid in the grill pan, and place it under the grill until brown.
2 Turn it over and do the same on the other side.
3 If you have an electric toaster, follow directions for your particular make.
4 When toast is cooked, do not lay it flat on plates or the kitchen table, for hot toast causes moisture to form and this would make it limp and soggy. Give toast a good tap on each side to let the steam out, then stand it up at once in a toast rack. If you have no rack, then support it against the back of the cooker until cold. Do not make too soon before breakfast for it spoils with waiting.
5 For really soft toast, spread with butter when it is cooked.

Continental breakfast

A plain breakfast of coffee, hot rolls, fruit and jam or marmalade is becoming more and more popular. In order to make sure the rolls really are crisp and fresh, allow about 10 minutes' heating in the oven. Croissants are fairly easy to obtain from good bakers.
To make good coffee and tea — see pages 277 to 278.

Cooking bacon

Preparation: 1 minute
No delay
Cooking: 3–8 minutes

Back, streaky, collar or gammon rashers are all recommended for frying. If you want thin rashers, ask for a No. 3 cut. Gammon rashers, however, are usually cut a little thicker.
If you prefer to grill bacon, choose just the same cuts as for frying and cook under a fairly hot grill.
To prevent gammon rashers curling, do not pre-heat the grill.

Fried bacon
1 Cut off the rind with kitchen scissors — this is often useful for the stockpot when making soup.
2 When using streaky bacon, be sure to cut out the bone from each side of the rasher.
3 If the bacon is very fat, snip the fat through at intervals so that it lies flat when cooking.
4 To get the best results, put the bacon into a COLD frying pan and arrange the rashers of bacon so that the lean overlaps the fat. This means that the lean is kept moist and well 'basted' by the fat.
5 Cook for a few minutes only for thin rashers, turning it until it is as crisp as you like it. There is no need to add fat to the pan, as bacon will make its own, unless very lean.

Grilled bacon
1 Use the grid of the grill pan and mushrooms, tomatoes, etc., can be cooked in the pan below.
2 It may be necessary to start the mushrooms and tomatoes with a knob of butter or margarine, and when half-cooked to put the grid with the bacon over. In this way they should then be ready to serve together.

Bacon and eggs

Preparation: few minutes
No delay
Cooking: few minutes

Secret of success
Have the fat sufficiently hot to set eggs quickly, but not so hot that it makes a crisp skin.

1 Fry the bacon in the pan as directed above, until as crisp as you like it.
2 If you have room in the pan, you can pull the bacon to one side and cook the eggs in the space that is left.
3 If not, transfer the bacon to a hot dish, keep hot in the oven.
4 Make sure there is enough fat in the bottom of the frying pan; if not, put in a little more.
5 Break the eggs into a saucer or a cup.

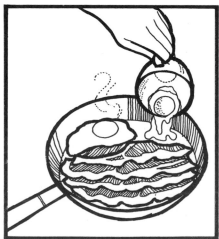

6 Put one egg in and allow it to set for a moment in the hot fat before adding the second.

7 Cook the eggs steadily until just set. If you like a crisp skin you can have a slightly higher heat.

8 If you like the type of fried eggs that are covered with a skin, spoon a little hot fat over the yolks while cooking.

Order of cooking foods for breakfast

Eggs, because they require the least cooking, are generally cooked last. The best order of cooking would be:

your *bacon* first, and keep hot if necessary;
mushrooms and *tomatoes* tend to put a sediment at the bottom of the pan, so if you plan to have these with eggs you can cook them in the pan after bacon, then wipe out the sediment, add a little more fat before putting in the eggs *or* they can be cooked in a separate pan;
fried bread leaves no sediment, so you can cook this after bacon, put on a dish to keep hot and then cook the *eggs*.

Bacon and mushrooms

Preparation: few minutes
No delay
Cooking: 10–15 minutes

There is no need to skin mushrooms — wash and dry, trim stalks.

To fry
1 Fry the bacon until cooked, remove from pan and keep hot.
2 Add a little fat if necessary before cooking mushrooms, then fry steadily for a few minutes.

To grill
1 Heat a little fat in the grill pan, turn the mushrooms in this and cook for 2–3 minutes.
2 Place the bacon on the grid of the pan, then complete the cooking.

Bacon and sausages

Preparation: few minutes
No delay
Cooking: 15 minutes

Allow enough time to cook sausages thoroughly; they take 10–15 minutes steady heating.

1 Cook the sausages first, either grilling or frying them, before cooking bacon.
2 Whether grilling or frying, remember to turn the sausages at regular intervals so they become evenly brown; kitchen tongs are the most efficient 'tool' to use.
3 Frozen sausages do not need defrosting before cooking.

Sausage cakes: add 1 egg to each 1 lb. sausage meat, together with a little chopped parsley; form into cakes and cook as sausages.

Bacon and tomatoes

Preparation: few minutes
No delay
Cooking: 8–10 minutes

Add a pinch of sugar to the tomatoes, as well as seasoning.

1 Cook tomatoes after bacon and eggs, since they tend to make the pan sticky, or cook as suggested above, before the eggs, and wipe out the pan.
2 When grilling, the tomatoes can be put in the pan under the bacon.
3 Canned peeled tomatoes are excellent with bacon. Heat these separately in a saucepan; the liquid from the can may be used, or saved to add to a stew.

Note. Canned tomatoes are generally plum-shaped; these have a particularly good flavour in cooking.

Bacon and scrambled egg flan

The picture below shows an interesting way to serve bacon and eggs. Make a flan case with short crust pastry, and bake until golden brown. Fry diced bacon in a little cooking fat; scramble eggs until set. Arrange in the flan and serve at once. This can be served for breakfast, but is even better for a light supper dish.

Bacon and scrambled egg flan

Potato cakes

Preparation: 10 minutes
Cooking: 4–5 minutes
Serves 4

Potato cakes are both an excellent way of using mashed potato, and an inexpensive and satisfying part of a breakfast meal. To save time, you can prepare them the night before.

8 oz. mashed potatoes	flour	*for frying*
salt and pepper	1 egg, *optional*	fat

1 Mash the potatoes, adding seasoning and a little flour if rather soft. For extra richness you can add an egg, then enough flour to make a consistency firm enough to handle.
2 Form the mixture into flat round cakes.
3 Coat in a little flour and fry in the hot bacon fat, or hot cooking fat, until crisp and golden brown.

Note. Dehydrated potatoes can be used to make potato cakes. Prepare as directions on the packet, but use slightly *less* liquid than usual.

Kippers

Preparation: few minutes
No delay
Cooking: approximately 5–10 minutes

Allow 1 large or 2 small kippers per person

Cut off the heads, then wash and dry kippers. Either cook under the grill, fry, or cook in hot water. The first method will appeal to those who like their kippers crisp, the last to those who like them soft and rather underdone.
Cook frozen kippers as fresh; there is no need to defrost these.

To grill
1 Heat the grill, put the fish on the rack, with a small knob of margarine on each fish.
2 Cook rapidly for about 5 minutes. You need not turn the fish.

To fry
1 Heat a little margarine in the frying pan, and fry the fish on the underside first for about 5 minutes.
2 Turn and cook for the same time.
When grilling or frying, serve on hot plates with any liquid left from cooking poured over.

To cook in hot water
1 Stand the kippers in a large jug, then pour over boiling water.
2 Leave for about 5 minutes. Drain, put on to hot plates and put a knob of margarine on top, or put under a hot grill for 1 minute.

Bloaters

These are prepared and cooked in the same way as herrings (page 52). They are, however, very salty, so no seasoning should be added while cooking.

Kedgeree

Kedgeree

Preparation: few minutes
No delay

Cooking: 10 minutes, plus time for cooking rice
Serves 2

Secret of success
Do not over-cook rice, etc., at stage 3.

4 oz. cooked smoked haddock	3–4 oz. cooked long grain rice	*to garnish* parsley sprigs
1 hard-boiled egg	pinch of cayenne pepper	lemon quarters, *optional*
	pinch of salt	

1 Flake the fish coarsely with a fork.
2 Slice the egg white, sieve the yolk and put on one side for garnishing.
3 With a fork, mix the flaked fish, sliced egg white, cooked rice and seasoning in a saucepan over moderate heat until hot, adding a little milk if necessary.
4 Pile the mixture into a hot entrée dish, garnish with the parsley and sieved egg yolk, and serve at once with lemon quarters, if liked.

To vary
Use a more generous amount of fish, i.e. about 12 oz. This dish will then be sufficient to serve 3–4.

Bacon, pancakes filled with apple sauce and scrambled eggs, see pages 232, 212 and 228

Top *Swiss roll made by the whisking method, see pages 255–7*
Centre *Fruit cake made by the rubbing in method, see pages 238–9*
Bottom *Chocolate cake made by the creaming method, see pages 242–252*

Cakes

Normally, if you are an accomplished cook, you may not bother to weigh very accurately. However, when making cakes it is important to *weigh* every ingredient. A well made cake has a perfect balance between fat, sugar, flour, etc., and if you add or subtract any of these, by design or accident, the quality of the cake may be spoiled. Naturally, when you have made the cake once or twice you can adjust the flavour to suit your own purpose. At the beginning of the book is an oven chart. It is stressed, under this, that the temperatures and setting are only approximate. It is particularly important to consult your own oven guide, to make sure that you are baking cakes at the temperature that is best in your own particular cooker.

Preparing tins

Tins you use for baking cakes are very important: look after them well.
1 Unless stated to the contrary, tins should be greased and then floured.
2 *To grease tins* use oil, melted fat or butter. To melt fat, stand in a cup or basin over hot water. Coat tins evenly with the oil or fat on a pastry brush. Never use more oil or fat than necessary.
3 *To flour tins* shake flour from a spoon or flour dredger. Tap the tin from side to side so that it becomes thinly coated with flour. Tap away any surplus flour.
4 For a rich fruit cake, or one rather inclined to stick, line with greaseproof paper. Stand the tin on the paper and draw round it, cut the paper and put into the bottom of the tin. Cut a strip of paper the length of the circumference of the tin, then cut it up about $\frac{1}{2}$ inch at $\frac{1}{2}$-inch intervals. This edge makes sure you will have a neat fold when it is put into the cake tin. Put into the tin with the cut edge towards the bottom. Press this firmly against the base of the tin. Grease the paper, but do not flour.
5 When tins are new, wipe out carefully, then grease efficiently — lard and cooking fat are both excellent. Put into a warm oven, heat gently. Remove and wipe away surplus fat with a soft cloth or kitchen tissue. Put the tins away.
6 After using the tins try NOT to wash them; instead wipe out with a soft cloth or kitchen tissue immediately you take out the cake.
7 If you wash tins, wipe dry, put into warm place for several hours before storing.
8 Cakes are easier to remove from tins and less likely to 'stick' if you wait a minute or two before removing, to allow them to shrink slightly away from the tin.

To test if cakes are cooked

1 With a light type of cake, the best method of testing is to press lightly in the centre; if the cake feels firm and there is no impression of your finger, then it is ready to come out of the oven.
2 The second test is to see if the cake has shrunk very slightly away from the sides of the tin.
3 With a rich fruit cake, press as described above and then take the cake out of the oven and listen very carefully. If no sound is heard then the cake is quite cooked.
4 You can insert a warm skewer into the cake; if it comes out sticky the cake is still uncooked.

Various methods of making cakes

There are various ways in which cakes can be mixed.

1 *Rubbing in method* (pages 238–9).
2 *Melting method*. This is generally used for gingerbreads (pages 240–1).
3 *Creaming method*. Use for a variety of light and rich cakes (pages 242–252 and 258).
4 *Whisking method*. This to many people is the most difficult. It does need care in incorporating the ingredients (pages 255–7).

To make cakes by rubbing in method

This is a very easy and not particularly 'temperamental' way of making cakes. Generally speaking, cakes made by this method should be eaten up fairly quickly as they are not meant to keep. Butter, margarine or cooking fat are suitable. White sugar should be used.

Types of cakes made by rubbing in method
1 Rock buns, jam buns and luncheon cakes.
2 Plain fruit cakes.

Rock buns

Preparation: 10 minutes
No delay
Cooking: 12–15 minutes
Makes about 12

Secret of success
Check the consistency carefully at stage 5. If too soft a mixture, the cakes spread badly; too stiff a mixture means dry cakes.

8 oz. flour (with plain flour use 3 level teaspoons baking powder)	4 oz. margarine *or* cooking fat 4 oz. sugar 4 oz. mixed dried fruit	1 *or* 2 eggs little milk sugar *for coating*

1 Sieve together the flour and baking powder, if used, into a large bowl.
2 Rub in fat until the mixture resembles breadcrumbs.
3 Add the sugar and dried fruit.

4 Stir in the egg or eggs, using a knife.
5 Stir the milk in gradually — you need approximately 4 tablespoons if using 1 egg, 2 tablespoons with 2 eggs. The mixture should drop from the knife if shaken very sharply.

6 Take up small portions of mixture between two forks. Put on to greased flat baking tins, allowing plenty of room for the cakes to spread.

7 Sprinkle with sugar before baking, if wished, or this can be done after baking.
8 Bake for 12–15 minutes near the top of a hot oven (425–450°F., Gas Mark 6–7). If baking two trays of buns, you may need to change them round halfway through cooking, or move the lower tray up in the oven after removing the top tray.
9 Cool for 2–3 minutes on the tray, as the buns are very crisp and short.
10 Sprinkle with sugar, if not already coated before baking, and lift on to a wire cooling tray.

Jam buns

Preparation: 10 minutes
No delay
Cooking: 12–15 minutes
Makes about 12

Use the same ingredients as for rock buns above, but omit the dried fruit, and use a little jam.

1 Method as for rock buns – until stage 3. Add sugar only.
2 When the mixture is on the baking trays, make a small 'dent' in the centre of each bun, using a fork or teaspoon.
3 Put a small amount of jam in the 'dent'.
4 Pull the cake mixture round the jam with a fork or spoon.
5 Bake as rock buns.

Luncheon cake

Preparation: 10 minutes
No delay
Cooking: 1–1¼ hours
Makes 12 slices

Use the same ingredients as for rock buns on facing page, but add a little extra milk.
This makes an excellent family cake, see picture below.

1 Method as for rock buns, but add about 5 tablespoons milk instead of 4, or 2½ instead of 2.
2 Grease and flour a 1-lb. loaf tin or 6-inch cake tin.
3 Put in the mixture, smooth flat on top.
4 Sprinkle with castor sugar.
5 Bake for 1–1¼ hours in the centre of a moderate oven (350–375°F., Gas Mark 4–5).
6 The cake is cooked when it feels quite firm, and has shrunk away from the sides. You may need to reduce the heat after 45 minutes if the cake is over-browning.

Date cake or cakes: use recipe as for rock cakes and luncheon cake, but instead of 4 oz. dried fruit use 4–6 oz. chopped dates. The grated rind of 1 lemon or orange adds flavour.

Larger cake (*as colour picture page 236*): use 12 oz. flour and all other ingredients in proportion (see rock buns and luncheon cake). Put into a 7½–8-inch cake tin and bake for nearly 1½ hours.

Streusel coffee cake

Preparation: 20 minutes – allow filling to cool
Cooking: 25–30 minutes
Makes 8–10 slices

Secret of success
As this is a 'crumbly' type of cake handle carefully at stage 12.

Eat when fresh.
A little icing sugar may be sieved over the top.

for the filling and topping
1 oz. flour
1 oz fine semolina
2 level teaspoons cinnamon
2 oz. demerara sugar
1½ oz. chopped nuts (almonds, walnuts *or* hazelnuts)

1½ oz. butter

for the cake
3 oz plain flour
3 oz. fine semolina
3 level teaspoons baking powder

pinch of salt
1 level teaspoon cinnamon
1 level teaspoon ginger
3 oz. castor sugar
2 oz butter
1 egg, beaten
6 tablespoons milk

To make the filling
1 Sift together flour, semolina and cinnamon.
2 Stir in the sugar and chopped nuts.
3 Melt the butter; stir into the other ingredients.
4 Set aside to cool whilst making up the cake.

To make the cake
5 Sift together the flour, semolina, baking powder, salt, spices and sugar.
6 Rub in the butter until the mixture is like fine crumbs.
7 Stir in the beaten egg and milk to make a very soft dropping consistency.
8 Have ready a shallow 7-inch square cake tin, greased and lined at the bottom with greased paper.
9 Spread half the cake mixture in the tin, and scatter a layer of filling over.
10 Cover with remaining cake mixture, level, then add rest of the topping mixture.
11 Bake in the centre of a moderate to moderately hot oven (375–400°F., Gas Mark 5) until firm, about 25–30 minutes.
12 Cool in the tin (about 10 minutes), turn out carefully, serve warm.

Left *Rock buns, Jam buns and Luncheon cake*
Right *Streusel coffee cake*

To make cakes by melting method

Types of cake made by melting method
Gingerbreads of all kinds, parkin.

1 Heat the ingredients together in a saucepan, but be careful not to boil too long or the mixture evaporates and the consistency of the cake is altered.
2 The flour should always be well sieved before adding the melted ingredients.
3 Beat fairly vigorously when adding the melted ingredients to the flour, etc.
4 Do not be worried by the fact that the mixture looks very 'wet'. You will find it is perfectly all right in cooking. On the other hand, do not be depressed by the fact that this type of cake may not rise very dramatically when cooking. It is quite permissible for it to be flat on top.
5 Butter, margarine, lard, dripping, cooking fat are all suitable.
6 White sugar (granulated or castor) or brown sugar can be used.

Spiced gingerbread

Preparation: 10 minutes
No delay
Cooking: 1¼ hours
Makes 8–10 slices

This cake makes a delicious dessert topped with apple purée and cream.

Secrets of success
Bake slowly at stage 4 so that the cake, with its high percentage of syrup and treacle, does not burn.
Store in an airtight container and leave for at least a day before cutting.

4 oz. margarine
2 oz. soft brown sugar
6 oz. black treacle
2 oz. golden syrup
8 oz. plain flour

½ level teaspoon salt
1 level teaspoon bicarbonate of soda
2 level teaspoons ground ginger

1 level teaspoon mixed spice
2 eggs
¼ pint milk

1 Put fat, sugar, treacle and syrup into a pan and heat gently until fat melts. Cool.
2 Meanwhile, sift dry ingredients into a bowl, make a well in centre and add eggs and milk.

3 Slowly pour in syrup mixture, stir, without beating, until ingredients are well blended.

4 Turn mixture quickly into a greased and paper-lined 8-inch square cake tin (page 237) and bake in the centre of a slow oven (300°F., Gas Mark 2) for about 1¼ hours. Test by pressing (page 237).
5 Remove from tin *when cool*.

Raisin gingerbread

Preparation: 12 minutes
No delay
Cooking: 45–50 minutes
Makes 8 squares

Secret of success
Like most gingerbread, this improves with storage.

٭ you can use up the white of egg for meringues, page 166.

4 oz. seedless raisins
2 oz. butter *or* margarine
4 tablespoons black treacle
2 oz. granulated sugar
5 oz. plain flour
½ level teaspoon bicarbonate of soda
pinch of salt
1 level teaspoon ground ginger
1 level teaspoon cinnamon
1 egg yolk٭
⅜ pint milk
glacé icing, *page 247*, made with 6 oz. icing sugar, etc.

1 Plump the raisins by covering with cold water, bring to boil, cover and leave to stand for 5 minutes; drain and dry.
2 Melt the fat, treacle and sugar together in a saucepan, then allow to cool.
3 Sieve flour, bicarbonate of soda, salt and spices together, make a well in the centre, add the beaten egg, milk and syrup mixture and beat until smooth.
4 Add the raisins.
5 Pour into a greased and lined tin 12 inches by 8 inches.
6 Bake in the centre of a very moderate oven (325–350°F., Gas Mark 3) for 45–50 minutes.
7 Remove paper when cool. Cover with glacé icing. Allow icing to set, then cut into squares.

Moist orange cake

Use the recipe for spiced gingerbread (page 240), but instead of ginger use exactly the same amount of orange marmalade. You can use the grated rind of an orange and ¼ pint orange juice (or orange juice and water) in place of the milk, to give a pronounced orange flavour.

Yoghourt ginger cake with pashka

The ginger cake recipe below is made as the basic recipe opposite, with the following adjustments:
a) use 2 oz. black treacle and 6 oz. golden syrup instead of the 6 oz. black treacle and 2 oz. golden syrup; mix with 5 oz. (¼ pint) natural yoghourt instead of milk; add 3 oz. chopped blanched almonds at stage 2.
b) bake as the recipe opposite and leave for at least 1–2 days before cutting; split and fill with the following:
blend 3 tablespoons thick cream with 2 teaspoons lemon juice, 2–3 oz. sugar, 6 oz. sieved cottage cheese, 1 oz. chopped blanched almonds, 1 oz. mixed peel (chopped), 1 oz. seedless raisins and the grated rind of 1 lemon. Strain through muslin for 24 hours, use this thick mixture as a filling.

Yoghourt ginger cake with pashka

Cooling trays

In several of the pictures in this book you will see cakes, scones, etc., shown on cooling trays.
If you intend to do any baking it is essential to have a tray of this type, for it enables the cakes to cool with air circulating around them, so they do not become heavy at the bottom.
The wire grid from a grill pan makes a very good cooling tray, although it is inclined to be rather small.

To make cakes by creaming method

Types of cakes made by creaming method
1 Light sponges and soft types of cakes.
2 Plain fine textured cakes like Madeira.
3 Fruit cakes such as Dundee.
4 Rich fruit cakes such as Christmas cake.

1 It is very important that the fat and sugar are creamed very well. In this type of cake you can use butter or margarine (some of the soft types of margarine cream very quickly), or the modern cooking fat or shortening.
2 Do not melt the fat. If it is very hard, you can warm the bowl by putting hot water into it for a minute or so, but if you melt the fat it is impossible to get as light a mixture as one would desire. If by chance you do melt fat and it becomes oily, put it into a cool place to set again.
3 Unless stated to the contrary, castor sugar is better in this type of cake.
4 When adding eggs, care must be taken not to put them in too quickly or the mixture is likely to curdle — this means it looks rather spotty and appears to be separating.
5 Do not over-beat the flour. Fold this in gently, preferably with a metal spoon.
6 You will find a spoon the easiest way of creaming fat and sugar, unless you care to use your hands. This is a professional method and certainly softens fat in a very short time.
7 Use a slow speed with a mixer. Add the flour by hand.

Victoria sandwich

Preparation: 15–20 minutes
No delay
Cooking: approximately 20 minutes

Quantities of ingredients are often written as the weight of eggs in fat, sugar and flour. If you wish, you can still continue to weigh in this manner, putting the eggs — still in their shells — in the scales in place of weights. You are fairly safe, though, in assuming that the weight of an average egg is 2 oz.

use this quantity of flour for 7- or 7½-inch tins. Use 8 oz. flour, etc. for 8- or 9-inch tins. Use 4 oz. flour, etc., for 6- or 6½-inch tins.

6 oz. flour (with plain flour use 1½ level teaspoons baking powder)*

6 oz. margarine *or* butter
6 oz. castor sugar

3 medium to large eggs (if the eggs are unusually small allow 1 dessertspoon water to each egg to make up the extra liquid)

1 Sieve flour (if using self-raising flour) or flour and baking powder together.
2 Cream the fat and sugar until soft and white.
3 Break the eggs into a cup to ensure each one is fresh before beating thoroughly in a basin.
4 Add a little of the beaten egg to the creamed mixture and stir carefully until thoroughly blended.
5 Add more egg and beat again — continue until all the egg is used. If the mixture shows any sign of curdling, stir in a little flour.
Or you may find you get a better result by the following: add a little egg, beat well, add a little flour and stir gently. Continue in this way, adding egg and flour alternately until thoroughly mixed.
6 Grease and flour two 7-inch sandwich tins carefully, and divide the mixture equally between them. Spread slightly away from the centre so that the two halves will be flat.
7 Bake for a good 20 minutes in a moderate oven (350–375°F., Gas Mark 4–5). If using a gas oven, put the tins side by side on a shelf just above the 2 rungs from the top of the oven, or put one under the other. With an electric oven or solid fuel, put one about the second rung from the top and one the second rung from the bottom, or have the tins side by side on the same shelf.
8 First look to see if the cake has shrunk slightly from sides of tin, then test by pressing gently but firmly on top and if no impression is left by the finger the cake is ready to come out of the oven. Wait about 2 minutes for cakes to set.
9 Turn out of the tins on to a wire sieve. It is quite a good idea to give the tins a sharp tap on the table before attempting to turn out the cakes, so loosening the cakes away from the sides and bottom of the tins.

Other flavours for Victoria sandwich

It is possible to flavour a Victoria sandwich in many ways. Care must be taken that when you add flavour you do not spoil the consistency. For example, in a chocolate cake, because you add cocoa your liquid content must be higher, so put in a little extra liquid. On the other hand, if you add coffee essence, etc., you must use a little extra flour.
If you wish to give an orange or lemon flavour, remember the finely grated rind adds flavour without spoiling the balance of the recipe (see opposite).

Chocolate Victoria sandwich

Preparation: 10–15 minutes
No delay
Cooking: 20–25 minutes
Makes 8 slices

This is a deliciously light chocolate cake.

Secrets of success
Read the comments opposite on making good sandwich cakes.

6 oz. butter *or* margarine
6 oz. castor sugar
3 eggs

6 oz. flour (with plain flour use 1½ level teaspoons baking powder)

1½ level tablespoons cocoa
1½ tablespoons warm water
cream *or* butter icing

1 Cream the butter or margarine and sugar until soft, light and fluffy.
2 Beat in the eggs a little at a time.

3 Sieve well the flour, baking powder, if used, and cocoa.
4 Fold in the sieved flour and cocoa, adding sufficient warm water to form a soft dropping consistency.

5 Divide the mixture, and turn it into the two 7-inch sponge tins. If you are at all worried about cakes 'sticking' to tins, line bottom with round of greased greaseproof paper.

6 Bake in a moderate oven (350–375°F., Gas Mark 4) for 20–25 minutes (page 242, step 8 for way of testing a sandwich cake).
7 Cool on a wire tray. Remove paper while warm.
8 Fill with cream or chocolate butter icing.

Coffee Victoria sandwich

Use basic recipe page 242.
Makes 8 slices

1 Choose small eggs. If you cannot get small eggs and so use medium ones, add an extra ½ oz. flour.
2 Add 3 dessertspoons coffee essence. Beat it with the eggs.
If preferred, sieve 2–3 level teaspoons instant coffee powder with the flour. Ordinary drinking-strength coffee does not impart sufficient flavour.

Orange Victoria sandwich

Use basic recipe page 242.
Makes 8 slices

1 Add the grated top rind of 1 or 2 oranges when creaming fat and sugar.
2 Add 2 tablespoons orange juice to the eggs and beat well.
3 Use 6½ oz. flour if using small eggs.
Use 7 oz. flour if using medium to large eggs.

Lemon Victoria sandwich

Use basic recipe page 242.
Makes 8 slices

1 Add the grated top rind of 1 lemon when creaming fat and sugar.
2 Add 2 tablespoons lemon juice to the eggs and beat well.
3 Use 6½ oz. flour if using small eggs.
Use 7 oz. flour if using medium to large eggs.

Victoria sandwich cake in one tin

You may wish to bake a sandwich cake in one tin, in which case you must use a lower temperature.

1 Put the mixture into a 7- or 8-inch cake tin and bake this in the centre of a very moderate oven (325°F., Gas Mark 3).
2 Allow 50 minutes for an 8-inch tin. Allow 60 minutes for a 7-inch tin.

A smaller tin, which gives a deeper cake, needs a longer baking time.

Cream filled sandwich cake

The Victoria sandwich cake on page 242 is very suitable for filling with cream, butter icing (page 245) and fruit. In the photograph opposite, a sandwich cake has been filled with cream and raspberries and topped with whipped thick cream and fruit. When fresh cream is not available you can make a very good mock cream, as given below.

Mock cream

Preparation: 8–10 minutes
No delay
No cooking

Secret of success
Do not add the milk too quickly otherwise the mixture will curdle (separate).

2 oz. soft margarine *or* butter	3 oz. icing sugar, sieved	1½ tablespoons milk

1 Cream the fat and sugar together until very soft and light.
2 Add the milk very gradually, about a teaspoon at a time, beating well as you do so.

Quick method of making cakes

Preparation: under 5 minutes
No delay
Cooking: 20–25 minutes
Makes 8 slices

With the modern whipped-up cooking fats and soft margarines it is possible to make a very good sandwich cake by incorporating all the ingredients at the same time.

To make a deeper cake use 6 oz. flour, etc.; the quantities, right, produce a really deep cake in a 6-inch tin.

4 oz. flour (with plain flour use 1½ level teaspoons baking powder)	4 oz. cooking fat 2 eggs	4 oz. castor sugar

1 Line the bottom of two 7-inch sandwich tins (or one 8-inch tin) with greased greaseproof paper.
2 Sieve flour and baking powder, if used, into a mixing bowl.

3 Add all other ingredients to the bowl, and using a wooden spoon beat for about 1 minute until well mixed. (Beating will not make the mixture heavy.)

4 Divide the mixture evenly between the tins (or place in tin).

5 Place the small tins side by side on the centre shelf and bake for 20–25 minutes or bake one 8-inch sandwich cake for 35 minutes in a moderate oven (375°F., Gas Mark 4).

6 When cold, fill with jam and sprinkle with castor sugar.

244

Decorations for sponge cakes

Decorations and fillings for sponge or light creamed mixtures need to be soft and delicate. Cream is excellent, so is butter icing and fudge icing: see the recipes below.

Butter icing

Preparation: 8–10 minutes
No delay
No cooking

Secret of success
Do not soften the butter by melting.
Other fats, i.e. margarine or soft cooking fat, can be substituted.

2 oz. butter

3–4 oz. icing sugar, sieved (to make a firmer icing use the larger quantity of sugar)

flavouring as individual recipe *or as below*

1 Cream the butter until very soft and white — it is essential not to warm it.
2 Work in the sugar and flavouring.

This is enough for a thick layer through the centre of a cake, 6–7 inches in diameter. Use double the amount for filling and topping, but at least three times the amount if coating the sides as well. If piping is added (as picture page 236), allow four times the amount.
Almond and other essences may be creamed with the butter, etc.
Chocolate: add a small quantity of sieved cocoa or chocolate powder to the creamed butter, etc.
Coffee: use a small quantity of concentrated coffee essence or instant coffee powder blended with water.
The picture on page 236 shows a chocolate cake (recipe pages 242 and 243) filled with butter icing.

Fudge icing

Although they cannot be described as butter icings, the modern high quality margarines and white shortenings make excellent soft icings — often called fudge icing. Use exactly the same quantities of fat as for butter icing. The Easter bonnet cake on the next page was decorated with this type of icing.

To vary
Chocolate: add a good dessertspoon chocolate powder or 1 oz. melted chocolate and a few drops of vanilla essence.
Coffee: work in a good dessertspoon coffee essence or 1 teaspoon soluble coffee powder dissolved in 2 teaspoons water. Do this gradually or mixture will curdle.
Lemon: add 2 teaspoons finely grated lemon rind and gradually beat in 1 dessertspoon lemon juice.
Orange: use 3 teaspoons finely grated orange rind and gradually beat in 1 dessertspoon orange juice.

Creamed filled sponge

Easter bonnet cake

Preparation: 40 minutes
Wait for cake to cool
Cooking: see Victoria sandwich,
page 242
Makes 10–12 slices

To toast coconut
Spread desiccated coconut on
baking trays and put in a
moderate oven (350–375°F.,
Gas Mark 4–5) for approximately
8–10 minutes, until golden
brown.

1 8- or 9-inch Victoria
sandwich, *page 242*
1 5- or 6-inch Victoria
sandwich, *page 242*

fudge *or* butter icing, any
flavour, *page 245*, but
use four times quantity

toasted coconut

1 Split the large sponge through the centre.
2 Make up the butter icing.
3 Sandwich the large cake together with butter icing.

4 Spread the top of the large cake with butter icing and press small cake into centre.
5 Cover sides and top with icing.
6 Press toasted coconut against all surfaces.

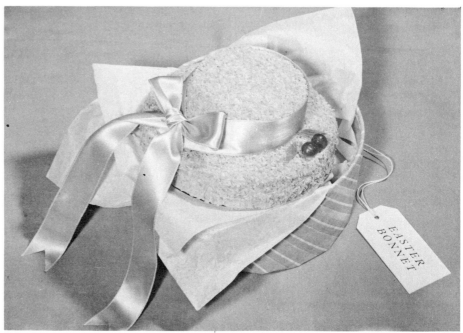

7 Tie a band of ribbon round the 'hat' and decorate with fruit or flowers.

American frosting

Preparation: 3–4 minutes
No delay, but remember you
must beat all the time the
frosting is cooking
Cooking: 15 minutes

American frosting is a complete
change from most other icings;
it is soft and delicious and it
never becomes hard.
This recipe is enough to cover a
6-inch cake, or to ice the top of
a 7-inch cake.

6 oz. castor sugar
1 egg white

2 dessertspoons water
¼ teaspoon cream of tartar

flavouring essence

1 Put ingredients, except flavouring essence, in a basin over a saucepan of hot water.
2 Stir over gentle heat until all the sugar dissolves.
3 Keep water in saucepan boiling gently. With a metal whisk, beat for 5–7 minutes, or until the mixture will hold a peak quite easily.
4 Remove mixture from the heat and continue beating until the icing becomes thick enough for it to be spread over the cake. It should be of a consistency that spreads easily, yet be thick enough to hold a peak.
5 Add the flavouring essence, and then use the icing on the cake immediately.

246

Simple piping with water icing

The veins on the cake below show the type of icing that can be done with water or glacé icing.

1 Use a No. 2 (medium) writing pipe and fit this at the end of a syringe or bag.
2 Press gently but firmly, and you will find you can control the flow of icing.
3 Make sure you have the cake at a convenient and comfortable height for working.
4 Put the cake on the board or plate on an upturned basin, to make it easy to turn as you work.

Autumn leaf

Preparation: 30 minutes
You must wait for cake to cool before icing, and for chocolate icing to set before completing cake.
Cooking: about 40 minutes for cake; allow few minutes' heating for icing
Makes 8 slices

Secret of success
You will notice rather more baking powder than usual in the ingredients. This is to compensate for the lack of creaming, which incorporates air into the mixture.

one-stage sandwich cake
4 oz. soft margarine
2 eggs
4 oz. castor sugar
4 oz. flour (with plain flour use 2 level teaspoons baking powder)

1 level teaspoon baking powder

for the chocolate glacé fudge icing
1 oz. soft margarine
3 tablespoons cold water

2 oz. milk chocolate
6 oz. icing sugar, sieved
2 oz. almonds, chopped *or* desiccated coconut

for the white glacé icing
1 oz. icing sugar, sieved
few drops warm water

To make the cake
1 Place all the cake ingredients in a mixing bowl.
2 Quickly mix together, then beat thoroughly with a wooden spoon (pressing the margarine to the sides of the bowl, if the fat has been refrigerated).
3 Place the mixture in an 8-inch sandwich cake tin, previously brushed with margarine and with the bottom lined with greaseproof paper.
4 Bake on the middle shelf of a very moderate oven (325–350°F., Gas Mark 3–4) for 35–40 minutes. Cool on a cake rack.
5 Cut out a paper pattern the shape of a leaf to the size of the cake, place on top of the cake and cut around (using any left-over cake for making a trifle).

To make the chocolate glacé fudge icing
6 Place the margarine, water and chocolate in a bowl, then place over a saucepan of boiling water.
7 Stir with a wooden spoon until the chocolate dissolves, and continue stirring until mixture thickens.
8 Remove the bowl, cool slightly and then beat in the icing sugar.
9 Continue beating until the icing is of a coating consistency.
10 Pour over the cake and press the chopped nuts or coconut around the sides.
11 Place on a cake-board. Allow this chocolate icing to set before continuing.

To make the white glacé icing
12 Place the icing sugar in a bowl and add a few drops of warm water; beat until smooth and of a piping consistency.
13 Pipe lines on the cake to resemble veins. Leave until set.

Autumn leaf

247

Honey frosting

Preparation: 4–5 minutes
No delay, but you must beat all
the time the frosting is cooking
Cooking: 15 minutes

2 egg whites   pinch of salt   8 oz. honey

1 Whisk the egg whites and salt until stiff.
2 Pour the honey over these in a steady stream — if thick warm the honey.
3 Beat for approximately 15 minutes until stiff. This can be done with an electric beater, in which case it takes about 6 minutes.
4 Use like American frosting.

Coating cakes with nuts

To coat the top of a cake with nuts, put nuts into a piece of greaseproof paper. Hold the edges so you make a narrow 'tunnel' and shake the nuts steadily over the cake. Press into the icing, etc., with a knife.
To coat the sides of a cake with nuts, put the chopped nuts on a long dish or piece of paper. Hold cake like a 'hoop', supporting top and bottom, and roll over the nuts — roll towards you, until sides are covered.

Other coatings for cakes

In addition to nuts, there are other coatings that may be used, for example:
Coconut: use either desiccated coconut from the packet, or toast this as suggested on page 246 (under Easter bonnet cake). Either coat the cake first with butter icing, jam, or whipped cream, and then with the coconut.
Chocolate: this can be grated chocolate or chocolate vermicelli (as shown in the coloured picture on page 236). Apply over whipped cream or butter icing.
Crushed biscuit crumbs: very crisp biscuit crumbs or crushed meringues make another excellent coating on cakes. They soften with standing, so apply over whipped cream or butter icing only a few hours before serving. Follow directions for coating under nut coating (above).

Small cakes

Do not bake small cakes for too long a period, for if you do you will find they become dry. The quick creaming margarine and fats are ideal for these cakes.

Quick creaming. Use the same ingredients as the recipes below, but tip all the ingredients into the mixing bowl and beat for 1–2 minutes. A little extra baking powder ($\frac{1}{2}$ teaspoon to 4 oz. self-raising flour) is a help to make the cakes rise.

Rich queen cakes

Preparation: 10–15 minutes
No delay
Cooking: approximately 12–15 minutes
Makes 12–15

Secrets of success
Do not bake too slowly.
Cream mixture well at stages 1–2.

4 oz. margarine *or* butter
4 oz. castor sugar
$\frac{1}{2}$ teaspoon vanilla essence
2 eggs

4 oz. flour (with plain flour use 1 level teaspoon baking powder)

2 oz. sultanas, halved
1 tablespoon hot water

1 Cream together the fat and sugar until light and fluffy and add the vanilla essence.
2 Beat in the eggs one at a time.
3 Fold in the sieved flour and baking powder, if used, then the sultanas and hot water.
4 Two-thirds fill greased bun tins with the mixture, and bake near the top of a moderately hot oven (400°F., Gas Mark 6) for 15 minutes.
5 Turn out and cool on a cake rack. Ice if liked (see page 245).

Economical queen cakes

Use above recipe, but reduce the margarine or butter and sugar to 2 oz. each. Bake near the top of a hot oven (425–450°F., Gas Mark 6–7).

Fairy cakes

This is the name given to very light fluffy cakes, which can have a little fruit in them if wished.
1 Use recipe for rich queen cakes, but instead of *all* flour, use 3 oz. flour and 1 oz. cornflour.
2 Use superfine margarine or butter.

Peach dessert cakes

Preparation: 20 minutes
Allow cakes to cool
Cooking: 12–15 minutes
Makes 12

Secrets of success
Handle the mixture carefully.
Cream thoroughly at stages 2–3.

5 oz. flour (with plain flour use 1¼ level teaspoons baking powder)
4 oz. butter *or* margarine

4 oz. castor sugar
2 eggs

for the filling and topping
¼ pint thick cream

12 canned peach halves, drained
12 glacé cherries

1 Sieve well the flour and baking powder, if used.

2 Cream fat and sugar until light and fluffy.
3 Add the well beaten eggs, one at a time, adding a tablespoon of flour with each to prevent curdling.
4 Fold in remaining flour with a metal spoon.

5 Put into 12 well greased deep patty or bun tins.
6 Bake towards the top of a moderately hot oven (400°F., Gas Mark 6) for 15 minutes, or until well risen and golden.
7 Turn out on to a wire tray.

8 When cold spread tops of cakes with cream, then put a peach half on each.
9 Decorate with more whipped cream and glacé cherries.

Honey cakes

Preparation: 15 minutes
No delay
Cooking: 10 minutes
Makes 12

Secrets of success
Handle the mixture carefully.
Cream thoroughly at stages 1–2.

4 oz. margarine
2 oz. sugar
2 tablespoons honey

1 egg
6 oz. flour (with plain flour use 1½ level teaspoons baking powder)

grated rind of 1 lemon
1 dessertspoon lemon juice
little milk

1 Cream margarine, sugar and honey until soft; add the well beaten egg.
2 Sieve the flour and baking powder, if used, together, stir into the margarine mixture with the lemon rind and juice.
3 Gradually add enough milk to make a soft consistency.
4 Put into paper cases and bake near the top of a hot oven (450°F., Gas Mark 7) for 10 minutes.
5 Cool on a wire tray.

Left *Madeira cake* Right *Light fruit cake*

Madeira cake

Preparation: 15 minutes
No delay
Cooking: 1¼ hours
Makes 8 slices

For a richer cake, use 6 oz.
butter, 6 oz. sugar and 3 eggs,
and bake for 1½–1¾ hours in a
very moderate oven.

Turn out on to a wire tray to
cool, as shown in the picture.

4 oz. margarine	2 eggs	little sugar
4 oz. sugar	1 teaspoon grated lemon rind	1 piece of candied lemon
8 oz. flour (with plain flour	milk *to mix*	peel *for top of cake*
use 2 level teaspoons		
baking powder)		

1. Cream together the margarine and sugar until soft and light.
2. Sieve flour and baking powder, if used, together.
3. Beat the eggs. Add eggs and flour alternately to margarine mixture, with lemon rind and enough milk to make a soft consistency.
4. Put into a greased and floured 7-inch cake tin, sprinkling a little sugar on top and put on the piece of lemon peel.
5. Bake for 1¼ hours in the centre of a very moderate oven (325–350°F., Gas Mark 3–4), lower the heat slightly after 1 hour if becoming too brown.

Genoa cake

Preparation: 15 minutes
No delay
Cooking: 1¼–1¾ hours
Makes 8 slices

For a richer cake, use 6 oz.
butter, 6 oz. sugar, 3 eggs and
8 oz. fruit, and bake for 1¼ hours
in a very moderate oven.

4 oz. margarine	2 eggs	6 oz. dried fruit
4 oz. sugar	1 teaspoon grated lemon rind	2 oz. chopped candied peel
8 oz. flour (with plain flour	milk *to mix*	little sugar
use 2 level teaspoons		
baking powder)		

1. Cream together the margarine and sugar until soft and light.
2. Sieve the flour and baking powder, if used, together.
3. Beat the eggs. Add the eggs and flour alternately to the margarine mixture, with the lemon rind and enough milk to make a soft consistency.
4. Add the fruit and peel.
5. Put into a greased and floured 7-inch cake tin, sprinkling a little sugar on top.
6. Bake for just over 1¼ hours in the centre of a very moderate oven (325–350°F. Gas Mark 3–4), lower the heat after 1 hour if becoming too brown.

Light fruit cakes

A tin with a loose bottom is
useful as it enables you to
remove the cake with ease,
see picture.

The Genoa cake recipe, above, gives a good basis for a light fruit cake. This can be varied in a number of ways:
1. Use all raisins, or all currants or all sultanas.
2. Turn it into an orange cake by using crystallised orange peel, instead of dried fruit, and grated orange rind, which should be mixed with the fat and sugar.
3. A richer fruit cake, resembling an economical Dundee cake, can be made by using up to 12 oz. of dried fruit. Never increase the amount of fruit *above* this, for the cake is too light in texture to carry the weight of the fruit.

Orange blossom date cake

Preparation: 15 minutes
Cool for 5 minutes
Cooking: 30–35 minutes
Makes 8–10 slices

Secret of success
Add the orange topping while
the cake is still warm.

8 oz. flour (with plain flour
use 2 level teaspoons
baking powder)
5 oz. lard *or* cooking fat
5 oz. sugar

3 eggs
2 tablespoons milk (sour
milk is excellent)
6 oz. dates
3 oz. walnuts *or* almonds

for the topping
3 tablespoons orange juice
4 oz. sugar
1 teaspoon grated orange
rind
whipped thick cream, *optional*

1 Sieve the flour or flour and baking powder.
2 Cream together fat and sugar until light and fluffy, add the beaten eggs gradually.
3 Add the sieved ingredients alternately with the milk, mixing well.
4 Chop the dates and nuts, then fold into the flour, etc.
5 Put into a greased 9-inch square tin. Bake in the centre of a moderate oven (350–375°F., Gas Mark 4–5) for 30–35 minutes. Cool for 5 minutes.
6 Remove the cake from the tin and place top side uppermost on a cake plate.
7 Boil the orange juice in a saucepan with the sugar and orange rind.
8 Pour over the warm cake; serve warm with whipped cream, if desired.

Caramel topped cake

Preparation: 12 minutes
No delay
Cooking: 1¼ hours
Makes 8 slices

Secret of success
Brown the topping very slowly
so that it does not scorch.

4 oz. margarine
2 oz. brown sugar
2 tablespoons golden syrup
4 oz. flour (with plain flour
use 1 teaspoon baking
powder)

2 eggs

for the caramel topping
1½ oz. margarine
1 oz. walnuts, chopped

1½ oz. brown sugar
1½ oz. desiccated coconut
generous 1 tablespoon milk
to bind

1 Cream together the margarine, sugar and golden syrup.
2 Add alternately the sieved flour and baking powder, if used, and the eggs.
3 Bake in a 6- or 7-inch tin lined with greased paper, for approximately 1¼ hours in the centre of a slow to very moderate oven (300–325°F., Gas Mark 2–3).
4 Cool slightly before turning out of the tin.
5 When cold, cover with the topping made by mixing all ingredients together and binding them with the milk.
6 Spread over the cake and put under a very *low* grill to brown.

Cherry cake

Preparation: 15–20 minutes
No delay
Cooking: 1¼ hours
Makes 8 slices

A cherry cake is considered a
difficult one to make. This recipe
will give you a rich cherry cake
with the cherries evenly
distributed. Shorten the cooking
time if using a loaf tin.

4–6 oz. glacé cherries
5 oz. butter *or* margarine

5 oz. sugar
3 large eggs and NO milk

8 oz. flour (it is better to use
plain flour and 1 level
teaspoon baking powder
only)

1 Halve and flour the cherries lightly (this helps to prevent sinking).
2 Cream fat and sugar until soft and light, then beat in the eggs gradually.
3 Fold in the sieved flour and baking powder and the cherries, together.
4 Put into a greased and floured 1½- or 2-lb. loaf tin or a 7-inch cake tin.
5 Bake the cake for approximately 1¼–1½ hours in the centre of a very moderate oven (325°F., Gas Mark 3), reducing the heat after 1 hour if necessary.

*Good and bad cherry cakes:
on the left the cherries are well
distributed, on the right they
have sunk to the bottom.
Reasons are: too wet a mixture,
too great an amount of raising
agent, so add no extra baking
powder and no extra liquid*

Less usual cakes by creaming method

When making these cakes remember the importance of careful creaming of the ingredients, as outlined on page 242.

Chocolate brownies

Preparation: 12–15 minutes
No delay
Cooking: 40–45 minutes
Makes 16

Secrets of success
Follow directions for mixing as basic recipe, page 242.

Colour picture opposite

4 oz. butter *or* margarine
6–8 oz. soft brown sugar
2 large eggs

3 oz. plain flour
1½ oz. cocoa
½ level teaspoon baking powder

2 oz. coarsely chopped walnuts
2 oz. halved walnuts
castor sugar

1 Cream the fat and sugar until light and fluffy, then gradually beat in the eggs.
2 Fold in the sieved flour, cocoa and baking powder, add the chopped walnuts.
3 Line the bottom of a 7-inch square tin with greased paper, grease the sides and put in the cake mixture; top with halved walnuts.
4 Bake in the centre of a very moderate to moderate oven (350°F., Gas Mark 4) for approximately 45 minutes, until firm to the touch.
5 Cut into squares while still warm and dust with castor sugar.

Spiced chocolate cake

Preparation: 12 minutes
No delay
Cooking: 1 hour
Makes 8 slices

Secret of success
Do not exceed amount of golden syrup in recipe, otherwise the cake will be heavy.

4 oz. margarine
4 oz. sugar
1 dessertspoon golden syrup
5 oz. flour (with plain flour use 1½ level teaspoons baking powder)

1 dessertspoon mixed spice
1 oz. chocolate powder
2 eggs

little milk
4 oz. sultanas
sieved icing sugar *to sprinkle*

1 Cream together the margarine, sugar and golden syrup.
2 Sieve the dry ingredients, and add to mixture, alternately with beaten eggs.
3 Lastly, add enough milk to give a sticky consistency, and the sultanas.
4 Put into a loaf tin and bake for approximately 1 hour in the centre of a moderate oven (375°F., Gas Mark 4).
5 Turn out and dust with sieved icing sugar.

Potato ring cake

Preparation: 20 minutes
Allow potatoes to cool
Cooking: 50 minutes–1 hour, plus time for cooking potatoes
Makes 8 slices

Secret of success
The boiled potatoes in this recipe give a fine texture, found in some Continental cakes made with potato flour. The potatoes must be dry and floury and well sieved (see stage 1 on the right).

4 oz. boiled potatoes
4 oz. butter *or* margarine
4 oz. castor sugar
grated rind of 1 lemon
3 large eggs

juice of ½ lemon
4 oz. plain flour
1 level teaspoon baking powder

to decorate
little sieved icing sugar
few halved glacé cherries

1 Rub the potatoes through a sieve.
2 Cream the fat, sugar and grated lemon rind until soft and light.
3 Separate the egg yolks and whites; beat the yolks with the lemon juice.
4 Add the yolk mixture very gradually to creamed mixture, beating well each time.
5 Sift flour and potato with the baking powder; whisk the egg whites.
6 Add the potato mixture and whisked egg whites to the rest of the ingredients, stirring gently until blended.
7 Put the mixture into a well greased and floured ring tin, or a greased and lined 7-inch round cake tin.
8 Bake in the centre of a moderate oven (350–375°F., Gas Mark 4–5) for 50 minutes in a ring tin, or 1 hour in a cake tin, or until firm to the touch.
9 Cool cake on a wire tray, dust with icing sugar and decorate with cherries.

Funny face cakes

Colour picture, page 254

The small cakes illustrated on page 254 can be made by the standard method on page 242, i.e. by creaming 4 oz. butter or margarine with 4 oz. castor sugar, gradually beating in 2 large eggs, then folding in 4 oz. self-raising flour, or plain flour sieved with 1 level teaspoon baking powder. If preferred, use the quick method of mixing on page 244, but use easy creaming margarine and 2 level teaspoons baking powder with 4 oz. plain flour. Bake the mixture in about 24 paper cases towards the top of a hot oven (425–450°F., Gas Mark 6–7) for 10–12 minutes. Top with glacé icing made with 10 oz. sieved icing sugar and 3 tablespoons lemon juice, and decorate with chocolate sweets, etc.

Chocolate brownies

Cakes made by the whisking method

This method of making cakes is used for the really light type of sponge. Many people consider this is the only true sponge. This method is also used in Genoese pastry — which is not like ordinary pastry but very similar to the sponge cake below, except that a larger percentage of butter is used (see page 286).

Many people find the whisking method a most difficult way of making cakes. The reason is that a rather high degree of skill is necessary in the way the flour, etc., is incorporated.

Below you will find details of the most popular method of making a sponge cake by whisking. If you find you are not entirely successful by this method I would suggest you follow the alternative way, i.e. as described in the three-layer sponge on page 256. In this the egg yolks and whites are beaten separately and then put together. As this recipe contains little fat the cake will be baked fairly quickly and you must watch to ensure there is no fear of it scorching.

When the cakes come out of the oven, wait for 2 to 3 minutes and then turn them out. Do NOT put them directly on to a cooling tray; they are better if put on a sheet of greaseproof paper, sprinkled with castor sugar and then put on the cooling tray.

Sponge sandwich

Preparation: 15–20 minutes
No delay
Cooking: 10–12 minutes
Makes 6–8 slices

Secrets of success
Whisk the eggs and sugar well.
Fold in the flour very gently;
too vigorous an action spoils the sponge.
Do not under-bake, or the cake will be heavy.
Do not over-bake, for this dries the sponge badly. Test as described in stage 8, right.

3 large eggs — at least 1 day old
4 oz. castor sugar

3 oz. flour (½ level teaspoon baking powder can be added with plain flour)

1 tablespoon hot water
1 oz. butter or margarine, melted, *or* 1 tablespoon oil, *optional*

1　Put the eggs and sugar into a large basin.
2　Whisk hard until thick enough to see the mark of the whisk in the mixture. If in a hurry, the eggs rise and thicken more quickly if whisked over hot water, but you will get a lighter result if you do NOT whisk over hot water.
3　Sieve flour and baking powder, if used, twice if possible.
4　FOLD in the well sieved flour carefully and gently with a metal spoon, using a gentle flicking movement. To make sure the flour is thoroughly incorporated blend from bottom of mixture all the time.
5　FOLD in water and, if using it, the melted fat or oil.
6　Grease and flour, or grease and coat with equal quantities of flour and sugar, two 7-inch sandwich tins.
7　Divide the mixture between them and bake for 10–12 minutes near the top of the oven — with gas it is a good idea to heat the oven on 8 then turn to 5–6 when the cakes go in. With electricity heat to 450°F., then re-set oven to 375–400°F. when the cakes go in.
8　Test by pressing *gently* the centre of the cakes. When firm they are cooked.
9　Remove from oven, leave for a minute, tap sharply, then turn on to a sieve or wire cooling tray. COOL AWAY FROM A DRAUGHT.

Sponge cake

Preparation: 15–20 minutes
No delay
Cooking: approximately 35 minutes
Makes 6–8 slices

1　Follow the recipe for sponge sandwich, above.
2　Put into one 7-inch cake tin, which should be prepared in the same way as the sandwich tins.
3　Bake in the centre of a very moderate oven (325°F., Gas Mark 3) for approximately 35 minutes.

Eggs and sugar can be whisked over a basin of hot water if you are in a hurry

Funny face cakes, see page 252

To make a Swiss roll

Preparation: 20–25 minutes
No delay
Cooking: 7–10 minutes

Secrets of success
Time the cooking very carefully.
If over-baked the roll cracks.
Make sure the jam is not too hot;
if it is it soaks into the cake.

1 For a large Swiss roll tin (approximately 9 inches by 14 inches), use ingredients for sponge sandwich on page 255.
2 For a small Swiss roll tin (approximately 7 inches by 11 inches), reduce ingredients by one-third.
3 Follow method of mixing on page 255.
4 Line the Swiss roll tin with well greased greaseproof paper.
5 You will find it easier to get a flat surface if you grease the tin slightly, under the paper.
6 To obtain neat corners to the paper, cut down these with scissors.
7 Pour in the mixture and bake near the top of a hot oven (425–450°F., Gas Mark 6–7) for approximately 7–10 minutes.
8 Test rather early during the cooking period the first time you make this in your cooker, since the roll will tend to crack if over-baked.
9 While the cake is cooking WARM the jam; this must not be too hot.
10 Have a sheet of greaseproof paper ready and sprinkle lavishly with castor sugar.
11 When the roll is ready, invert the tin over the sugared paper.
12 Remove the paper on the bottom of the cake. If this is at all difficult all you need to do is to brush it with cold water (on a pastry brush).
13 Cut off the crisp edges, spread the cake with jam.
14 To facilitate rolling, make a shallow cut in the roll about 1 inch from the end nearest you, then fold this over firmly.
15 Use the paper to help in rolling the sponge firmly.
16 Allow to cool away from a draught.

Cream Swiss roll: roll the paper inside the roll, or use a second sheet of paper and place on the sponge and roll. When cold gently unroll and fill with whipped cream.
Chocolate Swiss roll: instead of 3 oz. flour use $2\frac{1}{2}$ oz. flour sieved with 1 tablespoon cocoa. Roll with paper inside; when cold gently unroll and fill with whipped cream or butter icing (page 245).
Coffee Swiss roll: use basic sponge mixture on page 255, but add 1 teaspoon instant coffee, blended with 1 tablespoon of hot water and fold in instead of the plain hot water. Roll with paper inside; when cold unroll and fill with whipped cream or butter icing (page 245).

Three layer sponge

Preparation: 15 minutes
No delay
Cooking: 20 minutes
Makes 8 slices

Secret of success
The margarine must not be hot when added to the eggs and sugar. Melt this and then allow to cool.

2 eggs	few drops of cochineal	glacé icing, *page 247*
5 oz. sugar	1 dessertspoon sweetened	
3 oz. margarine	chocolate powder	*to decorate*
5 oz. self-raising flour	jam *or* butter icing, *page 245*	chopped nuts

1 Separate the eggs.
2 Beat the sugar with the yolks, then add the softened margarine.
3 Beat well, add the flour gradually.
4 Whip the egg whites until stiff, then fold into the cake mixture.
5 Separate into 3 portions. Colour one with cochineal, another with the chocolate powder and leave the third plain.
6 Turn into 3 well greased and floured 6-inch sandwich tins, and bake each for about 20 minutes in a moderate oven (350–375°F., Gas Mark 4–5).
7 When cold, sandwich the layers together with jam or butter icing, cover the top with water icing and decorate with chopped nuts.

Sponge fingers

Use either the recipe on page 255, or the one above, and bake in special sponge finger tins which should be greased and coated with equal quantities of flour and castor sugar. Dredge the sponge fingers with a little castor sugar before baking.

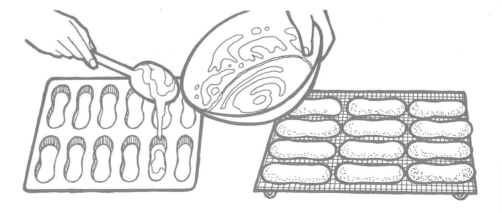

Pineapple party gâteau

Preparation: 30–35 minutes,
delay for cake to cool
Cooking: 20 minutes
Makes 8–10 slices

Secrets of success
The egg mixture should be really
thick before adding the cornflour.
Fold this in very gently and
carefully Do not over-whip the
cream.

3 eggs
pinch of salt
4 oz. castor sugar
3 oz. cornflour* (poor weight)

to decorate
pineapple jam
small can pineapple rings

cherries and angelica
¼ pint thick cream
boudoir biscuits

* if preferred use half cornflour and half self-raising flour, or plain flour with ½ teaspoon baking powder.

1 Separate the eggs (see page 227) and beat the whites stiffly with the salt.
2 Add the yolks and continue beating until the mixture is thick and creamy.
3 Add the sugar gradually, beating all the time, until the mixture is thick enough to hold the marks of the whisk for several seconds.
4 Carefully fold in the sifted cornflour, and turn into two 8-inch greased and floured sandwich tins.
5 Bake for about 20 minutes just above the centre of a moderate oven (350–375°F., Gas Mark 4–5). Test carefully by pressing firmly on top.
6 When cool, sandwich the sponge cakes together with pineapple jam, and if a sweet, rather than a cake, is desired, moisten with some of the pineapple syrup.
7 Brush the sides with warmed jam.
8 Arrange the pineapple slices on top, and decorate with glacé cherries, angelica and whipped cream.
9 Press boudoir biscuits (sponge fingers) against the sides and tie with ribbon.

Pineapple party gâteau

Rich fruit cakes

1. In many rich fruit cake recipes you will find plain flour and *no* baking powder or *relatively little* baking powder. *This is very important.* If you use too much baking powder it lifts the cake mixture but cannot carry the weight of fruit, which then sinks.
2. **To prepare fruit:** dried fruit is often very dirty, it can be rubbed in flour, but is better if washed in cold water then spread on flat trays and dried at room temperature. NEVER USE WET FRUIT in a cake. Allow it to dry for 48 hours before using.
3. **To blanch almonds:** put the almonds into a basin and pour over boiling water; leave for several minutes. The almonds can then be skinned and dried.
   To chop almonds: cut in pieces on a board or put into blender and switch on.
   To flake almonds: cut into thin neat shreds on a board.
4. Preparation of the tins is very important. As well as lining tins with paper as directed on page 237, tie a band of brown paper round the outside of cake tins.

Simnel cake

Preparation: 30 minutes. Cake must cool before decorating
Cooking: 2½–3 hours
Makes 12–14 slices

Secrets of success
Read the comments about creaming in similar recipe.
Do not brown the marzipan too quickly.
Keep the marzipan to be used for decoration covered in foil or polythene, so it does not become too dry.

8 oz. almond paste (marzipan), *page 260*
6 oz. butter
6 oz. castor sugar
grated rind of ½ lemon
1 oz. ground almonds
7 oz. plain flour

1 oz. cornflour
1 level teaspoon mixed spice
3 eggs
1 tablespoon brandy, optional
12 oz. currants *or* mixed fruit

2 oz. chopped candied peel
1 egg white

to decorate
glacé cherries
fondants *or* marzipan fruits *or* eggs, etc.

1. Roll out just under half the marzipan to about 6¾ inches in diameter.
2. Beat the butter and sugar until light and creamy, add the lemon rind and ground almonds and continue beating.
3. Sift the flour, cornflour and spice together.
4. Add these to the creamed mixture alternately with the beaten eggs and brandy, if used.
5. Add the currants or mixed fruit and candied peel.
6. Put half the mixture into a greased and lined 7-inch cake tin (see page 237), then cover this evenly with half the almond paste.
7. Place the remainder of the cake mixture on top.
8. Bake for 2½–3 hours in the centre of a very moderate oven (325°F., Gas Mark 3); reduce the heat to 300°F., or Gas Mark 2, after the first 1¼ hours.
9. When cool, brush the top of the cake with a little egg white, put the rest of the almond paste on top and brown under a moderate grill.
10. If wished, you can use some of the marzipan to form a plait round the edge.
11. Decorate cake with balls of almond paste or tiny eggs or glacé cherries, fondants or marzipan fruits, or with Easter chicks, see picture below.

Simnel cake

Dundee cake
(rich recipe)

Preparation: 20 minutes
No delay
Cooking: 2–2¼ hours
Makes 12–14 slices

Secrets of success
Do not add the eggs too quickly
otherwise the mixture will curdle.
Fold in the flour gently and
carefully; over-beating is NOT
good in this type of cake.
Watch the oven temperature
carefully the first time you bake
this cake.
See comment, stage 9, about
turning out the cake.

6 oz. margarine *or* butter
6 oz. sugar
3 eggs
8 oz. plain flour
1½ level teaspoons baking
 powder

1 teaspoon spice
2 oz. almonds, chopped
2 oz. cherries
1 lb. mixed dried fruit
2 oz. peel

2 tablespoons milk
2 oz. almonds, split
egg white *to glaze*

1 Cream the margarine or butter and sugar until soft and light.
2 Add the beaten eggs gradually.
3 Sieve the dry ingredients together.
4 Mix the chopped almonds, floured cherries, fruit and peel together.
5 Stir in the sieved ingredients and add enough milk to make a slow dropping consistency, then lastly put in the fruit.
6 Put into a greased and floured 8-inch cake tin.
7 Cover with split almonds, and brush with a little egg white to glaze.
8 Bake for 2–2¼ hours in the centre of a very moderate oven (325°F., Gas Mark 3), reducing the heat after 1½ hours if wished.
9 Cool slightly in the tin before turning on to a wire tray.

Rich Christmas cake

Preparation: 40–45 minutes
No delay
Cooking: 3–3½ hours
Makes 18–20 slices

Secrets of success
Ovens vary a great deal, so
check on your oven settings
most carefully when making this
rich fruit cake.
Look at the cake after about
1 hour – it should not have
changed colour much but be
very pale golden. If it is cooking
too quickly, reduce the heat.
Store for several weeks so the
cake may mature in flavour.

Christmas cake

8 oz. plain flour
½ level teaspoon salt
1 level teaspoon cinnamon
1 rounded teaspoon mixed
 spice
½ level teaspoon powdered
 nutmeg

4 oz. glacé cherries
4 oz. blanched almonds,
 page 258
8 oz. butter
8 oz. soft brown sugar
1 level tablespoon black
 treacle

5 eggs
2 oz. plain chocolate*
1 lb. seedless raisins
1 lb. sultanas
12 oz. currants
4 oz. chopped candied peel
3 tablespoons brandy

* this gives darkness to the cake without any pronounced chocolate flavour – if not desired use 1 oz. extra flour.

1 Sieve together the dry ingredients. Chop the cherries and almonds (see page 258 for preparing fruit).
2 Cream the butter and sugar until light and fluffy, stir in the black treacle.
3 Beat the eggs, add gradually to the creamed mixture.
4 Melt the chocolate, cool and fold into the mixture with the sieved dry ingredients, fruit, nuts, peel and brandy.
5 Turn the mixture into a greased and double-lined 9-inch cake tin (see page 237).
6 Bake in the centre of a very moderate oven (325°F., Gas Mark 3) for 1–1½ hours, then reduce the heat to 275–300°F., Gas Mark 1–2, for a further 1½–2 hours.
7 Allow cake to cool before removing from tin. When completely cold, store in an airtight tin until required.
8 Cover with marzipan and decorate (see page 260).

Royal icing

Royal icing is a rather crisp hard icing that you find on rich fruit cakes. It has the great advantage of keeping well without cracking or discolouring. It does tend to become hard with keeping, though this can be overcome to a degree, but not entirely, if you add 1 teaspoon glycerine (obtainable from a chemist) to each 8 oz. icing sugar.
Keep the basin containing Royal icing covered with damp paper or a damp cloth to prevent hardening on the surface. In this way you can prepare one batch for both coating and piping.

for the top only of a 7-inch cake – one layer and little piping:

8 oz. icing sugar	1 egg white	1 dessertspoon lemon juice

for the top and sides of a 7-inch cake – one layer and piping:

1¼ lb. icing sugar	2½ egg whites	1¼ tablespoons lemon juice

for the top only of a 9-inch round or 8-inch square cake – one layer and piping.

12 oz. icing sugar	1½ egg whites	1½ dessertspoons lemon juice

for top and sides of a 9-inch round or 8-inch square cake – one layer and piping.

2 lb. icing sugar	4 egg whites	2 tablespoons lemon juice

1 First sieve the icing sugar. If it is very hard it is easier if you roll this with a rolling pin between 2 sheets of greaseproof paper, and then rub it through a nylon sieve.
2 Whisk the egg whites lightly.
3 Gradually stir in the icing sugar.
4 Add the lemon juice and glycerine, if used.
5 Beat very hard with a wooden spoon until soft and white, approximately 10 minutes.
6 If using an electric mixer, do not over-beat otherwise you produce air bubbles.

Marzipan or almond paste

Preparation: approximately 10 minutes to make marzipan
No cooking

Marzipan should not be over-handled otherwise it becomes oily and sticky. Buy your ground almonds fresh, or in a wax container, so that they do not dry or become slightly bitter. Note point 10, on the right, very carefully.
Wrap any left-over marzipan so it does not harden on the outside.

for generous layer on top of a 7-inch cake:

2 oz. icing sugar	2 oz. castor sugar	egg yolk *to mix*
4 oz. ground almonds	few drops of almond essence*	

for top and sides of a 7-inch cake (thin layer).

4 oz. icing sugar	4 oz. castor sugar	2 egg yolks *to mix*
8 oz. ground almonds	few drops of almond essence*	

for generous layer on top of a 9-inch round cake or 8-inch square cake:

3 oz. icing sugar	3 oz. castor sugar	1½ egg yolks *to mix*
6 oz. ground almonds	few drops of almond essence*	

for top and sides of a 9-inch round or 8-inch square cake (thin layer):

6 oz. icing sugar	6 oz. castor sugar	3 egg yolks *to mix*
12 oz. ground almonds	few drops of almond essence*	

* the amount of almond essence should, of course, be increased proportionately.

1 Sieve the icing sugar (see recipe above).
2 Mix all ingredients together, adding enough egg yolk to make a firm mixture.
3 Knead thoroughly, but do not over-handle.
4 Use as required.

To coat a cake with marzipan

1 Brush away loose crumbs from the cake.
2 Spread the sides of the cake either with egg white or with sieved apricot jam.
3 Roll out the marzipan on a sugared board or table.
4 Measure the depth and circumference of the cake.
5 Cut a strip exactly the length of the circumference, plus about ⅛ inch – but to be 1 inch deeper than the cake. Use approximately half or just over half the total amount of marzipan. Cut a round of marzipan the size of the top of the cake.
6 Hold the cake on its side, then, just as if you were rolling a hoop, roll the cake along the strip of marzipan. If you do this firmly the marzipan sticks to the cake. Make sure the extra inch is at the top edge.
7 Turn cake on to the base again, seal the join firmly and press down the extra inch on top.
8 Brush the top with egg white or jam, and press the round of marzipan into position.
9 Tidy the sides by rolling a jam jar, or a rolling pin held upright, round the sides of the cake. Roll the top to give a neat edge – this makes icing the cake much easier.
10 If you are fairly practised in handling marzipan you will be able to put the icing on straight away. If, however, you feel that you have had to knead the marzipan a fair amount to make it pliable, it is much better to let this dry out for 48 hours, before icing the cake.
11 It helps the icing to adhere to the marzipan if you brush this with a little egg white before coating the cake with icing. Brush the cake with a thin layer of egg white, leave for 30 minutes then spread with the icing.

To coat a cake with icing

1 Lift the cake on to a cake board – if possible stand the cake on a turntable or upturned basin.
2 Use most of the royal icing and put it in one 'pile' on the top.
3 Spread icing away from the centre of the cake down the sides. Cover the whole of the cake before neatening icing. To spread icing easily use a broad-bladed palette knife and dip it in a jug of hot water. Shake knife reasonably dry but use while warm.
4 To neaten sides of the cake, hold the blade of the knife against the icing and gently, but firmly, draw round sides of cake, removing any uneven surplus icing – this should be returned to the basin. If your cake is on a turntable or upturned basin, you can then turn the cake round with your left hand while using the knife in your right hand.
5 To neaten top of the cake, hold either an icing spatula or the edge of the palette knife across the top of the cake, holding one end in each hand, and draw slowly across the cake to neaten the icing.
6 If piping, allow the flat icing to harden. Keep the rest of the icing in a basin covered with a damp cloth, so that it is soft enough for piping.

To pipe

When making an elaborate design, this should first be made on a piece of paper which can then be put on to the cake. If using your own design, prick through the paper to mark small holes on top of the cake. It is, however, possible to buy a transfer for icing on cakes and this is what has been used in the photograph.

Left *Decorative icing with a piping pen – useful for making fine lines and small rosettes*
Right *Piping with a syringe – hold at right angles to the cake to pipe down the sides*

To write lines

You will use a piping pen, syringe or bag. The pen and syringe are illustrated in the pictures above. The sketches show how to make a piping bag from greaseproof paper. Use a writing pipe No. 1, 2 or 3 and draw with this as you would with an ordinary pencil or pen. Keep the mixture flowing to get smooth writing.
You will not wish to invest in a number of pipes to begin with, and the most useful one is the rose pipe No. 8; this will give you small rosette shapes on the top of the cake, or the scroll and shell shapes shown in the second picture.
To make neat rosettes, hold the pipe fairly upright. To give a flowing design on the side, as in the second picture, hold your syringe more or less at right angles to the cake.

How to make an icing bag from greaseproof paper

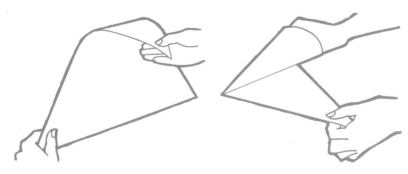

Golden Christmas cake

Preparation: 45 minutes
No delay
Cooking: 2½ hours
Makes 18–20 slices

Secret of success
The high percentage of candied peel, marmalade, etc., makes this a cake that is likely to scorch easily, so check oven temperatures carefully.

1 lb. seedless raisins
4 oz. candied lemon peel
4 oz. candied citron peel
4 oz. candied pineapple
4 oz. glacé cherries
4 oz. almonds
4 oz. walnuts
8 oz. butter

10 oz. castor sugar
4 eggs
4 level tablespoons orange marmalade
12 oz. flour (preferably half plain and half self-raising flour; 1½ level teaspoons baking powder with all plain flour)

1 level teaspoon salt
1 level teaspoon cinnamon
3 tablespoons milk
½ teaspoon vanilla essence

1 Plump the raisins by covering with cold water, bring to the boil, cover and leave to stand for 5 minutes. Drain and dry.
2 Chop peel and pineapple, halve cherries, blanch and chop almonds, chop walnuts and mix all together.
3 Cream the butter and sugar together until light and fluffy.
4 Gradually beat in the eggs, then stir in the marmalade.
5 Sieve the flour, baking powder if used, salt and cinnamon, and fold into the mixture alternately with the milk and vanilla essence.
6 Stir in the prepared fruit, turn the mixture into a greased and double-lined 8-inch tin (see page 237 for lining tins).
7 Bake in the centre of a very moderate oven (325°F., Gas Mark 3) for 2¼ hours. Reduce the heat to 275–300°F., Gas Mark 1–2, after 1½ hours.
8 Test carefully and remove from the tin when cool. Cover with marzipan and decorate as desired.

Valentine cake

Preparation: 20 minutes
No delay
No cooking – few minutes heating
Best if made 1 day beforehand
Makes 8–10 slices

Secret of success
Make the crumbs very fine to give a good texture to the cake. Work speedily on the damp icing, stages 9 and 10, to obtain the feathered effect in picture.

for the uncooked fudge cake
8 oz. sweet biscuits
4 oz. soft margarine
1 oz. castor sugar
1 tablespoon golden syrup
3 level tablespoons cocoa

little extra margarine *for brushing tin*

for the glacé icing
6 oz. icing sugar, sieved

2–3 dessertspoons hot water
few drops of red colouring

1 yard ribbon

To make the uncooked fudge cake
1 Put the biscuits on to a piece of greaseproof paper.
2 Cover with a second sheet of paper and roll very firmly until reduced to fine crumbs.
3 Put the margarine, sugar and syrup in a pan, melt but do not boil.
4 Put the cocoa and biscuit crumbs in a mixing bowl, add the melted ingredients and mix all together.
5 Brush the inside of a medium-sized heart-shaped tin with melted margarine, and press the mixture well down into the tin, smoothing the top with a palette knife.
6 Leave to set (preferably in a refrigerator) overnight. Turn out of the tin before icing.

To make the glacé icing and decorate the cake
7 Put the sieved icing sugar in a mixing bowl, stir in the hot water and mix to a coating consistency.
8 Place 1 tablespoon of the icing in a small bowl and add a few drops of red colouring on the tip of a skewer (see page 285); mix thoroughly.
9 Pour the white icing over the top of the heart cake, and, while still wet, pipe lines of pink icing (using a fine writing pipe (No. 1 or 2) and a syringe or bag) about ¾ inch apart across the cake.
10 Then with a pointed skewer or knife, draw lines at right angles across the pink icing to give a feathered effect.
11 When the icing has set, tie a ribbon around the sides.

Valentine cake

262

Nutty fritter cakes

Preparation: 10 minutes
Allow time for mixture to cool
and set
Cooking: 15 minutes
Makes 10 cakes

Secrets of success
These are unusual but easy to
make.
Sprinkle semolina gradually into
the milk, etc., see stage 3.
Allow mixture to set, stage 8.
A hot knife (dipped in hot water
and shaken dry) cuts the slices
at stage 9 very easily.

1 oz. walnuts
1 pint milk
¼ teaspoon salt
1 oz. castor sugar
4 oz. fine semolina
2 eggs, lightly beaten

¼ teaspoon vanilla essence
  or 1 teaspoon finely grated
  orange rind
little extra semolina *for
  coating*

2–3 oz. fat or oil *for frying*
apricot *or* black cherry jam

1 Chop the walnuts very finely.
2 Heat the milk with salt and sugar.
3 Sprinkle in the semolina and bring to the boil, stirring vigorously.
4 Cook for 2 minutes, stirring.
5 Remove from heat, leave to cool slightly then gradually beat in the eggs.
6 Reheat gently without boiling for 5 minutes, stirring as before.
7 Stir in vanilla essence or orange rind and the walnuts.

8 Turn mixture into a 1-lb. loaf tin, and leave in a cold place until firm.

9 Turn out of tin, cut into approximately 10 slices and coat each with dry semolina.

10 Melt fat or oil in a thick heavy frying pan to about 1 inch or less in depth; it must be less than half the depth of the pan.

11 When lightly smoking, lower in as many fritter cakes as the pan will hold.
12 Fry to a delicate brown, turning once.

13 Drain well on crumpled kitchen paper.
14 Serve hot with chunky apricot or black cherry jam.

To keep cakes

A light or rather plain cake is not meant to be kept for a very long time. Put it into a cake tin or airtight tin. If no tin is available, cakes keep very well wrapped in foil.
Do *not* put the cakes with bread, pastry or biscuits. They should be kept entirely apart.
Rich fruit cakes, like a Dundee cake, keep well for some weeks.
A very rich Christmas cake will keep for several months and its flavour is improved with keeping, so make this at least a month before required.

Making your own bread

Few things are more satisfying to eat than home-made bread, and certainly there is a great sense of achievement when once you have produced your own bread.

You may be surprised to find bread-making in a book for beginners but in fact it is a perfectly simple thing to make. All it requires is careful handling and patience. There are a few essential points to remember.

1 All the ingredients should be kept comfortably warm.
2 The word 'prove' means to rise, and this should be done in a warm place but not a hot one. The warming drawer of your cooker is a good place providing it is not too hot, but the bread will rise at ordinary room temperature quite well.
3 Do not be carried away with the kneading. You will see in *picture 3* how the 'heel' of your hand, i.e. the palm base, pushes the dough while the left hand pulls it firmly.
4 Many shops are now selling special bread flour. This is a strong type of flour which produces the best bread. If you cannot get this use ordinary plain flour.

Bread

Preparation: 40 minutes including time spent in kneading. Allow time waiting for dough to 'prove' Cooking: see opposite

This makes 3 1-lb. loaves

Secrets of success
a) Try to obtain right type of flour.
b) Keep utensils, etc., comfortably warm
c) Flours vary in the amount of liquid they absorb; make sure the dough is an elastic dough, see stage 6.
d) Do not try to prove in too high a temperature — room temperature is ideal, or an airing cupboard.
e) Careful kneading is important, see the way to test if it has been done correctly, stage 8.
f) Use a high temperature for cooking the bread, see stage 20.

3 lb. plain flour*
3 level teaspoons salt
1 oz. fresh yeast†

1 level teaspoon sugar
at least 1¼ pints tepid water

1 tablespoon oil *or* melted butter *or* lard, *optional*

* try to buy special strong flour.
† if using dried yeast see page 266.

1 Sieve flour and salt into a warm basin, then put in a warm place.
2 Cream yeast and sugar in another basin or jug if wished, add part of the liquid.
3 Either a) put this mixture into a well, made in the centre of the flour, giving a light dusting of flour over the top; or b) put a sprinkling of flour on top of the yeast in a jug or small basin.
4 Cover with a clean cloth, leave in a warm place for a good 15 minutes until the top is covered with bubbles.
5 If using method a), add the rest of the liquid and mix with the flour. If using method b), pour the yeast liquid on to the flour and then add the rest of the liquid (see picture below). If you add a tablespoon of oil or melted butter or lard to the liquid it does give a more moist loaf, but this is optional.

6 You may need a little more than the 1¼ pints, but make sure you have a soft dough.
7 Knead well until the dough is smooth and leaves the bowl clean.
8 To test, press with finger, if the impression comes out the dough is sufficiently kneaded.
9 Put to rise in a warm place for about 1½ hours then knead again.
10 Either cover with a tea-cloth, or put the dough into a very large plastic bag.
11 Put to rise in a warm place for about 1¼–1½ hours until about twice the size.
12 Put on to the floured board and knead again.

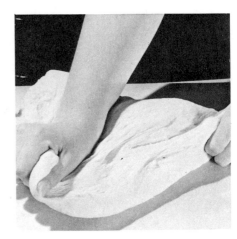

To make brown bread

Use the same recipe as on opposite page, but instead of 3 lb. ordinary flour use 1½ lb. ordinary flour and 1½ lb. stone ground or wholemeal flour. You will find that brown bread needs a little extra liquid.

Secret of success
Make a little softer than white bread.

Wholemeal bread

Use all stone ground or wholemeal flour.
You will need appreciably more liquid. The dough should be quite soft, so instead of kneading as in the pictures, you get a better result by beating it with a wooden spoon.

Secret of success
If you make the dough in wholemeal bread firm enough to knead, the bread is inclined to dry very rapidly.

Milk bread

Follow the basic recipe, but use milk to mix instead of water.

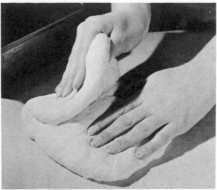

13 Form into loaves; this is the way to fold the dough to fit into a loaf tin.

14 This method gives a loaf that can be 'broken' into small rolls.

15 Put the dough into the warmed greased tins.
16 Make sure that they are only half-filled, because the bread will rise a great deal in both the final 'proving' and baking.
17 For a very crisp crust, brush the tops of the loaves or rolls with melted butter, margarine or a little oil.
18 If you wish for a rather soft crust, brush with a small amount of milk.
19 'Prove' for the final time — about 20 minutes.

20 Bake the loaves in the centre of a hot oven (425–450°F., Gas Mark 6–7) for the first 10 minutes. Reduce the heat to 375°F., Gas Mark 4, for a further 30–45 minutes, depending on size of loaves. Picture shows the dough risen but uncooked in the oven.

21 To test, tip the bread out of the tin on to a cloth, held in your hand.
22 Knock the bottoms of the loaves and they should sound hollow. If they do not, then put them back again into the tins, or, if you like the sides a little more brown, on to a flat baking sheet, and allow a few minutes longer in the oven.

Small rolls

Use the basic recipe or any variations, form into little rolls. These can be various shapes, or plaited, as the illustration. Bake towards the top of a very hot oven (450–475°F., Gas Mark 8) for 10–12 minutes.

Bread rolls

265

Looking after yeast

Yeast is a living organism, and, like a plant, it thrives under certain conditions and is destroyed with the wrong conditions.

Remember:
1 When you buy yeast it should look pale putty in colour and smell quite strongly.
2 It should crumble easily when you touch it.
3 If it is dark and hard in texture it is stale.
4 To keep yeast for 2 or 3 days put it into a refrigerator.

Dried yeast

If you have difficulty in buying fresh yeast, use dried yeast instead.
1 With dried yeast, mix with the sugar and a little tepid liquid.
2 Allow to stand in a warm place until soft — approximately 20 minutes, then cream.
3 Continue after this as for fresh yeast.
4 Makes of dried yeast vary, so follow instructions for each particular make — generally speaking 1 oz. fresh yeast is equivalent to 1 level tablespoon dried yeast.

Rich fruit raisin bread

Preparation: 25 minutes
Delay of 1 hour 20 minutes in 'proving'
Cooking: 40–45 minutes
Makes 2 loaves

Secret of success
Do not prove in too hot a place or over-handle the dough.

Fruit bread: This is made as raisin bread, but you can use a mixture of dried fruit and sugar instead of honey. Glaze with 1 tablespoon sugar dissolved in 1 tablespoon water when loaves come out of the oven.

approximately ½ pint water
  or milk and water
1 teaspoon salt

1 tablespoon honey
1 oz. lard
1 lb. plain flour

1 oz. fresh yeast
12 oz. — 1 lb. seedless
  raisins

1 Heat the liquid until just tepid.
2 Dissolve the salt and honey in the water.
3 Rub the lard into the flour.
4 Blend the yeast in the tepid water.
5 Make a well in the centre of the flour, pour in the liquid, beat well. If necessary, add a little more water to make a soft dough.
6 Prove for 45 minutes in a warm place (see pages 264 and 265).
7 Beat in the raisins and prove for 15 minutes longer.
8 Knead on a floured board.
9 Prove for 20 minutes, covered with greased polythene.
10 Divide into two, and put into two 1½–2 lb. loaf tins.
11 Bake in the centre of a moderately hot oven (400°F., Gas Mark 6) for 40–45 minutes.
12 Glaze with warmed honey (use a wet pastry brush) as soon as the loaves come out of the oven.

Wholemeal nut loaf

Breads without yeast

Bridge rolls

Preparation: 6—8 minutes
No delay
Cooking: 15 minutes
Makes 8

Secret of success
Keep the dough as moist as possible.

8 oz. plain flour*
3 level teaspoons baking powder*

½ level teaspoon salt
½ oz. lard
1 egg

¼ pint milk – *for use as required*

* or use self-raising flour plus 1 level teaspoon baking powder if possible.

1 Sieve together the plain flour, baking powder and salt.
2 Lightly rub in the lard.
3 Make a well in the centre, add the egg and some milk.
4 Fold in the flour gently to make an elastic dough, adding more milk if necessary.
5 Turn on to a floured board and divide into 8; shape into rolls.
6 Bake for 10—15 minutes on a lightly greased baking tin near the top of a hot to very hot oven (450—475°F., Gas Mark 7—8).
7 Cool on a wire tray.

Date and nut loaf

Preparation: 15 minutes
No delay
Cooking: approximately 1¼ hours
Makes 1 loaf

Secret of success
Use the full quantity of liquid; the bread looks moist but this is right.

2 oz. margarine
1½ oz. sugar
1 egg

8 oz. flour (with plain flour use 2 level teaspoons baking powder)
pinch of salt

4 oz. dates, chopped
1 oz. nuts, chopped
¼ pint milk and water

1 Grease a 1-lb. loaf tin.
2 Cream the margarine and sugar.
3 Beat the egg, add to the creamed mixture.
4 Sieve the flour, baking powder, if used, and salt; blend with the mixture.
5 Add the chopped dates and nuts. Stir in the milk and water gradually.
6 Bake in the prepared tin for about 1¼ hours in the centre of a moderate oven (350—375°F., Gas Mark 4—5). Test carefully.

Note. This loaf keeps well.

Wholemeal nut loaf

Preparation: 10 minutes
Cooking: 1¼—1½ hours
Makes a 2 lb. loaf

Secrets of success
Use sufficient liquid to make a slack dough.
Use the oven heat recommended to make the loaf rise well.

1 lb. wholemeal flour
2 level teaspoons baking powder

½ teaspoon salt
2 eggs
½ pint milk

2 oz. butter, melted
4 oz. walnuts, chopped

1 Sieve or mix the flour, baking powder and salt (some wholemeal flour is a little coarse for some sieves).
2 Beat the eggs lightly, then add to the dry ingredients together with the milk, melted butter and walnuts.
3 Mix to a soft smooth dough with a wooden spoon.
4 Grease and flour a 2 lb. loaf tin, or line the base with greased paper, then grease and flour the sides of the tin.
5 Put in the mixture and bake in the centre of a moderate to moderately hot oven (375—400°F., Gas Mark 5—6) for about 30 minutes; lower the heat to very moderate to moderate to complete the cooking.
6 This is delicious with cheese and salad.

To freshen stale bread

1 If bread has become stale, brush it with a little milk on the outside and put into a hot oven for a few minutes.
2 If you have a very stale loaf of bread it can be freshened by dipping the whole loaf in milk or water for approximately 1 minute. Lift out and crisp in the oven for approximately 15—20 minutes.

To make breadcrumbs

Preparation: few minutes
No delay
No cooking for breadcrumbs
Cooking for crisp toasted crumbs: about 30 minutes

1 Cut the crusts from stale bread.
2 Rub the crumb of the bread through a sieve, or, if preferred, against the coarse side of a grater, until fine breadcrumbs are made.

To toast breadcrumbs
1 Spread the crumbs out on baking trays, giving a thin layer.
2 Put into a very moderate oven (325°F., Gas Mark 3) for 30 minutes, until golden brown.
3 Cool, then store in jars or tins and use for coating fish, etc.

Left *Scones*
Right *Honey bread, Nutty raisin loaf and Honey muffins*

Honey bread

Preparation: 10–15 minutes
No delay
Cooking: 40–45 minutes
Makes 1 loaf

Secret of success
DO NOT OVER-bake otherwise
this is very dry.

2 oz. butter	8 oz. flour (with plain flour	¼ teaspoon salt
1 oz. sugar	use 1 teaspoon baking	¾ teaspoon mixed spice
2 tablespoons honey	powder)	1 egg
		2 tablespoons milk

1 Cream the butter and sugar together until light and fluffy.
2 Beat in the honey.
3 Sieve together the dry ingredients and add to the creamed mixture with the whisked egg and milk.
4 Put into a well greased tin, 4 by 5 inches, and bake in the centre of a moderate oven (350–375°F.; Gas Mark 4–5) for 40–45 minutes.

Nutty raisin loaf

Preparation: 20 minutes
No delay
Cooking: 1½ hours
Makes 1 loaf

Secret of success
Do not reduce the amount of
honey or milk if you wish the
loaf to keep well.

10 oz. seedless raisins	½ teaspoon salt	10 tablespoons honey
2 oz. walnuts, chopped	¼ teaspoon bicarbonate of	¼ pint milk
6 oz. white flour and 6 oz.	soda	1½ oz. butter, melted
wholemeal flour *or* 12 oz.	1½ oz. soft brown sugar	grated rind of 1 large
white flour (with plain	1 egg	orange
flour use 3 level teaspoons		
baking powder)		

1 Plump the raisins by covering them with cold water. Bring to the boil, cover and leave to stand for 5 minutes. Drain and dry.
2 Mix the raisins and nuts with 2 tablespoons flour.
3 Sieve the remaining white flour with the salt, bicarbonate of soda and baking powder, if used.
4 Mix in the wholemeal flour.
5 Add the sugar to the egg and beat thoroughly, beat in the honey, milk, butter and orange rind.
6 Add to the dry ingredients, mixing very lightly.
7 Stir in the fruit and nuts, pour the mixture into a 2-lb. greased and floured loaf tin, bake in the centre of a very moderate oven (325°F., Gas Mark 3) for about 1½ hours.

Note. This keeps for 7–10 days.

Honey muffins

Preparation: 6–8 minutes
No delay
Cooking: 25 minutes
Makes 6

Secret of success
This is a mixture that rarely
burns even if over-cooked, but
it DOES dry, so time the cooking
very carefully.

4 oz. flour (with plain flour	pinch of salt	1 egg yolk
use 1 teaspoon baking	scant 2 tablespoons milk	½ oz. lard, melted
powder)	1 tablespoon honey	

1 Sift the flour, baking powder, if used, and salt.
2 Mix the milk, honey and beaten egg yolk and stir into the dry ingredients with the melted fat.
3 Half fill six greased deep bun tins with the mixture, and bake in a moderately hot oven (400°F., Gas Mark 6) for 20–25 minutes until firm. Serve while warm, with butter.

To make good scones

Scones are very easy to make, and quite delicious when good. Remember:

1 A good scone dough should not be too stiff; it should leave one's fingers slightly 'sticky' when mixing, and be quite soft to handle.
2 Do not roll scones too much. Roll quickly then cut into required shapes.
3 Bake as soon as possible after preparing.
4 Use a really hot oven and bake near the top of the oven, unless recipe states to the contrary.
5 If you have any scones left, they can be reheated for a few minutes in the oven on the following day, or split and toasted.

The following is a good basic scone mixture.

Scone mixture

Preparation: 8 minutes
No delay
Cooking: 10 minutes
Makes 10–12

Secrets of success
Read the comments above – they are all very important.

If using sour milk, which is excellent for mixing scones, you can omit the cream of tartar – or if using baking powder use half the quantity only.

8 oz. flour*	1–2 oz. fat†	milk *to mix, see comment on left*
good pinch of salt	1 oz. sugar	

* with plain flour use EITHER 4 level teaspoons baking powder *or* 1 level teaspoon cream of tartar and ½ teaspoon bicarbonate of soda. With self-raising flour you can use half quantity raising agents above, but this is not essential.
† modern shortenings produce a light scone, or you can use margarine or butter.

1 Sieve together dry ingredients, then rub in the fat, add the sugar.
2 Mix to a SOFT rolling consistency with milk, roll out and cut into required shapes.
3 Put on to an ungreased tin (unless cheese, oatmeal or treacle are in the ingredients) and bake for approximately 10 minutes near the top of a very hot oven (475°F., Gas Mark 8).
4 To test if cooked, press at the sides; scones should feel firm to the touch.

Fruit scones: add 2–4 oz. dried fruit.
Cheese scones: omit sugar, add seasoning and 2 oz. grated cheese.
Honey or **syrup** or **treacle scones:** omit sugar and use same quantity of honey, golden syrup or treacle. Use slightly less milk to mix. Dried fruit can also be added.

Cheese and raisin muffins

Preparation: 8 minutes
No delay
Cooking: 20 minutes
Makes 6

4 oz. flour (with plain flour use 1 level teaspoon baking powder)	pinch of salt	1 oz. Cheddar cheese, grated
	¾ oz. lard *or* margarine	1 egg
	2 oz. seedless raisins	2 tablespoons milk

1 Sieve together the flour, baking powder, if used, and salt, into a mixing bowl.
2 Rub in the fat, add the seedless raisins and cheese, and finally break in the egg and add the milk, mixing to a fairly stiff consistency.
3 Put into six greased deep bun tins, and bake near the top of a moderately hot oven (400°F., Gas Mark 5) for approximately 20 minutes.

Griddle scones

Preparation: few minutes
No delay
Cooking: 4 minutes
Makes 10–12

To test if the plate or pan is the correct heat, drop a teaspoon of the mixture on this and if it goes golden brown within 1 minute the plate is ready.

4 oz. flour (with plain flour use either 2 teaspoons baking powder *or* ½ small teaspoon bicarbonate of soda and 1 small teaspoon cream of tartar)	pinch of salt	¼ pint milk
	1 oz. sugar	1 oz. margarine, melted, *optional*
	1 egg	

1 Sieve together the dry ingredients.
2 Beat in the egg, then the milk.
3 Lastly, stir in the melted margarine. This is not essential, but it does help to keep the scones moist.
4 Grease and warm the griddle, electric hot plate or frying pan. It is best to use the bottom of the frying pan – the part that usually goes over the heat.
5 Drop spoonfuls of the batter on to the plate.
6 Cook for about 2 minutes, then turn and cook for a further 2 minutes.
7 To test whether cooked, press firmly with back of a knife, and if no batter comes from sides and the scones feel firm, they are ready; cool on a wire sieve.

To vary
1 A little fruit can be added.
2 For ginger griddle scones, use 1 oz. semolina and 3 oz. flour together with ½ teaspoon powdered ginger.

To make choux pastry

Preparation: 15 minutes
Cooking: 25–30 minutes

Choux pastry is the mixture used for éclairs. It is quite an easy one to cook and prepare.

The choux pastry in the pictures has been made with modern shortening, which is very good; or you can use butter.

¼ pint water
1 oz. fat

1 teaspoon sugar
3 oz. plain *or* self-raising flour

2 whole eggs and 1 egg yolk *or* 3 small eggs

1 Put the water, fat and sugar into a saucepan.
2 Heat gently until the fat has melted.
3 Remove from the heat. Stir in the flour.

4 Return the pan to low heat and cook very gently but thoroughly, stirring all the time, until mixture is dry enough to form a ball and leave pan clean.

5 Once again remove pan from heat and gradually add eggs, beating well.
6 Do this slowly to produce a perfectly smooth mixture.

7 Allow to cool, then use for éclairs, choux buns, etc., see recipes below and opposite on colour page.

To make éclairs

Preparation: 40 minutes
Cooking: 25 minutes

The above amount makes about 12 good sized éclairs.

Make quite sure the éclairs are cold before slitting and filling. If you find there is a little uncooked mixture in the éclairs at stage 6, return to a very cool oven for a short time to 'dry out'.

ingredients as choux pastry, *above*
whipped cream

for the chocolate or coffee glacé icing
6 oz. icing sugar

2 teaspoons cocoa *or* 1 teaspoon instant coffee powder
little warm water

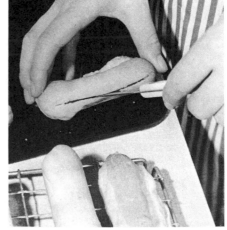

1 Insert plain pipe, ½ inch in diameter, into a cloth bag.
2 Half fill bag with choux pastry mixture, then pipe in narrow strips on to lightly greased baking tins.
3 Put the éclairs into a hot oven (425–450°F., Gas Mark 6–7) and bake for 20–25 minutes.
4 Open the door carefully after 15 minutes' cooking, and if the éclairs are browning rather quickly, lower the heat.

5 Take the éclairs out of the oven at the end of the cooking time and cool away from a draught.
6 Split into half, or make a cut down the side.
7 Fill with whipped cream and cover with coffee or chocolate glacé icing, made by blending all the ingredients together.

Ice cream gâteau St. Honoré

Ice cream gâteau St. Honoré

Preparation: 20 minutes
Cooking: 30 minutes
Serves 6

Secret of success
This depends upon perfect choux pastry, so follow points outlined opposite. Pipe the pastry carefully to give a neat shape.

for the pastry base
choux pastry, *page 270*
1½ oz. butter
3 oz. flour
little water to mix

for the glacé icing
3 oz. icing sugar, sieved
1 teaspoon coffee essence
little water *to mix*

for filling and decoration
whipped cream *or* butter icing, *page 245*
angelica
1 brick vanilla ice cream

1 *Make the choux pastry:* as directed on page 270.
2 *Prepare the pastry base:* rub the butter into the flour and bind to a firm paste with a little water.
3 Roll out to a ring shape, about 7 inches in diameter.
4 Place on a greased baking sheet and prick with a fork.
5 Put the prepared choux pastry into a forcing bag with a plain ½-inch nozzle, and pipe a ring of it at the edge of the short pastry.
6 Pipe the rest of the choux pastry into little bun shapes on another greased baking sheet.
7 Bake the pastry as directed on page 270.
8 *Make the glacé icing:* blend together the sieved icing sugar, coffee essence and a little water.
9 Fill the little choux buns with whipped cream or butter icing, and ice the tops with the glacé icing.
10 Attach the buns, with cream or butter icing, to the rim of the base.
11 Pipe between the buns with cream or butter icing, and decorate with leaves of angelica.
12 Just before serving, spoon in the vanilla ice cream.

Biscuits

The secret of good biscuits

1 Be sparing with liquid when you make biscuits — the drier the dough the more crisp and delicious they will be.
2 Do not bake them too quickly. Unless the recipe specifically states to the contrary, use the middle of a moderate oven, so that they cook steadily.
3 Put on to an ungreased tin — unless cheese, chocolate, oatmeal or syrup has been used in the biscuits.
4 Allow most biscuits to cool on the baking tin. In old recipes they were always baked TWICE — this is not essential, but if they soften slightly with keeping it will not hurt them to 'crisp-up' in a moderate oven.
5 Store away from cakes, pastry or bread.
6 You can knead a biscuit dough as much as you like.

Chocolate biscuits

Preparation: 10 minutes
No delay
Cooking: 10–15 minutes
Makes 20 biscuits

Secret of success
Knead well at stage 5, and use as little egg as possible.
This is an excellent basic chocolate dough. Make it into animal shapes for children and decorate with icing or currants, etc.

| 7 oz. plain flour | pinch of salt | 4 oz. castor sugar |
| 1 tablespoon cocoa | 4 oz. butter | beaten egg *to mix* |

1 Sieve the flour, cocoa and salt into a mixing bowl.
2 Add the butter, first by cutting it into small pieces and then by rubbing it into the dry ingredients with the fingertips, until the mixture resembles breadcrumbs.
3 Stir in the sugar.
4 Add sufficient egg to bind to a stiff dough.
5 Knead on a board sprinkled with a mixture of flour and cocoa. Roll into a circle as illustrated below.
6 Cut into the required shapes, prick with a fork and place on a greased baking tray. Bake in the centre of a very moderate oven (325–350°F., Gas Mark 3–4) for 10–15 minutes.
7 Cool on a baking tray for a time.
8 Put on to a wire tray and sprinkle with castor sugar.
9 Store in an airtight tin when cold, decorate as required.

Bourbon biscuits: cut the mixture into oblongs. Sprinkle with granulated sugar before cooking. When cooked and cooled, sandwich together with coffee-flavoured butter icing (page 245).

Rolling out chocolate biscuit dough

Top Chocolate biscuits see above
Left Brandy snaps, see page 276
Right Easter biscuits, see page 275

Semolina shortbread

Preparation: 10–15 minutes
No delay
Cooking: 15–20 minutes
Make 24 biscuits

Secret of success
Knead very well at stage 3.

Semolina gives a pleasing texture to many biscuits. Ground rice may be used instead – this gives a slightly more interesting flavour.
Do not add liquid to this mixture; knead the mixture well to bind.

Shortbreads – lemon, chocolate and almond

| 5 oz. plain flour | pinch of salt | 2 oz. castor sugar |
| 2 oz. fine semolina | 4 oz. butter *or* margarine | |

1 Sift together the flour, semolina and salt.
2 Cream the fat and sugar until soft and light, then stir in the dry ingredients.
3 Knead together lightly, then turn out on to a floured board and roll out to ¼ inch in thickness.
4 Cut into rounds with a 2-inch biscuit cutter, and prick with a fork.
5 Bake on lightly greased baking trays in the centre of a moderate oven (350–375°F., Gas Mark 4–5) for 15–20 minutes, or until pale golden in colour.
6 Sprinkle with castor sugar then cool on the baking trays.

Lemon shortbread crescents: add grated rind of 1 lemon to the creamed mixture. Cut into crescent shapes. Makes about 36.
Almond shortbread triangles: reduce flour to 4 oz. and add 2 oz. ground almonds and a few drops of almond essence to the creamed mixture. Cut into triangles. Makes about 24.
Chocolate shortbread fingers: sift ½ oz. cocoa with the dry ingredients and add a few drops of vanilla essence to the creamed mixture. Cut into fingers. Makes about 24.

Ginger nuts

Preparation: 5–6 minutes
No delay
Cooking: 15 minutes
Makes 12 biscuits

Secret of success
The rather complicated baking instructions mean the biscuits
a) spread out, and
b) crack well.

4 oz. plain flour	1 level teaspoon each mixed	2 oz. fat, butter *or* margarine
1 level teaspoon bicarbonate of soda	spice, cinnamon and powdered ginger	2 level tablespoons golden syrup
	1 oz. sugar	

1 Sieve all the dry ingredients together.
2 Melt the fat and syrup, and pour on to the flour mixture.
3 Roll into balls about the size of a walnut, and put on a well greased baking tin, allowing room between the balls, for as they cook they will spread.
4 Put the tin on the second shelf from the top of a moderately hot oven (400°F., Gas Mark 5–6) and bake for 5 minutes.
5 At the end of this time, transfer the tin to the middle of the oven and lower the heat to Gas Mark 4, or, if using an electric oven, switch OFF.
6 Cook in the middle of the oven for a further 10 minutes.
7 Cool on the tin.

Chocolate and vanilla refrigerator cookies

Preparation: 20 minutes
Allow time for dough to harden
in refrigerator
Cooking: 15–20 minutes
Makes 16 biscuits

Secret of success
Like most biscuits, this mixture
should be kept as firm in texture
as possible.

* this is better in this recipe than
self-raising flour.

4 oz. soft margarine	8 oz. plain flour*	3 tablespoons milk
4 oz. castor sugar	1 level teaspoon baking	2 oz. plain chocolate
1 egg yolk	powder	1 egg white *for brushing*
1 teaspoon vanilla essence		

1 Place the margarine and castor sugar in a mixing bowl and cream together until light and fluffy.
2 Add the egg yolk and vanilla essence and beat well.
3 Stir in the sieved flour and baking powder with 2 tablespoons milk.
4 Divide the mixture in half.
5 Wrap half in waxed or greaseproof paper, and leave in the refrigerator to chill.
6 Place the broken chocolate and remaining milk in a bowl over a saucepan of hot water and stir until dissolved.
7 Add to the second half of the biscuit dough and mix thoroughly. (See picture below.)

8 Wrap in waxed or greaseproof paper, and leave to chill in a refrigerator with the other half.
9 When required, remove from the refrigerator and roll into two oblongs 7 by 8 inches.
10 Cut each in half, making four rectangles.
11 Brush the tops with egg white.
12 Place a piece of waxed or greaseproof paper on a tray.
13 Put rectangles in alternate layers on the paper. Leave in refrigerator until firm.

14 Cut into ¼-inch slices. Place on a baking tray previously brushed with melted margarine.
15 Bake near the top of a moderate oven (350–375°F., Gas Mark 4–5) for 15–20 minutes. Cool on the baking tin.

Easter biscuits

Cooking: 15 minutes
Preparation: 15 minutes
Makes about 16–18

Secrets of success
Use the minimum of liquid.
Grease the tins very lightly as
you have currants in the mixture.

Colour picture, page 272

4 oz. margarine	8 oz. plain flour	4–5 oz. currants
4 oz. castor sugar	½–1 teaspoon mixed spice	1 egg

1 Cream the margarine and sugar until soft and light.
2 Sieve the flour and spice, add to the creamed mixture and knead very well, then add the currants.
3 Gradually work in enough egg to bind (if the egg is small you will need all of it plus a few drops of milk, but use as little liquid as possible).
4 Knead again firmly, then roll out to ¼ inch in thickness on a lightly floured board.
5 Cut into rounds and bake for 15 minutes in the centre of a very moderate oven (325–350°F., Gas Mark 3–4) until golden brown.
6 Cool on baking tray; store in an airtight tin (see colour picture page 272).

Brandy snaps

Preparation: 15 minutes
Cooking: 8–12 minutes
Makes 12–14

Secrets of success
Weigh the flour carefully, then take away 1 teaspoonful.
Time the cooking carefully.

Colour picture, page 272

2 oz. butter *or* margarine
2 oz. castor sugar

2 LEVEL tablespoons golden syrup
½–1 teaspoon ground ginger

2 oz. self-raising flour *or* plain flour with ½ level teaspoon baking powder

1 Put the butter or margarine, sugar and syrup into a saucepan.
2 Heat steadily until the fat has melted, then remove from the heat.
3 Sieve the ginger with the flour or flour and baking powder.
4 Stir into the syrup mixture in the saucepan.
5 Put teaspoons of the mixture on to well greased baking trays, allowing plenty of room for the mixture to spread out.
6 Put the first tray in the oven, but do not add the second tray for a few minutes (this makes it easier to deal with the biscuits when they come from the oven).
7 Bake near the centre of a very moderate oven (325–350°F., Gas Mark 3–4) until golden brown.
8 Remove first tray from oven, cool for just 2 minutes until easy to take off.
9 Roll the first biscuit round the greased handle of a wooden spoon, hold for a few seconds to set the shape, then put on to cooling tray. Continue, working quickly through each tray.
10 Allow to cool on a wire tray; store in an airtight tin.
11 These biscuits are delicious filled with whipped cream; do this just before serving them (see colour picture page 272).

Cheese crackers

Preparation: 7–10 minutes
No delay
Cooking: 7–10 minutes
Makes 12–18 biscuits

Secret of success
Knead the dough very firmly, otherwise it might break when rolled out so thinly.

1 oz. margarine *or* butter
3 oz. flour
salt and pepper

2 oz. cheese, finely grated
milk
cream cheese

olives
gherkins

1 Rub the fat into the flour.
2 Add the seasoning and cheese.
3 Bind with milk to a firm dough.
4 Roll thinly (paper thinness) and evenly, and cut into tiny shapes.
5 Bake on a lightly greased baking tin near the top of a hot oven (425–450°F., Gas Mark 6–7) for just about 7–10 minutes. Cool.
6 Top with cream cheese and sliced olives, gherkins, etc.

Quick shortbread fingers

Preparation: 10 minutes
No delay
Cooking: 30–35 minutes
Makes 12 biscuits

Secret of success
Work and knead ingredients very well at stage 2.
Keep oven temperature low when baking, so the biscuits keep pale in colour.

4 oz. soft margarine
2 oz. castor sugar

6 oz. plain flour

castor sugar *to sprinkle*

1 Place all the ingredients in a mixing bowl.
2 Knead together well with finger tips until smooth and pliable, making a firm smooth ball.
3 Turn out on to a lightly floured board. Divide into two portions.
4 Roll out and trim into two oblongs, about 8 by 2½ inches.
5 Place on a baking tray covered with greaseproof paper. Prick with a fork.
6 Bake above the centre of a slow to very moderate oven (300–325°F., Gas Mark 2–3) for 30–35 minutes.
7 Cut into fingers and sprinkle with castor sugar. Allow to cool on the baking tray for a few minutes, then on a wire tray.

Quick shortbread fingers

Hot and cold drinks

How to make perfect coffee

In these days many people make instant coffee and directions are given on the can or jar. Like all coffee, it should be freshly made so the flavour is at its best.

Buy only a small quantity at a time; if possible have it freshly ground. The ideal way is to buy coffee beans and to grind these as needed. For this you must have a coffee grinder. When choosing coffee, buy the best you can afford. Mocha coffee, which comes from Aden and Mocha, is generally considered to be the best, but you will find by experience which brands you prefer. If you like a strong flavour, choose coffee to which a little chicory has been added.

When you store coffee, take care that it is not near any strong-smelling foodstuffs, as it quickly absorbs other odours and is spoilt. When you open a can or a packet (if you have bought the vacuum-packed kind, and not had it freshly ground), transfer the coffee to a screw-topped jar. This keeps it fresh.

1 Use sufficient coffee; about 2 heaped tablespoons to each 1 pint water is correct.
2 Use freshly drawn water, as for tea making.
3 Never allow the coffee to boil with the water; bring it *just to boiling point*.
4 Add hot — not boiling — milk or cold milk to coffee, or thin cream.
  Breakfast coffee is usually a lighter roast than after-dinner coffee, and is sometimes known as 'American Roast'. For after-dinner, or black coffee, choose the darker kind, sometimes called 'Continental roast', which is stronger.

To make coffee in a jug

Preparation: few minutes
Infuse for a few minutes
Cooking: time for water to boil

1 Warm the jug to be used for making the coffee.
2 Put in the coffee, quantity as given above.
3 Pour over the freshly boiling water.
4 Give a brisk stir, cover and leave for a few minutes.
5 Strain into a second hot jug or directly into the coffee cups.
6 Keep the jug covered, to retain maximum heat for second cups.

To make coffee in a saucepan

Preparation: as above
Cooking: as above

Do not allow *coffee* to boil.

1 Put the water into a saucepan and bring to the boil.
2 Add the coffee — quantity as above.
3 Stir briskly and draw the pan away from the heat.
4 Cover, and leave to infuse for a few minutes in a warm place.
5 Strain into a hot jug, or directly into coffee cups.
6 If reheating the coffee in the saucepan make certain it does not boil.

To make coffee in a percolator

Preparation: few minutes
Leave to percolate
Cooking: time for water to boil

1 Put the cold water into the percolator.
2 Put the coffee into the basket; choose *medium ground coffee*.
3 Either stand the percolator on the cooker, or plug in if using an electric model.
4 Allow the water to come to the boil, reduce the heat *at once* so all the liquid percolates through the basket. A thermostatically controlled percolator can be set so the coffee percolates itself and never boils too fast.

To make coffee by the drip method

Preparation: few minutes
Time to drip through
Cooking: few minutes

1 Put the coffee into the top of the utensil. For quantity see above; choose a medium ground coffee.
2 Bring the water to the boil in a kettle.
3 Gradually pour the water over the coffee, allowing this to drip through into the lower container.

Stand the container on a hot plate (plate warmer) so the coffee keeps hot.
The Cona coffee-maker works rather on the principle above, although the water rises from the bottom container.

To make perfect tea

Preparation: few minutes
Infuse for a few minutes
Cooking: time required to boil
the water

Always warm the pot.

1 Fill the kettle with fresh water from the main water supply, then bring just to the boil before pouring over the tea.
2 Allow to infuse for 3–4 minutes before pouring.
3 Quantities of tea will vary according to personal taste, but the old ruling, one teaspoon for each person and one for the pot, is a good average amount.
4 Keep your teapot well washed out, but be certain, if using detergents, etc., that you rinse it well, otherwise this could spoil the flavour of the tea.

Both China and Indian (or other teas) may be served either with milk or with lemon, although it is more usual to serve China tea with lemon.

To make chocolate

Preparation: few minutes
Cooking: minute or so only

Do not boil the milk.

1 Blend cocoa or chocolate powder with a little cold milk.
2 Pour on the very hot milk and stir or whisk hard.
3 Add sugar to taste. Top with thick or thin cream, if desired.

As cocoa has a stronger flavour it is better to return the drink to the saucepan and heat gently for 2–3 minutes.
For a chilled chocolate drink, choose chocolate powder rather than cocoa.

To make milk shakes

Preparation: few minutes
No delay
No cooking for cold milk shakes;
time to heat milk for hot milk
shakes

It is possible to buy flavouring
syrups which are ideal for milk
shakes.

1 Put the syrup into a rather large container.
2 Add the hot or cold milk and whisk together sharply.
3 Pour into the glasses.
4 The photograph shows a spice milk shake where added flavour is given, with a little spice on top.
5 A richer milk shake can be made by using ice cream and whisking this with the cold milk. If using flavoured ice cream you have no need to use flavoured syrup.

The ideal way to make milk shakes is in an electric liquidiser. Put the hot or cold milk, flavouring (which can be fresh fruit or fruit syrup, etc.) into the goblet. Switch on for a minute until very light and fluffy. Ice or ice cream may be added to cold milk shakes.

Creamy egg nog

Preparation: 15 minutes. Allow
time after boiling evaporated
milk for it to cool (see page 174)
or to chill it thoroughly
No cooking
Serves 8–10

Secret of success
Whisk the egg yolks, etc., until
very fluffy at stages 2 and 3.

2 large cans evaporated milk
6 egg yolks
pinch of salt

3 oz. castor sugar
¼ pint sherry

2 tablespoons rum *or* cognac,
optional
little grated nutmeg

1 First chill then whip the cans of evaporated milk, if not already done.
2 Put the egg yolks into a bowl with salt and sugar; whisk well together.
3 Add the sherry and whisk again, then add the rum or cognac, if used, and whisk again.
4 Stir in the chilled and whipped evaporated milk, mixing well.
5 Pour into a large bowl. Sprinkle with a little grated nutmeg and serve.

Left *Creamy egg nog*
Right *Milk shake*

Preserves

To make perfect jam

1 Make sure the fruit is firm — over-ripe fruit causes jam to ferment or go mouldy.
2 Use the right proportion of sugar to fruit — this can be preserving, loaf or granulated sugar. Preserving sugar is economical and good. If a fruit is lacking in pectin, i.e. the natural setting quality of the fruit, you must add additional pectin in the form of lemon juice or commercial pectin.
3 Always simmer fruit gently BEFORE adding sugar. This softens skins and extracts the pectin.
4 Stir until sugar is dissolved — then boil steadily WITHOUT stirring until setting point is reached. ALLOW PLENTY OF SPACE IN PAN for jam to boil, without boiling over. It is better to make 2 batches of a smaller quantity than 1 large batch where you have insufficient room in the pan.
5 Test early for setting point, for if you boil beyond this the jam becomes sticky and spoiled. In the case of some fruits — oranges in particular — if you boil beyond setting point you 'lose' the jellying properties of the fruit and it will never set.
6 With whole fruit or peel do not pot immediately; allow jam or marmalade to cool slightly and thicken, then STIR and pot.
7 Always fill the jars to the top, for the less air space in the jar the less possibility there is of the jam fermenting.
8 Cover jam in jars while hot, with waxed circles and cellophane covers.
9 Store in a cool dry place.

To test if jam or marmalade has reached setting point

Always take the pan off heat as you test
There are three good ways of testing:
Method 1. Test with a sugar thermometer — jam sets at a temperature of 220°F.
Method 2. Stir preserve thoroughly with a wooden spoon, turn the spoon round to cool the jam adhering to it, then hold the spoon horizontally. If jam has set it will form a firm drop or flake on the edge of the spoon.
Method 3. Put a little on a cold saucer, cool it, and if adequately set it should wrinkle and feel firm.

Note. The approximate yield is given beside the recipes; if a much greater quantity of jam is produced then it is inadequately boiled and will not keep, and should be tipped back into the pan and re-boiled. Do not continually skim the jam. Wait until it reaches setting point, stir for a minute (this will get rid of quite a lot of the scum), then remove the remainder. A knob of margarine or butter put in when making the jam will not only safeguard the jam from burning in a thin pan but will help to prevent scum. Cooking times have not been given in the following recipes as these vary according to the ripeness of the fruit and the quantities used. Test early, as recommended above.

Apricot jam
(fresh fruit)

Makes 1⅔ lb. jam

Secret of success
Remember that lemon juice is essential here.

1 lb. apricots

1 tablespoon water, unless the fruit is under-ripe then 2 tablespoons

1 lb. sugar
½ teaspoon citric *or* tartaric acid *or* the juice of ½ lemon

1 Cut the fruit into pieces.
2 If desired, crack the stones and take out the kernels.
3 Put into a preserving pan with the water, and simmer until the fruit is soft.
4 Add the sugar and acid or lemon juice and boil rapidly until set.

Peach jam can be made in the same way.

Note. The stones of apricots or peaches may be cracked and the kernels added at stage 4, just before the jam sets.

Blackberry and apple jam

Makes 3½ lb. jam

Secret of success
Do not over-cook the fruit.

| 1 lb. cooking apples, weight after peeling and coring | 2 tablespoons water 1 lb. blackberries | 2 lb. sugar |

1 Put the apples and water into the preserving pan.
2 Cook gently until the apples are becoming soft.
3 Add the blackberries and continue cooking until all the fruit is soft.
4 Stir in the sugar, and continue stirring until dissolved.
5 Boil rapidly until the jam has set.

Blackcurrant jam

Makes just over 2 lb. jam

These proportions give a deliciously soft jam.

| 1 lb. blackcurrants | ¾ pint water | 1¼ lb. sugar |

1 Put the fruit and water into the pan, simmer until the blackcurrants are quite soft.
2 Stir in the sugar, then boil rapidly until set.

Cherry jam

Makes approximately 1½ lb. jam

Secret of success
Do not exceed this amount of sugar.
With Morello cherries, use half quantity of acid.

| 1 lb. stoned cherries, *or* nearly 1¼ lb. cherries before stoning | 12 oz. sugar | juice of ½ lemon or ½ teaspoon citric *or* tartaric acid |

1 Put the fruit, and stones tied in muslin, into the pan.
2 Simmer until the fruit is soft.
3 Stir in the sugar, lemon juice or acid, and continue stirring until dissolved.
4 Boil rapidly until set.

Damson jam

Makes 1 lb. jam with ripe fruit, just over 2 lb. jam with larger quantity of sugar and under-ripe fruit.

You may care to sieve the damsons at stage 2, to get rid of stones.

for ripe fruit

| 1 lb. damsons | 2 tablespoons water | 1 lb. sugar |

for under-ripe fruit

| 1 lb. damsons | ½ pint water | 1¼ lb. sugar |

1 Put the fruit and water into a pan.
2 Simmer until soft.
3 Add the sugar, stir until dissolved, then boil rapidly until set.

Gooseberry jam

Quantities as for damson jam, varying the quantity of sugar and water according to how ripe the fruit is found to be.

Greengage jam

Makes 1 lb. jam

Choose ripe fruit if possible, for true flavour.

| 1 lb. greengages, weight after stoning | 1 lb. sugar |

1 Use no water if fruit is ripe, 2 tablespoons water if under-ripe.
2 Stones of fruit can be cracked and kernels included.
3 Simmer fruit, then add sugar, stirring until dissolved.
4 Boil rapidly until set.

Plum jam

Makes 1 lb. jam

Choose fruit that is *just* ripe.

| 1 lb. plums | 1 lb. sugar |

1 Use no water if fruit is ripe, 2 tablespoons if under-ripe.
2 Follow the method for greengage jam.
3 If whole fruit jam is required, cut the plums in halves.
4 Put into a bowl, sprinkle sugar over, leave overnight. The next day proceed as usual.

Raspberry jam 1

Makes nearly 2 lb. jam

Do not over-cook.

1 lb. raspberries   1 lb. sugar

1 Heat the fruit until boiling.
2 Stir in the hot sugar — heated for a few minutes in the oven.
3 Boil rapidly until the jam has set. If the fruit is firm and fresh this should take only about 3 minutes' rapid boiling.

Strawberry jam 1

Makes 1⅔ lb. jam

Secret of success
Always add the lemon juice.

1 lb. strawberries   1 lb. sugar   juice of 1 lemon

1 Simmer the fruit until soft.
2 Add the sugar and lemon juice, and stir until dissolved.
3 Boil rapidly until set.

Recipes using commercial pectin

Raspberry jam 2

Makes 10 lb. jam
Choose slightly firm fruit.

4 lb. raspberries   5½ lb. sugar   1 bottle commercial pectin

1 Crush the raspberries. Add the sugar.
2 Heat slowly until the sugar is dissolved, stir occasionally.
3 Quickly bring to a full rolling boil.
4 Boil rapidly for 2 minutes, stirring occasionally.
5 Remove from heat and stir in the pectin.
6 Skim if necessary.
7 Allow to cool to prevent the fruit sinking.
8 Pot and cover in the usual way.

Quickly made strawberry jam 2

Preparation: 10–15 minutes
No delay
Cooking: 15 minutes

Makes 5½ lb. jam
Use *slightly* under-ripe fruit.

2¼ lb. strawberries   3 lb. sugar   ½ bottle commercial pectin
3 tablespoons lemon juice   knob butter *or* margarine

1 Hull the fruit (i.e. remove stalks). Crush, then add lemon juice and sugar.
2 Heat slowly until sugar has dissolved, stir occasionally, then bring quickly to a full rolling boil.
3 Boil rapidly for 2 minutes, stir occasionally, add butter or margarine.
4 Remove from heat and stir in the pectin. Skim if necessary.
5 Allow to cool slightly to prevent fruit sinking, pot and cover in the usual way.

To make jellies

The same basic rules apply, as for jam. The method is as follows:
1 Simmer fruit and water slowly until soft.
2 Strain through a jelly bag (obtainable from ironmongers) or several thicknesses of muslin over a hair sieve (not metal, as it might discolour the juice).
3 Measure the juice, add the sugar and stir over low heat until sugar dissolves.
4 Boil juice and sugar until thick, test and pot like jam.

Quantities

Fruit	Amount of water	Remarks
2 lb. blackberries and 2 lb. apples	1 pint	Do not peel apples. Wipe, cut in pieces but leave the peel and cores in, as these help to set jelly.
4 lb. apples 4 lb. redcurrants	1 pint 2 pints	As above. Wash fruit well. Shake fairly dry or, if rather damp, use a little less water.

Allow 1 lb. sugar to each 1 pint juice

Use a jelly bag to strain fruit juice

To make perfect marmalade

The rules are the same as for jam making – the fruit MUST soak well if so directed, and then be simmered very gently so that it really IS soft before adding sugar.

Seville or bitter orange marmalade

Makes 5 lb. marmalade.

Secret of success
Test marmalade early – it is easily over-boiled.

| 1 lb. oranges | 3 lb. sugar | juice of 1 large lemon |
| 3 pints water | | |

1 Cut or mince the oranges finely, removing the pips.
2 Soak the peel and pulp overnight in the water, together with the pips, which should be tied up carefully in a piece of muslin.
3 After soaking, put the fruit, water and pips in a covered pan, and simmer slowly until the peel is quite soft. This should take approximately 1½ hours.
4 Take out the bag of pips, stir in the sugar and lemon juice.
5 Bring the marmalade to the boil and boil rapidly in an uncovered pan until setting point is reached. This will take approximately 20 minutes.

To vary
For a less sweet and thicker marmalade, use either 2 pints water and 2 lb. sugar, or 2½ pints water and 2½ lb. sugar.

Lemon marmalade

Makes 4 lb. marmalade

| 1 lb. lemons (4 medium *or* 3 large) | 2½ pints water | 2½ lb. sugar |

Method as in recipe above.

To make mincemeat

1 It is absolutely essential the fruit is perfectly dry before making mincemeat.
2 If you have washed it, let it dry for 24 or preferably 48 hours before using.
3 A good cooking apple should be used.
4 Make certain your jars are clean and very dry.
5 Store in a cool, dry place.
6 The alcohol in the recipe is very important if you wish the mincemeat to keep.
7 If you do not intend to keep it for a very long time, you can substitute lemon and orange juice for the alcohol.
8 Do not cut down on the quantities of sugar, suet, etc.

Mincemeat

Preparation: 25–30 minutes. To be kept for several weeks
No cooking
Makes 3 lb.

Secret of success
Do not cut down on the amounts of sugar, brandy, etc., otherwise this will not keep.

4 oz. shredded suet or margarine, melted	4 oz. almonds, blanched, well dried and chopped	1 teaspoon mixed spice
4 oz. apple, grated	4 oz. chopped candied peel	½ teaspoon cinnamon
1 lb. mixed dried fruit	finely grated rind and juice of 1 large lemon	½ teaspoon grated nutmeg
4 oz. sugar, preferably brown		4 tablespoons brandy, whisky *or* rum

1 Mix all the ingredients together.
2 Put into dry jam jars and cover thoroughly. Use both wax circles and a thick cellophane or paper top.
3 Leave in a cool dry place.

To give added flavour to bought mincemeat

You may not have time to make your own mincemeat, and the bought preparation is very good – although not always as moist and rich as the recipe above. You can, however, give additional flavour if you tip the mincemeat into a basin and add a little rum, and perhaps a few chopped nuts and extra peel.

To make preserves in a pressure cooker

Follow your pressure cooker book, but remember the following points:
1 Because you lose very little liquid by evaporation, as in the ordinary jam recipes, you should cut the liquid down to approximately half in jams, and a third in marmalade.
2 You can cook the fruit under pressure, but when the sugar is added you must treat your pressure cooker like an ordinary preserving pan and boil with the lid off.
3 A pressure cooker, because it is of such solid construction, is a very good utensil for jam making.

Sweets

Making sweets at home

Many people have the idea that home-made sweets are very easy. In fact, until you have made them on several occasions they can be quite difficult, since you must reach the right temperature for different kinds of sweetmeat.

If you intend to make a lot of sweets, a sugar thermometer, as shown in sketch below, is an excellent investment.

Toffee apples

Preparation: few minutes
No delay
Cooking: see right
Makes 8

Secret of success
The easiest method of weighing golden syrup is to weigh saucepan and sugar together, then gradually pour in golden syrup and stop when the scales register a further 8 oz.

Always wrap toffee apples in waxed paper or foil if they are not to be eaten at once. This prevents the toffee becoming over-sticky.

8 oz. granulated sugar	8 apples	8 wooden sticks
8 oz. golden syrup		

1 Put the sugar and golden syrup into a strong saucepan.
2 Boil the sugar and syrup together, stirring at the beginning until the sugar is thoroughly dissolved.

3 Wipe apples and insert sticks into them.

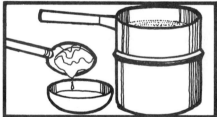 

4 Continue boiling the toffee mixture until the brittle stage. There are two ways to tell if it has reached this stage:
a) a sugar thermometer will register 310°F.
b) pour a few drops of the toffee mixture into cold water. Pour off the water and feel the toffee between thumb and forefinger. When the toffee is not quite ready, you will be able to press it into different shapes. When it is ready, it will be brittle and crack between your thumb and finger.
5 As soon as the toffee is nearly hard enough, be sure to take it off the heat while you test.

6 To dip apples, the toffee must be prevented from setting, so if using a double saucepan keep toffee over hot water. If you have boiled in an ordinary saucepan, stand this over a dish or baking tin of boiling water. Make sure that the cooker heat is turned right off.
7 Dip apples into hot toffee; if you want a thick coating dip once very quickly, hold for a moment above the pan, and then dip again. When the apple is no longer dripping, place on a buttered tin and allow to set.

To make toffee

The recipe above makes a good brittle toffee.
For a more creamy toffee
1 Add 1 oz. butter.
2 Boil as directed above, and when the toffee reaches the brittle stage pour into a buttered 6- or 7-inch square tin.
3 Leave to set, then break into pieces.

Fudge

Preparation: few minutes
Allow to set
Cooking: see method
Makes 1¾ lb.

Secrets of success
Stir fudge well during cooking;
it is inclined to burn.
Use the same care in testing as
is described on the previous
page for toffee.

1 lb. *either* granulated *or* loaf
   sugar
large can sweetened full-
   cream condensed milk

2 oz. butter.
2 tablespoons water

1 good teaspoon vanilla
   essence *or* 2 tablespoons
   cocoa *or* 3 tablespoons
   chocolate powder *or* 2
   tablespoons coffee essence

1 Put the ingredients into a strong saucepan.
2 Stir until the sugar has dissolved.
3 Boil steadily, stirring only occasionally, until the mixture has reached 238°F., or
   forms a soft ball when a little is dropped into a cup of cold water.
4 Remove from the heat, beat until the mixture starts to thicken, then pour into a tin
   greased with butter or oil.
5 When nearly set, cut into neat pieces with a sharp knife.

Almond and raisin candy

Preparation: 12 minutes
No delay
Cooking: varies a great deal
according to size of pan etc;
approximately 20 minutes
Makes 1 lb. 6 oz.

Secret of success
Stir this well during cooking; it is
inclined to burn.

Almond and raisin candy

2 oz. blanched almonds, *see*
   page 258
1 lb. granulated sugar

small can evaporated milk
1 oz. butter

2 oz. seedless raisins
few drops of almond essence

1 First chop the blanched almonds.
2 Put the sugar and evaporated milk into a strong saucepan and stir very slowly over a
   low heat until the sugar is completely dissolved. You can feel any grains of sugar
   with a wooden spoon. Add the butter.
3 Cook to soft ball stage (238°F. if you have a sugar thermometer) — when a teaspoonful
   dropped into a cup of cold water can be gathered up in the fingers to form a soft ball;
   then stir in the almonds and raisins.
4 Add a few drops almond essence, and stir the mixture until it thickens and looks
   slightly creamy.
5 Pour as quickly as you can into a lightly oiled tin. Do not delay, otherwise the mixture
   will set in the saucepan.
6 When partially set, cut into squares, but do not remove from tin until hardened.

Crystal fruit candy

Preparation: 12 minutes
No delay
Cooking: varies a great deal
according to size of pan etc;
approximately 20 minutes
Makes 1 lb. 6 oz.

Secret of success
Stir this well during cooking; it
is inclined to burn.

1 lb. granulated sugar
small can evaporated milk
1 oz. butter
1 teaspoon lemon juice

1 tablespoon golden syrup
1 tablespoon chopped
   angelica
1 tablespoon chopped glacé
   cherries

1 tablespoon glacé pineapple
   or apricots, chopped

1 Put the sugar and evaporated milk into a strong pan and heat slowly, stirring
   constantly.
2 When the sugar is dissolved, add the butter, lemon juice and golden syrup.
3 Stir well to blend, cook to soft ball stage (see above) then add rest of the ingredients
   and stir briskly until mixture is creamy, but not too thick to pour.
4 Pour as quickly as possible into a lightly oiled shallow tin.
5 When partially cooled, mark into squares.
6 When set, cut through to separate.

Raisin kisses

Preparation: 10–15 minutes
No delay
Cooking: 15 minutes
Makes about 15

2 oz. seedless raisins
2 egg whites
pinch of salt

4 oz. icing sugar
2 oz. walnuts or peanuts,
chopped

few drops of vanilla essence

1 Plump the seedless raisins by covering with cold water. Bring to the boil, cover and leave to stand for 5 minutes. Drain and dry.
2 Beat the egg whites, with a pinch of salt, until stiff, add half the icing sugar, beat again until the mixture stands in peaks.
3 Fold in the remaining sugar, the raisins, nuts and vanilla essence.
4 Place about 15 heaped teaspoonfuls well apart on a greased baking sheet, and, bake just above the centre of a moderate oven (375°F., Gas Mark 4) for 15 minutes.
5 Keep in an airtight tin away from cakes.

Uncooked sweets

Raisin crispies

Preparation: 5 minutes
No delay
Makes 16

Secret of success
Keep the heat very low at stage 1.

2 oz. butter
2 oz. marshmallows

2 oz. creamy toffee
4 oz. seedless raisins

2½ oz. rice breakfast cereal

1 Put the butter and marshmallows into a large saucepan.
2 Break up the toffee roughly, add it to the saucepan and stir this mixture over gentle heat until it has melted.
3 Stir in the raisins and rice cereal.
4 Pack the mixture into a buttered 8-inch round or square tin, press down well.
5 When set cut into 16 small squares, or triangles, before removing from tin.

Rum candies

Preparation: 15 minutes
No delay
Makes 18

Roll these with damp fingers at stages 4 and 5.

2 oz. golden syrup
3 oz. seedless raisins
2 oz. walnuts
4 oz. ice cream wafers

1 oz. icing sugar
½ oz. cocoa
2 tablespoons rum
2 oz. butter, melted

to coat
¾–1 oz. icing sugar
¾–1 teaspoon instant coffee
powder

1 To weigh syrup, flour the scale pan; pour in the syrup, which will then run easily from the scale pan.
2 Finely chop the raisins and nuts.
3 Crush the wafers into fine crumbs. To do this, put on greaseproof paper, cover with more greaseproof paper and roll with a rolling pin.
4 Combine the ingredients thoroughly with the hands.
5 Shape into 18 small balls, then roll in icing sugar mixed with instant coffee.
6 Store in an airtight container.

Coconut kisses

Preparation: few minutes
Allow to set.
Makes 18

small can full-cream
  condensed milk

4–5 oz. desiccated coconut

rice paper*

*obtainable from good stationers.

1 Mix the condensed milk with enough coconut to give a firm consistency.
2 Put the rice paper on to flat tins.
3 Put tiny spoonfuls of the coconut mixture on this; allow to harden in the air.
4 The mixture can be coloured by adding a few drops of cochineal or other vegetable colourings. When adding colourings, etc., it is very important to do this quickly. The easiest way is to dip the point of a metal skewer into the bottle and then allow the drops from the skewer to fall into the ingredients.

More uncooked sweets

Stuffed dates: stone dessert dates and fill with marzipan or royal icing page 260, mixed with chopped nuts and glacé cherries.
Chocolate marzipan truffles: make marzipan as page 260, and flavour with a little sieved cocoa and rum. You can add chopped nuts, sultanas, chopped cherries if wished. Do not have the mixture too stiff. Form into tiny balls, and roll in a mixture of sieved icing sugar and cocoa.
Uncooked coconut ice: make royal icing as page 260, using 8 oz. icing sugar, etc. Work in 2–4 oz. desiccated coconut and a little thick cream to make a slightly softer consistency. Press into a tin, leave until set, then cut into fingers or squares, if wished press half the coconut ice into a tin, colour the remainder pink, press on top, then cut.

To help when you entertain

Although tea is a less popular meal than in the past, it is a simple way to entertain. Make small sandwiches; scones or home-made bread (recipes pages 266–267); and have a fruit cake and/or gingerbread and a light sponge. Both a Victoria sandwich (recipe page 243) and Genoese pastry, below, can be made a day beforehand. Children will enjoy biscuits (see pages 273–276 and below). Genoese pastry can be decorated to turn it into a super gâteau which could be served for luncheon or dinner, and the biscuits given on this page would be very pleasant to serve with coffee after a meal.

Coffee walnut biscuits

Preparation: 15 minutes
No delay
Cooking: 10 minutes
Makes 24

Secret of success
Handle very firmly at stage 4.
Roll out firmly.

2 oz. walnuts	6 oz. plain flour	icing sugar *or* coffee butter
4 oz. margarine	1 teaspoon instant coffee	icing, *page 245* made with
4 oz. castor sugar	powder	4 oz. butter, etc.
	1 egg yolk	few chopped walnuts

1 Chop or mince the walnuts, or emulsify in the liquidiser – they should be very fine.
2 Cream margarine with the sugar, work in the flour, instant coffee and walnuts.
3 Work together firmly with your hands, then gradually add enough egg yolk to bind.
4 Roll out very thinly indeed – this must be done firmly so the biscuits do not break. Cut into 3-inch rounds.
5 Put on to lightly greased and floured baking trays, bake for 10 minutes in the centre of a moderate oven (350–375°F., Gas Mark 4–5). Cool on the tin.
6 Store in an airtight tin: serve dusted with icing sugar OR sandwich two biscuits with coffee butter icing and cover the top with a thin layer of coffee butter icing; decorate with chopped walnuts.
7 The butter icing must be put into the biscuits, and on top, *on the day they are being served*, but the biscuits themselves will keep for days in the tin.

Genoese sponge or Genoese pastry

Preparation: 15–18 minutes
No delay
Cooking: 16–18 minutes
Makes 8–10 slices

Secrets of success
Whisk eggs and sugar well at stages 1–3.
Fold in flour gently.
Cool butter or margarine, see stage 4.

3 large eggs	3 oz. flour (with plain flour	4 oz. butter, melted and
4 oz. castor sugar	use ½ teaspoon baking	allowed to cool
	powder)	

1 Put the eggs and sugar into a basin placed over a saucepan of hot water.
2 Whisk together until thick.
3 Take basin off the heat and continue to whisk until the egg mixture is cold.
4 FOLD IN the flour – which should be sieved with the baking powder, if used – then the melted butter. Here the use of butter is well justified, for if making this mixture a day or so before decorating it keeps very much better.
5 Put into two greased and floured 7- or 7½-inch sandwich tins; bake for approximately 16 minutes near the top of a moderately hot oven (400°F., Gas Mark 5).
6 This may be decorated as any ordinary sponge or light cake, but is ideal for filling and topping with fruit and whipped cream (see below).

Genoese sponge

286

A snack supper from the store cupboard

There may be occasions when you want to prepare a meal with the minimum of trouble. Here is a very satisfying snack meal; many of the ingredients could be used from your store cupboard. If you have a home freezer then you can store a good selection of perishable foods, meat, fish, etc.

The **Meat loaf** on page 74 (colour picture) can be prepared very rapidly. Take 1 lb. minced beef from freezer or refrigerator, blend with a good pinch seasoned salt; shake seasoned pepper; garlic salt; 2 eggs and 2 oz. breadcrumbs. Put into well greased loaf tin, cover with greased paper and bake for $1\frac{1}{2}$ hours in a very moderate oven.

Toasted meat loaf snack

Preparation: 10 minutes
No delay
Cooking: few minutes
Serves 6

Serve this when very freshly made.

4 oz. mushrooms *or* tomatoes	seasoning	16-oz. can corned beef loaf
little butter	6 slices sandwich loaf	*or* minced beef loaf
sugar		

1 Fry the mushrooms in a little butter; if you prefer tomatoes, slice and place in the grilling pan.
2 Sprinkle with a little sugar, salt and pepper.
3 Toast the bread slices on one side.
4 Divide the meat into 6 or 8 pieces.
5 Butter the untoasted side of the bread.
6 Spread with the meat, pressing it out to the edges.
7 Grill until the meat is hot and sizzling.
8 Cut diagonally, then garnish with mushrooms or tomatoes.

Piquant tuna snack

Preparation: 10 minutes
No delay
Cooking: few minutes
Serves 4

Secret of success
Do not over-cook the cheese topping, otherwise it will be tough.

4 slices of bread	2 tablespoons milk *or* thin	salt and pepper
can tuna fish	cream	
2 teaspoons concentrated	1 level teaspoon sugar	*to garnish*
tomato purée from a tube	little butter	parsley
or 2 medium tomatoes	3 oz. Cheddar cheese, grated	

1 Toast the bread slices on one side.
2 Mix the tuna, tomato, milk or cream and sugar (skin and chop fresh tomatoes).
3 Spread the untoasted side of the bread with butter, then cover with a generous amount of the tuna mixture; top with cheese, sprinkle with salt and pepper.
4 Toast until cheese has melted and fish is heated through.
5 Garnish each slice with a sprig of parsley, serve at once.

Fruit custard tarts

Preparation: few minutes
No delay
No cooking
Makes 9

large can peach *or* apricot	9 custard tartlets (bought	glacé cherries
halves	from pastrycooks)	

1 Open the can of peach or apricot halves, drain the fruit from the syrup.
2 Cut each piece of fruit in half.
3 Arrange two halves in each tartlet and put a cherry in between. Do not use too great a weight of fruit or the tartlets will break.

Cherry baskets

Preparation: 12 minutes
No delay
Cooking: few minutes for glaze
Serves 4

Secret of success
Make sure ice cream is very firm, or it melts and looks unattractive when baskets are complete.

2 sponge cakes	ice cream wafers	little thick cream
redcurrant jelly	about 8 oz. cherries, canned	strips of orange rind
4 small blocks ice cream	*or* cooked	

1 Split the sponge cakes through the centre, put on individual plates.
2 Spread with jelly and put the ice cream on top, then place wafers round the sides, shaping these if wishing to have the uneven edge of a basket.
3 Top with well drained cherries, cover with a glaze made by heating 2 good tablespoons of redcurrant jelly with the same amount of cherry juice.
4 Pipe or spread a little cream round the edges, and press strips of orange peel into position as handles. For details of piping see page 247.

Extra recipes for Christmas time

Christmas time always means rather a lot of cooking and in this book you will find recipes for traditional dishes such as roast turkey and Christmas pudding (pages 114 and 156). On this and the following page, however, you will find some less usual dishes to help make your Christmas entertaining successful.

Caramel or Viennese pudding

Preparation: 20 minutes
No delay — but better if allowed to stand
Cooking: approximately 2½ hours
Serves 6

For those who do not like, or cannot eat, rich Christmas pudding, and would like something different for Christmas Day, here is a recipe for a Caramel or Viennese pudding — which looks like a golden-coloured Christmas pudding — based on a custard mixture, and therefore suitable for invalids or children.

3 oz. loaf sugar	2 egg whites	2 oz. glacé cherries, chopped
3 tablespoons water	2 oz. sultanas	1 oz. crystallised peel,
1 pint milk	2 oz. nuts, chopped, *optional*	chopped
4 oz. bread, without crusts	1½ oz. castor sugar	2 tablespoons sherry,
4 egg yolks		*optional*

1 Put the loaf sugar and water into a strong pan, heat and stir until the sugar has dissolved, then boil steadily until dark brown; cool slightly.
2 Add the milk and heat without boiling until the milk has absorbed the caramel.
3 Pour over the diced bread.
4 Allow to soak for at least 30 minutes — but this could be done on Christmas Eve to save time on THE day.
5 Add all the other ingredients to the caramel mixture, beating the eggs very well before they are put in.
6 Pour into greased basin; steam gently WITHOUT BOILING for about 2½ hours.
7 Turn out and serve with the same sauces as for Christmas pudding.

Note. If making this for invalids omit the nuts which are sometimes found to be indigestible.

Crunchy fruit squares
(mince pies with a difference)

Preparation: 12 minutes
No delay
Cooking: 30 minutes
Makes about 18

Secret of success
Make sure the pastry *is* a firm consistency for this makes it *very crisp*, which gives the best result in this recipe.

Serve hot or cold. Delicious as a sweet with brandy butter, page 156.

for the crunchy pastry	3 oz. cooking fat	*to decorate*
2 oz. walnuts	about 6 tablespoons cold	icing sugar
12 oz. plain flour	water	about 18 canned *or* glacé
¼ level teaspoon salt		cherries
1 dessertspoon castor sugar	*for the filling*	
3 oz. margarine	1 lb. mincemeat	

1 Chop the walnuts finely.
2 Sift the flour, salt and castor sugar into a bowl.
3 Rub in the fats until the mixture resembles fine breadcrumbs, add the walnuts, mix to a *stiff* paste with the water.
4 Turn out on to a floured board, knead quickly until smooth then divide in two.
5 Roll out each piece into a rectangle, approximately 9 by 12 inches (or a little smaller than your baking tray) and put one on to a greased baking tray.
6 Spread with mincemeat to within ½ inch of the edges, moisten edges with water then cover with the remaining pastry.
7 Press the edges together to seal, then knock up with the back of a knife.
8 Bake just above the centre of a moderately hot oven (400°F., Gas Mark 5–6) for 30 minutes, or until pale golden.
9 Cut into squares while still warm, and dust the tops with sieved icing sugar. Put a cherry in the centre of each.

Party fruit cakes

Preparation: 15–20 minutes
No delay
Cooking: 20 minutes
Makes 24

4 oz. plain flour	4 oz. brown sugar	2 oz. glacé cherries
½ teaspoon baking powder	2 eggs	2 oz. mixed candied peel
½ teaspoon cinnamon	2 oz. seedless raisins	1 oz. nuts, coarsely chopped
2 oz. lard		

1 Sift together the flour, baking powder and cinnamon.
2 Cream the lard with the sugar until soft and light.
3 Add the eggs gradually and beat well.
4 Add the flour, etc., to the creamed mixture.
5 Cut the raisins and cherries into halves and the peel into small pieces, and add with the nuts to the cake mixture.
6 Half fill small paper cases.
7 Bake in a very moderate oven (350°F., Gas Mark 3), for approximately 20 minutes.

Star mince pies

Preparation: 25 minutes
Cooking: 20 minutes
Makes 12–18 (depending upon size)

Secret of success
This pastry can be kneaded a little more than an ordinary short crust.
Do not over-fill with mincemeat, otherwise it boils out in cooking.

Star mince pies

9 oz. plain flour
1 oz. cornflour
5 oz. butter *or* margarine
3 oz. castor sugar
1 egg
little water
8–10 oz. mincemeat

1 Sieve the flour and cornflour, rub in the butter or margarine.
2 Add the sugar and bind with the egg and a little water to give a firm rolling consistency; knead until quite smooth.
3 Roll out the dough and cut out 12 to 18 rounds for the bases of the tarts.
4 Put into the patty tins and fill with mincemeat.
5 Cut out 6 to 9 slightly smaller rounds for the lids for half the pies, then stamp out a star from the centre with a tiny cutter.
6 Brush the edges of the pastry with water, put the lids on half the pies and the stars on the others (see picture).
7 Bake for 20 minutes just above the centre of a moderately hot oven (400°F., Gas Mark 5–6). If the mincemeat appears to be drying, cover with foil.

Christmas cracker cookies

Preparation: 25 minutes
No delay
No cooking, just heating butter, etc.
Makes 12–15

Secret of success
Damp your fingers, before kneading mixture at stage 7.

Christmas cracker cookies

2 oz. walnuts
6 oz. raisins
2 oz. glacé cherries
8 oz. plain wafer biscuits
3 oz. brown sugar
3 level tablespoons cocoa
¼ teaspoon salt
3 oz. butter
3 tablespoons raspberry jam
3 tablespoons sweet sherry
1–1½ oz. coarse coconut *for rolling*

1 Chop the walnuts, raisins and glacé cherries into small pieces.
2 Break up the wafer biscuits into small crumbs. To do this, put the biscuits between two sheets of greaseproof paper and roll firmly.
3 Place the sugar, cocoa, salt and biscuit crumbs in a basin.
4 Add the chopped walnuts, raisins and cherries.
5 Place the butter, jam and sherry in a saucepan and heat until butter has melted.
6 Pour this mixture into the dry ingredients and mix all well together.
7 Knead mixture well with hand. Turn on to a board and form into a roll about 1½ inches in diameter.
8 Roll in coarse coconut, then wrap in greaseproof paper and chill until firm.
9 Cut into ½-inch slices.

Index

Acknowledgments

The author and publishers would like to thank the following for their co-operation in providing pictures for this book:

American Meat Institute: black and white photograph page 65
American Rice Council: Colour plate page 73
Australian Dairy Produce: black and white photograph page 215
Australian Dried Fruits: black and white photograph page 289
Batchelor's Foods Limited: black and white photograph page 35
J. Bibby and Sons Limited: black and white photographs, pages 188, 246, 255, 268, 270
Birds Eye Foods Ltd: black and white photographs, pages 118, 210
Blue Band Bureau: black and white photographs, pages 153, 158, 174, 189, 213, 245, 247, 259, 262, 275, 276
British Bacon Curers' Federation: Colour plate page 92; black and white photographs, pages 30, 31, 94, 95, 96, 219
British Egg Information Service: Colour plate, frontispiece, page 2; black and white photographs, pages 229, 234
British Meat Service: Colour plates page 56; black and white photographs, pages 82, 83, 84, 94, 105, 106, 225
Brown and Polson: Colour plate page 217
Butter Information Council: black and white photograph page 286
Cadbury Schweppes Foods Limited: Colour plates pages 150, 167, 253, 272; black and white photographs, pages 153, 166, 243, 273
California Prune Advisory Bureau: black and white photograph page 125
California Raisin Bureau: black and white photograph page 284
Campbell's Soups Limited: black and white photograph page 220
The Carnation Milk Bureau: black and white photographs, pages 81, 278
Cheese Bureau: black and white photograph page 89
Chicken Information Council: black and white photographs, pages 117, 121
Colman's Mustard: black and white photographs, pages 47, 80, 87, 206, 207
Colman's Semolina: black and white photographs, pages 22, 24, 164, 172, 176, 212, 215, 239, 263, 274
Cookeen: black and white photographs, pages 186, 189, 233
Cow and Gate: black and white photograph page 24
C.P.C. (UK) Ltd., Ocean Spray Cranberries: Colour plate page 110
Dutch Dairy Bureau: Colour plates page 218
Eden Vale Yoghourt: black and white photographs, pages 178, 241
Express Dairy Products: black and white photograph page 225
Farmer and Stockbreeder: black and white photograph page 115
Flour Advisory Bureau: black and white photographs, pages 70, 71, 77, 99, 119, 154, 159, 160, 161, 162, 165, 190, 193, 196, 223, 224, 240, 249, 264, 265, 266
Fruit Producers' Council: Colour plate page 127
Gale's Honey: black and white photograph page 268
Green Giant Corn: black and white photograph page 146
H.J. Heinz Company Limited: black and white photograph page 108
Herring Industry Bureau: black and white photographs, pages 26, 52
Kraft Foods Limited: black and white photographs, pages 26, 142, 205
Lawry's Foods Inc: Colour plate page 74
Lyons Maid Ltd: Colour plate page 271
MacFisheries Ltd: black and white photographs, pages 49, 120
Mushroom Information Service: black and white photographs, pages 138, 141, 148
National Milk Publicity Council: black and white photograph page 187
Nestlé Company: black and white photograph page 34
New Zealand Lamb Information Bureau: black and white photographs, pages 76, 77, 78, 90
Nor Prawn Advisory Bureau: black and white photograph page 27
Potato Marketing Board: black and white photographs, pages 54, 135, 136, 138, 139
Prestige Group Limited: black and white photographs, pages 69, 155, 197, 250
P.R. Visuals: black and white photographs, pages 124, 125, 144, 159, 170, 171, 202, 257, 258
Spillers Limited: black and white photographs, pages 23, 192, 238, 239
Spry Cookery Centre: black and white photographs, pages 45, 184, 185, 244
Stork Cookery Service: Colour plates pages 37, 109
Sunkist Growers: black and white photograph page 115
Syndication International: Colour plate page 236; black and white photographs, pages 102, 230
Tabasco Sauce: Colour plate page 74; black and white photograph page 87
Tala Icing Equipment: black and white photographs page 261
T. Wall and Sons Limited: Ice Cream: black and white photographs page 278
T. Wall and Sons (Meat and Handy Foods) Ltd: black and white photographs, pages 99, 211, 226
White Fish Kitchen: Colour plates pages 38, 55